CUBAN STUDIES 46

CUBAN STUDIES 46

ALEJANDRO DE LA FUENTE, *Editor*
LILLIAN GUERRA, *Book Review Editor*
(United States)
REINALDO FUNES,
Book Review Editor (Cuba)
CARY AILEEN GARCÍA YERO,
Associate Editor

UNIVERSITY OF PITTSBURGH PRESS

CUBAN STUDIES

ALEJANDRO DE LA FUENTE, Editor
CARY AILEEN GARCÍA YERO, Associate Editor

Manuscripts in English and Spanish may be submitted to Alejandro de la Fuente, Editor, Cuban Studies Program, Harvard University, 1730 Cambridge Street, Cambridge, MA 02138, USA. Maximum length is 10,000 words, including notes and illustrations. Please include an abstract of the article both in English and Spanish of no more than 200 words. Also include a short biographical paragraph of no more than 3 sentences. We prefer Chicago style (16th edition), but MLA style is also acceptable. *Cuban Studies* takes no responsibility for views or information presented in signed articles. For additional editorial inquiries, contact us at the address above or by e-mail at cubanstudies@fas.harvard.edu.

Review copies of books should be sent to the book review editor: Lillian Guerra, University of Florida, Department of History, 025 Keene-Flint Hall, Gainesville, FL 32611–7320, USA. For additional inquiries about book reviews, send e-mail to lillian.guerra@ufl.edu.

Orders for volumes 16–45 of *Cuban Studies* and standing orders for future volumes should be sent to the University of Pittsburgh Press, Chicago Distribution Center, 11030 South Langley, Chicago, IL, 60628-3893, USA; telephone 800-621-2736; fax 800-621-8476.

Back issues of volumes 1–15 of *Cuban Studies*, when available, may be obtained from the Center for Latin American Studies, University Center for International Studies, 230 South Bouquet Street, 4200 Wesley W. Posvar Hall, Pittsburgh, PA 15260.

Published by the University of Pittsburgh Press, Pittsburgh PA 15260

Library of Congress Card Number
ISBN 13: 978-0-8229-4512-3
US ISSN 0361-4441
10 9 8 7 6 5 4 3 2 1

Contents

Culture and Society

Economy

Premio Nacional de Artes Plásticas 2016　　309

Primary Sources

BOOK REVIEWS

History

Economy

Culture and Society

Nota del editor

Vuelvo a escribir esta nota introductoria en castellano, para facilitar el acceso a los lectores de la isla. Comienzo por compartir una grata sorpresa: el número de trabajos enviados desde Cuba —desde varios rincones de Cuba— se multiplica rápidamente, dando fe de que numerosos intelectuales y académicos residentes en la isla ven a *Cuban Studies* como una plataforma importante para diseminar sus resultados de investigación. A nombre de nuestro equipo editorial, agradezco a nuestros colegas en Cuba por darnos la oportunidad de leer y de evaluar sus trabajos. Una mención especial a los miembros de nuestro consejo editorial, algunos de los cuales han animado a varios autores jóvenes a publicar con nosotros.

Concluimos el numero 46 de *Cuban Studies* bajo el impacto de dos hechos potencialmente importantes para los estudios cubanos: el fallecimiento de Fidel Castro, líder histórico del proceso revolucionario cubano, y la elección de Donald Trump a la presidencia de los Estados Unidos. El fallecimiento de Fidel Castro produjo titulares y notas de prensa alrededor del mundo. Aunque su muerte, a los noventa años de edad, no sorprendió a nadie; a pesar de que llevaba casi diez años fuera del gobierno, al menos formalmente; y a pesar de que, además, en su cotidianidad los cubanos apenas hablaban de él, la muerte de Fidel Castro representa un momento simbólicamente importante, el ocaso inevitable de una generación cuya huella en la historia de Cuba ha sido y continuará siendo objeto de debate. Cualquier estudioso de nuestra historia sabe que el tiempo histórico de la nación cubana es frecuentemente medido en generaciones. No sé si esa generación será recordada como la "generación del centenario" —como la denomina la historia oficial cubana—, o si será recordada como la de-generación de dicho centenario. Tampoco está claro cuán importante y duradera, en el sentido profundo de los engranajes culturales de la cubanidad, será el impacto de esa generación. Los legados, contradictorios y complejos, del proceso revolucionario cubano y de sus líderes serán objeto de estudio y de polémica durante mucho tiempo.

Para muchos, Fidel Castro encarnó las ansias de justicia social y de afirmación soberana de todo un continente, de cara a la arrogancia imperial americana y de sus obsesiones anticomunistas. Para muchos otros, Fidel Castro fue un caudillo, megalómano y cruel, que traicionó los ideales puros de una revolución genuinamente popular, anclada en los reclamos cívicos de amplios sectores de la población. Lo que ninguna de las dos partes disputará es que no se puede estudiar el siglo XX cubano, o latinoamericano, sin mencionar a Fidel Castro. De hecho, hay procesos fundamentales de la pasada centuria, como la Guerra Fría o los procesos descolonizadores de África y Asia, que no pueden ser estudiados sin tener en cuenta las aspiraciones, acciones e influencias de Fidel Castro. Aunque los tiempos en los que los estudios sobre Cuba y su revolución versaban sobre su máximo líder han sido felizmente superados, hay muchos temas importantes de investigación que conectan, de una forma u otra, con Fidel Castro y con las distintas etapas de su larga vida. Los futuros presentes de Cuba tejerán sus propios pasados, reivindicando a algunos y condenando a otros. Es imposible predecir como evolucionarán dichos legados y como Fidel Castro será recordado. Cualquier lectura premonitoria de esos legados está inexorablemente anclada en el presente y es, por lo tanto, fundamentalmente equívoca.

Con irreflexividad característica, el presidente-electo Donald Trump reaccionó a la muerte de Fidel Castro con un "tweet" desprovisto del más elemental decoro presidencial. Esto tampoco sorprendió a nadie: el decoro no es precisamente una de las cualidades del presidente-electo, quien ha hecho una carrera política basada en el insulto, el sexismo, la xenofobia, la vulgaridad y el racismo. Con la elección de Trump, hay temas tradicionales de los estudios cubanos que adquieren vigencia renovada, como las relaciones entre Cuba y los Estados Unidos. En algún sentido perverso, Trump es un regalo. Para el nacionalismo cubano el Presidente Barack Obama representaba un reto imposible. El tradicional contraste entre una nación incluyente y fraterna (Cuba) y un país imperial, arrogante y segregado (Estados Unidos) se tambaleó ante el carisma, la franqueza y la crítica respetuosa (además de la melanina incómoda) que Barack y Michelle Obama desplegaron durante su visita a Cuba en marzo del 2016. Con la elección de Trump, el nacionalismo cubano regresa a una especie de antagonismo cómodo, que permite disimular o ignorar serios problemas al interior de la sociedad cubana. Un racista soez y grosero es un enemigo inmejorable. El nacionalismo siempre se alimenta de patrañas, mitos y caricaturas, pero es difícil imaginar una caricatura más eficaz que Donald Trump.

CUBAN STUDIES 46

DOSSIER: REREADING THE WORK OF LOURDES CASAL

COORDINATED BY IRAIDA H. LÓPEZ

RUTH BEHAR

Introduction: Looking Back and Forward

ABSTRACT

Lourdes Casal is one of the most important figures in contemporary Cuban history and also one of the most difficult to categorize. It is impossible to discuss the relationship between Cubans and Cuban Americans, and between Cuba and the United States, without being aware of her contributions. And yet because she was a woman, and moreover a black woman with Chinese heritage, and not just that, but a radical queer woman, and because she wrote both prose and poetry, devoting herself equally to scholarly work and creative work, she hasn't received the level of appreciation that she deserves. Especially in this moment of renewed relations between the United States and Cuba, it is imperative that Lourdes Casal be part of the emerging conversations about the interpretation of Cuban history. My introduction addresses the importance of Casal's work and engages with the critical essays included in this special volume.

RESUMEN

Lourdes Casal es una de las figuras más importantes de la historia cubana y también una de las más difíciles de categorizar. Es imposible hablar de la relación entre los cubanos y los cubanos-americanos, entre Cuba y los Estados Unidos, sin estar consciente de su obra. Pero porque fue mujer, y además mujer negra de herencia china, y mujer radical queer, y porque escribió prosa y poesía, y se dedicó a la investigación académica y a la obra creativa, por todo eso no ha recibido el reconocimiento que se merece. En este momento de nuevas relaciones entre los Estados Unidos y Cuba, es sumamente importante que Lourdes Casal forme parte de las conversaciones emergentes sobre la interpretación de la historia cubana. Mi introducción se enfoca en la importancia de la obra de Casal y examina los ensayos críticos incluidos en este volumen especial.

Lourdes Casal is one of the most important figures in contemporary Cuban history and one of the most difficult to categorize. It is impossible to discuss the relationship between Cubans and Cuban Americans, and between Cuba and the United States, without being aware of her contributions. And yet because she was a woman, and moreover a black woman with Chinese heritage, and not just that, but a radical queer woman, and because she wrote both prose and poetry, devoting herself equally to scholarly work and creative work, she hasn't received the level of appreciation that she deserves. Especially in this moment

3

of renewed relations between the United States and Cuba, it is imperative that Lourdes Casal be part of the emerging conversations about the interpretation of Cuban history. The question of historiography is key. Who is written into and out of the historical record, and why? The excellent papers collected here offer a much-needed and wonderfully multifaceted portrait of Lourdes Casal, revealing the productive tensions that inspired this scholar, writer, activist, and poet to speak in a range of voices, all of them memorable and significant. They demonstrate forcefully why she needs to be written into the record.

Born in 1938 in Cuba, and exiled to the United States in 1962, Casal died young at the age of forty-two in Cuba in 1981, and in that short life span she developed a sense of self that was deeply rooted in the idea of hybridity. While always aware that she had African and Chinese lineages, she identified with an almost mystical, sacred sense of Cubanness that draws heavily on José Martí's thinking. Trained as a social scientist in the United States, she developed a profound understanding of subjectivity from her social psychology training, as well as the sharp observation skills of a sociologist and the ethnographic listening skills of an anthropologist, which led her to undertake pioneering research on the lives of black Cubans in the United States.

But academic perspectives fell short for Casal. She pursued autobiographic analysis, writing about herself and her Cuban community in self-reflexive ways that call to mind the work of anthropologists such as Barbara Myerhoff, John Gwaltney, and José Limón, who have written about the meaning of home and homecoming.[1] She tried to construct a bridge to Cuba—a bridge between Cubans on the island and Cubans in the diaspora who believed in the possibility of a dialogue. She was perhaps the first "professional Cuban" to emerge after the Cuban Revolution, forging a career out of her search for her heritage and a lost home and the quest for a sense of belonging in Cuba. I consider Casal to have been an early proponent of auto-ethnography as scholarship.

Casal also felt a love of the Spanish language that led her to write poetry in her native tongue. Bilingual and bicultural, her work published in English in academic journals in the United States and poetry published in Spanish with Casa de las Américas, the most prestigious literary publisher in Cuba founded after the Revolution, Casal crossed borders, boundaries, and disciplines. She was a "scholartist"—a scholar and an artist—long before it was fashionable, and indeed at a time when these kinds of fusions were uncommon in academia.

But there were silences: her queer identity was kept under wraps in her public presentation of self. This was the price, other scholars have said, that she had to pay to reconnect with Cuba. Anti-gay politics in Cuba in the 1960s and 1970s were intense and unforgiving, with the existence of Unidades Militares de Ayuda a la Producción (UMAP) camps and continual discrimination and efforts to impose a heterosexual norm on the population with the Family Code.

To become a public revolutionary intellectual in Cuba in the 1970s, Casal had to stay in the closet. Among the rewards: she was buried in the Panteón de los Emigrados Revolucionarios de la Habana (February 3, 1981). But I was disappointed when I went to visit her grave—I found it too plain. I didn't want the words of José Martí engraved on it, but her own unforgettable words:

> I will remain forever a foreigner
> even when I return to the city of my birth.

At the same time, I wondered: do women's words ever appear on tombstones?

Casal revealed her sexuality by dedicating her most famous poem, "To Ana Veldford" (also known as Anna Veltfort), to a woman who was known to be a lesbian, a daughter of German parents who had settled in New York and then went to live in Cuba. Veltfort was in Cuba from 1962 to 1972, for ten years at the start of the revolution. She and Anna met in New York and Lourdes was drawn to the hybridity of Anna's identity, her ambiguous Cubanness and immigrant identity.[2]

For me, Lourdes Casal was a role model when I began a series of return trips to Cuba in 1991 that are ongoing to this day. I wrote a poem for her called "Prayer to Lourdes," where I confessed I didn't participate in the brigades:

> Lourdes, don't bother waking up to hear me.
> I wasn't there when you led the brigades.
> I was studying at Princeton in those years,
> a scholarship girl reading Marx behind ivy walls
> where dangerous ideas are kept in cages.[3]

I was a scholarship girl, my head in the clouds, and didn't hear of Lourdes and her work until after her death, though I did return to Cuba in 1979 for the first time during the brief thaw under Carter, and perhaps crossed paths with Lourdes on a street in Havana and didn't know it. She inspired me to think about bridges to Cuba. And as a writer, I felt inspired by her merging of research and poetry, her ability to be both a critical scholar as well as a lyrical speaker of eloquent truths that came from the heart. I also felt a certain affinity with her sense of hybrid identity, as I was seeking to give voice to the mix of Jewish and Cuban that is my heritage.

But despite these many points of connection, I realized, and said as much in my poem "Prayer to Lourdes," that for Lourdes Casal, culture and politics were thoroughly interwoven, at a moment when it was impossible to separate them because of the politicized relationship between the island and the diaspora. She became a passionate supporter of the Cuban Revolution and the political regime on the island. Her activism was expressed in her work with Grupo Areíto and the founding of the Antonio Maceo Brigade. She became, in a certain sense, a political proselytizer, encouraging young Cuban Americans to go to Cuba, to engage with the revolution, and do volunteer work, live out in practice the socialist ideal.

I found myself in a more ambiguous position, not wanting to take a political stand for or against, not wanting to choose between the island or the exiles, walking a tightrope. I tried to have empathy for Cubans on all sides (following the anthropological commitment to "being there" and witnessing and listening). I sought to separate culture from politics, believing that bridges could be established along the lines of shared culture and memory, and while not ignoring politics, at least giving it a secondary place in my interactions with fellow Cubans wherever they happened to be. With the restoration of ties between Cuba and the United States, it is time to rethink the relationship between culture and politics. Reflecting on the decisions that Casal made, over thirty years ago now in a different era, suddenly seems very timely.

The papers included here offer a fascinating new light on Casal's thinking about race, nation, and belonging in Cuba, and how these conceptions were deeply influenced by her experiences in the United States, which became a counterpoint to the homeland she both imagined and reclaimed in Cuba. They also gracefully show the interplay between Casal's autobiography and her aesthetics and politics.

Our contemporary concept of intersectional feminism seems to have been invented to understand Casal's work. As Laura Lomas shows, Casal worked in the space of the "in-between," both through her interdisciplinary pursuits as a scholar and poet, and through the way she continually saw feminism as entwined with struggles for black civil rights, working class struggles, and international decolonization movements. Casal's ability to inhabit borderlands and to seek to define them through lived experience connects her to other Latinas of color of her generation, including Gloria Anzaldúa, Cherríe Moraga, and Audre Lorde. As Lomas wisely suggests, Casal needs to be seen as part of "this group of queer-of-color foremothers," a thinker who helped to lay the foundation for the field of Cuban studies, through "interdisciplinary projects that continue to invigorate cultural criticism and theory."

Jenna Leving Jacobson illuminates the ways in which Casal developed a sense of her own blackness in exile. In the United States, Casal felt more defined by the color of her skin than by her cultural identity: "Mi color me define más que mi cultura." In the 1960s and 1970s, Lourdes Casal experienced both the cruel racism of American segregation and the hope for liberation and equality that the civil rights struggle was espousing. But the emphasis was on color, not culture, and Casal ultimately wanted to embrace her heritage, to move color into a secondary place. She wanted the familiarity of living among the orishas that she remembered from her childhood in Havana—culture as lived experience, as part of the everyday fabric of being.

Jacobson notes that Cuba was celebrating its African heritage as a means of bringing about racial equality through socialist revolution, while also engaging in military operations in Africa. Color and race were being officially erased. The elimination of private schools and a policy of integration on all levels of society would make racial difference an obsolete marker. Certainly it seems, as Jenna points out, that Casal was persuaded by this ideology—she viewed herself as the descendent of oppressed peoples, indigenous, African, and Chinese, who had reached a moment in history when they would gain true freedom and self-empowerment through participation in the revolution.

Naming the magazine she founded *Areíto*, acknowledging a Taíno heritage and a pre-Columbian ritual of collective dancing, was a way of claiming a history that preceded Spanish conquest, preceded the Cuban revolution—going to the source. This move memorialized the severe injustice upon which Cuba's racial politics had been built—the disappeared indigenous peoples and cultures whose bones had served as the bedrock for what would eventually become the Cuban nation.

In turn, naming the brigade after Antonio Maceo inscribed the important role of black Cubans in bringing about the fall of the Spanish empire in Cuba and beginning the process of seeking national independence. While most of the members of the brigade were white Cubans, giving pride of place to Maceo was a way of questioning their own white privilege, making it possible for them to return to the island under a noble cloak of hope for eventual racial integration through revolutionary commitment.

Jacobson's work shows us the crucial importance of key symbols in the thinking of Lourdes Casal and in her efforts to revise Cuban nationhood and give it a redemptive future. In this sense, it's possible to say that Casal was actively engaged in mythography—a mix of the mythological and the ethnographic.

And yet, as Yolanda Prieto shows, it is not mythography alone that Lourdes Casal embraced, but the nitty-gritty observational and statistical analysis of social science in her work on black Cubans in the United States. Yolanda has a very special perspective on this question, as she helped to complete the work that Casal began, and in addition she was a student of Casal's, so she also knew her as a teacher. Hopefully one day Yolanda will be inspired to write about Casal as an educator—and to give us more of a memoir about Casal—to share memories of how she taught, and how she interacted with students.

In the meantime, Prieto shows us how very pioneering was the research of Casal, who was studying black Cubans long before the existence of Afro-Latino studies. Paying attention to this minority of 3 percent among the Cuban influx in the early 1960s allowed Casal to understand the complex relationship between race and class and gender. She was able to show that the migration of black Cubans was miniscule because of their largely marginalized position in prerevolutionary Cuban society and because they feared racial discrimination in the United States. She was also able to observe how black Cubans initially identified more strongly as Cubans in Miami but over time came to identify in terms of race.

Casal was exceptional within her own group, coming from a middle-class family, and using education as a route to social mobility. Perhaps, I will dare to say, her own success as a scholar clouded her ability to see how racial discrimination and prejudice could be insidious. Social mobility might be attained, but the fear of a black nation and the prejudice toward interracial relationships could nevertheless continue unabated—even after years of revolution.

But my sense is that Casal was uneasy about her inclusion in the exile community that was so overwhelmingly white, and she sought to disentangle herself from the privilege she attained by choosing Cuba over the United States as her ultimate home, both in life and eventually in death. Home is not simply where you are born, but also where you are buried—the earth in Cuba took her back into itself, repatriated her.

Iraida H. López beautifully rounds out our appreciation and understanding of the work of Lourdes Casal by bringing our attention to the way Casal elaborated a notion of *mestizaje*—a notion I think would be interesting to compare and contrast to the idea of the "new mestiza" described by Gloria Anzaldúa in her iconic work on Mexican borderlands.[4]

López focuses on Casal's autobiographic writing, "Memories of a Black Cuban Childhood," as well as other texts where she was involved in the process of self-invention, both recalling and refiguring herself through the use of the personal voice.

"Too white" for Africa and "too black" for the United States, it is in Cuba that Casal finds she belongs. There, her color is the norm, *el color cubano*. Casal drew on her sense of a mestiza identity, though she used the Cuban term *mulata* to describe herself, a complex and symbolically loaded term that reaches into all levels of Cuban culture, finding its way into the poetry of Nicolás Guillén and becoming a rum brand as well.[5] She embraced the imperfect hybridity of this sense of identity, configuring Cuban nationhood as a model of convergence, a Cuba that is for all, in which differences are blended into the famous *ajiaco*, a social unity that rises above the distinctions that could pull everyone apart.

As López notes, for Casal it is at home that *mestizaje* happens, unfolds, becomes real, in the cultural conjuncture of her Chinese great-grandfather, an indentured worker, and her Afro-Cuban great-grandmother, a *mulata*, and a descendant of slaves who practices Santería, who has not lost her bond with Africa. The pictures of the ancestors hang together on the walls, meshing, creating a space for an intersecting history of exile from China and Africa and forced labor in Cuba, a place of suffering that eventually becomes a place of belonging.

This sense of home is definitely not unique on the island—the history that Lourdes Casal recounts is multiplied numerous times, for marriages among Chinese men and black women were very common, given that white women didn't want to marry Chinese men, while black and *mulata* women were more willing, not sharing the same prejudice, and hoping for the economic mobility that the work ethic of "los chinos" promised.

It is out of the intersection of lived oppressions, and overcoming them through revolutionary change, that Casal envisions an ideal of *mestizaje* that might offer liberation and a renewed sense of home on a larger scale, a national scale. Hers is a hopeful vision of *patria*—founded on the notion of cultural mixing and fusion, on tolerance and acceptance, and on a redemptive sense of history. It was an uneasy kind of belonging, as envisioned by a woman who in her poetry described herself as remaining a foreigner even when returning to the city of her birth.

The legacy Lourdes Casal left us is a great one, and I am grateful that the scholars in this volume, along with others, are reclaiming her work and assessing it with fresh eyes. Lourdes died much too young, unfortunately. She believed in the Cuban revolution, naively perhaps but with great sincerity, and she was always brave, calling for reconciliation between Cubans on the island and in the diaspora when you could get murdered for doing so. Had she been a man, there'd be a monument in her honor by now, in Havana and Miami. Instead, all she has is a plain tombstone in the Colón cemetery. I doubt President Obama heard of her, and yet she paved the way for the historic opening he spearheaded. Lourdes Casal was there first. Let's not forget.

NOTES

1. Barbara Myerhoff, *Number Our Days* (New York: Touchstone, 1980); John Gwaltney, *Drylongso: A Self-Portrait of Black America* (New York: Random House, 1980); José Limón, *Dancing with the Devil: Society and Cultural Politics in Mexican-American South Texas* (Madison: University of Wisconsin Press, 1994).

2. For an illuminating analysis of the relationship between Anna Veltfort and Lourdes Casal, see Frances Negrón-Muntaner and Yolanda Martínez-San Miguel, "In Search of Lourdes Casal's 'Ana Veldford,'" *Social Text* 25, no. 3 (Fall 2007): 57–84.

3. Ruth Behar, "Prayer to Lourdes," in *Bridges to Cuba/Puentes a Cuba*, 20th anniversary ed., ed. Ruth Behar (Ann Arbor: University of Michigan Press, 2015), 23.

4. Gloria Anzaldúa, *Borderlands/La Frontera: The New Mestiza* (San Francisco: Aunt Lute Books, 1987).

5. Nicolas Guillén, "Mulata," first published in his collection *Motivos de son* (Havana: Rambla, Bouza y Co., 1930). Also see Raúl Rubio, "Materializing Havana and Revolution: Cuban Material Culture," *Studies in Latin American Popular Culture* 24 (2005): 161–177.

LAURA LOMAS

On the "Shock" of Diaspora: Lourdes Casal's Critical Interdisciplinarity and Intersectional Feminism

ABSTRACT

The exiled intellectual Lourdes Casal experienced in 1960s and 1970s New York a "shock" that led her to reconsider her anti-Castro position and to become aware of her condition as an Afro-descendent, a feminist, and Marxist, especially after returning from serving on a student delegation to Africa and after traveling to Cuba in 1973. Like other postcolonial lesbian-of-color feminists publishing in this period, she interrogated dichotomies and introduced interdisciplinary approaches to her writings about Cuban culture and society. Casal theorized the crossroads and the borderlands of discursive categories such as race, gender, sexuality, language, class, age, nationality, and religion before Kimberlé Crenshaw's influential concept of intersectionality became common-place in feminist and antiracist cultural studies and calls our attention to the effects of *décalage*, a French philosophical term for the temporal and spatial gaps within social formations. By examining Casal's writings and their reception, this essay argues that Casal contributed to the building of interdisciplines such as Cuban studies. A critical, bilingual, gendered-subaltern diasporic intellectual of color such as Casal has played a key role in the interpretation of Cuba's revolutionary culture and considers how Casal enacts strategies for rebuilding a post–Cold War and postcolonial intellectual dialogue between the United States and Cuba.

RESUMEN

Lourdes Casal, intelectual cubana exiliada en Estados Unidos, experimentó en la urbe nuyorquina de los años sesenta y setenta un "shock" que le llevó a declinar su posición anti-Castrista y a adoptar un criterio de conciencia de afrodescendiente, feminista, y marxista, especialmente a partir de su vuelta del África y de su visita a Cuba en 1973. Como otras feministas postcoloniales y lesbianas que comenzaron a publicar en los años setenta, Casal cuestionaba las dicotomías e introdujo una metodología interdisci-plinaria en los estudios de la cultura y sociedad cubana. Casal teorizaba la cruzacalle y el espacio fronterizo entre las categorías discursivas, es decir, entre raza, género sexual, orientación sexual, idioma, clase, nacionalidad, y eso mucho antes que el concepto de Kimberlé Crenshaw —la interseccionalidad— se volviera común en los estudios feministas y antiracistas. También subraya los efectos de *décalage*, término filosófico francés que refiere a las brechas temporales y espaciales dentro de las formaciones sociales. A través de una lectura de sus ensayos y del debate sobre su transformación ideológica, este trabajo destaca la contribución casaliana a los campos interdisciplinarios, como por ejemplo los estudios cubanos. Enfatiza el papel que una intelectual negra crítica, diaspórica, bilingüe y subalterna ha jugado en la interpretación de la cultura revolucionaria cubana y considera como Casal pone en practica estrategias ejemplares para construir un diálogo intelectual, poscolonial y post-Guerra Fría, entre Estados Unidos y Cuba.

Criticism is love.

José Martí, "Echegaray"[1]

> To be critical of one's culture is not to betray that culture. We tend
> to be very righteous in our criticism and indictment of the dominant
> culture and we so often suffer from the delusion that, since Chicanos
> are so maligned from the outside, there is little room to criticize those
> aspects from within our oppressed culture which oppress us.

Cherríe Moraga, *Loving in the War Years*[2]

Cuban diaspora intellectual Lourdes Casal's writing imbricates theory and practice, aesthetics and politics, perspectives on the island and the diaspora, in a body of work that straddles divergent political affiliations and articulates a pioneering form of interdisciplinary Cuban, diaspora, and Afro-Latin@ studies. Casal herself transforms from exiled college student sharing the Catholic Church's critique of the 1959 revolution, to a radicalized "new left" intellectual committed to the Cuban revolution and to the struggle for "una nueva cultura."[3] An advocate of the reestablishment of diplomatic relations between Cuba and the United States who contributed to a shift in policy whereby exiled Cubans and their families could revisit the island, Casal was the first exile authorized to return to the Havana of her youth in 1973, and lies buried there.[4] Yet the reader of her poetry knows that any "return" in the fullest sense of that word had become impossible for her precisely as a result of her years as a New Yorker. Part of the transformation of her consciousness includes a keen awareness of her queer location—that is, a perennial sense of difference or marginality—with respect to the norms of the social and cultural formations in which she made her home. As a result, she came to live in a state of constant becoming, of dwelling and thinking from the uncomfortable site of the border. This place, which I refer to as an "in-between state" in the larger project from which this chapter derives, proves uniquely generative for developing new interdisciplinary interrogations of gendered, racialized, and postcolonial hierarchies.

A border-crosser in terms of academic disciplines and literary form in addition to physically moving across borders as a migrant, Casal did not limit herself to a single literary genre, language, or discipline. Neither, finally, did she restrict herself to like-minded interlocutors, which could easily exacerbate a permanent sense of living as "a stranger among the stones," a famous line from Casal's most anthologized poem, "Para Ana Veltford."[5] Casal fearlessly criticized authorities and senior colleagues (such as Casa de las Américas and Martí Studies Center director Roberto Fernández Retamar and Harvard professor of government Jorge I. Domínguez), with whom she nonetheless maintained working relationships and enduring friendships. Dwelling on the margins, Casal was "too *habanera* to be *newyorkina* / too *newyorkina* to be—even to become again—anything else," per the oft-cited closing lines of her most widely anthologized poem.

As a professor of social psychology, Casal pioneers approaches that are harbingers of the most innovative scholarship in interdisciplinary fields of Cuban, Africana, Latina/o, feminist, and postcolonial studies today. Casal's social science supplements her creative writing and humanities-based work in the form of poems, stories, film reviews, personal essay and interpretation. This supplementation among her modes of writing interweaves her autobiographical prose, her short fiction, and her social science, keeping each of her multiple genres connected to her own and others' struggles and transformations, in and beyond the university.[6] Casal's insistent relation of her various kinds of writing to the politics of her location in Cuban and in US society makes it possible to think of Casal as a "specific intellectual" in opposition to Marx's concept of the intellectual as "bearer of universal values."[7] Michel Foucault defines the specific intellectual as "the person occupying a specific position," defined by a class background, but also by conditions of life and work, and by the structures of power governing the struggle over what counts as "truth."[8] Like Foucault, Casal eschewed public self-identification with homosexual labels and did not associate liberation with publicly speaking about her sexual orientation.[9] Instead Casal focused her intellectual struggle and activism on plotting alternatives to persistent forms of Eurocentric, male, and imperial domination.

Formally Casal's commitments result in a hybrid interdisciplinary style that moves beyond the expert's "objective" stance, to draw on first-person narration, oral histories, and poetry to challenge disciplinary borders and to introduce sometimes unspeakable ground-breaking perspectives. For example, Lourdes Casal's sociological and historical essay "Race Relations in Contemporary Cuba," published in 1979 as part 2 of a volume coedited with Anani Dzidzienyo in London, shows how her family participated in the silencing of race consciousness by refusing to speak openly about the so-called *guerrita*, or torture and massacre of thousands of black Cubans affiliated with the Partido Independiente de Color (PIC) in 1912, a topic that was silenced in pre- and post-revolutionary Cuba. In a riveting retelling of this personal coming to consciousness, Casal risks appearing as a traitor to her own family, and to her country because she reveals their complicity in the gentleman's agreement, as she states, "not to speak of 'disagreeable' things concerning race":

A grand-uncle of mine was assassinated, supposedly by orders of Monteagudo, the rural guard officer who terrorized blacks throughout the island. Chills went down my spine when I heard stories about blacks being hunted day and night; and black men being hung by their genitals from the lamp posts in the central plazas of small Cuban towns.[10]

The first-person account of whispered transmission about gruesome violence that affected her grandparents' generation conveys the personal stake that Casal had in her research on contemporary race relations in Cuba as a "bicultural scholar" in the social sciences.[11] Casal's literary work and social science give "hard data" the tone, sound, and accent of her family members. Making recourse to this collage of academic and literary writing exemplifies a key continuity with other feminists of color who transformed the form of academic prose by introducing first-person narrative, popular culture, and poetry alongside social scientific scholarship and criticism.[12] Anticipating a contemporary ongoing effort to break the silence around racism in Cuba in conjunction with the centennial anniversary of the 1912 massacre of Afro-Cubans in 2012, Casal's essays on racism in Cuba in the late 1970s join other precursors in forging the field of Afro-Cuban and Afro-Latina/o studies.[13] Although readers of Latina/o literature know Lourdes Casal primarily as an exiled poet of the Cuban diaspora, her full oeuvre includes studies of race and gender relations in Cuba and in the diaspora, representations of Chinese and African diasporas in Cuba and transnationally, and a feminist and postcolonial critique of the U.S.-based academic's relationship to her object of study.

Casal's work anticipates an interdisciplinary, intersectional feminism.[14] Her writing across the humanities and social sciences divide exemplifies a tradition popularized by her contemporaries—Caribbean and Chicana queer or lesbian feminists Audre Lorde, Gloria Anzaldúa, and Cherríe Moraga.[15] This contemporary queer-of-color theory provides a framework for perceiving a subtle, yet quite radical intersectional and anticolonial black feminist discourse in Lourdes Casal's work. Although Casal only defined herself privately as a lesbian, Yolanda Martínez San Miguel has illustrated how Casal creates rebellious nonconformist female-gendered characters that make it possible to read her corpus as informed by queer perspectives.[16] Intersectional feminism—as defined by the legal scholar Kimberlé Crenshaw—criticizes legal and social discourses that tend to elide the perspectives of those occupying simultaneously nondominant positions within sexual, racial, class, and other hierarchies.[17] Casal's texts reveal her awareness of the "triple discrimination" faced by women of color, something that she experienced, in her words, as a

"Black, a woman and Latina."[18] As a scholar whose work intertwines poetics and politics, Casal theorizes in the utopian fashion that we have learned to associate with the work of her Cuban queer-of-color successor, José Muñoz, who tirelessly imagined ways to move beyond the limits of a restrictive here and now.[19]

The "Shock" of Diaspora: Casal's Shifting Self-Definitions

Casal's process of becoming or self-transformation, catalyzed by experiences of difference during her travel and residence outside of Cuba, facilitated a dramatic shift in her politics. This shift begins with a trip to Africa where she arrived at a more complex understanding of the heterogeneity of blackness and of her homeland.[20] Casal's "pequeño-burguesa" middle-class parents sent her to the private Universidad Católica de Santo Tomás de Villanueva, where she enrolled and became perhaps the only black and the only female student in chemical engineering. Changing majors, she pursued studies in psychology, without finishing her degree, likely due to the delay in awarding private university degrees beginning in 1959, and eventual closure of private institutions of higher learning as part of reforms instituted in 1961.[21] Casal nonetheless distinguished herself as a brilliant student, an award-winning essayist and a collaborator in various student organizations and periodicals such as *La Quincena, Insula*, and the student newspaper, *El Quibú*.[22] At this stage, as a good Catholic complying with the expectations of her family, Casal perceived communism as "the devil," and Casal retrospectively includes herself among the "confused catholics" who wept after the nationalization of all of Cuba's major private businesses in 1960.[23]

A trip to several countries in Africa as part of a CIA-sponsored anti-Communist delegation in June 1962 led Casal to question her political stance and to rethink her understanding of blackness and of Africa.[24] She worked with "counterrevolutionary" organizations, such as the Directorio Revolucionario Estudiantil (DRE), through which she had an opportunity to participate in this delegation that sought to share an anti-Communist critique of Cuba with emerging postcolonial republics including Egypt, Senegal, Rwanda, and Nigeria.[25] In her narratives of this experience, Casal undergoes a classic Caribbean reencounter with Africa in which, despite her black ancestry and her initiation into the Afro-Caribbean Yoruba religion known as Regla de Ocha or Santería, she describes how Nigerian youths pointed to her and labeled her in Yoruba as "white," which led her to recognize her Cubanness, and to begin to rethink her politics.[26] Casal comments in her report on the trip that, in fact, Africans had many other more urgent concerns besides the critique of communism that her sponsors wanted her to emphasize. In the essay "Africa frente al problema cubano," Casal recounts one Senegalese's unforgettable comment: "Si yo tengo hambre y el diablo me da pan, me lo como. Pero el pan de Rusia y el pan de Francia y hasta el pan del diablo, cuando me los haya comido, se convertirán en mi carne, carne africana" ("Africa frente el problema Cubano" 14). Casal reads this comment as the African student's rejection of the false dilemma of either a "socialist" or a "democratic" European solution to Africa's problems stemming from a longstanding legacy of colonial violence. The Africans perceived the reduction of their situation to this dichotomy as "absurd," according to Casal, for they instead placed much greater emphasis on the need to search for African forms of expression, forms of political organization, and social-economic institutions, according to their own needs and traditions. This profoundly anticolonial critique in 1962 reflects Casal's observation of a continental African desire to revalorize their own culture and reverse the effects of European colonial domination. Casal's report also notes strong similarities between Cuba and the African countries she visited. It echoes the decolonial vindication of Latin America in her early essay "Problemas hispanoamericanos"—now with a diasporic consciousness—and foreshadows her late critique of lingering racism and sexism in Cuba and in the Cuban diaspora, even after the strides made by the 1959 revolution.

Upon returning from the trip to Africa, she found herself in conflict with the leaders of the Consejo Revolucionario, which was responsible for coordinating anti-Castro counterrevolutionary efforts from Miami. The Consejo (which had funded the trip) wanted her to prepare a report on the trip to Africa to reflect the idea that "communism horrified the Africans."[27] The experience of seeing herself as different in Africa, and of seeing her report censored by her sponsors led her to begin to complicate her original political position and self-definition in light of the shock of diaspora.[28]

Upon her relocation to New York City, Casal's subsequent encounter with black and Puerto Rican civil rights, anti-war, and other social movements at the end of the 1960s further pushes Casal to articulate the specificity and complexity of her point of view as a black Cuban woman. In terms of writing about race in Cuba from a black perspective, Lourdes Casal's sociological and historical essay "Race Relations in Contemporary Cuba," mentioned above, reveals her daring critique of a tendency dating to the early republic to suppress race-consciousness and to silence conversations and awareness about the problem of antiblack violence. As noted above, Casal breaks the silence around the 1912 massacre and exposes the suppression of the memory of the PIC. Her essay contributes to a tradition of writing and documentary work designed to foment precisely this kind of critical self-reflection about racism and other lingering forms of coloniality in Cuba and in the diaspora.[29]

Remarkably, Casal's articulation of her black subjectivity is always intersecting with other categories of difference such as sexuality, class, language and gender. For example, she furthermore articulates her affiliation with blackness in English and as an effect of what I am calling the "shock" of diaspora, for it is in New York and Newark that she "had to learn to assert her Blackness . . . particularly as a Hispanic Black."[30] In her canny first-person essay entitled "Memories of a Black Cuban Childhood," in which she reflects on her childhood in Havana and describes her transformation after relocating to the United States, Casal grounds the critique of Cuban "criollo" discourse in her experiences in the United States at this particular historical moment:

In the US during the 60s, I was forced to look at my Blackness with different eyes. I had become accustomed to considering myself *una mulata* in a mulatto country, in a quintessentially mulatto culture. *The US was a shock.* Here I had to learn to assert my Blackness somehow—even or particularly as a Hispanic Black—in a country where Black and white were defined in opposition to one another and where any attempt to avoid the dichotomy seemed to be some kind of betrayal.[31]

The sudden insufficiency of the definition of herself as a "*mulata* in a mulatto country" upon entering the effervescence of black, Puerto Rican, feminist, and anti-Vietnam rebellions of the 1960s and 1970s reveals the effect of the "shock" of diaspora. In particular, Casal becomes conscious of how her "Hispanic Black" self-definition in English troubled the dominant racial binary of the United States by calling attention to the heterogeneity and multilingualism of the African diaspora, including in the United States. In contrast, black and post-colonial consciousness, among other movements, prompted Casal to assert her blackness, over and against the common Cuban practice that she learned at home: to not speak of race, and most especially of 'disagreeable' things concerning race. With the personal anecdote quoted above, she interrogates the suppression of critical remembering of antiblack violence in Cuba as someone who lived the effects of this self-censorship. In this and other late writings on contemporary race relations in Cuba, she makes clear that the suppression of this history that occurred after 1912, and in the 1940s when she was growing up, had left an entrenched traumatic legacy. The passage above indicates an awareness of how her position might meet with the accusation of betrayal of the nation or of the revolution (in Cuba), and of "the race" (which could refer to any racialized group marked by a shared history of oppression at the hands of people privileged by colonialism) in the United States, much like Cherríe Moraga and Gloria Anzaldúa had encountered from Chicano nationalists. Simply by referring to herself as "Black," Casal violated the mandate from José Martí institutionalized after 1961, that in revolutionary Cuba there was no longer white or black, only Cuban.

Casal's contemporaries also began at this juncture to articulate a third-world feminist critique of dichotomies and their role in enabling violence, which also met with traumatic repercussions, if not death threats as in the case of Casal.[32] According to Anzaldúa, dualism and dichotomies undergird the violent projects headed up by European men and their descendants: "Western culture made 'objects' of things and people when it distanced itself from them, thereby losing 'touch' with them. This dichotomy is the root of all violence."[33] Chicana feminists Moraga and Anzaldúa in particular decry the way queer women who refuse to defer to the masculinist, heterosexist hierarchies of nationalist anti-colonialism find themselves accused of betraying their people and their race: "Ever since [the period of Cortés], brown men have been accusing [La Malinche] of betraying her race, and over the centuries continue to blame her entire sex for this 'transgression.'"[34] In the 1980s, Chicana feminist theory began to theoretically respond to the misogynist discourse that blamed the conquest of the Mexican nation on Hernán Cortés's mistress and translator, La Malinche. By extension, insubordinate women—especially women exploring their sexuality or loving women—became emblematic as traitors to *la raza*: "the potential accusation of 'traitor' or 'vendida' is what hangs above the heads and beats in the hearts of most Chicanas seeking to develop our own autonomous sense of ourselves, particularly through sexuality."[35] It is notable that La Malinche's mastery of two languages contributed to this masculinist definition of her as threatening or treacherous, given that Casal also moved easily between English and Spanish, defining her ethnicity or race as "Black," but with the adjective "Hispanic" that alludes to her ethno-linguistic difference in Anglo-centric North America. Anzaldúa proposes queerness as another way of knowing and pursuing justice without making recourse to dichotomies: To be queer is "a path of knowledge—one of knowing (and of learning) the history of oppression of our *raza*. It is a way of balancing, of mitigating duality."[36] According to Audre Lorde, Afro-Caribbean lesbian feminist of Cariacou, the attempt to acknowledge and then change "that piece of the oppressor which is planted deep within each of us" reveals the possibility of deconstructing racial or gendered hierarchies by acknowledging that such dichotomies are never hermetic, and no "identity" is pure.[37] Third world, Chicana, and Afro-Caribbean queer feminist theory parallels Casal's attention to how dichotomies elided internal heterogeneity and provided an apology for colonial violence.

Casal also recognizes her debt to black power, Puerto Rican student movements, anti–Vietnam War and civil rights movements, to global processes of decolonization, and to New York City counterculture, in describing her process of radicalization. In an interview with Margaret Randall, Casal foregrounds her affiliation with a woman-of-color feminism that speaks from a position subject to intersecting discrimination: "I did not fit anywhere in the United States. Because I'm Black, a woman and Latina, three things that brought me triple discrimination. . . . I found myself asking myself what I was doing [in the United States]. But it wasn't my voice alone doing the asking. Black student leaders, with whom I participated in the struggles against racial discrimination or against the war in Vietnam; they were asking me too. So I had left Cuba, where a revolution was taking place, and had come to suffer a process of radicalization inside the US. Because that is what it was, a process of personal radicalization."[38] Speaking of herself as simultaneously occupying categories that signal difference in terms of language, race, and gender, Casal shares the vocabulary of intersecting discrimination that continues to shape feminist discourse in the twenty-first century. Casal's prose and poetry articulates the concerns she knew the most intimately, those of Afro-Cubans, of Chinese Cubans, of Afro-Latina/o migrants, and of women of color generally, all of whom lacked adequate representation in the leadership of revolutionary nationalist or civil rights movements.

After her initial opposition to the Castro government that propelled her into exile, she was invited by the Instituto Cubano de Amistad con los Pueblos (Institute of Friendship with the Peoples, or ICAP) to return to Cuba on a trip that fundamentally changed her view of the Cuban revolution and led her to help launch the progressive Cuban diaspora magazine *Areíto*, in 1974. With an eye to reopen a dialogue between Cubans living outside and Cubans on the island, Casal helped to found the Antonio Maceo Brigade, through which fifty-five Cuban Americans returned to the island between December 1977 and January 1978 and thereafter.[39] These negotiations and moves toward restoring diplomatic relations contributed to the release of political prisoners in 1978–1979.[40] Casal's multiple trips to Cuba and support of the restoration of relations and travel by Cubans violated the exile-nation dichotomy and thus appeared as a betrayal to some militant anti-Castro members of the Cuban exile community.[41] Casal puts into practice a critique of the dichotomies that define national, racial, sexual, linguistic, and other politicized borders. Casal and other progressive Cubans experienced firsthand the threat of violent reprisals against those who dared to transgress the borders between the United States and Cuba.

Having edited a dossier of documents on Cuban poet Heberto Padilla's case in 1971, coedited a 402-page report on the Cuban minority in the United States with Rafael J. Prohías (1980), and published with Yolanda Prieto a pioneering study on Black Cubans in the United States, Casal established herself as a scholar and activist who was willing to break the silence around both political repression, sexism, and racism, if not homophobia. Casal enriched emerging interdisciplinary fields of study from her multiple, intersecting positions, yet has remained relatively invisible because of how her work straddles different, often opposing, readerships.[42] Casal contributes to what we now call Latina/o, Caribbean, and Cuban studies by questioning the dominant narrative of a homogeneous, white-identified, and model-minority Cuban exile group. Casal and Prieto's pioneering study of black Cubans notes how overrepresentation and the ideology of "exceptionalism" among whites and professionals in the earliest phases of Cuban migration tended to isolate Cubans from contact with New York Puerto Ricans in West New York and to lead to outright tension with Puerto Ricans on the island. In her essay "Cubans in the US" published in *Nueva Generación* (1972), she interjects a critical note to the resounding success story of the Cuban exile community by revealing how this narrative dismissed the heterogeneity and hierarchies within the Cuban exile group.[43]

Lourdes Casal's great contribution through her social science is to insist on the complexity and heterogeneity of the Cuban diaspora, a point William Luis underscores in publications where he cites Casal.[44] She notes how the myth of the Cuban model minority foreclosed solidarity among minority groups, and tended to disavow the difficulties faced by black, working-class Cubans and Cuban women of color in particular.[45] During the period in which she was a graduate student in social psychology at the New School for Social Research (she defended her doctoral dissertation in 1975), Casal had already begun to develop an argument about ethnicity, class, and gender as fundamental facts of sociopolitical life in the United States, including in revolutionary Cuba, and in the Cuban exile enclave. Casal's experience in the diaspora—including perhaps her identification not with the bourgeoisie of New York City, but as a working graduate student and one of very few faculty of color at Rutgers University–Newark—pushed her to participate in movements of working-class people of color happening all around her.[46] The Newark Puerto Rican riots of nearly ten thousand in 1974 to protest police abuse happened while Casal was teaching in Newark. Inside Rutgers, Puerto Rican students, staff, and faculty struggled to change curriculum, to recruit Latina/o students and faculty, and to have office space for community outreach and education programs in Newark, where over one-fourth of blacks and Puerto Ricans lived in poverty.[47] In 1977, Assata Shakur (JoAnne Chesimard) was arrested on the New Jersey Turnpike and convicted by an all-white jury of murdering a state trooper, although no physical evidence indicated that she had been the shooter. She escaped from prison in November 1979.[48] As the world transformed around her, Casal translates this dramatic historical effervescence into a call for "U.S. Latinos" to become aware of global struggles for decolonization and civil rights.[49] Her poetry records how the military junta's deposing of Chile's democratically elected President Salvador Allende in 1973 crushed her remaining hopes for changes through electoral reform.[50] Her reflections on a conference on Women and National Development at Wellesley, published in the major feminist journal *Signs*, interwove her feminist, racial consciousness and postcolonial perspectives to critique the notion of "objective" or "pure" academic work: "the definitions of development and even the status of women *are* political."[51] Her intersectional feminism and interdisciplinarity led her to interrogate the conditions of knowledge production and to speak critically about the political implications of academic discussions from her perspective as a woman of color from a politically controversial, postcolonial island.

I Was a Paradox: A Black *Cubana* in 1970s New York

> I caused a problem because it was impossible to understand how a radical black woman was also a Cuban exile. I was a paradox. What was a black Cubana doing in the middle of the effervescence of the 1970s?
> Lourdes Casal[52]

Lourdes Emilia de la Caridad Casal y Valdés (1938–1981) would have been sixty-six years old when I first started teaching at Rutgers University–Newark in 2002, where she taught undergraduate and graduate courses in the Psychology Department between 1972 and 1979.[53] But her life ended too quickly, when she was only forty-two, having returned to Havana exhausted by diabetes, and perhaps also terrified by death threats. In this same year, her progressive Cuban collaborators Carlos Muñiz Varela and Eulalio José Negrín Santos were assassinated by anti-Castro Cuban exile groups in San Juan, Puerto Rico, and Union City, New Jersey, respectively.[54] Her health and the stress of this historical moment in the North may have prompted her to plan to spend one month in Cuba. There her health deteriorated, and she remained until her death in February 1981 in Havana, where she is now buried next to José Martí's mother in the Panteón de los Emigrados Revolucionarios in the Cementerio Colón.

Neither the official version of Casal's uncomplicated return to the embrace of the *patria* that emerges in Cuban functionaries' discourses at her funeral, nor the portrait of her Marxist turn as one dubious "conversion" among many (and perhaps even a major error, according to her friends at the Instituto de Estudios Cubanos), fully captures in my mind how the shock of diaspora propelled Casal toward an uncompromising intersectional, interdisciplinary feminist and postcolonial critique. Casal's friend María Cristina Herrera at the IEC, and her former classmate Leonel de la Cuesta, coedited *Itinerario ideológico* (1982), the most complete anthology of Casal's writings to date. A debate about this anthology with ramifications for how we should remember Casal emerges in *Areíto* and demonstrates how Casal's intersectional commitments often surpassed the ability of any single readership to take stock of the implications of her feminist intervention and interdisciplinary method.[55]

While *Itinerario ideológico* gathers and disseminates Casal's scattered essays, stories, and poetry from her earliest to her deathbed writings, this volume depicts a partial view of Casal's life work.[56] The volume represents Casal's ideological shifts as "conversions" thus inscribing her within a religious framework. The anthology includes selections from her 1973 short fiction, which as the editors rightly judge, exceeded the bounds of Soviet-influenced socialist realism favored by the Cuban government in the 1970s. An editorial by the Consejo de Dirección—most likely drafted by Casal's friend and collaborator Marifeli Pérez-Stable—of *Areíto* critically reviews Herrera and de la Cuesta's anthology. While *Areíto* recognized the value of republishing Casal's early writings on Félix Varela and José Martí through her later work on the Caso Padilla, *Areíto*'s review notes how the anthology fails to represent Casal's writing life objectively, for the volume leaves out the key texts specifically from Casal's period of affiliation with the Cuban revolution (1977–1981). Casal's early texts usefully demonstrate her longstanding interrogation of the role of the intellectual in processes of revolutionary change. Among the late works not included in the anthology are the introduction to *Contra Viento y Marea: Grupo Areíto* (1978) and her critique of Roberto Fernández Retamar's influential essay, "Calibán," both of which illuminate Casal's revindication of critical perspectives informed by the "shock" of Cuban diaspora.[57]

While I agree with Areíto's Consejo de Dirección that the *Itinerario ideológico* seems lopsided, it is also true that the official Cuban burial ceremony in Havana elides indispensable elements of Casal's critical preoccupations. During the official internment of her body in the Mausoleum for Emigré Cubans, the director of Casas de las Americas, Roberto Fernández Retamar, praised Casal's revolutionary, patriotic self-sacrifice of herself for others. Lourdes Casal's poem "Cada uno tiene su Moncada" alludes to her commitment to a historical task that might include risking her life for a difficult-to-achieve revolutionary cause. But Retamar's characterization diminishes Casal's major contribution of articulating her perspective as a black Cuban feminist and focuses only on the conventional, much less threatening notion of her self-sacrifice: "Her sensitivity brought her to the discriminated black, the violated Vietnamese, to 'the poor of the earth,' with whom she forged a brotherhood, and for whom she suffered and struggled."[58] This portrayal of Casal as a self-sacrificing *criollo* or mestiza leader, in a tradition dating to Martí, tends to invisibilize Casal's blackness (and her gender and sexuality). It tends to distance her from the darker-skinned, suffering masses as if they were unnamed victims, not interlocutors, collaborators, made up of people like Casal. Retamar misrepresents Casal as suffering for someone or some group different from herself, as if she were not also black (and Chinese), and as if in Cuba the African-descended no longer faced particular forms of oppression, and therefore, could not legitimately speak of racism post-1961, the year of successful reforms to integrate public spaces, the workforce, and education, major achievements that led the Cuban government to proclaim that racism was no longer an issue in Cuba. Ironically, Retamar's failure to acknowledge or comment on Casal's groundbreaking English-language sociological studies of black Cubans in the diaspora and of race and gender relations in Cuba, resonates with the US-based critics who expressed dismay at Casal and Rafael Prohías's call to acknowledge a distinct category of a "Black Cuban" group in Miami, of people of color who suffered racism and discrimination at the hands of the white society and of white Cubans.[59] Casal's willingness to criticize racism in the white-dominant Creole cultures of Cuba and the United States leads her also to redefine the intellectual history of Cuba and of Latin America through critically interpreting a major thinker such as Roberto Fernández Retamar.

Lourdes Casal's Critique of Cuban Studies and of Roberto Fernández Retamar's "Caliban"

Throughout her career, Casal never refrained from articulating critical views in order to constructively contribute to the body of knowledge that became Cuban Studies, even when she differed from those in positions of relatively greater power. She had extraordinary mastery of so many bodies of knowledge related to Cuba that she prepared formidable book reviews and critically engaged—and thus made original contributions to—emerging interdisciplinary fields such as Cuban and Latin American studies at the point of their inception. In an essay entitled "The Development of Cuban Studies in the US," she exposed weaknesses in recent books about the Cuban revolution by citing the missing archives or research that would provide a more nuanced or complex understanding of the historical period or political processes in question. In this review of historiographies of Cuba, Casal shows how each book betrays its partisan views of the 1959 Cuban revolution and corrects at least four "gross errors of fact."[60] She exposes the "virulent anti-Communism" and "low-level psychologizing" of Jaime Suchlicki's history, *Cuba: From Columbus to Castro*; she observes how the Trotskyite filter of Samuel Farber's *Revolution and Reaction in Cuba, 1933–1960*, leads him to minimize the differences between Batista and Castro by problematically reducing them both to versions of Napoleon Bonaparte. Casal suggests Herbert S. Dinerstein cannot possibly capture the full history of the Cuban Missile Crisis because he only consults the newspaper *Hoy*—of the Partido Socialista Popular (or "old" Communist Party in Cuba)—and fails to consult *Revolución*, the organ of the 26th of July Movement, in his *The Making of a Missile Crisis*. Even when Casal endorses diaspora critic Louis Pérez's *Army Politics in Cuba, 1898–1958* as a model of careful scholarship that usefully explains the 1933 Cuban sergeants' revolt as an attempt to redress racism, she nonetheless takes him to task for not discussing further the role of the newly reconstituted (white-led) armed forces, linked as they were to extranational (and specifically US) military authorities, in the 1912 Race War.[61]

Casal's friend and contemporary Ana Veltfort notes in a 2007 interview that Casal had a penchant and a gift for exercising her critical faculty in print, even or especially when her friends—the people who wrote letters of recommendation for her, the people who had the task of publicly memorializing her—became the object of her critical investigation. Veltfort attributes this to both Casal's interest in broaching "taboo" subjects and to her deft diplomatic skill:

[Casal] did seem to want to be able to discuss things that were taboo on both sides of the big divide. The only way that she could make this work was by cultivating a very ambiguous persona—by making herself accessible and palatable to people with very diverse politics. She could talk with rabid right-wingers and orthodox Cuban government officials. She was a magnet for bringing people together, an able diplomat.[62]

A brilliant if ambiguous diplomat, Casal maintained close friendships with interlocutors of all political persuasions, even as she adopted a method of critical examination of both pro- and anti-Castro positions. Jorge I. Domínguez, professor of government at Harvard, memorialized Lourdes Casal by sharing with *Areíto* a letter of recommendation he wrote on her behalf in which he acknowledged their ideological differences: "Lourdes is a marxist—one of the most provocative, profound and subtle I know. . . . It is a pleasure to struggle intellectually with her."[63] Casal published a review in the *Wilson Quarterly* while holding the very fellowship she likely earned with the help of Domínguez's letter of reference, in which she points out a major limitation of Domínguez's book *Cuba: Order and Revolution* (1978).[64] By the same token, Casal's publicly acknowledged commitment to a Marxist revolutionary project did not mean that she would refrain from critically assessing leading Cuban government intellectuals and the Latin American intellectual tradition.

In her essay "Lo que dice Calibán" in response to Roberto Fernández Retamar, Casal raises a crucial question that still remains urgent today: How is it possible for the Cuban revolutionary society to continue to critically acknowledge and redress elitist and racially marked structures that "live on in the Republic" in Martí's formulation, even with the many advances of Cuban society since 1959? The hypothesis that guides many of Casal's writings from her doctoral dissertation to the end of her career presumes that the 1959 revolution is as yet incomplete. She claims that Retamar's influential article "Calibán" perhaps does not go far enough to define a Marxist aesthetic that might continue to acknowledge the proletarian, the racialized and gendered subaltern response to globally expanding bourgeois culture that—not surprisingly—continued to characterize aspects of the post-1959 revolutionary culture. Casal pushes Retamar's embrace of Calibán and his critique of the intellectual Ariel even further, suggesting the need "to assume our Caliban-esque condition, to brandish like a weapon, to wear like a feathered headdress of pride that which has been attributed to us as an insult: our character as a mixed people, radically *other* with respect to Europeans, although we have learned to speak their language, which serves us now to curse."[65] This passage, which does not appear in the edited reprint of Casal's interpretation of Retamar's influential essay in *Areíto* in 1984, acknowledges that in a sense Casal too speaks as a Caliban-esque figure and embraces a radical otherness to European or "white" culture that moves beyond the more palatable dichotomies of American-European or New-Old worlds.

Casal suggests that Retamar's famous essay, in its revision of José Enrique Rodó's reading of Shakespeare's *The Tempest*, backs down from a key implication of its own argument, that the culture of our América is not that of highly decorated salons, but of rebellious indigenous, African, and other radical intellectuals who allied themselves with them, as Retamar seems to claim in his essay "Calibán."[66] But Casal clarifies that the culture of "nuestra América" pertains to "the oppressed, in terms of class, and not in terms of geographic or national origin."[67] Indeed, Casal critically revises Martí's romanticizing of the autochthonous *mestizo* and redresses a tendency among Latin American writers to lose sight of a class critique while emphasizing New World cultural and aesthetic difference:

The question is not one of autochthony, spontaneity or novelty of things American, because the American, like the European, hides class differences behind general terminology, differences that thus become more entrenched. It is possible to affirm that, as dominant American classes have been almost completely penetrated by the ideologies and cultural forms of metropolitan dominant classes, what is American, by definition, is the culture elaborated by the oppressed masses, the culture where, like Caliban, we use the language of the oppressors, but transformed into a hybrid language, fused with indigenous, black and Chinese elements as a result of the mestizaje that defines who we are.[68]

Casal redefines "nuestra América" as the culture that does not derive from the elite, European-identified classes but from the creativity of the oppressed, working-class African, Asian, and indigenous, or some mestizo form therefrom, that in turn transforms language by hybridizing it. Making a groundbreaking observation of how racialized groups bear double or triple forms of oppression that reflects her acute awareness of the political significance of her often invisibilized perspective, Casal suggests that the revalorization of national culture contributes to a revolutionary project only insofar as it also engages questions of class transnationally and in light of imperial geopolitics. Casal privileges her radicalized "mestizo" over a romanticized and depoliticized view of the New World or "lo americano." Instead, she insists on the salience of race, class, and gender critique as indispensable knowledge in those sites where light-skinned and heterosexual masculine privilege still holds true, both in metropolitan centers and in the periphery. In light of her definition of a category of a gendered subaltern or a black Cuban subjectivity, it is fascinating that Casal nevertheless takes distance from the category of "la raza" in José Vasconcelos's sense, for she sees it as debilitating an international class critique and as slowing the process of forming alliances among differently racialized groups. By emphasizing a proletarian transnational socialist rather than nationalist culture in the post-revolutionary context, Casal echoes the communist DuBois, the revolutionary Langston Hughes, and the José Martí who admired and legitimized the transnational anarchist and working-class–identified Lucy Parsons.[69]

Retamar's response to Casal, which appeared in *Areíto* in 1981 after her death, sidesteps Casal's effort to broach the taboo subject of the prevailing European-descended and formerly class-privileged majority of revolutionary Cuba's leadership, and more broadly, of the region's political and intellectual elites in the 1970s and 1980s. Retamar belittles Casal's serious critique and its anti-racist implications by recalling the "accidental" publication of the article, and the "slightly absurd history" behind it that she mentions to him in correspondence. In insisting that Casal erroneously describes "nuestra América" as "really, the culture of the proletariat, socialist culture," Retamar sidesteps some of her most daring points, limiting himself to criticizing her main argument with extensive quotations from Lenin and Armando Hart Dávalos. To Casal, Retamar's "Calibán" does not fully clarify the relationship between class and culture, because in part Retamar writes as a "man of transition," that is, a product of a prerevolutionary tradition of letters formed in the context of a plantation economy and of dominant, yet unacknowledged, anti-African racism. To Casal, Retamar valiantly attempts to define a Marxist aesthetic, yet remains draped in the "out-of-date vestments" of a transition to a radically non-Eurocentric revolutionary culture.[70]

Moreover, Casal asserts the critical legitimacy and privileged vision of oppressed, in-between, and mixed minority groups, including Latinas/o who speak in Spanglish, precisely because a diaspora tradition sees single-issue, single-nation, or race-based organizing as a tool to prevent organized solidarity across borders of nation, language, and culture. Casal sees alliances across borders as necessary to undermine privileged national intellectual elites:

Perhaps it may be precisely in the interior of the United States, upon observing the evolution and destiny of movements of colonized minorities within this country who may see themselves and see with striking clarity the paradox: mobilization on "cultural" bases of oppressed ethnic groups entails various pitfalls. For example, the idolizing of "la raza," the genealogy of which takes us back to Vasconcelos, impairs a classist perspective, weakens (or makes impossible) the alliance with other oppressed groups—even among

Hispanics—and feeds a series of mystifications that obfuscate the struggle against the dominant classes.[71]

Even as Casal acknowledges the insufficiency of race as analytic, especially when it functions as essence pertaining to a single nation or finding expression in a single language, she defines the experience of racialization inside empire—what she refers to elsewhere as the "shock" of diaspora—as a source of insight into how national or racial categories can obfuscate a transnational, class-informed critique. Precisely at the moment she claims her "Hispanic Blackness," or what we might think of in Juan Flores and Miriam Jimenez Román's term as "Afro-latinidad," Casal begins to fully appreciate and make visible the factor of *décalage*—the time lag or spatial gap that marks the distance between the changed economic and political structures post-revolution and lingering consciousness and cultural beliefs that do not yet reflect revolutionary principles. The fictively antiracist nation and the white-privileged male-dominant Cuban elite (both on the island and in exile) often define themselves through elision of the gaps or denigration of the forms resulting from contact and contamination.

Casal, perceiving the gap, living in it, begs for translation and attention to *décalage*.[72] Casal uses this exact term to critically examine superstructural forms in which the revolution had not (yet) successfully generalized antisexist, antihomophobic, and antiracist consciousness as part of its revolutionary project. Casal's use of this term to explain the persistent hierarchies of class, racism, and masculinism in revolutionary society looks forward to Brent Hayes Edwards's deployment of this term for thinking about creating international collectivities in the African diaspora, or across gaps of geopolitical power, culture, and language.[73] Even as Casal transgressively left her place of exile and her youthful training in Catholic petit-bourgeois values in order to return to a struggling Caribbean country which had (or has) yet to come to grips with its racism, sexism, and homophobia, Casal's poetry, stories, and social science demonstrate her distance from the stilted, forced bourgeois rituals in which her family engaged as part of a brown professional class.[74] On the other hand, Casal's support for Cuba's revolution exists in tension with her outspoken feminist and antiracist history of publications and public speaking. Both her embrace of the revolution and her critique of it remain part of her legacy, albeit muffled by the silence of her subaltern position with respect to the revolution's antihomophobic discourse and institutions.[75] Casal's prescient intersectional critique crystallizes precisely at the time when her own liberal beliefs enter into crisis and historical forces propel her toward Cuba's revolutionary project.

I have suggested that Casal, like other Latina and "Third World" feminists of color, such as Gloria Anzaldúa and Cherríe Moraga of the US-Mexico borderlands, or Afro-Caribbean poet and essayist Audre Lorde, theorized the crossroads and the borderlands of discursive categories such as race, gender, sexuality, language, class, age, nationality, and religion before Kimberlé Crenshaw's influential concept became commonplace in feminist and antiracist cultural studies. Casal rightly belongs to this group of queer-of-color foremothers, just as we begin to recognize her contributions to Cuban, Cuban diaspora, and Afro-Cuban studies. Marked by her enduring experiences of displacement in the center of a capitalist empire, Casal declares the impossibility of ever fully returning or fully belonging here or there, even as she embraces Cuba's right to exist and makes Cuba her final destination.

The Intersectional Feminist and Diaspora Intellectual as Dangerous Individual

For Casal, an imminent shift in US-Cuban relations had direct implications for the way Cuban migrants might conceive of themselves as much more heterogeneous than was available in dominant representations of the Cuban exile community as model minority. An editorial in *Areíto* invites the Cuban diaspora—in North America or in other countries—to see itself as heterogeneous in racial, gender, and political terms, that is, not completely unified in its support for a US agenda or in idealizing the straight, male, and light-skinned dominant culture still prevalent in the United States, the Caribbean, and Latin America in the 1970s. In only its second year of publication, 1975, *Areíto* published "On the Reestablishment of Relations with Cuba," in which the editors conclude optimistically, "The end to Cuba's isolation is only a matter of time, perhaps just a few months."[76] While the projected dates are off, the implications of a shift in Cuban relations usefully recasts the "reluctant minority" of Cubans in the United States as a migrant Latina/o group like others that came before or afterward, a claim that another *Areíto* contributor and one of Casal's collaborators in Grupo Areíto, Román de la Campa, makes in his memoir.[77] The editorial conjures the Cuban exile community as a racialized group, whose status as such is "due to intense psycho-social forces, along with economic, historical and political causes."[78] Moreover, it contests the myth of a univocal exile community that tended to distort the Cuban diaspora's perceptions of its reality, according to an editorial to which Casal likely contributed: "The obsession with blocking Cuba, fed by exile media, only impedes us from analyzing the reality around us and acting upon that reality in consequence. Furthermore, this approach prevents us making common cause with segments of the North American people committed to change."[79] *Areíto*'s editorial positions the Cuban diasporic subject to see itself like others of racialized groups engaged at the time in black and brown civil rights and emancipatory movements—i.e., as subject to institutionalized discrimination. To acknowledge a divergence from a univocal, upwardly mobile, politically conservative Cuban exile group effectively criticizes the model minority myth, and turns toward dialogue and solidarity with migrant and racialized groups that were calling for radical changes within the United States and to US foreign policy in Latin America and the Caribbean.

By excavating examples of Lourdes Casal's formidable intellect, by adumbrating her arguments and expanding the scope of our knowledge of her ideological itinerary, I have proposed that Casal engages in interdisciplinary writing that now defines African diaspora, Latina/o, and feminist studies. In 1971, when Casal was on the verge of abandoning her anti-Castro exilic position for the quirky combination of feminist Marxism and socialism that she began to adopt after returning to Cuba in 1973, she affirmed the radical necessity of critique that arises through fearless intellectual struggle with ambiguity, and challenges us to also consider the no-man's-land of a politics that critically redefines the existing political traditions. In 1971, Casal calls our attention to a female-gendered intellectual and to her disruptive, probing function in both democratic and socialist societies:

the critical function of the intellectual, her fundamentally radical labor that places everything in question: the hard-headedness with which she insists—if she is a legitimate intellectual—upon analyzing all the aspects of a problem, upon seeking understanding of a problem in all of its ambiguity and confusion; her refusal to allow herself to be influenced by simplistic or manichean formulas, which always have the virtue of being the most convenient for maintaining 'peace and quiet' in society: all these characteristics make the intellectual a dangerous individual for the establishment of any regime, from Athenian democracy to Socialist Cuba.[80]

The work of New York Afro-Cuban diasporic feminist Lourdes Casal invites us to mourn and honor the groundbreaking interdisciplinarity and the refusal of dichotomies that accompanied Casal's assertion of the intellectual as a "dangerous individual," a term that we have come to associate with Michel Foucault's work on governmentality, and which Casal claims for her critical project. Casal's interstitial location in-between states brushes against the grain of Manichean white-black, male-female, English-Spanish, queer-straight, island-exile, democracy-socialism, nation-diaspora dichotomies. Incarnating the orisha who navigates the entry into the crossroads of exile or sickness and facilitates restoration, Casal contributed critical brilliance and diplomatic prowess to the process of opening a dialogue between the US and Cuban governments, a process that may come to fruition forty years later. But will Casal's politics, her practice of vigilant self-critique, her frank acknowledgement of racism in contemporary Cuba and the United States, and the confident articulation of non-heteronormative desire and feminist values be audible in a future

Cuba? And more challenging still, will her commitment to Latin America's sovereignty and self-determination continue to define the politics of Latina/o diaspora cultures?

NOTES

1. "Criticar es amar." Martí, "Echegaray," fragmentary notes to speech delivered at Liceo Artístico y Literario de Guanabacoa on June 21, 1879; reprinted in *Obras completas* 15:94.

2. Moraga, *Loving in the War Years*, 108.

3. "Lo que dice Calibán," *Areíto* 6.24 (1980): 44–46; reprinted in *Areíto* 9.36 (1984): 115–116. It is important to note that the reprinted 1984 version of this essay leaves out six paragraphs and incorporates changes Casal could not have authorized throughout. Unless otherwise noted, all translations are mine.

4. Roy S. Bryce-Laporte's beautiful obituary for Lourdes Casal in a volume which she helped to conceptualize but died without seeing invokes Casal's "spirit of daring and determination" as an Afro-Caribbean migrant scholar, which manifested even in her choice about where to die.

5. "Para Ana Veltford," *Areíto* 3.1 (1976): 52; reprinted in *Palabras juntan revolución*, 60–61; and *Norton Anthology of Latino Literature*, trans. David Frye, 1189–1190, translation modified. As Yolanda Martínez-San Miguel and Frances Negrón-Muntaner note, the last name was misspelled "Veldford" in the posthumous book. In an interview with the author and Iraida López in August 2015, Albor Ruiz commented that in fact the poem was untitled and the dedication mistakenly became known as the title.

6. See Iraida López's discussion in this dossier of the intimate relationship between Casal's "Memories of a Black Childhood" and her short fiction, "Los zapaticos me aprietan" and "Juegos," in which she draws on the same autobiographical memories in essay and in autobiographical fiction about her Chinese- and African-descended ancestors.

7. Foucault, "Truth and Power," 132.

8. Ibid.

9. Foucault, *History of Sexuality: Volume 1*, 159, speaks ironically about the injunction to discourse about sexuality that is a legacy of Christian asceticism and of Freudian psychology, both traditions with which Casal was intimately familiar: "Let us consider the stratagems by which we were induced to apply all our skills to discovering [sex's] secrets, by which we were attached to the obligation to draw out its truth, and made to feel guilty for having failed to recognize it for so long. . . . The irony of this deployment is in having us believe our 'liberation' is in the balance."

10. Casal, "Contemporary Race Relations in Cuba," 12.

11. According to the Rutgers University–Newark Annual Report of 1977, Casal presented a paper at the annual meeting of the International Studies Association in Toronto, February 1976: "The Bicultural Scholar in the Social Sciences" (Rutgers University Archives).

12. The classic texts that initiate this phase of Latina feminist writing include *This Bridge Called My Back: Writings by Radical Women of Color*, ed. Gloria Anzaldúa and Cherríe Moraga (1981); Moraga, *Loving in the War Years* (1983); Anzaldúa, *Borderlands/La Frontera* (1987). Black and Caribbean feminist contributions from this same period include Hull, Bell-Scott, and Smith, eds., *All the Women Are White, All the Blacks Are Men, but Some of us are Brave* (1982). Cf. Priya Kandaswamy, "Gendering Racial Formations," and Vanessa Pérez-Rosario, "Latina Feminist Theory and Writing," forthcoming in the *Cambridge History of Latina/o Literature* (2018).

13. See Tomás Fernández Robaina, *El Negro en Cuba*, and more recently, *Antología cubana del pensamiento antirracista*, which does not mention Lourdes Casal; Roberto Zurbano Torres,

"Cuba: doce dificultades para enfrentar al (neo)racismo," and Gloria Rolando's three-part documentary on the Partido Independiente de Color. Precursors to this contemporary effort include books by Rafael Formoselle and Aline Helg.

14. In addition to "Revolution and Conciencia: Women in Cuba," in which Casal studies masculinism in post-revolution Cuban society, see Casal's brilliant critique in "Reflections on the Conference on Women and Development: II."

15. Audre Lorde begins to publish her poetry with *The First Cities* (1968), *Cables to Rage* (1970), and *From a Land Where Other People Live* (1973), so she precedes Casal, who begins to publish her short stories and poetry in 1973. Anzaldúa and Moraga's *This Bridge Called My Back* (1981) coincides with Casal's poetry *Palabras juntan revolución* (1981).

16. See, for example, Yolanda Martínez-San Miguel's essay, "Fantasy as Identity," on Casal's inscriptions of queer and antiracist subjectivity. I am grateful to Yolanda for her groundbreaking work on Casal and for comments and suggestions from her and others on this chapter in Rutgers's "Archipelagos" seminar at the Center for Cultural Analysis, 2015–2016.

17. Kimberlé Crenshaw, "Mapping the Margins."

18. Jorge I. Domínguez, Harvard University professor of government, in discussion with the author and Iraida López, May 2016. Lourdes Casal interviewed by Margaret Randall in *Breaking the Silences* 124.

19. Muñoz, *Cruising Utopia.*

20. Casal, "Africa ante el problema cubano"; rpt. *Itinerario ideológico.*

21. Casal uses the Marxist term *pequeño-burguesa* (petit bourgeois) to identify her family's class position, due to her father's status as a medical doctor of color in "Los zapaticos me aprietan," *Los fundadores*, 34. This story suggests both the material comforts and certain psychic anguish that her privileged yet subaltern status created for Casal and her family, while they lived in the working class and black-dominant neighborhood of Havana, Los Sitios. In the yearbook, or Memoria, of Santo Tomás de Villanueva, Casal appears to the be only woman and the only person of color in the Department of Chemical Engineering.

22. "Problemas Hispanoamericanos" (for which Casal was awarded first place in the Concurso Literario), "El liberalismo del Padre Varela" (for which Casal was awarded second place in the Concurso Literario), "La mujer cristiana," and "Pio XII and el comunismo," first appeared in *Insula.* I am grateful to Ricardo Luis Hernández Otero for his detailed recovery of the early articles Casal published in university magazines such as *La Quincena, Insula,* and *El Quibú.*

23. Casal, "Entrevista with Susana Lee," 125.

24. de la Cuesta, "Perfíl," 5.

25. The Directorio Revolucionario Estudiantil (DRE) had two distinct iterations: first, in Cuba, as an anti-Batista student organization in which university students in Havana were active; second, as a group founded and funded by the Central Intelligence Agency in Miami, Florida. It is likely Casal was active in both iterations; the second group sponsored Casal's trip to Africa, according to Alberto Müller, who was interviewed by the author and Iraida López, June 2016. On CIA's role in founding the DRE in Miami, see CIA, "Directorio Revolucionario Estudiantil (DRE). doi: http://www.maryferrell.org/archive/docs/013/13958/images/img_13958_2_300.png.

26. In Casal, "Memories of a Black Cuban Childhood," (62), Casal reports how her companion in the delegation explained to her a translation of the scene in which Nigerian children were pointing at Casal and making comments that affected her deeply: "'You know . . . the children back there at the school . . . they were calling you white.' I almost collapsed, as if hit by a thunderbolt. White? They were calling me white?"

27. Casal, "Entrevista con Susana Lee," 126, my translation.

28. *Cuba nueva* published Casel's report, which conveys her sense that Africans had many concerns, but Communism wasn't one of them. But the leaders of the Consejo recalled and destroyed the publication. The revised published version placed her report after an article written by

the president of the Consejo. This experience in Miami led Casal to distance her position from the extreme right in Miami. Silvia Pedraza and Jorge I. Domínguez (2012) mention the effects of the trip to Africa and participation in social movements of the 1960s and 1970s as influential in Casal's transformation.

29. See Devyn Spence Benson, *Antiracism in Cuba*, for a generative history of anti-racist movements on the island. Although she notes the crucial role of *afrocubanas*, especially filmmaker Sara Gómez, the book cites Casal's 1979 essay without discussing her significance in detail, perhaps because Casal published her antiracist essays primarily in English and outside of Cuba.

30. Casal, "Memories of a Black Cuban Childhood," 62. In keeping with terminology introduced by members of Black power movements at the time, Casal used the capitalized form of this adjective, which I'm quoting here. In order to emphasize Casal's eventual interrogation of the notion of race as a category with some biological or scientifically significant basis, I don't maintain this capitalization throughout.

31. Ibid., 62, my emphasis. Antonio López mentions this essay by Casal in *Unbecoming Blackness*. We are all indebted to Iraida H. López, for disseminating this essay after learning about it from Mirtha Quintanales. I am also grateful to Iraida for curating this dossier and including this essay, which I first presented as the keynote address at the 2nd Biennial Latina/o Literary Theory and Criticism Conference, at John Jay College of Criminal Justice on April 23, 2015. I am grateful to Richard Pérez and Belinda Linn Rincón for that invitation.

32. See Chandan Reddy's useful history of the emergence of this so-called third world perspective in the context of student-of-color movements that resulted in the creation of an Ethnic Studies Department at San Francisco State University, in *Freedom with Violence*.

33. Anzaldúa, *Borderlands/La Frontera*, 59.

34. Moraga, *Loving in the War Years*, 99–100.

35. Moraga, *Loving in the War Years*, 103.

36. Anzaldúa, *Borderlands/La Frontera*, 41.

37. See Moraga's discussion of the feminist Malinchista in "A Long Line of Vendidas," 113, and Lorde's evocation of Paulo Freire in "Age, Race, Class and Sex," 123.

38. Lourdes Casal interviewed by Margaret Randall in *Breaking the Silences*, 124.

39. During secret "back channel" negotiations that included a meeting in New York's Pierre Hotel in 1975, Cuban Americans such as the Democratic leader Bernardo Benes helped to negotiate an opening of the island to Cuban family members in the diaspora, and New York-based Cubans sent letters appealing to the president and to Congress to restore opportunities for travel by exiled Cubans to the island. Kornbluh and LeoGrande mention the secret three-hour meeting at the New York Pierre Hotel in July 1975 in *Back Channel to Cuba*, 139. On Maceo brigades, see Teishan Latner, *Cuban Revolution in America*.

40. On Bernardo Benes's role, see especially Catherine Loiacano, "A 'Community' Divided," who cites the letter from the "New York Cubans," and gives the figure for released political prisoners as five thousand.

41. Nancy Morejón notes in her interview with Ruth Behar: "Nowadays it's easy to talk, but back then there were bombs and threats and more threats and more bombs, and anonymous notes, 'I'm going to cut your tongue out,' and 'I'm going to kill you because you went to Cuba'" (*Bridges to Cuba*, 135).

42. For example, in her essay "Literature and Society," she makes this critique of the repression of intellectuals in Cuba with a typically Casalian chiasmic rhetorical structure and mode of thinking: "Any presentation of the panorama of the first ten years of the Revolution as a paradise of freedom for writers and artists is false. However, it is also false to maintain a negative view of the impact of the Revolution on literature and culture in general" (458).

43. Casal and Prieto, "Cubans in the US," *Nueva Generación* (1972): 14n5.

44. William Luis, *Dance Between Two Cultures* and chapter in *Cambridge History of Latina/o Literature*.

45. Casal and Prohías, *Cuban Minority in the U.S.*, 7.

46. Casal likely witnessed or heard about the 1967 Newark rebellion, the black student take-over of Conklin Hall on the campus where Casal began teaching as an adjunct, and her poem, "Columbia, Sorbona. Primavera 1968," documents Casal's awareness of a radical impatience in pursuit of change through the global rebellions of 1968, which took root near her at Columbia University with the takeover of Hamilton Hall, located between the New School and her residence in Washington Heights.

47. Casal's hiring may in fact respond to the students' demands for more black and Latin@ faculty and curriculum during this period. See Elizabeth Parker and Yesenia López's exhibit, "Newark '74: The Puerto Rican Riots—An Unexamined History," www.GardenStateLegacy.com Special Nov. 2014. The history of these riots is still being written. I am indebted to Olga Jiménez de Wagenheim's oral histories and personal account of this period in conjunction with an exhibit at Dana Library organized by the Latina/o Studies Working Group, at Rutgers University–Newark on February 3, 2016. The Rutgers University archives of the Newark Provost's inactive files document the struggles of the Federación Estudiantil Latino Americano (FELA) and the Puerto Rican Orga-nization (PRO) for office space, for more Latina/o faculty and staff, and for a Puerto Rican Studies and Latin American Studies Program, record groups N1/A0/4 and N1/A0/8 in Rutgers University Archives and Special Collections.

48. Latner, *Cuban Revolution in America*.

49. Casal, "Recognizing Our Roots," 40.

50. Cf. Casal, "Conversación en Pittsburgh," where she refers to how the assassination of Allende and others overshadowed an academic conference in Pittsburgh and augured "la muerte del sueño liberal (the death of the liberal dream)," *Palabras juntan revolución*, 63.

51. Casal, "Reflections on the Conference on Women and Development: II," *Signs* 3.1 (1977): 317.

52. "Yo causaba un problema porque no se entendía cómo una negra radical era también una exiliada de Cuba. Era una paradoja. ¿Qué hacía una negra cubana en el medio de la efervescencia de los setenta?" "Entrevista con Susana Lee," *Areíto* 9.36 (1984): 126.

53. According to Rutgers University–Newark course catalogues between 1972 and 1979, Casal was instructor for the 200-level Introduction to Social Psychology, and two upper-level courses: History and Modern Viewpoints in Psychology ("a critical study of schools of psycho-logical thought including behaviorism, learning theory, psychoanalysis, gestalt psychology, cog-nitive psychology, existentialism and Russian psychology") and Laboratory in Social Psychol-ogy, according to the *Bulletins of the Newark College of Arts and Sciences* for 1972–1973 and 1974–1975.

54. According to David Vidal, Negrín died at the hands of anti-Castro militants affiliated with a vigilante terrorist organization that referred to itself as Omega 7, which was a counterpart of Co-mando Cero, a parallel organization in San Juan, Puerto Rico. These groups assumed responsibility for thirteen bombings in the Northeastern region, including the killing of former Chilean ambas-sador Orlando Letelier, in Washington, DC, and a bomb, detonated before takeoff at JFK airport on March 25, 1979. These terrorist organizations carried out attacks on Cubans in exile who supported dialogue and family reunification. In Orwellian fashion, the terrorist groups were subsections of the two principal organizations in New Jersey: the Bloc of Cuban Revolutionary Organizations and the Cuban Nationalist Movement. Miguel de Dios Unanue, a Cuban reporter, received death threats for attempting to investigate the terrorist organizations on US soil. David Vidal, "In Union City, Memories of the Bay of Pigs Don't Die," *New York Times*, December 2, 1979, E9. Casal was working on a book about US-sponsored terrorism among Cuban exiles at the time of her death.

55. *Areíto* was founded by Casal and other progressive Cuban exiles to form connections among and give voice to a geographically scattered and heterogeneous Cuban and Latin American diaspora. The journal highlighted politically progressive Cuban, Latina/o, and Latin American culture in poetry, stories, and reportage in order to chart the heterogeneity of Cubans in exile. Taking its title from colonial chronicler Fernández de Oviedo's *Historia general y natural de las Indias, Areíto* refers to a way the original inhabitants of Cuba would commemorate the past in the present in order to define a collective future. The *areíto*, we learn, was a festivity of excess, a performance, and a story, feared by the European Catholic colonizers who sought to eradicate this Taíno practice of collective cultural self-preservation in the sixteenth century. See Jenna Leving Jacobson's essay in this volume for a description of the journal.

56. Because Casal dedicated herself to many editorial projects, journalism, and co-authored essays, we might erroneously assume that Casal's writerly corpus consists of only one single-authored book of poetry and one volume of stories. A complete bibliography is forthcoming in the anthology of Casal's writings edited by López and myself.

57. In 1981, *Areíto*'s Consejo de Dirección included Max Azicri, Emilio Bejel, Lourdes Casal, Marifeli Pérez-Stable, Yolanda Prieto, Eliana Rivero, Albor Ruiz, and José Ramón Villalón. The essay, "El Instituto de Estudios Cubanos o los estrechos límites del pluralismo," appears in *Areíto* 9.33 (1983): 4–6. *Contra Viento y Marea: Grupo Areíto*, which won an "extraordinary" Casa de las Américas Award in 1978, traces the emergence of the magazine *Areíto* in conversations among young liberal and progressive Cuban youth in Union City, New Jersey, who began to connect with peers engaged in similar discussions about Cuba and the Revolution across the United States, from Madison, Wisconsin, to San Juan, Puerto Rico. The Comité de Redacción for this collectively written book included Román de la Campa, Lourdes Casal, Vicente Dopico, and Margarita Lejarza.

58. "Su sensibilidad la llevó al negro discriminado, al vietnamita agredido, a 'los pobres de la tierra,' con los que se hermanó y por los que padeció y luchó," in "Palabras de Roberto Fernández Retamar en el entierro de la compañera Lourdes Casal, el 3 de febrero de 1981," *Areíto* 7.26 (1981), 5. Casal, "Cada uno tiene su Moncada," *Palabras juntan revolución*, 69.

59. An article in the first issue of Areíto, for example, notes a controversy that erupted around a short section of the study entitled "The Invisible Cubans," which argues that black Cubans constitute "a highly at-risk group, potentially a victim of double or triple discrimination (in the case of poor black Cubans)" (Prohías and Casal, 101), due to housing discrimination which they faced at the hands of white Cubans and white non-Cubans. Prohías and Casal note that "there seem to be certain normative forces within the Cuban refugee community tending to deny the existence of racial problems in pre-revolutionary Cuba (Rogg 1972) and among exiles" (98).

60. Casal, "The Development of Cuban Studies," 253.

61. See discussion in Casal, "Race Relations in Contemporary Cuba," 13–14 and 25n21.

62. Veltfort, quoted in Martínez-San Miguel and Negrón-Muntaner, 76.

63. Jorge I. Domínguez, "To Abe Lowenthal," Nov. 14, 1977; reprinted in "Testimonios," *Areíto* 7.26 (1981): 18.

64. Casal asks the simple question: how can he sustain a critique of a Marxist-Leninist revolution when he makes not a single reference to either Marx or Lenin? See her "Review of Jorge I. Domínguez, *Cuba: Order and Revolution.*"

65. Casal, "Lo que dice Caliban," 44.

66. Fernández Retamar, "Calibán: Apuntes," 77.

67. Casal, "Lo que dice Calibán," 45.

68. Ibid.

69. See Lomas, "'El negro es tan capaz como el blanco': José Martí and the Politics of Late-Nineteenth Century Latinidad."

70. While Casal would agree with Retamar who echoes José Zacarías Tallet (and José Emilio Pachéco) that we are all in transition, Casal also concurs with Ernesto "Che" Guevara in this critical re-reading of Retamar's famous essay in which she notes that Retamar is limited by his privileged formation: "Heredero de una vertiente culturalista de larga tradición en las letras américanas, tradición que arranca en el siglo diecinueve, y culmina en él. . . . [E]s obvio que no ha logrado desembarazarse de los viejos ropajes y el producto es un híbrido que nos deja insatisfechos, porque se le ven las forzadas costuras" (Casal, "Lo que dice Calibán," 45–46). In other words, the process of becoming differs significantly depending on the locus of departure, and that locus is marked by color, language, class and educational training, gender, etc. Casal makes ironic reference to Retamar's poem, "Ud. tenía razón, Tallet," 33. Thanks to Rafael Rojas for pointing me to this poem.

71. "Quizás sea precisamente en el interior de los Estados Unidos, al observar la evolución y destino de los movimientos de las minorías colonizadas dentro de este país que pueda verse con meridiana claridad la paradoja: la movilización sobre bases 'culturales' de los grupos étnicos oprimidos entraña varias trampas. Por ejemplo, la idolización de 'la raza,' cuya genealogía puede trazarse a Vasconcelos, desvirtúa la perspectiva clasista, debilita (o imposibilita) la alianza con otros grupos oprimidos —aún hispanos—, y da pábulo a una serie de mitificaciones que dificultan la lucha contra las clases dominantes," in Casal, "Lo que dice Calibán," 115–116.

72. Casal, "Revolution and conciencia: Women in Cuba," 183; and Casal, "Race Relations in Contemporary Cuba," 24. See Robyn Grant's award-winning undergraduate honors thesis, "But who will do the dishes: Negotiating socialism with femininity in *Mujeres* magazine, Cuba, 1961–1965," for a mention of Casal's theorizing of the relations between Marxism and feminism in "Revolution and conciencia." Thanks to Jacqueline Loss for pointing me to Grant's thesis.

73. While Brent Hayes Edwards complicates the conventional Marxist use of the term *décalage* in *The Practice of Diaspora* (14), his emphasis on the heterogeneity of the African diaspora echoes Casal's adaptation of Louis Althusser's deployment of this term to refer to the lagging behind of consciousness and cultural forms, despite economic and political changes in the wake of revolution.

74. See Casal, "Los zapaticos me aprietan," and "Salvador en cuatro tiempos," which includes a vignette on Susana, a woman who carries a dildo in her purse.

75. Yolanda Martínez-San Miguel and Frances Negrón-Muntaner call attention to Casal's marked silence, and her epistolary expressions of a desire to acknowledge the violent homophobia of Cuba, in their indispensable interview and essay, "In Search of Lourdes Casal's Ana Veltford."

76. "Sobre el reestablecimiento de relaciones con Cuba: Editorial," *Areíto* 2.1–3 (1975): 2.

77. de la Campa, Román, *Cuba on My Mind: Journeys to Severed Nation* (2001), 3, 7, 106–122.

78. "Editorial," 3.

79. Ibid.

80. Casal, "Opinión," *Nueva Generación*; reprinted in *Itinerario Ideológico*, 66.

BIBLIOGRAPHY

Anzaldúa, Gloria. *Borderlands/La Frontera: The New Mestiza*. San Francisco: Aunt Lute Books, 1999.

Anzaldúa, Gloria, and Cherríe Moraga, eds. *This Bridge Called My Back: Writings by Radical Women of Color*. New York: Kitchen Table Women of Color Press, 1981.

Behar, Ruth, ed. *Bridges to Cuba/Puentes a Cuba*. Ann Arbor: University of Michigan Press, 1995.

Benson, Devyn Spence. *Antiracism in Cuba: The Unfinished Revolution.* Chapel Hill: University of North Carolina Press, 2016.

Bryce-Laporte, Roy S. "Obituary to a Female Immigrant and Scholar: Lourdes Casal (1938–1981)." In Delores M. Mortimer and Roy S. Bryce-Laporte, eds. *Female Immigrants to the United States: Caribbean, Latin American and African Experiences.* Washington, DC: RIIES Occasional Papers No. 2, Research Institute on Immigration and Ethnic Studies, Smithsonian Institution, 1981. 349–355.

Casal, Lourdes. "Africa ante el problema cubano." *Cuba nueva* 1 (1962): 11–17.

_____. "Cubans in the United States: Their Impact on US-Cuba Relations," Martin Weinstein, ed., *Revolutionary Cuba in the World Arena.* Philadelphia: Institute for the Study of Human Issues, 1979.

_____. "Cubans in the US." *Nueva Generación.* 3–4. 24–26 (1972): 6–20.

_____. "The Development of Cuban Studies in the US." *Latin American Research Review.* 13.1 (1978): 248–254.

_____. "Entrevista con Susana Lee." *Areíto* 9.36 (1984): 124–127.

_____. "For Ana Veltford." Trans. David Frye. Ilan Stavans et al., ed. *The Norton Anthology of Latino Literature.* New York: W.W. Norton and Co., 2011. 1189–1190.

_____. "Literature and Society." *Revolutionary Change in Cuba,* ed. Carmelo Mesa-Lago. Pittsburgh, PA: University of Pittsburgh Press, 1971. 447–469.

_____. "Lo que dice Calibán." *Areíto* 6.24 (1980); reprinted slightly abridged, *Areíto* 9.36 (1981): 115–116.

_____. "Memories of a Black Cuban Childhood." *Nuestro* 2.4 (1978): 61–62.

_____. "On Popular Power: The Organization of the Cuban State during the Period of Transition." *Latin American Perspectives* 2.4 (1975): 78–88.

_____. "Opinión." Editorial *Nueva Generación* 22–23 (1971); reprinted in *Itinerario ideológico,* 65–68.

_____. "Race Relations in Contemporary Cuba." Anani Dzidizenyo and Lourdes Casal, *The Position of Blacks in Brazilian and Cuban Society.* London: Minority Rights Group, 1979.

_____. "Recognizing Our Roots." *Nuestro* (April 1977): 39–40.

_____. "Reflections on the Conference on Women and Development: II." *Signs* 3.1 (1977): 317–319.

_____. "Review of Jorge I. Domínguez, *Cuba: Order and Revolution.*" *Wilson Quarterly* (Spring 1949): 148–149.

_____. "Revolution and *Conciencia*: Women in Cuba." Carol R. Berkin and Clara M. Lovett, eds. *Women, War and Revolution.* New York: Holmes and Meier Publishers. 1980. 183–206.

_____. "Revolution and Race: Blacks in Contemporary Cuba" Working Papers, Woodrow Wilson International Center for Scholars, 39. Washington, DC: Woodrow Wilson Center, Latin American Program, 1979. 1–29.

_____. *Images of Cuban Society among Pre- and Post-revolutionary Novelists.* Doctoral Dissertation, New School for Social Research, 1975.

_____. *Itinerario ideológico: Antología.* Miami: Instituto de Estudios Cubanos, 1982.

_____. *El caso Padilla: Literatura y revolución en Cuba.* Miami: Ediciones Universal, 1971.

_____. *Los fundadores: Alfonso y otros cuentos.* Miami: Ediciones Universal, 1973.

_____. *Palabras juntan revolución.* Havana: Casa de las Américas, 1981.

Casal, Lourdes, with assistance of Yolanda Prieto. "Black Cubans in the United States: Basic Demographic Information." Delores M. Mortimer and Roy S. Bryce-Laporte, eds. *Female Immigrants to the United States.* 314–348.

Casal, Lourdes, and Rafael J. Prohías. *The Cuban Minority in the US: Preliminary Report on Need Identification and Program Evaluation.* Boca Raton: Florida Atlantic University, 1973; reprinted in New York: Arno Press 1980.

Consejo de Dirección de Areíto. "El Instituto de Estudios Cubanos o los estrechos límites del pluralismo." *Areíto* 9.36 (1984): 120–122.

Consejo de Dirección y la Brigada Antonio Maceo, 3 de febrero de 1981. "Homenaje a Lourdes Casal." *Areíto* 7.26 (1981): 6.

Crenshaw, Kimberlé. "Mapping the Margins: Intersectionality, Identity Politics, and Violence against Women of Color." *Stanford Law Review* 43.6 (1991): 1241–1299.

DeCosta-Willis, Miriam. *Daughters of the Diaspora: Afra-Hispanic Writers*. Kingston: Ian Randle Publishers, 2003.

De la Campa, Román. *Cuba on My Mind: Journeys to a Severed Nation*. London: Verso 2000.

De la Cuesta, Leonel. "Perfil biográfico." María Cristina Herrera and Leonel Antonio de la Cuesta, eds. *Itinerario ideológico: Antología*. Miami: Instituto de Estudios Cubanos, 1982.

Domínguez, Jorge I. "To Abe Lowenthal" (Nov. 14, 1977); reprinted in "Testimonios," *Areíto* 7.26 (1981): 18.

———. "Reshaping the Relations between the United States and Cuba." *Debating US-Cuban Relations: Shall We Play Ball?* Eds. Jorge I. Domínguez, Rafael Hernández, and Lorena Barbería. London: Routledge, 2012.

Edwards, Brent Hayes. *The Practice of Diaspora: Literature, Translation and the Rise of Black Internationalism*. Cambridge: Harvard University Press, 2003.

Fermoselle y López, Rafael. *Política y color en Cuba*. Montevideo: Ediciones Geminis, 1974.

Fernández Retamar, Roberto. "Palabras de Roberto Fernández Retamar en el entierro de la compañera Lourdes Casal, el 3 de febrero de 1981," *Areíto* 7.26 (1981): 4–5.

———. "Otra conversación con Lourdes Casal." *Areíto* 9.36 (1981): 117.

———. "Ud. tenía razón Tallet: Somos hombres de transición." *Antología personal*. México, DF: Siglo XXI, 2007. 33–35.

———. *Calibán y otros ensayos: Nuestra América y el mundo*. Havana: Editorial Arte y Literatura, 1979.

———. "Caliban: Notes Toward a Discussion of Culture in Our America." *Caliban and Other Essays*. Trans. Edward Baker, foreword by Fredric Jameson. Minneapolis: University of Minnesota Press, 1989. 3–45.

Fernández Robaina, Tomás. *Antología cubana del pensamiento antirracista*. Camagüey: Editorial Acana, 2015.

———. *El negro en Cuba: Apuntes para la historia de la lucha contra la discriminación racial (1900–1958)*. 2nd ed. La Habana: Editorial Ciencias Sociales, 1994.

Flores, Juan and Miriam Jiménez Román, eds. *The Afro-Latin@ Reader: History and Culture in the United States*. Duke University Press, 2010.

Foucault, Michel. "Truth and Power." *Power/Knowledge: Selected Interviews & Other Writings 1972–1977*. Ed. Colin Gordon. Trans. Colin Gordon, Leo Marshall, John Mepham, and Kate Soper. New York: Pantheon Books. 109–133.

———. *The History of Sexuality: Volume 1, An Introduction*. Trans. Robert Hurley. New York: Random House, 1978.

Grant, Robyn. "But who will do the dishes: Negotiating socialism with femininity in *Mujeres* magazine, Cuba, 1961–1965." Undergraduate honor's thesis, 2011. University of Notre Dame. http://genderstudies.nd.edu/undergraduate-program/writing-prizes/thesis-award-recipients/.

Grupo Areíto. *Contra viento y marea: Grupo Areíto*. Habana: Casa de las Américas, 1978.

Helg, Aline. *Our Rightful Share: The Afro-Cuban Struggle for Equality, 1868–1912*. Chapel Hill: University of North Carolina Press, 1995.

Herrera, María Cristina. "Lourdes Casal." *Oxford Encyclopedia of Latinos and Latinas in the United States*. Suzanne Oboler and Deena González, eds. Oxford: Oxford University Press, 2005. 274–275.

Hull, Gloria T., Patricia Bell-Scott, and Barbara Smith, eds. *All the Women Are White, All the Blacks Are Men, but Some of Us Are Brave: Black Women's Studies*. Old Westbury, NY: The Feminist Press, 1982.

Kandaswamy, Priya. "Gendering Racial Formation." *Racial Formation in the Twenty-First Century*. Ed. Daniel Martinez HoSang, Oneka LaBennett, and Laura Pulido. Berkeley: University of California Press, 2012. 23–43.

Kornbluh, Peter, and William M. LeoGrande. *Back Channel to Cuba: The Hidden History of Negotiations between Washington and Havana*. Chapel Hill: University of North Carolina Press, 2014.

Latner, Teishan, *Cuban Revolution in America: Havana and the Making of a United States Left, 1968–1992*. Chapel Hill: University of North Carolina Press, 2018.

Loiacana, Catherine. "A 'Community' Divided: Cuban-American Attempts to Influence Jimmy Carter's Cuba Policy, January 1977–May 1978." *American Diplomacy* (September 2010). http://www.unc.edu/depts/diplomat/.

Lomas, Laura. "'El negro es tan capaz como el blanco': José Martí and the Politics of Late-Nineteenth Century *Latinidad*." Jesse Alemán and Rodrigo Lazo, eds. *The Latino Nineteenth Century*. New York: New York University Press, 2016.

López, Antonio. *Unbecoming Blackness: The Diaspora Cultures of Afro-Cuban America*. New York: New York University Press, 2012.

López, Iraida H. "De *Alacrán Azul* a *Apuntes posmodernos*: Exilio, etnicidad y diáspora cubana." *Revista Iberoamericana* 70.207 (2004 April–June): 455–71.

Lorde, Audre. "Age, Race, Class and Sex: Women Redefining Difference," paper first presented at the Copeland Colloquium, Amherst College, 1980; reprinted in *Zami, Sister Outsider, Undersong*. New York: Quality Paperback Book Club, 1993. 114–123.

Luis, William. *Dance Between Two Cultures: Latino Caribbean Literature Written in the United States*. Vanderbilt University Press, 1997.

———. "Cuban American Counterpoint: The Heterogeneity of Cuban American Literature, Culture, and Politics." In *Cambridge History of Latina/o American Literature*, edited by John Moran González and Laura Lomas. Cambridge: Cambridge University Press, forthcoming.

Martí, José. *Obras completas*. 28 vols. Havana: Editorial de Ciencias Sociales, 1963–1973.

Martínez-San Miguel, Yolanda. "Fantasy as Identity: Beyond Foundational Narratives in Lourdes Casal," *Cuban Studies* 45 (2017): 91–114.

Martínez-San Miguel, Yolanda, and Frances Negrón-Muntaner. "In Search of Lourdes Casal's 'Ana Veltford'" *Social Text* 92 (2007): 57–84.

Moraga, Cherríe. *Loving in the War Years: Lo que nunca pasó por sus labios*. Boston: South End Press, 1983.

Muñoz, José. *Cruising Utopia: The Then and There of Queer Futurity*. New York: New York University Press, 2009.

Pedraza, Silvia. "Cuba's Refugees: Manifold Migrations." *Cuban Communism: 1959–2003*. Eds. Irving Louis Horowitz, Jaime Suchlicki, 11th ed. New Brunswick, NJ: Transaction Publishers, 2003. 308–328.

Pérez, Louis A. *Army Politics in the Cuban Republic, 1902–1958*. Pittsburgh: University of Pittsburgh Press, 1976.

Pérez-Rosario, Vanessa. "Latina Feminist Theory and Writing." *Cambridge History of Latina/o Literature*. Cambridge: Cambridge University Press, 2018.

Randall, Margaret. "Lourdes Casal." *Breaking the Silences: An Anthology of 20th-Century Poetry by Cuban Women*. Vancouver: Pulp Press, 1982.

Reddy, Chandan. *Freedom with Violence: Sexuality and the US State*. Durham, NC: Duke University Press, 2011.

Vasconcelos, José. *La raza cósmica: Misión de la raza iberoamericana, notas de viajes a la américa del sur.* Paris: Agencia Mundial de Librería, 1920.

Zurbano, Roberto. "Cuba: Doce dificultades para enfrentar al (neo)racismo o doce razones para abrir el (otro) debate." *Universidad de la Habana* 273 (2012): 266–277.

JENNA LEVING JACOBSON

Race and Reconciliation in the Work of Lourdes Casal

ABSTRACT

This essay explores constructions of racial identity in Lourdes Casal's work leading up to, and with, Grupo Areíto and the Brigada Antonio Maceo. Casal's conceptualizations of race were deeply informed by national and historical notions of identity and belonging. Evidenced in the texts examined here, Casal draws from her African and Chinese ancestry while also identifying with Cuba's indigenous heritage. By considering the composition of her own racial identity at a moment in which Lourdes Casal labored for a reconciliation between herself, her diasporic community, and her island homeland, this essay also proposes a historical comparison to the current moment of possible rapprochement between two countries still struggling with racism.

RESUMEN

Este ensayo indaga sobre la construcción de la identidad racial en la obra de Lourdes Casal, específicamente durante la época del Grupo Areíto y la Brigada Antonio Maceo. La forma en que Casal conceptualizaba la identidad racial se informaba profundamente por las nociones nacionales-históricas de identidad y pertenencia. Evidente en los textos estudiados en el presente ensayo, Casal se apoya sobre sus descendencias africana y china, mientras también asume una identificación con la herencia indígena de Cuba. Al considerar la composición de su propia identidad racial mientras Lourdes Casal luchaba por una reconciliación entre su isla natal, su comunidad diaspórica y sí misma, este ensayo también propone una comparación histórica para algunas de las problemáticas apremiantes del momento actual del posible acercamiento entre dos países que todavía lucha con el racismo.

In the thick of the media storm that followed the December 17, 2014, announcements of intentions to normalize US-Cuban diplomatic relations, *The Root* published a piece that circulated widely titled "Black Cubans: Restoring US Ties Is Cool, but America, Keep Your Hang-Ups About Race at Bay." Aside from relying on some problematic generalizations, the article communicated two familiar arguments: first, Cuba's racial "hangups" aren't as dangerous as the racism that plagues the United States, and second, it highlights the historically assumed primacy of nationalism over race as constitutive of Cuban identity. Moreover, the article's interviews of black Cubans (almost exclusively

39

of folks who were not living in Cuba) were framed by this new potential for reunification of the Cuban communities in the United States and on the island. But recent events are not the first steps toward such reunification, nor did the December 17 announcements introduce the notion that race has played a troubling part in Cuba's encounters with its North American diaspora. As is well-documented, the first post-1959 *reencuentro* between the island and exile communities—the formation of the Brigada Antonio Maceo and subsequent Dialogues in the late 1970s—took place primarily as a result of Lourdes Casal's individual commitment to reestablishing a relationship with her homeland. As a means of exploring the role of race in those first significant encounters between the two communities, this essay will discuss constructions of racial identity in Casal's work leading up to, and with, Grupo Areíto and the Brigada Antonio Maceo, and accordingly serve as a historical comparison for some of the pressing questions of this moment of transition.[1]

In complement to the other contributions to this dossier, it is warranted to first pause to consider the ways in which Lourdes Casal composed her own racial identity, and the extent to which the contours of that composition conditioned her notion of a national, Cuban identity. One may instinctively recall that famous final verse from her most studied and recited poem, "Para Ana Veltfort," in which the poetic voice qualifies her marginality as:

> demasiado habanera para ser newyorkina,
> demasiado newyorkina para ser,
> —aún volver a ser—
> cualquier otra cosa (61).[2]

This expression of an uneasy duality has proven easy to lift, cite, and study independently from her other creative and academic work where she was likewise concerned with her identity. But doing so has restricted scholarly examination of a hybridity that should complicate the simple, deceptively stable, homeland-exile binary.[3] As will be illustrated, Casal's writing draws from her African and Chinese ancestry, while also assuming an identification with an indigenous heritage as, I propose, her own conceptualizations of racial identity were deeply informed by an understanding of national and historical notions of identity and belonging.

Having enjoyed the privileges of a middle-class upbringing and a private education in Cuba, Lourdes Casal developed a sense of her own blackness in exile;[4] it was the place where "mi color me define más que mi cultura." As described in the Spanish-language epilogue to her 1978 English-language essay "Memories of a Black Cuban Childhood," the personal experience of first noticing her skin color and hair texture in the United States, paired with her dedication to civil rights activism, became an entry point to creative, scholarly, and

solidarity work on black issues (61–62).[5] While her political radicalization facilitated an ideological reconnection with revolutionary Cuba, it is important to
remember that Casal was critical not only of the discrimination she witnessed
and experienced in the United States, but also of her homeland's misremem-
bering of its own troubled history. In reference to the 1912 massacre, she wrote
of the "conspiracy of silence" that erased the violence committed against black
Cubans, including her own family members. Afro-Cuban bodies were wiped
out, as was the memory of their massacre, kept as what she called "unspeakable secrets" of the country's history (Dzidzienyo and Casal, *The Position of
Black People*, 12). Though the critiques are framed historically rather than in
confrontation with lingering postrevolutionary racism, her indignation toward
the suppressing of her homeland's historical memory becomes problematic,
given that her attention to questions of race permitted certain erasure of issues
such as homophobia and censorship, taboo in Cuba's political climate of the
1970s. And Casal engages with these difficult, complex questions of race, arguably at the expense of other aspects of her own identity that would have been
more dangerous at the time, and that would afford her no political currency
toward her broader agenda of reintegration with Cuba. The renegotiation of her
blackness, activated by confronting direct discrimination in her US exile, along
with the deep process of ideological radicalization that precipitated her activism, enabled Casal to mobilize her racial difference for political gain on the island. Because while being black in the United States meant a violent struggle,
revolutionary Cuba was publicly celebrating its African heritage as part of both
its official mythology of racial equality through socialist revolution, along with
a simultaneous campaign to justify military interventions in Africa (as well as
connect with larger, more global cultural movements of the 1970s). This is to
underscore the irony of how the blackness that became so important to defining
her Cubanness was strongly cultivated in exile.

During the process of her political turn to the radical left, and therein her
turn to revolutionary Cuba, Casal also explored her Afro-Cuban identity in her
creative writing by returning to her childhood, mining her memories for evidence of these roots. Throughout *Palabras juntan revolución*, her collection of
poems posthumously published in 1981, she alternately juxtaposes the dominant landscapes of her life: the Havana of her childhood with the New York of
her young adulthood. She reconstructs her homeland by writing the domestic
spaces and practices of her childhood, marked by quotidian spirituality, family
rituals, and beliefs. She describes the presence of Eleggua and Ebbo the "mensajero de mi madre con sus palomas y signos y viejas encantaciones [. . .] me
protege," visits from Obbatalá "con sus ropajes blancos," and from Yemayá,
who brought sounds that frightened "a mis ojos infantiles" (Casal, *Palabras*,
14, 13, 106). Her Havana childhood inscribed with Afro-Cuban traditions is
not exoticized, but domesticized; the orishas are present at birthday parties,

at dances, and in the family home. Casal carefully relies on the safely remote frame of childhood to explore the problems of race and class that will trouble her in the adult moment of its writing. And by establishing the lived connection between her origins and specifically Cuban blackness, Casal further solidifies her national belonging through poetically constructing a black identity.

Casal's writing furthermore recuperates her Chinese ancestry, telling the story of Chinese migration to Cuba in the short story "Los fundadores: Alfonso," where she narrates her family history as a national history, as a way of celebrating her own ancestors' nearly forgotten protagonism in Cuban history (Casal, *Los fundadores*, 17–37). Casal makes intentional reference to the Taiping Rebellion as a revolution against "la aristocracia imperial [. . .] a la propiedad privada [. . .] a los terratenientes" in affirmation of "la reforma agraria, a la igualdad de la mujer" and of "un milenarismo revolucionario [. . .] Los Taipings creían que su misión era crear un cielo en la tierra—el reino de la Gran Paz, que proclamaron solemnemente en Nanking, al tomarla en 1853" (Casal, "Los fundadores," 23). Casal structures the text to situate herself and her family history into a larger teleology of revolution beyond a specifically Cuban nationalism, but within a grand narrative congruent to that of the socialist utopia and Socialist New Man imagined in her contemporary notions of heroism, again, employing her racial identity to position herself politically. Not an insincere gesture of her ideology at that moment, Casal moved to recuperate her Cubanness through an articulation of her race, specifically here by reclaiming revolutionary roots in her Chinese ancestry.

She makes a similar rhetorical move by assuming her homeland's indigenous patrimony, despite never biographically identifying any native Taíno or Siboney genealogy. In an untitled poem, Casal's poetic voice meditates over the feeling of belonging to her homeland, stating:

> Vivo en Cuba.
> Siempre he vivido en Cuba,
> aún cuando he creído habitar,
> muy lejos del caimán de la agonía
> siempre he vivido en Cuba. (Casal, *Palabras*, 105)

This Cuba she belongs to is not the "isla fácil" of "soberbias palmas," but

> la que asomó en el hálito indómito de Hatuey, la que creció
> en palenques y conspiraciones,
> la que a empellones construye el socialismo,
> la del heroico pueblo que vivió los sesenta
> y no flaqueó,
> sino que oscura,

calladamente,
ha ido haciendo la historia
y rehaciéndose. (Casal, *Palabras*, 105)

The poetic description asserting that Cuba is an island remaking itself and its history through revolution is the very homeland with which Casal attempts to poetically identify, by racially conflating herself with a glorified heritage of indigenous and slave resistance, and writing a place for herself in the deepest, most resilient place of its history. This glorification of indigeneity is evident in another poem in the collection entitled "Areíto por Carlos Muñiz," composed in tribute to her fellow exile, murdered by counterrevolutionary terrorists in 1979.[6] By calling the text an *areíto*, her voice incorporates the Taíno ritual to honor a comrade who had collaborated on the important publication of the same name that Casal initiated as a project intended to pave a path toward reunification for such sympathetic exiles like Lourdes Casal and Carlos Muñiz.

Casal's ideological radicalization in the United States—the turn toward revolutionary Cuba as a place of greater identification than any community in which she found herself in exile—propelled her political activism and scholarship. For this work, she was identified and officially invited to visit Cuba in 1973. Following this first return visit, she initiated *Areíto* as a space for like-minded exiles to rethink the Revolution and their relationship to the lost homeland. The first issue of the magazine featured an interview with Casal where she describes her personal obsession with Cuba and belief in "el hecho innegable de la sobrevivencia de la revolución" (Casal, "2 semanas," 22). That very issue of *Areíto* opened with a declaration of the journal's political and intellectual disposition: "Entendemos que ese proceso revolucionario ha sentado las bases para una sociedad más justa e igualitaria y se ha enraizado de tal forma en la sociedad cubana como para hacerse irreversible" (Grupo Areíto, 1.1, 1). This proclaimed irreversibility of the Revolution confirms Casal and the *Areíto*'s editors' acceptance of the binary perception of Cuban national and political identity, one is found either *dentro o fuera*, with or against the historical progress made by the Revolution.[7] And they now wanted to work within the Revolution. The desperation to locate the *Areíto* project in the longer narrative of national Cuban history is a desire consistently articulated in its pages. In a 1978 issue, the editors reflect on the organization of the Brigada Antonio Maceo to remind readers of their objective to "reinsertarnos en la historia de nuestro pueblo" (Grupo Areíto, "¿Por qué?," 4). It was the intention of the *Areíto* editors to place themselves, or rather, to re-place themselves, within the national, historical narrative of Cuba's Revolution. That is, the political stance of the publication was one that accepted a notion of "authentic" Cubanness tied to participation in the Revolution. The leftist politics of Casal and others actively involved in early issues of *Areíto* was stressed with the specific intention of reclaiming that authenticity.

One significant way in which Lourdes Casal articulated this identity and political stance was with the very act of naming the project *Areíto*. By appropriating its name from the Taíno ritual of collective dance, the magazine's discursive effort to reclaim cultural and political belonging is evidenced by the title's identification with pre-Colombian origins on the island. In that first 1974 issue, an essay entitled "¿Qué es el Areíto?" described the practice of combining music, song, dance, and pantomime "aplicado a las liturgias religiosas, a los ritos mágicos, a las narraciones epopéyicas, a las historias tribales y las grandes expresiones de la voluntad colectiva" qualifying as "la máxima expresión de las artes musicales y poéticas de los indios antillanos" (29). *Areíto* therein assumed a kind of surrogate expression of indigeneity and collectivity rooted in the country's deepest, most epic origins. The magazine's table of contents included a citation from Gonzalo Fernández de Oviedo's *Historia general y natural de las Indias* (1855) that became a standard to the journal, referring to the island's indigenous Taíno population, reading: "Tenían estas gentes una buena y gentil manera de memorar las cosas pasadas y antiguas, y esto era en sus cantares y bailes, que ellos llaman areíto, que es lo mismo que nosotros llamamos bailar cantando [. . .], es su libro o memorial que de gente en gente queda de los padres a los hijos y de los presentes a los venideros."[8] The insistence on *Areíto's* belonging to a historic tradition of cultural practices native to Cuba, particularly those practices aimed at the transmission of history and memory, and significantly, the publication's place in the formation of that native archive, was a central claim of *Areíto's* project. This insistence on national belonging is what, in my view, guided Lourdes Casal's interest in inscribing her exile community into that tradition.

Along with their rhetorical staging of belonging to Cuba's indigenous tradition with *Areíto*, Lourdes Casal and Grupo Areíto consistently returned to the device of historiography to insist on their Cubanness, asserting that, "Somos cubanos, y es precisamente la fuerza de nuestra identidad nacional la que nos impulsa en una nueva búsqueda [. . .] Nuestra tradición nacional está íntimamente enraizada en Cuba, su historia, sus héroes, sus mártires y su pueblo" (Grupo Areíto, 1.1, 1). The force of their claim on national identity as a historic one led to their claiming of common national heroes explicitly in the naming of the Brigada Antonio Maceo, the first brigade of Cuban exiles to visit the island after 1959. As an homage to the nineteenth century *mulato* hero of independence, the symbolic charge of Maceo's name echoes Casal and Grupo Areíto's anxiety to reintegrate in the national historical narrative. The Brigade organizers wanted their name to communicate various messages: "Nuestra voluntad de mantener una continuidad con la historia de nuestra patria, con sus figuras históricas, con sus héroes revolucionarios. Nuestra rebeldía contra una decisión ajena y contra las circunstancias históricas que nos arrancaron del suelo patrio" (Grupo Areíto, "¿Por qué?," 5). They chose a name aligning Cuba's War of Independence with their own protest against the embargo that had tried to keep them from trying to understand the reality of the Revolution. The Brigada Antonio Maceo leaders chose to label themselves with an expression of reverence for Maceo with whom they identified not only for his patriotism, but also for the depth of his revolutionary thought. And the claiming of the *mulato* general's name intentionally underscores the Brigade's position of racial equality, both as a point of pride in the Revolution, and of contempt in exile.[9]

Lourdes Casal would have understood the historic power behind the Antonio Maceo moniker—a power historian Rebecca Scott described in calling Maceo a "hero to thousands of Cubans and a model for African American activists" (Scott, *Degrees of Freedom*, 173) and "an icon of black masculinity and bravery" with his name being cited alongside that of Toussaint Louverture in the hagiography of black struggle (76). This particular brand of Black-Atlantic heroism spoke not only to Casal and Grupo Areíto's commitment to the African American civil rights struggle, but Antonio Maceo's name was also significantly charged with the kind of mythology already centrally anchored in the Revolution's official discourse. The Brigade claimed their tribute to Maceo as "nuestra conmemoración de la Protesta de Baraguá, cuyo centenario celebramos este año 1978" (Grupo Areíto, "¿Por qué?," 5). This was a significant appropriation of Cuban revolutionary history given that the story of the Baraguá protest is remembered mythically as Maceo's noble opposition to a peace treaty that would end the Ten Years' War without abolishing slavery or achieving independence from Spain. Official Party rhetoric has thusly framed Cuba's ideological intransigence as an "eterno Baraguá." In racial terms, the political trope of the *mambí* determined as an origin of future emancipation constructs parallel mythologies between black liberation and national liberation, all the while holding on to the narrative of national-historic heroism, a narrative scheme already shown to parallel Lourdes Casal's writing. And despite its racial composition being mostly white, the Brigade carrying Antonio Maceo's name represented an exile population committed to reintegration with the Revolution, and with their native country's national history under such racialized terms.

I return, in conclusion, to the earlier suggestion that Casal's potentially problematic exploitation of race for political advantage, as silencing other aspects of her identity undermines any gain in a complicit condoning of institutionalized homophobia and censorship. While it is not my intention to reduce contradictions to an indication of insincerity, or discount the tensions present in her creative and scholarly oeuvre, it is important to recognize that the presence of race in this sample of Casal's writing, as her work in *Areíto, Contra viento y marea*, and efforts in organizing the Brigada Antonio Maceo as well as subsequent Dialogues, reflect an absence of other issues of identity politics relevant to both her personal and political interest.[10] Lourdes Casal wrote about race as it related to her own national belonging. Her autobiographical fiction recovers her Chinese ancestors' foundational role in Cuba's history while incorporating Afro-Cuban cultural practices. And her poetry (her collection's very title intimates that hers are the words that bring revolution together) likewise locates a personal narrative within the Revolution's grand historical narrative, cast in a figure of hopeful reintegration.

But race was also central to the historical-narrative argument constructed by Casal, Grupo Areíto, and the Brigada Antonio Maceo, specifically with the aim of reunification of the Cuban communities on and off the island. Her treatment of race, in the context of her personal experience and ideological positioning with respect to the Revolution's socialist programs, remains relevant to the current moment of proposed rapprochement between two countries still struggling with racism. Her understanding of racial identity and belonging were also deeply embedded in the Cuban practice of historicizing national identity, a facet that we cannot overlook when discussing the question of race. And it is with this in mind that I proffer placing further critical pressure on the categories deployed when we talk about Cuban identity in the context of reconciliation and return, along with a commitment to continued work on Lourdes Casal. The recent attention given to her life and work is not only profoundly merited, but of great importance to the field of Cuban studies across disciplines.

NOTES

1. In 1973, Cuban diplomats invited Lourdes Casal, then a PhD student at the New School for Social Research in New York, to the island to observe the accomplishments of the Revolution. She came back enthusiastic, and shortly thereafter began planning the publication of *Areíto*, a journal intended to provide a space for exiles to rethink the Revolution and to reflect critically on their experiences in exile, as well as their struggles to define their identity. The very first edition of *Areíto* included an interview with Casal where she explains her obsessive interest in the Cuban Revolution, and that she returned to the island because of "el querer saber, interpretar y comprender bien lo que pasa allí en Cuba." Casal defends the Revolution against accusations that her hosts controlled her visit and restricted her from seeing the reality of life for Cubans on the island. She credits the Revolution's accomplishments and explains the improvements she observed to the rationing system, definitively asserting "el hecho innegable de la sobrevivencia de la revolución" (see Lourdes Casal, "2 semanas en Cuba"). This first edition of *Areíto* also opened with a declaration of the journal's political and intellectual disposition: "Entendemos que ese proceso revolucionario ha sentado las bases para una sociedad más justa e igualitaria y se ha enraizado de tal forma en la sociedad cubana como para hacerse irreversible." The publication's criticism and analysis developed from this framework of accepting the Revolution (an impossibility for the hard-line Cuban exile community) with the hope that "al acercarnos a lo cotidiano de Cuba logremos una dimensión nueva en nuestro pensamiento y nuestros sentimientos como cubanos" (see Grupo Areíto, *Areíto* 1.1). The sympathies for and identification with the daily struggle of the

Cuban Revolution articulated here lay the groundwork for their eventual return to the island. The group decided that the next step in reconciling with their homeland would be the composition and publication of a book-length testimony of their memories, experiences, and confessions. Having laid much of the foundation in subsequent visits, and in directing the journal, Lourdes Casal was a driving force behind the project. Having met while working on *Areíto*, Casal, Román de la Campa, Vicente Dopico, and Margarita Lejarza decided to further explore the roots and character of this political and cultural movement that was developing among their community and in the pages of their magazine. Before returning to the island at the end of 1977, they would edit *Contra viento y marea*, first published by Casa de las Américas in Havana in 1978. (Later publications of the book would include 1979 editions by both Siglo XXI in Mexico City and Editorial Universitaria in El Salvador, as well as a 1980 publication by Alfa-Omega in São Paulo, translated by Leda Rita Cintra Ferraz.) The publication of *Contra viento* accomplished Grupo Areíto's bridge-building effort, and from December 22, 1977, to January 14, 1978, fifty-five Cuban exiles returned to the island as the first contingent of the Brigada Antonio Maceo. This was the first official return visit of exiles to the island, not with the aim to dismantle the Revolution but to potentially become part of it. Marking a transition in Cuba's relationship with its community abroad, the Cuban government and its institutions organized this historic event. Cuba's Instituto Cubano de Amistad con los Pueblos (ICAP) was the primary organizer and host of the Brigade and the participants were granted permission to travel by then US President Jimmy Carter. It should be noted that, though instrumental in its organization, Lourdes Casal did not participate in the Brigade. Casal did not qualify to join because she had been old enough at the time not to be able to claim "decisión familiar" as her reason for leaving, as well as because of her early support for counterrevolutionary activities.

2. This citation comes from the version titled "Para Ana Veldford" published in Casal's collection of poems *Palabras juntan revolución*. The poem was originally published as "Para Ana Veltfort" in *Areíto* in 1976. (For a discussion of the alterations of the poem's title, see Frances Negrón-Mutaner and Yolanda Martínez-San Miguel, "In Search of Lourdes Casal's 'Ana Veldford.'") Cited on and off the island, the poem has become a sort of unofficial anthem for the returning exiles who, no matter where they are,

> para siempre permanecer[án] extranjer[os],
> aún cuando regrese[n] a la ciudad de la infancia,
> carg[an] esta marginalidad inmune a todos los retornos
> (Casal, "Para Ana Veldford," *Palabras*, 61.)

This lament admits to a lack of belonging and a longing, however impossible, to recuperate it. Casal's "retorno" through poetry, however, was recognized by the Premio Casa de las Américas, the first Casa literary prize awarded to an exile in the poetry category. This visible recognition, as well as the publication of an exile's voice on the island, is a significant gesture of acceptance by an official organ of the Revolution.

3. Reducing Lourdes Casal's legacy to four lines of poetry, even when exalting their metonymy of the national reunification that she struggled for, erases the complexities expressed in her writings, not to mention the complex realities of her lived experiences. The tensions between nostalgia, so heavily charged in recitations and reappropriations of that final verse, and lingering questions related to identities, politics, patriotism, and the relationship between art and Revolution, signal a latent discomfort in the canonization of her poem. Along with the continued proliferation of the presence of "Para Ana Veltfort" in US anthologies such as *Bridges to Cuba* in 1995 and *The Latino Reader* in 1997, it also appears in Cuban collections like the 1999 *Las palabras son islas* (Jorge Luis Arcos). The final verse of the poem is also evoked as a dedicatory epigraph in *La espada y la pared*, Gustavo Eguren's 1985 novel in which a Cuban exile returns to the island. Ena

Lucía Portela uses the line "Una extraña entre las piedras" in her 1999 short story collection. After her passing, Miguel Barnet, Eliseo Diego and Jesús Díaz, among others, wrote tributes to Casal, recognizing her place as a Cuban writer and thinker. Casa de las Américas instituted their "Premio Lourdes Casal," and in his eulogy delivered in Havana and then published in Casa's journal, Roberto Fernández Retamar extolled her as a "compañera," "patriota," and "revolucionaria," validating her national belonging for "la tierra cubana, por la que Lourdes tanto y tan abnegadamente luchó, acoge hoy en su seno a una de sus nobles hijas. Ella murió, como dijera Martí, 'en brazos de la patria agradecida.'" With words from such prominent cultural figures representing ideological officialdom, Lourdes Casal's legacy was politically consecrated to the project of dialogue and reconciliation, as she was to the Revolution. This is a primary reason for which I believe Casal has not been adequately studied, and why her legacy has been allowed a certain simplification, despite her evident resistance to any single identity or ideological category. For example, Jesús Díaz sentimentalizes the repentant exile character, Ana, in his 1985 film *Lejanía*. But Cucu Diamantes downright misquotes the famous verse in the 2012 road movie *Amor crónico*, and reduces it to a cliché expression of biculturalism with its particular history—and the political, ideological charge of that history—nearly absent from its utterance. Such re-appropriation of "Para Ana Veltfort" sanitizes Casal's legacy and attempts to smooth out the wrinkles of complexity written into her constructions of national identity.

4. Casal (1938–1981) left Cuba in 1961 after graduating from La Universidad de Villanueva and was a leader in the reunification of the Cuban community, a commitment she made in both her academic and political work. Despite the foundational role she played in the formation and organization of the Cuban exile community interested in reuniting with revolutionary Cuba, her biographic profile differs significantly from the familiar narrative of the Peter Pan generation. From 1957 to 1958, while still a university student, Casal established contacts with members of Fidel Castro's 26th of July Movement who also identified with the Catholic groups to which Casal belonged. She participated in anti-Batista activities, and upon the triumph of the Revolution, she was linked to the Directorio Revolucionario Estudiantil. But as Leonel Antonio de la Cuesta describes, "arrinconados por los comunistas, los católicos revolucionarios pronto pasaron a la oposición y ello determinó que después de conspirar dentro del país Lourdes se viera forzada a salir al exilio" (5). As a leader of the Consejo Revolucionario Cubano, Casal then traveled to Africa on a trip sponsored by the CIA before completing her graduate work in New York. This trip, or her "African pilgrimage," surprisingly initiated her turn back to Cuba as it "confirmed that home, for better or worse, was not in Nigeria, or anywhere else, but in Cuba. And that regardless of the different places that my ancestors had come from (China or Galicia or the ancient land of the Yorubas), my roots had been solidly planted in the island of my birth." Casal, "Memories," 62.

5. As discussed in Iraida López's essay included in this dossier, Casal's "Memories" explores the components of her racial identity and how that identity, in the context of her US exile, made her more essentially Cuban: "In Cuba, I knew who I was. I knew I came from Spaniards, Africans, Chinese in a complex mixture and blending of oppressed and oppressors, of masters and slaves, of rapists and raped, but a mixture which I felt was somehow identical to the mélange which constituted Cuba itself. I was *cubana*. And to me the essence of being Cuban was the cultural and racial mixture of which I felt I was a perfect example. In the US during the 60s, I was forced to look at my Blackness with different eyes. I had become accustomed to considering myself *una mulata* in a mulatto country, in a quintessentially mulatto culture. The US was a shock. Here I had to learn to assert my Blackness somehow" (61). In an interview with Ruth Behar in *Bridges to Cuba*, poet Nancy Morejón, who knew Lourdes Casal prior to her exile and then again when she began to return to the island, commented on the process of Casal's so-called discovery of her race: "It was only in the United States that Lourdes noticed what color she was, what kind of hair she had that she was a woman." See Ruth Behar and Lucía Suárez's "Two Conversations with Nancy Morejón," in *Bridges to Cuba/Puentes a Cuba*, Ruth Behar, ed. (Ann Arbor: University of

Michigan, 1995), 135. Evidently, Casal's racial self-discovery was intimately tied to her political radicalization.

6. Carlos Muñiz Varela, a then twenty-six-year-old member of Grupo Areíto and participant of the Brigada Antonio Maceo, was brutally murdered in San Juan on April 28, 1978. Following the murder, counterrevolutionary terrorist groups Omega 7 and Comando Cero publically threatened the same fate to other pro-Dialogue exiles. A martyr to those exiles, the second contingent of the brigade was named after Muñiz and there is a Carlos Muñiz Varela school in Bauta, Cuba. *Areíto* used Muñiz's death, and other acts of terrorism, such as the murder of thirty-seven-year-old Eulalio José Negrín on November 25, 1979, in Union City, New Jersey, as a way not only to condemn the violence against them, but also to reconfirm the objectives of the Brigade and advocate Dialogue between Cuba and its community abroad. See journalist and ICAP functionary Luis Adrián Betancourt's book documenting Muñiz's murder, *¿Por qué Carlos?* (La Habana: Editorial Letras Cubanas, 1981). For *Areíto*'s official response to the assassination, see "El Diálogo y la desesperación de los terroristas," *Areíto* 5.19–20 (1979), 9–11.

7. This is the recognizable reference to Fidel Castro's oft-quoted speech "Palabras a los intelectuales," delivered in 1961 at the National Library to Cuba's most important intellectual figures, where he famously declared that "dentro de la Revolución, todo; contra la Revolución, nada."

8. Grupo Areíto, *Areíto* (1974–1985).

9. Grupo Areíto also detailed the racism they personally observed and experienced in the United States in both the pages of its magazine and in testimonies included in their book, *Contra viento y marea*. Contributors to the book recounted confrontations with racist attitudes and discrimination in exile, given that positioning themselves as both victims—suffering in exile as well as in ideological alignment to the Revolution's anti-US discourse—was fundamental to the case for their repatriation. The book includes a section in its first chapter, "Prehistoria de la radicalización," entitled "El racismo: experiencia directa" in which contributors recount their personal confrontations with racist attitudes and discrimination in exile: "Me encontré con la realidad de que 'Cuban, Puerto Rican; a spick is a spick; it does not matter.' Es decir, que mi intento de escapar de la discriminación identificándome como cubano fallaba porque para aquellos racistas todos los hispanos éramos *spicks*, e igualmente despreciables" (Grupo Areíto, *Contra viento*, 57).

10. Laura Lomas's essay in this dossier unpacks some of these central tensions, and credits the feminist, queer perspective in her writing, as well as points to some of her public critiques of revolutionary leadership on the island. Yolanda Martínez-San Miguel also points to a "deseo lésbico que está simultáneamente inscrito y silenciado en sus textos" (Martínez-San Miguel, "Releyendo a Lourdes Casal").

WORKS CITED

Behar, Ruth, and Lucía Suárez. "Two Conversations with Nancy Morejón," *Bridges to Cuba/ Puentes a Cuba*. Ed. Ruth Behar. Ann Arbor: University of Michigan, 1995. 129–139.

Betancourt, Luis Adrián. *¿Por qué Carlos?* La Habana: Editorial Letras Cubanas, 1981.

Casal, Lourdes. "2 semanas en Cuba." *Areíto* 1.1 (1974): 20–27.

———. "Los Fundadores: Alfonso." *Los Fundadores: Alfonso y otros cuentos*. Miami: Ediciones Universal, 1973. 17–37. [This story was also published in *Exilio* 6.1 (1972): 109–117.]

———. "Memories of a Black Cuban Childhood." *Nuestro* (April 1978).

———. "Para Ana Veldford." *Palabras juntan revolución*. Havana: Ediciones Casa de las Américas, 1981.

Castro, Fidel. "Discurso pronunciado como conclusión de las reuniones con los intelectuales cubanos, efectuadas en la Biblioteca Nacional el 16, 23 y 30 de junio de 1961." http://www.cuba .cu/gobierno/discursos.1961/esp/f300661e.html.

De la Cuesta, Leonel Antonio. "Perfil biográfico." *Itinerario ideológico: antología de Lourdes Casal*. Eds. María Cristina Herrera y Leonel Antonio de la Cuesta. Miami: Instituto de Estudios Cubanos, 1982.

Dzidzienyo, Anani, and Lourdes Casal. *The Position of Black People in Brazilian and Cuban Society*. London: Minority Rights Group, 1979.

Eromosele, Diana Ozemebhoya. "Black Cubans: Restoring US Ties is Cool, but America, Keep Your Hang-Ups about Race at Bay." *TheRoot.com*, January 21, 2015. http://www.theroot.com/articles/culture/2015/01/black_cubans_discuss_the_restoration_of_us_ties_and_how_their_experiences.html.

Fernández Retamar, Roberto. "Palabras de Roberto Fernández Retamar en el entierro de la compañera Lourdes Casal, el 3 de febrero de 1981." *Areíto* 7.26 (1981): 4–5.

Grupo Areíto. *Areíto* 1.1 (1974): 1.

———. *Contra viento y marea*. Havana: Casa de las Américas, 1978.

———. "¿Por qué Antonio Maceo?" *Areíto* 4.3–4 (1978): 4.

———. "¿Qué es Areíto?" *Areíto* 1.1 (1974): 29.

Grupo de Investigación Areíto. "El diálogo y la desesperación de los terroristas." *Areíto* 5.19–20 (1979): 9–11.

Martínez-San Miguel, Yolanda. "Releyendo a Lourdes Casal desde su escritura en queer." *80 grados*, October 16, 2015. http://www.80grados.net/releyendo-a-lourdes-casal-desde-su-escritura-en-queer.

Negrón-Mutaner, Frances, and Yolanda Martínez-San Miguel. "In Search of Lourdes Casal's 'Ana Veldford.'" *Social Text* 92, no. 25.3 (2007): 56–84.

Scott, Rebecca J. *Degrees of Freedom: Louisiana and Cuba after Slavery*. Cambridge, MA: Harvard University Press, 2009.

YOLANDA PRIETO

Lourdes Casal and Black Cubans in the United States: The 1970s and Beyond

ABSTRACT

This article looks at the work of Lourdes Casal as a social scientist. In particular, I examine a research project that she undertook with a colleague, Rafael Prohias, on Black Cubans in Miami. They studied a sample of Black Cubans in Miami and analyzed the 1970 US Census information for that population. The article here describes the methodology used in the study and the characteristics of the sample. One of the major findings is that, in the 1970s, Miami Cubans overwhelmingly identified themselves as Cubans first, Black second. In terms of social psychology, this identification gave Black Cubans social gains. After the untimely deaths of both Casal and Prohias, Joaquin Carrasco, a student of Prohias, completed the Miami manuscript. I then finished an article that Casal had started, based on that full research project, for a Smithsonian publication. I base the discussion of the article that follows on Casal's Smithsonian article. The article also features a section on Cuban migration to the United States since the 1980s and the place of Black Cubans in these migratory movements.

RESUMEN

Este artículo explora el trabajo de Lourdes Casal como científica social. En particular, examina una investigación que ella llevó a cabo con un colega, Rafael Prohias, sobre los afrocubanos en Miami. Los dos estudiaron una muestra de afrocubanos en Miami y analizaron la información del Censo de 1970 sobre esa población. Este artículo describe la metodología del estudio, así como las características de la muestra. Uno de los hallazgos principales es que, en los años setenta, los afrocubanos en Miami abrumadoramente se autoidentificaban como cubanos primero y como afrodescendientes después. Desde el punto de vista de psicología social, esta identificación les daba ganancias sociales. Después de las tempranas muertes de Casal y Prohias, Joaquín Carrasco, un estudiante de Prohias, completó el manuscrito del estudio. El artículo que sigue termina el que Casal había comenzado, basado en la investigación completa, para una publicación de la Institución Smithsonian. También está incluida una sección sobre la migración cubana a los Estados Unidos desde 1980 y el lugar de los afrocubanos en esos movimientos migratorios.

Lourdes Casal is known mostly as a creative writer and a public intellectual, but another important aspect of this multifaceted woman was a social scientist. Casal graduated with a degree in chemical engineering from the Catholic

51

University of Villanueva in Havana, Cuba. But her interest in the social sciences was evident since she was very young. She took psychology courses at the University of Havana. After leaving Cuba for exile in 1962, she enrolled at the New School for Social Research in New York City (now known as New School), where she completed a doctorate in social psychology. She taught psychology at the City University of New York and later at Rutgers University in Newark, New Jersey.

Lourdes Casal's numerous creative writings were mainly about Cuba, her homeland and the source of her identity. As a social scientist, she focused her research on race and gender, in both Cuba and the United States. Casal studied the fate of US minorities, particularly Cubans. In 1974, along with Rafael Prohias, another Cuban-born scholar, she coordinated and published *The Cuban Minority in the United States* (Prohias and Casal 1973). This report was a comprehensive, national study on the needs of Cubans in the United States, in particular of those who were not as successful as other Cuban exiles of the 1960s.

Casal and Prohias also collaborated on a study on Black Cubans in the United States. They studied a Miami sample of Black Cubans and compared their findings to the information in the 1970 US Census. Their seminal work in this area was interrupted by tragedy twice—once when Prohias died in 1974, and again with Lourdes's death in 1981.

The study on Black Cubans in the United States originated with Rafael Prohias's dissertation project, which would have been presented to the Sociology Department at Indiana University. Prohias's dissertation was incomplete at the time of his death, and Joaquín Carrasco, a student and research assistant of Prohias, performed the statistical analyses and completed the first manuscript. This study, an unpublished report, was progressively placed in a wider context, and the second manuscript, as it stands, was mainly the work of Lourdes Casal, who won a Ford Foundation grant to undertake the study (Casal, Prohias, Carrasco, and Prieto 1979). Later, Casal wrote an article based on that study, "Black Cubans in the United States: Basic Demographic Information," which was published by the Smithsonian Institution (Casal and Prieto 1981). I had by then become her collaborator and was asked by the editors to conclude the article after her untimely death.

Unfortunately, the original report is no longer available at the Ford Foundation. Thus, for the purposes of this work, I discuss the article just mentioned, which is derived from the report. Although it was already published in 1981, I highlight some of the findings because they represent an example of rigorous empirical study of Black Cubans in the United States during the early Cuban migration. Even though the study uses a Miami sample, the findings can be generalized because they are very similar to the information contained in the

1970 US Census, particularly a special computer run on Black Cubans conducted for the Cuban Refugee Center.

Black Cubans in the United States: Basic Demographic Information

Black Cubans were severely underrepresented in the Cuban migration of the 1960s to the United States. A special computer run from the 1970 Census (the first to separate Hispanics into nationalities) that was carried out for the Cuban Refugee Center revealed that roughly 3 percent of Cubans who had arrived in the United States since the 1960s were Black, although Blacks and mulattos represented 27 percent of Cuba's population in that country's 1953 census (Casal and Prieto 1981, 314; De la Fuente 2001, 303; US Census Bureau 1970). At least two factors are relevant for trying to understand that underrepresentation. First, Blacks were concentrated in the lower strata of the Cuban population, and the early migration was mostly composed of upper- and upper-middle-class Cubans. Second, Blacks were among the beneficiaries of significant improvements in terms of education, employment, and general access to opportunity brought about by the 1959 Cuban Revolution. Also contributing to the low percentage of Blacks in the migration was the fear of encountering racial oppression and discrimination in the United States.

I briefly discuss general trends in employment, education, income, and the socio-psychological characteristics of Black Cubans in the United States by drawing on two data sources: the US 1970 Census and the Casal and Prohias Miami sample.

The Miami Sample

A total of 265 Black Cuban households were identified in the Miami-Dade area over the period from September 1970 to October 1971. Of those 265 households, 100 were selected at random. One of the most interesting challenges encountered in the work was how to determine who was Black. The social construction of race—namely, the difference between the phenotypical and the cultural bases for racial identification—is beyond the scope of this article. But Lourdes addressed this issue in her article:

From a purely cultural standpoint, the range of skin color and the overall racial mix is much greater in any Caribbean country than in the United States. There are a sizable number of individuals whose own racial identification is closely tied to their racial visibility and their class position. In other words, not all individuals considered racially Black may in fact have developed a racial identity, and in many cases they may simply reject it when faced with the opportunity of "passing." Clearly, it became necessary to make sure that we were in fact dealing with individuals who, as a matter of self-identification shared racial and ethnic characteristics. For that reason all potential respondents in the study were asked a filter question about whether they considered themselves Black or not. Of 265 households approached only 6 individuals did not consider themselves Black and were therefore excluded. (Casal and Prieto 1981, 327–330)

Defining the universe of Black Cubans in the Miami area was a problem because there was not a comprehensive data source on Cubans that included racial group membership. All possible sources, including the Immigration and Naturalization Service, the Cuban Refugee Program, the school system, and religious organizations were thoroughly searched. Again from Lourdes's account:

We began by contacting members of the only known organization of Cuban blacks that has operated in the area in the last few years. Through them we obtained a membership list from which we were able to locate 87 households of potential respondents. In addition, we conducted a personal survey of the 44 largest Cuban organizations in the area, and requested names of black Cubans. We also enlisted the cooperation of approximately 150 business establishments requesting names of customers judged to be both black and Cuban. Once contact was established with a black Cuban, he or she was asked to submit a list of other black Cubans in the area. Of the 265 households that were located through this process, we selected 100 at random, and a total of 128 individual interviews were completed fitting our criteria. (329–330)

A restriction was introduced in the screening of respondents. Only individuals who had an acquaintance with occupational, organizational, social, and other areas of interaction in both Cuba and the United States were selected. This ensured strict comparability of occupational change and exposure to their society of origin and community of destination. The following were the criteria for individuals to be interviewed:

- They were adults.
- They had declared themselves to be both Black and Cuban.
- They had arrived in the United States no earlier than January 1959.
- They had been working for at least one calendar year both in Cuba (before their departure) and in the United States.

The characteristics of the Miami sample differed little from the US Census demographics for Black Cubans in the United States. One difference, though, is worth noting: the Miami sample shows a lower representation among both men and women of college degree holding, and a high concentration of Black women with just elementary education. The researchers interpreted this to mean that perhaps lesser-educated Cubans (particularly women) stayed in the Miami area, whereas those with better educational backgrounds tended to emigrate from the South.

Labor-Force Participation and Education

In 1970, the number of Cubans in the civilian labor force, number of employed persons, and level of unemployment were very similar between white and Black Cubans, but there were some differences. As table 1 shows, Black men showed lower rates of incorporation into the civilian labor force, a lower percentage of employed persons, and higher unemployment rates than did white men. The differences were not dramatic. It is interesting, though, that when we look at the census figures for women, the situation is inverse. Black Cuban females were in the labor force in greater numbers, had higher employment rates, and had lower unemployment rates than did white Cuban women. Even though the Miami sample showed a high concentration of Black women with only elementary school education, in the 1970 census, a greater percentage of the Black female population as compared to other groups from Cuba was engaged in professional, technical, and kindred jobs (US Census Bureau 1970). This probably reflects the great weight that Black Cuban women gave to education, particularly to the use of education as a tool for social mobility among a visible group of middle-class and professional Blacks in prerevolutionary Cuban society, of which Lourdes Casal was an example. In terms of overall labor-force participation, in 1970, Black Cuban women outdid not only their Cuban counterparts but *all* US female groups except for African American females.

As table 2 shows, Black Cubans in the United States on average had fewer years of formal education than did their white counterparts. For example, only 37.7 percent of Black men versus 48.4 percent of white men had completed high school or acquired some higher education. For women, these figures were 33.7 and 41.9, respectively. Two other differences by race noted in by the census are worth mentioning. The percentage of female-headed households among Black Cuban families, at 21.8 percent, was twice the corresponding rate for white Cubans. Black Cubans also had a significantly higher percentage of male family heads older than age 65. This intriguing indicator could not be readily interpreted. It might reflect the "older" character of the Black Cuban

TABLE 1. Cubans in the United States: Employment indicators by race and gender

	Men			Women		
Labor-force participation	*Employment*	*Unemployment*	*Labor-force participation*	*Employment*	*Unemployment*
Black 78.2%	73.8%	4.4%	55.8%	52.7%	3.1%
White 82.7%	79.7%	3%	50.5%	47%	3.5%

Source: 1970 US Census.

TABLE 2. High school graduation rates and higher: All US Cubans and the Miami sample

	Women		Men	
	All US Cubans	Miami sample	All US Cubans	Miami sample
Black	33.7	37.7	37.7	37.7
White	41.9	23.4	48.4	37.7*

Note: This figure is the same for black females in the United States, black males and females in the Miami sample, and white males in the Miami sample. I recalculated all percentages and reached the same results. The similarities between census figures and the Miami sample may explain this. Source: US 1970 Census and Miami sample.

population at the time, or it could be related to the existence of extended family patterns with "grandfather"-headed families, or indicate that more restrictions were imposed on younger men who were seeking to emigrate from Cuba (US Census Bureau 1970).

The differences discussed in occupational distribution and educational attainment were translated into income differentials. The median family income for all Cubans in the United States in 1970 was $8,690, for white Cubans, $8,720, and for Black Cubans, $7,971 (US Census Bureau 1970).

Social Psychological Characteristics

One of the most interesting discussions in the article is about the social psychological dimension of the study of Black Cubans. A couple of findings from the sample are worth stressing:

- Black Cubans in Miami tended to identify primarily as Cubans, and only secondarily as Blacks. Their interactions took place primarily within the Cuban community and they had few contacts with African Americans. They tended to agree more with items emphasizing Cuban self-sufficiency and economic and cultural survival than with items emphasizing Black self-sufficiency and economic and cultural survival.
- The longer the time spent in the United States, the greater was a respondent's tendency to identify racially. Racial militancy also increased with time spent in the United States, and militancy has a negative relationship with age and income (the higher the income, the lower the militancy; the lower the age, the higher the militancy).

To further explore the degree of identity construction and assimilation, the effects of twelve independent variables were studied. The variables ranged from traditional, structural ones (e.g., age, time in United States, religion, education, income level, rural and urban origin, occupation) to social psychological factors (e.g., ethnic identity, racial identity, self-reported experience with discrimination, racial militancy). Findings were arrived at through responses to ethnic and identity scales.[1]

The study concluded that Black Cubans in Miami-Dade overwhelmingly identified as Cuban first and Black second. From a psychological perspective, Casal stated:

Whenever individuals share more than one ascribed characteristic, they can selectively manipulate their own identity orientation. Black Cubans, faced with the two possible choices of being considered black and Cuban, selectively chose to identify as Cubans in order to maximize their relative advantages for mobility and status achievement. An environment as ethnically diverse as Miami's seemed to both facilitate and encourage black Cubans' first identification as Cubans. (Casal and Prieto 1981, 331–35)

Questions remain for Black Cubans: Where do they belong? In which community do they feel comfortable? In which community are they accepted? Casal and Prohias found that early Black Cuban migrants tended to live in the geographies between the white Cuban community and the African American community. This confirms that Black Cubans define themselves as Cuban first, given the strength of nationalism in the process of their identity formation in Cuba, but they also may feel ambivalent about rejecting their identity as Blacks altogether.

Cuban Migration to the United States since the 1980s

"Black Cubans in the United States," researched in the 1970s, precedes the waves of Cuban migration since the 1980s: the Mariel boatlift, the *balsero* exodus, and the legal and illegal migration from Cuba since the 1990s (see Aguirre 1976; Bach 1980; Pedraza 1996; Portes and Rumbaut 1996; Aja 1999; Aguirre and Bonilla Silva 2002; Grenier and Pérez 2003; Prieto 2009; Portes and Puhrmann 2014). "Black Cubans in the United States" reveals the characteristics of the early Cuban exodus to the United States. The differences between white and Black Cubans among early Cuban migrants were not dramatic; the Black Cubans who migrated in the 1960s and 1970s had mainly professional, educated, middle-class Blacks in Cuba.

How did successive waves of Cuban migrants change the composition of the Cuban population in the United States? The subsequent waves differ from earlier ones in that, generally speaking, they did not involve people from the prerevolutionary upper or middle classes. Most migrants in those groups are more representative of Cuban society as a whole, with a significant number of people who had been marginalized by Cuba's sociopolitical process. For the most part, these new migrants were younger than earlier exiles and, at least in the beginning of the 1980s, heavily male. A notable difference between migrants of the 1980s until the present and the early exiles of the 1960s and 1970s is race. For example, studies on the Mariel boatlift report that between 20 percent and 40 percent of migrants identified themselves as Black on arrival in the United States (Bach 1980, 40).[2]

After Mariel, between 1980 and 1993, there was limited immigration from Cuba. The next massive wave of migrants came in the summer of 1994, with the *balsero* exodus, when masses of people left the country by boats and home-made rafts. The Cuban government openly allowed those who wanted to leave to do so. In general, these migrants came from the poorest sectors of Cuban society and had been most hurt by the Special Period of the 1990s.

The chaos of the 1994 migration led to lengthy conversations between the United States and Cuba in which the United States agreed to grant twenty thousand visas a year for Cubans who emigrated. Cubans who presented proper documentation were randomly selected and then interviewed by the US embassy in Havana for approval. Before changes to migration laws in Cuba in 2013, prospective travelers needed to obtain authorization from the Cuban government to exit the country, but that is no longer the case.

Current migration from Cuba, especially from the 1990s on, is different still from that of earlier periods. Even if most migrants are opposed to the Cuban government, most of those leaving Cuba today cite economics as their primary reason for leaving. They come from all sectors of society and include the poor, but also many professionals who were raised and educated in contemporary Cuba—a brain drain.

Even though the number of Black Cuban migrants has increased, especially from the 1980s until the present, they still account for a low proportion of migrants overall. The reasons for less migration by Black Cubans may be similar to the reasons discussed for early Black migration, especially fear of racism and discrimination in the United States. The differences in "migratory propensity between blacks and whites may be the result of a greater sense of satisfaction among black non-emigrants with the present-day political system in Cuba" (Aguirre and Bonilla Silva 2002, 322).

There is a selectivity in the Black Cuban migration to the United States. This applies to both the early and the more recent waves of migrants. Many of the Black and white migrants in Aguirre and Bonilla Silva's study had similar characteristics. Black and white would-be emigrants "are different from their counterparts in the general Cuban population but are similar to each other in family income, education, employment, their use of the mass media. . . . Stayers, both black and white, may not have the resources, opportunity, networks, or interest to leave the country" (Aguirre and Bonilla Silva 2002, 319). Also, the US lottery visa system provides a means to screen both Black and white would-be migrants for employment history, education, and other factors that prevent migrants from becoming a burden to US society.

How have migrants from the 1980s to the present fared in US society? Many have assimilated as previous exiles did. Others are moving in that direction, particularly professionals who have arrived legally since the 1990s. But many have encountered difficulties. Black *marielitos* found it very hard to adjust. Not only did they lack relatives in the United States; they also experienced racial discrimination in the United States (De la Fuente 2001, 305). In a recent article about "the bifurcated enclave," Portes and Puhrmann (2914, 122–23) argue that "Mariel . . . shifted the mode of incorporation of Cuban arrivals in the United States from positive to negative. . . . Because of its social and racial composition, the image that Cubans had carved in the US public opinion also suffered a marked deterioration . . . from a 'model minority' and the 'builders of Miami' to just another Third World minority forcing its way, unwelcome, into US shores."

Discussion

Early Black Cuban migrants to the United States were not dramatically different from their white counterparts in terms of socioeconomic characteristics or education. Rather, their identification as Cuban first and Black second reflects the strong role that nationalism played, and continues to play, in the formation of Cuban identity. But does this signify absence of intergroup conflict? Were race relations harmonious between Black and white Cubans? What are the reactions of white and Black Cubans now?

Devin Spence Benson (2012, 20) argues that a generally accepted notion that the Cuban Revolution is antiracist and the exile community is racist has endured for more than fifty years. In 1959, the revolutionary government began a campaign to eliminate racial discrimination. As Benson states, "A central component of this plan included defining racism as counterrevolutionary and establishing the ideal that revolutionaries could not be racist" (20). The revolutionary government implemented some measures intended to eliminate racism. Examples are the integration of white spaces such as beaches and recreational facilities. Perhaps most important, Blacks were given educational, political, and employment opportunities. Not all Cubans were happy with these changes, especially middle- and upper-class white Cubans, who decided to emigrate, among other things, because of the racial politics of the revolution. Postrevolutionary racial relations have been complex, and over time, many Blacks accused the government of racism and discrimination. Aguirre and Bonilla Silva (2002, 321) contend that in Cuba there is racial discrimination in interpersonal relations and institutionalized discrimination. An example of this is housing. In a case study of Pilar Atarés, a poor neighborhood in Havana, housing conditions for the population were considered very precarious. More than half of interviewed residents live in *ciudadelas*, especially predominantly

Black migrants from Oriente province (Iñíguez 2014). Also, it is interesting that so many political dissidents are Black, perhaps indicating that racism and race relations fuel social discontent.

In Miami, the racial discourse of white exiles during the early migration often included denials of racism in prerevolutionary Cuba. And just as the revolutionary government pursued the goal of "unity" between the races, the exiles chose to prioritize anticommunist goals over racial division (Benson 2012, 21). As Benson puts it, "In both places, the ensuing silence about racial equality and the pretense to know what was best for Afro-Cubans suggests more similarities than differences across the ninety miles separating the island and Key West."

When I did my research on Cubans in Union City, New Jersey, I interviewed Black Cubans. My main objective was to learn whether they had faced racism and discrimination. Most of the Black Cubans that I interviewed had arrived in the 1960s and 1970s. When I asked Doris, a light-skinned Black Cuban woman, if she had ever been discriminated against in Union City on the basis of her race, she said:

Never. I came to Union City in 1968, and I was always accepted by both white Cubans and Americans. My children are darker than I am, and they got an education here and grew up here without any problems. Only once, my eldest son was the victim of a verbal racist attack. An Italian American student in school called him a "black spic" and they fought physically. I'm sure that among the students there were tensions, but maybe it was more tensions between the Cubans and the Americans, not specifically racial tensions. (Interviewed on June 8, 2008)

Did racial relations change between Black and white Cubans in the more recent waves of Cuban migration? It appears that the emphasis on national identity is strong among Blacks now too. But this national identity among more recent Black Cuban migrants encompasses various levels. For them, *Cuban* (especially among the young, the more educated, and artists) means "African," and they proudly display it, sometimes with music or in the way they dress or wear their hair. When I asked Ariel if he felt more Cuban than Black, he said that he feels Cuban but in a "different" way. When older Black Cubans choose to be Cuban first, he explained, they are trying to gain socially:

That is how the old guard sees it. I am Cuban by choice, and my definition of Cubanness is very inclusive. It includes my African ancestry, the Spaniards, the homosexual, the communists. I have acquired this identity through an intellectual process, by studying my history with all that it entails. (Interviewed on July 7, 2008)

In my research in Union City, I never detected animosity among white Cubans toward Black Cubans, especially toward those Blacks who were professional and well educated. Some authors contend, however, that, among the more re-cent Cuban migrants, especially Black Cubans, will polarize (Dixon 1988, 236). The poor, the dark-skinned, the high school dropouts—these individuals will continue to be marginalized (Llanes 1982, in Dixon 1988, 237). Dixon brings us back to the issue of social location for newly arrived Blacks: In which community will they live? White Cuban? Black American? Having credentials to belong in both, "Will they be accepted in either, both or none? If they are rejected by both the Black-American and the Cuban American communities, will they develop their own marginal and polarized sub-community?" (Dixon 1988, 237).

We need more of the kind of research that Lourdes Casal and Rafael Pro-hias undertook. As is evidenced in this article, other authors have carefully studied the topic of Black Cubans in the United States. However, Casal and Prohias researched a sizable sample of Black Cubans in Miami. We need more empirical evidence of how the Cuban races are faring. Unfortunately, the cor-pus of studies on Cubans in the United States lacks substantive discussions about race. Casal's work holds lessons for greater American society as well. This country continues to be ripped apart by racial conflict. Casal's pioneering work about one "invisible" minority group serves as an example of the careful, committed social science research that she hoped would allow us to see clearly what the problems are in order to progress beyond them. May we honor her commitment, continue to do the work, and demonstrate that her faith was not misplaced.

NOTES

1. The ethnic and racial identity scales used in this project were constructed by Prohias and Carrasco from items already used in the Gary Area Project, 1969, Institute for Social Research, Indiana University. They were mainly based on concrete referents to everyday interaction situa-tions rather than to attitudinal dispositions.

2. The gender and racial composition of the migrants has changed after the 1990s. The mi-gration has become more complex with more women, families, and white persons coming. The lottery visa system probably favors whites because they have more relatives and contacts in the United States.

REFERENCES

Aguirre, Benigno E. 1976. "Differential Migration of Cuban Social Races: A Review and Interpre-tation of the Problem." *Latin American Research Review* 11 (1): 103–124.

Aguirre, Benigno E., and Eduardo Bonilla Silva. 2002. "Does Race Matter among Cuban Immi-grants? An Analysis of the Racial Characteristics of Recent Cuban Immigrants." *Journal of Latin American Studies* 34 (2) : 311–324.

Aja Diaz, Antonio. 1999. "La emigración de Cuba en los años noventa." *Cuban Studies* 30: 1–25.

Bach, Robert L. 1980. "The New Cuban Immigrants: Their Background and Prospects." *Monthly Labor Review* 103: 39–46.

Benson, Devin Spence. 2012. "Owning the Revolution: Race, Revolution, and Politics from Havana to Miami." *Journal of Transnational American Studies* 4 (2): 1–30.

Casal, Lourdes, with the assistance of Yolanda Prieto. 1981. "Black Cubans in the United States: Basic Demographic Information." In D. Mortimer and Roy S. Bryce-Laborite, *Female Immigrants to the United States: Caribbean, Latin American and African Experiences*, Research Institute On Immigration and Ethnic Studies Occasional Paper No. 2. Washington, DC: Smithsonian Institution.

Casal, Lourdes, Rafael Prohias, J. Carrasco, and Yolanda Prieto. 1979. *Black Cubans in the United States*. Report presented to the Ford Foundation, January.

De la Fuente, Alejandro. 2001. *A Nation for All: Race, Inequality, and Politics in Twentieth-Century Cuba*. Chapel Hill: University of North Carolina Press.

Dixon, Heriberto. 1988. "The Cuban American Counterpoint: Black Cubans in the United States." *Dialectical Anthropology* 13: 227–239.

Grenier, Guillermo J., and Lisandro Pérez. 2003. *The Legacy of Exile: Cubans in the United States*. New Immigrant Series. Boston: Allyn and Bacon.

Iñíguez, Luisa, ed. 2014. *Las tantas Habanas: Estrategias para comprender sus dinámicas sociales*. Havana: Editorial UH.

Llanes, José. 1982. *Cuban Americans: Masters of Survival*. Cambridge, MA: Abt Books.

Pedraza, Silvia. 1996. "Cuba's Refugees: Manifold Migrations." In Silvia Pedraza and Ruben G. Rumbaut, eds., *Origins and Destinies: Immigration, Race and Ethnicity in America*, 263–279. Belmont, CA: Wadsworth Publishing.

Portes, Alejandro, and Aaron Puhrmann. 2014. "A Bifurcated Enclave: The Peculiar Evolution of the Cuban Immigrant Population in the Last Decades." In *Un pueblo disperso: Dimensiones sociales de la diáspora cubana*, by Jorge Duany, 122–123. Valencia: Aduana Vieja Editorial.

Portes, Alejandro, and Ruben G. Rumbaut. 1996. *Immigrant America: A Portrait*. Berkeley: University of California Press.

Prieto, Yolanda. 2009. *The Cubans of Union City: Immigrants and Exiles in a New Jersey Community*. Philadelphia: Temple University Press.

Prohias, Rafael, and Lourdes Casal. 1973. *The Cuban Minority in the United States: Preliminary Report on Need Identification and Program Evaluation*. Boca Raton: Florida Atlantic University, Cuban National Planning Council.

US Census Bureau. 1972. *US Census of the Population 1970, Special Run for the Cuban Refugee Center*. Washington, DC: US Census Bureau.

IRAIDA H. LÓPEZ

Entre el ideal de la nación mestiza y la discordia racial: "Memories of a Black Cuban Childhood" y otros textos de Lourdes Casal

RESUMEN

El presente artículo aborda las ideas de Lourdes Casal sobre la discriminación racial y el mestizaje en Cuba a través de sus artículos académicos, sus cuentos y, sobre todo, su ensayo autobiográfico "Memories of a Black Cuban Childhood" (1978). A diferencia de otros autores que, en las décadas de 1960 y 1970, hicieron hincapié en el vigor del racismo en la isla, Casal resalta en sus estudios las posibilidades de la integración racial. Pero si bien celebró los éxitos de la Revolución cubana para eliminar legalmente la discriminación racial, tampoco ignoró los desafíos pendientes para alcanzar una "verdadera cultura mestiza". El potencial del mestizaje es clave para entender el pensamiento de Casal sobre Cuba y su propia subjetividad. Si bien se atiene al mestizaje como intrínseco a la identidad nacional cubana, Casal lo asume subrayando el componente negro de la mezcla racial. Su experiencia diaspórica, que la expuso a diferentes constructos de lo racial tanto en los Estados Unidos como en África, influyó en su reformulación del concepto, llevándola a realzar la negritud dentro de los límites del mestizaje. Se trata de un mestizaje activista que en lugar de encubrir las diferencias, las trae a colación.

ABSTRACT

Through a review of her academic essays, short stories, and autobiographical essay "Memories of a Black Cuban Childhood" (1978), this article addresses Lourdes Casal's ideas about racial discrimination and mestizaje. In contrast with other authors who in the 1960s and 1970s called attention to the robust racism on the island, Casal in her work stresses the possibilities of racial integration. She celebrated the successes that had been legally achieved in Cuba under the revolution at the same time that she denounced the remnants of racism. There was much that still needed to be overcome to reach a "true mulatto culture". The potential of *mestizaje* is key to an understanding of Casal's thoughts about race in Cuba and her own subjectivity. Although she adheres to *mestizaje* as intrinsic to Cuban national identity, Casal highlights the Black, devalued component of the racial mixture. Her diasporic experience, which exposed her to various constructs of race both in the United States and in Africa, had a major impact on this reconceptualization of race. Instead of concealing the differences, her advocacy of *mestizaje* brings them to the fore.

Quisiera empezar por esbozar dos escenarios paradigmáticos extraídos de sendos textos autobiográficos escritos por autores afrodescendientes del exilio. En el primer texto, una mulata cubana proveniente de la clase media, tras experimentar la diferencia racial tanto en los Estados Unidos como en el África Occidental, llega a la conclusión de que Cuba provee el espacio idóneo para asumir a plenitud su identidad racial, la cual es producto tanto de la sangre africana, china y europea que corre por sus venas como de su peripecia vital. Ella es un exponente de lo que algunos llaman, siguiendo a Nicolás Guillén, "el color cubano" como resultado del mestizaje, esta vez en una triple dimensión. El texto al que aludo es un ensayo en primera persona de Lourdes Casal (1938–1981), "Memories of a Black Cuban Childhood" —dado a conocer poco más de dos años antes de su muerte prematura— escrito cuando ya la autora viajaba con frecuencia a su tierra natal. El ensayo apareció en abril de 1978 en la revista *Nuestro* (1977–1987), que a la sazón editaba la periodista y dramaturga Dolores Prida en Nueva York, la "patria" adoptiva de Casal.

El segundo texto nos sumerge retrospectivamente en una sociedad insular compuesta de castas en cuya base se concentran los negros y los mulatos. Nos golpea con un universo regido por una arraigada segregación racial, en cuyos predios un niño pobre descendiente de jamaicanos se erige en la figura abyecta por antonomasia, condenada inexorablemente al menosprecio general. El personaje abandona la isla y años más tarde retorna para abanderar la lucha contra el persistente prejuicio racial en la Cuba revolucionaria, con fatídicas consecuencias. La Cuba en la que intenta reinsertarse ha decretado el fin de la discriminación y, por consiguiente, la batalla es no solo ociosa, sino también desafiante y arriesgada. El autor se ve obligado a abandonar la isla una vez más y ha permanecido en el exilio. Las memorias donde se aprecia esta otra atmósfera infeliz son *Pichón: Race and Revolution in Castro's Cuba* (2008), de Carlos Moore.

A grandes rasgos, los textos señalados se sitúan en los dos polos de las interpretaciones sobre el papel que ha jugado la raza en la historia cubana. Mientras que uno se regodea a primera vista en la armonía del mestizaje, el otro delata la larga historia de animosidad entre las razas. Debido a la marcada diferencia, estos relatos autobiográficos parecieran devenir caja de resonancia, al otro lado del estrecho de la Florida (se trata de textos publicados en los Estados Unidos), de las tensiones que rodean el tratamiento del tema racial entre los investigadores. En su libro *A Nation for All: Race, Inequality, and Politics in Twentieth-Century Cuba* (2001), Alejandro de la Fuente profundiza en las opiniones discrepantes sobre los prejuicios raciales en la isla a lo largo del siglo XX. Por un lado, hay quienes subrayan la naturaleza racista de la sociedad prerrevolucionaria, descorriendo el velo de la opresión a la que estaban sometidos los de piel oscura. Por otro lado, hay quienes resaltan el progreso de los afrodescendientes tanto bajo la república como en la etapa posterior, gracias a las oportunidades que obtuvieron paulatinamente. De la Fuente califica estas visiones como "the dominance of racism" y "the possibility of racial integration" respectivamente, de forma que se establece una bifurcación en la apreciación e interpretaciones de los conflictos raciales, cada lado enfatizando lo que percibe como la tónica sobresaliente del asunto.[1]

Aunque el estudio de este historiador se circunscribe a la isla, dichas tendencias afloran de forma análoga entre los abocados a pensar sobre el mismo tema en el exilio, como sugieren de cierta manera los textos autobiográficos de Casal y de Moore. El presente trabajo trata sobre la inserción compleja y ambivalente de Casal en dicho panorama. Si bien Casal pareciera acogerse en ocasiones al mestizaje complaciente que celebra la mezcla racial que opera como un crisol de razas, en realidad ese mestizaje está intervenido por una visión analítica y crítica, cultivada durante un largo periodo de tiempo. Dicho mestizaje militante se pone de manifiesto en algunos de sus escritos.[2] A causa de sus vicisitudes en la diáspora, Casal somete a revisión el discurso sobre la identidad nacional cubana sin renunciar al mismo.

Es conveniente ubicar a Casal sobre el trasfondo resumido por de la Fuente porque su obra tiende un puente, de cierta manera, entre esas tendencias aparentemente incompatibles. Para corroborarlo, es conveniente evaluar el tratamiento del tema de marras tanto en sus ensayos académicos como en su literatura, en especial en el relato autobiográfico. Este último proporciona el medio para reclamar una identidad negra y al mismo tiempo forjar una imagen tamizada por la mitopoética de la nación cubana, una imagen que se acopla a los ideales de la reconciliación racial en Cuba. Es indispensable apuntar que su propuesta se aviene a lo que Zuleica Romay Guerra denomina "la unidad de las diversidades", que tolera y acepta las diferencias raciales y étnicas, entre otras, y no "la unidad rasa e indiferenciada" que escamotea las antedichas diferencias en aras de un ideal.[3] Dicha propuesta, sin dejar nunca de incitar al análisis y la reflexión, corresponde al modelo del mestizaje como un relato que aúpa la nación, es decir, como "expresión del persistente anhelo de unidad de la nación".[4]

El lugar desde el cual se erige tal puente nos remite a la posición "otra" de Casal, al margen de los encasillamientos. Se trata de una localización que han resaltado, desde distintos ángulos, algunas académicas que en los pasados años se han aproximado a su variada obra: Miriam DeCosta-Willis, Laura Lomas, Yolanda Martínez-San Miguel (en colaboración con Frances Negrón-Muntaner, en uno de sus ensayos sobre Casal) y Eliana Rivero. Para la primera, dicho enfoque se origina en las coordenadas geográficas dentro de las cuales se orientan sus textos literarios. Estos oscilan entre La Habana y Nueva York como metáforas de representación de una subjetividad que transgrede los lindes de un territorio circunscrito por la geografía insular, a la que es común superponer una nacionalidad igualmente circunscrita. Para la segunda, se deriva de su proto-latinidad, la cual se adelanta al discurso contestatario, feminista y/o afrolatino de más reciente factura (ver el artículo de Lomas en el Dossier). Para la tercera, proviene de su escritura "en queer", caracterizada por las alusiones, en su ficción, a sexualidades alternativas, lésbicas en particular, que se desvían de la heteronormatividad, y a otras categorías de análisis que producen una "nota discordante".[5] Y para la cuarta, se origina en su dominio de dos ámbitos culturales diferentes, lo cual se evidencia en los múltiples referentes literarios, musicales y de otros tipos plasmados en su narrativa.[6]

Las cuatro apuntan, y yo suscribo su criterio, al cuestionamiento de categorías heredadas que, debido al entrecruce de perspectivas, Casal asumió implícitamente al esquivar conceptos y paradigmas que consideró inadecuados o insuficientes para la exploración cabal de la subjetividad, las relaciones sociales y diversas coyunturas. No podían darse por sentado las hipótesis corrientes en el análisis social, como observó en más de una ocasión, sin reajustarlas en cada caso para que mantuvieran su validez. Esa otredad se concretó igualmente en el acercamiento a su patria después de haberla abandonado a raíz del triunfo de la Revolución de 1959 y en su apuesta por el diálogo entre los cubanos años después, cuando el antagonismo a ultranza y la controversia apasionada en torno a Cuba se llevaban la palma.[7] Casal nadaba contra la corriente, resistiéndose al yugo de las normas.

La noción de mestizaje se vincula correlativamente a categorías indeterminadas debido al sincretismo y la fluidez racial que connota. Casal adopta el mestizaje como símbolo de la nación caribeña, pero lo hace desde una postura crítica que aprovecha la elasticidad implícita en el concepto. Por otro lado, el mestizaje se constituye asimismo en una vía para superar la dicotomía racial imperante en los Estados Unidos, es decir, para diferenciarse con respecto a la codificación de las razas en el imperio. Entre estos dos ejes se desempeñaba Casal, aunque el primero —su relación con Cuba— haya recibido más escrutinio que el segundo.

La cuestión racial en la ensayística de Casal

La polifacética y carismática Lourdes Casal incursionó tanto en el campo académico como en la creación literaria, además del periodismo. Siendo muy joven, colaboró asiduamente con publicaciones periódicas de perfil cristiano en Cuba, como *La Quincena* y *Quibú*, este último órgano oficial de la Universidad Católica de Santo Tomás de Villanueva, donde estudió. En *La Quincena* publicó, cuando apenas contaba diecinueve años de edad, "Derechos civiles y discriminación racial en los E.U.", un artículo que revela su interés en este tema desde su juventud y que anticipa inquietudes posteriores.[8] En el exilio, Casal se destacó como activista y cofundadora de organizaciones inequívocamente a favor del diálogo entre los cubanos de ambas orillas. Las actividades de la revista *Areíto*, la Brigada Antonio Maceo, y el Círculo de Cultura Cubana, organizaciones, en especial la primera, con las que Casal se vinculó, estaban enfrascadas en la reafirmación o la recuperación simbólica de lo cubano a través del aprendizaje sobre la actualidad cubana, la promoción de la cultura isleña en los Estados Unidos y la participación directa en la Cuba de los años sesenta y setenta. Fue también cofundadora del Instituto de Estudios Cubanos, el cual mantuvo una actitud más crítica hacia la revolución. En septiembre de 1973, según Norberto Fuentes, ella fue la primera exiliada en recibir la autorización del gobierno cubano para viajar a su tierra natal,[9] dedicándole una buena parte de sus investigaciones a la isla.

En lugar de reclamar una verdad absoluta, Casal asumió *avant la lettre* una posición instigada por las certezas parciales antes de que el posmodernismo le diera primacía al concepto. Esta actitud se refleja en lo que escribió.[10] Sus publicaciones en el campo de la literatura y los estudios literarios van desde *El caso Padilla* (1972) y sus artículos en revistas como *Alacrán Azul, Nueva Generación, Exilio, Ínsula, Cuba Nueva* y *Areíto* (la cual ayudó a fundar), que representan toda una gama de disciplinas y de posiciones políticas dentro del exilio cubano, hasta el poemario *Palabras juntan revolución* (Premio Casa de las Américas, 1981) y la colección de cuentos *Los fundadores: Alfonso y otros cuentos* (1973). Su tesis de doctorado en psicología social en el New School of Social Research gira en torno a las implicaciones sociológicas de la novela de la Revolución cubana. Y varios de sus trabajos académicos, incluida la disertación, se concentran en los temas de la raza y del género, a menudo en relación con el proceso revolucionario. Entre los mismos se encuentra "Black Cubans in the United States: Basic Demographic Information", que contiene los resultados de una investigación pionera, en la que colaboró Yolanda Prieto, sobre la población negra en el exilio posrevolucionario (ver el artículo de Prieto en el Dossier).

La mayoría de los trabajos académicos de Casal sobre Cuba, publicados en la década del 1970, abordaron el impacto del proceso revolucionario en parcelas significativas de la realidad social: ¿qué aportaba el estremecimiento político y social más extraordinario y convulsionante del siglo XX cubano a un mejor entendimiento de la dinámica entre las razas y los géneros (mujeres y hombres) en la isla y de la literatura insular? ¿Cómo o hasta qué punto habían cambiado las reglas del juego dados los objetivos radicales del momento? Entre los dedicados al estudio del género se destaca "Revolution and *Conciencia*: Women in Cuba", el cual gira alrededor de la urgencia de transformar la conciencia de género por encima de los cambios que venían constatándose en la infraestructura. Casal propugna la adopción de estrategias adecuadas para lograr la liberación de la mujer en un entorno como el cubano, con su propio bagaje cultural, pues insistía también en la necesidad imprescindible de no pasar por alto, en este y otros campos, las diferencias resultantes del devenir histórico. A pesar de los avances en la incorporación de la mujer a la fuerza de trabajo, el nuevo Código de la Familia, aprobado en 1975, y las crecientes oportunidades de estudio, aún perduraban los estereotipos (como el de equiparar a la mujer con la maternidad) y la labor doméstica. De ahí que faltara mucho por superar. Aunque Casal siente optimismo en cuanto al futuro, pues consideraba que ya habían empezado a dinamitarse las bases del machismo, conminaba a seguir vigilando y escudriñando el proceso. Poniendo el énfasis en los logros, Casal, sin embargo, no deja de ser cautelosa en su valoración, como hace paralelamente en sus artículos sobre la raza. Para ella, la legislación por sí sola no podría erradicar la desigualdad.

Prueba del vivo interés de Casal por el tema racial es el trabajo presentado en el Woodrow Wilson Center del Smithsonian titulado "Revolution and Race: Blacks in Contemporary Cuba". Este ensayo, esencial para comprender el pensamiento de Casal sobre las relaciones interraciales en la isla, se propone explicar por qué la dirigencia cubana había rechazado la implementación de programas del tipo de acción afirmativa que hubieran combatido frontalmente los prejuicios hacia el negro. En su opinión, había que empezar por plantear el estudio de los afrodescendientes en Cuba con empirismo, sistematicidad e imparcialidad. Hasta ese momento, dicho estudio estaba contaminado por factores ideológicos que tergiversaban los resultados, pues tampoco se utilizaban los indicadores apropiados para su análisis en una sociedad en transición como la cubana. Para colmo, había serias contradicciones entre los enfoques empleados, pues estos estaban influidos o por el nacionalismo negro en los Estados Unidos, que promovía la autodeterminación, o por el marxismo, el cual "reducía" todo análisis al conflicto de clases.[11] Con su notable capacidad de síntesis, Casal resume apretadamente estas dificultades en la introducción de su ensayo sobre la intersección entre raza y revolución. El ensayo revela las inquietudes que compartía Casal con los intelectuales que denunciaban el arraigo del racismo en Cuba, a la vez que advierte sobre la imposición de conceptos de otras latitudes supuestamente ajenos a la cubana.

Casal emplaza en su texto a escritores como Carlos Moore y lo acusa de obviar la autoctonía de lo cubano. (Igual lo haría con Eldridge Cleaver en un artículo publicado en *Areíto* sobre la intervención cubana en Angola.) Al referirse a las críticas dirigidas a la política racial de la revolución, o más bien a su carencia, Casal alude al nacionalismo afroamericano, señalando que aplican la lógica de la dicotomía racial existente en los Estados Unidos directamente a la realidad cubana, desatendiéndose de las diferencias:

They fail to recognize the possibility which Cuba embodies: the historical prospect of a true mulatto culture, emerging from the blending furnaces of the independence wars and finally crystallizing in the process of redefinition of "lo cubano" (of what Cuban means) in the transition to socialism and away from cultural colonization".[12]

Más que aseverar que las diferencias raciales ya estaban superadas, Casal apuesta por el potencial que emana de la lucha social, lo cual la insta a seleccionar cuidadosamente el léxico: "the *possibility* which Cuba embodies[,] . . . the historical *prospect* of a *true* mulatto culture[,] . . . the process of *redefinition* of 'lo cubano'" en la transición hacia el socialismo. Se trataba mayormente de una posibilidad, una expectativa y un anhelo. El mestizaje dejaría de ser una mera herramienta retórica al servicio de la patria para convertirse en simiente capaz de germinar bajo el amparo de la igualdad, contribuyendo a renovar la cubanía. Era esa dificultosa transición dilucidada, en sus distintas facetas, por Casal la que la lleva a la conclusión de que la transformación que había desatado la revolución traería como consecuencia una mayor fusión de las razas:

The deep social transformation ushered in by the Revolution, including the elimination of all forms of institutionalized discrimination (separate social clubs, separate "walking routes" in the parks of small Cuban towns, elimination of private schools, etc.) has meant increased opportunities for mingling of the races, which has accelerated the process of "mulattoization" of Cuba.[13]

El mestizaje que formaba parte esencial de la nación cubana desde la colonia se aceleraría como resultado de esta coyuntura. Casal llega incluso, como otros que reflexionaron sobre el tema, a reprobar el epíteto *afrocubano* por considerarlo redundante.[14] La estudiosa detecta en la sociedad revolucionaria tendencias que redoblan la identidad mulata del pueblo cubano, como una mayor aceptación del matrimonio interracial y una disminución de prejuicios entre los jóvenes. Su optimismo, derivado de varios estudios sobre la cuestión racial publicados por aquellos años, la lleva a la conclusión que "twenty years after the triumph of the Revolution, Cuban people—White and Black alike— seem to have accepted Cuban culture as a *mulatto* culture".[15] En su opinión, tratar de separar el sustrato afro de lo cubano suponía un gesto inútil dadas no solamente la demografía y la cultura, sino también el proceso histórico que propició su fundación y desarrollo.

Como hiciera en su ensayo sobre la situación de las mujeres en Cuba, Casal hace hincapié en ello, alegando que, además de denunciar la discriminación, hay que identificar las fórmulas aptas para impugnarla. Esta actitud estaba en conformidad con las ideas martianas de "Nuestra América" (1891) que ella exploró en artículos publicados en su juventud, como "Problemas hispanoamericanos" (1957). En ellos exhortaba a conocer desde adentro y a honrar la auténtica realidad de los pueblos latinoamericanos, propuesta sobre la que vuelve una y otra vez en relación con el entorno cubano.[16] En "Revolution and Race: Blacks in Contemporary Cuba", Casal conviene con la vertiente de la promesa de la integración racial señalada por de la Fuente, pero bajo la revolución. Como el Nicolás Guillén de "Tengo" ("Tengo, vamos a ver, lo que tenía que tener", concluye el hablante poético en su célebre poema, publicado en 1964), la escritora aplaude el progreso que representaba el cese de la más lacerante segregación racial, cese que, al eliminar las restricciones estructurales, convirtió legalmente a los negros en "sujetos de la Revolución" con igualdad de derechos, deberes y oportunidades.[17]

Sin embargo, no olvidemos que Casal argumenta en sus ensayos sobre la necesidad de arremeter contra ciertas actitudes, prácticas y prejuicios que, en el plano superestructural, perduraban (y siguen perdurando) como vestigios de la discriminación racial, vestigios contra los cuales había que luchar en términos patrios. No obstante su convicción en el progreso obtenido, la actitud crítica de la académica es incuestionable. De forma paralela a la del ensayo mencionado más arriba, Casal afirma que los prejuicios y rezagos del pasado distan mucho de haberse extirpado. Rebate la simplificación de establecer una relación directa entre la base material y la superestructura, pues las mejoras en la primera no conducen automáticamente a adelantos en la última. Para ella, ya se había enarbolado oficialmente la lucha que culminaría —era esto lo que aventuraba— en la erradicación de los prejuicios, pero no había duda de que quedaba mucho por conquistar debido, en particular, a la relativa autonomía del pensamiento racista.

A pesar de su perseverante crítica en los ensayos sociológicos, en sus textos de corte autobiográfico Casal apuesta por el horizonte de igualdad y reconocimiento a una identidad racial hacia el que, según ella, se encaminaba Cuba bajo la revolución. En el corpus comentado hasta ahora Casal hacía gala de un discurso correspondiente a las ciencias sociales enraizado en la realidad empírica, aunque no desprovisto de opiniones y datos personales explícitamente reconocidos como tales. En los textos que siguen, busca legitimidad en el literario, el cual le ofrece la vía para desplegar los imaginarios cubanos sobre la raza.

La preocupación por la raza en las "escrituras del yo"

"Memories of a Black Cuban Childhood" es el único ensayo que Casal escribió en torno a su identidad racial explícitamente desde el punto de vista autorreferencial. En este breve ensayo autobiográfico, Casal se confiesa. Y la confesión, como escribiera María Zambrano, es "la máxima acción que es dado ejecutar con la palabra".[18] Además, en algunos de los cuentos reunidos en *Los fundadores: Alfonso y otros cuentos*, hay un llamativo componente autobiográfico que acomete el tema de la raza. Todos estos textos forman parte de las "escrituras del yo" que la autora publicó en vida. Aproximarse a los textos literarios de Lourdes Casal desde la óptica racial provee elementos adicionales para decantar su posición ante un tema espinoso para la nación caribeña tanto hoy como en los años sesenta y setenta, un periodo en el que Casal va desde su rechazo abierto a la revolución hasta su empatía con los cambios que esta promovió y su retorno a Cuba. Como académica, Casal hurga en el tema racial y se manifiesta consciente de las numerosas tensiones que lo asedian. Y en sus "escrituras del yo", adopta un imaginario simbólico yuxtapuesto al mestizaje como crisol de razas, también desde una postura crítica que se percata de las diversas aristas del concepto. Despliega su mirada inconforme en todos los casos.

Veamos primero los cuentos de *Los fundadores*, en algunos de los cuales Casal abordó el tema de la raza y el mestizaje. Este libro se publicó en 1973 y, por lo tanto, los textos que contiene fueron escritos antes del primer viaje a Cuba de Casal. Ya a partir del epígrafe (o "justificación"), el libro apunta a la cubanidad como una "superposición". Todo el epígrafe privilegia la mezcla cultural, concluyendo, en su acostumbrado estilo coloquial y desenfadado, que "sólo en Cuba pondríamos a Afrodita a comer pitihayas [*sic*] y ofreceríamos olelé a San Pascual Bailón". Casal reúne en el espacio de un enunciado a la diosa del amor de la mitología griega, una fruta de origen americano, a un fraile franciscano al que la tradición popular ponía a bailotear cada vez que oraba, y un ofrecimiento (*olelé*) cuya procedencia parece ser el Congo. Al rematar el epígrafe con las palabras "Yo soy cubana. Vale", suscribe, en el plano personal, el concepto de la hibridez racial, étnica y cultural que permea la amalgama de elementos de extracción indígena, hispana y africana.

Es esta idea del mestizaje, al hilo con la tradición insular, la que marca casi toda la colección y que aparece en interacción con lo social. Desde este ángulo, al reclamar la identidad mulata Casal no hacía más que revalidar su identidad nacional, desde el punto de vista personal, gesto que formaría parte de un proyecto colectivo a partir de mediados de la década de 1970 (ver el ensayo de Leving Jacobson en el Dossier sobre las posibles motivaciones de dicho proyecto).

Aunque este es un libro de creación literaria, como señalaba arriba algunos de sus textos tienen un innegable carácter testimonial que los convierte en escrituras del yo, en los cuales la tenue frontera entre la ficción autobiográfica y el testimonio, sin desaparecer del todo, es más bien porosa. El texto inicial, titulado "Los fundadores: Alfonso", es una especie de oda a los ancestros chinos de la autora, partiendo desde la importación de los culíes a mediados del siglo XIX. Se hace un recuento del Barrio Chino de La Habana a través de las memorias de una bisnieta cuya función es recordar dicha historia. Su abuela le cuenta la historia de su bisabuelo Alfonso, quien contrajo nupcias con una mulata, hija de negra de nación y despalilladora en una fábrica de tabacos. La familia sobrevive las guerras de la independencia de Cuba y poco a poco se abre paso en la república. Dividida en varios segmentos, la historia de Alfonso se va reconstituyendo a partir de tres voces complementarias: la de un narrador omnisciente que se dirige a Alfonso con un *tú*, la de la bisnieta que se expresa con un *yo*, y la correspondiente al pasado histórico, en tercera persona y en tono impersonal. De esta forma polifónica, la autora convierte en un relato ficticio e histórico a la vez su ascendencia china (y negra) desde una perspectiva femenina, la cual tratará asimismo, en primera persona, en "Memories of a Black Cuban Childhood".

No es casual que a "Los fundadores: Alfonso" le siga el cuento "Los zapaticos me aprietan", en el que la autora recrea escenas sugerentes de una fiesta infantil celebrada en 1945. La que narra, que bien pudiera ser la bisnieta del culí chino del cuento anterior, en este frisa los siete años de edad, como hubiese tenido la pequeña Lourdes en esa fecha, y abandona Cuba dieciséis años más tarde, al igual que la autora. Obviamente, hay en este cuento ciertas huellas autobiográficas que le dan pábulo a Casal a ejercer la crítica sobre "el petit burgeois [*sic*] cubanensis" que ella conocía bien, ya que su familia ocupaba una holgada posición social.[19] Su padre era médico y dentista y la madre, maestra. Su linaje social se comprueba en su álbum fotográfico, el cual registra los hitos y rituales correspondientes al mismo: fiestas de cumpleaños, la primera comunión, la celebración de quinceañera y los estudios universitarios.[20]

"Los zapaticos me aprietan" se dedica a parodiar las prácticas insípidas de ese sector de la pequeña burguesía cubana en las fiestas infantiles, como las declamaciones, bailes y tonadas de niños, a las cuales la narradora se resiste. El título alude a unos versos que los niños cubanos tenían la costumbre de memorizar. Como se trata de "un testimonio", la crítica se dirige a una burguesía que comprende a parte de la población negra a la que su familia pertenecía.[21] Se trata de un sector demográfico que se amolda a las prácticas culturales de la élite blanca y que con ello silencia, figurada pero fallidamente, su condición racial. Fallidamente no solo porque los valores prevalecientes le impiden olvidar su origen, sino también porque se veía apremiada a exagerar el estilo de vida de la pequeña burguesía cubana para poder "pasar",[22] convirtiéndose así en una especie de remedo que llama la atención sobre sí mismo. Sin embargo, su acceso a ciertas ventajas sociales por su posición de clase contribuía a que pudiera sortear los efectos más deletéreos de la discriminación. El relato está escrito desde el punto de vista de un narrador que ha superado esa tendencia, inscribiendo a la vez cierta distancia. Este texto es una especie de representación de ese mestizaje que aspira a la "unidad rasa e indiferenciada", como apuntaba Romay, porque con esas prácticas se pretendían borrar las diferencias.

FIGURA 1. Casal de niña. Cortesía de Marifeli Pérez-Stable

La crítica social y racial se evidencia en otro cuento titulado "Juegos", también ambientado en los años de la niñez de Casal. Construido igualmente alrededor de un "yo", el texto esboza el despertar de la conciencia de clase de la joven narradora, cuando "creía que los problemas de desnutrición en el barrio de Los Sitios [en Centro Habana, donde efectivamente creció Casal, en una casa espaciosa y cómoda cerca de la calle Infanta] podían resolverse repartiendo diariamente un queso crema y una Malta Hatuey a cada niño".[23] Para la autora, la pobreza la podía remediar exclusivamente un cambio social, revolucionario, de grandes proporciones que combatiera las raíces del problema, no la acción filantrópica dirigida a atenuarla. El cuento, sobre las relaciones de la niña con amistades blancas del barrio cuyas familias ocupaban un escalafón social menos privilegiado, le sirve a la escritora para ilustrar la velada inequidad racial. Aunque el personaje repara en las diferencias sociales y hace lo indecible por mitigarlas, una de sus amigas la excluye de un agasajo, alegando que "es una mulatica pretenciosa, que se cree mejor que nadie porque su padre es médico".[24] Pese a semejante ventaja en la estratificación social, no se le perdona su supuesta pretensión debido al color de la piel: a la "mulatica" hay que ponerla en su lugar, acotando sus ínfulas. Tales actitudes atentan contra el pretendido silencio acerca de la raza, silencio que Casal combatió a diestra y siniestra, entre otras asumiendo la negritud.

Este cuento de la colección sugiere una toma de conciencia del problema racial de manera más prominente, pero aun así sin la crítica ríspida y desapacible que se vislumbra en los textos fustigadores de otros. No obstante, "Juegos" sugiere que Casal se propuso denunciar, desde principios de los años setenta, la existencia de una "sociedad racializada" en la Cuba republicana, tildada así porque en sus procesos socioculturales intervenían continuamente "el aspecto racial y su significado social".[25] Por ese motivo, como veremos seguidamente, en su ensayo autobiográfico no es el mestizaje al uso el que, como emblema de la nación cubana, colorea su autofiguración. Ese término, *autofiguración*, es el que ha propuesto José Amícola en *Autobiografía* para referirse a la forma en que los textos autobiográficos generan una imagen moldeada por diversas estrategias de representación. El concepto tiene la ventaja de alejarnos de la representación candorosa y transparente, pues se trata de una estampa que uno quiere proyectar dentro de lo posible, lo deseado y lo aconsejable.

Mientras que los anteriores son relatos autorreferenciales, ambientados en la etapa prerrevolucionaria, que dejan entrever la relación de Casal con el tema de la raza, "Memories of a Black Cuban Childhood" es un texto singular que contiene un rotundo reconocimiento a la negritud cultural de la autora a partir del género autobiográfico en el que la protagonista, la narradora y la autora convergen, según las expectativas clásicas de esta categoría literaria.[26] Tal reconocimiento culmina con una vuelta a la Cuba mestiza. Aun así, es imprescindible anotar que la primera parte del ensayo subraya los aspectos menos ensalzados y más disminuidos del mestizaje, es decir, la negritud. Los retratos de sus antepasados, que colgaban de las paredes de la casa de su abuela, la hacen detenerse en el bisabuelo chino y en su cónyuge mulata, ambos sobrevivientes de interrelacionadas formas de esclavitud, las dos de naturaleza racial.

No obstante, mientras que su abuela hacía frecuentes referencias a su padre chino, apenas mencionaba a su progenitora, sobre la cual meramente sabía que era hija de una esclava y un hombre blanco. Este es un silencio que le preocupa. En otra parte, Casal denuncia silencios similares, en la conciencia colectiva, relacionados con la opresión de la raza negra, como los que ocurrieron durante "la guerrita del 12", diminutivo que le resta importancia a la gesta. Son precisamente esas incógnitas las que la perturban, empujándola a formular "obsesivamente" (su palabra) preguntas sobre las relaciones entre las razas y sobre su propia subjetividad.[27]

La religión afrocubana forma parte de la autofiguración de la autora. De-

FIGURA 2. Carmela López Garrido, la abuela. Cortesía de Marifeli Pérez-Stable

bido al predominio de la cultura yoruba entre los esclavos, la narradora da por sentado que sus ancestros procedían del territorio habitado por dicha etnia. Gracias a la madre recibe de herencia los atávicos códigos de la santería. Es ella la que inicia a la niña en la Regla de Ocha, exhortándola a llevar los collares de Obatalá y Yemayá, entre los orishas a los que más tarde invocaría en por lo menos cinco de sus poemas.[28] La narradora recuerda vívidamente, según relata, escenas de los ritos y las ceremonias de origen yoruba con una mezcla de admiración y sobrecogimiento, al tanto de su connotación ancestral.

Lo interesante de este ensayo en el que exalta el mestizaje color café sobrepuesto a la nacionalidad cubana es que le sirve al mismo tiempo para poner el énfasis en su negritud, como anuncia el título, no para amputarla o diluirla en tintes más claros. A través de las estrategias narrativas que utiliza, Casal subraya la magnitud del componente africano. El mestizaje oscuro le sirve asimismo para rescatar la parte más silenciada de su historia familiar y, por extensión, la nacional, tanto por el lado racial como por el de la genealogía femenina que traza. De esta manera, Casal asume el mestizaje críticamente. En su aproximación al mestizaje, el ensayo se distancia de la identidad heredada producida por la repetición y la performance, tal y como ha argumentado Judith Butler en *Gender Trouble*, y adopta la "desobediencia" por la manera en que se subvierte esa identidad al hacer resaltar un elemento comúnmente amortiguado, pero vital.

Una vez reafirmada esa negritud cultural (o mestizaje "subido de color"), producto de sus experiencias en los Estados Unidos ("Here [in the United States] I had to learn to assert my Blackness somehow—even or particularly as a Hispanic Black"),[29] la narradora describe el periplo que recorrió hasta llegar de vuelta a una Cuba mestiza. Con su tez canela, nariz roma y cabello ensortijado, Casal personifica lo que se considera el prototipo racial de la nación mestiza, máxime cuando se toman en cuenta sus experiencias contrastantes en los Estados Unidos y en África.

Confiesa en el ensayo que durante los sesenta se sintió obligada a definirse como negra (y como hispana, signos de una doble opresión) en los Estados Unidos debido a la reinante dicotomía racial en aquella época. Es entonces que sus raíces se convierten en un problema que había que atender. Luego, durante un viaje a Nigeria, tierra de sus antepasados yorubas, descubre de que pese a su familiarización con la cultura de este país, sobresale en ese medio debido a la pigmentación de su piel, más bien clara en comparación con la de sus ciudadanos. Demasiado pálida para África y demasiado oscura para los Estados

FIGURA 3. Hacia el final de su vida. Del documental *Los que se fueron*, de Estela Bravo

Unidos, Casal concluye que debido a la sangre española y africana y china que corre por sus venas, solo en Cuba puede ella ser quien es, únicamente allí se le acepta por lo que es.[30] Casal asume ese potencial del mestizaje que viola las fronteras raciales y que había identificado en "Revolution and Race" como aspiración y lo hace suyo, aquí y ahora. En Cuba, según su propia valoración, Lourdes sabía quién era:

In Cuba, I knew who I was. I knew I came from Spaniards, Africans, Chinese in a complex mixture and blending of oppressed and oppressors, of masters and slaves, of rapists and raped, but a mixture which I felt was somehow identical to the mélange which constituted Cuba itself. I was *cubana*. And to me the essence of being Cuban was the cultural and racial mixture of which I felt I was a perfect example.[31]

La mezcla racial se erige entonces en epítome de lo cubano. Aunque desde sus propias premisas que redefinen "desobedientemente" el mestizaje, Casal elabora una autofiguración ostensiblemente acorde con la versión prevaleciente sobre la nación cubana desde el siglo XIX. En otro ensayo afirma sin ambages: "As a Cuban of mixed ancestry (white, black, and Chinese), I considered myself to be like Cuba—a mulatress in an essentially mulatto country".[32] El uso del pretérito indefinido pudiera dar la impresión de que se trata de una acción ya concluida, pero la resolución contradice tal impresión. Al final del ensayo llega a la conclusión de que "home, for better or worse, was not in Nigeria, or anywhere else, but in Cuba".[33] A diferencia de otras memorias que presentan a Cuba como la distopía (por ejemplo, las ya mencionadas, de Carlos Moore; *Antes que anochezca*, de Reinaldo Arenas; y *Mapa dibujado por un espía*, de Guillermo Cabrera Infante), en Casal Cuba representa el sitio donde mejor se *es*, a sabiendas, sin embargo, de la imposibilidad de los retornos: "Nunca se regresa a Ítaca. / Las razones son obvias. / (Heráclito y su río / entre otras cosas). / La ciudad recobrada / es invariable y dolorosamente, / otra".[34] A pesar de los obstáculos, esa Cuba un tanto idealizada en estas páginas autorreferenciales sigue siendo el mejor de los sitios. Arriba a esa idea después de su trayectoria a través de diferentes constructos de identidad racial que no armonizan con la nacional, pero que le confirman la preeminencia y problematización del factor racial mano a mano con el nacional.

No deja de ser curioso que este texto dirigido hacia Cuba haya sido escrito y publicado en inglés, otra señal del espacio ambidiestro —todavía por estudiarse adecuadamente, en relación dialéctica— en el que se desenvolvía Casal. El ensayo es relevante no solamente por resumir preocupaciones medulares de la autora sobre su identidad racial, sino por el momento en que sale a la luz. Poco más de un año antes de su publicación, Casal escribía en su cuaderno de apuntes:

De una manera inesperada, pero "normal", es decir, sin sobresaltos, siento que los fragmentos (hasta ahora en pugna) de mi vida empiezan a caer en su lugar, a convertirse en una estructura coherente.

No hay un plan maestro, solo este responder dialécticamente al entorno, este imperceptible fabricarse de una biografía en el crisol de la historia.[35]

Lo que expresa en "Memories", entonces, debe aceptarse como el testamento de una Casal madura y congruente con las vivencias que la han marcado. Es el fruto de un momento en el que, sin negar la posibilidad de cambios futuros al hacer camino al andar, se ve a sí misma habiendo alcanzado la paz interior como la culminación de un proceso de "desfragmentación". Lamentablemente, la enfermedad renal que la llevó a la muerte le impondría nuevos retos.

El mestizaje frente al racismo denunciado por otros

El texto autobiográfico de Casal alude a las tensiones en torno a la raza que salen a la superficie en sus propios artículos académicos y en los cuentos comentados más arriba, tensiones que caracterizaron las relaciones entre los diferentes sectores en Cuba durante el siglo XX, sin exceptuar los años sesenta. Este último es un periodo que si bien legisló el fin de la desigualdad racial, a la vez dictaminó el cierre en Cuba tanto de los clubes privados de las clases privilegiadas como las sociedades para cubanos "de color" que proveían de servicios a este grupo subalterno y que jugaron, junto con las organizaciones religiosas, un importante papel en la conservación del legado africano.[36] Dichas entidades habían dejado de cumplir su función, de acuerdo con la retórica oficial, como resultado de la superación de la desigualdad racial y de la lucha de clases lograda por la revolución, responsable de los estertores del racismo y la eliminación de las jerarquías sociales.[37]

Pero los críticos no han cesado de señalar que las medidas adoptadas para eliminar la subalternidad racial en sectores importantes como la educación, el trabajo y el ocio no fueron acompañadas de una campaña que arremetiera contra los prejuicios y los estereotipos que irrumpían en el plano de la cotidianeidad. Es también durante esta época que las religiones populares, como la santería que profesaba la madre de Casal, empiezan a practicarse solo soterradamente.[38] Esta es precisamente la dinámica que motivó a otros escritores negros como Carlos Moore y Walterio Carbonell, alarmados por la condena a la invisibilidad de la población afrocubana en una sociedad mestiza, a presionar a los líderes de la revolución a que prestaran atención inaplazable al palpable problema racial que arrastraba Cuba desde la colonia. El racismo, alegaban tanto Moore como Carbonell, requería una atención especial. La discusión sobre programas de acción afirmativa respondía a este objetivo respecto al cual Casal no se mantuvo al margen. Al comentar en uno de sus ensayos las objeciones de la política oficial cubana a dichos programas paliativos, Casal reconoce que pese a los avances obtenidos por la revolución hacían falta "medidas compensatorias", no especificadas en el texto, que socavaran los obstáculos que subsistían en la lucha por la igualdad.[39]

Este era un tema sobre el que había desacuerdos. En sus memorias, Moore describe sus esfuerzos para fomentar, junto a otros críticos como Carbonell, una actitud combativa, argumentando que la discriminación y la desigualdad debían enfrentarse aisladamente, como parte de una campaña diseñada adrede para erradicarlas del cuerpo social.[40] A esta opinión se adherían otros líderes negros que después se vincularon a la oposición fuera de Cuba, como Juan René Betancourt y Bencomo, presidente en el exilio de la Federación Nacional de Sociedades Negras de Cuba, quien cuestionaba la desproporcionada presencia de blancos entre los líderes de la revolución.[41] Moore cita palabras de Betancourt sobre lo contraproducente de sofocar el debate acerca del problema racial en Cuba.[42]

Al mismo tiempo, Betancourt denunciaba las exclusiones y el escaso interés que demostraban las organizaciones de exiliados por la cuestión racial.[43] Todos estos líderes advertían que el primer vocablo del binomio *afrocubano* estaba lejos de ser relevante en cualquiera de los dos ambientes. Casal compartía inquietudes similares, pero sus propuestas parece que fueran idiosincrásicas, especialmente en lo que se refiere a considerar el peso de los esquemas mentales de largo arrastre y la especificidad de la cultura cubana. Quizás su formación como sicóloga social influía en esto. Aunque al leer las expresiones sobre la prioridad concedida a lo cubano o lo africano a uno le pareciera que hubiese sido imposible delinear un común denominador, seguramente se trataba de una cuestión de énfasis. Casal le daba preeminencia a lo cubano, pero condenaba la supresión del debate sobre la raza.

A todo ello contribuía su trayectoria vital. Es posible que debido a su posición como mujer y como feminista en un orden social transido por el patriarcado, como una exiliada ideológicamente de izquierda en una comunidad en la que la cláusula constituía un oxímoron, como mulata en un país donde no se contemplaban los términos medios, y como homosexual en entornos intransigentes, Casal tuviera una perspectiva paradójicamente privilegiada para valorar los tonos grises y el aporte de distintos puntos de vista al análisis de un conjunto. A lo mejor por ello, en medio de ese haz de tensiones, mientras otros priorizaban la lucha radical contra "the dominance of racism" o la discordia racial en la sociedad, Casal fluctuaba entre condenar la desavenencia y ponderar "the possibility of racial integration" —las frases acuñadas por de la Fuente para referirse a la Cuba republicana, pero cuyas implicaciones sobrevivieron en la Cuba revolucionaria. Muy bien informada y experimentada sobre la profunda discriminación racial en Cuba, en su ensayo autobiográfico (así como en algunos de sus artículos) aparece especialmente la segunda opción. En el mismo se declara negra, pero también, y tal vez sobre todo, mulata. Su mulatez, sin embargo, pone en entredicho el mestizaje diluido que se constituye en preceptivo o convencional, ese que pudiera empujar al sector negro o mulato, como la familia del cuento de Casal, a tratar de "pasar" por blanca valiéndose del mimetismo. Al realzar su negritud, Casal se distancia y simultáneamente ensalza y enriquece el mestizaje que ha persistido como símbolo de la nación cubana.

NOTAS

El primer borrador de este trabajo fue presentado en la reunión del Cuban Research Institute de Florida International University celebrada en febrero de 2015 como parte de una mesa organizada por Jenna Leving Jacobson dedicada a Lourdes Casal. Con excepción del artículo de Laura Lomas, que añadimos más tarde por su evidente aporte, los demás trabajos de este Dossier se presentaron originalmente allí. Comprobar el interés de una nueva generación de académicos en Casal me motivó a proponerles el presente dossier a los editores de *Cuban Studies/Estudios cubanos*.

1. de la Fuente, *Nation for All*, 6.

2. Como señalan Telles y Garcia, en "*Mestizaje*", al encomiar la mezcla de las razas, el mestizaje puede suscitar el espejismo de la igualdad entre las razas y la ilusión de que no hacen falta reformas en pos de la igualdad racial (132). No es este el mestizaje acrítico que promovió Casal.

3. Romay Guerra, *Elogio de la altea*, 47.

4. Ibíd., 62. Sobre la base ideológica del mestizaje ver especialmente el capítulo "Mito, sociedad y racialidad en Cuba" (37–85) de la misma obra, el cual alude al sistema esclavista, el colonialismo y el poder del mito para potenciar la naturalización de las diferencias como parte de un proyecto hegemónico.

5. Martínez-San Miguel, "Releyendo a Lourdes Casal", s.p.

6. Rivero, "(Re)Writing Sugarcane Memories". Un fragmento de este artículo sobre el despliegue de biculturalismo en Casal fue publicado en traducción al español en el volumen editado por Ambrosio Fornet, *Memorias recobradas*.

7. González Echevarría, *Cuban Fiestas*, 113–120. El autor no escatima sus críticas al movimiento cubano progresista en los Estados Unidos de los años setenta y ochenta, con una salvedad. A Lourdes Casal le prodiga grandes elogios, aduciendo su inteligencia, simpatía y don de gentes, a pesar de tener una apariencia física que sobresalta al hijo del crítico, ya fuera por su color o su figura. Pero tan importante como estas virtudes tal vez haya sido la formidable capacidad de Casal para entablar una discusión civilizada y hasta amistosa con personas que provenían del amplio espectro de posiciones políticas en torno a Cuba, las cuales estaban generalmente en abierta contienda. Esa habilidad la llevó a interactuar con grupos y organizaciones que profesaban las más disímiles opiniones. Las anécdotas sobre Casal resaltan lo mucho que atesoraba el diálogo y su rechazo vertical a la agresión, ya que esta descartaba la viabilidad del intercambio civilizado. Ella misma se expresó al respecto en "Los límites del pluralismo".

8. El investigador Ricardo Luis Hernández Otero, del Instituto de Literatura y Lingüística de La Habana, ha documentado minuciosamente la etapa formativa de Casal en Cuba. A él le agradezco el haberme dirigido hacia las revistas en las que publicó Casal antes de salir de Cuba, cuando frisaba los veinte años. La colaboración asidua de Casal en *La Quincena*, que dirigía el padre Ignacio Biaín, desde agosto de 1956 hasta abril de 1959 permite apreciar su curiosidad ilimitada por una variedad de temas aparte del catolicismo, el que contaba entre sus prioridades. La joven Casal estaba a cargo de una columna titulada "Ciencia y Tecnología", la cual comentaba las noticias principales del momento en este campo del saber. La democracia y el liberalismo, el comunismo,

el compromiso del escritor, el teatro, los partidos políticos, y la poesía y el espíritu franciscano también fueron blancos de su mirada inquisidora. "Derechos civiles y discriminación racial en los E.U". refleja intereses que desarrollaría posteriormente sobre el desfase entre lo que establece la ley y lo que se practica, esta vez respecto al sufragio durante los primeros años del movimiento por los derechos civiles en el país del norte. Asimismo, entre lo que se predica y lo que se ejercita, pues Casal critica la falta de caridad de los católicos en las actitudes discriminatorias.

9. Casal, "Ganar hermanos", 70. Esta es una de dos entrevistas de Noberto Fuentes con Casal que publicó *Revolución y cultura*.

10. Ver Casal, "Descarga No. 1", un testimonio sobre su primer viaje a Cuba publicado en *Areíto* en 1975. Casal comienza por cuestionar la validez del testimonio por ser un género literario que adolece de subjetividad, anticipándose a las críticas que con seguridad le lloverían en aquella época de polarización, pero aun así, dice, cada testimonio aporta un dato a la totalidad, aporte que debemos tomar en cuenta para reconstruir un todo (19).

11. Casal, "Revolution and Race", 4.

12. Ibíd., 14.

13. Ibíd., 19.

14. Fernández Robaina explica en *Identidad afrocubana* (75–76) que el término *afrocubano* apenas se incorporó al habla popular por el papel primario que juega la nación, siendo utilizado principalmente por algunos estudiosos del tema negro como Fernando Ortiz y Gustavo E. Urrutia.

15. Casal, "Revolution and Race", 24.

16. Herrera y de la Cuesta, *Itinerario ideológico*, 13–19. En este ensayo, publicado por primera vez en la revista *Ínsula* en 1957, Casal sigue de cerca las ideas elaboradas por Martí en "Nuestra América", lamentando la admiración por lo foráneo entre los pueblos de Latinoamérica, señal de los hábitos mentales inculcados por el colonialismo.

17. Romay Guerra, *Elogio de la altea*, 78.

18. Zambrano, *La confesión*, 31.

19. Casal, *Los fundadores*, 34.

20. Mi agradecimiento a Marifeli Pérez-Stable por proporcionarme las fotografías del álbum familiar de Casal.

21. Casal, *Los fundadores*, 34.

22. Casal, "Entrevista", 125.

23. Casal, *Los fundadores*, 47.

24. Ibíd,, 49.

25. Romay Guerra, *Elogio de la altea*, 28.

26. Este es uno de los textos de Casal que ha sido recuperado . Ella misma no hizo ningún esfuerzo por dejar un registro de lo que escribió y de lo que estaba escribiendo cuando se agravó su enfermedad, lo cual dificulta la recopilación de sus escritos.

27. Casal "Race Relations", 12. Al igual que su "Revolution and Race", este es un artículo clave sobre el tema.

28. Casal, *Palabras juntan revolución* 13, 14, 20, 29, 106.

29. Casal, "Memories", 62.

30. Entre los homenajes aparecidos en *Areíto* después de su muerte en 1981, el de Jesús Díaz destaca también esta cualidad: "La mano de Lourdes es china, es negra, es blanca, es decir, es cubana" ("Homenaje", 7). Por su parte, Miguel Barnet resalta, con un tono benévolo, sus ancestros chinos y africanos, que "la hacían así, elegante, sofisticada, directa, llana, barroca. Pero sobre todo limpia y humilde, como si los oráculos del *I Ching* y el *Ifá* hubieran preservado para ella las fórmulas más preciadas" (16).

31. Casal, "Memories", 62

32. Casal, "Race Relations", 12.

33. Ibíd., 62.

34. Casal, *Palabras juntan revolución*, 59.

35. Esta entrada tiene la fecha del 20 de febrero de 1977. Doy las gracias a Vivian Otero por haber compartido con Lomas y conmigo algunas páginas del cuaderno de apuntes de Lourdes. Otero vivió durante un tiempo en el apartamento que ocupaba Casal en el barrio de Washington Heights, en Nueva York, en momentos de mucha efervescencia dentro de la comunidad cubanoamericana progresista. Los fines de la década del 1970 son los años de la fundación de la Brigada Antonio Maceo, el diálogo con el gobierno cubano que culminaría con el retorno de "la comunidad", la liberación de presos políticos, y la apertura de la agencia de viajes Marazul, dedicada entonces casi exclusivamente a los vuelos de la comunidad cubanoamericana. Al morir Casal, sus amigos y colaboradores más cercanos se repartieron algunas de sus pertenencias. Gracias a Otero asimismo por compartir abiertamente con nosotras sus memorias de esa época.

36. Carbonell, "Birth of a National Culture", 200.

37. de la Fuente, *Nation for All*, 281–284.

38. Ibíd., 290–295.

39. Casal, "Race Relations", 21. No es solamente en Cuba donde el tipo de programa de acción afirmativa ha sido combatido, sino en otros como Brasil y Guatemala, en los cuales el largo proceso del mestizaje se supone que haya borrado las diferencias raciales (Telles y Garcia, "*Mestizaje*", 132). Ver también la crítica al mestizaje de Sawyer, Peña, y Sidanius en "Cuban Exceptionalism", especialmente las páginas 95–96.

40. Moore, *Pichón*, 177–183.

41. Spence Benson, "Owning the Revolution", 9.

42. Moore, *Pichón*, 180.

43. Betancourt envía desde Nueva York una carta fechada el 24 de marzo de 1961 a José Miró Cardona, entonces presidente de la Junta Revolucionaria Democrática, en la que se queja de no haber recibido respuesta a su solicitud de membresía, descuido que Betancourt atribuye al "problema negro". Agradezco a Spence Benson una copia de esta carta reveladora que forma parte del Cuban Heritage Collection de la Universidad de Miami. La misma historiadora explica en *Antiracism in Cuba* (134–137) que para los miembros de la Junta lo importante era la lucha por la recuperación de la democracia y, junto con ella, la armonía racial que supuestamente existía en Cuba antes de 1959.

BIBLIOGRAFÍA

Amícola, José. *Autobiografía como autofiguración: Estrategias discursivas del yo y cuestiones de género*. Buenos Aires: Beatriz Viterbo Editora, 2007.

Arenas, Reinaldo. *Antes que anochezca*. Barcelona: Tusquets, 1992.

Barnet, Miguel. "Testimonios". *Areíto* 7, no. 26 (1981): 16–17.

Bravo, Estela, dir. *Los que se fueron*. Instituto Cubano de Radio y Teledifusión, 1980.

Butler, Judith. *Gender Trouble: Feminism and the Subversion of Identity*. New York: Routledge, 1990.

Cabrera Infante, Guillermo. *Mapa dibujado por un espía*. Barcelona: Galaxia Gutenberg, 2013.

Carbonell, Walterio. "Birth of a National Culture". En *AfroCuba: An Anthology of Cuban Writing on Race, Politics and Culture*, editado por Pedro Pérez Sarduy y Jean Stubbs, 195–203. Melbourne: Ocean Press, 1993.

Casal, Lourdes. "Black Cubans in the United States: Basic Demographic Information". Con la colaboración de Yolanda Prieto. En *Female Immigrants to the United States: Caribbean, Latin American and African Experiences*, editado por Delores M. Mortimer y Roy S. Bryce-Laporte, 314–348. Washington, DC: Smithsonian Institution, 1981.

———. "Descarga No. 1". *Areíto* 2, nos. 2–3 (1975): 19.

———. "Entrevista con Lourdes Casal" (por Susana Lee). *Areíto* 9, no. 36 (1984) (número extraordinario por el décimo aniversario de la revista): 124–126.

———. *Los fundadores: Alfonso y otros cuentos*. Miami: Ediciones Universal, 1973.

———. "Ganar hermanos (Entrevista a Lourdes Casal)" (por Norberto Fuentes). *Revolución y Cultura* 77 (enero 1979): 70–74.

———. "Images of Cuban Society among Pre- and Post-Revolutionary Novelists". PhD diss., New School for Social Research, New York City, 1976.

———. "Lourdes Casal: Hay mucho que hacer" (por Norberto Fuentes). *Revolución y Cultura* 92 (abril 1980): 70–74.

———. "Los límites del pluralismo". En *Itinerario ideológico: Antología de Lourdes Casal*, editado por María Cristina Herrera y Leonel Antonio de la Cuesta, 119–123. Miami: Instituto de Estudios Cubanos, 1982.

———. "Memories of a Black Cuban Childhood". *Nuestro* (abril 1978): 61–62.

———. *Palabras juntan revolución*. La Habana: Casa de las Américas, 1981.

———. "Problemas hispanoamericanos". En *Itinerario ideológico: Antología de Lourdes Casal*, editado por María Cristina Herrera y Leonel Antonio de la Cuesta, 13–19. Miami: Instituto de Estudios Cubanos, 1982.

———. "Race Relations in Contemporary Cuba". En *The Position of Blacks in Brazilian and Cuban Society*, editado por Anani Dzidzienyo y Lourdes Casal, 11–27. London: Minority Rights Group, 1979.

———. "Revolution and *Conciencia*: Women in Cuba". En *Women, War, and Revolution*, editado por Clara Lovett y Carol Berkin, 183–206. New York: Holmes & Meier, 1980.

———. "Revolution and Race: Blacks in Contemporary Cuba". Working Paper No. 39. Latin American Program, Woodrow Wilson International Center for Scholars, Smithsonian Institution, Washington, DC, 1979.

Casal Valdés, Lourdes. "Derechos civiles y discriminación racial en los E.U". *La Quincena* 3, no. 16 (1957): 12–13, 48–51.

Casal, Lourdes, y Marifeli Pérez-Stable. "Sobre Angola y los negros de Cuba". *Areíto* 3.1(1976): 32–33.

DeCosta Willis, Miriam. "Lourdes Casal: Identity and the Politics of (Dis)location in Lourdes Casal's Narratives of Place". En *Daughters of the Diaspora: Afro-Hispanic Writers*, 194–201. Kingston: Ian Randle Publishers, 2003.

de la Fuente, Alejandro. *A Nation for All: Race, Inequality, and Politics in Twentieth-Century Cuba*. Chapel Hill: University of North Carolina Press, 2001.

Díaz, Jesús. "Homenaje a Lourdes Casal". *Areíto* 7, no. 26 (1981): 7–8.

Fernández Robaina, Tomás. *Identidad afrocubana, cultura y nacionalidad*. Santiago de Cuba: Editorial Oriente, 2009.

González Echevarría, Roberto. *Cuban Fiestas*. New Haven, CT: Yale University Press, 2010.

Guillén, Nicolás. "Tengo". En *Tengo*. Santa Clara: Universidad Central de Las Villas, 1964. http://cvc.cervantes.es/literatura/escritores/guillen/poemas/poema_15.htm.

Herrera, María Cristina, y Leonel Antonio de la Cuesta. *Itinerario ideológico: Antología de Lourdes Casal*. Miami: Instituto de Estudios Cubanos, 1982.

Martí, José. "Nuestra América". En *José Martí: Páginas escogidas*, editado por Roberto Fernández Retamar, 1:157–168. La Habana: Editorial de Ciencias Sociales, 1974.

Martínez-San Miguel, Yolanda. "Releyendo a Lourdes Casal desde su escritura en queer". *80grados* (2015). http://www.80grados.net/releyendo-a-lourdes-casal-desde-su-escritura-en-queer/.

Martínez-San Miguel, Yolanda, y Frances Negrón-Muntaner. "En busca de la 'Ana Veldford' de Lourdes Casal: exilio, sexualidad y cubanía". *Debate Feminista* 17, no. 33 (2006): 166–197.

Moore, Carlos. *Pichón, a Memoir: Race and Revolution in Castro's Cuba*. Chicago: Lawrence Hill Books and Chicago Review Press, 2008.

Rivero, Eliana. "Lourdes Casal o la experiencia del biculturalismo". En *Memorias recobradas: introducción al discurso literario de la diáspora*, editado por Ambrosio Fornet, 68–73. Villa Clara, Cuba: Ediciones Capiro, 2000.

———. "(Re)Writing Sugarcane Memories: Cuban Americans and Literature". En *Paradise Lost or Gained? The Literature of Hispanic Exile*, editado por Fernando Alegría y Jorge Rufinelli, 164–182. Houston: Arte Público Press, 1990. https://www.questia.com/read/91502384/paradise-lost-or-gained-the-literature-of-hispanic.

Romay Guerra, Zuleica. *Elogio de la altea o las paradojas de la racialidad*. La Habana: Fondo Editorial Casa de las Américas, 2012.

Sawyer, Mark Q., Yesilernis Peña y Jim Sidanius. "Cuban Exceptionalism: Group-Based Hierarchy and the Dynamics of Patriotism in Puerto Rico, the Dominican Republic, and Cuba". *Du Bois Review* 1, no. 1 (2004): 93–113.

Spence Benson, Devyn. *Antiracism in Cuba: The Unfinished Revolution*. Chapel Hill: University of North Carolina Press, 2016.

———. "Owning the Revolution: Race, Revolution, and Politics from Havana to Miami, 1959–1963". *Journal of Transnational American Studies* 4, no. 2 (2012): 1–30.

Telles, Edward, y Denia García. "*Mestizaje* and Public Opinion in Latin America". *Latin American Research Review* 48, no. 3 (2013): 130–152.

Zambrano, María. *La confesión: Género literario*. Madrid: Siruela, 1995.

HISTORY

ANA AMIGO

Identidad, modernidad, ocio: Jardines urbanos de La Habana en el siglo XIX

RESUMEN

Pese a constituir uno de los centros urbanos más modernos y activos de su tiempo, La Habana del siglo XIX nunca encarnó la imagen capitalista de la metrópolis industrial. En este sentido, los jardines urbanos que desde principios de siglo se fueron constituyendo en la ciudad, supusieron un espacio de ocio neutralizador, no de la contaminación ni de la enajenación tecnológica, sino de los profundos conflictos identitarios que atravesó la población cubana al tratar de calibrar sus deseos de independencia con la pertenencia hispánica al antiguo régimen. Incluso aquellos espacios verdes que fueron establecidos por las autoridades y se integraron, por tanto, dentro del proyecto colonial, fueron capaces de cuestionar a varios niveles tanto las limitaciones impuestas por las autoridades, como aquéllas desarrolladas por la propia élite urbana para preservar sus privilegios de clase. Asimismo, el mito colonial de lo exótico, proyectado por los extranjeros visitantes, se adaptó perfectamente a las condiciones ambientales de La Habana, acabando por convertirse en uno de los principales significantes de la emergente identidad cubana, todavía vigente en la actualidad.

ABSTRACT

A big part of the traditional features associated with urban modernity—industrial pollution, dehumanization, alienation from the immediate environment—do not apply to Havana. Quite the opposite. A great deal of Cuba's phantasmagoria during the nineteenth century was a continuous feedback mythology based on the colonial trope of the Exotic. For that matter, smoke did not asphyxiate Havana's dwellers, identity issues did. Its delicate relationship with the Spanish metropolis, the increasing commercial and political links with the United States of America, and the permanent fear of a slave revolution, led to a profound identity crisis. Within that process, the exotic images of the city were embraced and spread as part of a new identity in the making. In this article, I argue that urban gardens—even when they were part of the colonial agenda—played a decisive role in defining and legitimizing Havana's attributes and personal notions of modernity through leisure expressions. They became a counterbalancing scape, a liminal venue where a certain degree of permeability towards the fossilized urban hierarchies was allowed.

87

Aire fresco

Los jardines urbanos de La Habana constituyeron uno de los escenarios simbólicamente más densos a la hora de analizar la negociación de una identidad
moderna en Cuba. En mi opinión, incluso aquéllos que fueron establecidos
por las autoridades y se integraron, por tanto, dentro del proyecto colonial,
fueron capaces de cuestionar a varios niveles tanto las limitaciones impuestas por las autoridades, como aquéllas desarrolladas por la propia élite urbana
para preservar sus privilegios de clase. En este sentido, los jardines urbanos se
convirtieron en un espacio neutralizador, no de la contaminación ni de la enajenación industrial, sino de los profundos conflictos identitarios que atravesó
la población habanera durante el siglo XIX. En busca de esa nueva identidad,
estos espacios liminales se apropiaron del mito colonial de lo exótico y acabaron por convertirlo en significante de la ciudad.

Durante el siglo XIX, dos de los tópicos más frecuentados en el entorno
urbano fueron la contaminación y la celeridad de la vida metropolitana. Anthony Vidler recopila en la siguiente cita los críticos más importantes del popular concepto de alienación: "The estrangement of the inhabitant of a city too
rapidly changing and enlarging to comprehend in traditional terms; the estrangement of classes form each other, of individual from individual, of individual
from self, of workers from work. These refrains were constant from Rousseau
to Marx, Baudelaire to Benjamin" (Vidler 1994, 11–29).

En este sentido, el ejemplo de Londres es bien conocido gracias a las dis-
quisiciones teóricas de John Ruskin, quien no sólo abordó aquellas nubes del
siglo XIX en términos estéticos, sino que, en su opinión, el humo y la contaminación constituían un problema de dimensiones éticas. En una de sus conferencias sobre este tema, Ruskin confesaba: "The reader would not doubt observe,
throughout the following lecture, my own habit of speaking of beautiful things
as 'natural,' and ugly ones as 'unnatural'" (Ruskin 1884, 66).

¿Pero qué ocurre cuando, como de hecho sucede en un gran número de
casos (Sennett 1978, 135), nos encontramos ante una capital que no responde a
los parámetros de la ciudad industrial? ¿Cómo podemos encajar La Habana en
el discurso canónico de la ciudad decimonónica? Es bien sabido que el binomio de azúcar y esclavitud propició en la ciudad un crecimiento desmesurado
y sin precedentes a partir de 1800. Sin embargo, la industria azucarera estaba
localizada en el interior, junto a las plantaciones de caña, mientras que la capital quedaba reservada a las transacciones comerciales, la burocracia peninsular
y un mínimo porcentaje de actividades industriales. Por otra parte, el clima del
trópico hacía innecesario el uso de calefacción.

En cuanto al devenir acelerado de la ciudad, un gran porcentaje de la población blanca de La Habana había delegado su fuerza de trabajo en los esclavos, por lo que puede decirse que, en términos generales, el tono de la ciudad

FIGURA 1. *La Habana en* 1875. Archivo Nacional de la República de Cuba

era bastante más pausado comparado con otros núcleos urbanos del momento. Así pues, una gran parte de estas semióticas o características vinculadas al capitalismo —polución, automatismo, alienación del entorno inmediato— no pueden aplicarse a La Habana del siglo XIX, a pesar de que la circulación de capital era, paradójicamente, la principal actividad de esta ciudad.

En 1851, la escritora sueca Fredrika Bremer escribía: "No comprendo dónde están los fogones ni qué hacen con el humo. La atmósfera de la ciudad es transparente como el cristal" (Bremer 1980, 27). Tales circunstancias llamaron especialmente la atención de los viajeros británicos, como es el caso de J. M. Phillipo, debido al incremento de la industria en Inglaterra:

The atmosphere of Cuba, as everywhere within the tropics, except when the high winds prevail, is so unpolluted, so thin, so elastic, so dry, so serene, and so almost inconceivably transparent and brilliant, that every object is distinct and clearly defined as if cut out of the clear blue sky. (Phillippo 1857, 441)

Este tipo de aproximación de los extranjeros a La Habana disparó la aparición de un imaginario colectivo que orbitaba en torno a descripciones estrictamente sensoriales de la ciudad, contradiciendo el lenguaje asociado al progreso que venimos analizando hasta ahora. En 1841, C. Barinetti escribía:

Havanna is one of the most delightful places I ever saw. The brilliancy of the sky, the commanding view of the sea, the gaiety of the evergreen environs, the spacious basin with its forests of mast, evincing the extensive trade of the place, and a kind of prosperity which shows itself at every step, render that city highly agreeable and interesting. (Barinetti 1841, 120)

Este tipo de lecturas paradisíacas de La Habana, además, se acopló perfectamente a los parámetros retóricos de las guías de salud norteamericanas de mediados de siglo: "It is an Eden to see and inhale the breath of this fair isle— though the new Adam and Eve be of colour least prayed for in our 'Paradaise Regained'" (Willis 1853, 277). En el popular *Stranger in the Tropics*, C. D. Tyng se atrevía a asegurar que el clima tropical de Cuba era el más indicado para aquellos que sufrían enfermedades de pulmón (Tyng 1868), a pesar de que hacía ya catorce años que Hermann Brehmer había demostrado que la cura para la tuberculosis consistía en un régimen de aire fresco en las montañas alpinas (Warren 2006, 457–576). En el contexto de las políticas americanas post anexionistas —tras el intento de anexión fallido liderado por el venezolano Narciso López, planeado en Nueva York, y llevado a cabo por él mismo y otros filibusteros de origen cubano— este tipo de sesgos beneficiaban en gran medida la promoción de Cuba como destino turístico.

Dicho aspecto ha sido muy bien estudiado por J. P. Leary, quien asegura que, en términos generales, las guías de viaje americanas publicadas tras la tentativa de López en 1851, transitan dos estilos retóricos opuestos: la celebración paradisíaca o la ironía que suscita el encuentro con una realidad decepcionante (Leary 2009, 130). Efectivamente, La Habana no siempre fue un destino ideal o edénico. No obstante, incluso cuando las descripciones de la ciudad eran negativas y gravitaban hacia el tópico urbano de Babilonia (Tinkler-Villani 2005), solía recurrirse al discurso de la enfermedad o a las tormentas tropicales, de tal forma que el régimen descriptivo de lo sensorial permanecía vigente dentro del contexto de estos fenómenos naturales.

Las epidemias tropicales fueron usadas frecuentemente como tropo infernal (Edmon 2005). En el caso de La Habana, el cólera resultó especialmente nocivo para la ciudad. Su brote más devastador, acaecido en 1833, no sólo despertó un sinfín de literatura científica sobre el tema, sino que, de hecho, acabó por convertirse en uno de los principales argumentos para la regeneración social y urbana (Ramos 1994). Por otra parte, los relatos sobre huracanes terminaron formando parte del imaginario colectivo del Caribe debido a la tradición oral que se transmitía de generación en generación (Pérez Jr. 2001, 7–8), constituyendo una afirmación de pertenencia bastante consolidada. Sin embargo, tal y como hemos dicho, las descripciones de estas tormentas estaban ligadas a la celebración natural del entorno:

Cuando eran las siete de la noche reinaba una oscuridad profunda, alumbrada a intervalos por la luz rojiza de los relámpagos; una lluvia copiosa, con que jugaba el huracán, azotaba los edificios, mientras que las ramas de los árboles y las tejas de los techos volaban por el aire estrellándose contra los objetos que encontraban a su paso. Aturdían el fragor de los truenos y el ruido del viento entre las olas, en las calles y en las quiebras de los cerros, al través de los cuales se percibían, de vez en cuando, los cañonazos con que los náufragos imploraban la compasión impotente de los que en tierra apenas podían guarecerse contra la rabia del huracán. El terror de las gentes, el espanto con que aguardaban el rayo que había de venir a calcinarlas, o la ráfaga que había de arrastrar los escombros de sus casas; todo se reunía para dar a aquella escena lúgubre un carácter de horror capaz de helar la sangre en las venas del hombre más valeroso. (Borrero 1869, 15)

En definitiva, aunque La Habana cumplía todas las condiciones económicas para ser considerada una ciudad moderna —capitalista—, su clima y, especialmente, las peculiares características de la producción de azúcar, hicieron que su apariencia externa no se ajustase a las características de otras grandes metrópolis industriales del momento. Esto provocó el desarrollo de un tipo de literatura en torno a la capital cubana basada en la percepción sensorial de la naturaleza, frente a los regímenes escópicos y tecnológicos que predominaron en el desarrollo del imaginario de la ciudad decimonónica (Simmel 2002, 11–19; Benjamin 2006, 69).

El mito de lo exótico

En 1800 el poeta alemán Novalis adelantó de forma muy clarividente la ansiedad que provocaría al hombre su separación de la Naturaleza, un temor del que Occidente ya no se desprendería jamás:

The old world began to decline. The pleasure-garden of the young race withered away, up into more open, desolate regions, forsaking his childhood, struggled the growing man. The gods vanished with their retinue. Nature stood alone and lifeless. (Novalis 1977)

La ecuación Naturaleza = Dios, así como sus derivados en escenarios incorruptos de la Biblia, fueron temas que, desde su conquista, habían sido asociados con la isla de Cuba, y que en el contexto de la industrialización del siglo XIX cobraron una fuerza renovada:

A blight fell upon Cuba on the day when Columbus came, with lofty spiritual professions, and first trod its soil. Filled with admiration, he exclaimed, "I know not where first to go, nor are my eyes ever weary of gazing on the beautiful verdure. The singing of the birds is such that it seems as if one would never desire to part from hence. There are flocks of parrots that obscure the sun, and ether birds of many kinds, large and small; and trees, also, of a thousand speeics, each having its peculiar fruit, and all of marvelous flavour. ("Three Weeks in Cuba by an Artist" 1853, 161)

Teodoro Adorno reflexionó sobre este particular en su *Teoría Estética*, exponiendo que la visión de la naturaleza como elemento indómito y liberador del curso de la evolución humana se intensificó en el siglo XIX cuando "la urdimbre social se halla tan apretadamente tejida que quienes en ella viven temen la muerte por asfixia" (Adorno 1983, 91). Siguiendo estas observaciones, Jens Andermann añadía que, en la dinámica del capitalismo y el progreso,

ese goce sin inversión, sin trabajo, en una figura de resonancias religiosas a la vez que históricas y políticas, es a un mismo tiempo tentación, invitación a un peligroso desvío de la disciplina crítica al pantanoso terreno de la inmediatez (*Eigentlichkeit*), y promesa radical de liberación de las cadenas de subjetividad burguesa y occidental. (Andermann 2008, 1)

Y he aquí una cuestión fundamental: en el contexto de esta tradición retórica, la ideología colonial tiende a separar y, más importante, a excluir los conceptos de naturaleza y cultura, de caos y claridad (Bhabha 1994, 124), aunque este axioma funcione exclusivamente a nivel teórico, tal y como demuestran la mayoría de las iniciativas coloniales. En el caso de Humboldt, por ejemplo, la sensibilidad estética que le produjo la naturaleza de Cuba tuvo una gran repercusión en su discurso científico posterior (Dettelbach 1999, 475). Es más, algunos teóricos postcoloniales más radicales como Jill Casid, llegan a proponer que el paisaje tropical es en realidad una creación artificial fruto de la proyección estética del siglo XVIII (Casid 2005, 8). Sea como fuere, lo cierto es que la problemática de lo exótico sigue siendo hoy en día muy compleja, pues todavía no ha sido abordada como entidad autónoma, permaneciendo dentro de discursos relativistas que no llegan a abarcar su entera complejidad (Agzenay 2015, 2).

En este sentido, lo que hace verdaderamente modernos a los jardines de La Habana decimonónica, es que en ellos se reproduce un discurso colonial de lo exótico que ha sido asimilado por sus habitantes, a través del cual se reconcilian dos elementos tradicionalmente expresados como contrarios: la modernidad y la percepción sensorial de la naturaleza. Es decir, la diferencia que encontramos en La Habana con respecto a los espacios ajardinados de otras urbes coetáneas radica en la paradoja de que sus jardines y paseos se presentaron, de forma absolutamente deliberada, como imagen de lo exótico, y que este producto fue consumido mediante la percepción sensorial (Besse 2011, 14), una sinestesia que adelanta muchas de las experiencias de ocio vigentes en la actualidad, como el recurso de la autenticidad escenificada (MacCannell 1999, 121): ofrecer al visitante lo que espera encontrar en el lugar, reduciendo la alteridad a una fórmula de consumo a través de la retórica de lo exótico (Han 2012, 14). Hasta ahora hemos hablado de lo exótico como filtro externo a través del cual La Habana es observada desde fuera, pero, ¿cómo fue el proceso

FIGURA 2. William Henry Hurlbert, *Gan-Eden; or, Pictures of Cuba*. Boston: John P. Jewett and Company, 1854

de acogida de esta retórica, por otra parte de una gran sugestión estética, por los habitantes de la ciudad? El hecho es que, en un contexto de debilidad o fragilidad identitaria como se vive a mediados del siglo XIX, el imaginario paradisíaco construido por los extranjeros fue reproducido hasta sus últimas consecuencias por los habitantes de Cuba (Barcia Zequeira 2002, 21). Se trataba, pues, de un flujo bidireccional de lectura y escritura de la ciudad, que acabó por contaminarse mutuamente (Álvarez-Tabío Albo 2000, 16).

Esto no sólo afectó a las dinámicas urbanas, sino que acabó empleándose en ocasiones como símbolo distintivo de la identidad cubana. Un caso anecdótico que refleja muy bien este trasvase es el de Francisco P. de Coimbra. En una carta escrita en castellano a Domingo del Monte y firmada en Nueva York el 21 de noviembre de 1840, el cubano añade una posdata en inglés:

How do you like my Seal?—A Palm—yes, a palm is the emblem of Cuba—The Land of Palms. Every one choose arms; but I prefer a Palm according to my democratic principles and because I wish that every one may say "That fellow is a native of Cuba." (Academia de la Historia de Cuba 1930, 196)

De hecho, algunas de las descripciones más exóticas y sensoriales de La Habana del siglo XIX fueron realizadas por cubanos:

A este punto de su narración llegaba mi tia cuando entramos en el paseo de Tacón. El sol se ocultaba envuelto en hermosos cendales de oro; la palmera, la magoa, la jagua, y los graciosos matorrales de rosa altea, agitados por la brisa de la tarde, se balanceaban dulcemente; las aves, que habian estado silenciosas durante el calor del dia, cantaban alegremente rebuscando su nido, meciéndose sobre la débil y perfumada rama que debia servirles de asilo, y protegerles contra el rocío de la noche. Algunas jóvenes sentadas á sus ventanas, contentas y risueñas, dirigían al través de las rejas miradas que brillaban como estrellas, y nos saludaban agitando sus blancas manos. Otras, recostadas voluptuosamente en sus quitrines, gozaban desdeñosamente de la dulzura del aire y de la hermosura de la naturaleza. (Merlín 1844, 47–48)

El empleo de este tipo de oratoria para afirmar la identidad cubana también provocó rechazo en muchos intelectuales del momento. Así, tanto el relato de la *Condesa de Merlín* (Veráfilo 1844), como algunas guías americanas del tipo de *Gan-Eden, or, Pictures of Cuba*, publicada en Boston en 1854, fueron inmediatamente contestados:

Sin embargo, despúes de leer el libro de cabo á rabo, se vé bien que si el autor no hace reserva ninguna en la aplicacion de esos sonoros y dulces epítetos á Cuba física, á Cuba tal cual salió de las manos de su Creador, la hace y mucho respecto á la Cuba social y política. (Mendive y García 1855, 5)

Así pues, queda claro que la naturaleza, en el contexto ético, estético y material de la modernidad, jugó un papel importantísimo como aliada en la expiación de los terrores que despertaba la industria (Duguid 2010, 45). En este contexto, la retórica de lo exótico encontró un medio muy favorable de desarrollo, que, por otra parte, la ciudad de La Habana, en un giro sorprendentemente moderno, supo muy bien como emplear en beneficio propio.

Ornato y policía

Sin embargo, no todo fueron alabanzas por parte de los visitantes extranjeros. Existen también muchos testimonios de rechazo que descreditan la imagen paradisíaca de La Habana. En una ocasión, el corresponsal de *Harper's Monthly Magazine* ponía el grito en el cielo al comprobar que las plantas de la ciudad estaban siempre secas y los jardines mal cuidados. Aunque su visita tuvo lugar en el mes de agosto, época de lluvias en Cuba, lo cierto es que las inundaciones podrían ser causa de la falta de ornato en los espacios ajardinados, y encontramos más de un crítica extranjera a este respecto ("Life in Cuba" 1871, 350). Incluso aquellos que a su llegada quedaban maravillados con la capital cubana, tardaban poco en advertir la mala gestión de sus residuos orgánicos:

Should I like Havannah? To be sure: who would not be charmed by his first experience of life in the tropics? What is the brightness of the sea and sky, even in Italy, compared with the glittering waves and blazing stars of this glowing region? What is the rank growth of elms and oaks even in moist England, compared with the teeming life of this torrid vegetation? Somehow, however, is spite of the raptures into which travelers new to the world, and especially those from dreary Yankeeland, are apt to fall, the country about Havannah, on a first glance, presents itself as singularly flat and bare, and the town itself, after a few hours' evidence, suggests the definition of a "city of smells and noises". (Gallenga 1873, 55)

Aunque La Habana no fuese una ciudad industrial al estilo de las grandes ciudades europeas o estadounidenses, tal y como hemos visto, la contaminación urbana radicaba en problemas de salubridad e higiene básicos. En primer lugar, la congestión intramuros facilitaba el contagio de epidemias y hacia muy difícil mantener la calidad y potabilidad del agua de la Zanja, después Acueducto de Fernando VII (Segre 1997, 277):

En realidad, La Habana de la época de Cecilia Valdés era una ciudad sucia en extremo, poco saludable y con escaso atractivo para quienes no disponían de bienes, una abrumadora mayoría. Las aguas malolientes a que aludieron viajeros con sentido crítico, llevaban a sus calles basura, desechos de la alimentación y detritus que atentaban contra el olfato y la salud del vecindario; la de beber, la extraían de pozos y ríos distantes, para conservarla en aljibes de dudosa higiene. En la zanja principal, que llegaba al centro desde la Chorrera, se bañaban personas o animales. (González 2012, 61–62)

Y no sólo la calidad del agua suponía un tema conflictivo, sino también su cantidad. En 1854, por ejemplo, el Ayuntamiento se dirigió al ramo de acueductos alertando sobre la escasez de agua para todo el vecindario de La Habana (*Expediente promovido por el ayuntamiento . . .* 1854). En época de lluvias, cuando el agua no era precisamente escasa, se producían continuas inundaciones debido a la mala gestión del pavimento y el alcantarillado.

Por otra parte, La Habana experimentó constantes problemas con la iluminación urbana, lo cual afectaba a la ciudad a varios niveles: seguridad, ornato, ocio. Teniendo en cuenta que un alto porcentaje de su vida social tenía lugar de noche —*The real social life of Havana is revealed, however, after dark* (F. H. Taylor 1879)—, las dificultades con el alumbrado fueron una de las mayores preocupaciones de sus habitantes.

No obstante, para examinar los problemas de ornato y policía en La Habana, es preciso retroceder a las primeras planificaciones oficiales de los barrios extramuros en el año de 1819. Recientes estudios como *Beyond the Walled City: Colonial Exclusion in Havana*, de Guadalupe García, han insistido en la tradición historiográfica de la existencia de dos ciudades separadas por la muralla y, sobre todo, en el uso de estos barrios como estrategia urbana para exiliar a las clases menos favorecidas (García 2016, 5). Aunque este argumento tiene gran parte de verdad, la planificación y desarrollo de los barrios extramuros resultó ser un proceso mucho más complejo en el que, por una parte, no todas las autoridades implicadas fomentaron las políticas de exclusión y, por otra, siempre se tuvo claro que la prioridad era unificar las dos secciones de la ciudad en la medida de lo posible, incluso proponiendo desde fechas muy tempranas el derribo de la muralla.

Con respecto a este momento histórico, se ha sugerido en varias ocasiones la idea de que el subteniente Antonio María de la Torre dirigió todo el proceso del trazado de los barrios extramuros e, inclusive, que fue el encargado de redactar unas ordenanzas municipales para La Habana en 1817, las cuales incluirían por primera vez la noción de dichos barrios. No obstante, estos axiomas no han sido esgrimidos mediante testimonio documental (Weiss 2002, 341; Venegas Fornias 1990, 15; Chateloin 1989, 111), y de hecho los materiales consultados denotan una jerarquía de trabajo bastante más complicado (Amigo, en prensa). La búsqueda de las ordenanzas de 1817 no ha dado frutos por el momento. Lo único que puede apuntarse al respecto es que entre los años de 1640 y 1855 rigieron en La Habana los mismos estatutos, que fueron reimpresos en el año 1827 por el gobierno insular (Pedroso 1827).

En cuanto al papel que hubo de desempeñar Antonio María de la Torre, por el momento sólo puede certificarse que a él le fue encomendado el dibujo de sendos planos de los barrios extramuros —con fines militar y urbanístico, respectivamente—, enviados a la regencia en diciembre de 1819. Fue ésta la materialización gráfica de dos años de especulación y trabajo de campo en los que la intervención del director del cuerpo de ingenieros por aquellos años, Antonio Ventura Bocarro, del coronel Mariano Carrillo, del segundo jefe de brigada Félix Lemaur y del Agrimensor General de Florida, Vicente Nicolás Pintado, resultó absolutamente decisiva, a pesar de haber quedado sus nombres alejados de todo crédito.

Así pues, en diciembre de 1819 el Capitán General recibió cuatro ejemplares del *Plano de una parte de La Habana y sus barrios extramuros*, firmados por Antonio Maria de la Torre, junto a una memoria de los mismos realizada por Antonio Ventura Bocarro (Bocarro 1819). En esta memoria, Bocarro se

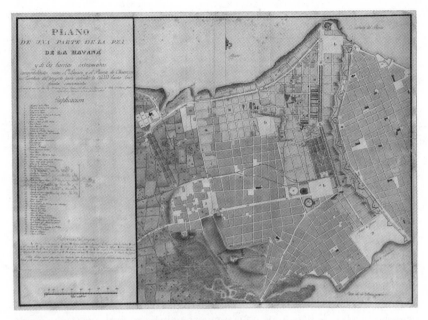

FIGURA 3. *Plano de una parte de la Pza. de La Habana y de los barrios extramuros.* 1819. Ink-on-paper drawing. Cartoteca, Archivo General Militar de Madrid

lamenta sobre la interferencia que todas las construcciones irregulares de la zona habían tenido en la búsqueda de un diálogo visual coherente entre sendas partes de la ciudad, así como de la dificultad de lidiar continuamente con la promiscuidad existente entre lo público y lo privado.

Un aspecto muy relevante de esta planificación fue el gran número de innovadoras medidas que proponía. Sin embargo, la gran mayoría nunca fueron llevadas a cabo, y las que sí lo hicieron hubieron de esperar varias décadas. Entre las reformas que proponía el plan de 1819, encontramos una gran plaza ajardinada en el Campo de Marte, un paseo para el uso exclusivo de peatones, así como baños dulces y salados de uso público y gratuito.

En síntesis, podríamos afirmar que pese a la imagen paradisíaca comercializada por La Habana, la gestión ineficaz de sus residuos orgánicos, especialmente a partir del crecimiento descontrolado de sus barrios extramuros, generó una gran preocupación que acabó por manifestarse en un innovador plan urbano de los mismos. Sin embargo, la intervención extramuros tardó muchas décadas en asemejarse al proyecto de 1819, presentando en ocasiones viviendas de muy mala calidad y, más importante para el tema en cuestión, grandes deficiencias en materia de salubridad urbana. No obstante, tal y como veremos en el desarrollo de este trabajo, las iniciativas de tipo higienista, especialmente aquellas relacionadas con el esparcimiento, acabaron por emerger de forma casi orgánica en la ciudad a pesar de la legislación vigente.

Los primeros "jardines sociales": del Jardín Botánico a la Quinta de los Molinos

Desde comienzos del siglo XIX aparece en Cuba una marcada tendencia a promover las iniciativas botánicas, ya fuesen de tipo científico o con un perfil más didáctico. Sin duda, las excursiones de Alexander von Humboldt a la isla (Humboldt 1856) habían establecido un precedente muy importante. Su empresa, como tantas otras de la época, constituía un síntoma obvio de la expansión económica europea (Pratt 2010, 211) que tenía sus orígenes en las expediciones ilustradas (Wagner, Dickhaut, and Ette 2015). En el caso del proyecto hispánico, tal y como Daniella Bleichmar ha demostrado, las expediciones botánicas y su legado visual jugaron un papel decisivo a la hora de apoyar el proyecto colonial (Bleichmar 2012). La exploración y análisis de los recursos naturales del Caribe, así como la publicación de estos estudios, facilitó la publicidad y legitimación del imperio, así como el nacimiento de los primeros programas ecologistas de Occidente, como respuesta a la deforestación del trópico (Grove 1996). Esta rama de la empresa colonizadora también había sido exitosamente demostrada en las colonias francesas (Osborne 1994), inglesas y, en última instancia, desarrollada por todas potencias europeas con dominios en ultramar (Mitchell 2002, 5; Sluyter 2002).

Y es aquí donde el problema de la modernidad vuelve a aparecer en escena. Para Walter D. Mignolo, la colonialidad y la modernidad constituyen dos caras de una misma moneda, tratándose de fenómenos codependientes que constantemente se retroalimentan (Mignolo 2010, 9). En este sentido, mi propuesta es que el Jardín Botánico de La Habana supuso una estrategia imperial que, no obstante, entrañaba un propósito descolonial (39), esto es, crear un espacio rehabilitador (Francis and Hester Jr. 1991) en el marco de una legislación urbana altamente restrictiva en términos de socialización y modales públicos (Valdés 1842).

Inaugurado en 1817 (Puig-Samper, Valero 2000, 60), el primer Jardín Botánico de La Habana contaba con varias fuentes, una pequeña glorieta y un laberinto (94–95). Las noticias confirman que tan sólo un año después de su inauguración, en 1818, la gente había comenzado a reunirse en este espacio para recoger hierbas y plantas medicinales (95). Se crea así un punto de reunión informal fuera del marco legislativo, en el cual pudieron desarrollarse formas alternativas y más naturales de socialización (Cosgrove 1984, 18). Asimismo, al estar prohibidos los carruajes dentro del jardín, las mujeres encontraron un espacio legítimo donde caminar y realizar un ejercicio físico que generalmente no les estaba permitido debido a las restricciones morales.

La reclusión e inmovilidad de la mujer cubana, en este sentido, supuso uno de los síntomas más evidentes de los conflictos identitarios que padeció la isla durante el siglo XIX. Visitantes americanas como Julia W. Howe se escandalizaban con la situación de la mujer blanca en La Habana: "They of the lovely sex meanwhile undergo, with what patience they may, an Oriental imprisoment" (Howe 1860, 43).

Lo que obviamente trataba de evitarse era la interacción entre estas mujeres y los esclavos y libertos dentro del debate de las políticas de blanqueamiento iniciadas a finales del siglo XVIII y refrendadas por José Antonio Saco en la década de los años treinta (Guevara 2006, 106), de tal forma que el asunto acabó por convertirse en un elemento central de discusión acerca de la identidad cubana moderna. En 1864, *El amigo de las mujeres* se veía obligado a publicar lo siguiente:

Varias veces se han ocupado los periódicos de la capital del grave asunto de hacer bajar de sus carruajes á las damas habaneras en las horas del paseo y suplicarles que adopten la bella costumbre de caminar por las espaciosas alamedas, que hace tantos años parecen estar diciendo a gritos: —Señoras mías, hagan usted el favor de ponerme encima los pies. Pero ni por esas han accedido ellas á tan prudente petición, y hé aquí que es necesario que en este periódico se inicie la cuestión de nuevo, á fin de que se lleve ante el tribunal de quienes intervengan su justicia. (*Las mujeres en el paseo* 1864, 7)

Junto con la posibilidad de caminar libremente, el Jardín Botánico comenzó a ofrecer otros entretenimientos muy populares entre los habitantes de la ciudad. En 1827 el artista Juan Bautista Vermay, director de la Academia de San Alejandro, construyó al fondo del mismo un pequeño teatro denominado *Diorama,* donde se celebraron numerosas representaciones dramáticas, así como el primer baile de máscaras celebrado en La Habana durante el carnaval de 1831 (Roig de Leuchsenring 1939, 64*; Plano del terreno que ocupa el Jardín Botánico . . .* 1839). La paradoja del Diorama no sólo reside en que fue edificado en el seno de una institución supuestamente científica, sino que, además, nunca tuvieron lugar en él representaciones que propiamente hicieran uso de la tecnología del diorama.

Como decimos, desde los años treinta tuvieron lugar en su interior funciones de las compañías dramáticas española y francesa establecidas en la ciudad (Ramírez 1891, 31), así como eventos de carácter más diplomático como el baile conmemorativo en honor a la jura de la infanta María Isabel Luisa en octubre de 1833 (Ferrety 1833, 31).

En abril de 1838 fue autorizado el uso de los terrenos del Jardín Botánico para instalar la nueva terminal de ferrocarril: el depósito de Villanueva (Puig-Samper, Valero 2000, 183). Entre 1839 y 1840, la Escuela de Botánica y todas aquellas plantas susceptibles de replantarse fueron reubicadas en la Quinta de los Molinos, casa de verano de los capitanes generales construida bajo el mandato de Miguel Tacón (184–185). A mitad de este proceso de transición, en el año de 1839, encontramos como ya algunas autoridades locales confirman las funciones lúdicas que venimos examinando, dirigiéndose a los terrenos del ex Jardín Botánico como Jardín Social (López 1839).

Una vez finalizado este traslado, el Diorama permaneció en uso algunos años más. En 1839 fue ocupado por la *Academia de declamación y Filarmónica de Cristina (*Roig de Leuchsenring 1939, 64*) y tenemos noticias de que en 1842 había pasado a ser propiedad de Luisa Long, quien ofrecía en su interior funciones dramáticas (Documentos que se relacionan con Luisa Long* 1842). En ocasiones Long alquilaba el espacio para exhibiciones de tipo circense como las organizadas por Otto Motty Kisley y su hijo en 1843:

Los señores Otto Motty Kisley e hijo con el mayor respeto a VE exponen, que han llegado a esta capital con la intención de dar funciones gimnásticas, de fuerzas físicas, equilibrios, etcétera en el teatro del Diorama. (*Sobre el permiso concedido a los señores Otto Motty Kisley e hijo* . . . 1843)

No obstante, el edificio del Diorama sufrió siempre muchos contratiempos en su mantenimiento. Constantemente había que reparar sus techos y pintar goteras. El marido de Luisa Long, Enrique Dalton, realizó algunas reformas de las más importantes durante el verano de 1844 (*Documentos que se relacionan con Don Enrique Dalton* . . . 1844), pero el devastador huracán de ese mismo año volvió a causar graves daños en el edificio (*Documentos que se relacionan con Don Ramón de la Riva Agüero* . . . 1845).

Una vez reubicado en la Quinta de los Molinos, cuyos jardines habían sido diseñados como laberintos al estilo francés —*In the vicinity of the former is the governor's villa, with its gardens laid out in the style of Versailles, and presenting beautifully picturesque effects*— (Phillippo 1857, 563) son muy pocas las crónicas que se refieren al jardín botánico por su nombre institucional. Lo más común es que fuese confundido con el jardín particular, aunque también abierto al público, propiedad del Capitán General.

El inglés Joseph John Gurney, se refería en 1840 al conjunto formado por el Jardín Botánico y los jardines de la Quinta de los Molinos como "a place of constant public resort" (Gurney 1840, 210). Por su parte, Tyng recordaba la prohibición de usar carruajes en su interior, tal y como ocurría en la primera ubicación del jardín:

The latter is a villa for the use of the Captain General during the heat of summer. The grounds of the villa, and those of the adjoining Botanical Garden, are open to visitors every day (driving is not permitted), and form a delightful promenade, where the luxuriant vegetation of the tropics can be seen in a great and admirably arranged variety. (Tyng 1868, 91)

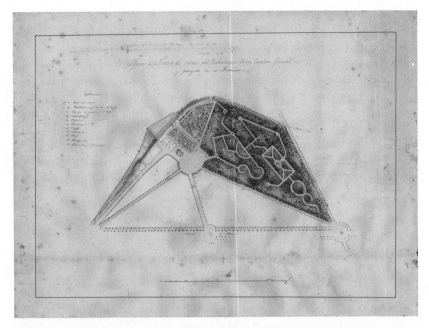

FIGURA 4. *Plano de la Casa de recreo del Excelentísimo Señor Capitan General y proyecto de un laberinto*, ca. 1837. Ink-on-paper drawing. Cartoteca, Archivo General Militar de Madrid

Henry Wikoff, manager y supuesto autor de las *cartas* de Fanny Ellser, describía el espacio como un paraíso inescrutable con tintes estéticos que remiten de nuevo al discurso de lo exótico:

We'll follow the crowd to the Tacon Garden, some very prettily laid-out grounds enclosing the summer residence of the captain governor [. . .] a beautiful moonlight, we sauntered down an *allée*, that looked too inviting to resist; we pursued it till we found ourselves in a sweet garden, where we wandered wondering and delighted. At every turn a new and agreeable surprise; a *jet d'eau*; a gurgling waterfall, with its moss and grottos; we ascended terraces, sat down in arbors, wound through thick-leaved groves, and while astonished at our presumptuous intrusion, we wondered if it had an owner, as we saw no house, heard no keepers or servants, nor the barking of some vigilant dog: all was silent and silent and enchantingly on the bright moonlight. [. . .] I had no idea where we were, whether on public or private property. [. . .] I thought of the magical gardens in the Arabian Nights. (Wikoff 1845, 44)

A medida que pasaron los años, el verdadero uso de los jardines no pasó inadvertido a los miembros locales de la Real Academia de Ciencias Médicas, Físicas y Naturales de Cuba. En 1868, F. A. Sauvalle, autor de la famosa *Flora*

Cubana, criticaba duramente el fracaso científico y la vergüenza pública que suponía el Jardín Botánico de La Habana (Puig-Samper, Valero 2000, 207).

¿Por qué, entonces, un proyecto que se declaraba fracasado fue capaz de sobrevivir más de ochenta años? Mi hipótesis es que la creciente clase alta de La Habana, así como la gran afluencia de turistas, encontraron en estos jardines un espacio alternativo de recreo que suponía, especialmente para la mujer, una tregua a los estrictos códigos sociales impuestos por una sociedad cuya principal preocupación era mantenerla biológicamente separada de la población negra masculina, fomentando una serie de conductas muy restrictivas (Costales 1854; Torre 1860). Por otra parte, incluso las autoridades locales más liberales tenían verdaderos problemas para incentivar los jardines de recreo sin el amparo institucional que ofrecía la supuesta vocación científica del Jardín Botánico.

En este sentido, el popular formato de entretenimiento del *pleasure garden* (Coke, Borg 2011; Edelstein 1983) suponía un elemento bastante complicado de encajar en el marco moral católico de la España decimonónica. Su mera tra-

FIGURA 5. *Havana: In the Botanical Gardens.* Smith Collection, vol. 2; Anon. Cuba, Havana. Victoria and Albert Museum

ducción literal, "jardín de placer," resultaba inadmisible. En 1834, tan sólo un mes después de la apertura en Madrid del Jardín de las Delicias, Mariano José de Larra criticaba ferozmente la falta de afluencia de público a este espacio, que según él podría ser muy beneficioso para la civilización y socialización del país (Larra 1834)[1].

En el caso de La Habana, sin embargo, las cuestiones de género, raza e independencia incrementaban esta problemática, por lo que los jardines públicos eran considerados mucho más peligrosos que en la península. El nivel de restricción era tal, que a veces incluso publicaciones relacionadas con la botánica eran aprovechadas para incluir relatos de tinte pseudo-erótico en la prensa local: "Al referirnos Linneo los amores de las plantas, y al descubrirnos los misteriosos agentes de su fecundación, llevados en las alas de los vientos, ¿quién no creería estar leyendo la amorosa historia de Céfiro y Flora?" (Piña 1857, 181).

Así pues, el Jardín Botánico de La Habana apoyaba el proyecto colonial y, al mismo tiempo, acogía una serie de fenómenos que encarnaban una fuerte resistencia al dominio hispánico, relejo de una sociedad en cambio. La inclusión paulatina de elementos de ocio como el diorama, el paseo femenino, las funciones de teatro o los bailes de máscaras, fueron poco a poco desplazando su papel como institución científica.

Jardines privados: el Tívoli y la Quinta del Obispo

En una fecha tan temprana como 1819, el Capitán General José Cienfuegos se refería al Jardín de Gervasio —del que no conservamos más noticias— como un obstáculo importante para el diseño de nuevos sistemas defensivos que el gobierno estaba planeado (*Informe sobre la necesidad . . .* 1839). Más avanzado el siglo, en la década de 1830, existió un jardín llamado Tívoli junto a la calzada de Belascoaín, donde se presentaban hombres incombustibles, fieras, figuras de cera, fuegos artificiales y justas medievales (Ramírez 1891, 32). Así solicitó Antonio Bruzón su apertura en 1833, inicialmente pensada para el Campo de Marte:

El exponente, señor, es propietario de un espacio de terreno situado en el Campo de Marte, al lado del paseo [. . .] este terreno es el más a propósito para hacer en él un edificio cómodo y elegante, que sirva para un establecimiento de honesta diversión a personas decentes y sea también un adorno para el mismo paseo. En esta población de tan brillante sociedad como la de La Habana se echa de menos un sitio donde el público disfrute a la vez de las delicias del campo y de los goces de la ciudad; ninguno hay que reúna estas ventajas con mas proporción que el indicado por su localidad, extensión y elementos para planificar un tívoli semejante a los que en Europa hermosean a algunas ciudades. (*Documentos y plano demostrativo . . .* 1833)

Sin embargo, en lo que a jardines privados se refiere, la verdadera estrella de este período fue la Quinta de Palatino, también conocida por los Jardines del Obispo o la Quinta de Peñalver (Murray 1856, 58). En palabras de W. H. Hulbert, este jardín resultó ser "extremely popular among American and North European visitors" (Hurlbert 1854, 61).

De hecho, la mayoría de las descripciones de este parque las encontramos en la literatura extranjera, de lo cual deducimos que la mayoría de sus consumidores debieron de ser visitantes:

We were engaged to breakfast with the British consul; but, before going to his house, we availed ourselves of the cool air of the early morning, in order to visit "El jardin del Obispo"—the villa and gardens of the late archbishop—which are quite as worthy of inspection as those of the Governor Tacon. The objects which chiefly attracted us there, were the shady avenues of mango trees, a living alligator kept in a small reservoir, and the greater rarity, in a tropical climate, of a cold stream of clear water, in which it was a luxury to bathe. (Gurney 1840, 206)

Aunque quizá el punto de inflexión de toda esta secuencia que venimos evaluando sea la aparición en escena del naturalista y empresario bohemio Benedikt Roezl, quien, tras haber viajado por toda Europa y varios estados sureños de Norteamérica, había entrado en contacto con una amplia selección de jardines públicos y de entretenimiento. Antes de llegar a La Habana en 1867 residió algunos meses en Nueva Orleans, donde en aquel momento se estaba produciendo un tremendo desarrollo de este tipo de espacios de recreo (Douglas 2013).

En 1871, Roezl realizó una petición al gobierno español para que le dejasen remontar la administración del Jardín Botánico de La Habana. Su argumento fue que, salvo aquellas personas que tenían aspiraciones científicas, los ciudadanos de La Habana no podían encontrar nada agradable en su visita a esta institución, sugiriendo la introducción del cobro de boletos para así financiar diversas atracciones de feria y un jardín zoológico anexo:

En la Habana pueden hallarse recursos para establecer y sostener un jardín botánico en su debida forma, agregándole uno de aclimatación y zoológico. El jardín botánico servirá para las ciencias, á los hombres ilustrados; el de aclimatación para los agricultores, y el zoológico en general para todos los visitantes, siendo de grande atractivo para el pueblo, á quien servirá de inocente distracción y recreo. (Roezl 1872, 505)

Obviamente la propuesta cuestionaba el *statu quo* colonial del Jardín desde múltiples ángulos, por lo que nunca fue aprobada, pero en ella quedan reflejadas una serie de realidades sociales y urbanas que fueron negadas por las autoridades a lo largo de todo el siglo XIX. En un régimen social que exigía cada vez más espacios de legitimación a través de diversas manifestaciones del ocio, no debe sorprendernos que algunas dinámicas de entretenimiento modernas fuesen filtrándose naturalmente en ámbitos más conservadores de la ciudad.

Ajardinamiento de enclaves públicos: La Plaza de Armas y el baile de la Retreta

El tema del ajardinamiento de espacios inicialmente diseñados con finalidades defensivas como el glacis de la muralla, las faldas de la Cabaña o, en este caso, la Plaza de Armas, se venía practicando en La Habana desde mediados del siglo XVIII, tal y como describía el historiador José Martín Félix de Arrate. En estas zonas, militarmente obsoletas, se fueron plantando árboles, y comenzaron a servir de destino predilecto para el paseo, ya fuese a pie o en volante (Venegas Fornias 1990, 11).

La Plaza Mayor o Plaza de Armas constituía el *locus genui* de la villa hispanoamericana, a partir del cual se trazaban los ejes determinantes del crecimiento inmediato. Este enclave, monopolio de las funciones representativas, aglutinaba en un sólo espacio simbólico la sede de gobierno, la iglesia matriz y el ejercicio de mercado, atrayendo de manera centrípeta el resto de las actividades colectivas, permanentes o esporádicas. En los años treinta del siglo XIX Miguel Tacón remodeló el palacio de gobierno y trasladó los presos a la nueva cárcel, donde comenzó a celebrar sus reuniones (Pérez de la Riva 1963, 40). De este modo exorcizaba muchas de las connotaciones militares de la plaza, que adoptó tras estas reformas un cariz menos severo y propicio a los encuentros sociales.

José de la Concha continuó el acondicionamiento de La Plaza de Armas. En 1851 ordenó la unificación de las cortinas edilicias y la eliminación del espacio ocupado por el *glacis* de la Real Fuerza para la apertura de una calle "ó mejor dicho se prolongase la llamada de O'Relly que pasa por un costado de la Plaza de Armas para facilitar entre esta y el muelle de Caballería el tránsito público, quedando de este modo separado de los edificios particulares el Cuartel de la Fuerza y dando á la vez al monumento del Templete el decoro, la belleza y la ostentación correspondientes" (Concha 1851,1–2).

A pesar de lo moderno de esta intervención, el gobernador dejó claro su fuerte deseo de subrayar los valores fundacionales en el "depósito de memoria" (Azúa 2004, 178) de La Habana, última capital colonial del reino: "conviniendo pues en todos los tiempos y mucho más en las circunstancias políticas en que se halla el país fortalecer estos recuerdos históricos y religiosos" (Concha 1851, 2).

Sin embargo, hacía ya muchos años que la Plaza de Armas era fundamentalmente reconocida por su jardín, al que acudían cada noche tanto locales como extranjeros: "We forgot to state that in front of the Captain-General's Palace there is a beautiful garden of flowers and shrubs, in the midst of which stands a monument in honor of Columbus" ("A Flying Visit to Havana" 1852).

FIGURA 6. *Plaza de Armos* [*sic*] *from the Palace.* Smith Collection, vol. 2; Anon. Cuba, Havana. Victoria and Albert Museum

En la famosa obra *Notes on Cuba*, publicada en 1844, la plaza y el baile de la retreta aparecen descritos como un verdadero jardín de entretenimiento:

And when night set in, the citizens flock to the Plaza des [*sic*] Armas, to listen to the military band that plays there several nights in the week. It is situated in front of the Captain-General's mansion, and is laid out in four small parks enclosed by low iron railings and is traversed by two wide walks paved with smooth stone, while another of like width surrounds the whole, with numerous benches, some extending the whole length of the sides, offering to the pedestrians an agreeable lounge. A few trees are planted in the parks, so arranged as not to intercept the view; while fountains, pouring out constant streams into their reservoirs, serve the double purpose of watering the garden and cooling the air. The whole has a pleasing effect, whether seen by day, with its green sward and neatly trimmed orange trees, its prim-looking sagus, and graceful palms. (Wurdemann 1844, 26–27)

La sofisticada sociedad habanera evadía una vez más las limitaciones morales y se apropiaba de las instituciones oficiales para elaborar sus propios discursos urbanos:

Nous voulons parler de l'aspect féerique que prend la Plaza de las Armas, au moment du concert militaire. Au-dessous d'un massif de superbes palmiers de l'espèce dite Royale, qui s'élèvent au centre de cette magnifique place, un orchestre d'élite y exé —cute, pendant près de deux heures, les mor— ceaux les plus exquis des répertoires européens. Mais la partie essentielle de ce spectacle, c'est la foule immense d'élégants et d'élégantes, qui ne cessent de circuler le long des quatre côtés de ce vaste carré ver-doyant. A ce moment, les hommes ont revêtu leur toi lette du soir, savoir, le frac en drap noir et le gilet blanc: ils ont également remplacé le chapeau de paille—Panama par le feutre noir de France ou d'Angleterre. Pour ce qui est des dames, elles sont aussi plen-didement habillées que si elles allaient à un bal de cour: presque toutes sont détiolletées; elles sont éblouissantes de bijoux d'or, de perles et de diamants. Parfois, quelques— unes, même des plus fashionnables, entremêlent dans leurs cheveux, qui ressemblent à du satin noir, un certain nombre de ces insectes brillants que l'on ne rencontre que sous les tropiques, et dont l'éclat égale celadu saphir, du rubis et de l'émeraude. (Olliffe 1852, 82–83)

Y cerrando el círculo retórico que venimos presentando hasta ahora, es ne-cesario recordar que la plaza exhibía unos determinados arreglos florales y paisajísticos, de manera que extranjeros como Hurlbert pudieran reconocer (revisualizar) en ellos el producto de consumo que, una vez de regreso a casa, podían a su vez capitalizar:

A charming place, suggesting recollections more charming still of lovelier places, of the gardens of King Agib, and on the courts wherein "Ganem, the Distracted Slave of Love," recited extemporaneous verses to the dark eyed Alcolomb. (Hurlbert 1854, 43)

En este sentido, Paul Niell recientemente sugirió que esta imagen trataba de comunicar una interpretación borbónica de la plaza, ejerciendo su poder me-diante la construcción de un espacio que inspirase tranquilidad social, lealtad y florecimiento económico (Niell 2015, 46). Sin embargo, aunque sí es cierto que el añadido de los jardines en la plaza —hacia 1834— podrían de alguna manera relacionarse con una nueva imagen de la corona española, considero que el uso de este espacio —los bailes, la iluminación de gas, los adornos florales, o la venta de chocolates y refrescos— tienen un claro componente de modernidad que es complicado vincular a los valores del antiguo régimen sostenidos por la metrópolis.

Así pues, tras el proyecto fallido de 1819, observamos la fascinante di-námica urbana que se produce en La Habana: la toma y resignificación de espacios, ya sean institucionales o privados, mediante la fórmula capitalista del *pleasure garden* y la estética foránea de lo exótico. En mi opinión, este es claramente el caso de la Plaza de Armas, nodo institucional de la ciudad de día y "ameno jardín que parece destinado a los amorosos misterios" una vez que la jornada terminaba (Andueza 1841, 43).

La Habana del siglo XIX nunca encarnó la imagen tradicional de la ciudad capitalista, pese a constituir uno de los centros urbanos más modernos de su tiempo. El mito colonial de lo exótico, proyectado por los extranjeros visitantes, se adaptó perfectamente a sus condiciones ambientales, siendo finalmente incorporado al nuevo acervo de significantes que la sociedad cubana empleó para manifestar su nueva identidad en el contexto del ideario independentista y anexionista. En este sentido, los jardines urbanos de La Habana, amén de boicotear el sistema colonial desde dentro mediante las iniciativas de ocio, supusieron un espacio de altísima relevancia a la hora de gestar y proyectar esta nueva identidad. No obstante, en el inocente acto de basar su identidad en la mirada del Otro, la Isla quedó atrapada en un cliché que perdura en nuestros días y que deja al margen muchas de las facetas esenciales de su idiosincrasia. Mediante la puesta en marcha de un régimen escópico para el consumo de la experiencia sensorial, se legitimaba de alguna forma el eje vertical en el cual la *visión*, la industria y la producción eran superiores a la naturaleza o la acción de consumir, facilitando simbólicamente la inminente transición entre la administración colonial y la intervención del país vecino a partir de 1898.

NOTA

1. Aunque en Madrid sí que encontramos varios ejemplos de jardines de este tipo, la mayoría gozaron de poco éxito, especialmente los anteriores a la primera mitad de siglo. El Jardín de Tívoli, abierto en 1821, fue desarticulado ocho años después por falta de consumidores (Cruz 2011, 188). A partir de 1860 el negocio de los jardines públicos remontó ligeramente en la capital de la metrópolis con la apertura del Jardín del Paraíso, los Jardines del señor Price, el Eliseo madrileño, el Jardín de la Alhambra, los jardines orientales y los famosos Campos Elíseos, que tras apenas quince años de vida fueron ocupados por el nuevo Barrio de Salamanca (Ariza 1988).

OBRAS CITADAS

Academia de la Historia de Cuba. 1930. *Centón epistolario de Domingo Del Monte, tomo IV*. La Habana: Imprenta El Siglo XX.
Adorno, Theodor W. 1983. *Teoría estética*. Barcelona: Ediciones Orbis.
Agzenay, Asma. 2015. *Returning the Gaze: The Manichean Drama of Postcolonial Exoticism*. Oxford, Inglaterra: Peter Lang.
Álvarez-Tabío Albo, Emma. 2000. *Invención de La Habana*. Barcelona: Editorial Casiopea.
Amigo, Ana. En prensa. "Más allá de la muralla: Nacimiento y desarrollo de los barrios extramuros de La Habana (1771–1844)." *Anales de Historia del Arte*.
Andermann, Jens. 2008. "Paisaje: Imagen, entorno, ensamble." *Orbis Tertius* 13 (14): 1–7.
Andueza, José María de. 1841. *Isla de Cuba pintoresca, histórica, política, literaria, mercantil e industrial: Recuerdos, apuntes, impresiones de dos épocas*. Madrid: Boix.
Ariza, Carmen. 1988. *Los jardines de Madrid en el siglo XIX*. Madrid: Editorial El Avapiés.
Azúa, Félix de, ed. 2004. *La arquitectura de la no-ciudad*. Pamplona: Universidad Pública de Navarra.

Barcia Zequeira, María del Carmen. 2002. "Sociedad imaginada: La isla de Cuba en el siglo XIX." *Contrastes: Revista de Historia Moderna*, no. 12: 21–42.

Barinetti, Charles. 1841. *A Voyage to Mexico and Havana; Including Some General Observations on the United States*. Nueva York: n.p.

Benjamin, Walter. 2006. *The Writer of Modern Life: Essays on Charles Baudelaire*. Cambridge, MA: Belknap Press of Harvard University Press.

Besse, J. M. 2011. "L'espace du paysage: Considérations théoriques". En *Teoría y paisaje: Reflexiones desde miradas interdisciplinarias*, editado por Toni Luna e Isabel Valverde. Barcelona: Observatorio del Paisaje de Cataluña. http://www.catpaisatge.net/cat/documentacio_coedi_2 .php\nC:\Users\Federico\AppData\Roaming\Mozilla\Firefox\Profiles\njal2u9s.default\ zotero\storage\IEPNBZNK\documentacio_coedi_2.html.

Bhabha, Homi K. 1994. *The Location of Culture*. Vol. 6. Londres: Routledge.

Bleichmar, Daniella. 2012. *Visible Empire: Botanical Expeditions and Visual Culture in the Hispanic Enlightenment*. Chicago: University of Chicago Press.

Bocarro, A. V. 1819. *Memoria correspondiente al plano de la delineación ejecutada por el Real Cuerpo de Ingenieros en los barrios extramuros de esta ciudad para el ensanche de esta, de orden de S.M. y disposición del Excmo. Señor D. José Cienfuegos Presente Gobernador y Capitán General de esta Isla* (AGMM, Colección general de documentos, 4-1-1-6, Fols. 1–7).

Borrero, Filomeno. 1869. *Recuerdos de viajes en América, Europa, Asia y África en los años de 1865 a 1867*. Bogotá: Imprenta Ortiz Malo.

Bremer, Fredrika. 1980. *Cartas desde Cuba*. La Habana: Editorial Arte y Literatura de la Ciudad de La Habana.

Casid, Jill H. 2005. *Sowing Empire: Landscape and Colonization*. Minneapolis: University of Minnesota Press.

Chateloin, F. 1989. *La Habana de Tacón*. La Habana: Editorial Letras Cubanas.

Coke, David, and Alan Borg. 2011. *Vauxhall Gardens: A History*. New Haven, CT: Yale University Press.

Concha, J. de la. 1851. *El Capitán General pide la ejecución de algunas obras del Cuartel de la Fuerza para la apertura de una calle al tránsito público* (AGMM, Ultramar, Caja 2819, Carpeta 176.1.3, Documento 40, Fols.1v–2v).

Cosgrove, Denis E. 1984. *Social Formation and Symbolic Landscape*. Londres: Croom Helm.

Costales, Manuel. 1854. *Educación de la muger*. La Habana: Establecimiento Tipográfico La Cubana.

Cruz, Jesús. 2011. *The Rise of Middle-Class Culture in Nineteenth-Century Spain*. Baton Rouge: Louisiana State Universiy Press.

Dettelbach, Michael. 1999. "The Face of Nature: Precise Measurement, Mapping, and Sensibility in the Work of Alexander von Humboldt." *Studies in History and Philosophy of Biological and Biomedical Sciences* 30 (4): 473–504.

Documentos que se relacionan con doña Luisa Long sobre un permiso que solicita para reparar los techos de una casa. Año de 1842. (ANRC, Licencia para fábricas, Legajo 6, Expediente 1277, Doc. 1, Fol. 1rº).

Documentos que se relacionan con Don Enrique Dalton sobre un permiso que solicita para hacer varias obras. Año de 1844. (ANRC, Licencia para fábricas, Legajo 10, Expediente 2330, Doc. 1, Fol. 1rº).

Documentos que se relacionan con Don Ramón de la Riva Agüero, sobre un permiso que solicita para reparar un teatro. Año de 1845. (ANRC, Licencia para fábricas, Legajo 11, Expediente 2610, Doc. 2., Fol. 1r)

Documentos y plano demostrativo del terreno que ha denunciado don Antonio Bruzón en el Campo de Marte, lindando con el paseo y la estatua de Carlos III. Año 1833. (ANRC, Gobierno General, Legajo 1, Expediente 11, Doc. 1). La cursiva es mía.

Douglas, Lake. 2013. "Pleasure Gardens in Nineteenth-Century New Orleans: 'Useful for All Classes of Society.'" En *The Pleasure Garden, from Vauxhall to Coney Island*, editado por Jonathan Conlin, 150–76. Philadelphia, PA: University of Pennsylvania Press.

Duguid, Stephen. 2010. *Nature in Modernity : Servant, Citizen, Queen or Comrade*. Nueva York: Peter Lang.

Edelstein, T. J. 1983. *Vauxhall Gardens*. New Haven, CT: Yale Center for British Art.

Edmon, R. 2005. "Returning Fears: Tropical Disease and the Metropolis." En *Tropical Visions in an Age of Empire*, 175–194. Chicago: University of Chicago Press.

Expediente promovido por el ayuntamiento sobre la escasez de agua para el servicio del vecindario de La Habana, 1854. Ramo de acueductos (ANRC, Intendencia General de Hacienda, legajo 804, expediente 117).

Ferrety, Juan Agustín de. 1833. *Relación de los festejos que se han hecho en la siempre fidelísima ciudad de La Habana, los días 14, 15, 16 y 17 de octubre de 1833 con motivo de celebrar la jura de S. A. R. La Infanta Doña María Isabel Luisa de Borbón, como heredera de La Corona de España*. La Habana: Imprenta del Gobierno y Capitanía General.

"A Flying Visit to Havana." 1852. *New York Daily Times*.

Francis, Mark, and Randolph T. Hester Jr., eds. 1991. *The Meaning of Gardens: Idea, Place, and Action*. Cambridge, MA: MIT Press.

Gallenga, A. 1873. *The Pearl of the Antilles*. Londres: Chapman and Hall.

García, Guadalupe. 2016. *Beyond the Walled City: Colonial Exclusion in Havana*. Oakland: University of California Press.

González, Reynaldo. 2012. *Contradanzas y latigazos*. La Habana: Editorial Letras Cubanas.

Grove, Richard H. 1996. *Green Imperialism: Colonial Expansion, Tropical Island Edens, and the Origins of Environmentalism, 1600–1860*. Cambridge: Cambridge University Press.

Guevara, G. R. 2006. "Inexacting Whiteness: *Blanqueamiento* as a Gender-Specific Trope in the Nineteenth Century." *Cuban Studies*, no. 36: 106.

Gurney, Joseph John. 1840. *A Winter in the West Indies, Described in Familiar Letters to Henry Clay, of Kentucky, by Joseph John Gurney*. Londres: John Murray, Albemarle Street.

Han, B. 2012. *La sociedad del cansancio*. Barcelona: Herder Editorial.

Howe, Julia W. 1860. *A Trip to Cuba*. Boston: Ticknor and Fields.

Humboldt, Alexander. 1856. *The Island of Cuba*. Edited by J. S. Trasher. Nueva York: Derby & Jackson, 119 Nassau Street.

Hurlbert, William Henry. 1854. *Gan-Eden; or, Pictures of Cuba*. Boston: John P. Jewett and Co.

Larra, Mariano José de. 1834. "Jardines Públicos." *La Revista Española, Periódico Dedicado a La Reina Ntra. Sra.*, no. 256: 597–98.

Leary, John Patrick. 2009. *Cuba in the American Imaginary: Literature and National Culture in Cuba and the United States, 1848–1958*. Nueva York: New York University Press.

"Life in Cuba." 1871. *Harper's New Monthly Magazine* (August), 350–365.

MacCannell, D. 1999. *El turista: Una nueva teoría de la clase ociosa*. N.p.: Melusina.

Mendive, R. M. de, y J. de J. Q. García, eds. 1855. *Revista de La Habana, periódico quincenal de ciencias, literatura, artes, modas, teatros, &, con litografías y grabados*. La Habana: Imprenta y Encuadernación del Tiempo.

Merlin, La Condesa Mercedes de. 1844. *Viaje a La Habana*. Madrid: Imprenta de la Sociedad Literaria y Tipográfica.

Mignolo, Walter D. 2010. *Desobediencia epistémica: Retórica de la modernidad, lógica de la colonialidad y gramática de la descolonialiad*. Buenos Aires: Ediciones del Signo.

Mitchell, W. J. T., ed. 2002. *Landscape and Power*. Chicago: University of Chicago Press.

"Las mujeres en el paseo." 1864. *El amigo las mujeres*, no. 7: 7.

Murray, Amelia M. 1856. *Letters from the United States, Cuba and Canada*. Vol. 2. Londres: John W. Parker and Son West Strand.

Niell, Paul. 2015. *Urban Space as Heritage in Late Colonial Cuba: Classicism and Dissonance on the Plaza de Armas of Havana, 1754–1828.* Austin: University of Texas Press.

Novalis. 1977. *Hymns to the Night and Other Selected Writings.* Indianapolis, IN: Bobbs-Merrill.

Olliffe, Charles. 1852. *Scènes américaines: Dix-huit mois dans le Nouveau Monde (1850–1851) par Charles Olliffe.* Paris: Amyot, Libraire, Rue de la Paix, 8.

Osborne, Michael A. 1994. *Nature, the Exotic, and the Science of French Colonialism.* Bloomington: Indiana University Press.

Pedroso, Pedro de. 1827. *Ordenanzas municipales de La Habana.* La Habana: Imprenta del Gobierno y Capitanía General.

Pérez, Louis A., Jr. 2001. *Winds of Change: Hurricanes and the Transformation of Nineteenth-Century Cuba.* Chapel Hill: University of North Carolina Press.

Pérez de la Riva, Juan, ed. 1963. *Correspondencia reservada del Capitán General Don Miguel Tacón con el gobierno de Madrid: 1834–1836.* La Habana: Biblioteca Nacional José Martí.

Phillippo, James Mursell. 1857. *The United States and Cuba.* Londres: Pewtress & Co.

Piña, Ramón. 1857. "Botánica: El sueño de las plantas." *Revista de La Habana* 3: 181–190.

Pratt, Mary Louise. 2010. *Ojos imperiales: Literatura de viajes y transculturación.* México, DF: Fondo de Cultura Económica.

Puig-Samper, Miguel Ángel, y Mercedes Valero. 2000. *Historia del Jardín Botánico de La Habana.* Madrid: Consejo Superior de Investigaciones Científicas.

Ramírez, Serafín. 1891. *La Habana artística: Apuntes históricos.* La Habana: Imprenta del E. M. de la Capitanía General.

Ramos, Julio. 1994. "A Citizen Body: Cholera in Havana (1833)." *Dispositio* 19 (46): 179–95.

Roezl, Benedikt. 1872. "De los jardines botánicos en general, y en particular de la formación de uno botánico, de aclimatación y zoológico." *Anales de la Real Academia de Ciencias Médicas, Físicas y Naturales de La Habana* 8: 501–506.

Roig de Leuchsenring, Emilo. 1939. *La Habana: Apuntes históricos.* La Habana: Municipio de La Habana.

Ruskin, John. 1884. *The Storm Cloud of the Nineteenth Century.* Londres: Sunnyside, Kent, G. Allen.

Segre, Roberto. 1997. *Havana. Two Faces of the Antillean Metropolis.* Chichester, Inglaterra: John Wiley & Sons.

Sennett, Richard. 1978. *El declive del hombre público.* Barcelona: Ediciones Península.

Simmel, G. 2002. "The Metropolis and Mental Life." En *The Blackwell City Reader.* Mahwah, NJ: Wiley-Blackwell, 11–19.

Sluyter, A. 2002. *Colonialism and Landscape: Postcolonial Theory and Applications.* Lanham, MD: Rowman & Littlefield.

Sobre el permiso concedido a los señores Otto Motty Kisley e hijo para dar funciones de fuerzas y equilibrios en el teatro del Diorama. Año de 1843 (ANRC, Gobierno Superior Civil, Legajo 996, Expediente 34389, Doc. 1, Fol. 1rº).

Taylor, Frank H. 1879. "Street Scenes in Havana." *Harper's New Monthly Magazine* 58 (347): 682–687.

"Three Weeks in Cuba by an Artist." 1853. *Harper's New Monthly Magazine* 6 (32): 161–175.

Tinkler-Villani, Valeria, ed. 2005. *Babylon or New Jerusalem? Perceptions of the City in Literature.* Amsterdam: Rodopi.

Torre, José María de la. 1860. *Nuevo tratado de urbanidad, etiqueta y buenas maneras, con aplicación a los usos y costumbres de la Isla de Cuba.* La Habana: Imprenta Militar.

Tyng, C.D. 1868. *The Stranger in the Tropics: Being a Hand-Book for Havana and Guide Book for Travellers in Cuba, Puerto Rico, and St. Thomas; with Descriptions of the Principal Objects of Interest, Suggestions to Invalids, by a Physician. Hints for Tours and General Dire.* Nueva York: American News Co.

Valdés, Gerónimo. 1842. *Bando de gobernación y policía de la isla de Cuba*. La Habana: Imprenta del Gobierno y la Capitanía General por S.M.

Venegas Fornias, Carlos. 1990. *La urbanización de las murallas: Dependencia y modernidad*. La Habana: Editorial Letras Cubanas.

Veráfilo. 1844. *Refutación al folleto intitulado "Viage a La Habana" por la Condesa de Merlín*. La Habana: Imprenta del Gobierno y Capitanía General.

Vidler, Anthony. 1994. "Psychopathologies of Modern Space: Metropolitant Fear from Agoraphonia to Estrangement." In *Rediscovering History. Culture, Politics, and the Psyche*, edited by Michael S. Roth, 11–29. Stanford, CA: Standford University Press.

Wagner, Peter, Kirsten Dickhaut, and Ottmar Ette, eds. 2015. *The Garden in the Focus of Cultural Discourses in the Eighteenth Century*. Trier: Wissenschaftlicher Verlag Trier.

Warren, Peter. 2006. "The Evolution of the Sanatorium: The First Half-Century, 1854–1904." *Canadian Bulletin of Medical History / Bulletin Canadien d'Histoire de la Médecine* 23 (2): 457–476.

Weiss, Joaquín E. 2002. *La arquitectura colonial cubana, siglos XVI al XIX*. La Habana: Letras Cubanas; Sevilla: Junta de Andalucía, AECID.

Wikoff, Henry. 1845. *The Letters and Journal of Fanny Ellsler, Written before and after Her Operatic Campaign in the United States. Including Her Letters from New York, London, Paris, Havana*. Nueva York: Henry G. Daggers.

Willis, N. Parker. 1853. *Health Trip to the Tropics*. Nueva York: Charles Scribner.

Wurdemann, John G. *Notes on Cuba, Containing [. . .], with Directions to Tavellers Visiting the Island, by a Physician*. 1844. Boston: James Munroe and Co.

MARÍA ELENA MENESES MURO

Los esclavos embargados: Movilidad, espacios y trabajo en la Guerra de los Diez Años

RESUMEN

El artículo presenta un análisis de la administración de la fuerza de trabajo esclava confiscada por el Estado español como resultado de la política de embargo de bienes, implementada en Cuba entre 1869 y 1878. El procesamiento de fuentes documentales inéditas atesoradas en el fondo Bienes Embargados del Archivo Nacional de Cuba, permite develar aristas de un tema poco explorado por la historiografía cubana. La intención principal del texto es desentrañar las complejidades que caracterizaron la gestión administrativa alrededor del embargo de esclavos, así como las distintas racionalidades e intereses militares, económicos, jurídicos y políticos que convergieron en ese proceso durante la Guerra de los Diez Años. Al mismo tiempo, se expondrán estrategias identificadas de esclavos interesados en lograr posibles cambios dentro de su estatus de embargado, bien en los espacios de confinamiento o a partir de los oficios asignados.

ABSTRACT

This article presents an analysis of the administration of slave manpower by the Spanish state as a result of the policy of *embargo de bienes*, implemented in Cuba between 1869 and 1878. The processing of unpublished documentary sources archived in the Seized Property collection of the National Archive of Cuba allows for the unveiling of issues related to a theme little explored in Cuban historiography. The main intention is to unravel the complexities that characterized admininstration related to the slave embargo, as well as the distinct rationales and military, legal, economic, and political interests that converged in this process during the Ten Years' War. At the same time, we identify strategies of slaves interested in achieving possible changes to their status, as well in spaces of confinement or in assigned occupations.

Si un elemento caracteriza la producción historiográfica sobre Cuba en los últimos decenios, es el sostenido y creciente interés por el estudio de las problemáticas asociadas a la esclavitud de hombres y mujeres de origen africano. En un país de inmigración y, aún más, de esclavitud —como lo define el historiador Oscar Zanetti Lecuona—, las preocupaciones en modo alguno no son fortuitas ni de reciente data. Desde diversos campos disciplinares —etnología,

113

antropología, demografía histórica y economía— un conjunto de investigadores plantearon problemas esenciales del fenómeno esclavista a lo largo de la vigésima centuria.

No obstante los avances, con respecto a la evolución del régimen de servidumbre en el contexto de la Guerra de los Diez Años quedan aún parcelas del conocimiento por explorar. Entre estas destaca la ausencia de ángulos de análisis dirigidos al proceso por el cual pasaron a ser administrados por el Estado español centenares de esclavos de la geografía insular como parte de la política de embargo de bienes, decretada el 15 de abril de 1869 en las planas de la *Gaceta de La Habana* a todos aquellos individuos clasificados de infidentes.[1]

Los reclamos y enfoques historiográficos sobre dicha temática provienen, como generalidad, de estudios acerca de los modos de expropiación y el impacto político económico del procedimiento de confiscación de propiedades en virtud del cual se desplazó parte del patrimonio cubano hacia manos españolas.[2]

No se trata sólo de advertir la existencia lógica de una confiscación de esclavos a sus propietarios, víctimas del embargo, sino de entender las problemáticas que generó ese proceso en lo relativo a los cambios de las formas administrativas del régimen esclavista.

Si bien no era la primera vez que se instituía semejante legislación en la isla, el origen de este tipo de procedimiento, a diferencia de otros dispuestos por causas judiciales administrativas, estaba orientado a salvaguardar la integridad de la nación hispana, tras el inicio de la Guerra de los Diez Años y el objetivo confeso de privar de recursos materiales a la naciente revolución independentista. La política de embargo implicó en la práctica modificaciones en las formas de organizar e implementar el trabajo en los espacios urbano y rural. Grupos de siervos de todo el país dejaron de ser administrados por particulares para pasar a manos del Estado con experiencia previa a la guerra en la gestión administrativa sobre la mano de obra, tanto esclava como de los llamados emancipados. A cargo de las instancias estatales, incluso, operaron los Depósitos Judiciales de esclavos, que se gestionaban a cuenta de algunos ayuntamientos o de instituciones como la Junta de Fomento, hasta que a finales de la década del cincuenta el Gobierno Superior Civil asumió esas funciones.

Ahora bien, este conocimiento en la gestión de embargados tuvo su diferencia con respecto a la política instrumentada en el decurso de la década bélica. Como bien advierten Aisnara Perera y María de los Ángeles Meriño, los litigios en los juzgados habaneros y santiagueros que generaban órdenes de embargos de siervos, estaban mediados como norma por causas financieras: reclamación por pesos, quiebra mercantil, ruina de un hacendado, una testamentaría dilatada, una querella verbal o un juicio criminal.[3] Queda claro, por tanto, que existía la experiencia estatal en estos menesteres de depósitos y explotación de la mano de obra embargada, pero no es menos cierto que la guerra impuso su sello a la dinámica experiencial de los magistrados de la corona.

En el orden político las causales no se sostenían por lo general en los litigios financieros, sin que por ello desparecieran, sino en las circunstancias de un conflicto militar de objetivos independentistas, inéditos hasta ese momento. El traspaso de bienes no sólo significó la creación de instancias burocráticas para la implementación del cuerpo legislativo que demandó el acto de expropiación, sino también una nueva movilización jurisdiccional de dichos esclavos.

He aquí la importancia de mostrar la complejidad que asumió un proceso donde confluyeron tantas racionalidades como intereses militares, económicos, jurídicos y políticos acerca del esclavo como bien embargado. Algunas interrogantes se imponen: ¿Qué significaba ser un esclavo embargado en el contexto de la guerra? O, en otro sentido: ¿Cómo se estructuró e implementó la administración de la fuerza de trabajo esclava embargada entre 1869 y 1878? Sin dudas, tales preguntas, imposibles de develar todas sus aristas en el número de páginas que abarcan este artículo, exigen del historiador un estudio detenido y profundo. Esto no implica que adelantemos algunas ideas orientadas a situar en la palestra historiográfica el tema del esclavo embargado, en estrecha relación con el movimiento físico geográfico, las estrategias de poder trazadas con el objetivo de regular su ordenación y disposición por parte de las instancias estatales, así como las reacciones de las propias individualidades esclavas ante los cambios en su estatus de vida.

Tampoco se trata de incursionar, desde una perspectiva de estudio comparado, en otras experiencias relacionadas con embargos de esclavos fuera de Cuba. El proceso al que nos acercamos presenta rasgos específicos propios de concepciones y prácticas jurídicas que se instrumentan en un contexto de guerra anticolonialista. El tema presenta importancia *per se* y avanzar en su conocimiento mediante el procesamiento de la abundante información inédita existente, será un excelente punto de partida para entender la dinámica de un fenómeno multifacético acontecido en circunstancias especiales, con lógicas procedimentales ajustadas únicamente a los imperativos bélicos insulares y que, por tanto, hacen viable y legítima la singularidad de su estudio.

Racionalidades administrativas en conflictos: Del *Consejo Administrativo de Bienes Embargados* a la *Junta de la Deuda del Tesoro*

La articulación de la compleja red burocrática encargada de sofisticar los controles sobre los esclavos tuvo como soporte inicial tres puntales. La instancia rectora de la política de embargo radicaba en el Consejo Administrativo de Bienes Embargados.[4] La responsabilidad ejecutiva del cumplimiento de las normativas prescritas por el Consejo descansaba en los gobernadores y tenientes gobernadores, presidentes de las Juntas de Embargo jurisdiccionales. En la base de la legalidad radicaban los depositarios, figura jurídica a cargo de la custodia, conservación y administración de las propiedades embargadas. Dicha estratificación jerárquica operó de múltiples formas de acuerdo con los intereses contrapuestos alrededor de los "usos" de la fuerza de trabajo esclava.

A modo de ejemplo resulta interesante la conducta seguida por el Gobernador Político del Departamento de Puerto Príncipe, quien presumía de ser la máxima instancia con respecto al destino de los esclavos de su jurisdicción. De tal suerte, en octubre de 1871, dispuso la entrega de todos los llamados esclavos útiles del ramo de Bienes Embargados al capitán del partido de Camujiro para el establecimiento de una trocha entre los fuertes situados en la localidad. El comportamiento de dicha autoridad fue severamente impugnado por Carlos de la Torre, inspector del Negociado de Bienes Embargados, en comunicación dirigida al Capitán General de la isla. De la Torre recordaba a la máxima autoridad que los fueros correspondientes a las distintas dependencias del Estado debían ser respetados, por tanto, a la sección de hacienda le pertenecía el control sobre las formas de empleo de la mano de obra esclava embargada.

El inspector, al razonar el acto de entrega de "sus siervos" como parte de las prestaciones de servicios que por el ramo de hacienda se extendían a las restantes dependencias estatales, reclamaba al capitán del partido de Camujiro la remuneración a aquella del importe de jornales o alquileres de los esclavos de Bienes Embargados.[5] Inclusive, dado su interés en delimitar jurídicamente las facultades con respecto a la administración de los embargados, advertía en el texto:

los servicios q. de más a otras dependencias se prestan deben ser remunerados, por ello corresponde q. por el ramo de Guerra se abone al de Hacienda, tanto en el presente caso como en cuantos puedan ocurrir, el importe de jornales o alquileres de los esclavos de bienes embargados ocupados en los antedichos trabajos de la trocha y q. para en lo sucesivo q. siempre q. por Guerra se necesite la prestación de la Hacienda presida antes la concepción de la autoridad competente y solo en casos especiales q. no permitan espera o demora será cuando por Guerra dicte la medida excepcional de la q. deberá dar cuenta con causas.[6]

En el marco del contexto de crisis económica, reducidos drásticamente los presupuestos del Estado y priorizados estos hacia el aprovisionamiento de los cuerpos de ejército, el negociado de hacienda buscaba asegurar una fuente de ingresos rentable. En tal caso, un bien encarecido como el esclavo se presentó como pieza de indudable valor para el fisco, sobre todo en la medida en que se prolongaba el conflicto colonial y con él la crítica situación del tesoro español.

En la argumentación del inspector del Negociado de Bienes Embargados se revela también, curiosamente, el alcance del calificativo esclavo embargado en no pocas ocasiones asociados por los funcionarios como esclavo del Estado. Desde el punto de vista jurídico el embargo y, posteriormente, la administración estatal no implicaron el derecho de propiedad sobre los siervos confiscados, en tanto este continuaba residiendo en sus propietarios de origen. De hecho, en los distintos tipos de documentación oficial que registra el itinerario seguido por el siervo una vez embargado, el nombre del dueño figuraba como uno de los indicadores con que se distinguía.

No obstante, la naturaleza de la tutela ejercida sobre los esclavos abarcaba y regulaba aspectos importantes que determinaron en buena medida el curso cotidiano de sus vidas. En el gobierno colonial radicaba la asignación de los tipos de trabajo a realizar, los espacios físicos de residencia, así como las instancias oficiales o arrendatarios particulares a quienes eran adjudicados. Inclusive, retomando el caso del inspector Carlos de la Torre, para algunos se trataba de sus siervos.

En torno a los controles sobre la movilidad espacial de los esclavos se detonaron también otros puntos de conflicto registrados en varios expedientes del fondo Bienes Embargados. Próximo a cumplirse el primer año del decreto de embargo de bienes, el Capitán General Antonio Fernández y Caballero de Rodas ofició el 16 de febrero de 1870, hasta donde se ha podido comprobar, el primer traslado de esclavos hacia la capital colonial. En este caso se trataba de los que se encontraban sin ubicación en las jurisdicciones de Santiago de Cuba y Puerto Príncipe. A finales de ese mismo año, otra resolución emitida el 21 de diciembre ampliaba el margen movilizador al ordenarse el envío "a disposición del Consejo Administrativo" de "todos los esclavos de ambos secsos [*sic*] pertenecientes a Bienes Embargados que sean útiles para el trabajo."[7]

El hecho en sí parece expresar, en primer término, una lógica económica de quienes dispusieron el reforzamiento regular de las dotaciones del occidente de la isla con fuerzas embargadas destinadas al incremento de la producción azucarera y con ella las fuentes de ganancias para el sostenimiento de una guerra revitalizada a partir de 1872, con la exitosa campaña de Guantánamo. Asimismo, se aseguraba el control de la mano de obra esclava, la cual, de permanecer en las unidades productivas del centro oriente, corría el riesgo de ser liberada por el avance impetuoso de las fuerzas libertadoras.

El análisis de la historiadora estadounidense Rebecca Scott sobre la estructura demográfica de la población esclava en la década de 1870 demostró la resistencia de la institución esclavista, fundamentalmente, sobre la base de la concentración de la fuerza de trabajo en los principales emporios azucareros del país. Como bien planteaba la autora, en regiones como Puerto Príncipe y Santiago de Cuba se manifestó la disminución poblacional luego del inicio de la revolución independentista: la liberación, la muerte o "emigración," estaban entre los factores que condicionaron la reducción del número de esclavos. Las cifras mostradas por Scott revelaron, en efecto, el incremento en la distribución de esclavos en las zonas de Matanzas y Santa Clara.[8] Ahora bien, quedaban por determinar entre las causales propiciadoras de las tendencias que aportaban los datos, el impacto de la administración estatal de los esclavos embargados.

He aquí un punto de encuentro necesario al que sólo acudirá con algunos adelantos, no por breves, menos importantes para entender la complejidad de un proceso con incidencia tanto en el orden demográfico como económico.

Entre las fuentes representativas que permiten determinar la dinámica en la movilidad de la población embargada, se sitúan los listados de esclavos elaborados por los administradores depositarios de los bienes. En efecto, algunos conteos comienzan a mostrar el desplazamiento regional a partir de la ejecución de los decretos de Caballero de Rodas. En cuanto a las jurisdicciones de Bayamo y Puerto Príncipe, las cifras ascienden al número de 184 y 117 respectivamente, para un total de 301 embargados trasladados hasta el mes de marzo de 1871.[9]

La racionalidad económica operada en el reordenamiento de la fuerza de trabajo se confirma tras el examen de un valioso documento donde Jorge Crabb, inspector de ingenios de Colón, informa al Consejo Administrativo el estado de los haberes devengados a los trabajadores de las unidades productivas pertenecientes a Domingo Aldama, expropiadas por decreto del 16 de julio de 1869. El documento aludía a los ingenios más importantes administrados por la entidad, en cuanto a posibilidades de capitalización en la región matancera.

Llama la atención que, a tan solo un año del primer decreto de remisión de esclavos, el monto de los llegados a los ingenios San José, Concepción, Santa Rosa, Santo Domingo y Armonía, ascendieran a 310. En modo alguno era una mera cifra. Las autoridades prestaban especial cuidado a la hora de distinguir a la dotación propia de los enclaves de las "cuadrillas de trabajadores" trasladadas. El expediente contenía, en cada caso, las variables siguientes: nombre, nación, edad, dueño, salario devengado. Válido resaltar el registro del Concepción, donde se estimaba también la jurisdicción de procedencia. Según muestran las cifras, de un total de 75 embargados, el 34,4 por ciento se transportó de la región principeña.[10]

El reforzamiento de las plantaciones occidentales a partir de la movilidad esclava fue advertido, con razón, por el *Boletín de Colonización* del 15 de abril de 1876:

Desde que la insurrección invadió el Departamento Oriental y parte del Central, casi todas las dotaciones que existían en los ingenios, cafetales y haciendas de crianzas de los mismos, fueron trasladadas a las Villas y al Departamento Occidental, y con el auxilio de ellas se fomentaron multitud de ingenios cuyos productos, en aumento gradual como era consiguiente, vinieron a acrecentar la cifra de exportación de azúcares.[11]

No obstante, las resoluciones de la máxima autoridad son reflejo de una lógica centralizadora, reforzada con la creación el 9 de agosto de 1872 de la Junta de la Deuda del Tesoro, a la cual pasaron las funciones del Consejo en lo relativo a los bienes embargados, hecho este que marcó un segundo momento en el proceso de institucionalización de la política de embargo.[12] Claro está, en la medida que el desplazamiento geográfico de la fuerza confiscada alcanzaba mayores dimensiones, estas máximas estructuras requerían de dispositivos de fiscalización más afinados, sobre todo en cuanto al control de los organismos funcionales. Las atribuciones otorgadas a los representantes de las oficinas de rentas locales abrían márgenes de oportunidades excelentes para maniobrar a favor de sus intereses.

Baste citar la reclamación cursada por la Junta de la Deuda del Tesoro, en agosto de 1874, al Administrador General de Hacienda de Santa Clara con motivo de averiguar con que autorización se había efectuado la subasta pública mediante la cual fueron dados en alquiler varios esclavos, algunos, ahora adjudicados a Don Antonio de los Ríos. El hecho en sí refleja la violación de la circular emitida el 8 de julio con motivo del traslado hacia la capital de todos los embargados del Departamento Central que no pertenecían a dotaciones de las fincas que estuviesen arrendadas por la junta.

Las discordias entre las autoridades se tornaron complejas cuando entraron en el forcejeo los arrendatarios particulares, quienes habían adquirido la mano de obra en base a su planificación económica. A tenor de los procesos de arrendamiento por la administración de rentas de Santa Clara antes aludidos y la misiva central ordenando la remisión de los grupos de esclavos a la capital, varios inquilinos se negaron a cumplir dicha ley, respaldando su accionar en la legalidad que había presidido el convenio.[13]

Las exiguas garantías ofrecidas a los arrendatarios que se beneficiaron de la política de embargo de bienes no sólo se hicieron explícitas como resultado de los conflictos de poder dirimidos entre las autoridades estatales, sino también en la propia realidad de la legislación. Bastaba que un propietario abandonase las filas de la revolución para tomar la vía del orden español, en tal caso, sus bienes debían ser devueltos pues se trataba de un individuo que supuestamente habría de comenzar a prestar sus servicios a la madre patria. De ahí los pliegos de reclamaciones y sugerencias que llegaban a la mesa del Capitán General con cierta frecuencia.[14]

De tal suerte, resulta comprensible el mayor énfasis en la fiscalización sobre las atribuciones de los organismos municipales, quienes al retener los esclavos embargados disponían así de un medio económico para su sustento.

El arrendamiento de esclavos generó, al mismo tiempo, conflictos con la Junta Central Protectora de Libertos a partir de la firma de la Ley Moret.[15] El asunto medular abarcó el cumplimiento del artículo décimo sexto que fijaba el cobro del impuesto por cada esclavo comprendido en la edad de once a sesenta años. Nuevamente salta a la vista la problemática jurídica del alcance que en la práctica cotidiana tuvo el término esclavo embargado, es decir, un esclavo administrado por el Estado ante la expropiación de su dueño pero, en muchos casos, vinculado directamente a un arrendatario particular. Algunas preguntas se imponen entonces: ¿Quién debía abonar el gravamen?, ¿qué relación existió entre la Junta de la Deuda del Tesoro (a cargo de los embargados) y la Junta Protectora (a cargo de los libertos)?

Pudiera citarse la comunicación del Presidente de la Junta Protectora de Libertos de San Juan de los Remedios, el 5 de octubre de 1874, al propietario Don Luis de Lavalet del partido de Guaracabulla. Este individuo tenía en arrendamiento a varios esclavos embargados y se negaba a cumplir el pago del impuesto de setenta y cinco centavos que demandaba la secretaría, pues no tenía órdenes superiores al efecto. Cierto es que en el pliego de condiciones para el arrendamiento no se informaba nada al respecto, por tanto, no es de extrañar se viera en obligación alguna.[16]

En efecto, el 19 de octubre se reiteró la comunicación cursada el 21 de septiembre por el Vicepresidente de la Junta Central Protectora de Libertos al Presidente de la Junta de la Deuda del Tesoro donde se afirmaba que el cumplimiento del abono correspondía a su administración "como hecha cargo de los esclavos pertenecientes a infidentes." Al mismo tiempo le exigía "dar las ordenes necesarias, para que a la presentación de los recibos de que se trata, sean satisfechos, o en su defecto, se sirva ver el mejor medio de que se hagan efectivos."[17]

El cobro de los recibos no sólo se dificultaba en varios partidos de dicha jurisdicción, sino también en los de Trinidad. Meses después, el 17 de febrero de 1875, el Presidente de la Junta de Libertos cursaba al Administrador de Rentas de Trinidad el reclamo de la suma de treinta y cinco pesos con veinticinco centavos por el impuesto sobre cuarenta y siete esclavos embargados. Dado el caso, en abril de 1875 la Junta de la Deuda informó al Administrador de Rentas de Trinidad el acuerdo por el cual debía pagarse a la Junta de Libertos, siempre y cuando fuera "por cuenta de los productos de los bienes de los infidentes que se expresan en la relación que adjunta usted a su oficio fecha 5 del mes de marzo."[18]

Ahora bien, ¿eran todos los esclavos embargados por el Estado bien recibidos en calidad de arrendamiento? Desde luego que sí, siempre y cuando fueran funcionales. El cumplimiento de la normativa sobre el movimiento humano permite ilustrar la racionalidad económica de la cual formaba parte integrante el examen de los índices de salud corporal de la "mercancía" que se debía trasladar, en ocasiones, no sólo en dirección a la zona occidental. En un oficio del Administrador Depositario de Bienes Embargados de Puerto Príncipe cursado el 15 de abril de 1872 al Teniente Gobernador de Victoria de las Tunas se corrobora este proceder. La inspeccionada, en este caso, era la esclava Rita de la Caridad quien, residiendo en la localidad de Nuevitas, figuraba en los libros de bienes embargados de Puerto Príncipe. Al parecer, por tal motivo, la Junta Local de Bienes Embargados de Victoria de Las Tunas había ordenado su remisión hacia la ciudad principeña. El resultado del examen practicado por el Administrador Depositario fue el siguiente:

La enunciada esclava es completamente inutil por manca y coja ó sea liciada (sic) de las piernas y un brazo, lo que le hace no servir absolutamente para nada por cuya razón no debio hacerse mención de ella en Nuevitas para su remisión a esta Ciudad, pues solo ha servido para originar gastos que ella no puede ni podrá remunerar con ninguna clase de servicios, sino que por el contario hay que sostenerla sin esperanzas de provecho alguno.[19]

Ante esta realidad, el Teniente Gobernador demandó la consulta del Administrador especial de Bienes del Estado en La Habana al tiempo que informó a la Hacienda de Puerto Príncipe la inutilidad de la esclava. Planteada la lógica del régimen de servidumbre en base a la producción de bienes de consumo, resultaba alarmante el caso de la esclava Rita, quien con su traslado había producido el gasto de doce pesos con cincuenta centavos.[20]

Itinerarios del embargo: Entre reclamaciones y estrategias

En estrecho vínculo con la movilidad espacial se revela otra arista de análisis vinculada a las estrategias implementadas para controlar, en términos físicos, las colectividades de esclavos ahora en manos del Estado. ¿Contaba la infraestructura estatal con locales suficientes dada las condiciones de guerra? En este sentido, se impuso la refuncionalización de espacios ya creados entre los que se encuentran las cárceles, asilos y depósitos de cimarrones a cargo de las oficinas de rentas locales. Este dispositivo es importante, tanto para entender como instituciones correctoras de comportamientos se rediseñan para la reclusión de seres presuntamente necesitados del constante disciplinamiento, pero también permite conocer cómo entre los propios esclavos embargados existían estrategias para evadir la reclusión a partir del conocimiento de la funcionalidad prístina de la institución de encierro a la que se le confinaba, diferente a la del barracón o casa de sus propietarios.

En casos excepcionales, las lecturas de los nuevos inquilinos sobre la transformación de los símbolos que identificaban a dichas entidades llegaban en forma de sutiles reclamos a las más altas esferas del poder colonial. Tal fue la conducta seguida por la esclava Tomasa Zaldívar al ser depositada junto a otros tres en la Cárcel de Guanabacoa en 1869. A diferencia de sus compañeros, pudo reclamar sus derechos ante el Capitán General en una misiva fechada el 11 de junio.

Más allá de la autoría del texto, los términos en que se redacta traslucen una serie de inquietudes, estados de ánimo y dominio de los derechos que le asistían. El cuestionamiento lanzado sobre la base de la breve pero enfática pregunta: "¿Por qué yo estoy aquí si no he hecho nada malo?," revela la percepción clara que tenía de la función del entorno carcelario. Pero la esclava de Ramón Zaldívar llegó más allá de las súplicas al proponer, sobre la base de una solicitud claramente calculada, el tipo de espacio en que debía ser colocada. Debido a que en la que hablaba "no hay delito," le correspondía un depósito que fuese particular. De tal suerte, se presentaba la casa de Pablo Suárez, vecino de la localidad y necesitado de sus habilidades puesto que "sus pequeños hijos se han quedado sin el alimento necesario."[21]

Aunque la legislación examinada sobre el arrendamiento de la mano de obra embargada no refiere la existencia de una autogestión laboral por parte del esclavo, tampoco es de desdeñar tal posibilidad. Sobre todo en casos como el anterior, referidos a esclavas domésticas cuya fuerza de trabajo no era destinada a trabajos en campos de caña o en el servicio militar, es factible que se les diera autonomía para gestionar dónde y con quién alquilarse. Claro está, siempre y cuando los indicadores de rentabilidad quedaran incólumes. Tal margen de acción era usual en los esclavos litigantes en la ciudad de Santiago de Cuba, quienes como norma no eran ubicados en el depósito judicial e inclusive podían solicitar empleos mediante anuncios en la prensa.[22]

En cuanto a la legitimidad de la cárcel habanera como depósito de esclavas, vale destacar que el artículo séptimo de las reglas para normar el trabajo de las sindicaturas capitalinas —elaboradas en 1865— confería a las que se encontraban en litigio el Hospital de San Francisco de Paula o la Casa de Beneficencia. Ahora bien, distinta fue la situación de las embargadas. En ello influyó la poca disponibilidad de espacios que fungieran como depósitos transitorios ante el desplazamiento geográfico hacia la capital. A modo de ejemplo, según refiere el oficial Melchor Gastón al jefe de la Sección de Administración encargada de la jurisdicción de Puerto Príncipe, hasta abril de 1874 se habían trasladado 542 embargados desde dicha localidad.[23]

No cabe dudas de que entre el acto de confiscación y el destino de los embargados existió un circuito de movilidades y encierros que ofreció coberturas de tácticas para mejorar las condiciones de vida e incluso para alcanzar la libertad que en ocasiones fueron aprovechadas. Uno de los espacios que constituyó por excelencia depósito de estos esclavos fue el *Asilo de San José* de La Habana, hasta donde se ha podido constatar, entre 1870 y 1877.[24] El asilo fungió como espacio transitorio donde los esclavos aguardaban la hora de la subasta pública y la adjudicación de los arrendatarios.

Llaman la atención las regulaciones en la distribución espacial. De acuerdo con lo estipulado en el artículo 42 del *Reglamento para el régimen y gobierno interior del Asilo de San José* de 1874, en el establecimiento convergían los negros del Depósito Judicial de esclavos y cimarrones, de la Junta Protectora de Libertos, y de la Junta de la Deuda del Tesoro. En condición de esclavos, resulta lógico que el apartado, para evitar contagios de "conductas desviadas," estipulara que "estarán estos individuos en completa separación de los asilados."[25]

En cuanto a los de la junta, conjuntamente con el historial de embargo, que debía contener entre sus referencias el nombre del dueño, la edad, nación y oficio, los esclavos eran registrados en el Expediente de Arrendamiento que llevaba el inspector del Negociado de Arriendos. Curiosamente, según documenta el "Cuaderno de notas del expediente formado para el arrendamiento de los esclavos de bienes embargados . . .," ante la ausencia de fuentes de información que acreditaran las edades, estas eran instituidas, en primer lugar, por el testimonio del propio siervo, en caso de su desconocimiento, el administrador del asilo junto a otro empleado del establecimiento procedía a su cálculo aproximado.[26]

El hecho de que el esclavo embargado tuviera el poder de decisión de fijar su condición etaria le permitía incidir en su propia situación. Atendiendo al grado de conocimiento y de astucia del interrogado, este podía registrase en un rango de edad susceptible de recibir los beneficios de la Ley Moret.

Algunos historiadores han señalado las irregularidades en cuanto a los censos y registros de la población esclava posteriores a 1868.[27] Ahora bien, quedan por precisar las especificidades que asumen esas anomalías en el contexto específico del embargo de esclavos. Es decir, se está en presencia de un proceso donde convergen múltiples estrategias desplegadas ante los continuos arrendamientos, que incluyen posibles márgenes de maniobras alrededor de las prescripciones de la Ley Moret.

Se trataba, sin dudas, de casos insólitos, donde la redistribución de la fuerza de trabajo confiscada complejizó el ejercicio del control sobre las estadísticas necesarias para la aplicación de la ley. En las ardides empleadas en el proceso de adjudicación de edades entraron también en juego los intereses de los arrendatarios, claro está, desde presupuestos distintos a los del hombre esclavizado. Para aquellos significaba, sobre todo, un cálculo que atribuía la rentabilidad de la mano de obra en adquisición, por lo cual no es de extrañar que el tema de la construcción etaria suscitara controversias.

En particular, llaman la atención las misivas cursadas en febrero de 1873 por la sociedad de comercio de la ciudad de La Habana Sres. Domenech y Compañía a la Junta de la Deuda. El contenido en discusión era el artículo décimo del pliego de condiciones para el arrendamiento de ingenios, en virtud del cual el Estado estipulaba el pago a la junta de diecisiete pesos mensuales por cada esclavo otorgado en alquiler que no integrase las dotaciones de los enclaves azucareros. Dado que la Ley Moret excluía del sistema de servidumbre a los nacidos posterior a la publicación del decreto y los que arribaban a los sesenta años de edad, era deber de la junta, en opinión de los arrendatarios, reglamentar el abono mensual en relación a la edad útil del esclavo. La enmienda al contrato estaba precedida del análisis de la estructura por edades del inventario de plantaciones realizado por las autoridades en los ingenios matanceros Santo Domingo, Santa Rosa, Santo José y Colombia:

Existen en la finca numerosos siervos que pasan de los 60 años y existen también otros no menos numerosos que por su poca edad constituyen lo propio que aquellos una verdadera carga para el arrendatario. Claro es y evidente que por esas dos categorías de siervos no puede ni debe pagarse arrendamiento alguno; es más que es contra derecho satisfacer renta por lo que lejos de proporcionar utilidad da solo gravamen y de aquí que se necesario que se fije por V. E. la edad a que han de reputarse útiles los siervos para los efectos del pago de esos alquileres [. . .].[28]

Al mismo tiempo, sobre la base de esta lógica, los administradores demandaban la rectificación de las edades asignadas a los esclavos arrendados, puesto que era "indudable que muchos [. . .] han ingresado en la dependencia de bienes embargados sin que les acompañara ningún antecedente respecto a su edad." E incluso, las asignadas en el inventario carecen "de verdad y certeza." El reajuste de las cifras, recomendaban, debía implementarse a partir de un examen físico a cargo de "personas prácticas en conocimiento de dotaciones de fincas," nombradas por los demandantes y la junta.[29]

¿Quiénes empleaban el recurso de la mentira en el cálculo aproximado de las edades? Ya fuesen los funcionarios estatales, quienes podían registrar al esclavo en una escala etaria favorable a las rentas del fisco, o los inquilinos, en aras de librarse de estas, lo cierto es que, una vez más, salta a la vista el estado incompleto del registro historiable del siervo embargado y el amplio grado de improvisación en la actuación de las autoridades a la hora de adjudicar las edades.

El caso tuvo un cierre favorable para los arrendatarios pues, según el acuerdo de la junta fechado el 12 de febrero de 1873, el alquiler comenzó a abonarse por los esclavos que estuvieran en un rango etario entre diez a sesenta años, claro está, previa clasificación según los padrones u otro tipo de documentación legal.[30]

La documentación consultada hasta el momento no apunta a una regularización legal de dicha resolución para casos similares al anterior. Es de resaltar que en las tasaciones realizadas en el Asilo de San José eran los esclavos menores de ocho años los que se registraban sin jornal. Sin embargo, en otras ocasiones, a partir de los seis años se declaraban aptos para el trabajo, las hembras avaluadas en cuatro pesos mensuales y los varones en seis respectivamente.[31]

Circunstancias como las expuestas evidencian la complejidad que subyace tras el acto de tasación. A pesar de la estructuración burocrática destinada a fiscalizar el empleo de la fuerza de trabajo embargada, es notoria la ausencia de una reglamentación que normara quiénes y cómo se debía establecer el valor de los esclavos. Efectivamente, no fueron pocos los casos en que los embargados fueron dados en alquiler sin que mediara la figura del perito tasador. Y es que en coyunturas como la analizada resulta complejo poder estandarizar, en ocasiones, la aplicación de determinadas normativas. La escasez creciente de brazos destinados a las faenas agrícolas y la amenaza que supuso la política independentista para su estabilidad, fueron coyunturas aprovechadas por determinadas autoridades para proceder bajo las reglas del mercado de oferta y demanda. El expediente de embargo del ingenio Santa Rita, situado en la jurisdicción de Colón y perteneciente al infidente Tomás Rodríguez Ruiz, deviene ejemplo de ello.

Como resultado de la tasación de la dotación, remitida por el presidente de la Junta de Vigilancia de Colón en abril de 1872, el oficial a cargo del Negociado de Arriendos —inconforme al efecto— razonaba que, "dadas las actuales circunstancias" donde los esclavos cobran un "valor extraordinario," no se deben admitir "unos jornales tan bajos; el más alto no escede [*sic*] de veinte pesos y el más bajo no pasa de dos pesos al mes, comprendiendo el primero de dichos sueldos, la edad de veinte a sesenta años y el segundo de ocho a quince."

El modo de fijar los jornales que había determinado el oficial sólo tuvo en cuenta la condición etaria y el sexo de los esclavos que habían sido trasladados por el Consejo Administrativo de Bienes Embargados hacia el enclave. Algunos de estos fueron revalorizados en el triple del precio estipulado con anterioridad. Se trataba entonces de un proceder conforme al patrón de las subastas públicas y mucho más beneficioso que "perfectamente legal, evitaría los perjuicios traídos por las tasaciones, no siempre ajustadas a la razón ni hechas con la imparcialidad requerida."[32]

La práctica seguida con los depositados en el ingenio Santa Rita, tuvo su continuación bajo la Junta de la Deuda del Tesoro. En abril de 1873, la oferta elevada por la sociedad de comercio Srs. Domenech y Compañía revalorizó nuevamente los servicios de los cincuenta y cinco esclavos. Dado el caso, Julián Zulueta, uno de consejeros más influyentes de la junta, aprovechó la coyuntura para exigir al arrendatario Don Ventura Mantecón la suma de mil pesos en vez de los 735 devengados mensualmente, puesto que "se le concedieron los negros a un tipo menor del que puede obtenerse en el mercado."[33]

Pese a lo apuntado con anterioridad, otros puntos a destacar donde los administradores de bienes confiscados prestaban especial cuidado eran el oficio y las tachas físicas que poseían los embargados. El primero de dichos indicadores cualitativos era en extremo representativo a los fines de los estimados de tasación y renta realizados con motivo de las subastas públicas. En su estudio resulta relevante la relación de esclavos a arrendar que se expedía de forma periódica en el Asilo de San José.[34] Su apartado *Observaciones* revela el examen físico y verbal al que era sometido el esclavo una vez depositado en el asilo.

Dicho establecimiento devino hospicio para aquellos esclavos que, "defectuosos" para las faenas agrícolas o domésticas, eran depositados temporalmente con vistas a la rehabilitación de sus padecimientos. De ahí que en las "Observaciones" se revelen las tachas más comunes: enfermos del pecho, quebrados, medios locos o con úlceras, lo cual no impidió su tasación. En determinadas ocasiones, los cuidados requerían atención especializada. En estos casos la política seguida por la Junta de la Deuda del Tesoro era depositarlos en el Hospital de San Francisco de Paula o en otro establecimiento similar según la jurisdicción de la que se tratase. Los gastos que se generaban, claro está, corrían a su cuenta.

Tomemos como muestra la realizada el 14 de enero de 1876 al lote de esclavos pertenecientes a Don Miguel Acosta Barañano, de la jurisdicción de Puerto Príncipe. Joaquín Hernández resultó tasado en diecisiete pesos, a pesar de que el vocal de la junta que ejercía como tasador lo presentara como enfermo y necesitado de trabajo poco activo. Planteaba la existencia de "úlcera sobre un tobillo" y que "si no se mantiene en quietud hasta curarse no se curara jamás." Por su parte, el alegato de la lavandera Petronila, tasada en diez pesos, no fue tan creíble para el observador: "dice q. está quebrada de las dos ingles, ombligo y pecho, le fije 10 pesos por tener un hijo pequeño y he dispuesto q. se reconozca por el médico del Asilo dando cuenta de oficio [sic]."[35] Claro está, este tipo de información salvaba a las autoridades de reclamaciones de futuros arrendatarios.

La posibilidad de registrar por sí mismo su oficio fue otro ardid que utilizó el esclavo como medio para ascender o, simplemente, mejorar su estatus de vida hasta donde le fuera posible.[36] Una de las razones que propiciaba ello era, justamente, el estado incompleto de la información que llegaba a las dependencias habaneras. En un contexto de conflicto bélico y crisis económica acrecentada con el paso de los años, el personal de las oficinas de rentas locales no daba abasto para cumplir con la burocracia que generaba el acto de tramitar la confiscación de centenares de propiedades.

Sin poder constatar con certeza las posibles mediaciones en el acto de clasificación de la "mercancía," es ostensible el interés de algunos de los enlistados en la citada tasación por mostrarse como "buen sastre, buen cocinero, criado y algo de zapatero."[37] O, como el esclavo Santos Valdés, quien, luego de registrarse inicialmente por el vocal de la junta en trabajo de campo, de alguna manera se la ingenió para convencer a otro oficial del Negociado de Arriendos con el firme propósito de cambiar su destino. Según la nueva relación, el esclavo Suárez aparecía desempeñándose en otros oficios. El cambio se explica al final del documento: "sabe también aserrar maderas, de albañilería y de cocina," y, por tal motivo, al considerar esas habilidades de más provecho, advertía que "se le ha variado al hacer la publicación en los periódicos." Fuese empleado en las faenas agrícolas o en otro de los oficios manifestados, lo cierto es que era imposible para las autoridades la confirmación de su testimonio en los lugares donde había servido, ya que se trataba de un embargado de la juris-dicción de Puerto Príncipe.[38]

Otra de las estrategias de los recluidos en los depósitos de la capital eran las posibilidades de establecer mediaciones a partir de la creación de vínculos de amistad con particulares. Baste citar los lazos tejidos entre la esclava Ca-ridad Correas, embargada a la propietaria Elvira Céspedes, con Doña María Belén Delgado y Mercedes Busto tras la petición elevada por Correas a la Junta de la Deuda del Tesoro con motivo del patronazgo sobre su hija María una vez regulada la Ley de Vientres Libres.

La carta del 31 de agosto de 1875 fue redactada por Mercedes Bustos, quien también debió hacer la entrega de la misiva en las oficinas centrales de la junta en la ciudad de La Habana.[39] Bustos era parte integrante del círculo de personas de condición libre que le merecían confianza a la esclava a la hora de tratar asuntos personales y hacer valer sus derechos legales. Cercanía que también confería a María Belén Delgado, esposa del administrador del Asilo de San José y a quien la demandante recomendaba el cuidado de la pequeña.

Llaman la atención los calificativos mediante los que se representaba a la figura del patrono en la carta. Ya fuesen ideados por la esclava o por la escri-bana, lo cierto es que ambas debieron compartir el modelo del protector. Junto a la familiaridad que debía inspirar en el esclavo, se articulaba la capacidad del patrono para educar al liberto. Ciertamente, María era destinada bajo el cuidado de Belén Delgado sobre la base de "su enseñanza y demás de su seczo [*sic*]," credenciales fuertes para la época con vistas a lograr un mejor destino para su prole.[40] Detrás de este tipo de cuidado aludido en la carta, subyacen las estrategias trazadas por padres esclavizados para facilitar la movilidad social de sus hijos, una vez que podían recibir los beneficios de la Ley Moret explí-citos en su artículo séptimo: "enseñanza primaria y educación necesaria para ejercer un arte o un oficio."[41]

Los vínculos fraternos entre la esclava y la posible patrona de su hija eran el resultado de un proceso de acercamiento entre ambas, mediado por la solicitud que hiciera María Belén Delgado a la Junta de la Deuda con motivo del arrenda-miento de Caridad y sus dos hijos depositados en el Asilo de San José en enero de 1875. Si bien el contrato se prolongó entre los meses de febrero y noviembre de dicho año, fue suficiente para que la esclava lograse que la obligación con-traída por Belén Delgado en cuanto a la manutención, vestimenta, calzado y asistencia médica, excediera dichos límites en el caso de su hija María.[42]

Con respecto al papel ejercido por Mercedes Bustos como intermediara en la petición de Caridad, pudiera sugerir una suerte de sustitución del Sín-dico Procurador, aunque hasta la fecha no se ha localizado ninguna regula-ción legal al respecto. Empero, resulta interesante como la práctica de acudir a representantes particulares se registra en varios expedientes. Tal fue la conducta seguida por Guadalupe Tellez, perteneciente a los bienes embargados a Doña Josefa Tellez de Bayamo. En esta ocasión, se trataba de una esclava hospitalizada en San Francisco de Paula como consecuencia de antiguos y graves padecimientos. Dado el caso, acudió a Luis M. del Monte, quien en su nombre demandó al Vicepresidente de la Junta de la Deuda del Tesoro el patronazgo de su primogénita Demeteria por parte de Doña Mercedes Dovarganes de Rodil.[43]

En alusión a la citada ley, la carta, fechada el 12 de julio de 1875, expone nuevamente las cualidades del patrono: "persona que le inspire completa fe, que de ella cuide, le inculque sanos principios de moralidad y la eduque con arreglo a su condición."[44]

A diferencia de las madres esclavas cuyas hijas eran patrocinadas por sus mismos amos, la inestabilidad que marcó la vida de muchas embargadas, dispuestas en alquiler a distintos licitadores por cortos períodos de tiempo, trajo consigo el alejamiento de su prole. Tales fueron los casos de las esclavas Caridad y Guadalupe, antes mencionadas. Sin embargo, en el segundo de estos resultó complejo el acceso al patronazgo de la liberta. Y es que otro punto distintivo se asocia justamente con la acreditición etaria de los llamados vientres libres.

¿Cómo acceder a la partida de bautismo de Demeteria asentada en la jurisdicción de Bayamo? Probablemente, dicha interrogante precedió a la actitud de Mercedes Dovarganes al acudir ante el Licenciado D. Domingo Rosan, puesto que la Junta de la Deuda se negaba a otorgar la cédula de vecindad hasta tanto no fuera calificada su edad y así justificar la cesión de la párvula. El 18 de octubre de 1875 el médico y cirujano certificó la edad de seis años y medio "pues aún no ha mudado la primera dentición."[45]

Lo más significativo, empero, es que desde agosto de 1875 hasta mayo de 1876, cuando reclamó el auxilio conjunto de la Junta Protectora de Libertos de La Habana, fue Dovarganes quien demandó a la Junta de la Deuda el cumplimiento de la petición de la esclava Guadalupe sobre la libertad de su hija Demeteria.

Curiosamente, en otras ocasiones, el hecho de ser un "esclavo del Estado" en el contexto de la guerra brindó la posibilidad de restablecer lazos familiares dentro de los propios marcos jurídicos. El caso de los hermanos Mateo y Ledia Tellez es uno de ellos. Al obtener su libertad, Mateo se había trasladado a La Habana, probablemente con la expectativa de mejorar sus condiciones de vida. Mientras, su hermana continuaba en la ciudad de Bayamo como esclava de Doña Mercedes Tellez.

Una vez que le fueron embargadas sus propiedades a la infidente Tellez en enero de 1870, el solicitante del alquiler de la embargada Ledia, en posesión de Don Rafael Caiña, fue su hermano. Mateo elevó su reclamo al Administrador Principal de Rentas el 23 de septiembre de 1876. Luego de cumplidos los trámites pertinentes y de informar la Colecturía de Rentas de Bayamo que la esclava de trece años apenas aportaba cuatro pesos como resultado de sus labores por cuenta propia, el administrador decidió acceder a la solicitud del hermano. Una vez más se imponía la racionalidad económica del fisco, mucho más apremiante en un contexto de guerra donde las fuerzas libertadoras se encontraban en las fértiles llanuras de Matanzas, con las correspondientes destrucciones de las riquezas que les proporcionaban ganancias a España. De ahí los términos de la aceptación del alquiler de la esclava Tellez a cargo de su hermano residente en La Habana y de los rejuegos para posibles desplazamientos de otros embargados. El 20 de octubre el oficial del Negociado informaba que "en esta Capital podría producir en alquiler por lo menos 12 pesos oro mensuales por lo que el Negociado considera conveniente la traslación de dicha esclava a esta ciudad."[46]

Y a continuación le orientaba al Colector de Rentas de Bayamo que

a la mayor brevedad posible remita, relación de todos los esclavos que en aquella Ciudad se encuentran alquilados con espresion [*sic*] del alquiler que cada uno devenga mensual y nombre de los infidentes a quien pertenece para en vista de lo que producen proponer lo que mejor convenga al fisco.[47]

En rigor, estamos en presencia de situaciones donde los controles legales sobre las movilidades de los esclavos embargados, mucho más sofisticados en la medida que avanzaba la década bélica, podían ser transgredidos por estructuras administrativas intermedias de la administración colonial, en busca del aprovechamiento de la fuerza de trabajo a cargo del Estado en unidades productivas o en el ejército. Pero, en otro orden, los propios esclavos embargados aprovecharon sus nuevos espacios de reclusión, así como los márgenes de movilidad como bien alquilado dentro o fuera de una región determinada. Los nuevos vínculos creados le permitieron disponer de información y de intermediarios, instancias ambas facilitadoras de reclamos de mejores oportunidades de destinos, bien dentro de su condición esclava o, en los casos de mayor conocimientos, habilidades y asesoramientos, la obtención de la libertad, valiéndose de las regulaciones de las políticas coloniales con respecto al esclavo, en particular de la denominada Ley de Vientres Libres.

Más que proceder a generalizaciones a partir del procesamiento de ejemplos como los expuestos, se trata de advertir la existencia de variantes de comportamientos y de estrategias de esclavos refrendados en la documentación existente. Acercarse al "rostro humano de la historia" y escrutar los márgenes de acción esclava sobre las normativas impuestas, obligan a establecer ciertas pautas en el orden metodológico que permitan avanzar hacia la definición de enfoques más plurales y complejos. Tales acercamientos, empero, prefiguran la existencia de movilidades que discurren más allá de la sombra de los barracones. A la postre, se asiste a una historia donde perviven relaciones de poder, conflictos y negociaciones, inmersas en un proceso independentista y entre los estertores de un sistema abocado a su desintegración definitiva.

NOTAS

1. La política de embargo de bienes define el conjunto de edictos, circulares y ordenanzas que regularon, desde el punto de vista jurídico, el proceso de expropiación y administración de los bienes de toda clase retenidos. Si bien de forma oficial debe tenerse en cuenta la publicación de la *Gaceta de La Habana*, lo cierto es que desde el día primero, el Capitán General Domingo Dulce, en un contexto de fuertes presiones de la élite integrista habanera, remitió dos circulares al gobernador político de La Habana con la orden de embargo inmediato de dieciséis individuos, conspicuos representantes de la Junta Central Republicana de Cuba y Puerto Rico, con sede en Nueva York. Al respecto véase, Alfonso W. Quiroz: "Costes socioeconómicos de la Guerra de los Diez Años: insurrección cubana independentista y represión oficial española (1868–1878)", en José G. Cayuela (coord.): *Un siglo de España: centenario 1898-1998*, Ediciones de la Universidad de Castilla- La Mancha, Cuenca, 1998, 245–282. Para el análisis de las líneas de acción del Cuerpo de Voluntarios, a partir de la composición e intereses de grupo de su directiva integrista, consúltese: María Dolores Domingo Acebrón: *Los voluntarios y su papel contrarrevolucionario en la Guerra de los Diez Años en Cuba, 1868–1878*, L' Harmattan, Paris, 1996, 42–112. Una visión de conjunto sobre el integrismo insular puede leerse en la obra de Mercedes García Rodríguez: *Con un ojo en Yara y otro en Madrid. Cuba entre dos revoluciones*, Editorial de Ciencias Sociales, La Habana, 2002.

2. Véanse: Julio Le Riverend: *Historia económica de Cuba*, Edición Revolucionaria, La Habana, 1974; María del Carmen Barcia Zequeira: *Burguesía esclavista y abolición*, Editorial de Ciencias Sociales, La Habana, 1987; Inés Roldán de Montaud: *La Hacienda en Cuba durante la Guerra de los Diez Años (1868–1880)*, Instituto de Cooperación Iberoamericana, Sociedad Estatal Quinto Centenario, Instituto de Estudios Fiscales, Madrid, 1990; Alfonso W. Quiroz: "Costes socioeconómicos de la Guerra de los Diez Años: Insurrección cubana independentista y represión oficial española (1868–1878)," *ob. cit.*; Alfonso W. Quiroz: "Corrupción, burocracia colonial y veteranos separatistas en Cuba, 1868–1910," *Revista de Indias* 61, no. 221, 2001; Jorge Ibarra Cuesta: *Marx y los historiadores ante la hacienda y la plantación esclavistas*, Editorial de Ciencias Sociales, La Habana, 2008, Mercedes García Rodríguez: *ob. cit.*.

3. Aisnara Perera y María de los Ángeles Meriño: *Estrategias de libertad: un acercamiento a las acciones legales de los esclavos en Cuba (1762–1872)*, Editorial de Ciencias Sociales, La Habana, 2015, 1:180.

4. La creación del Consejo Administrativo de Bienes Embargados se decretó el 17 de abril de 1869 y el 20 se promulgó otra resolución que, de conjunto con la anterior, fijaron las funciones de este órgano como las de los gobernadores, tenientes gobernadores y depositarios. El Consejo fue dirigido por el gobernador político de La Habana, Dionisio López Roberts, hasta el 31 de agosto de 1869. Al asumir el cargo Antonio Fernández y Caballero de Rodas, recién nombrado Capitán General, delegó sus funciones en el intendente general de Hacienda José Emilio de Santos. Con un grado de autonomía impresionante en cuanto a facultades resolutivas para la gestión de los embargos, se auxiliaba en el cuerpo de consejeros y vocales. En la curiosa composición estaban representados exponentes de los sectores financiero, industrial y comercial. Juan Atilano Colomé, Mamerto Pulido, Segundo Rigal, José Antonio Cabarga, Bonifacio Blesa Jiménez y Nicolás Martínez Valdivielso, demarcaron la representación mayoritaria del Comité Español, el Casino Español de La Habana, así como la plana mayor de los cuerpos de voluntarios. Al mismo tiempo, se integraron figuras del universo plantacionista al estilo de Juan Francisco Poey y Aloy, Joaquín

Pedroso y Echevarría y José Eugenio Moré. Para información detallada sobre la estructuración, el funcionamiento y atribuciones del Consejo, véase: *Datos y noticias oficiales referentes a los bienes mandados a embargar en la Isla de Cuba por el Gobierno Superior Político*, Imprenta del Gobierno y Capitanía General, Habana, 1870. Consúltense los cargos que detentaban algunos de sus miembros en las secciones de Hacienda y de Gobierno del Consejo de Administración de la isla, así como en el Ayuntamiento habanero, en: *Guía de Forasteros de la Isla de Cuba*, Habana, Imprenta del Gobierno y Capitanía General, (1871-1873) (1876-1878).

5. "Dispuesto por el ramo de guerra para que los negros útiles de bienes embargados existentes en el depósito fuesen a trabajar en trabajos de la trocha de los fuertes situados en Camujiro," Archivo Nacional de Cuba (ANC), Fondo *Bienes Embargados*, leg. 148, no. 66.

6. Ibíd.

7. "Correspondencia de Bienes Embargados," ANC, Fondo *Bienes Embargados*, leg. 204, no. 1.

8. Rebecca J. Scott, *La emancipación de los esclavos en Cuba: La transición al trabajo libre 1860–1899*, Editorial Caminos, La Habana, 2001. Véase específicamente el capítulo 4, La adaptación, 1870–1877.

9. "Expediente formado para que se remitan a disposición de este Consejo los esclavos embargados que carezcan de ocupación en los puntos en que se hallen": ANC, Fondo *Bienes Embargados*, leg. 150, no. 30; "Relación de los esclavos embargados que se remiten a disposición del Consejo del Ramo, los cuales han sido clasificados por la Inspección de Puerto Príncipe," ANC, Fondo *Bienes Embargados*, leg. 208, no. 5.

10. "Documento referente a ingenios," ANC, Fondo *Bienes Embargados*, leg. 205, no. 23.

11. *Boletín de Colonización* 4, no. 7, Comisión Central del Ramo en la Isla de Cuba, Habana, 15 de abril de 1876, 6.

12. Con el surgimiento de la Junta de la Deuda se complejizaron las atribuciones de la red burocrática encargada de administrar las propiedades confiscadas. La junta asumió las funciones de clasificar los embargos según la clase y calidad de lo embargado, de administrar los bienes y arrendar dichas propiedades a individuos solventes. Al mismo tiempo, se redujo considerablemente el aparato burocrático. Presidida por el Gobernador Superior Civil como máximo rector y por el Intendente General de Hacienda en calidad de vicepresidente, se componía de quince individuos representantes del comercio, la industria, la propiedad, la banca española, la administración pública y la deuda del Tesoro. Algunos de sus integrantes más sobresalientes fueron Julián Zulueta y Amondo, Ramón Herrera y Francisco Feliciano Ibáñez. Para mayor información, véase: Mariano Cancio Villaamil: "Situación económica de la Isla de Cuba. Exposición dirigida al Excmo. Sr. Ministro de Ultramar," Imprenta de Miguel Ginesta, Madrid, 1875, en Vidal Morales y Morales, *Colección Facticia*, 17:77; *Disposiciones relativas a bienes embargados e incautados a los infidente*, Almacén de papel y efectos de escritorio, de Castro, Hermanos y Compañía, Habana, 1874, 58–82.

13. "Incidente promovido en reclamación de que sean remitidos a esta capital varios esclavos de diferentes infidentes. Santa Clara," ANC, Fondo *Bienes Embargados*, leg. 208, no. 43, no. 44.

14. Varios legajos del fondo *Bienes Embargados* del ANC contienen este tipo de documentación encabezada tanto por arrendatarios como por propietarios confiscados, entre los primeros se encuentran las "Dudas de Don Francisco Vilabrú, vecino de La Habana, planteadas a la Junta de la Deuda el 23 de diciembre de 1872 con motivo de las condiciones para el arrendamiento de los ingenios." Para Vilabrú, quien se manifestaba en términos de justicia, resultaba indispensable que la junta encontrase alguna fórmula garante de la vigencia del contrato ante la devolución del bien arrendado a su legítimo dueño. Ya fuese por medio de una indemnización o de la adjudicación de otra unidad productiva, el inquilino debía quedar satisfecho ante la inversión de capitales realizada. Véase también: "Expediente general de arrendamiento de los ingenios San José, Concepción, Santa Rosa, Santo Domingo, Armonía y Desempeño," leg. 141, no. 1.

15. Aprobada por las Cortes españolas en julio de 1870. Conocida también como Ley de Vientres Libres, otorgaba la libertad jurídica a los esclavos mayores de sesenta años de edad y los hijos nacidos de madres esclavas luego de la publicación de la ley, al tiempo que los niños nacidos entre septiembre de 1868 y la emisión de la normativa eran adquiridos por el estado mediante el pago a sus dueños de 125 pesetas. Véase Hortensia Pichardo, *Documentos para la Historia de Cuba*, Editorial de Ciencias Sociales, La Habana, 1975, 1:383–386.

16. "Reclamación de la Junta C. P. de Libertos a la Junta del Tesoro por el retraso en el cobro del impuesto a los arrendatarios de esclavos comprendidos en la Ley Moret," ANC, Fondo *Bienes Embargados*, leg. 208, no. 64.

17. Ibíd.

18. "Expediente sobre reclamo de la Junta de Libertos de $35.25 por impuesto de 75c. por cada esclavo de los 47 embargados de Trinidad," ANC, Fondo *Bienes Embargados*, leg. 200, no. 42. En la documentación localizada aparece la "Relación de los recibos de la Junta de Libertos a cargo de la Admón. de Rentas de Trinidad que pertenecen a esclavos embargados a infidentes," elaborada el 27 de febrero de 1875. "Don Antonio de Armas (1 esclavo), Juan O-bourke (2), José Ybargollin (6), Miguel Martínez (2), Alonso Primellas (padre) (1), Alonso Primellas (hijo) (3), Benjamín Primellas (1), Caridad Cruz (1), Francisco Molina Adan (1), Luis Molina Adan (1), J. R. Limoni (2), Tomas P. Betancourt (sus herederos) (22), Manuel A. Molina (2), José Nodal (2)." Ibíd.

19. "Expediente formado para averiguar a quien pertenece la esclava Rita de la Caridad," ANC, Fondo *Bienes Embargados*, leg. 148, no. 54.

20. Ibíd.

21. "Correspondencia de Bienes Embargados," ANC, Fondo *Bienes Embargados*, leg. 204, no. 70.

22. Sobre los esclavos litigantes de Santiago de Cuba, véase: Aisnara Perera y María de los Ángeles Meriño: *Estrategias de libertad: un acercamiento a las acciones legales de los esclavos en Cuba (1762–1872)*, 1:195. Los márgenes de una cierta autonomía laboral fueron advertidos por Rebecca Scott al plantear el caso de la esclava Domitila, embargada a Liberato Leiva y Arnau del distrito de Yaguaramas. Véase, Rebecca J. Scott: *Grados de libertad: Cuba y Luisiana después de la esclavitud*, Editorial de Ciencias Sociales, La Habana, 2006, 118.

23. "Expediente instruido por haber pedido el Excmo. Gobernador Gral. una reclamación de los esclavos embargados en Puerto Príncipe," ANC, Fondo *Bienes Embargados*, leg. 148, no. 65.

24. Establecido en la segunda mitad del siglo XIX como Taller general de artes y oficios por el gobierno español. Entidad que les proporcionaba a los jóvenes huérfanos, desvalidos, o con conductas delictivas no sólo hospicio sino también medios de enseñanza para reincorporarlos a la sociedad en calidad de hombres útiles y reformados. El establecimiento se sostenía con los productos de los propios talleres y con los alquileres de los esclavos del Depósito Judicial, cuya administración tenía a su cargo la dirección de la institución. Véase *Guía de Forasteros de la Isla de Cuba*, 159.

25. *Reglamento para el régimen y gobierno interior del Asilo de San José*, Imprenta de la Viuda de Barcina y Compañía, Habana, 1874, 8.

26. "Cuaderno de notas del expediente formado para el arrendamiento de los esclavos de bienes embargados que se encuentran en el Asilo de San José," ANC, Fondo *Bienes Embargados*, leg. 197, no. 12.

27. Para mayor, véanse Manuel Moreno Fraginals, Herbert S. Klein y Stanley L. Engerman: "El nivel y estructura de los precios de los esclavos de las plantaciones cubanas a mediados del siglo XIX: Algunas perspectivas comparativas," *Santiago* (Santiago de Cuba), no. 63, septiembre–diciembre, 1986, 97-121; Scott, *La emancipación de los esclavos en Cuba*, 102–103.

28. "Expediente general de arrendamiento de los ingenios San José, Concepción, Sta. Rosa, Sto. Domingo, Armonía y Desempeño," ANC, Fondo *Bienes Embargados*, leg. 141, no. 1. El último de estos enclaves azucareros pertenecía a los bienes de J. E. Angarica, embargados en el

año 1869. El proceso de arrendamiento y adjudicación a la sociedad de comercio Sres. Domenech y Compañía se llevó a cabo el 13 de enero de 1873 por término de seis años. "Promovido para la subasta de arrendamiento y adjudicación de los ingenios de Bienes Embargados," ANC, Fondo *Bienes Embargados*, leg. 209, no. 21.

29. "Expediente general de arrendamiento de los ingenios San José, Concepción, Sta. Rosa, Sto. Domingo, Armonía y Desempeño," ANC, Fondo *Bienes Embargados*, leg. 141, no. 1.

30. Ibíd.

31. "Cuaderno de notas del expediente relativo al embargo de los bienes del infidente Tomás Rodríguez Ruiz," ANC, Fondo *Bienes Embargados*, leg. 160, no. 13.

32. Ibíd.

33. Ibíd.

34. Como generalidad las relaciones se elaboraban por la "Sección Administración. Negociado de Arriendos" de la Junta de la Deuda del Tesoro.

35. "Expediente general de subastas de esclavos embargados, procedentes del Asilo San José," ANC, Fondo *Bienes Embargados*, leg. 199, no. 16.

36. El historiador Alejandro de la Fuente se refiere, en el orden metodológico, a la necesidad de tener en cuenta, dentro de los marcos jurídicos establecidos por la metrópoli, las estrategias extralegales empleadas por los propios esclavos, así como el uso a su favor de los recursos legales e institucionales. Véase Alejandro de la Fuente, "La esclavitud, la ley, y la reclamación de derechos en Cuba: Repensando el debate de Tannenbaum," *Debate y perspectivas: Cuadernos de historia y Ciencias Sociales*, no. 4, Fundación Mapfre Tavera, Madrid, diciembre 2004, 67.

37. Ibíd.

38. "Expediente formado por el negociado para el arrendamiento de veinte y cinco esclavos pertenecientes al infidente incautado D. Miguel Acosta Barañano de Puerto Príncipe," ANC, Fondo *Bienes Embargados*, leg. 199, no. 7.

39. En el escrito figura la petición de la esclava Caridad a nombre de su hija Caridad. No obstante, en las relaciones de esclavos a arrendar del Asilo de San José aparecen como descendientes María de siete años de edad y Tomás de uno. Justamente, la primera se registra como solicitada tener al servicio. Ambas coincidencias, junto al hecho de que tanto María como Tomás habían sido arrendados con anterioridad por Doña María Belén Delgado, apuntan a un error de Mercedes Bustos al escribir el nombre de la esclava. Seguramente debió confundirlo con el de su madre.

40. "Expediente promovido por la morena Caridad Correas solicitando que su hija Caridad sea entregada a Dª Belén Delgado," ANC, Fondo *Bienes Embargados*, leg. 154, no. 8.

41. Pichardo, *Documentos para la Historia de Cuba*, 384.

42. "Expediente sobre alquiler de la esclava Caridad Correas y sus hijos María y Tomas de D. Elvira Céspedes," ANC, Fondo *Bienes Embargados*, leg. 156, no. 43.

43. "Promovido por la morena Guadalupe Tellez solicitando le sea entregada a D. Mercedes Dobarganes su hija Demeteria," ANC, Fondo *Bienes Embargados*, leg. 157, no. 1.

44. Ibíd.

45. Ibíd.

46. "Expediente promovido por Mateo Telles solicitando la traslación a esta Capital de su hermana Ledia de la infidente Da Merced Telles," ANC, Fondo *Bienes Embargados*, leg. 69, no. 47.

47. Ibíd.

DEVYN SPENCE BENSON

Sara Gómez: Afrocubana (Afro-Cuban Women's) Activism after 1961

ABSTRACT

This article examines the ways black and *mulato* Cubans in the late 1960s and early 1970s continued to fight against racial discrimination despite the official end of the 1959 revolution's antidiscrimination campaign and announcement that racism no longer existed in Cuba. By focusing on the work of Sara Gómez (1943–1974), the first black woman filmmaker at the National Cuban Film Institute (ICAIC), the article shows how Gómez highlighted the experiences of Afro-Cubans and encouraged the revolution to live up to its antiracist and feminist goals. Gómez explored themes related to class divisions, racial discrimination, and gender inequalities and used the lens of her camera and ethnographic techniques to narrate histories about everyday lives in revolutionary Cuba. The article analyzes three of Gomez's lesser-known documentaries to reevaluate how censorship, antiracism, and feminism worked in Cuba in the late 1960s and early 1970s.

RESUMEN

Este artículo examina las formas en que los cubanos negros y mulatos a finales de los años sesenta y principios de los setenta siguieron luchando contra la discriminación racial a pesar del final oficial de la campaña contra la discriminación en 1960 y el anuncio por lideres de la revolución de 1959 que el racismo ya no existía en Cuba. Dentro de una enfoque en las obras de Sara Gómez (1943–1974), la primera cineasta negra en el Instituto Cubano de Arte e Industria Cinematográficos (ICAIC), el ensayo muestra cómo Gómez subrayó la historia, cultura, y política de afrodescendientes en Cuba y promovió el proyecto revolucionario al enfatizar espacios en Cuba dónde no había llegado la visión de una nación para todos. Gómez exploró temas relacionados a la división de clases, discriminación racial, e inequidades de género y usó el lente de su cámara y técnicas etnográficas para narrar historias sobre las realidades de la vida revolucionaria. El ensayo analiza tres documentales menos conocidos de Gómez para reevaluar el funcionamiento de la censura, el antirracismo y el feminismo en Cuba a finales de los años sesenta y principios de los setenta.

In the 1964 documentary *Iré a Santiago* (I'm Going to Santiago), Afro-Cuban director Sara Gómez celebrated Santiago de Cuba's black history. She employed wide shots of the eastern city's colonial streets, cathedral, and university while explaining to her audience that "the first blacks [in Cuba] were brought to Santiago and General Antonio Maceo was born here." In doing so, she emphasized the city's rich past and Afro-Cuban contributions to the nation. But in 1964, Gómez was not only aware of Santiago's past; she also had a stake in its future—a future marked by the dynamic social changes of the 1959 revolution, including both an antidiscrimination campaign and a movement to integrate women into the workforce. In fact, the documentary's narrator claimed that "history is beginning again in Santiago [with the revolution]," as images of Afro-Cuban women outfitted with batons, drums, and marching band uniforms moved across the screen. As the only woman and one of three black directors working at the National Cuban Film Institute (Instituto Cubano de Arte e Industria Cinematográficos, or ICAIC) in the 1960s, Gómez routinely stood out by producing documentaries that showcased the daily experiences of blacks and *mulatos* in revolutionary Cuba—she showed blacks in neighborhoods, factories, and rural areas participating in and questioning the new government's policies. This work sat in stark contrast to the contradictory images proliferating revolutionary visual culture that simultaneously welcomed blacks into the new nation and portrayed Afro-Cubans as in need of salvation and reform to be ideal citizens.[1] It also challenged recent moves by state cultural institutions, ICAIC included, to position blackness in the past, as folklore.[2] Gómez's claim that history was beginning again in Santiago mirrored statements made by revolutionary leaders who imagined 1959 as a new start for the island; however, the young filmmaker saw Cuba's renewal, its revolution, in the lives of Afro-Cuban men and women in Santiago, Guanabacoa, and other sites far removed from the accepted centers of white, male power.

Like other Cubans, blacks and *mulatos* negotiated the changing landscape of revolutionary Cuba throughout the 1960s. New legislation like the Agrarian and Urban Reform Laws, coupled with moves to reduce telephone and electricity rates and provide educational scholarships and health care to working-class and rural Cubans, meant that less than a year after the ouster of President Fulgencio Batista in 1959, life in Cuba had changed dramatically.[3] In the midst of these reforms, revolutionary leaders announced a campaign against racial discrimination in March 1959 that targeted informal segregation practices in schools, social clubs, and parks, constructed a lasting narrative that revolutionaries could not be racists, and sought to fulfill the promises of nineteenth-century patriots by creating a Cuba without blacks, or whites, only Cubans. By 1960 when Fidel Castro led the Cuban delegation to the United Nations meeting in New York and met with Malcolm X in Harlem's Hotel Theresa, revolutionary leaders proclaimed to the world the success of their antidiscrimination campaign and invited African Americans to Cuba to see the island's racial paradise.[4] Shortly afterward, public debates about lingering racism became taboo as Cuban leaders focused the national lens on defending the revolution from

US aggression—this move left little public space for dissent. According to the existing literature, this silence continued until the 1990s, when economic crisis led to another wave of vocal Afro-Cuban activism against worsening inequalities and employment discrimination in the new tourist industry. Much of the current work on race in Cuba traces this familiar arc about antiracist activism on the island. A rich body of scholarship exists about nineteenth-century slavery, slave rebellions, abolition, and Afro-Cuban participation in the Cuban wars of independence.[5] Similarly, black and *mulato* activism and national political participation during both the Cuban republic (1902–1958) and the first years of the revolution has received considerable attention.[6] More recently, anthropologists, sociologists, and political scientists in Cuba and the United States have analyzed racial tensions following the fall of the Soviet Union in 1989 and theorized about the "return of racism" after decentralizing economic reforms.[7] However, there remains an accepted gap in knowledge about revolutionary changes in the late 1960s and 1970s.[8] In particular, more research is needed on how black and *mulato* Cubans who stayed on the island (and did not move into exile) found creative ways to have public and private debates about racial inequality despite the 1960 declaration that racial discrimination had been eliminated and repeated state attempts to silence public conversations about lingering racisms in favor of national unity. Many of these Afro-Cubans, like filmmaker Sara Gómez, found outlets for addressing discrimination and fighting for racial equality in literature and the arts.[9]

Young black women, including prominent Afro-Cubanas like poets Georgina Herrera and Nancy Morejón, literary critic Inés María Martiatu Terry, and Gómez, played influential roles in these late 1960s conversations, yet the literature about the period is dominated by responses by black men. Books by and about black activist-intellectuals such as Juan R. Betancourt, Carlos Moore, Walterio Carbonell, and Pedro Perez Sarduy are well known.[10] Some of this is because the international press picked up their works and published them outside of Cuba. Despite this trend, as Paula Sanmartín noted in her recent book *Black Women as Custodians of History*, the 1959 revolution was, in fact, a revolution in black women's writings. After 1959, Afro-Cuban women used the education and openings provided by the new government to move from being the subjects to the objects or the creative voices of Cuban literature and poetry.[11] Black women (of various classes), like the former domestic-turned-poet Herrera and the middle-class documentary director Gómez, experienced and reinvented Cuba's revolution in the late 1960s. Their lives and works illuminate tensions between opportunity and censorship in post-1959 Cuba, but they also show how despite official government silences on domestic racism, black and *mulato* Cubans never lost sight of the revolution's promise of racial equality.[12] Moreover, with the founding of the Federation of Cuban Women and the rise of the state-backed women's movement in Cuba after 1959, it becomes even more important to recover the work of black female activists who pushed an intersected agenda. Using the case study of Sara Gómez, with special attention to her lesser-known short documentaries, this article reevaluates how censorship, antiracism, and feminism worked in Cuba in the late 1960s and early 1970s.

* * *

Sara Gómez Yera was born to a middle-class black family in Havana in 1943. Raised by her paternal grandmother and four aunts, she grew up surrounded by Afro-Cuban professionals, including family members who played in the Havana Philharmonic Orchestra, and attended dances at black recreational societies like the Porvenir and El Club Progreso. These associations, along with her education at the Conservatory of Music in Havana, where she studied piano before the revolution, led her to make films that questioned class and race distinctions among all Cubans, including blacks and *mulatos*. Claiming that she did not want to be a "middle-class black girl [*negrita*] who played the piano," Gómez experimented with journalism—she wrote for the youth magazine *Mella* and the supplement for the Communist Party paper, *Noticias de Hoy*—before taking a position at ICAIC as assistant to the famed director Tomás Gutiérrez Alea in 1961. From then until her premature death from an asthma attack in 1973, she directed fifteen short documentaries and one feature film as ICAIC's first female director, and the only black woman, in a space that had barred women prior to 1959.[13]

Film historian Susan Lord writes that Gómez is both simultaneously "claimed and dis-claimed."[14] She is well known among Western film scholars; they have analyzed her work, especially her 1977 feature film *De cierta manera* (One Way or Another), as one of the first pieces of non-Western feminist film coming out of the so-called third world to denounce patriarchy and machismo. Other film critics have talked about her use of innovative techniques that epitomized the 1960s film style of imperfect cinema, in which directors intentionally left films aesthetically imperfect to encourage audience interaction and promote social debates. For example, Gómez shot *De cierta manera* in 16 mm and intermixed documentary-style footage with fictional shots while putting trained actors into scenes with nonactor locals going about their everyday lives.[15] Until recently, however, Gómez was largely unknown on the island of her birth. The National Film Institute remained virtually silent about Gómez's career until it dedicated a special edition of *Cine Cubano* to her life in 1989.[16] And other than *De cierta manera*, which was released to international acclaim after her death, ICAIC censored her documentaries, leaving them untouched in the institute's archives until 2007, when a special colloquium, *Sara Gómez: Multiple Images: The Cuban Audiovisual from a Gendered Point of View*, celebrated Gómez and pushed for the digitalization of her short films.[17]

Still, few of these newer works about Gómez have contextualized her work as an extension of Afro-Cuban political activism in the republic and a response to the 1959 revolution's antidiscrimination campaign.

Importantly, this lack of public acknowledgment about Gómez's work is not indicative of her influence during the period, but a reflection of the limited distribution of certain types of black art and the narrowing space for public debates about race in the 1960s. Afro-Cuban author and literary critic (and close friend of Gómez) Inés María Martiatu Terry rightly categorized Gómez's documentaries as a type of "political cinema" that "reflected the extraordinary moment that they lived in and the political tensions of the time." One of the ways Gómez accomplished this was by showcasing black and *mulato* neighborhoods and how they changed or remained the same as a result of revolutionary programs. Some scholars have incorrectly suggested that her attention to working-class Cubans of African descent was a result of her own background and "marginalization." However, as Martiatu explains, Gómez was not from a poor black family; rather, she was raised by four aunts—a piano professor, a painter, a dentist, and a dressmaker. Gómez was a member of the small but highly educated black middle class, and she focused her films on how the revolution affected Afro-Cubans, especially black women.[18] As a part of a group of black intellectuals, Gómez, like her friend Martiatu, worked to develop a black consciousness on the island by inserting Afro-Cuban history, culture, and politics into the revolutionary narrative.[19]

Cubans of African descent faced considerable challenges in their demands to tackle lingering racism during the first decade of the revolution. In addition to Castro's public claims that racial discrimination had been eliminated and his dismissal of black critics as ungrateful, in June 1961 (two months after declaring the Marxist Leninist nature of the Revolution) the young leader declared: "Within the Revolution, everything! Outside of the Revolution, nothing!" In this speech, titled "Some Words to the Intellectuals," Castro argued that artists and intellectuals had creative freedom to do whatever work they desired, but the revolution had the right, and a weightier right, to review (and prohibit if necessary) any art form that would damage the ideology of Cubans: "We have the responsibility to lead the people and to lead the Revolution, especially in the midst of a revolutionary struggle."[20]

The speech did not mention socialism or try to validate its claims with Soviet ideology; instead, Castro depicted the revolution as a battle for the re-education or decolonization of Cuban minds. In addition to being an attempt to unify the country after the Bay of Pigs attack in April, Castro's speech was also part of a series of meetings and public fora among intellectuals, ICAIC, and the National Culture Council (CNC, Consejo Nacional de Cultura) in response to the censuring of the film *P.M.* (1961). Directed by two young filmmakers, *P.M.* was a short documentary, less than ten minutes, showing Afro-Cubans partaking in the nightclub scene in Havana. A British traveler to the island described the film as follows: It showed black and *mulato* Cubans "drinking, arguing, loving, quarrelling, [and] dreaming. A blurred negress stands in front of the lens, and the camera moves back to take in the whole jostling, sweating scene . . . the only sound is the roar of so many Cuban voices, the clink of glasses and ice from the bar, and the music."[21] More pointedly, Bob Taber highlighted the difference between the Cubans portrayed in the film and the revolution's famous literacy campaign martyr: "I didn't see a single Conrado Benítez among them, with a rifle in one hand and a book in the other."[22] Contemporary scholars continue to dispute why the revolution banned *P.M.* Some argue that ICAIC and the CNC found its focus on black nightlife counter-revolutionary and in conflict with the celebratory rhetoric that had consumed the island since the April 1961 defeat of US-backed forces in the Bay of Pigs Invasion. Others see the banning as the first step in what would soon be a state-supported censorship campaign that valued only positive portrayals of the revolution for both domestic and international consumption.[23] Susan Lord concludes that "the story of *P.M.* is more than a story of the censorship of a film that coincidentally has black content; it is a story about the struggle over how to tell the story about race."[24] Surely not a coincidence, the censuring of art featuring Afro-Cuban life, the closing of black social clubs that had existed since the late nineteenth century, and ICAIC's later choice not to screen any of Sara Gómez's documentaries reflected Cuban conflicts over who was allowed to represent blackness and what images of blackness were considered revolutionary.[25] The state's distaste for *P.M.* centered on the fact that blacks in the film, while obviously working class—later interviews even identified them as revolutionaries—did not accept the new government's plans to reform them. The Afro-Cubans caught on camera for *P.M.* saw little reason to give up their nightly leisure activities, nor did they fit into the parameters of appropriate revolutionary blackness, which valued clean-cut and grateful workers and *brigadistas*.[26] Instead, the dancers were individuals who, like Gómez, dared to pursue their own destiny and definition of the revolution.

Sara Gómez's fifteen short documentaries dialogued with many of these and other pressing questions facing Cuba in the 1960s. She explored themes related to class divisions, racial discrimination, and gender inequalities and used the lens of the camera and ethnographic techniques to tell stories about the realities of revolutionary life. Gómez directed her first solo documentary, *Iré a Santiago*, in 1964, three years after the *P.M.* controversy (before this she had been assistant director for two other short documentaries).[27] *Iré a Santiago* narrates the history of Cuba's largest eastern city, Santiago, from the perspective of black and *mulato* Cubans, who composed a large percentage of the city's population at the time. The film begins with and is titled after a quotation from the Spanish author Federico García Lorca's 1930 poem "Son de Negros en

Cuba" (Blacks Dancing to Cuban Rhythms): "When the full moon rises, I'm going to Santiago. I'm going to Santiago in a carriage of black waters." Some years later, Compay Segundo, a member of the Buena Vista Social Club, put the poem to music. Compay Segundo's song resonates in the background of the film's opening scene while the camera tracks a *mulata* woman strolling into the center of the city.[28] Gómez frequently began her documentaries with images of Afro-Cuban women doing routine tasks such as cutting cane, cooking, walking to market, or dancing. These panoramic moving shots, always accompanied by Cuban music, were one of the ways the director foregrounded the experiences of black and *mulata* women in her work and positioned them as central to the building of a new Cuba. Although she did not interview any Cubans in *Iré a Santiago*, the young director achieved an intimate feeling with the protagonists in the documentary by using the camera to follow them into their homes and into other private moments, such as a scene in which a young black couple is on a date.

Gómez revealed the diversity of Cuba's black population and highlighted diasporic cultural practices linking Cuba to Haiti by dedicating a quarter of *Iré a Santiago* to tracking a funeral procession for Esperanza, the president of a "French" society. "In Santiago, there are blacks who call themselves French," she says, "because their ancestors arrived in Cuba when white planters fled Haiti to escape the neighboring island's revolution which had freed its slaves." And even as the documentary notes that there are no longer any French in Cuba and that the coffee plantations that they owned have long disappeared, Gómez employs footage of over fifty Afro-Cubans marching behind Esperanza's casket to demonstrate the cultural significance that black social clubs, like the French society, had in structuring life in Santiago.

Gómez continues to draw attention to black social clubs in *Guanabacoa: Crónica de mi familia* (Guanabacoa: Chronicle of My Family, 1966)—this time through the example of members of her own middle-class family who attended dances at elite Afro-Cuban societies before the revolution.[29] The documentary offers an inside portrait of black refinement and culture through images of her uncles playing music in locales ranging from Central Park to the Philharmonic Orchestra in Havana. Gómez combines views of well-dressed aunts attending Catholic mass with still studio portraits of other family members at different moments in their lives—including pictures of babies in white christening gowns and wedding party photographs. One by one she introduces her family, and acting as the narrator, she remembers "*mulato* cousins in nice suits and visiting uncles with hard collars and houses where clarinets were kept in leather cases." Watching the documentary it is clear the young director has fond memories of her childhood in her grandmother's home and the black cultural practices (art, music, and religion) that she learned there. Gómez continues to emphasize her family's class status by describing how her aunts did not attend public dances because they were "decent women." Instead, she explains, they supported events and dances at El Progreso and El Porvenir—two Afro-Cuban black societies—that Gómez says were clubs only for "certain blacks."

Combined with the scenes of the French society in *Iré a Santiago*, Gómez's accounts of Afro-Cuban associations in *Crónica de mi familia* reflect on the controversial closing of black and *mulato* social clubs in the early 1960s. As the new government began to integrate and abolish elite white societies and recreational facilities, it faced the question of what to do with similar organizations for people of African descent. These mutual-aid societies had existed since the late nineteenth century and served as spaces for middle- and upper-class Afro-Cubans not only to gather and network but also to push for social and political change.[30] But most private clubs (both black and white) were gone by the mid-1960s when Gómez made this documentary, since revolutionary leaders and some Afro-Cubans saw little need for black and *mulato* social clubs after the 1959 racial integration campaign. Therefore, mentioning these clubs in her films, in a positive way no less, while highlighting her middle-class roots, is likely one reason Gómez's works were not screened in Cuba when they were made. *Crónica de mi familia*, however, was not a simple statement in support of Afro-Cuban clubs. Because while Gómez warmly remembered the dances her family members had attended, she also acknowledged that the societies were exclusive and only for "certain blacks." At the end of the short film, Gómez shows her favorite cousin, Berta, leaving her kitchen, where she had been sitting moments before surrounded by relics of the Virgin Mary and Catholic saints, and walking out of her house. The documentary ends, much like *Iré a Santiago* began, following an Afro-Cuban woman, this time her cousin, down an unpopulated street. The narrator concludes, asking, "Will we have to fight against necessity of being a better and superior black? To come to Guanabacoa and accept a complete or total history; a complete picture of Guanabacoa and to tell it all." With these words, Gómez recognized and questioned the tensions between working- and middle-class blacks, something the revolution's antiracist campaign often failed to do. These documentaries suggest that she saw something to be admired in the popular French society of Santiago and the refined clubs of Guanabacoa, but she also questioned how Afro-Cuban associations perpetuated class hierarchies. In trying to paint a "complete picture" of black Cuba—using case studies from cities outside of Havana—Gómez's work marked continuities between pre- and postrevolutionary life. She celebrated her family's history, even as she felt compelled not to be a "middle-class girl who played the piano" and struggled to meld her own class background with revolutionary ideals. She insisted on using routine images of black life, including its contradictions (such as shots of Catholic religious idols sitting next to Santería orishas or 26th of July Movement paraphernalia in the background of a French society's funeral procession) to portray Afro-Cubans as normal human beings. In doing so, Gómez built on the work of previous Afro-Cuban activists and challenged notions of grateful, simplistic, revolutionary blackness seen in other aspects of popular culture while positioning black cultural practices as a part of present-day Cuba, not the far-off past.

* * *

By 1968, Gómez was using her camera to expose contradictions in the government's claims to have eliminated racism, and her work stands out as an example of the ways Afro-Cubans continued debates about discrimination past the official end of the campaign. In a series of three documentaries about the Isle of Pines, renamed the Isle of Youth after the revolution, the now-seasoned short-film director examined the experiences of Cuban youth (who were disproportionately black and *mulato*) sent to reform camps for deviant behavior.[31] However, spaces for critiquing the revolution continued to decrease as the decade progressed. More than four hundred intellectuals from seventy countries gathered in Havana in January 1968 for Cuba's first Culture Congress. The meeting, which celebrated the growth of a revolutionary and anti-imperialist consciousness in the developing world, was a congress of contradictions. On the one hand, the Cuban government invited foreign intellectuals (often paying for their travel) and presented them with an image of cultural openness and opportunity on the island. Domestically, however, Congress marked the beginning of a five-year interlude Cuban historians have characterized as the "gray period" in Cuban culture because of the limits placed on what was considered revolutionary art.[32] According to Martiatu, one of the topics challenged at the Congress was the work of black intellectuals, like Walterio Carbonell, who had fought to insert the history of Africa and blacks in Cuba into the public school curriculum. Revolutionary leaders accused Carbonell, along with other Afro-Cubans, of fomenting "black power." As a result, revolutionary leaders "seized" his book, *Crítica: Cómo surgió la cultura nacional* (Critique: How to Build a National Culture, 1961) and sent Carbonell to a reform camp to cut cane.[33] Similarly, in 1968 the minister of education called Gómez and two colleagues, black playwright Tomás González and ethnologist Alberto Pedro Díaz, into his office under the suspicion "of organizing activities diverging from the Revolution's ideological line and encouraging black power" as well.[34] These charges point to the shrinking space for intellectual creativity in the late 1960s, and to the ways that the revolutionary government targeted some Afro-Cuban activists as counterrevolutionaries.

Race added an additional layer to the contradictions of the 1968 Cultural Congress and raised the stakes for black and *mulato* intellectuals who questioned the new government. The three Afro-Cuban directors at ICAIC each experienced this period in different ways. When describing a film that he had made that was considered "inopportune" and therefore not released in Cuba until years later, Sergio Giral said, "That was hard to take, because I've always felt a sense of political and social responsibility and wanted what I do to serve the revolutionary process. You exercise a form of self-censorship in not wanting to destroy the cake by sticking your fingers in it too much."[35] Giral's comment, though brief, explains why slavery and the lives of blacks in the nineteenth-century colonial period became the content of the majority of his films. Rather than risk having his work not shown, he chose topics that featured Afro-Cubans and educated audiences about blackness, without intervening into contemporary affairs. Giral had a long and successful career in Cuba until the 1990s when he moved into exile for economic reasons. In contrast, the second black director at ICAIC, Nicolas Guillén Landrián, nephew of the national poet Nicolas Guillén, made documentaries questioning contemporary issues explicitly, using banned Beatles music in the background of one and poking fun of Castro in another. Revolutionary leaders jailed Guillén Landrián, and after attempts to "rehabilitate" him with excessive electric shock therapy failed, the young director escaped into exile as well.[36] In this high-risk environment, only Gómez directed films that showed the lingering inequalities on the island and demanded that the revolution meet its own social justice claims. And while she did not face the physical persecution that Guillén Landrián encountered, likely because she remained committed to revolutionary goals even as she highlighted their failings, ICAIC did not screen Gómez's documentaries about youth reform camps at the time when they might have been most useful.[37]

Gómez completed a series of three documentaries questioning why so many black and *mulato* youth were sent to reform camps on the Isle of Youth, including *Una isla para Miguel* (An Island for Miguel, 1968), *En la otra isla* (On the Other Island, 1968), and *Isla del Tesoro* (Treasure Island, 1969). In these pieces, she took on the role of ethnographer and mixed interviews with teenagers on the island with statements from revolutionary leaders describing the purpose of the reform camps. In *En la otra isla*, Gómez questioned a seventeen-year-old dark-skinned girl named Maria about her family in Havana and her daily schedule at the camp. Maria explained how she has seven brothers and sisters and that her mother was a prostitute before the revolution. "But now she is no longer working on the street," Maria stated in reference to a new program that had provided former prostitutes with opportunities to attend school and later obtain employment.[38] The young girl proudly described her goal to become a hairdresser and outlined her daily routines. These included studying political culture in the morning and straightening black hair with a hot comb in the afternoon. Other than the somewhat unsettling image of a white, blonde Cuban instructing Maria on how to straighten black hair (there are seemingly no black female revolutionary leaders to mentor young black girls on hair care), Gómez's overall portrayal of Maria is hopeful and the teenager seems genuinely happy with the education she is receiving on the island. It remains unclear, however, how Maria arrived on the Isle of Youth. Martiatu notes that Gómez was interested in learning more about the island because it had been featured prominently in the Cuba press as a utopia where young people could construct a revolutionary consciousness without the bourgeoisie prejudices of adult Cubans. But revolutionary authorities sent kids to the island if they got into trouble with the law, if they failed to show the appropriate ideological formation, or if their parents could not care for them. Because these reasons were often linked to socioeconomic status, Martiatu said that once on the island Gómez encountered a disproportionately high number of working-class black and *mulato* youth.[39] By showing how social inequalities of the past invaded and were reproduced on the Isle of Youth, Gómez challenged the revolution's claims to have eliminated racial discrimination and provide equal opportunities to Afro-Cubans.

In another interview, Rafael, a young dark-skinned black man, explained to Gómez how he had studied music for two and a half years at the National Art Institute. Opera was his specialty and he sang the part of tenor. Rafael described his love of music and the numerous concerts he gave in Havana until the "problems" began:

RAFAEL: Then the problems started.
GÓMEZ: Which ones?
RAFAEL: Problems with some of the *compañeras* [women] in the group. A lot of them didn't want to work with me anymore. It didn't feel right to be working in a scene with me anymore. I didn't know why; what was happening to me?
GÓMEZ: Did they not like you because you came from the National Art Institute or because of your political formation?
RAFAEL: No, I don't think so.
GÓMEZ: Were they political problems? What type of problems?
RAFAEL: [Looking directly at Gómez] I think the problem was race.
GÓMEZ: They were prejudiced against you? . . . Weren't they revolutionaries?
RAFAEL: Yes . . . [pause] They were revolutionaries, some not, but most were, but the fundamental problem was to tell you more concretely that the only black man was me . . . [pause] Look, Sara, this wasn't about color. It was about aesthetics. They needed someone to work with a white woman in love scenes in the opera. And imagine it . . . [pause] if I might have to give her kiss? When I took this problem of race to my supervisor, they said maybe it was there before, but, not now; that it must have been some error.

After this dialogue, Gómez cut to images of Rafael performing agricultural work, before a final close-up of him speaking again. Nodding his head affirmatively, he said, "I have confidence in the revolution that things will get better. So, now I'm doing agriculture, I'm doing something to help the revolution . . . being on the island has helped me a lot, they treat me well, and it is not like there. . . . [pause] I have a question for you, Sara. Do you think one day, a black man could sing *La Traviata*?"[40] This uncomfortable exchange highlights how many of the contradictions inherent in the 1959 campaign to eliminate racial discrimination followed Cubans into the late 1960s. On the one hand, Rafael benefitted from the opportunity to break into a predominantly white space of opera singing having studied and worked with the National Opera in the early 1960s, something that would likely not have been available before 1959. On the other hand, the public silence around continued racism after 1961 not only left him with few spaces to denounce the discrimination against him, but it also led him to feel ashamed of what happened to his career and internalize it as his fault that white women did not want to sing with him. Martiatu concludes that Rafael both accepted his punishment and punished himself; the island acted as space of "purgatory" for him.[41] As Rafael completed his "reform" through agricultural work, he distanced himself from his earlier goals and hoped that the revolution would accept him as a hard laborer since it refused to accept him as a cultural laborer, as a black opera singer. But his final shy question to Gómez, which he proposed with a small smile and without looking at her face, reveals that he still hoped that he might one day sing an Italian opera for a Havana audience, even as he was hesitant to believe that day would come any time soon.

In choosing to highlight the stories of youth like Maria and Rafael, Gómez suggested that there were things that revolutionaries could learn from the supposed deviants of society. As she told Rafael during their discussion, "The Revolution can't do everything for you. You have to make it, the Revolution, yourself."[42] These young men and women were not delinquents to Gómez. Rather their perseverance, commitment to revolutionary equality, and willingness to sacrifice for Cuba positioned them as potentially more revolutionary than the Cuban authorities who were unwilling to see past their race and class status. With this understanding, it becomes clear why the opening frame of *La isla para Miguel* (coming before the title and credits) quoted Frantz Fanon's *Wretched of the Earth*: "These vagrants, these second-class citizens, find their way back to the nation thanks to their decisive, militant action."[43] Gómez's documentary reminded viewers that Afro-Cubans were not vagrants or second-class citizens; rather, they had something significant to contribute to the nation. For Gómez, asking the tough questions about the contradictions in the revolution's programs and documenting on film the moments when the new government benefited Cubans and when it failed them was not a simplistic endeavor, but it a necessary one. She implicitly disagreed with authorities who questioned the usefulness of art to the revolution when she wrote: "Didactic cinema is a necessity, not a specialty. Many of us came to this vocation with the revolution and . . . always express ourselves in revolutionary terms." Gómez saw herself as a revolutionary and imagined her craft as a space in which she could use the camera as a weapon to fight against injustice. As she explained in 1970, artists had certain responsibilities to Cubans and to the revolution. "We [filmmakers] have a vast public, including urban workers, rural campesinos, children and adolescents . . . for them and with them we have to make films without making concessions. Films that touch on their interests. Films that are capable of expressing contradictions. And that have as a goal helping all of us . . . Is this overly ambitious? Will we achieve it? This has to be the goal."[44] In this way, while her documentaries showed the places where revolutionary rhetoric did not meet its own expectations, especially in relation to marginalized groups like blacks and women, she also always left a space for those issues to be resolved.[45]

* * *

In one of the last documentaries made before her death in 1974, Gómez assessed the changes in gender roles after the revolution, but like her other pieces this one also paid special attention to black women. Using ethnographic techniques, *Mi aporte* (My Contribution, 1972) interviewed male and female workers in the Camilo Cienfuegos sugar refinery and examined how they managed shifting gender roles once more women were working and more men were expected to complete household chores. Cuban women had participated in the anti-Batista coalition in the 1950s and continued to be politically active during the revolution's earliest years.[46] This participation was centralized in August 1960, when Vilma Espín created the Federation of Cuban Women (FMC) to facilitate women's organizing in response to a call from Fidel Castro for women to join the revolution. From its original membership of seventeen thousand in early 1961, the FMC expanded to more than two million members by 1975 and represented approximately 77 percent of women over the age of fifteen. But it was not until the late 1960s that women were incorporated in larger numbers into the labor economy. The urgent economic needs in Cuba and the desire to mobilize Cubans for the ten-million-ton sugar harvest in 1970 pushed the government to work tirelessly to bring women into the economy. In response, almost two hundred thousand new female workers volunteered for sugar production and other agricultural work. Women also worked part-time in factories and got managerial positions and administrative positions in small retail outlets. Of the four thousand new managers named in 1968, 90 percent were women.[47] Similar to the campaign to eliminate racial discrimination that resulted in the relatively quick integration of public spaces like schools and social clubs, the high numbers of women who began working alongside men in factories led to anxieties that gender norms were changing too quickly or not fast enough. *Mi aporte* intervenes into this highly contested social issue through interviews with workers, FMC officials, and a focus group of women intellectuals. In doing so, it highlights the double duty that many working women faced and exposes

Cuban men's perceptions and stereotypes about women workers while also examining how racial and class inequality affected black women workers.

Mi aporte begins by contrasting the official "positive" version of what women are experiencing in the workplace with a much more complicated reality. As the FMC hymn plays in the background, popular Cuban television personality Consuelo Vidal interviews a group of women about their jobs in the factory. Each one says that she enjoys her new position and has not had any trouble with her new male *compañeros*. An Afro-Cuban woman named Zenaida cheerily notes that both she and her husband leave for work at 3 a.m. and 6 a.m., respectively, while their children get up, eat, and dress themselves before going to the state-provided childcare and school on their own. Vidal asks the woman if she is overwhelmed by cooking and cleaning for her family at the end of a long work day and the woman grins and says of course not, my husband helps me with all the chores:

CONSUELA VIDAL: You've never had problems with your husband?
ZENAIDA: No.
CONSUELA VIDAL: Because you took on a job?
ZENAIDA: No.
CONSUELA VIDAL: Does he help you?
ZENAIDA: Yes, when I wash, he cooks.
CONSUELA VIDAL: He hangs out clothes? Really?! (Laughter)[48]

Filled with music, laughter, jokes, and positive demeanors, the opening scene of *Mi aporte* paints a utopic portrait of the lives of women workers who are fulfilled, supported, and respected by their male counterparts just as the FMC intended.

Gómez contrasts the sheer joy pictured in this opening scene with an interview with a male worker inside the factory who is critical of what he calls women's "absenteeism" from work:

We do not agree with what you suggest. . . . There are problems here and very serious problems in some occasions. The *compañeras*, because they lack the habit of tough work—work generally carried out by men—their behavior is not the best. There are cases of constant absenteeism, poor habits at work, abusing the unhappy men who work around them through paternalism, if you will, since the men do their own work and part of the work the *compañeras* should be doing, because the poor *compañeras* cannot put in the physical effort required by the task they must complete. Then, the men help them.

The unnamed man's commentary reiterates common tropes about female workers—that they are not as strong as men and that they lack discipline. Oddly, he calls men doing women's jobs paternalism and implies that women are taking advantage of men's chivalry by not working as hard. During another point in the documentary he recounts the story of a pregnant woman who sleeps during work hours:

The problem of paternalism. . . . We had a very interesting case of a *compañera* who was pregnant. Then, when it was time for her shift, she made her little round. And calmly, after two or three hours, she hid in a place she had prepped with her coat and her little blanket and her pillow and to sleep she goes. Then, the *compañeros* who more or less worked in the same area, in the same zone, did the work for her. . . . Their stance did not help her, or them or the Revolution, it helped nobody. And if this *compañera* was here, it was not because factory work was indispensable to her, but because it was a need of the Revolution, a need of the nation for women to swarm massively to work to solve all the labor force problems we have.

By contrasting these two episodes (the interviews with contented female workers and those with the disgruntled male workers), Gómez again shows how the revolution fails to live up to its ideals. Similarly, she juxtaposes the "official narrative" shown in the opening clip of the television show—seen in the interview outside of the factory—to the grittier daily experiences and tensions inside the building. Viewers would have left *Mi aporte* questioning the success of programs to incorporate women into the workforce and seeing how traditional gender norms had an impact on how both men and women understood and used humor to deal with anxieties about each other's new roles. For instance, that the women in the opening scene all laughed at the image of Zenaida's husband washing and hanging clothes suggests that women were not quite comfortable with men as domestic laborers. And not only did the male worker seem to easily accept that women were not physically capable of working in the factory because they were weaker than men; he also chuckled while telling his story about the pregnant woman and her doing her "little round" and laying our her "little blanket." His laughter and use of the diminutive suggest a belief that while cute and playful, most women severely misunderstood what real work should be. In the end, Gómez uses these scenes from *Mi aporte* to reveal that even as revolutionary programs had altered the physical spaces inhabited by men and women, they had yet to change Cuban hearts and minds.

One of the most striking aspects of *Mi aporte*, however, is the way the documentary analyzes gender, race, and class together to make an intersected critique of how revolutionary programs continue to be at odds with some working-class black women's realities. In the second half of the documentary Gómez rides along as FMC representatives visit the homes of women who have "abandoned" their jobs to see what problems they are facing and if they can be encouraged to return to work. The camera zooms in on a white, middle-class FMC official as she converses with a dark-skinned black woman about why she has not been at work. The woman explains that she wants to work, but that she cannot because the school where her children are assigned is too far away for her to drop them off and get to work on time. The mother also tells Gómez that she had relayed this information to the official before and asked them to switch her children to a different school location, but they refused. The FMC official tries to explain that it is impossible to move the children halfway through the year and suggests that the black woman accept the intern that they have hired to take her kids to school and feed them lunch. However, the black mother finds this option unsatisfactory "because unless I drop him off at school, I can't go to work. Because maybe he says yes, that he's going to school. But when it comes down to it, he goes with the other kids to the river [ignoring the intern]. And one is left with the preoccupation that maybe he drowned, or a machine killed him. I can't be calm at work, it's the truth. And I need to go work." By providing this example of the concerned black mother, Gómez pushes back against two notions: that Afro-Cuban women do not want to work and participate in the revolution, and that Afro-Cuban women are not good mothers and are lacking "culture" when it comes to raising their children. Instead, Gómez portrays the FMC official as unfeeling and unrelenting in her desire for the woman to work despite uncertain childcare conditions. During an interview with another black woman, Gómez's stance on the needs of female revolutionaries becomes even clearer. This Afro-Cuban interviewee looks directly into the camera and says: "My problem is the following: I'm alone at home. I do all the household chores at home. I recognize the need that the Revolution has for labor and for all the *compañeros* to help the Revolution, I'm a member of the Federation and I would like to help the Revolution. When they generate the necessary conditions, then I will go to work."

Both of the women interviewed say that they are the "heads of household" suggesting that they are not married and do not have partners to coparent with. Despite this, they both have clear expectations about how they want to parent and who they trust to supervise their children. Gómez challenges stereotypes about Afro-Cubans while also pushing the revolution to live up to its promises by showcasing women's, particularly working-class black women's, struggles merging revolutionary needs with personal ones. Similar to the ways that Gómez represented Maria and Rafael's stay on the Isle of Youth, the black and *mulata* women in *Mi aporte* are not counterrevolutionaries or women in need of reform; instead, it is the system that needs to be revolutionized to meet the needs of all its citizens. More important, it is clear that these Afro-Cuban woman are aware of the limits of the revolution and feel comfortable telling FMC officials and Gómez's camera about the conditions they require before they can become the contented and excited workers featured in the documentary's propaganda-like opening scene.

Gómez concludes the documentary with two focus groups that further complicate how *Mi aporte* challenges gender, racial, and class privileges and offers an inside look into continued (albeit nonpublic) debates about sexism, racism, and classism in revolutionary Cuba. The first focus group begins with a title screen asking, "Are we creating the conditions for the formation of the new woman? Some reflections on the subject." Gómez joins this conversation with three other professional young women (Lucía Corona, from the National Center of Scientific Investigations, Mirta Valladares, from the School of Industrial Design, and Gladys Eques, from the School of Journalism) as they discuss the difficulties of fulfilling the roles of mother and intellectual. Interestingly, and a sign of changing times and an evolution in Gómez's self-presentation to the world, this is the first time she appears on camera with the Afro hairstyle that she began wearing shortly after Stokely Carmichael's 1967 visit to the island. During the conversation it becomes clear that these privileged, educated, professional women face many of the same problems as the working-class black women Gómez interviewed previously. But, in addition to lamenting the fact that men never miss work when their children are ill, but that as women they might have to take off a month to tend a sick child, they also debated potential solutions to these problems. One woman, Lucía, suggests they should give up motherhood all together. The three others disagree and debate about the possibility of reeducating their sons by not raising them in a macho way. Mirta points out, however, that this would lead her son to be teased at school:

If I educate my son in that way, taking away the prejudice of household chores, he will find, when he goes to school or with his friends on the streets, many contradictions. Because the first thing he will stumble upon is the little friend who will say: "Oh no, no, I don't scrub [dishes], because that is a girl's thing. My mom has told me. That's a girl thing."

Despite these limits, all the women were in agreement that things were changing and that the revolution had given them "weapons" to fight these battles: "The revolution gives us weapons so we can grow," they said. For the four professionals, the fact that Gómez was making the documentary and they were sitting in the room having a discussion about gender norms was progress toward a more equitable society.

The second focus group takes place in the ICAIC private screening room with women who had just finished watching the film.[49] The heterogeneous group of Cubans (young, old, white, black, various classes) debated the points of the documentary and unlike the four professionals it appears that these women did not know each other before the screening. Yet, despite their unfamiliarity with one another, the group has a heated debate about the documentary and the filmed discussion between Gómez and her friends. They were especially disturbed by a point in the conversation among the professional women when Lucía says that she only wants to work and create, to be an individual, and that she does not want to have a family or get married. The audience felt that Lucía was too extreme and was closing herself off to opportunities that she might want to have later in life. They disagreed with the proposition that a woman had to renounce all her femininity or maternal desires to be taken seriously as a worker, intellectual, or artist. They also criticized her for being selfish and not advocating for all the other women who had children and families and needed the revolution's support to work. This interaction is telling because it marks the type of feminism that some Cuban women desired in the early 1970s. The women in the audience wanted to be able to work and to be mothers and they fully expected the revolution and Cuban men to respect and support those goals. The audience also had choice words for the "unenlightened *compañero*" who thought that women used pregnancy as an "excuse" to be lazy—they found that he was an example of men who "call themselves revolutionary, but won't let their women work." And some of the audience members shared stories about other revolutionary men who failed to accept and support women's moves into the workforce with refreshing honesty that suggests that they did not feel the need to censor their comments.

In the end, as in her other documentaries, Gómez's argument in *Mi aporte* is multifaceted. She applauds the revolution for opening up a space for dialogue about gender norms and giving women "weapons" to fight their battles —this is both a literal and a figurative reference, since women joined militias shortly after 1959. However, similar to her analysis of the Isle of Youth, the revolution fell short of its promises and women still experienced discrimination. In particular, she disagreed with the portrayal of poor black women as uninterested in joining the workforce as good revolutionaries and used the film to draw attention to the social inequities (lack of childcare and the prevalence of female-headed households) that prevented some black women's participation.

Despite the lived reality behind Gómez's evaluation of the limits of social change in Cuba, *Mi aporte* encountered strong resistance from the FMC. Martiatu recalls the response by Vilma Espín, president of the FMC:

It was a critical documentary and the Federation thought it was going to be celebratory of the Federation and it wasn't. And when Espín saw that it was made by a black woman, she (well, here everyone is very authoritative) wanted to kill her. I'm the only one Sara told what she said: "You made this film this way because you were raised by maids and you had everything, but you don't understand the problem at all," Espín said. And she was the president of the Federation of Women, heroine of the Sierra Maestra, married to Raúl Castro, etc. And Sara was a nobody next to her. She called Sara a counterrevolutionary. She pointed the finger at her, and like Cubans say, you know what happened next. They didn't show anything that Sara made after that.[50]

That Espín thought that Gómez was critical of the revolution's incorporation of women because of her class background (to clarify, her family did not have maids) shows how much revolutionary authorities misunderstood the young director's feminist and antiracist project.

Conclusions

Sara Gómez passed away at the age of thirty-one on June 2, 1974, from an asthma attack that robbed Cuba of one of its great revolutionary artists and activists. Her funeral was attended by her family and close circle of friends, including a collection of young people who would later become—and were already in the process of becoming—some of the most famous writers, poets, and playwrights of Cuba, including Inés María Martiatu, Pedro Pérez Sarduy, Georgina Herrera, Nancy Morejón, and Manulo Granados. Many of her contemporaries remember the day of her funeral in clear detail both because of their anguish at their loss, but also because of a violent rainstorm that began as Gómez was being buried. Martiatu recalls:

We were together and crying, and we all got wet when at the exact moment that they were going to bury Sara, the sky broke in a surprising rain shower. A torrential *aguacero* and there wasn't anyway for us to move, no one did anything. The *aguacero* was so strong, and so much water fell in so little time that the streets of the cemetery filled up and the water ran over the gutters. . . . A goodbye from Ochun and Yemaya, probably. When Sara was under the ground the rain stopped as quickly as it had begun.[51]

Later the group returned to Manulo Granados's home to console one another, to cry, and to say goodbye to Gómez with rum and rumba. In many ways, Martiatu's memories of this day epitomize Gómez's life. A life surrounded by friends, caught up in the storm of revolutionary change, sometimes being unable to move, and other times rushing forward to redefine Cuba. It seems fitting that an *aguacero* would accompany Gómez's funeral given that her work often strove to cleanse Cuba of its limitations and shine the fierce sunlight that comes after such a storm on the inconsistencies of revolutionary change.

Gómez is one of the critical missing links between Afro-Cuban activism during the early twentieth-century republic and today. Many of the new black and *mulato* antiracist organizations, especially women's groups like the Afro-Cubanas Project established in 2010 by Martiatu and Daisy Rubiera, found inspiration in Gómez's documentaries and films. Despite the accepted narrative that debates about racial equality were silenced after 1960 and did not begin again until the 1990s, documentaries like *Iré a Santiago*, *Crónica de mi familia*, *La otra isla*, and *Mi aporte* demonstrate that pioneering filmmakers like Gómez were still pushing revolutionary leaders about contested social issues into the early 1970s; and her interviewees and film discussants did so as well. That so many men and women were willing to speak candidly about their lives, struggles, dreams, and fears living in revolutionary Cuba encourages historians to take another look at how censorship worked in practice in this period and how all Cubans defined their revolution.

In particular, Gómez's career with ICAIC also highlights how blacks and *mulatos* challenged the official declaration that racial discrimination had been eliminated and fought state attempts to silence public debates about lingering racism. Cuban conversations about racism did not end after 1961; instead, they were reconstructed in areas outside of the public sphere, in art, poetry, literature, and film. Additional research is needed on the seemingly large role black and *mulata* women artists played in this continued struggle and the ongoing transnational connections they invoked. Still, Gómez's work suggests that an emerging antiracist Cuban feminism was a part of the discussions taking place during this period. Her determination to feature all sorts of Afro-Cuban women on camera in respectful rather than stereotypical ways is a reminder that official discourses about blackness were not the only ones available. What other hidden transcripts, to use James C. Scott's term, might be hiding in the archives of 1970s revolutionary Cuba?[52]

Gómez believed in a "perfectible revolution" and used her art and her own intersected positionality as a black woman to push the revolution in a more equitable direction. Martiatu notes that Gómez was not against revolutionary projects like the Isle of Youth or the FMC, but that she thought that "they could have been realized more coherently."[53] But, as seen in how Espín reacted to *Mi aporte*, this vision of a revolution in progress was not always looked at favorably. Martiatu concludes, "ICAIC had very special politics with Sara. They left her to make her documentaries, but they didn't exhibit them. They didn't show the documentaries. They didn't appear at the film festivals, but she worked and kept working and working."[54]

After Gómez's death, her colleague Tómas González wrote that when he first met Gómez her hair was straight "under the neocolonial process of a relaxer," but that by 1973 she sported a small Afro. "Hers was the first natural black head in my country. A Revolution inside of a Revolution!" he claimed. This comment invokes Castro's claim that women's entrance into the workplace was a revolution inside of the revolution, but it does so in a way that highlights Gómez's contributions to Cuban national debates about blackness and Afro-Cubans' role in the revolution in the late 1960s and 1970s. Even knowing that her films would not be shown publicly for decades, Gómez continued to write and direct innovative scripts about pressing social concerns often mixing narratives about racism, sexism, and class hierarchies together in ways that raised more questions than answers. In doing so, she captured the dynamic changes of the period and created an archive of everyday experiences of revolutionary life that existing film studies scholarship on her techniques of imperfect cinema have yet to uncover.

NOTES

1. I discuss the contradictory nature of the 1959 revolution's antidiscrimination campaign in *Antiracism in Cuba: The Unfinished Revolution* (Chapel Hill: University of North Carolina Press, 2016). Excerpts of this article were published previously in *Antiracism in Cuba.*

2. For additional information on the ways revolutionary cultural institutions imagined blackness and African cultural practices as a part of the Cuban past, see Alejandro de la Fuente's discussion of the creation of the Department of Folklore in 1960, *A Nation for All: Race, Inequality, and Politics in Twentieth-Century Cuba* (Chapel Hill: University of North Carolina Press, 2001), 285–296. For a discussion of how, unlike her ICAIC colleagues, Gómez's films were not about "the 'past' of racial identity," see Susan Lord, "Acts of Affection: Cinema, Citizenship, and Race in the Work of Sara Gómez," in Lessie Jo Frazier and Deborah Cohen, *Gender and Sexuality in 1968: Transformative Politics in the Cultural Imagination* (New York: Palgrave Macmillan, 2009), 175.

3. On reforms in the early 1960s, see Louis A. Pérez Jr., *Cuba: Between Reform and Revolution*, 2nd ed. (Oxford: Oxford University Press, 1995), and Marifeli Pérez-Stable, *The Cuban Revolution* (New York: Oxford University Press, 1999).

4. Benson, *Antiracism in Cuba*, 153–197.

5. For nineteenth-century slave rebellions, see Robert L. Paquette, *Sugar Is Made with Blood: The Conspiracy of La Escalera and the Conflict between Empires over Slavery in Cuba* (Middletown, CT: Wesleyan University Press, 1990); Gloria García, *Conspiraciones y revueltas: La actividad de los negros en Cuba, 1790–1845* (Santiago de Cuba: Editorial Oriente, 2003); Matt Childs, *The 1812 Aponte Rebellion in Cuba and the Struggle against Atlantic Slavery* (Chapel Hill: University of North Carolina Press, 2006); and Aisha Finch, *Rethinking Slave Rebellion in Cuba: La Escalera and the Insurgencies of 1841–1844* (Chapel Hill: University of North Carolina Press, 2015). For additional reading on slavery and abolition in Cuba, see Rebecca J. Scott, *Slave Emancipation in Cuba: The Transition to Free Labor, 1860–1899*, 2nd ed. (Pittsburgh, PA: University of Pittsburgh Press, 2000); Franklin W. Knight, *Slave Society in Cuba during the Nineteenth Century* (Madison: University of Wisconsin Press, 1970); Julio Angel Carreras, *Esclavitud, abolición, y racismo* (Havana: Editorial de Ciencias Sociales, 1989); and Olga Portuondo Zúñiga, *Entre esclavos y libres de Cuba colonial* (Santiago de Cuba: Editorial Oriente, 2003). For the Wars of Independence, see Ada Ferrer, *Insurgent Cuba: Race, Nation, and Revolution, 1868–1898* (Chapel Hill: University of North Carolina Press, 1999); Mark A. Sander, *A Black Soldier's Story: The Narrative of Ricardo Batrell and the Cuban War of Independence* (Minneapolis: University of Minnesota Press, 2010); David Satorious, *Ever Faithful: Race, Loyalty, and the Ends of Empire in Spanish Cuba* (Durham, NC: Duke University Press, 2013); and Robert C. Nathan, "The Blood of Our Heroes: Race, Memory, and Iconography in Cuba, 1902–1962" (PhD diss., University of North Carolina–Chapel Hill, College Park, 2012).

6. For Afro-Cubans in the republic, see Aline Helg, *Our Rightful Share: The Afro-Cuban Struggle for Equality, 1886–1912* (Chapel Hill: University of North Carolina Press, 1995); Alejandro de la Fuente, *A Nation for All: Race, Inequality, and Politics in Twentieth Century Cuba* (Chapel Hill: University of North Carolina Press, 2001); Robin Moore, *Nationalizing Blackness: AfroCubanismo and the Artistic Revolution in Havana, 1920–1940* (Pittsburgh, PA: University of Pittsburgh Press, 1997); Alejandra Bronfman, *Measures of Equality: Social Science, Citizenship, and Race in Cuba* (Chapel Hill: University of North Carolina Press, 2004); Frank Andre Guridy, *Forging Diaspora: Afro-Cubans and African Americans in a World of Empire and Jim Crow* (Chapel Hill: University of North Carolina Press, 2010); Melina Pappademos, *Black Activism in the Cuban Republic* (Chapel Hill: University of North Carolina Press, 2012); and Devyn Spence Benson, *Antiracism in Cuba: The Unfinished Revolution* (Chapel Hill: University of North Carolina Press, 2016).

7. See Mark Q. Sawyer, *Racial Politics in Post-Revolutionary Cuba* (Cambridge: Cambridge University Press, 2006); Esteban Morales Domínguez, "Un modelo para el análisis de la problemática racial cubano," *Catauro: Revista cubano de antropología 4*, no. 6 (2002), 70; Morales, *Desafíos de la problemática racial en Cuba* (Havana: Fundación Fernando Ortiz, 2007); Alejandro de la Fuente, "The New Afro-Cuban Cultural Movement and the Debate on Race in Contemporary Cuba," *Journal of Latin American Studies 40* (2008): 714; Sujatha Fernandes, *Cuba Represent! Cuban Arts, State Power, and the Making of New Revolutionary Cultures* (Durham, NC: Duke University Press, 2006); L. Kaifa Roland, *Cuban Color in Tourism and La Lucha* (Oxford: Oxford University Press, 2010); Jafari Allen, *¿Venceremos? The Erotics of Black Self-making in Cuba* (Durham, NC: Duke University Press, 2011); Andrea Queeley, *Rescuing Our Roots: The African Anglo-Caribbean Diaspora in Contemporary Cuba* (Gainesville: University Press of Florida, 2015); Marc Perry, *Negro Soy Yo: Hip Hop and Raced Citizenship in Neoliberal Cuba* (Durham, NC: Duke University Press, 2015).

8. See Lillian Guerra, *Visions of Power in Cuba: Revolution, Redemption, and Resistance 1959–1971* (Chapel Hill: University of North Carolina Press, 2012) for an example of more recent scholarship about 1960s and 1970s Cuba.

9. For examples of research beginning to fill this gap, see Alejandro de la Fuente, ed., *Grupo Antillano: The Art of Afro-Cuba* (Pittsburgh, PA: University of Pittsburgh Press, 2013), and Jesús J. Barquet, ed., *Ediciones El Puente en la Habana de los años 60: Lecturas críticas y libros de poesía* (Chihuahua, Mexico: Ediciones del Azar, 2011).

10. See Juan René Betancourt, *El Negro: ciudadano del futuro* (Havana: Cárdenas y Cía., 1959), and Walterio Carbonell, *Critica: Cómo surgió la cultura nacional* (Havana: Ediciones Yaka, 1961). As Guerra discusses in *Visions of Power in Cuba*, these books had limited circulation in Cuba and were ultimately banned by the revolutionary leadership. After leaving Cuba for exile, Moore and Betancourt continued to push revolutionary leaders to tackle lingering prejudices and racism, especially in the government. See the following works printed in the international press for examples: Carlos Moore, *Castro, the Blacks, and Africa* (Los Angeles: Center for Afro-American Studies, University of California, 1988); Carlos Moore, *Pichón, A Memoir: Race and Revolution in Castro's Cuba* (Chicago: Lawrence Hill Books, 2008); Juan René Betancourt, "Castro and the Cuban Negro," *The Crisis: A Record of the Darker Races* 68, no. 5 (May 1961); Juan René Betancourt, *Sociología integral: La superación científica del prejuicio racial* (Buenos Aires: Editorial Freeland, 1964); and more recently Pedro Pérez Sarduy and Jean Stubbs, eds., *Afro-Cuban Voices: On Race and Identity in Contemporary Cuba* (Gainesville: University Press of Florida, 2000).

11. Paula Sanmartín, *Black Women as Custodians of History: Unsung Rebel (M)others in African American and Afro-Cuban Women's Writing* (Amherst, NY: Cambria Press, 2014).

12. I say "domestic racism" because throughout the late 1960s and 1970s Cuba became very involved and had much success in international antiracist and decolonial struggles. See Piero Gleijeses, *Conflicting Missions: Havana, Washington, and Africa, 1959–1976* (Chapel Hill: University of North Carolina Press, 2002).

13. For information about Gómez's background, see Michael Chanan, *Cuban Cinema* (Minneapolis: University of Minnesota Press, 2004), 341–352, and Inés María Martiatu Terry, "Una isla para Sara Gómez," unpublished transcript of an address given at Fiesta del Caribe in 2007. She directed fifteen shorts while working at ICAIC, among them *Iré a Santiago de Cuba* (1964); *Excursión a Vueltabajo* (1965); *Guanabacoa: Crónica de mi familia* (1966); *Y . . . tenemos sabor* (1967); *Una isla para Miguel* (1968); *Y la otra isla* (1968); *La isla del tesoro* (1969); *Poder local, poder popular* (1970); *Un documental a propósito del tránsito* (1971); *Mi aporte* (1972); *Año uno* (1972); *Sobre horas extras y trabajo voluntario* (1973); and the feature film *De cierta manera* (1977), which was later finished and released after her death. Many of these short documentaries are available on YouTube.

14. Susan Lord, "Temporality and Identity in Sara Gómez's Documentaries," in *Women Filmmakers: Refocusing*, ed. Jacqueline Levitin, Judith Plessis, and Valerie Raoul (New York: Routledge, 2003), 251.

15. For additional reading on imperfect cinema, see Chanan, *Cuban Cinema*, 305–331.

16. See the special issue of *Cine Cubano* on Sara Gómez: no. 127 (1989).

17. *Sara Gómez: Imagen múltiple: El audiovisual cubano desde la perspectiva de género* (Havana, November 1–3, 2007). For additional information about Gómez's documentaries and their censorship, see Haseenah Ebrahim, "Sarita and the Revolution: Race and Cuban Cinema," *European Review of Latin American and Caribbean Studies/Revista Europea de Estudios Latinoamericanos y del Caribe*, no. 82 (April 2007): 107–118.

18. Martiatu, "Una isla para Sara," 1. The Swiss film ¿*Donde está Sara Gómez?* (2006) by Alessandra Muller inappropriately portrays Gómez as someone who grew up in poverty and fails to recognize her middle-class roots and university-educated background.

19. By the late 1960s, some Afro-Cuban intellectuals had begun to form study groups to read and discuss a variety of issues including the ways race and blackness were being discussed by revolutionary leaders. Frequently meeting in each other's homes or in the National Library, this group included writers, artists, filmmakers, and poets like Nancy Morejón, Georgina Herrera, Manuel Granados, Sara Gómez, Pedro Pérez Sarduy, Rogelio Martinez Fure, Nicolás Guillén Landrián, and Walterio Carbonell. Some of these intellectuals also published with the independent press, *El Puente*, until it closed in 1965. See Maria Isabel Alfonso, "Ediciones El Puente y dinámicas raciales de los anos 60: Un capítulo olvidado de la historia literaria cubana" *Temas 70* (2012): 110–118, and Barquet, *Ediciones El Puente*. Additional research is needed on how these Cuban black consciousness activists were influenced by and had an impact on other Caribbean notions of black consciousness or Negritude and US versions of black nationalism in the late 1960s and 1970s.

20. Fidel Castro, *Palabras a los intelectuales* (Havana: National Cultural Council, 1961).

21. Nicolas Wollaston, quoted in Chanan, *Cuban Cinema*, 134.

22. Bob Taber, "En defensa de PM," in *El caso de PM: cine, poder y censura*, ed. Orlando Jiménez Leal and Manual Zayas (Madrid: Editorial Colibrí, 2012), 14.

23. For additional reading on this debate, see Chanan, *Cuban Cinema*, 133–136; Lillian Guerra, *Visions of Power in Cuba: Revolution, Redemption, and Resistance, 1959–1971* (Chapel Hill: University of North Carolina Press, 2012), 162–164 and 342–344; Susan Lord, "Acts of Affection," in *Gender and Sexuality in 1968*, 184–185; and José Quiroga, *Cuban Palimpsests* (Minneapolis: University of Minnesota Press, 2005), 251. Guerra, in particular, describes how five years later, black filmmaker Nicolás Guillén Landrián made a film resembling *P.M.* titled *Los del baile* (Those of the dance); it showed Afro-Cubans dancing and drinking in the streets of Cuba during the day. Saying that "it might well have been called *A.M.*," she describes how revolutionary leaders also banned this film for its supposed "counterrevolutionary" content, 343.

24. Susan Lord, "Acts of Affection," in *Gender and Sexuality in 1968*, 184–185.

25. There remains debate about whether Gómez's documentaries were screened publicly or not. Martiatu claims that the documentaries were not shown widely and that they were censored. Similarly, Ebrahim in "Sarita and the Revolution" notes that Cuban censors prohibited the showing of "*Crónica de mi familia*" (1966) after it was completed, p. 111. Whereas Cuban filmmaker Rigoberto López says that while the documentaries did not get the circulation they deserved, he did attend a screening at ICAIC. I find that the answer is somewhere in between. The documentaries were likely shown to small groups at ICAIC, especially other employees (López worked there at the time as an assistant), and directors could host private showings to get feedback on their work (this will be discussed later for Gómez's *Mi aporte* in which she filmed the post-film discussion session and later includes it in the final cut). But there is little evidence that Gómez's documentaries interrogating revolutionary programs were screened publicly or widely in Havana or anywhere else in the late 1960s and 1970s.

26. See Benson, *Antiracism in Cuba*, 198–230.

27. Sara Gómez Yera, *Iré a Santiago* (1964), Instituto Cubano de Arte e Industria Cinematograficos.

28. Betto Arcos, "Interview with Francisco Repilado aka Compay Segundo," *Global Village—Pacifica Radio KPFK 90.7 FM,* http://www.pbs.org/buenavista/musicians/bios/compay_interview_eng.html.

29. Sara Gómez Yera, *Crónica de mi familia* (1966), Instituto Cubano de Arte e Industria Cinematograficos.

30. For Afro-Cuban social clubs in the twentieth century, see de la Fuente, *A Nation for All*; Guridy, *Forging Diaspora*; Pappademos, *Black Activism in Cuba*; and Benson, *Antiracism in Cuba*.

31. By 1968, Gómez had completed six short documentaries at ICAIC.

32. For additional reading on the censorship in the late 1960s, see Alberto Abreu Arcia, *Los juegos de la escritura o la reescritura de la historia* (Havana: Casa de las Americas, 2007); Barquet, *Ediciones El Puente*.

33. Lord, "Acts of Affection," 185; Martiatu, "Una isla para Sara," 13.

34. As told to Martiatu in "Una isla para Sara," 14.

35. Pedro Pérez Sarduy and Jean Stubbs, *AfroCuba: An Anthology of Cuban Writing on Race, Politics, and Culture* (New York: Ocean Press, 1993), 266.

36. See Lillian Guerra, *Visions of Power in Cuba*, for more information on Guillén Landrián.

37. Martiatu also noted that Gómez had influential protectors at ICAIC. Interview with author, spring 2010. Like other historians of 1960s Cuba, I rely heavily on oral histories and interviews to recount the experiences of revolutionary Cuba. In addition to the limited archival materials available to North American researchers for 1960s Cuba, the perspectives of blacks and *mulatos* are additionally marginalized in the written record. I met Inés María Martiatu Terry through my work with the AfroCubanas project. She was one of the cofounders of the black and *mulata* women's organization in Havana. Over a course of days, we talked about her work at ICAIC, Gómez, and the group of young black intellectuals who met, worked, and made art during this period.

38. In 1961, the revolution began a program to rehabilitate prostitutes. It lasted five to six years and was organized to deal with the forty thousand prostitutes who had existed on the island in 1959. See Pilar's testimony in Oscar Lewis, *Four Women: Living the Revolution* (Urbana: University of Illinois Press, 1977), 237–319, for an account of someone who participated in this process.

39. Interview with author, spring 2010. Martiatu, "Una isla para Sara," 15.

40. Sara Gómez Yera, *En la otra isla* (1968).

41. Martiatu, "Una isla para Sara," 17.

42. Sara Gómez Yera, *En la otra isla* (1968).

43. Ibid. The original Spanish quotation is from the Spanish edition of Fanon, *Los condenados de la tierra* (1963).

44. Sara Gómez Yera interview in "Los documentalistas y sus concepciones," *Pensamiento crítico* 42 (July 1970): 94–96.

45. Martiatu, "Una isla para Sara."

46. For women's participation in the revolution, see Michelle Chase, *Revolution within the Revolution: Women and Gender Politics in Cuba, 1952–1962* (Chapel Hill: University of North Carolina Press, 2015).

47. See "Introduction," in Lewis et al., *Four Women*, ix–xxxviii.

48. Sara Gómez Yera, *Mi aporte* (1972).

49. This is one of the private ICAIC screenings referred to earlier where audiences saw the documentary even though it was not widely circulated.

50. Interview with author, spring 2010.

51. Martiatu, "Algo bueno e interesante con Manolo Granados en el patio del resturante El Patio y la ventanita del oro," *Afro-Hispanic Review* 24, no. 1 (Spring 2005): 29–30.

52. James C. Scott, *Domination and the Arts of Resistance: Hidden Transcripts* (New Haven, CT: Yale University Press, 1990).

53. Martiatu, "Una isla para Sara," 15, 18.

54. Interview with author, spring 2010.

TAKKARA BRUNSON

"In the general interest of all conscious women": Race, Class, and the Cuban Women's Movement, 1923–1939

ABSTRACT

This article examines the evolution of racial and class dynamics in the women's movement during the 1920s and 1930s. In particular, it traces the evolution of the feminist leadership between the 1923 First National Women's Congress and 1939 Third National Women's Congress, with specific consideration of how elite and middle-class white organizers formed alliances with black women from a range of class backgrounds. Though scholarship has emphasized the increasing collaboration of elite and working-class women in support of suffrage, labor reform, and social welfare programs during the rise of popular movements in this period, this article argues that race played a critical role in how many feminists reimagined their platform. By 1939, black female leaders emphasized their disparate experiences before national audiences while attempting to unify all Cuban women on behalf of democratic reform. The article thus shows how African-descended women helped build a cross-racial political alliance that would demand institutional reform during the 1940 Constitutional Assembly.

RESUMEN

Este artículo examina la evolución de la dinámica racial y de clase en el movimiento de mujeres durante las décadas de 1920 y 1930. En particular, traza la evolución del liderazgo feminista entre el Primer Congreso Nacional de Mujeres de 1923 y el Tercer Congreso Nacional de Mujeres de 1939, con una consideración específica de cómo los mujeres blancas de la burguesía y la clase media formaron alianzas con mujeres negras de diferentes orígenes. A pesar de que la erudición ha enfatizado la creciente colaboración de las mujeres de la burguesía y la clase trabajadora en apoyo del sufragio, la reforma laboral y los programas de asistencia social durante el ascenso de los movimientos populares en este período, este artículo argumenta que la raza jugó un papel crítico en cuántas feministas imaginó su plataforma. Hacia 1939, las mujeres negras enfatizaron sus experiencias dispares ante las audiencias nacionales mientras trataban de unificar a todas las mujeres cubanas a favor de la reforma democrática. El artículo muestra así cómo las mujeres negras ayudaron a construir una alianza política a través de grupos raciales y que exigiría una reforma institucional durante la Asamblea Constituyente de 1940.

159

In April 1939, Santa Clara poet and teacher María Dámasa Jova gave a speech entitled "La situación de la mujer negra en Cuba" at the Third National Women's Congress. The forty-three-year-old woman of African descent argued that "the black mother suffered most because she was the mother of the marginal black child, the prostitute, the little newspaper vendor, the gang of robbers, the great number of unemployed and illiterate, and the ill-mannered black child." She went on to assert that discrimination within schools undermined social equality, as they trained black girls to become ironers rather than professionals. "When the black woman is conceded her rights and when there is a [sizable] percentage of black women in shops and offices, one can rest assured that women in Cuba are united in the struggle for their overall betterment and in the interests of mothers and children," she determined.[1] She insisted that any movement for democratic reform must include a commitment to securing the rights of women and children of African descent.

Dámasa Jova critically examined the role of white feminists in Cuban society.[2] She stressed that "the problem of racial discrimination calls the attention of white women to the situation of black women."[3] "One must note," she explained, "that in this fight for the vindication of the white woman, she holds the greatest responsibility in being able to reject her unjust privileges. She must fight for a redistribution of resources by rejecting her privileges so that the black woman might receive her rights."[4] She thus implored white female attendees to act on their stated commitment to racial solidarity.

Dámasa Jova's speech is a striking indictment of Cuban democracy and its failure to realize the principles of racial equality put forth by the independence movement and the 1901 Constitution. Equally significant is her participation in the congress. The first two national women's congresses—which took place in 1923 and 1925—included few women of African descent in attendance. Delegates and organizers did not discuss racial discrimination. The 1939 Third National Women's Congress, however, featured black women as executive committee members, delegates, and presenters. Women of African descent put forth an analysis of Cuban womanhood that emphasized the intersection of gender discrimination with anti-black racism and class exploitation. This article examines these shifting dynamics from three angles: how discussions of class and race evolved during each congress as white and black feminists built alliances; the transformation of black women's activism during the 1920s and 1930s that led them to emerge as leaders within national organizations; and African-descended women's efforts to address racial discrimination as part of the national feminist platform during the 1939 congress. These dynamics demonstrate shifts in Cuban political culture more broadly, including how black women helped forge an intersected political coalition leading up to the 1940 Constitutional Assembly.

Recent studies demonstrate a growing interest in the Cuban women's movement during the Republican era.[5] While scholars have explored the lives of a primarily elite and middle-class white leadership, acknowledging the presence of individual black (and) laboring women, few have discussed how race shaped the evolution of the movement.[6] The political and economic turmoil of the 1920s led many white feminists to collaborate with poor and African-descended women in order to attain suffrage rights, and the national women's congresses presented opportunities for women to articulate a common agenda. This article contributes to the study of women's activism in Latin America by focusing on evolving discussions of race and cross-racial alliances; it highlights the utility of an intersectional analysis that takes into account the contributions of a range of social groups.[7] Cuban women's history has focused on the efforts of activists to achieve voting rights and family law reform, establish social welfare programs, and challenge government corruption. But much work needs to be done on how women activists engaged racial politics, including how racial dynamics prompted collaboration and dissention.

Black women's participation in the women's movement buttressed their commitment to racial advancement. The historiography on black political activism has tended to focus on how men negotiated the contradictions between racism and anti-black racism that shaped Cuban nationalism.[8] This article explores how women of African descent participated in struggles for racial equality and highlights the ways in which gender and sexuality shaped black activist strategies. Elite blacks formulated a project of racial uplift that promoted thrift, education, sexual morality, and patriarchal authority as a strategy to counter assumptions of black inferiority.[9] Often, black men and some black women reinforced gendered racial ideologies put forth by white cultural elites: they derided African-descended women as the carriers of immorality and cultural backwardness within the community of color. Women of African descent resisted racial stereotypes through their writings and activism. During the early decades of the republic, most black women activists emphasized "women's issues" as mothers and laborers, with rare references to race, in order to adhere to nationalist discourses of racial egalitarianism.[10] I contend that, by the 1930s, black women forged a modern feminist discourse that challenged the rhetoric of racial equality. Black feminists' visions of reform, as such, occasionally challenged black men's perspectives on women's sexuality and racial improvement.

Women of African descent sat at the intersection of women's activism and black (men's) club activism. At no time during were all black women of one mind about which political philosophy would best help them improve the social status of women. Indeed, while some individuals pursued reform primarily through elite black associations and women's groups, others joined radical labor and communist organizations. Both groups of black women forged strategic alliances with white women with the goal of achieving racial *and* gender reform. Certainly, building coalitions across racial (and class) differences created moments of tension. And following the conclusion of the 1939 Congress, the vision of racial solidarity put forth by Dámasa Jova remained unresolved. Yet many women of African descent who moved between black, feminist, and labor organizations rose to national prominence as political leaders by the close of the decade. The alliances they helped forge would be critical to securing the antidiscrimination clause of the 1940 Constitution.

Race, Class, and the Emergence of a National Woman's Movement

During the early years of the republic, white elite and middle-class women activists utilized state reforms that targeted the family to insert themselves into the national public sphere as citizens. They asserted that their moral superiority as enlightened caretakers qualified them to shape policies regarding education, family law reform, and women's labor. However, they lacked the social power necessary to build a movement for profound reform. This resulted, in part, from a lack of cohesion among women's organizations. Groups like the Comité de Sufragio Femenino, Partido Popular Feminista, and Partido Nacional Feminista organized in 1912 to advocate for women's participation in electoral politics.[11] Five years later, women established the Club Femenino de Cuba to end prostitution and advocate for the establishment of women's prisons and juvenile courts, in addition to political rights. Organizations such as the Asociación de Damas Isabelinas focused on charity endeavors, particularly public health care programs and policies affecting children. While this community of privileged white urbane women held varying perspectives on how to enact legal reform, they upheld the nationalist rhetoric of racial equality by adopting a race-neutral discourse regarding women's issues.

In practice, most white feminists maintained a sense of racial superiority to their black counterparts. As an example, photographs published in feminist publications like *Aspiraciones* and *Revista de la Asociación Femenina de Camagüey* featured only white women from established families. White feminists excluded black women from writing for their magazines and becoming members of their early organizations.[12] At the same time, elite black women formulated their own political agenda that often found agreement with white feminists' concerns while responding to black sociocultural life.[13] They published a regular "Páginas Feministas" column in the black magazine *Minerva: Revista Universal Ilustrada* between 1910 and 1913, and they formed the Club Feminista "Minerva" in January 1911. The exclusion of women of African descent from elite white women's organizations is unsurprising given the fact that blacks faced exclusion from most elite white civic clubs.[14]

These dynamics would begin to change by 1923. Members of the Club Femenino, under the leadership of white feminist journalist Pilar Morlon de

Menéndez, invited women's organizations from across the island to attend the First National Women's Congress. They also invited male public officials. Delegates from thirty-one women's associations attended and represented a range of political viewpoints. Several black women participated, though they did not present or serve as major leaders. The women in attendance aimed to exert some influence over national policy as they addressed "the problems that affect the individual, family, home, and country."[15] Presenters discussed women's political participation, children's rights, abolishing the adultery law, labor rights, the white slave trade, public welfare, and women's education. The congress's final resolutions included obtaining suffrage rights and legal rights, in addition to forging political campaigns to transform the court and prison system, establish social welfare programs at the national level, fight against vice, and educate laboring women. White feminist organizers thus promoted reformist approaches rather than revolutionary transformations; they spoke on behalf of poor women as self-appointed leaders regarding all "women's issues."

The presidency of Gerardo Machado y Morales buttressed many feminist objectives while broadening political discussions to recognize the concerns of multiple social groups. In 1924, the Liberal Party candidate proposed a political "Platform of Regeneration" to revive the nation. He promised to end government corruption, ensure economic development, and bolster the rights of workers, blacks, and women.[16] During Machado's first term (1925–1928) he instituted public works programs and social services, and he expanded the educational system. Machado even spoke at the 1925 Second National Women's Congress, during which he agreed to support the idea of women's suffrage. He also supported the community of African descent by promoting blacks to government positions and financially supporting black civic clubs. By 1926, political elites of the Conservative, Popular, and Liberal parties felt so strongly about his accomplishments that they declared their unified support for Machado.[17]

Machado inaugurated his presidency during a pivotal year for popular class organizing. Student activist Julio Antonio Mella founded the Partido Comunista de Cuba (PCC) in Havana.[18] The labor movement expanded in size and influence, as trade unions consolidated to form a single national organization—the Confederación Nacional de Obreros Cubanos (CNOC). Both the PCC and CNOC began to devote full attention to the "black question" and "woman question" as part of a global conversation that took place at labor conferences.[19] Leaders increasingly framed their rights in relation to Marxist critiques of labor, which emphasized the exploitation of workers by the oligarchic class and US imperialism. They argued that capitalism relied on the division of the proletariat into gendered and racial subdivisions of labor, thereby creating women's work that was distinguished from men's work and discriminating against Cubans of African descent.[20] These perspectives extended throughout the labor movement. By 1938, the Partido Agrario Nacional circulated a manifesto that argued "Cuban women have shouldered tremendous responsibilities without having rights. The Party demands legal reform of maternity rights, minimum wages and eight-hour work days, the right to organize, no discrimination against black women, and equal rights with men."[21] Such actions highlight how popular-class organizations forged an intersectional analysis of social discrimination.[22]

By 1924, white feminist leaders sought alliances with women of the popular classes as they debated legal reform. Organizers of the national women's congresses attended a board meeting of the Havana tobacco stemmers guild, and they found themselves "pleasantly surprised to see the degree of cultural advancement among laboring women."[23] The elite feminist leaders, having observed interactions among "women from different races," determined that workingwomen were the future of Cuban politics. Subsequently, the 1925 Second National Women's Congress included laboring women among its attendees who represented seventy-one organizations from Havana, Matanzas, Camagüey, Nuevitas, Santa Clara, and Pinar del Río. Two women of African descent presented: tobacco stemmer Inocencia Valdés and physician María Julia de Lara. The black historian Angelina Edreira and educator Rosa Pastora Leclerc attended as *vocales*.[24] Delegates addressed themes similar to the first congress through a race-neutral analysis of Cuban womanhood. They advocated for the establishment of more home schools, women's commerce, and physical education. They also addressed disease, drug abuse, and abortion rights. However, in the process of collaborating with laboring women, elite white leaders expanded their platform to emphasize material issues affecting poor families: equal pay between men and women, health care centers for women, and affordable food options.

Inocencia Valdés represented the Havana Tobacco Workers' Union.[25] She addressed the difficulties that laborers faced due to the current economic crisis. The crash of the economy during the 1920s led to the failure of both the sugar and tobacco industries. Falling wages and unemployment forced the already poor workers to face starvation and struggle to pay their rent. As Valdés presented the grim reality of tobacco laborers, she emphasized that the main problem lay in the limited employment opportunities available to women. Cuban women, she explained, had few choices beyond the tobacco and domestic service industries:

For many years, Cuban women had no doors open to her (except for, of course, domestic occupations), which [the tobacco industry] provided. Perhaps this has been the main motive or reason to explain the poor wages women have always earned for their work in the tobacco fields—forcing our sisters to find other sources to meet the specific needs of every proletarian home, as they become victims of their employers' greed. Later, when other industries were established in Cuba, that is, new fields opened to women's work, poor remuneration continued, despite what they naturally expected.[26]

Valdés called upon the congress delegates to help create educational opportunities for her colleagues. She suggested that association members establish schools to provide working women with the intellectual development necessary to obtain better-paying positions and "demonstrate that the Cuban woman is capable of doing the same as her sisters of other countries, countries where women shine at the same level as men."[27] Valdés's discussion of workers who fell victim to "greedy" employers exemplified the language through which labor activists criticized capitalism and class inequities. Upon concluding the congress, attendees announced in their official bulletin their support for women tobacco stemmers. Their final summary highlighted the need for laws that protected women workers "in all orders," and called for the establishment of night schools to prepare poor women for work.[28]

Though Valdés represented the Havana Tobacco Workers' Union, including the tobacco stemmers sector, which was dominated by black women, she did not mention race. Neither did doctor María Julia de Lara in her speech on venereal diseases.[29] There are at least two possibilities for this occurrence. First, in 1925, major labor organizations had only begun to address the ways in which racial discrimination affected blacks. Critiques of racism had not yet become standard within discourses of the labor movement. Second, most white feminist associations did not incorporate race and the experiences of African descendants in their analyses of sociopolitical reform. Both women's speeches highlight how black women sought to improve their rights and material conditions while affirming the nationalist rhetoric of racial equality.

Ultimately, elite white feminists' conflicting perspectives on class inequities led to fractures within the movement. Most attendees emphasized the traditional family structure as critical to ensuring national morality. They determined poverty should be alleviated through education, social welfare, and forming married households rather than challenging class hierarchies. White lawyers Margot López of Havana and Ofelia Domínguez Navarro of Santa Clara disrupted this approach by calling for equal rights for illegitimate children. *El Mundo* reported that "an incident arose" when white feminist Dulce María Borrero de Luján pushed delegates to act on behalf of illegitimate children. As the newspaper explained, "[Borrero de Luján] asked for the just protection of maternity under any circumstance and later, a fierce discussion emerged in the executive committee of the congress about certain comments that were aroused by the delegation of Camagüey."[30] When most of the delegates rejected proposals to grant illegitimate children equal rights, radical white feminists including López, Domínguez Navarro, and Borrero de Luján walked out of the congress.[31]

Some white feminists who walked out subsequently expanded their organizational platforms to recognize the particular experiences of black (and) laboring women. The radical feminist organization, the Alianza Nacional

Feminista (ANF), recruited women of African descent as they sought to mobilize women in support of suffrage rights. Headed by Domínguez Navarro, the call of the ANF in 1928 elucidated this strategy: "Companions of all races, of all social classes, you, white as Martí and Aragamonte, you, black as Moncada and Maceo . . . What do we desire? That the right to suffrage is conceded to us plainly and without restrictions."[32] ANF leaders, rather than uphold the rhetoric of racial equality, acknowledged racial distinctions. This broad conceptualization of womanhood appealed to many black women—a large percentage of whom worked as tobacco stemmers—who joined the mainstream feminist movement en masse.[33]

Black women like Rosa Pastora Leclerc entered into national politics through such organizations. The Cárdenas educator attended the 1923 First National Women's Congress. She joined the ANF shortly after its founding. Leclerc and Domínguez Navarro later became disillusioned when many wealthy members struggled to "grasp more advanced problems beyond charitable and social issues," which prohibited them from attacking matters that hurt workingwomen.[34] The two women left the ANF to form the Union Laborista de Mujeres (ULM) in 1931. The ULM recruited a divergent contingent of feminists—including Inocencia Valdés—who denounced bourgeois capitalism and advocated for a classless society.[35] They supported other groups that organized on behalf of workingwomen, fought for the rights of illegitimate children, and "espoused socialist revolution."[36] Radical women thus built a multiracial cadre of activists who centered on the rights of laboring women.

Women of the ULM joined the anti-Machado movement that erupted in 1933. Despite the president's early successes, he incited protests across the island when—feeling confident in his support from political elites and the US Embassy—he revoked his pledge to not run for reelection and amended the Constitution of the Republic so that he could serve until 1934. The ULM joined other popular and middle-class youth organizations that considered his decision to serve a second term an indefensible violation of his earlier promise. Women spoke at strikes and provided legal defense for jailed activists; they proposed motions to have corrupt public officials dismissed from their positions. Machado actively, and often brutally, targeted threatening political factions. He ordered law enforcement to target the ULM. Police stormed the group's offices and interrupted new member orientations. Such actions did little to quell the women's activities. Leclerc helped mobilize the ULM student branch and was among those imprisoned for supporting the guerrillas. Eventually, women of the organization came to oppose suffrage as "an accommodation" with the repressive Machado administration.[37] They broke from moderate feminist groups like the Partido Demócrata Sufragista, Club Femenino, and Lyceum Lawn and Tennis Club that advocated for suffrage.

Black women's alliances with white labor and feminist leaders reflected a multiracial coalition that continued to evolve following the 1933 Revolution.[38] Elite white women appealed to women of African descent as they began preparations for the Third National Women's Congress. In October 1933, the organizing committee issued a call to all Cuban women through the pages of the black social column of *Ahora*. They wrote the following: "It is necessary to begin, without delay, a work of reconstruction that is oriented in the sense of creating among ourselves a spirit of solidarity, and a clear understanding of our responsibility in the future. It is absolutely necessary that we be able to perform our civil and political rights effectively."[39] The committee expressed its particular interest in partnering with women of the black civic organizations Club Antilla, Unión Fraternal, Orientación, Atenas, Deportivo La Fe, Juventud Selecta del Cerro Jóvenes del Vals, and Club Maceo. Organizing members invited the female readers of the column to an upcoming meeting at the home of activist Justina Sandó Tellez. While the next congress would not meet for six years, white and African-descended women advocated for legal and social welfare reforms through a range of organizations. In the process, questions about women's citizenship led women of African descent to reevaluate the tenets of racial advancement put forth by black civic club members.

The Transformation of Black Women's Activism during the 1920s and 1930s

Black women's activism during the early years of the republic reflected a range of perspectives informed by their class, regional, and political backgrounds. Labor leaders like Inocencia Valdés, Teresa García, and Eudosia Lara organized strikes to receive higher wages and improved working conditions in the tobacco industry.[40] They joined unions and formed worker's congresses. Elite and upwardly mobile women, due to practices of racial exclusion from elite white organizations, advocated for reform primarily through black civic associations. They served as members of auxiliary branches of male-headed clubs; they submitted articles, letters, and poetry to black publications throughout the island. Their activities highlighted black elites' commitment to the ideology of racial advancement—which emphasized moral respectability, thrift, hard work, and education—that limited women's formal leadership and denigrated poor blacks that formed unmarried unions or practiced African cultural traditions.[41] Neither group of women contested incidents of racial discrimination in their writings during this period. In fact, only women of the black political party, the Partido Independiente de Color (PIC), explicitly challenged anti-black racism in their writings and political organizing. Most women of African descent affirmed the nationalist rhetoric of racial equality by emphasizing "women's issues" as caretakers and laborers, and they rarely made reference to race.

By the 1920s, it became clear that elites' emphasis on respectability and racial advancement was not enough to protect them from discrimination. Despite declaring their moral virtue and cultural superiority over poor blacks, elites of African descent confronted prejudice in social spaces that included restaurants and hotels, as well as housing. They faced exclusion within parks where racial segregation was the established practice; violating these practices resulted in violence on several occasions.[42] In 1928, black journalist Gustavo Urrutia lamented that "decent" families were unable to lease units in "skyscrapers" and modern apartment buildings of Havana.[43] Families of African descent who possessed the financial means to socialize and live in the most fashionable establishments and neighborhoods frequently found themselves restricted from entry.

Elite and upwardly mobile blacks were not alone in their struggle with racial discrimination. Indeed, poor families of African descent faced an additional set of challenges due to their socioeconomic status. Blacks' control of farmland—as both renters and owners—decreased 50 percent between 1899 and 1931 as foreign investors took over the sugar industry.[44] African descendants who worked in the factories and agricultural sectors were usually excluded from the most skilled positions and restricted to wage labor. They were underrepresented as laborers within the expanding civil service, transportation, and telephone industries. The decline of Cuba's economy during the late 1920s exacerbated these circumstances, as falling wages and rising unemployment left persons of African descent, and Cubans in general, in a precarious financial situation. High unemployment often caused black women to support themselves and their families by working in the informal sector as laundresses, domestic servants, street vendors, and prostitutes.

Elite blacks writing during the period developed a divergent view of political activism that reflected generational perspectives: having grappled with higher rates of unemployment than older elites, they were more attuned to socioeconomic inequities. For example, Urrutia expressed the frustrations of many black activists when he rejected the nationalist rhetoric of a single Cuban race and instead emphasized the distinct experiences of two racial groups—whites and the "colored race."[45] This younger generation of leaders also insisted that elites abandon outmoded gender norms in favor of "new" and "modern" expectations that endorsed women's civic participation. Feminists like Catalina Pozo Gato, journalist Calixta María Hernández de Cervantes, and lawyer Cloris Tejo took to the black press to promote women's political rights and to contest the economic marginalization of African-descended women. Educator Consuelo Serra and University of Havana professor Ana Echegoyen de Cañizares promoted social reform through their articles on motherhood, spirituality, and pedagogy. These actions reflected the rise of a new cohort of black feminists.

Central to black feminist discourses of the late 1920s and 1930s was a vision of social reform that centered the experiences of black women. Pozo Gato, unlike her feminist predecessors, cast off race-neutral discussions of womanhood. She challenged black men's assertions that women held the community of African descent back due to "uncivilized" practices like "witchcraft." Instead, she decried racial discrimination in employment. She complained that black women who received training as dentists, pharmacists, lawyers, and doctors worked as dressmakers in stores controlled by "Poles" (Polish workers and business owners), earning a "vexing salary" that forced them to stay poor. As identified by Pozo Gato, cultural values did not explain why many families of African descent lived in poverty. The true problem lay in the fact that black women did not have the same possibilities as their "white sisters."[46]

Black feminists' attention to economic disparities occasionally led them to critique the elitism of African-descended men who admonished poor black women. A notable instance of conflicting views arose at the 1938 National Convention of Black Societies, one of several conventions organized periodically by civic club leaders to help coordinate their organizations' objectives and activities. Cloris Tejo attended the convention. Several discussions left Tejo infuriated with those whom she labeled the "black aristocracy." For one, delegates proposed a ban that would prohibit minors under the age of twelve from selling newspapers in the streets. Tejo explained that, while "not in favor of children engaged in the sale of newspapers," she recognized that their work provided a necessary income for their households.[47] Thus, she could not allow their parents to be judged negatively for allowing their children to work or for parents to feel forced to abandon their children out of financial necessity. Tejo accused the convention members of failing to acknowledge the stigma placed on the black mother and father.

The approach of women like Tejo resembled those of their white feminist counterparts who asserted their political authority within the realm of education and social welfare.[48] Elite black women of Havana established the Asociación Cultural Femenina (ACF) in 1935 to carry out this vision of feminine civic duty. Founded by Consuelo Serra, the apolitical organization focused on "the civic and cultural betterment of women."[49] Its membership consisted of a highly selective and privileged group of women. Its leaders included Serra, who served as the ACF president in 1935, Catalina Pozo Gato, Ana Echegoyen de Cañizares, and educators Adela García de Falcon and Dr. Juana Oliva Bulnes. Members provided typing classes for poor girls and organized social events such as dances. The ACF's focus on social events, cultural development, and instruction for uneducated women demonstrates that its members did not completely abandon racial advancement strategies. In addition, their connection to Havana's educated black community suggests that, though concerned with problems affecting all black women, they continued to distinguish themselves from African-descended women who formed part of the laboring poor. Moreover, while members did not mention race in their manifesto, that they established an organization for black women suggests they continued to experience exclusion from elite white women's organizations, or at least saw the importance of spaces exclusively for elite women of African descent.[50]

Black feminist activists of the 1930s, similar to previous generations, emphasized their civic duties as feminine caretakers. Yet they reinterpreted patriarchal gender norms to emphasize their formal leadership beyond auxiliary branches of male-headed civic clubs. Women gained the right to vote in 1934. Subsequently, Calixta María Hernández de Cervantes articulated a political vision in which women "were incorporated into the grooves of the electoral machine" as full citizens.[51] She argued that the Cuban woman, having participated in the fight for national independence, had "earned the right to penetrate the political arena in order to contribute with the support of her militancy the resolution of the grave problems that presented themselves on the horizon of *cubanidad*."[52] She questioned if women should "affiliate themselves with parties controlled by men or those which had been exclusively formed and run by women."[53] Hernández recognized that women took a risk in building political alliances with men when she reflected on the difficult union between the women's political organization Alianza Nacional Feminista (National Feminist Alliance, or ANF) and the political party Conjunto Nacional Democrático (National Democratic Group, formerly the Partido Conservador). The Conjunto leaders broke from their partnership with the ANF in order to form a separate party and maintain their right to make their own decisions. Despite this political conflict, Hernández maintained that women should not isolate themselves from men.

Elite black men like Manuel Machado cautioned that suffrage created a new and important problem for "the thinking and disgruntled youth of the current age, especially the black woman younger than thirty years.'" He criticized that wealthy and middle-class white women had never forged "a radical and sincere work base, an apostolic identification between the 'lady' and the cook, a fraternal 'tete-a-tete' between the 'señorita' and the nubile family."[54] Machado suggested that women of African descent participate in electoral politics while remaining cautious of "pseudo representatives"—especially given that "the vast majority of our women are domestics and that almost all of the 'haves' are bureaucrats." He asserted that blacks must ensure that exploitative employers not fire women for not casting votes in their favor, as many men already experienced.

As Machado anticipated, black feminists' engagement with the women's movement remained troubled by racial hierarchies. Women of African descent struggled to publish in national periodicals such as *Carteles* and *El Pueblo*. Instead, they published articles primarily within the black press. Black columnist

Gustavo Urrutia helped address this dilemma in 1933, when he advertised that white feminist magazine editors Berta Arozarena de Martínez Márquez and Rene Méndez Capote de Solis had reached out to him in order to recruit black women to contribute to their magazine.[55] The editors sought to rectify divisions between white and black feminists by recruiting women of African descent for their recently formed writers' association. "We white women," Arozarena and Méndez explained in their announcement, "and you black women work separated by the color line that ruins us both." They continued, "We recognize in you all of our strengths and weaknesses and call you to our side without requiring conditions."[56] No document that I found indicates whether black women did indeed become members of the writers' association. That Arozarena and Méndez chose to reach out to black women highlights that some white women were aware of the racial divisions within the feminist movement and attempted to bridge such divisions.

Black women continued to forge alliances with white (and) laboring women, as many expanded their leadership beyond black civic clubs to include national women's groups. ACF associates like the well-known doctor María Ignacia Matehu joined the central committee of the Unión Nacional de Mujeres (UNM), a group established "to fight for the national liberation of Cuba and organize women to obtain their just social valorization."[57] In 1937, ten radical activists, among them the *mulata* and cigar stemmer union leader Teresa García, white poet María Villar Buceta, and student organizer Edith García Buchaca (future leader of the Unión Radical de Mujeres and the Partido Socialista Popular), announced their decision to join the Unión Revolucionaria after becoming "disillusioned with the compromises of President Laredo Bru's government."[58] These individuals also worked with professional black women, including Felicita Ortiz and Consuelo Silveira, who entered the communist movement through labor unions. Perhaps the most prominent communist leader was pharmacist Esperanza Sánchez of Oriente Province, who served as the only black woman elected as a delegate of the 1940 Constitutional Assembly.

By the late 1930s, African-descended women's intersectional analysis of social discrimination could be found in public political discourse nationally. In December 1937, the Club Femenino Ejemplar (an auxiliary branch of the Hermandad de los Jóvenes Cubanos, established in 1936) formed to "improve the physical and intellectual capacities of women." Its members established a school for women of all race and classes.[59] Ofelia Domínguez Navarro linked racial oppression to gender discrimination during a December 1938 presentation before the Spanish club, El Pilar. She asserted that, despite the "pretend equality" that many Cubans espoused, the black race "remain[ed] constitutionally separated, isolated from the integral development of our society."[60] She explained, "We cannot deny that our black [female] companion suffers the most iniquitous of preteritions."[61] While Domínguez Navarro put forth a theoretical examination of racial and gender discrimination, the Federación de Mujeres Auténticas (a branch of the communist organization, the Partido Revolucionario Cubano) proposed legal reforms to address these inequities. Their demands included the "intervention of the state in the administration of factories, establishments, workshops, etc. for the purpose of eliminating the exploitation of workers, for those who suffer the obsession of accumulating money." The Federación de Mujeres Auténticas also called for the "electivity of the rights of women of color, which our former constitution guarantees and will have to guarantee, but which have never been fulfilled in regards to their right to work in establishments, factories, and workshops."[62] The organization thus proposed a populist vision of reform that emphasized the responsibilities of the government to protect the rights of African-descended women.

Women of African descent emerged as "black brokers" who formed strategic alliances that enabled them to advance issues they deemed important on a national scale.[63] Those who emphasized their particular experiences with racism, sexism, and class exploitation recognized the need for a broad approach for political activism. Calixta Maria de Hernández and Consuelo Serra bridged feminist issues with elite black politics as part of this strategy. Esperanza Sánchez and Felicita Ortiz believed the ideas espoused in communist organizations offered solutions to address social inequities through progressive social reforms. While women of African descent held a range of political perspectives, they consistently collaborated with white women from elite and laboring class backgrounds to achieve reform.

Black Women and the 1939 Third National Women's Congress

Similar to the First and Second National Women's Congresses of 1923 and 1925, the Third Congress operated under the assumption that Cuban women were responsible for ensuring national progress as mothers and wives. Yet articles published by black women activists prior to and during the Congress revealed philosophical transformations within the women's movement.[64] For one, the Congress's platform served the dual purpose of incorporating a diverse range of individuals into the women's movement. No longer solely comprised of and planned by white elite and middle-class members, the Third Congress brought together more than 2,000 women delegates from all backgrounds: urban and rural, white and black, the rich and the laboring poor, professional and nonprofessional (including factory workers, domestic laborers, and *campesinas*), and women of various political and religious affiliations. Because of this, dialogues during the event featured a range of perspectives on womanhood in relation to political representation and social equality. In addition, Congress organizers addressed the particular experiences of the black women for the first time; they emphasized racial unity, included racial discrimination on their list of social issues, and asserted the legal rights of black women as workers. As participants committed to these efforts, black feminists helped build a cross-racial political alliance that would demand institutional reform during the 1940 Constitutional Assembly.[65]

Perhaps to prevent the clashes that took place during the 1925 Congress, leaders established upfront their inclusive intensions: "This women's movement will rise above all circumstantial religious or racial distinctions, constituting us as a force capable of guaranteeing the rights of women and children, the peace and progress of Cuban society."[66] If the women's movement was to be successful in obtaining social equality, race had to be acknowledged and discussed so that it addressed the multiplicity of women's concerns. Committee members and delegates circulated articles and interviews from a variety of national and regional newspapers and journals that appealed to women of all social backgrounds. They consistently stated their concern with what they felt was a failure of the government to protect women and children. Moreover, they insisted that all women be given the opportunity to advocate for themselves within public institutions as the equal of their male counterparts. As explained by black Oriente Province delegate Catalina Causse Vda. de Mercer: "It is not a question of blacks or whites, rather it is in the general interest of all conscious women, their duty and responsibility, to obtain a post in the collective movement for social betterment on behalf of our children."[67]

That Causse rejected the "question" of distinct black or white interests is not surprising considering that women of African descent played a major role in the development of the Congress. The executive committee included prominent black professionals and activists from throughout the island. Consuelo Silveira, a black Havana labor leader, served as the committee's vice secretary of finance. Ana Echegoyen de Cañizares was selected as the secretary of correspondence. The executive committee also included several women of African descent as *vocales*: Teresa García from the Havana Tobacco Workers' Union, educator and historian Angelina Edreira, domestic worker and union leader Elvira Rodríguez, Catalina Pozo Gato, pharmacist Esperanza Sánchez Mastrapa from Gíbara (Oriente Province), and educator and writer María Dámasa Jova from Santa Clara. Importantly, conference organizers aimed to create an atmosphere where women would leave their political leanings behind, yet many women represented the interests of social groups affiliated with labor unions and political organizations.

María Patrocinado Garbey Aguila was at once uncharacteristic and representative of the black women who attended the Third National Women's Congress. A prominent activist committed to social equality, Garbey held the rare position for a woman as the long-time president of the Centro Cultural Martín Morúa Delgado (Martín Morúa Delgado Cultural Center), the black civic club in Santiago de Cuba.[68] In 1914, she attended the National Labor Convention as a representative of "Cuban women from Oriente Province."[69] She brought her public leadership to the 1939 National Women's Congress to advocate for the betterment of Cuban women. For Garbey, the realization of the National Women's Congress (which she referred to as the National Feminist Congress) signified "a significant step forward taken by the Cuban woman" in her evolution. As she explained, "that which results will be helpful for women themselves and, as consequence, for our country."[70]

Garbey's endorsement of the Congress was certainly in sync with other black civic clubwomen who expressly affirmed its mission. Indeed, women of African descent frequently organized other black women on behalf of the feminist movement. Elite black women of Havana (associated with the Sociedad Antilla Sport Club) held an assembly for black women (sponsored by the Federación de Sociedades Negras de la Provincia de la Habana) to identify issues affecting black women "to be brought to the Women's Congress."[71] Attendees represented the civic organizations La Unión de Bauta, El Progreso de Guanabacoa, and Vedado Social Club. Women of the civic club Luz de Oriente hosted a similar meeting to discuss the "main problems that affect the black women of Oriente."[72] They aimed to compile a list of issues that concerned black women that would interest "white women as much as women of color."[73] The clubwomen's suggestive evocation of both white and black women claimed the possibility that black women's equality would lead to "a better future for [all] Cuban women."[74]

Such directives, black clubwomen asserted, supported a Cuban nationalist cause. In February of 1939, women of the Federación of Sociedades Negras published an article entitled "La Mujer en General y la Mujer Negra en Particular" in the national communist newspaper *Noticias de Hoy*.[75] Signed by members of the organizing committee of the Asamblea Provincial de Mujeres Negras—and elite clubwomen Mercedes Ruis de Andrade, Digna Ferrera González, Francisca Romay Valdés, feminist writer Cloris Tejo Hernández, and committee secretary Esther Torriente Moncada—the brief, yet loaded, manifesto carved out a particular place for black women in contemporary political debates as they addressed constitutional reform. Their language was straightforward and passionate, and it targeted racial intolerance. The women assailed:

[W]e cannot deny or ignore that sensitive developments—which have occurred in our Nation since before the foundation of the Republic—have created a painful situation in which one finds the highest percentage of exploited women, battered mothers, and lack of food to prepare and to educate men capable of conceiving a radiant future of justices and of laying the foundations for a society of brotherhood, peace, and love—where they find shelter from petty racial prejudice and economic inequalities that currently impede man's life. [. . .] That is why, despite our great ideological values, we hold in our minds a poor ethnic classification based on the absurdity of racial superiority or inferiority.[76]

Thus, to complete their "duty as women," they intended "to fight tenaciously so that the black woman might take her place in the National Women's Congress as women." The writers of "La Mujer en General" employed rhetorical strategies utilized by a variety of black activists: they focused the discrepancies between racism and the nationalist rhetoric of racial equality as they addressed the contributions of black women to state reform. Torriente Moncada and her peers maintained that such "inconsistencies" should not prevent women of African descent from joining the movement, as it was dangerous for them to "remain indifferent to the call to [all] Cuban women." Importantly, they spoke as "Cuban women, as conscientious mothers," committed to political redevelopment. Additionally, the clubwomen recalled the slave woman who, "in a gesture of humanity," offered "the fruits of her love" to the independence cause.[77] By denying ethnic differences among Cubans and reiterating black women's role in the independence movement, the organizing committee members of the Asamblea Provincial de Mujeres Negras appealed to a vision of racelessness that remained an aspiration.[78]

Perhaps the sight of so many women of African descent who served as organizing members and delegates alarmed some white women, or white women may have resented the prominent position that racial discrimination held in the Congress agenda. A few weeks before the opening celebrations, *Oriente*, one of the major regional newspapers of the eastern province, printed a letter from black activist Pastora Causede de Atiés directed to other black women of Santiago de Cuba. She responded to claims that "the development of assemblies with large numbers of black women in attendance" resulted in racial prejudice within the women's movement.[79] Causede emphasized the stake that black women held in the movement: "Us [black women] we're struggling, we're applying the pressure that these key organizations need and appealing to women from the highest positions to the most humble." Causede put in plain words that black women were "initiating a series of acts" to alleviate their own issues since their efforts had "not been matched" by their white counterparts.[80]

The author could have replicated the language of unification to appeal to those put off by the discussions of race at the National Women's Congress. Yet she purposefully pointed out the dilemmas confronted by black women of the eastern province within their daily lives. Causede astutely observed:

There is only one real thing that exists: the black woman has responded to this clarion call because her problems have not been resolved; because it is difficult to enroll her children in some schools; because apart from making a physical, monetary, and intellectual effort it is difficult to achieve her desires; [. . .] because she does not have the right to hold public offices as more than a simple typist after many recommendations; because neither as a worker can she occupy a post in public establishments nor as a cook or nanny.[81]

Causede highlighted the limitations that she and her peers faced as mothers and workers—realities that illustrated the persistence of racial discrimination within society. She, like activists and intellectuals who argued that capitalist exploitation perpetuated black women's marginalization, underscored the racialization of labor and argued that skin color determined one's access to employment. Racism, then, was more than an economic or social problem; it violated the individual freedoms entitled to every Cuban. Additionally, she determined that "[t]he years of fighting" that black men incurred during childhood were hardly rewarded as adult laborers, a compensation "always postponed." Not unlike black women's marginalization within employment, a black man might devote "the best years of his life to acquire a degree of proficiency," yet his training never seemed enough for "a post-occupancy as judge or in our courts or Justice of the Diplomatic or Cuban consular."[82] If the Congress did not address these issues, Causede worried that the men and women of her community would be left behind in a developing society.[83]

The Congress thus presented a moment to address these social inequities, outline a plan for legal reform, and galvanize white women in opposition to anti-black racism. Analyses of black women's experiences highlighted the intersection of racial, class, and gender oppression; they also called attention to a range of broader issues that included access to health care and social services, equal pay and fair working conditions, and women's political representation. Women of African descent drew from these issues as they helped mobilize a large constituency of activists from across the island. The communist newspaper *Noticias de Hoy* estimated that 2,000 women gathered in the Teatro Nacional for the opening presentations. As a reporter observed, the venue "was completely full; even the hallways and spaces between seats were occupied by an indefinable number of women, who on this occasion, have been able to give full demonstrations of their collective desire for redemption and mutual cooperation for the achievement of their ends."[84] Notably, "women of all races and origins" could be observed throughout the theater.[85]

Maria Dámasa Jova's "La situación de la mujer negra en Cuba" is the only available document in which a delegate specifically addressed the experiences of black women at the 1939 Third National Women's Congress.[86] However, by placing it alongside the congress's conclusions summarized by the executive committee, we can better grasp how leaders of the women's movement integrated matters affecting the black woman into their agenda for legal reform. During the final discussions of the congress, attendees outlined a detailed proposal to submit to the 1940 Constitutional Assembly that reified their commitment to "women and children's improvement," in addition to "Cuban peace and progress."[87] One section, entitled "La mujer y los prejuicios raciales," presented fifteen points that they wanted the delegates to take into consideration. The attendees explicitly based their suggestions for political reorganization on

Article I of the Constitution, which they cited: "All Cubans are equal before the law, and the law does not recognize exemptions or privileges."[88] The attendees' proposals included the creation of a "body of congress capable of fighting against all forms of racial prejudice, to vigorously oppose acts of discriminatory injustice against the black race in all activities of civic life, creating a bureau of statistics and research to that effect." Such a body would establish racial quotas for labor and education; it would enforce strict penalties for those professors and judges who discriminated against blacks, in addition to those who violated blacks' rights within private schools, as well as public places like parks, walkways, cabarets, and hotels. The women also called for the elimination of assigning racial descriptors when filling official documents, "except in cases where required for personal identification." Finally, the women proposed an anti-racism campaign to be carried out through the radio, the press, conferences, and "especially in primary schools."[89]

No doubt, attendees recognized the centrality of this doctrine to Cuba's legal order, as their desire for solidarity and absolute equality across racial, professional, and regional differences constituted a central tenet of the Congress's discourse. The delegates of the National Women's Congress understood that racial discrimination had persisted because of the government's failure to implement and enforce legislation for those who violated the Constitution. Therefore, the majority of the points featured in the proposal put forth new policies—such as maternity laws and public school curriculum reform—that addressed discrimination within the legal system, employment, education, and public places. These policies stood in line with reform issues identified within labor unions, the Communist Party, and the Federación of Sociedades Negras (Federation of Black Societies).[90]

It is difficult to fully comprehend elite white leaders' responses to African-descended women's calls for social reform. Certainly, white women's incorporation of anti-racial discrimination policies into the final resolution highlights their willingness to endorse black women's demands in order to advance their own political goals. Yet the publication of radical feminist Mariblanca Sabás Alomá's *El Pueblo* article, "Black Women in the Women's Congress," reveals the tensions that continued to shape processes of cross-racial collaboration. Weeks after the conclusion of the Third National Women's Congress, Sabás Alomá lauded the efforts of black women to mobilize on behalf of women's issues. African-descended socialist Angel César Pinto Albiol responded with indignation.[91] Pinto Albiol questioned Sabás Alomá's right to speak on behalf of black women. He also accused her of racism, questioning her use of terms like *mestizo* and suggesting she harbored anti-miscegenation attitudes. Sabás Alomá responded by expressing concerns with sexual relationships between black women and white men—particularly, exploitative relationships in which white men fathered illegitimate children they then left to live in poverty. She determined that, through such exchanges, white men helped weaken the "pure" black race. Sabás Alomá's exchange with Pinto Albiol suggests how some elite white women maintained ideas of racial inferiority that contributed to black women's marginalization.

Ultimately, the activism of women of African descent at the intersection of black civic clubs and women's organizations highlights the overlapping nature of political activity among movements for legal reform. Leaders and activists of each movement increasingly utilized discussions of a black female experience to mobilize Cubans across social divisions. Moreover, women of African descent often centralized their experiences as they entered into white feminist organizations. Their strategic collaborations with white women in national political organizations—especially in the Communist Party—would continue to expand throughout the 1940s. Thus an analysis of transformations within the feminist movement shows how race and gender informed Cuban state formation following the ratification of the 1940 Constitution.

NOTES

1. María Dámasa Jova Baro, "Ponencia presentada en el III Congreso Nacional de Mujeres" (Havana, 1939). Cited in Esperanza Méndez Oliva, *El estirpe de Mariana en la Villas* (Santa Clara, Cuba: Editorial Capiro, 2006).

2. Ibid.

3. Ibid.

4. Ibid.

5. K. Lynn Stoner, "On Men Reforming the Rights of Men: The Abrogation of the Cuban Adultery Law, 1930," *Cuban Studies* 21 (1991): 83–99; Stoner, *From the House to the Streets: The Cuban Women's Movement for Legal Reform* (Durham, NC: Duke University Press, 1991); Julio César González Pagés, *En busca de un espacio: Historia de mujeres en Cuba* (Havana: Ediciones de Ciencias Sociales, 2003); María del Carmen Barcia, *Capas populares y modernidad en Cuba, 1878–1930* (Havana: Fundación Fernando Ortiz, 2005); Raquel Vinat de la Mata, *Las cubanas en la posguerra (1898–1902): Acercamiento a la reconstrucción de una etapa olvidada* (Havana: Editora Política, 2001); Esperanza Méndez Oliva and Santiago Alemán Santana, *Villareñas camino a la emancipación* (Havana: Editora Política, 2008); Michelle Chase, *Revolution within the Revolution: Women and Gender Politics in Cuba, 1952–1962* (Chapel Hill: University of North Carolina, 2015); Tiffany A. Sippial, *Prostitution, Modernity, and the Making of the Cuban Republic, 1840–1920* (Chapel Hill: University of North Carolina Press, 2013).

6. Recent studies that address these themes include Takkara Brunson, "Constructing Afro-Cuban Womanhood: Race, Gender, and Citizenship in Republican-Era Cuba, 1902–1958" (PhD diss., University of Texas at Austin, 2011); Brunson, "'Writing' Black Womanhood in the Early Cuban Republic, 1904–1916," *Gender and History* 28, no. 2 (August 2016): 480–500.

7. See, for instance, James Sanders, "'A Mob of Women' Confront Post-Colonial Republican Politics: How Class, Race, and Partisan Ideology Affected Gendered Political Space in Nineteenth-Century Southwestern Colombia," *Journal of Women's History* 20, no. 1 (Spring 2008): 63–89.

8. Aline Helg, *Our Rightful Share: The Afro-Cuban Struggle for Equality, 1886–1912* (Chapel Hill: University of North Carolina Press, 1995); Alejandro de la Fuente, *A Nation for All: Race, Inequality, and Politics in Twentieth-Century Cuba* (Chapel Hill: University of North Carolina Press,

2001); Alejandra Bronfman, *Measures of Inequality: Social Science, Citizenship, and Race in Cuba* (Chapel Hill: University of North Carolina Press, 2004); Frank Guridy, *Forging Diaspora: Afro-Cubans and African Americans in a World of Empire and Jim Crow* (Chapel Hill: University of North Carolina Press, 2010); Melina Pappademos, *Black Political Activism and the Cuban Republic* (Chapel Hill: University of North Carolina Press, 2012); Devyn Spence Benson, *Antiracism in Cuba: The Unfinished Revolution* (Chapel Hill: University of North Carolina Press, 2016). Scholars who utilize an intersectional analysis or focus on women of African descent include Carmen Montejo Arrechea, *"Minerva*: A Magazine for Women (and Men) of Color" in *Between Race and Empire: African Americans and Cubans before the Cuban Revolution* (Philadelphia: Temple University Press, 1998); Dawn Duke, *Literary Passion, Ideological Commitment: Towards a Legacy of Afro-Cuban and Afro-Brazilian Women Writers* (Lewisburg, PA: Bucknell University Press, 2008); Maria del Carmen Barcia Zequeira, *Mujeres al margen de la historia* (Havana: Editorial de Ciencias Sociales, 2009); Daisy Rubiera Castillo and Ines Martiatu Terry, eds., *Afrocubanas: Historia, pensamiento, and prácticas culturales* (Havana: Editorial de Ciencias Sociales, 2011); Karen Y. Morrison, *Cuba's Racial Crucible: The Sexual Economy of Social Identities, 1750–2000* (Bloomington: Indiana University Press, 2015); and Maikel Colón Pichardo, *¿Es fácil ser hombre y difícil ser negro? Masculinidad y estereotipos raciales en Cuba (1898–1912)* (Havana: Casa Editorial Abril, 2015).

9. When using the term *elite*, I refer to those affiliated with black civic clubs and the black press. While few elite black households reached the level of wealth that affluent white families attained, their advanced education and political connections made them privileged in comparison to the average family of African descent.

10. Takkara Brunson, "'Writing' Black Womanhood in the Early Cuban Republic, 1904–1916," *Gender & History* 28, no. 2 (August 2016): 480–500.

11. Fondo Donativos y Remisiones, No. 6, Caja 622; Fondo Registro de Asociaciones, Exp. 11886, Leg. 400, Archivo Nacional de Cuba (ANC).

12. There is no evidence that indicates that white feminists reached out to black women, nor are they mentioned in the rosters of the organizations cited above. The black press does not feature activities that African-descended women attended.

13. See Carmen Montejo Arrechea, *"Minerva*: A Magazine for Women (and Men) of Color"; del Carmen Barcia Zequeira, *Mujeres al margen de la historia*; Castillo and Martiatu Terry, *Afrocubanas*; Duke, *Literary Passion, Ideological Commitment*; Brunson, "'Writing' Black Womanhood in the Early Cuban Republic."

14. These organizations appeared after the 1910 Morúa Amendment banned race-based organizing. The three national women's organizations appeared in the year that blacks affiliated with or believed affiliated with the black political party, the Partido Independiente de Color, protested and were met with a massacre. I have found no evidence of these or the black feminist club responding to the massacre.

15. Pilar Morlon de Menéndez, "El Primer Congreso Nacional de Mujeres," *Revista Bimestre Cubana* (1923): 123.

16. Pérez, *Cuba: Between Reform and Revolution*, 258; Stoner, *From the House to the Streets*, 76.

17. Guridy, "Racial Knowledge in Cuba," 169–188; Whitney, *State and Revolution in Cuba*, 55.

18. The first communist organization in Cuba was founded in 1923.

19. Alejandra Bronfman also notes that the PCC led campaigns against the white supremacist organization, the Ku Klux Klan Cubano in 1928 and 1932, while the CNOC routinely called for the inclusion of black workers into all labor sectors. See *Measures of Equality*, 152–155.

20. See Juan Marinello, "La cuestión racial en el trabajo, la inmigración y la cultura" (Criterios de Unión Revolucionaria, March 10, 1939).

21. Partido Agrario Nacional, Sección Femenina, "Manifiesto a la mujer" (Havana: Impresos Sabin, 1938). Also see Serafín Portuondo, "Sobre el problema negro," *El Comunista*, November 1939; Marinello, "La cuestión racial."

22. Robert Whitney, *State and Revolution in Cuba: Mass Mobilization and Political Change, 1920–1940* (Chapel Hill: University of North Carolina Press, 2002), 53.

23. "Las despaliladoras en el Congreso de Mujeres," *Diario de la Marina*, April 3, 1925, p. 4.

24. "Reglamento del Segundo Congreso Nacional de Mujeres," *Comisión redactora de la memoria del Segundo Congreso Nacional de Mujeres* (Havana, 1925), 15.

25. See Pedro Luis Padrón, *La mujer trabajadora* (Havana: n.p., 1972), 22–23.

26. Inocencia Valdés, "El trabajo femenino en la industria tabacalera," *Comision Redactora de la Memoria del Segundo Congreso Nacional de Mujeres* (1925): 194–196.

27. Ibid.

28. "Conclusiones," *Comisión Redactora de la Memoria del Segundo Congreso Nacional de Mujeres* (1925): 646–648.

29. Lara, "Lucha contra las enfermedades," 373.

30. "Las sesiones del Congreso de Mujeres," *El Mundo*, April 19, 1925, 12.

31. Stoner, *From the House to the Streets*, 69. Debate is highlighted in *Diario de la Marina*, "Segundo Congreso Nacional," April 1, 1925, 8; "Las sesiones del Congreso de Mujeres," *El Mundo*, April 19, 1925, 12.

32. González-Pagés, *En busca de un espacio*, 86.

33. Led by Afro-Cuban female labor leaders Eudosia Lara and Inocencia Valdés, women's tobacco stemmers unions helped mobilize thousands of black women who demanded higher wages, maternity regulations, and improved working conditions. See González Pagés, *En busca de un espacio*, 86.

34. Interview with Ofelia Domínguez Navarro, Archivo del Instituto de Historia (AIH) 3/54.1/1–8.

35. They changed their name to the Unión Radical de Mujeres in 1933. Stoner, *From the House to the Streets*, 116.

36. Fondo Registro de Asociaciones, exp. 8622, leg. 298, ANC.

37. Stoner, 75; see 116–126 for an overview of women's activism in the anti-Machado movement.

38. Frank Guridy, "'War on the Negro': Race and the Revolution of 1933," *Cuban Studies* 40 (2009): 49–73.

39. Raúl Suárez-Mendoza, "A la Mujer Cubana," *Ahora*, 20 October 1933. Also see Raul Suárez-Mendoza, "La mujer piñarena y sus clubs femeninos," *Ahora*, October 21, 1933.

40. Padrón, *La mujer trabajadora*.

41. Pappademos, *Black Political Activism*; Guridy, *Forging Diaspora*; Spence Benson, *Anti-racism in Cuba*, 72–92.

42. Guridy, "'War on the Negro'"; Guridy, "Racial Knowledge in Cuba"; de la Fuente, *A Nation for All*.

43. de la Fuente, *A Nation for All*, 160.

44. Ibid., 106.

45. Alejandra Bronfman, *Measures of Equality: Social Science, Citizenship, and Race in Cuba, 1902–1940* (Chapel Hill: University of North Carolina Press, 2003). Also see Tomás Fernández Robaina, *El negro en Cuba, 1902–1958: Apuntes para la historia de la lucha contra la discriminación racial* (Havana: Editorial de Ciencias Sociales, 1990); Guridy, "Racial Knowledge in Cuba."

46. Dra. Catalina Pozo Gato, "La negra cubana y la cultura: Para el escritor Gerardo del Valle, en indagación," *Diario de la Marina*, November 30, 1930.

47. Cloris Tejo, "En torno a la convención de sociedades negras," *Adelante* 3 (June 1938): 5.

48. Stoner, *From the House to the Streets*; González Pagés, *En busca de un espacio.*

49. Fondo Asociaciones, leg. 111, nos. 23246–23248, ANC.

50. Guridy, *Forging Diaspora*, 151–194; Spence Benson, *Antiracism in Cuba*, 153.

51. "Feminismo: La mujer y la política," *Adelante*, September 1935.

52. Ibid.

53. Ibid.

54. Manuel Machado, "El voto femenino," *Adelante*, July 1935.

55. Gustavo Urrutia, "Mujeres nuevas," *Diario de la Marina*, February 15, 1933.

56. Ibid.

57. Fondo Donativos y Remisiones, leg. 16, exp. 159, ANC.

58. "Declaraciones sobre la Unión Revolucionaria," *MD* 13 (March 25, 1937): 10–11, in K. Lynn Stoner, *Cuban and Cuban-American Women: An Annotated Bibliography* (Lanham, MD: Rowman and Littlefield, 2000), 38.

59. "Club Femenino Ejemplar," *MD* 46 (December 13, 1937): 13, 16, in Stoner, *Cuban and Cuban-American Women*, 37.

60. Ofelia Domínguez Navarro, "La mujer y la discriminación racial," 3/28.1/30-32, Archivo del Instituto de Historia de Cuba.

61. Ibid.

62. Declaration of the Federación de Mujeres Auténticas.

63. See Pappademos, *Black Political Activism*, 42.

64. See Stoner, *From the House to the Streets*, 162.

65. de la Fuente, *A Nation for All*, 210–258.

66. María Núñez, "Postura de la mujer cubana frente al Congreso Femenino que se celebrará en la Habana," *Diario de Cuba*, March 12, 1939.

67. Catalina Causse Vda. de Mercer, "Congreso Femenino," *Diario de Cuba*, March 29, 1939.

68. Registro de Asociaciones, leg. 2455, exp. 10, Archivo Histórico Provincial de Santiago de Cuba.

69. María Patrocinado Garbey Aguila, "Una opinión sobre el Congreso Femenino," *Diario de Cuba*, March 12, 1939.

70. Ibid.

71. "Asamblea Femenino auspiciada por la F. de Sociedades Negras," *Noticias de Hoy*, March 11, 1939.

72. Garbey Aguila, "Una opinión sobre el Congreso Femenino."

73. Ibid.

74. "Gran actividad de la mujer oriental para el Congreso," *Noticias de Hoy*, April 7, 1939.

75. "La mujer en general y la mujer negra en particular," *Noticias de Hoy*, February 18, 1939.

76. Ibid.

77. Ibid.

78. Similarly, black elite women of Havana (associated with the Sociedad Antilla Sport Club) held an Assembly for Black Women (auspiciada por la Federación de Sociedades Negras de la provincia de la Habana) to discuss "all the problems that affect the Black Woman los cuales serán llevados ordenamente al Congreso Femenino." Delegates attended from the civic clubs La Unión de Bauta, El Progreso de Guanabacoa, and Vedado Social Club. "Asamblea Femenino Auspiciada por la F. de Sociedades Negras," *Noticias de Hoy*, March 11, 1939.

79. Pastora Causede de Atiés, "Congreso Femenino," *Oriente*, April 5, 1939.

80. Ibid.

81. "Congreso Femenino."

82. Ibid.

83. Ibid.

84. "Brillante inauguración del congreso femenino," *Noticias de Hoy*, April 20, 1939.

85. Ibid.

86. The "Conclusiones" presented at the end of the conference references a speech given by the Afro-Cuban educator and Santiago de Cuba resident Serafina Causse, but I have been unable to locate this document.

87. "Conclusiones," AIH Registro General 10.6/76.

88. "Conclusiones."

89. "Conclusiones," AIH Registro General 10.6/76.

90. Ibid.

91. For a brief biography on César Pinto Albiol, see Spence Benson, *Antiracism in Cuba*, 89.

CULTURE AND SOCIETY

LESTER TOMÉ

The Racial Other's Dancing Body in El milagro de anaquillé *(1927): Avant-Garde Ballet and Ethnography of Afro-Cuban Performance*

ABSTRACT

El milagro de anaquillé (1927), a ballet project with libretto by Alejo Carpentier and music by Amadeo Roldán, originated at the intersection of avant-garde art, *afrocubanismo*, and ethnography. Inspired by the aesthetic experimentation of Les Ballets Russes and Les Ballets Suédois in Europe, Carpentier and Roldán adopted ballet as a vehicle for introducing avant-garde trends in Cuba. Their work referenced two revolutionary ballets: *Rite of Spring* and, more important, *Parade*. Seeking to restage an Abakuá ritual, their project illustrated the artistic output of *afrocubanismo* as well as the movement's ethnographic approach to the study of black culture. The libretto, which depicted a conflict between a US filmmaker and a group of Abakuá celebrants, critiqued the colonialist caricatures of the racial other's dancing body in cinema and ballet. In doing so, it contributed to a concurrent repudiation of colonialist films in Latin American intellectual circles. Amid pivotal changes in cultural anthropology, the libretto also alluded to the ideological entanglement of anthropology and coloniality. It obliquely represented the lopsided interactions—mediated by class, race, and education—between ethnographers and subjects. In formulating such political messages, *Milagro* made adept use of caricature, irony, metatheatricality, nonrealist representation, and other techniques from the avant-garde tool kit for critical interrogation of reality.

RESUMEN

El milagro de anaquillé (1927), proyecto de ballet de Alejo Carpentier (libreto) y Amadeo Roldán (música), surgió de la encrucijada entre arte vanguardista, afrocubanismo y etnografía. Inspirados por la experimentación estética de Les Ballets Russes y Les Ballets Suédois en Europa, Carpentier y Roldán adoptaron el ballet como un vehículo para introducir tendencias vanguardistas en Cuba. Milagro hizo referencia a dos ballets revolucionarios: *La consagración de la primavera* y, sobre todo, *Parade*. Al recrear un ritual abakuá, este proyecto ilustró la producción artística del afrocubanismo, así como el acercamiento etnográfico de tal movimiento al estudio de la cultura negra. En torno al conflicto dramático entre un cineasta estadounidense y un grupo de practicantes abakuás, el libreto condenó las caricaturas colonialistas en cine y ballet de un otro racial en tanto cuerpo danzante. De esta manera, *Milagro* intervino en una campaña crítica en

185

círculos intelectuales latinoamericanos ante un cine de índole colonialista. En diálogo con desarrollos claves en el campo de la antropología cultural, el libreto también aludió al alineamiento ideológico entre antropología y colonialidad. Implícitamente, el texto representó las relaciones asimétricas —determinadas por jerarquías de clase, raza y educación— entre etnógrafos y sujetos en el trabajo de campo. Para formular tales postulados políticos, *Milagro* hizo uso de la caricatura, el metateatro, la representación no realista y otras técnicas de interpretación crítica de la realidad típicas de la vanguardia.

In the gruesome closing scene of Alejo Carpentier's 1927 ballet libretto *El milagro de anaquillé*, two Afro-Cuban deities strangle a North American movie director who in the process of filming an Abakuá ritual has desecrated the altar. Directions for the mise-en-scène insist that the characters should look monstrous and move like robots. Carpentier imagines the divinities as gigantic puppets shaped like cylinders. The filmmaker is no less fantastic—wearing a mask that doubles the size of his head.[1] These physiognomies, typical of futurist theater, make the avant-garde affiliation of the text apparent. In fact, the ballet was one of the earliest outcomes of the adoption of avant-garde vocabularies by Cuban artists in the 1920s. Meanwhile, the recreation of an Abakuá ceremony made the ballet one of the initial expressions of *afrocubanismo*, the groundbreaking movement that reclaimed the island's black traditions as an undeniable component of Cuban culture and incorporated them in the production of music, literature, and art of nationalist character.[2] Carpentier and Amadeo Roldán, the composer of the ballet's score, researched Abakuá music, dance, and religion through direct observation in fieldwork. In this regard, their collaboration holds additional historical value as one of the earliest efforts in the modern ethnography of Afro-Cuban culture.

In the late 1920s, Cuban artists' espousal of avant-gardism expressed more than a desire to explore new aesthetic possibilities. These advocates of innovation aimed to transform society itself. They called for a revolution in education, the arts, politics, and the economy to overcome the handicaps that had frustrated the nation's development since the instauration of the Republic in 1902. Illustrating the intelligentsia's view that national renovation should take place on all fronts, in 1927 the Minorista Group called for improving the situation of the working classes, reforming public education, strengthening democracy and the electoral system, achieving political and economic autonomy from the United States, and introducing to Cuba "the most recent doctrines, theories and practices in the sciences and the arts."[3] Conceived that same year, *Milagro* epitomized two of the points from the Minorista Group's public declaration, to which Carpentier added his signature. In addition to proposing a cutting-edge spectacle up to date with international trends in avant-garde theater, the project delivered overt denunciation of US interventionism in Cuba. Carpentier dubbed *Milagro* an "anti-imperialist" ballet on account of the libretto's representation of the US filmmaker as an authoritarian intruder unwelcomed by the work's Cuban characters.[4] The Afro-Cuban topic of the ballet amplified its political resonance. As Carpentier observed, the mere fact of showing serious interest in Afro-Cuban traditions, let alone validating them as a source of nationalist art, was a confrontational gesture in a country where disenfranchisement of blacks and censure of their culture were the status quo.[5]

Rather than focusing on *Milagro*'s statements against US interventionism and in favor of national recognition of Afro-Cuban culture, this article stresses other political implications of the ballet. Equally prominent in the libretto is the question of observing and representing the native subject through a colonialist gaze. Pointing his camera at characters from the Cuban countryside, the US filmmaker symbolized the proliferation of narratives depicting colonial and neocolonial bodies as exotic or savage in the expanding medium of cinema. *Milagro* lampooned the actions of the filmmaker and, through an ending that culminated in his fatal punishment, took a firm stance against the production of such discourse. Carpentier and Roldán also responded critically to the very same medium of ballet, whose own tradition of exotica had promoted similar objectification of non-European bodies and locales. In embracing a political theme and a caustic avant-garde vocabulary, *Milagro* negated the hedonistic exotica of the Orientalist ballets that had been in vogue early in the century to instead affirm a revolutionary vision of this theatrical genre. Furthermore, *Milagro*'s postcolonial perspective on the hegemonic observation of the subaltern other extended to the practice of ethnography, which, as noted already, was Carpentier and Roldán's method to gain knowledge of Abakuá performances.[6] As argued here, the libretto embedded a commentary on the problematic fieldwork interactions that arose as part of the ethnography of *afrocubanismo* when members of a predominantly white cultural elite studied the religious rituals of working-class blacks.

Before examining the ideological arguments brought to the fore by *Milagro*, this article considers a fundamental question: why did Carpentier and Roldán, having no experience in the production of ballets and working in a country with no institutions in this medium, adopt the genre? I bring attention to how ballet, which in Europe had gained the status of a fashionable outcome for artistic innovation, afforded Carpentier and Roldán an exciting vehicle to advance the adoption of avant-garde art in Cuba and, simultaneously, to showcase black music, dance, and ritual as suitable materials for developing a nationalist theater. It was Carpentier's impressive familiarity with developments in modernist and avant-garde ballet that enabled him to model *Milagro* after works from the repertoire of Serge Diaghilev's Ballets Russes and Rolf de Maré's Ballets Suédois.[7] In particular, I trace his inspiration for *Milagro* to *Parade* (1917), the iconoclastic product of the collaboration among Jean Cocteau,

Pablo Picasso, Erik Satie, and Léonide Massine for Les Ballets Russes. Ballets like *Parade* revealed to Carpentier an arsenal of tools that could be used effectively in the articulation of political messages. Embracing the aesthetics of the avant-garde was a political declaration in itself: a disruption of the status quo, a nonconformist gesture in line with the revolutionary spirit of the Minorista Group. But, going beyond a general formulation of antiestablishment sentiment, *Milagro* was able to enounce a specific indictment of colonialist ideology by effectively manipulating the expressive potential of avant-garde ballet and futurist theater, with which it shared its attention to contemporary life, critical outlook of reality, broadening of choreographic sources, incorporation of popular entertainment, and juxtaposition of incongruous materials. In building a mordant satire of coloniality, the ballet also engaged subversive devices of avant-garde performance such as nonrealist representation, caricature, and metatheatricality.

In arguing for the relevance of *Milagro* in the Cuban artistic corpus of this period and in connection to the politics of cinema, ballet, and ethnography, this article takes into consideration and adds to existing analyses of this piece by Frank Janney, who has examined the libretto in his study of Carpentier's early works, and Vicky Unruh, who has considered the libretto in her investigation of Latin American avant-garde production. Their interpretations of *Milagro* highlight a clash between modernity and tradition as the ballet's central theme. In Janney's view, the narrative is a parable of the triumph of the genuine culture and religious beliefs of Afro-Cubans over the power of capitalism and commercialism, symbolized by the US filmmaker. Along similar lines, but stressing the technological dimension of this conflict and its implications for art and performance, Unruh reads the libretto as a confrontation between commercial art based on mechanical reproduction, as exemplified by cinema, and the socially transcendent, living performance that the Abakuá ritual represents.[8] In different ways both scholars point out the significance of *Milagro*. Janney identifies in it seeds of the monumental novels that Carpentier would write later. Meanwhile, Unruh warns against assuming that a work like *Milagro* is too minor or unconventional to be relevant. This is because avant-gardism, being essentially experimental, manifested in a multifarious number of media and formats, often unorthodox.[9] My case for the value of *Milagro* is consistent with her proposition that pieces like this one staged meaningful interventions in aesthetic, cultural, and social debates—even if by other standards ballet librettos are considered an inconsequential literary subgenre. The truth is that the libretto did not constitute a rarity in the work of Carpentier. The piece was part of a group of seven different ballet projects envisioned by the writer around the same time. Those ballet projects, in turn, belong next to an assembly of ten other works from his early career, including poems, songs, an oratorio, an opera for puppets, and other musical pieces, in which he collaborated as a poet and librettist with Cuban and French composers. Authored between the late 1920s and the late 1930s, all these pieces fused elements of avant-garde art and Afro-Cuban folklore.[10] Such output attests to how Carpentier regarded writing for the stage and the concert hall a substantive form of artistic expression and participation in the cultural trends of the era.

This analysis of *Milagro* attempts to situate the work of one of Latin America's most important literary figures in new contexts. In view of Carpentier's investment in ballet, I seek to provide a more detailed understanding of his connection to the medium, sources of balletic references, pioneering efforts to cultivate the genre in Cuba, and active involvement in what at the time was a pivotal international development in this art: the transition from exotica to avant-gardism. I also attempt to illuminate Carpentier's engagement with avant-garde art as a method of cultural and political action. As Unruh observes, the Latin American avant-garde movement of which Carpentier was a participant might have emerged in close dialogue with European models, but it distinctively heeded the region's own cultural concerns and produced a thoughtful inquiry into the Latin American experience.[11] Contributing to this argument, I define *Milagro* as Carpentier's intervention in a debate, unfolding in the 1920s, about colonialist representations of Latin Americans and other non-Western subjects in cinema—which sheds light on the writer's critical position toward the discourse of Western civilization and non-Western barbarity. In ballet, a choreographic art, Carpentier found an ideal medium for creating a subversive parody of colonialist films since, as explained here, cinema's construction of savagery relied on Darwinist representations of dance, gesture, and human movement. The libretto appropriated and satirized the kinetic and narrative codes of barbarity on celluloid, while bringing attention to the staged, performative nature of exotica and primitivism.

Finally, in providing insight into Carpentier's anthropological study of Afro-Cuban culture, the case of *Milagro* permits us to reassess his endeavors as an ethnographer and gain a more nuanced judgment of their worth. While the ethnographic activities of Carpentier's early career have been commonly disqualified as immature, problematic, and of limited value, studies by Anke Birkenmaier and Emily Maguire have contributed a deeper knowledge of not only the challenges but also the merits of the writer's anthropological work.[12] I advance that discussion by highlighting the pioneer character of some of Carpentier's ethnographic methods. The very notion of attending Afro-Cuban ceremonials assiduously, as Carpentier did, was revolutionary at a time when rigorous fieldwork and participant observation were just beginning to claim the status of a scientific method. Also novel were his plans to stage an Abakuá ritual and feature knowledgeable Afro-Cuban dancers in it, which prefigured a performance-based approach to ethnography that would be realized by US anthropologists such as Zora Neale Hurston and Katherine Dunham in the 1930s.

Certainly, Carpentier's ethnography of Afro-Cuban culture was ridden with the skewed power dynamic between a white intellectual in the role of anthropologists and marginalized blacks in the position of observed subjects. But, in *Milagro*, Carpentier seemed to acknowledge this critical limitation through an incipient form of ethnographic reflexivity, for, as argued here, the US filmmaker's violation of the Abakuá ritual symbolized the librettist's own interference with Afro-Cuban ceremonials during his preliminary fieldwork for the ballet. Moreover, his use of ethnography to develop a critique of Western misrepresentation of the racial other paralleled new anthropological approaches, as epitomized in the work of Franz Boas, that opposed the study of non-Western cultures from a Eurocentric perspective.

Experiments in a Fashionable Medium: Ballet Librettos of Avant-Garde Inspiration

Carpentier's attraction to the avant-garde movement in Europe, so clearly displayed in his journalism from the 1920s, holds the key to understanding his interest in producing ballets. Born in 1904, Carpentier initiated his literary career in 1922, at age eighteen, with contributions for magazines and newspapers in Havana. Already in 1923, the young author was writing frequent articles about Satie, Picasso, Cocteau, and other avant-garde artists for publications such as *Chic*, *Social*, and *El Diario de la Marina*.[13] His columns provided enthusiastic commentary on the freshest developments in music, painting, theater, and literature in Paris and other European cultural centers. Aiming to be more than a reporter of the avant-garde's latest tendencies, he co-organized with Roldán two concerts of modernist music in Havana—the first one in 1926 and the second one the following year—and in this way became responsible for the first performances in Cuba of works by Igor Stravinsky, Claude Debussy, Maurice Ravel, Francis Poulenc, and Sergei Prokofiev.[14] Additionally, Carpentier joined other local writers in founding *Revista de Avance*, a journal created with the purpose of informing readers about the artistic and intellectual trends of the day in Europe, Latin America, and also Cuba, where avant-garde art had begun to take root.[15] By then, some of the island's composers were starting to incorporate modernist techniques in their creations. Roldán and Alejandro García Caturla, the best exponents of this development, had studied the music of Poulenc, Darius Milhaud, and Manuel de Falla.[16] At that same time, Cuban visual artists were also advocating for the adoption of revolutionary aesthetics. In 1927, painters Víctor Manuel and Antonio Gattorno, who had traveled to Paris to learn the Fauvist, expressionist, cubist, and surrealist styles, presented the first local exhibitions of works that featured these new vocabularies.[17]

Being at the center of avant-gardism, ballet did not go unnoticed for a generation of Cuban artists emulating the novelties in European music and visual arts. In the years following the 1909 debut of Serge Diaghilev's Ballets Russes in Paris, ballet achieved a reputation for embodying the modernist and avant-garde aesthetics to which Cuban artists aspired. Diaghilev famously turned ballet into a medium for collaboration between revolutionary artists from various fields. The scores for Les Ballets Russes of Satie, Stravinsky, Poulenc, Milhaud, de Falla, and Prokofiev represented innovative developments in music. Similarly, the ballet decors and costumes of Picasso, Georges Braque, Henri Matisse, and Giorgio di Chirico, among other painters, embodied trends such as cubism, surrealism, and constructivism. Keeping up with these novelties, the choreographers working for Diaghilev expanded the genre's stylistic range. As Lynn Garafola sustains, during and after World War I, Les Ballets Russes assumed a style of performance linked to the tenets of futurist theater. Choreographers moved away from naturalist narratives and favored, instead, scenarios that incorporated discontinuity, synthesis, and depersonalization. At the same time, they loosened their adherence to the vocabulary of classical ballet to experiment with movement styles that stressed angularity and mechanization, or that borrowed elements from circus, sports, and popular entertainment.[18] In *Les noces* (1923), for example, Bronislava Nijinska staged a villagers' wedding using stark mechanistic motions that made the characters look like automatons. Meanwhile, in Massine's *Pas d'acier* (1927) the dancers manipulated hammers, levers, and pulleys in an ode to labor in the industrial age. These developments marked a radical departure from prewar works by Les Ballet Russes such as *Cléopâtre* (1909), *Schéhérazade* (1910), and *Le Dieu bleu* (1912), which, as explained later in this article, had been choreographed in an Orientalist vein and followed conventional narratives and means of representation.

During a childhood trip to Paris in 1913, Carpentier had enjoyed the opportunity to witness a rehearsal of Les Ballets Russes's *Firebird* (1910), a Russian folktale featuring music by Stravinsky, choreography by Mikhail Fokine, and designs by Léon Bakst. Later, he had seen presentations in Havana of Ana Pavlova, who visited Cuba several times between 1915 and 1919. But neither *Firebird* nor Pavlova embodied avant-garde ballet—Fokine's work belonged to Les Ballets Russes's more conventional repertoire, and Pavlova's performances reflected her traditionalist stance of opposition to experimentation.[19] While these early encounters with ballet planted the seeds of Carpentier's love of the medium, it was by reading about this dance genre that he was drawn to its avant-gardist expressions. He kept abreast of events in European ballet through French publications on modern art that arrived to Havana.[20] Not only did he read those magazines with devotion; he also used them as sources for his own secondhand reports on Les Ballets Russes's seasons, as illustrated by a 1923 piece for *La Discusión* in which he wrote excitedly about *Les noces* within just one month of its premiere in Paris.[21] His increasing fascination with ballet became evident the following year in a series of articles for *Chic* in which he discussed contributions to the genre by Stravinsky, Ravel, Satie, and Picasso.[22] In another sign of enthusiasm for the medium, he and Roldán ordered ballet scores from abroad and studied them in detail, as was the case with Stravinsky's *Rite of Spring*.[23]

Soon after, Carpentier and Roldán sought to follow in the footsteps of the modernist and avant-garde artists who had made ballet a cutting-edge genre. If for Roldán ballet was a vehicle for musical experimentation, for Carpentier it represented a literary outlet that permitted its own measure of originality. In the mid-1920s, having published only his articles for newspapers and magazines— and very far from becoming the prominent novelist recognized with the Cervantes Award in 1977 and nominated for the Nobel Prize in 1979—Carpentier was eager to participate in the artistic life of the time as more than a journalist.[24] Writing scenarios for a stimulating form of spectacle enabled him to express his own creative voice. Despite librettos not carrying the greatest literary weight, in Europe respected figures were authoring and legitimizing them as a dramatic subgenre. From 1920 to 1925, Rolf de Maré's Ballets Suédois staged productions in which the librettos by Cocteau, Paul Claudel, Blaise Cendrars, and Luigi Pirandello featured prominently. The scenarios went from representing aspects of contemporary life to depicting surrealist environments. The significance of literary material was the most evident in Cocteau's *Les mariés de la Tour Eiffel* (1921), a work that mixed dance and spoken drama.[25] Conscious of the literary potential of librettos, Carpentier equated avant-garde ballet to a form of plastic, dramatic or choreographic poetry in chronicles in which he gave consideration to the work of librettists. In a 1923 article about Les Ballets Suédois's *L'Homme et son désir* (1921), he declared that Claudel's libretto for this spectacle was among the author's most original creations. He highlighted the producers' classification of the ballet as a *poème plastique*. The following year, Carpentier judged that the most significant work of that troupe's season had been *La jarre* (1924), a choreographic satire conceived by Pirandello. Similarly, in an extensive 1925 essay on Cocteau, he explained how the author's signature "aesthetic of the commonplace" had come to life masterfully in *Les mariés de la Tour Eiffel* and the "surrealist choreographic poem" *Parade*.[26]

Performances in Havana of the theater troupe of Duvan Torzov, in 1924, catalyzed Carpentier's interest in writing for the stage. Witnessing Torzov's production of the revue *La Chauve-Souris*, he came the closest to experiencing first hand the innovative theatrical spectacles being conceived in Europe. The revue's revolutionary elements triggered his excitement. He lauded the production as a form of total theater that integrated words, music, and decors into an expressive *gesamtkunstwerk*. His description of the performance pointed to qualities of synthesis and dynamism typical of Filippo Tommaso Marinetti's concept of futurist theater. Proposing Torzov's piece as a model for a "Cuban synthetic theater," Carpentier prompted local artists to cultivate what would be a "completely new art" in the country. He called them to coopt the aesthetic elements of avant-garde spectacles. The novel Cuban productions, as recommended by him, would fall within a collaborative template by incorporating music, dance, visual arts, and literary ideas, while also adhering to the premises of directedness, distillation, dynamism, originality, and economy of means.[27] Going further, he identified potential themes in Cuban colonial history and folklore, as captured in the nineteenth-century drawings of Víctor Patricio de Landaluze and Frédéric Mialhe—an approach that, in fact, he would follow in *La rebambaramba*, the first of his own ballet librettos.

Not long after issuing this call for developing a Cuban experimental theater, Carpentier approached local composers and designers with the purpose of interesting them in producing ballets. In a letter to García Caturla dated March 15, 1927, he expressed eagerness to collaborate with him: "For a while I have been obsessed with the idea of finally outlining three or four scenarios of Cuban ballets, to subject them to your judgment and Roldán's."[28] Noteworthy is the fact that by this point Carpentier had already engaged Roldán in plans for a ballet. The previous year, they had begun work on *La rebambaramba*.[29] Its comedic libretto, set in colonial Havana, presents the competition of three suitors—a clumsy soldier, a clever free black, and a jealous coachman—for the love of a beautiful biracial woman. The narrative takes place against the backdrop of Three Kings' Day carnival, when, according to colonial tradition, slaves paraded their dances in the streets of the city.[30] Caricaturist José Hurtado de Mendoza was brought onboard as the designer of sets and costumes. Throughout 1927 Carpentier worked on other ballet projects, including *Milagro*, again in collaboration with Roldán and Hurtado de Mendoza. He also invited García Caturla to compose music for a ballet depicting the entrance of an itinerant circus to a Cuban provincial town, with the action revolving around the colorful cortege of musicians, clowns, and elephants marching through the streets to announce the circus's arrival.[31] Three other ballet projects from this period are more difficult to date with precision. Carpentier undertook them before leaving for Paris in self-exile in March 1928, but there is no documentation establishing the exact year of each one's conception. Among them was *La hija del ogro* (The Ogre's Daughter), in association with Roldán and painter Adia Yunkers. In this farce, a girl elopes with her beau from the castle of her father, who is an ogre. The monster chases them as they come across a traveling circus and, later, a movie set where Charles Chaplin comes to the lovers' rescue.[32] Moreover, Carpentier entertained plans for a ballet titled *Azúcar* (Sugar), which would "express, by means of a dynamic performance, the convulsive life of the sugar mill, the labor of the men, and the blind activity of the machines."[33] Less is known about his ideas for *Mata-cangrejo* (Crab-Killer), another ballet project attributed to this period.[34] The correspondence between Carpentier and

García Caturla reveals plans for yet another ballet, *El embó*, whose title refers to an Afro-Cuban funerary ritual.[35]

In summary, within the span of a few years Carpentier envisaged seven ballet projects.[36] According to the records preserved to date, he completed the librettos for three of them: *La rebambaramba* and *Milagro* (for both of which Roldán finalized the music), and *La hija del ogro* (which, in contrast, did not originate a score). Judged on their own terms, these texts show Carpentier's surprising mastery of the ballet libretto as a literary subgenre with its own possibilities and challenges. As he explained to García Caturla, a librettist had to bear in mind the imperatives of the theatrical spectacle as a whole. Accordingly, the writer saw himself in a procreant role that influenced all aspects of the production. Finding an appropriate subject was not sufficient: the plot had to lend itself to stylized choreographic representation, spark the imagination of the painter in charge of sets and costumes, and contain actions and environments befitting to inspired musicalization. For this reason, he explained that even if a libretto could be distilled into "fifty lines," it had to encapsulate "the true quintessence of many ideas."[37] The scenarios for *La rebambaramba* and *Milagro* did justice to this complex task. They introduced vivid characters, picturesque backdrops, and narratives conducive to the showcase of music and dance. Well-developed concepts animated each ballet, which sought to provide both entertainment and social commentary. For instance, *La rebambaramba* dazzles with its colorful depiction of carnival in Havana, while, in the subversive tradition of Cuban *teatro bufo*, it indicts patriarchal, racist, and colonialist ideology in nineteenth-century Cuba.[38] In addition to creating rich content and attending to the multiple requirements of a theatrical production, Carpentier succeeded at infusing his ballets with "a high level of Cubanness" while capturing "the esprit of the day"—a quest to package national character in avant-garde form that he shared with other Cuban artists of his generation.[39]

None of these works reached the stage at the time, at least not in choreographic form. Orchestral suites of *La rebambaramba* and *Milagro* premiered in symphonic concerts in Havana on August 12, 1928, and September 22, 1929, respectively. But the absence of dance ensembles in Cuba rendered the choreographic productions unfeasible. Nevertheless, the librettos and scores hold historical significance as pioneer efforts to produce ballets locally (although visiting European dancers had presented ballet in Cuba since the nineteenth century, no Cuban ballets had ever been created). Three decades later, choreographers Alberto Alonso and Ramiro Guerra would finally stage *La rebambaramba* and *Milagro*, but their productions, which did not engage Carpentier in direct collaboration and reflected the artistic climate of a different period, are not considered in the present discussion.[40]

Critical Interpretations of Contemporary Life in Avant-Garde Ballet:
From *Parade* to *Milagro*

While presenting distinctively Cuban content, *Milagro*'s amalgamation of ex-pressionist, cubist, futurist, and surrealist traits revealed Carpentier and Rol-dán's desire to exhaust the possibilities of avant-garde art. More specifically, *Milagro* evidenced a dialogue with the revolutionary dance aesthetics modeled by Les Ballets Russes and Les Ballet Suédois. The Abakuá ceremony refer-enced *Rite of Spring* (1913), the legendary ballet with music by Stravinsky, choreography by Vaslav Nijinsky, and designs by Nicholas Roerich that had scandalized Paris with its irreverent recreation of an ancient sacrificial ritual in pagan Russia. Not only did *Rite of Spring* provide an antecedent for center-ing a ballet narrative on the theme of ritual; it also led Carpentier and Roldán to engage with Afro-Cuban culture through a modernist sensibility. Their ac-quired Stravinskian perspective on rhythm pushed them to listen to the island's black music with fresh ears, growing aware of its sophistication. The writer reasoned that the polyrhythmic richness that had made Stravinsky's compo-sition so revolutionary already existed, in an even superior manifestation, in Afro-Cuban music. For Carpentier, thus, black musical traditions were ripe for being repackaged as innovative products.[41] Consistently, Roldán's score for *Milagro* integrated Afro-Cuban sources and progressive composition tech-niques. Carpentier's description of this music suggested a strong parallel with the harsh sonority of *Rite of Spring*. "Nothing in it sought to caress or se-duce the listener," he indicated. Harmonically, it was "one of Roldán's severest scores," creating the effect of a sonic environment "angular and linear, [in the] color of steel, with no trace of flattery."[42]

The influence of *Rite of Spring* on Carpentier is not surprising to those familiar with his oeuvre. His final novel, *La consagración de la primavera* (1978), borrowed its title from the iconic ballet—the novel's main character, a Russian ballerina, arrives to Cuba after having danced with Les Ballets Russes and, not unlike Carpentier himself with *Milagro*, stages a singular produc-tion of Nijinky's ballet with Afro-Cuban dancers. Yet, another of Les Ballets Russes's works, *Parade*, was more fundamentally influential in the concep-tion of *Milagro*. *Parade*'s premiere in 1917 had ushered a new era in ballet, as Carpentier noted in an article from 1929 about the aesthetic evolution of Les Ballets Russes.[43] While some of the early modernist productions of Diag-hilev's troupe had spoken in the languages of primitivism, neo-romanticism, and symbolism, *Parade* established ballet's adoption of even more innovative trends. Carpentier had paid special attention to *Parade* in various columns that predated his work on *Milagro*. His chronicles from 1924 repeatedly character-ized that ballet as an example of Satie's, Picasso's, and Cocteau's innovations. One of those texts explained that *Parade* embodied a new musical aesthetics in which simple melodies wedded daring harmonic effects. Another essay, about the rise of cubism, indicated that Picasso's designs for the ballet were deservingly notable.[44] Yet another article, concerned with futurist art, rightly observed that *Parade* had been a realist attempt to capture the street life of Paris in all its banality.[45] This comment demonstrated familiarity with the producers' original vision; an essay by Guillaume Apollinaire in the souvenir program for the premiere of *Parade* had explained the multiple elements of the piece precisely in terms of their realist function.[46]

Cocteau's libretto for *Parade* introduced a theater-within-a-theater scenario, a metatheatrical situation in which the spectators contemplated the dancers in the act of performing for an imaginary street crowd. A magician, a mime, acrobats, and a *cheval jupon* (two clowns disguised as one horse) perform on the street, trying in vain to entice onlookers to enter the auditorium where they are about to present a variety show (a show that *Parade* does not depict in the end). Interspersed with their dances are the numbers of two greedy managers who advertise the show with grandiloquence that betrays the banality of the planned music-hall event. The actions on the stage cited lowbrow attractions that the audience could recognize from films, variety acts, and circus and magic shows playing in Paris at the time. Cocteau's ironic look at these popular entertainment genres celebrated their commonplace poetry while exposing their tackiness and commercialism. The emphasis was on the mundane occurrences, apathetic encounters, and vacuous publicity that defined the city's street life. Among the ballet's most spectacular elements were the managers' costumes, which Picasso designed in the shape of enormous contraptions akin to three-dimensional cubist collages (fig. 1). Satie's score, of surrealist and futurist orientation, was equally memorable for blending such disparate ingredients as classical music, a jazz number, and the everyday noises of modern machinery (e.g., typewriters, telegraphs, sirens, engines, klaxons). Meanwhile, the choreography borrowed heavily from popular entertainment, as it was most evident in the dance of the Little American Girl. Her pantomime reproduced actions and gestures from silent films—movements that, in the context of a ballet, exhibited the surrealist quality of a familiar object placed in an unfamiliar environment.[47]

In paying attention to the life of the times, *Parade* broadened the range of ballet's subject matter and inaugurated a trend that inspired various works of Les Ballets Russes and became the hallmark of Les Ballets Suédois's productions.[48] Until then, ballet had been concerned with romantic, exotic, or mythical subjects while embodying autocratic and bourgeois ideologies. In groundbreaking fashion, *Parade* departed from that model of narrative to convey, instead, a nonconformist perspective on modern life and its alienating values. Cocteau's music-hall managers, depicted as deceitful automatons driven by a desire to profit, both epitomized and denounced the soullessness of capitalism.

FIGURE 1. *Parade's* American Manager. Design by Pablo Picasso. Souvenir program of Les Ballets Russes, Paris Opera (May 8, 1920). Bibliothèque National de France

In the original libretto, the French Manager beckoned passersby to buy tickets with empty promises to change their equally empty lives: "If you want to become rich—if you feel sick—if you have attacks for languor—ENTER [. . .] Boredom is lying in wait for you! You are sleeping without being aware of it! Wake up! Enter, enter!" Similarly, *Parade's* American Manager advertised the show as the solution for the crowd to alter their apathetic experience of life: "IT IS A CRIME to kill your own curiosity [. . .] Are you dead? NO? Then you must LIVE! Make sure you get this idea through your head! A timid man is a DEAD man."[49]

Just as *Parade* took its inspiration from the contemporary, *Milagro* rendered a picture of the present. To do so, it relied on similar signifiers of a dynamic modernity. *Parade's* imagery of skyscrapers, machinery, cinema, and jazz was ingeniously recontextualized in *Milagro's* setting, in which each of these elements reappeared (as detailed in the analysis of the libretto that follows below). But *Milagro's* own depiction of the present extended beyond a futurist display of the accoutrements of twentieth-century architecture, technology, and popular entertainment. The notion that ballet could question the status quo in contemporary life, as originated in *Parade*, paved the way for Carpentier to utilize the genre as a means of social and cultural critique. In this regard, Carpentier epitomized the Latin American artists' interest in turning avant-garde artistic production into a platform for reflecting critically on the social and cultural issues of their nations.

The setting of *Milagro*'s narrative in a sugarcane plantation immediately establishes the ballet's Cuban character and references sugar production as the backbone of the country's economy. The view of a sugarcane field, palm trees, and rural huts, elements all contemplated in Carpentier's indications for the decors, celebrate fixtures of the island's rural landscape. Types easily recognizable as local conform the majority of the dramatis personae and reinforce the national specificity of the work: sugarcane cutters, *guajiros* (Cuban peasants), and, as part of the Abakuá ritual, an *iyamba* (priest) and a *diablito* (*ireme* ceremonial dancer). The music and dance numbers consolidate the ballet's nationalist flavor. In contrasting a Spanish-derived *zapateo* and the eminently African Abakuá ceremonial, the libretto showcases the broad spectrum of Cuban culture and makes a statement about its hybrid roots—as such, it prefigures Carpentier's meticulous analysis of the country's European and African musical genealogies in his seminal treatise *La música en Cuba* (1946).

Milagro's storyline revolves around a US filmmaker (the Business Man) determined to make a movie in the Cuban countryside. He travels with two fellow North Americans (the Flapper and the Sailor) whom he employs as actors. First, he films them in an improvised toreador scene, surrounded by a group of Cuban peasants. Later, he attempts to shoot an ill-concocted Tarzanesque sequence with the two actors appearing against the backdrop of an unfolding Afro-Cuban ritual. Rather than undermining the Cubanness of the ballet, the presence of these three North American figures suggests the political reality of a country subject to US interventionism. Presiding over the stage, the silhouette of a sugar mill acts as a reminder of the North American control of the island's economy, while the doings of the Business Man, a self-interested bully, constitute an allegory of the authoritarian and exploitative North American actions in the country.

Before further discussing other ways in which *Milagro* interrogates contemporary reality and formulates a critique of coloniality, it is essential to review its narrative in detail, which provides an opportunity for establishing the libretto's aesthetic affiliation to avant-garde art and performance. That affiliation often manifests in the form of a stylistic debt to *Parade*. *Milagro* borrows from that ballet's themes and imagery while incorporating avant-gardism's favored devices of absurdity, hyperbole, juxtaposition, caricature, grotesquerie, satire, and metatheatricality. The libretto's indications for the mise-en-scéne include clear directions for realizing the experimental set, costumes, and choreography along that line. The set's most prominent features would have been the Peasant's and the Iyamba's huts, in the style of the rudimentary dwellings typical of the Cuban countryside. However, those conventional buildings were expected to appear against a backdrop in which lines and planes intersected with the geometric quality of an avant-garde design. Like a "vegetable fence," the uniform sugarcane field would have extended across the stage, forming a horizontal band of green interrupted by the vertical lines of equidistant palm trees. Proclaiming the futurist love of industrial motifs, the "geometric hulk" of a sugar mill was supposed to dominate the horizon. Carpentier imagined its three "very exaggerated" chimneys shooting upward into the theater's ceiling as disproportionate columns that contributed an expressionist accent. Thick black letters would have covered the chimneys, introducing the sort of typographic element popular in cubism. An equally avant-garde sensibility informs Carpentier's suggestions for the costumes and choreography. The Business Man and the Twins (two Afro-Cuban deities) would have appeared in masks, looking "unreal and monstrous," and dancing "like automatons." Such masked, grotesque, robotic characters were the currency of futurism, which jettisoned psychological drama in favor of a theater of impersonality and automatism. A mechanistic style would have marked, too, the demeanor of the eight Sugarcane Cutters, who were called to perform with "perfect synchronicity, executing the same gestures simultaneously." Speed, another of futurism's fixations, would have defined the dancing of the Sailor, the Flapper, and the Diablito, characters all directed to display a "frenetic rhythm." As other avant-garde ballets, the libretto projects a hotchpotch of dance styles: a Cuban *zapateo*, a jazz number, a Spanish dance pastiche, and Afro-Cuban dances.

The one-act libretto unfolds swiftly in eight short scenes. As the narrative progresses, an atmosphere of surrealist absurdity congeals out of incongruous juxtapositions that take place at every turn—industry and countryside, foreign and local characters, a skyscraper and rustic huts, jazz and Cuban music, commercial cinema and religious ritual.

The ballet opens with the Peasant's return to his hut after a day of work. He pushes a wheeled toy horse that succumbs under disproportionally large saddlebags. (The appearance of these and other disproportionate objects throughout the libretto creates an expressionist effect.) With the day's work done, the Peasant begins to plays the guitar. A group of farmers assemble and perform the *zapateo*, a foot-stomping dance that epitomizes Cuban rural culture. Just at this point, the Business Man enters the stage under the form of an accretion of artifacts that obscure his human shape. He wears an enormous cap and a mask twice the size of his head, and carries strange signs, a bicycle air pump, a film camera, a tripod, and extravagant parcels all at once. (The Business Man, like the two Managers of *Parade*, is defined as a profiteering entrepreneur by its very name, and he is, like one of the Managers, an American. His dehumanized, monstrous figure also hints at *Parade*'s Managers, who wore ten-feet-tall cubist constructions that integrated disparate articles; see figure 1. The collage-like American Manager, for instance, donned a gigantic top hat; had a skyscraper, a cloud, and flags attached to his back; and carried a megaphone and a placard.)

The peasants, intimidated by the Business Man's appearance, stop dancing. The Business Man surveys the grounds as the potential location for a movie. He feels the muscles of the peasants as if they were livestock. Satisfied, he approaches the fore and shouts: "OK!" The interjection triggers a "rhythmic explosion" of jazz music. (What follows resembles *Parade*'s jazz number, in which the character known as the Little American Girl performed a hectic pantomime allusive of silent films' actions. In full-speed motion, she moved across the stage as if riding a horse, assaulting a train, playing cowboys and Indians, cranking up a car, pedaling a bike, taking photographs, sailing in a boat, swimming, dancing a ragtime, impersonating Charlie Chaplin, and so on. Along similar lines, Carpentier imagines *Milagro*'s jazz scene as a number in which American types flood the stage with frenzied and disjointed commotion, evoking the world of cinema, and introducing American iconography.) The "Yankee" Sailor and the Flapper, amateurish actors of the planned movie, enter the stage dancing an inarticulate, fast-paced black bottom. While they dance, the Business Man gets himself busy with the "furious activity" of transforming the location into a movie set. He attaches flashy signs in English to the Iyamba's hut. They read, "Bar," " Ice Cream Soda," and "Wrigley Chewing Gum." In the process, he covers an icon of St. Lazarus that presides over the hut.[50] Somewhere else he hangs another sign: "Church of the Rotarian Church." Next, he operates an air pump to make an inflatable skyscraper grow rapidly out of the sugarcane field. (This is another connection to *Parade*'s American Manager, whose most distinguishable feature was the skyscraper protruding from his back.) The air pump explodes on the final note of the black bottom.

After readying the set, the Business Man continues his frantic work. He mounts the camera on its tripod and hands Spanish costumes and props to the actors: decorative comb, mantilla, and shawl for the Flapper, and toreador's flag, cape, and cap for the Sailor. Next he gives tambourines to the stupefied peasants, forcedly engaging them as extras. The shooting begins: surrounded by a circle of tambourine-playing peasants, the American duo performs a grotesque Spanish dance that mimics a bullfight. By the duet's end, the Flapper-Bull kneels in an imploring gesture at the feet of the Soldier-Toreador, who threatens to kill her with a sword. (By then, it has become clear that *Milagro* shares *Parade*'s scorn for the crassness, amateurism, and commercialism of certain forms of popular entertainment, cinema in this case.)

As the filming of the pseudo-Spanish scene is about to come to an end, the Iyamba and a group of black Sugarcane Cutters arrive from the fields. They ruin the shooting by walking in front of the camera. Enraged, the Business Man throws a fit, but the black workers pay him no heed. Finding his hut covered with signs in English, the Iyamba takes them down and throws them off stage. He restores the image of St. Lazarus. The Business Man tries to protest but a chilling look from the Iyamba keeps him at bay.

Soon after this, the Iyamba begins preparations for a ritual by setting a number of ceremonial objects on a bench. The black men form a circle around the bench and crouch, with knees and elbows touching the ground. The Diablito, an officiating masked figure, comes out of the hut dancing energetically (figure 2). He jumps over the prostrated men while running a black rooster along their backs. Next, the Diablito places a pot with the ritual meal in the center of the circle. He spreads gunpowder around it. As the powder burns, he dances over the red flames and around the pot. The worshippers join in the ritual. They try to reach the pot, but the Diablito guards it furiously. After sev-

FIGURE 2. "El ñáñigo," iconic drawing of an Abakuá ireme or diablito by Víctor Patricio de Landaluze in *Tipos y costumbres de la Isla de Cuba* (1881). Boston Public Library's Rare Books Collection

eral attempts, one of the men advances to the center of the circle and runs away with the pot. The Diablito pursues him in a ceremonial dance.

The Business Man, who has been observing the ritual with growing interest, jumps at the opportunity to incorporate it into his film. He chooses new costumes for the two actors. The Sailor puts on a tiger skin and necklaces. The Flapper wears a Hawaiian grass skirt and decorates her hair with flowers. The Business Man directs the actors to join the ritual. However, the participants block them angrily. Determined to carry out his plan, the filmmaker brandishes the camera tripod like a spear and tries to physically impose authority on the black men. The Iyamba and the Diablito confront him. Using magical powers, they conjure fire under the intruder's nose. Blind with rage, the Business Man wields his tripod and smashes the altar. The worshipers are about to jump at him when a mysterious force paralyzes them. The Twins, Afro-Cuban deities, materialize as gigantic black puppets with bulging eyes and cylindrical bodies. Performing an ominous dance of heavy steps, they inch their way toward the terrified Business Man, magically wrap a cord around his neck, and strangle him with abrupt gesture. The skyscraper deflates. The sugar mill's siren wails somberly. The peasants, the Sailor, and the Flapper freeze, as the black worshipers raise their arms to the sky and the curtain descends slowly.

The Racial Other's Dancing Body under the Colonialist Gaze: Cinema and Ballet

The characters and situations in *Milagro* bear the mark of a long history of colonialist practices of observation, appropriation, and representation of non-European cultures. Initially manifested in Carpentier's oeuvre by way of the libretto's acerbic critique of cinema, the question of how Europeans and North Americans perceive and interact with the cultures of their colonies, former colonies or neo-colonies would become a motif of his work. In later years, the novels *Los pasos perdidos* (1953), *El siglo de las luces* (1962), and *La consagración de la primavera* (1978), in which European and North American travelers negotiate their immersion in Latin American environments, would attend to that concern. Carpentier's own hybrid identity fueled his curiosity about intercultural encounter and translation. Born in Switzerland to a French father and a Russian mother but raised in Cuba, he cultivated equally fervent interests in Europe and the Caribbean, and shifted fluidly between insider and outsider positions in reference to both regions' cultures—often taking the role of interlocutor between them, as when he reported on the European avant-garde for Cuban readers or lectured about Cuban music for French audiences.[51]

Early in his youth, Carpentier developed an appreciation of the cultures of territories with a history of colonialism. From uncritical acceptance of the identification of Europe with civilization and of Latin America, Africa, and

Asia with barbarity, primitivism, and underdevelopment, he moved to a position that countered such colonialist hierarchy with a defense of the rich cultures of the latter regions. An initial indication of this transition appeared in his 1923 review of René Maran's *Batouala*, a novel that garnished considerable attention for fictionalizing the crude conflict between an African tribe and European colonists. Commenting on the novel, a nineteen-year-old Carpentier reiterated the stereotypical classification of Africans as "savages." He attributed the disastrous events of the literary narrative as much to the European characters' exploitative greed as to the African characters' "rudimentary mentality" and "coarse morality." While restating these racist tropes, the review attested to Carpentier's nascent concern with the question of how, in scenarios of colonialism, groups in opposite positions of power articulated schematic representations of each other. As it is, Carpentier proposed that the novel's primary theme was the incapacity of the two sets of characters to mutually regard themselves outside their preconceptions. If, in the novel, for the Africans a European doctor is a witch, "for the colonizer, Batouala [the African protagonist] is a simple beast that must be treated as such."[52]

The fact that, four years later, Carpentier chose to denounce the cultural classifications of coloniality in a ballet about cinema was revealing, on the one hand, of cinema's new dominant role in disseminating narratives of the exotic and barbaric, and, on the other hand, of the salient place of dance in those narratives. Building on the public's fascination with racial otherness and moving image technology, and banking in on mass reproduction and international commercialization, cinema had quickly become the medium par excellence for reproducing the discourse of non-European primitivism. Films extended the possibilities for the Western public to fulfill its curiosity about other races and cultures. The new technology could easily record non-Western bodies performing culturally specific behavior in their local environment. Now, the spectacle of otherness could be constructed with a sense of immediacy never achieved before. Movies such as Gaumont's *Customs and Manners in Senegal* (1910), Pathé Frères's *Madagascar: Manners and Customs of the Sakalava* (1910), and the Tahitian, Japanese, Javanese, and Cambodian installments of Gaston Méliès's "Round the World Films" (1912–1913), turned travelogues into a popular genre of the incipient industry. Many of these movies fictionalized non-European cultures and locations according to stereotypes of primitivism and savagery. Osa and Martin Johnson's *Cannibals of the South Seas* (1912), filmed in Malekula, and Méliès's *Captured by Aborigines* (1913), set in Australia, traded in characterizations of the natives as cannibals and rapists.[53]

In *Milagro*, the Business Man's attraction to the Abakuá ritual bespoke cinema's obsession with the non-Western dancing body. The camera's capacity to capture human movement, coupled with the potential of dance for representing cultural difference, resulted in a proliferation of exotic dancing bodies on the celluloid. In the United States, one of the earliest applications of the new technology had been the filming of Plains Indians' ceremonial dances, as illustrated by Thomas Edison's *Buffalo Dance* (1894) and *Circle Dance* (1898). Fatimah Tobing Rony contends that films commonly portrayed the racial other as a subject that gestured and danced—communicating through physical actions rather than language. In these depictions, kinetic exoticism and verbal inarticulateness worked together to signify the supposedly lower evolutionary stage of Africans, Polynesians, Native Americans, and other colonial subalterns. Reinforcing the construction of a primitive physicality, the non-Western subject was often caught in camera minimally dressed and executing actions like crouching and jumping, which situated him as evolutionarily close to apes. Darwinist theories that deemed posture and movement markers of evolution were appropriated in the representation of race, as it was evident in chronophotographic films by Félix-Louis Regnault from the 1890s that compared the walking and running of West Africans and Europeans. An advertisement for *Cannibals of the South Seas* made these associations apparent through the montage of the film's title, with its reference to cannibalism, and images of black men that included, in the background, a dancer holding a spear and striking a primitivist posture (figure 3). Even when the camera recorded authentic performances of dances and rituals, as was the case with Edison's movies and might have been with the hypothetic filming of an Abakuá ceremony in rural Cuba, the final product often generated a cultural gulf between the performers and their Western audiences. Decontextualized and unexplained, the performances appeared as aberrant behavior at odds with Western notions of civilization.[54]

By the time Carpentier worked on *Milagro*, the colonialist discourse of European and North American cinema had become an object of condemnation in Latin American circles. In Mexico, a country that the librettist visited in 1926 right before writing the libretto, the denunciation of Hollywood's stereotypes of the region had reached diplomatic proportions. The administrations of Venustiano Carranza (1917–1920) and Plutarco Elías Calles (1924–1928) demanded that Hollywood studios put an end to their offensive depictions of Mexicans.[55] Coinciding with Carpentier's stay in that nation, poet Gabriela Mistral intervened in the debate. Mistral, writing from Europe, reported that the cinemas of Paris and Brussels regularly projected US films that caricaturized Mexicans as "tribal" and "animalistic" people: physically weak and ugly, and inclined to violence, laziness, cowardice, alcoholism, and lechery. Grasping cinema's efficacy in shaping public opinion, she argued that such movies were poisonous propaganda that distorted the world's view of Mexicans and, by extension, other Latin Americans.[56] Between June and July, her article appeared in *El Universal* (Mexico), *El Mercurio* (Chile), and *Repertorio Americano* (Costa Rica). Its broad diffusion spoke to the resonance that the issue had beyond Mexican borders. It is plausible that Carpentier's trip to Mexico

PROFITS AND PLEASED PATRONS
follow everywhere

MARTIN JOHNSON'S CANNIBALS
of THE SOUTH SEAS

It's a positive, proven S.R.O. producer and a magnet for new patrons. Read the testimony on next page.

FIGURE 3. Advertisement for Osa and Martin Johnson's *Cannibals of the South Seas* in *Moving Picture World* (June 1919). Museum of Modern Art Library

informed his choice of topic for the ballet libretto one year later. The writer, who moved in Mexican artistic circles and made the acquaintance of the likes of painter Diego Rivera, acknowledged the trip to have been artistically and politically stimulating.[57] With Hollywood's stereotypes of Mexicans occupying the attention of the intelligentsia, press, and government, Carpentier must have grasped, as Mistral, the relevance of the debate for all Latin American countries.

Milagro, then, should be contextualized as Carpentier's contribution to this regional protest of colonialist cinema. As such, it was not an isolated instance of the writer's involvement in the debate, which went beyond the allegory in the ballet libretto. He conveyed his explicit disapproval of this form of cinema in an article from 1931 that lambasted a French documentary about Mexico for its negative stereotypes of the country. Its display of indigenous people naked portrayed a rudimentary Mexico. Expressing bitterness for the "negative power" of foreign films to misrepresent the region, Carpentier stressed how vital it was for Latin Americans to make their own documentaries: "If to make films about ourselves we rely on foreigners, we can be certain of always being betrayed and deformed."[58] Aware that this problem was not confined to Latin America, that same year the writer published an article that condemned a film about Africa that he had watched in Paris. The documentary's depiction of groups living between the Niger River and Lake Tanganyika reiterated tropes of savagery: "[The producers] can't manage to rid their words of a vague ironic tone, when they tell us about [the Africans'] magical practices, their sense of mystery, their concept of divinity, their laws, their witchdoctors, diviners and healers. As if in this realm primitive men gave more proof of barbarity than the children of [Western] countries do in some of their most usual actions."[59] Carpentier argued that the filmmakers, coming from nations that had fought one another barbarously only a few years earlier, during World War I, had no right of claim to cultural superiority. For Carpentier, as for other intellectuals of his generation, the war's atrocities put in doubt the alleged role of Europe as the world's beacon of civilization, thus prompting a negation of the dualist opposition of Western development and non-Western barbarity.

The ritual scene in *Milagro* cites the representational codes of this category of movies, taking advantage of the ways in which the Abakuá ceremonial, framed as an archetypal vignette of primitivism, can meet the clichés of colonialist cinema. The black participants corporealize the discourse of barbarity by performing Africanist dances and exposing their bodies half-naked. They suggest backwardness when they crouch in a circle around the fire, while the Diablito jumps vigorously over the flames. Extraordinary ceremonial objects—such as the rooster, magic sticks, a feathered drum, and the Diablito's otherworldly mask—further place the ritual in counterpoint with Western notions of civilization. Carpentier cites yet another convention of primivitist cinema: the racial antithesis between natives and white actors. In their attempt to perform with the ceremony as their backdrop and donning the cartoonish grass skirt and tiger skin, the Flapper and the Sailor create a blackface spectacle of racial difference.

Subversion of the codes of colonialist cinema makes *Milagro* a postcolonial satire. The libretto appropriates and turns around a key element of colonialist representation, caricature, to expose the unethical and false character of this type of cinema. If European and North American filmmakers commonly relied on caricature to portray other cultures, now *Milagro* subjects those filmmakers' practices to the same reductionism, distilling them into a schematic picture of unscrupulous behavior. The Business Man's actions, scripted and exaggerated, stand as commonplaces of exploitative filmmaking, while his ersatz, simplistic construction of Spanish and Tarzanesque scenes reveals itself as a platitude of commercialism. And, just as celluloid caricatures dehumanized Africans, Asians, Polynesians, and Latin Americans by making them alternatively risible and intimidating, the libretto strips the Business Man of his humanity, turning him into a freak that causes both laughter and fright. In appearance and demeanor, he comes across as simultaneously ridiculous and monstrous. (As indicated earlier, avant-garde ballet and futurist theater provided Carpentier with the necessary elements to construct this caricature; the physiognomy and behavior of the Business Man had its equivalent in the hyperbolic, grotesque music-hall managers from *Parade*).

In another subversive twist, Carpentier attributes an empowering role to magic and religion. This point is central to the ballet, as implied by its title (The Miracle of Anaquillé). The libretto claims a link to medieval miracle plays in which divine intervention remedies misfortune and injustice when saints come to the aid of troubled believers—although in the libretto the assisting divinities are Afro-Cuban. As Rony contends, the depiction of ritual and magic in colonialist cinema served to reinforce the savage image of the natives.[60] From the perspective of Western modernity, the invocations and divinations of Africans were nothing more than obscurantism. Accordingly, the Business Man sees in the Abakuá ceremony only a futile cult that suits his plans for a colorful film scene. But this contemptuous view of Afro-Cuban religion carries deadly consequences. The filmmaker's profanation of the ritual unleashes magical forces that seal his fate. In Unruh's interpretation, the triumphant intervention of the Twin deities amounts to a statement about the superior cultural value of authentic Afro-Cuban religion in relationship to the falsehood and sterility of colonialist cinema.[61] But the significance of this gesture is also political. What in colonialist discourse denoted atavistic behavior ranking low in the scale of cultural evolution, in *Milagro* becomes a fantastic element that endows the subaltern subject with the power to affirm his culture and sovereignty.[62] This aspect of the libretto prefigured the political, *real maravilloso* theme of Carpentier's novel *El reino de este mundo* (1949)—in which runaway slave Mackandal appears to have the power to change shape into an animal and use this supernatural gift to promote slave rebellion during the Haitian Revolution.

Milagro's revisionism of colonialist discourse extends beyond the sphere of cinema. It also targets ballet's own relationship with exotica. Before becoming an iconic institution of the avant-garde, Les Ballets Russes had achieved much of its fame thanks to peculiar embodiments of orientalism. The troupe's Slavic dancers were in and of themselves exotic for Parisian audiences who saw in Russians a people from outside the cultural confines of Europe, hailing from the continent's borderland with Asia. Furthermore, the ensemble's early repertoire showcased lurid spectacles noted for their representations of the "Orient" such as *Cléopâtre* (1909), *Schéhérazade* (1910), *Thamar* (1912), and *Le Dieu bleu* (1912). Archetypically, *Schéhérazade*'s story, taken from *The Arabians Nights*, took place in a harem. Bakst's decadent decors and risqué costumes (fig. 4), Fokine's fleshly choreography, and Nikolai Rimsky-Korsakov's voluptuous music reiterated Orientalist commonplaces of sexual hedonism and bacchanalian excess. The ballet's attraction rested on erotic imagery whose performance was permissible only if marked as exotic behavior. In Orientalist fashion, Les Ballet Russes's performance of sexual desire attributed a reprehensible morality not to the European spectators for whose pleasure it was intended, but to the fictional Asian bodies of the narrative.[63] An article from 1929 sheds light on Carpentier's disapproving outlook on such racialization of non-European

FIGURE 4. *Schéhérazade.* Designs by Léon Bakst. Souvenir program of Les Ballets Russes, Paris Opera (May 26, 1914). Bibliothèque National de France

subjects. Reacting to this brand of ballet, Carpentier eloquently stated that the time was past for productions in which "décors and dancers swam in a golden sauce of orientalism." He rejected a formula marked by "an invasion of silver turbans and indigo negroes, seraglios and temples, Samarkand envoys and Persian pointed sleepers, unrestrained exoticism and all the colors of the palette." He welcomed, as an alternative, Les Ballets Russes's embrace of futurism, cubism, and other avant-garde trends.[64]

Just as Les Ballets Russes's output had transitioned from exotica to avant-gardism, Carpentier's own ballet projects quickly evolved from the postcard style of *La rebambaramba* to the astringent aesthetic of *Milagro*. Predating *Milagro* by one year, *La rebambaramba* features characters, situations, staging indications, and choreographic scenarios that fall under the picturesque style of Cuban *costumbrismo*. Through the magnification of local color, that libretto parallels the exotic character of Orientalist ballet. It seduces with its vibrant views of Havana's colonial architecture, flamboyant recreation of an Afro-Cuban carnival, and sexually alluring mixed-race female protagonist. It must be noted, however, that under its glossy postcard surface *La rebambaramba* embeds a critique of the ideologies of patriarchy, racism, and colonialism of Spanish-ruled nineteenth-century Cuba.[65] With *Milagro*, Carpentier proposed an interpretation of ballet that, while maintaining a political orientation, jettisoned facile exoticism and embraced an experimental aesthetic.

A declaration by Roldán illuminates the discarding of exoticism as more than an adjustment of the librettist and composer to the evolving stylistic paradigms of ballet. Their decision evinced a political response to another manifestation of the problematic link between coloniality and exotica: the classification of non-Western artists as purveyors of the exotic. Roldán struggled with the fact that in Europe his music was primarily appreciated for its colorful quality. He complained, "The music [from the Americas] up to now has been accepted in Europe mainly upon the basis of its outlandish flavor [. . .] with the accommodating smile with which grown people face a child's mischief, without giving it any real importance." In view of this, the musician clarified that a distinctive feature of his symphonic works, the integration of Afro-Cuban instruments, had a purpose more ambitious than producing a colorful sound. In his opinion, using those instruments to obtain "an easy local color" was not "artistically serious." He defended incorporating them in the orchestra, instead, for their richness of sonority and rhythmic precision, which highlights an experimental ethos in line with the modernist expansion of form and technique, as well as with the avant-gardist embrace of popular culture. Roldán asked that his music be judged "not on account of its exotic qualities," but by the same standards of compositional originality applied to European artists.[66] Seen in this light, *Milagro* was a defiant gesture to any international expectations that Latin American artists limited themselves to producing colorful vignettes of their milieu. The librettist and composer's appropriation of the artistic tools of the avant-garde proved that Latin Americans could operate on the same cutting-edge terms as Europeans rather than confine themselves to reproducing the conventional images that the metropolis associated with their region.

What is more, *Milagro* avails itself of the artistic devices of the avant-garde to launch its attack on the production of exotica. Taking an antipodal stance against realism and naturalism, avant-garde art generated nonrealist forms of representing the world, such as cubism, that brought attention to the inner workings and artifice of all artistic representation. For audiences, this entailed taking critical distance from the artwork as an image of life and, thus, interrogating the methods and intention of artistic representation. Unruh demonstrates that such capacity of avant-garde art for examining the representational process proved to be extremely attractive for those Latin American artists invested, for reasons ranging from the purely aesthetic to the overtly political, in producing a critical discourse of the aesthetic and ideological establishment.[67] Operating in this manner, *Milagro* seeks to expose the fabricated character of the exotic representations of the racial other in colonialist cultural production. At first glance, the picturesque *zapateo* of the farmers and spectacular dances of the Abakuá might have seemed choreographic equivalents of Orientalist ballet and colonialist cinema for a hypothetical spectator. Yet *Milagro*'s avant-garde aesthetic disrupts this view by pointing to the performativity of exotica. The projected decors situate the Cuban dances in a strange environment of expressionist, futurist, and surrealist fixtures that destabilizes any illusion of realism. The set, with its flattened sugarcane field, disproportionate sugar mill, and nonsensical skyscraper, would have made the spectator aware of the incongruity between things and their artistic images, of the disparity between reality and its theatrical rendition. Placed in this context of theatrical artifice, the exoticism of dance and dancers would have appeared, too, as stylized performance, as yet another manipulation of reality through art. This was precisely the premise behind avant-garde ballet's approach to folkloric material, as explained by Lynn Garafola. Those works from the post-Orientalist phase of Les Ballets Russes such as *Chout* (1921) and *Le Renard* (1922) that incorporated folklore (specifically, Russian folklore) placed emphasis on situating the ethnic material not as an actual representation of reality but as a product of a primitivist imagination to be observed through ironic distancing.[68]

The presentation of the Abakuá ritual within a metatheatrical framework permits *Milagro* to address in an even more transparent fashion the questions of how exotica is constructed, what relationship it holds to reality, and how colonialist cultural production represents the racial other.[69] Through the adoption of this favorite resource of avant-garde performance (another nod to *Parade*, which also deployed metatheater), Carpentier shows his adeptness at promoting critical spectatorship. The presence of the filmmaker's camera makes the

Abakuá ceremony appear as theater within the theater or, more exactly, a potential movie scene within a ballet. In a classic alienation effect, á la Bertolt Brecht, the libretto generates two perspectives of the ritual and presses the audience into contemplating the difference between both: the ritual itself, as hypothetically performed in an authentic setting, and its (mis)representation through the lens of the camera. Such metatheatrical staging prompts spectators to imagine the transformation of the religious event into screen entertainment, and to consider the manipulation of the black dancers as an exotic human backdrop for ridiculous North American actors in a grass skirt and a tiger skin. *Milagro* forcefully denaturalizes the spectacle of exoticism in the film scene envisioned by the Business Man.

Staging an Afro-Cuban Ritual: The Politics of Ethnography

As much as avant-garde art postulated nonrealist representation, in *Milagro* the intended contrast between an Abakuá ceremony and what would have been its Tarzanesque rendition rested on a realist staging of the ritual. It was by attempting a truthful recreation of the ceremony that Carpentier and Roldán could set themselves apart from filmmakers and choreographers who caricaturized non-European dance expressions. Accordingly, an extensive two-year period of dedicated research anteceded their work on the ballet. Starting in 1925, and following in the footsteps of Cuban anthropologist Fernando Ortiz, the librettist and composer studied black music and dance through direct observation.[70] Carpentier's accounts of this research are fragmentary but contain enough details to align it with the emerging practice of ethnographic fieldwork, which Ortiz had pioneered in Cuba almost at the same time that European cultural anthropologists such as Bronislaw Malinowski and Marcel Mauss established participant observation as the core methodology of their discipline.[71] Later in his life, Carpentier frequently reminisced of having attended "countless" Afro-Cuban dance and music events during those years, including rituals in the rural periphery of Havana and ceremonies that unfolded overnight. In these fieldwork activities, he was accompanied by Ortiz or Roldán (the musician took copious notes with the purpose of capturing motifs for his scores and developing an accurate system for transcribing the ways of beating, shaking, and scraping the various Afro-Cuban percussion instruments).[72] As part of his research, Carpentier also worked with informants. He referred to having visited at least two Abakuá priests in their homes: one in the town of Regla, across the bay from Havana, and another one in a remote mountainous spot in the Santiago de Cuba region.[73]

Casting Carpentier in the role of anthropologist might appear far-fetched. However, as Anke Birkenmaier and Emily Maguire have established, ethnography occupied a pivotal place in the writer's early production.[74] Ultimately,

Carpentier led a monumental career in journalism, literature, and criticism next to which his ethnographic endeavors stood as short lived, apparently negligible efforts of youth. From a contemporary perspective, they appear to be a dilettante's work: undertaken without rigorous training, lacking precise methods, and oriented toward artistic rather than scientific production. But Carpentier was active in this field during a period, from the mid-1920s to the mid-1930s, when conducting ethnographic research did not necessarily presuppose having acquired the formal instruction that later came to be associated with the academic discipline of cultural anthropology. James Clifford rightly observes that at the time cultural anthropology had yet to achieve the status of a social science with distinct research methods.[75] The training and methodologies of contemporary Cuban ethnographers corresponded with this. Ortiz, whose professional training had been as a lawyer, was a self-taught ethnographer. So was Lydia Cabrera, an artist by training who during those years overlapped with Carpentier at Afro-Cuban rituals and more than two decades later made fundamental contributions to the documentation of Afro-Cuban religion with her books *El Monte* (1954) and *La sociedad secreta Abakuá* (1958).[76] In this regard, what looks like amateurism in Carpentier's anthropological work was, to an important extent, a reflection of historical limitations of the discipline, to which, as Maguire indicates, he and other Cuban ethnographers responded with necessarily experimental approaches.[77]

Carpentier's experimentation was palpable in the varied outcomes of his anthropological research. On the one hand, he wrote strictly ethnographic and musicological texts about aspects of Afro-Cuban culture and, particularly, the Abakuá. The articles in this category—"Lettre des Antilles" (1929), "La musique cubaine" (1929), "Cuban Magic" (1930), and "Images et Prières Nègres" (1933)—appeared in international periodicals that customarily featured ethnography alongside fiction, journalism, and criticism.[78] On the other hand, his anthropological work also took the form of literary texts that approached the black themes typical of *afrocubanismo* through the lens of avant-garde aesthetics. The best known among these works is the novel *Écue-Yamba-Ó* (1933), which, as Birkenmaier argues, followed an ethnographic model of writing visible in the strong impetus to document Afro-Cuban culture through both descriptions and photographs.[79] Similarly, Thomas Anderson details that knowledge acquired in fieldwork found expression in a handful of poems that Carpentier authored early in his career, including "Liturgia" and "Juego santo," both from 1927, which evoked the images and sounds of Abakuá celebrations.[80] As part of this group of anthropologically inspired literary products, *Milagro* holds certain cues for assessing the level of exhaustiveness and even pioneer character of Carpentier's ethnographic studies, while also contributing a rare glimpse into the fraught relationship between the anthropologist and the subjects he observed in fieldwork. An examination of the ballet from these perspectives clarifies certain aspects of the anthropological work of Carpentier and, by extension, the other ethnographers of afrocubanismo.

The issue of achieving accuracy in the choreographic recreation of the Abakuá ritual is key to appraising the significance of *Milagro*, concerned as this project was with critiquing filmic and balletic distortions of non-European cultures. Later in life, Carpentier famously disavowed the representations of black traditions in his texts from the 1920s and early 1930s. He acknowledged that his ethnographic observations had been incomplete and that his understanding of certain Afro-Cuban cultural expressions was often erroneous. He explained that, not just for him but also for Ortiz and other ethnographers, researching the field of Afro-Cuban music, dance, and religion meant charting unexplored terrain, trying to understand traditions on which no scientific work had been previously done. Offering an example of the limitations of that work, Carpentier conceded that the music of Roldán was an inaccurate ethnographic record. In his scores, "the elements of that vast sonority of the Afro-Cuban realm are all mixed together" without distinction between a Yoruba hymn and an Abakuá ceremonial dance.[81] Carpentier also recognized the imperfectness of his own portrayal of Afro-Cuban traditions in *Écue-Yamba-Ó*: "Everything that was deep, truthful and universal about the world that I tried to depict in the novel had remained outside the scope of my observation."[82]

Compounded with the disciplinary limitations of early twentieth-century ethnography, this negative self-assessment reinforces the disqualifying perceptions of Carpentier's anthropological work as inept or of limited value. Yet *Milagro* attests to the librettist's desire for exhaustiveness in documenting the Abakuá ritual of initiation. Even if in retrospect he denied the validity of his research, Carpentier asserted that the descriptions of Abakuá rituals in *Milagro* and *Écue-Yamba-Ó* were, in fact, precise representations of ceremonies he had observed. His self-acknowledged failure to fully understand the cosmology and culture that those rituals encapsulated did not preclude him from accurately recording the events' structure, participants, dances, liturgical objects, and other formal elements. In the preface accompanying the publication of the ballet libretto in 1937, he affirmed that *Milagro* had incorporated, "without any modifications, the choreographic ritual of [Abakuá] initiation ceremonies." He ratified this idea in the preface to the 1977 reprint of *Écue-Yamba-Ó*, in which he stood by the description of the Abakuá ceremony in the novel: "While not aspiring to be scientific, [it] reflects reality quite accurately."[83] In fact, the portrayal of the ritual in the libretto closely corresponds with Cabrera's detailed documentation of the Abakuá initiation rite.[84] Carpentier did not record the totality of the ceremony, which extends for almost a full day and, for the most part, is open only to members of Abakuá groups. Instead, the ballet depicts the one section of the ritual that an outsider like Carpentier could have observed: the dances leading to the communion meal, which are performed in public. In essence, the scene in *Milagro* is similar to the performance of those dances as described in Cabrera's study, although Carpentier presents them in a schematic manner that obeys to a libretto's demand for synthesis. Keeping this in mind, the discrepancies between the two accounts are minor and could be understood as a result of the distinct aim of each text and the different scope of their supporting fieldwork—Cabrera's text is scholarly in nature and she authored it after more than two decades studying the ritual.[85]

In contrast to the textual accounts of the ritual in Carpentier's ethnographic articles and first novel, the ballet libretto proposes an experiment in staging the ceremony. Even though literary documentation could prove more permanent than a transient work for the stage, performance held the promise of capturing the ritual holistically by integrating dance, gesture, music, and costumes. In 1927, this was a revolutionary proposition that augured the research-to-performance ethnography of African diaspora traditions established by Zora Neale Hurston with *The Great Day* (1932) and Katherine Dunham with *L'Ag'Ya* (1938)—respective stagings of the Bahamian and Martinican dances that these anthropologists assiduously studied.[86] Like Hurston and Dunham, who sought to cast their works with Caribbean dancers, Carpentier aimed to integrate native performers in the production of the ballet.[87] He envisioned a staging not with professional performers, but actual "dancers from the people, knowledgeable of the folkloric rituals [and] capable of dancing what they knew through ancestral tradition."[88] Admittedly, this proposition conformed to practical considerations about producing the ballet in a country where there were no professional dance ensembles. Engaging black performers would have been opportune, too, to compensate for Carpentier's lack of mastery of the liturgical dances—which he had observed but not physically learned. However, regardless of its practical nature, such solution strategically advanced the ballet's stance against the colonialist representation of non-Western cultures. The librettist must have understood how employing a cast of knowledgeable Afro-Cuban dancers could bring into relief the contrast between a living black tradition and the portrayal of this type of event in colonialist cultural production.

In her study of Hurston's *The Great Day*, Anthea Kraut takes stock of some of the challenges in research-to-performance ethnography. To be dealt with is the problem of authenticity in representation. Hurston's staging of the Bahamian Fire Dance in *The Great Day* consisted of an ethnographically informed adaptation of the original, which, by force, had to be modified to satisfy the demands of the theatrical medium. The transposition of a nontheatrical performance tradition for the stage requires taking the material out of its original context and extricating it from its social function. In the end, the dances and rituals studied in this manner enter the theater under artistic form, conforming to spatiotemporal conventions and modes of emplotment dictated by a theatrical logic. For an anthropologist in Hurston's situation, who had to assume responsibilities typical of a choreographer, the line between ethnographic documentation and artistic invention got blurred. As far as choreographic credits were a concern, the fact that her staging involved native dancers raised a question about their input in the production, pointing to issues of authorship and ownership. Hurston, who sought to remain as close to the ethnic material as possible, defended the genuineness of the staging. But according to Kraut, her proclamation of authenticity, no matter how bona fide, had a commercialist connotation in that it constituted a strategy for marketing the show. In the end, independent of the production's degree of faithfulness, Hurston possessed limited ability to shape the work's reception: audiences interpreted *The Great Day* in terms of the exoticism and primitivism attributed to black dancing bodies.[89]

Since Carpentier and Roldán did not stage *Milagro*, it is difficult to predict how similar issues would have played out in rehearsals and performances. The libretto and stated production plan, while containing some clues, prompt more questions than answers. Conceptually, however, *Milagro* could offer apt solutions to issues of reception and authenticity. As argued already, the ballet created a model for critical spectatorship of the Abakuá ritual that negated the consumption of this ethnographic material as exotica. At the same time, by framing the ritual within an avant-garde environment that raised awareness of the constructedness of artistic representation, the ballet could circumvent debates about ethnographic authenticity. In fact, it opened the door to discussing the performativity of authenticity in performance-to-research anthropology. Going beyond these points, one may question how the collaboration between the producers and the cast of Afro-Cuban dancers would have unfolded, and, considering Carpentier and Roldán's distinction from the dancers in terms of racial identity and social status, what the politics of their relationship would have been. Without enough information to address these queries in a hypothetical context of rehearsals and performances, one could, instead, consider them in relationship to the librettist and composer's fieldwork.

Paradoxically, Carpentier's quest for accurate information about the Abakuá ritual could hardly take place outside the same matrix of colonialist ideology that *Milagro* condemned. In anthropology, the nexus between the observer and the observed had been traditionally characterized by lopsided power dynamics between educated white scientists from the imperial metropolis and nonwhite natives of the colonies assumed to be rudimentary. In the context of *afrocubanismo*, this asymmetric contact manifested in a divide between white intellectuals representative of the Cuban cultural elite such as Carpentier, Ortiz, and Cabrera, and the marginalized working class Afro-Cubans that they turned into a subject of study. The issue of racial relations lay at the heart of *afrocubanismo*. Through their research and artistic production, members of this movement advocated for rethinking the Cuban nation as a multiracial space inclusive of whites and blacks, and with a hybrid culture rooted both in

Europe and in Africa. However, although clearly questioning racial relations at the scale of nation, these ethnographers and artists' own personal interactions with Afro-Cubans remained unexamined or, at best, elusively documented. The lack of commentary on this matter can be understood as another consequence of the theoretical stage of anthropology in the 1920s and 1930s, when the practice of reflexivity had not yet crystallized into a mechanism for acknowledging and redressing the politically skewed interactions that take place in fieldwork. Maguire rightly observes that the details of participant observation and contact with informants are rare if not inexistent even in Ortiz's texts, despite his status as the most sophisticated of the island's ethnographers at the time.[90] Similarly, the specifics of Carpentier and Roldán's fieldwork interactions are, for the most part, lost to the historical record. In "Images et Prières Nègres," Carpentier hints at the complexity of his racially mediated work with informants, but he takes no more than one sentence to address the thorny issue; he indicates that Abakuá priests in the vicinity of Havana "showed themselves distrustful of whites" interested in studying their religion.[91]

The sparseness of information about interracial tensions in fieldwork makes the more significant an anecdote from the research process for *Milagro* that Carpentier related more than a decade later, in 1939. According to the writer, he and Roldán had shown up to an Abakuá initiation ritual with the purpose of gathering material for the ballet. The composer took copious notes and transcribed musical motifs directly onto music sheets until the performance came to an unexpected halt:

All of a sudden, we noticed that an atmosphere of discomfort and hostility took hold of the festivity. An extraordinary *diablito* in red and blue hid in the *cuarto fambá* [the altar room]. The drums became silent. The worshipers gave us chilling glances.

"What are you writing down?" asked the iyamba, who had seen Roldán at work.

"Nothing . . . The music," the composer replied.

"And what for are you writing the music down?"

"For composing some *danzones*," affirmed Amadeo to avoid getting into a more complex explanation [of plans for a ballet].

But the answer did not satisfy the *obón* [iyamba].

"If you want to avoid a tragedy, put away the notebook and pencil. No one comes here to compose *danzones*."

In spite of the suggestion that we went somewhere else, we stayed at the festivity trying to record the rhythms and words in our brains.[92]

The story sheds light on how ethical problems and disagreements with subjects could mark the fieldwork of ethnographers who studied Afro-Cuban ceremonials. The incident captured in the anecdote was not an isolated example. Elsewhere Carpentier noted that frictions about data collection emerged repeatedly: "As we have experienced on *many occasions*, [the Abakuá] oppose the notation or phonographic recording of their ritual music, which they consider a profanation of their secrets."[93] While in his anecdote Carpentier made no reference to the racial and social rift that informed the conflict, it is implicit that such separation was at the heart of it. In more than one way, he and Roldán stood out as strangers among what was, in all likelihood, an assembly of working-class Afro-Cubans. Racial distinctions were prominent. Of French and Russian ancestry, Carpentier was white. And Roldán, the son of a Spaniard and a mixed-race Cuban woman, had fair skin that allowed him to pass as white. Their status as intellectuals with an education strongly rooted in European culture further distanced them from a popular community that practiced an African-rooted religion. Homeschooled by his foreign parents, Carpentier spoke French and, as detailed earlier, was well versed in European literature, music, and art. Meanwhile, Roldán had enjoyed extensive training as a violinist in the Madrid Conservatory. Even in terms of nationality the writer and the composer contrasted with the Abakuá group. Carpentier had been born in Lausanne and Roldán in Madrid. Judging from the testimony of literary critic Juan Marinello, some of Carpentier's contemporaries saw him more as Franco-Cuban than as integrally Cuban.[94] Roldán's national identity could have been perceived as equally undefined. Having grown up in Spain, he had lived in Cuba for only eight years by the time the episode took place.[95]

It is remarkable how much Carpentier and Roldán's field-work anecdote resembled the confrontation of the US filmmaker and the Afro-Cuban worshippers in *Milagro*. Analogously to the characters of the ballet, the participants in the anecdote were set apart by the marked differences of racial identity and social status pointed above. Both in real life and in the libretto those differences informed relations of power and resistance between the involved actors. Carpentier and Roldán, as the filmmaker, recorded the Abakuá ritual without consent and, even after a warning from the priest, insisted on doing so. Also as the filmmaker, they sought to appropriate elements of the ritual for an artistic enterprise of their own, a ballet that, not unlike the North American's movie, put forward a representation of Afro-Cubans by outsiders. Meanwhile, the iyamba, as the priest in the ballet, resisted the intruders' observation and threatened them with violent retaliation. The close parallel between the field-work incident and the scene in the libretto strongly supports the notion that real-life experience inspired *Milagro*, which complicates an interpretation of the ballet as a critique of coloniality. How is it possible to reconcile *Milagro*'s denunciation of the colonialist discourse of racial otherness with its own reproduction of colonialist dynamics in fieldwork? Given the resemblance between the actions of the fictional filmmaker and those of the authors of the ballet, it seems evident that Carpentier wrote the libretto with an understanding of the similarities between colonialist cinema and anthropology. Not just an archetype of a certain class of filmmaker, the Business Man stood, too, as an avatar of Carpentier and Roldán in their roles as ethnographers. By assigning such dual identity to a character constructed as an anti-hero, the librettist hinted at the ethically problematic overlap between the behavior of the filmmaker and the practices of ethnographers.

Similarly to the travelogue, safari, and explorer genres in cinema, anthropology had developed in dialogue with imperialist history. Victorian explorers, missionaries, and government officials such as George Grey, Thomas Williams, and Francis Galton, who acted as propagators of British imperialism, produced accounts of African, Australian, and Polynesian cultures that gave fodder to the theories of racial determinism and social evolutionism that came to dominate anthropological theory in the nineteenth century.[96] Born from the colonialist enterprise, those theories, in turn, lent themselves to legitimizing European colonial ruling as an expression of the alleged superiority of Europeans, or as part of a civilizationist project directed to the supposed advancement of those societies deemed barbaric and inferior.[97] In disciplinary terms, the same logic normalized the ethnographer's position of superiority in relation to the groups he studied. Only a few years before the creation of *Milagro* had anthropology begun to abandon the evolutionist and eugenicist theories that posited the cultural and racial supremacy of Europeans. This shift had started at the turn of the century with Franz Boas's proposition that societies should be analyzed through the lens of their own history and culture, which implied the dislodging of Eurocentric perspectives from anthropological research. In a corollary of it, fieldwork emerged as the essential methodology of cultural anthropology. Through systematic participant observation, as Malinowski demonstrated in *Argonauts of the Western Pacific* (1922), ethnographers could achieve a detailed understanding of other cultures and the natives' own points of view. The transformation in anthropological paradigms outlined here found expression in the study of black culture in Cuba, something patent in the reorientation of Ortiz's research over the initial decades of the new century. From having first examined black culture from a criminological standpoint that linked Afro-Cuban religion to illegal behavior in *Los negros brujos* (1906), Ortiz moved toward affirming the value of Afro-Cuban culture in his works on music from the 1920s to the 1930s, and overtly negating racism and the very concept of race a decade later in *El engaño de las razas* (1946).

The contradiction between *Milagro*'s indictment of the Business Man and Carpentier and Roldán's own fieldwork practices could be understood against this background of shifting anthropological principles. Proceeding in tandem, the repudiation of Eurocentrism and the endorsement of fieldwork pointed to an eventual revolution in the politics of participant observation. To conduct fieldwork while negating Eurocentrism would mean, ultimately, renouncing colonialist ideology and, therefore, questioning the position of power of ethnographers relative to the subjects they observed. But such postcolonial conception of fieldwork, which would take decades to evolve, remained unformulated at the time that Carpentier and Roldán studied the Abakuá rituals, between 1925 and 1927. By then, the professionalization of participant observation had merely begun with Malinowski's publication of *Argonauts* in 1922 and Mauss's inception of the Institut d'Ethnologie in Paris in 1925. *Milagro* was typical of this transitional moment. It shared the Boasian opposition to the representation of non-Western cultures from a Eurocentric standpoint—expressed as primitivism and exoticism in cinema.[98] At the same time, the ballet reflected the incomplete development of fieldwork procedures that constituted an alternative to colonialist ethnography. Seen in the context of Cuban anthropology, *Milagro* evinced, too, signs of transition. Expectedly, since Carpentier and Roldán entered ethnography under Ortiz's guide, the ballet was indicative of the shift from criminology to cultural anthropology in the study of Afro-Cuban traditions. In similar fashion, the librettist and composer's ethnographic methods were idiosyncratic of the 1920s in that their problematic limitations revealed how far Cuban anthropologists still were from establishing a radical critique of racism of the sort that Ortiz articulated in the 1940s.

Locating Carpentier and Roldán's ethnography in a context of critical changeover in anthropology does not seek to justify the questionable interactions described in their fieldwork anecdote. However, this contextualization illuminates the historical significance of a libretto that recognizes the problematic resemblance between the modus operandi of the Business Man and colonialist practices in ethnography. In itself, such an acknowledgment evidenced shifting values in anthropology by suggesting the ethical invalidity of ethnographers' authoritarian treatment of subaltern groups. To this extent, *Milagro* embedded a provocative if veiled commentary on ethnography. Written with awareness of the politics of fieldwork, the libretto did not go as far as making them explicit for a general audience. Carpentier's anecdote, published thirteen years after the genesis of the ballet, illuminated those politics only in retrospect. Had the ballet been staged at the time of its conception, most spectators would have missed its allegory of ethnography, but not those figures of *afrocubanismo* who engaged in fieldwork. Researchers like Ortiz and Cabrera, and artists who frequented Afro-Cuban rituals in search of material for their nationalist artworks, would have grasped the parallel between their ethnographic activities and the Business Man's actions. In other words, *Milagro* invited a reflection on the ideological underpinnings of fieldwork among precisely those who should consider them critically. Inasmuch as the field of anthropology had not yet developed a theory of reflexivity and postcolonial critiques of its practices, it is notable that a novice ethnographer's ballet libretto hinted at the racial tensions and conflicting interests that characterized the contact with subjects. *Milagro* could be seen as a seminal point in Carpentier's trajectory toward articulating more explicit postcolonial assessments of anthropology—which manifested, eventually, in the already cited critiques of documentaries on Mexico and Africa, as well as in his later disavowal of his own ethnographic work.

As Carpentier and Roldán's proposition in avant-garde ballet, *El milagro de anaquillé* constituted a gesture to bring Cuban artistic production up to date with cutting-edge artistic trends that had recently flourished in Europe. On the surface, the librettist and composer's embrace of ballet and avant-gardism appeared to reiterate a Eurocentric logic by which Latin American artists and nations ought to follow aesthetic dictates and definitions of development from Old World metropolises. However, *Milagro* evidenced the much more complex and critical relationship of the region's artists to discourses of Eurocentrism and coloniality. For Carpentier and Roldán, adopting avant-garde vocabularies served a purpose larger than catching up with the latest artistic innovations from Europe. For them, the disruptive techniques of avant-garde art, so well suited for interrogating reality and the very same process of artistic signification, became a toolkit for producing a political piece that questioned Western representations of cultural and racial otherness. By showcasing these authors' adept manipulation of the elements of avant-garde ballet, theater, and music in function of an incisive critique of colonialist spectacles of primitivism and exotica, *Milagro* also opposed pre-established assumptions about the scope of Latin American artistic production. Carpentier and Roldán claimed for themselves the status of modernizers commonly reserved for artists from European cultural centers, while rejecting any colonialist expectations on Latin American artists to produce works that reinscribed the assumed exoticism of the region. Similarly, the ballet contested the geographically and racially pre-assigned classifications of civilization and barbarity in the colonialist discourse of European cultural domination.

Milagro reflected profound artistic and political transformations in Cuba and abroad at the time of its creation, sometimes in pioneer fashion. Not only did the piece spearhead the espousal of avant-gardism among the island's artists; it was also an early expression of the cultural production of *afrocubanismo*. At the same time, it channeled the peaking anti-imperialist sentiment and protest of US interventionism among the Cuban intelligentsia at the time. Furthermore, *Milagro* illustrated cinema's popularization and conversion into the preeminent medium for reproducing narratives of primitivism and exotica, while also standing as a manifest to the growing opposition of Latin American intellectuals to the latter phenomenon. Moreover, Carpentier and Roldán's project attested to ballet's creative resurgence, shift from exotica to avant-gardism, and international proliferation in the early twentieth century. Finally, *Milagro* remains a testament to historic reformations in the arena of cultural anthropology. As such, it embodied the contradictions that marked a period of change in that discipline. Carpentier and Roldán's fieldwork study of

Afro-Cuban rituals corresponded with the ascendance of participant observation as a data-collection method, while their ballet prefigured the research-to-performance approach to ethnography. In exposing and mocking the Western construction of non-Western exoticism, their proposed staging of the Abakuá ceremony coincided with the Boasian turn in anthropology, which spurned Eurocentric biases in the interpretation of cultures. But even as anthropologists were beginning to rebuff colonialist theories of social evolutionism and racial determinism, the creators of *Milagro* could not fully overcome ethico-political faults rooted in the supremacy of the ethnographer in colonialist anthropology. Positioned by their racial identity and social status in a hegemonic relation vis-à-vis Afro-Cuban subjects, Carpentier and Roldán banked in on this lopsided dynamic to gather material for the ballet. And yet the questionable character of this form of anthropological authority did not escape the author of the libretto. Self-criticism, expressed in the text's veiled parallel between an unscrupulous filmmaker and an ethnographer, did not redeem Carpentier and Roldán's research tactics but, in keeping with the pioneer character of the ballet, opened the door to reflecting on the power disparities of fieldwork.

NOTES

This study was supported through fellowships from the National Endowment for the Humanities and Harvard University's David Rockefeller Center for Latin American Studies. Grants from Smith College provided additional support for research trips to Havana. I thank these institutions for their funding. I also thank Graciela Pogolotti, Rafael Rodríguez Beltrán, Armando Raggi, and Xonia Jiménez from the Fundación Alejo Carpentier for facilitating my access to the author's papers and other archival materials. I am grateful too for the valuable feedback received from this journal's anonymous reviewers and colleagues at the Boston Workshop for Historians of Latin America and the Caribbean, led by Kirsten Weld. Additionally, I am indebted to Lynn Garafola and Justin Crumbaugh for exchanges on topics related to this article.

1. A. Carpentier, "Un ballet afrocubano," *Revista Cubana* (Havana) 8, nos. 22–24 (April–June 1937): 145–154.

2. See R. Moore, *Nationalizing Blackness: Afrocubanismo and Artistic Revolution in Havana, 1920–1940* (Pittsburgh, PA: University of Pittsburgh Press, 1997).

3. "Declaración del Grupo Minorista," *Social* (Havana), June 1927, 7.

4. A. Carpentier, "El recuerdo de Amadeo Roldán," *Carteles* (Havana), June 4, 1939, reproduced in *Obras completas* (Mexico City: Siglo XXI, 1986), 9:426.

5. Carpentier is quoted in P. Tovar, "Ideas y sonidos de Alejo Carpentier: La danza de las palabras," in *Alejo carpentier: América, la imagen de una conjunción* (Barcelona: Anthropos, 2004), 55.

6. In attributing a postcolonial character to *Milagro*, this article connotes a critical relationship to coloniality not merely in terms of Cuba's political status as a former colony of Spain—or a neocolony of the United States at the time of the libretto's creation. Rather, the term *postcolonial* is used to define opposition to what Aníbal Quijano calls "coloniality of power": a long-lasting global social order and hierarchical system of cultural and racial classification that, having transcended the politico-territorial domination of colonies and neocolonies under European colonialism and Western imperialism, continues to situate certain nations, cultures, and racially defined groups in

relationships of subordination to Europe and the West. A. Quijano, "Coloniality and Modernity/ Rationality," *Cultural Studies* 21, nos. 2–3 (2007), 168–171.

7. Establishing a historical and aesthetic distinction between modernism and avant-gardism aids in clarifying the nomenclature followed in this article. Given that modernism comprehends avant-gardism, a distinction could be debatable and the elements of any given ballet (i.e., choreography, music, libretto, sets, and costumes) could be labeled individually as modernist or avant-gardist. In general, I consider avant-garde ballets those that espoused cubism, futurism, surrealism, constructivism, and other radical artistic trends that flourished in Europe beginning around 1910 and extending into the 1930s. Almost all works of Les Ballets Suédois fall in this category, as do several of the works of Les Ballets Russes after World War I. Meanwhile, modernist ballet is a broader field that includes such cutting-edge pieces as well as other works that, despite being revolutionary for their time, were not as radical in their break with tradition. Most of the prewar primitivist and neo-romantic repertoire of Les Ballets Russes exemplifies a modernist sensibility distinguishable from avant-garde radicalism. Even though distinctions between modernism and avant-gardism are specific to genre, for the sake of consistency here I follow a similar criterion (based on historical periodization and degree of aesthetic radicalism) to differentiate between modernist and avant-garde art, theater, and music. Carpentier expressed interest in both modernist and avant-garde artistic production, but it was the latter that he found the most fascinating.

8. In Janney's opinion, *Milagro* introduces a construction of archetypal characters that embody the collective, manifest in Carpentier's novels. F. Janney, *Alejo Carpentier and His Early Works* (London: Tamesis Books), 26–32; and V. Unruh, *Latin American Vanguards: The Art of Contentious Encounters* (Berkeley: University of California Press, 1994), 64–66.

9. Unruh, *Latin American Vanguards*, 2–3, 8.

10. Carpentier's poems "Liturgia," "Marisabel," and "Juego santo" were musicalized by García Caturla in 1928. That same year, Carpentier and the French composer Marius-François Gaillard created *Yamba-O*, a *tragédie burlesque* for voices and orchestra, followed in 1929 by *Poèmes des Antilles*, a cycle of nine songs for soprano and piano. A third collaboration with Gaillard resulted in *La Passion noire* (1931), an oratorio for vocal soloists, chorus, and large orchestra with an Afro-Cuban percussion section. Additionally, Carpentier worked with Edgar Varèse in *Canción de la niña enferma de fiebre* (1930) for soprano and orchestra. Together with Robert Desnos, he devised the libretto for another piece by Varèse: *The One All Alone*, an ambitious surrealist work for the stage that the composer did not complete. During this same period, Carpentier also wrote the libretto for the comic opera for puppets *Manita en el suelo* (1937), whose scoring Roldán did for the most part, but without finishing it before his death. Carpentier's final musical project, with Milhaud, was *Incantations* (1939), for unaccompanied male voices. For an analysis of this body of work, see A. Birkenmaier, *Alejo Carpentier y la cultura del surrealismo en América Latina* (Madrid: Iberoamericana-Verveurt, 2006), 181–196; C. Rae, "In Havana and Paris: The musical activities of Alejo Carpentier," *Music & Letters* 89, no. 3 (2008); and T. F. Anderson, *Carnival and National Identity in the Poetry of Afrocubanismo* (Gainesville: Univesity Press of Florida, 2011), 49–78.

11. Unruh, *Latin American Vanguards*, 3, 22–23.

12. Birkenmaier, *Alejo Carpentier*; and E. Maguire, *Racial Experiments in Cuban Literature and Ethnography* (Gainesville: University Press of Florida, 2011).

13. For examples, see A. Carpentier, "La música rusa en París," *Chic* (Havana) 12, no. 96 (August 1923): 30; "Las enseñanzas de Satie," *Chic* 13, no. 105 (May 1924): 34–35; "Cocteau y sus teorías sobre el teatro," *El Heraldo* (Habana), October 7, 1924, 7; "El arte múltiple de Picasso," *Social* 10, no. 9 (September 1925): 29; and "Música nueva: Francis Poulenc," *Diario de la Marina* (Havana), October 23, 1927, 44.

14. Rae, "In Havana and Paris," 378–382.

15. C. Ripoll, "La revista de *Avance* (1927–1930): Vocero de vanguardismo y pórtico de revolución," *Revista Iberoamericana* 30, no. 58 (1964): 261–282.

16. Roldán and García Caturla gained exposure to modernist music through their studies with Spanish conductor Pedro Sanjuán. See H. Orovio, *Cuban music from A to Z* (Durham, NC: Duke University Press, 2004), 90–91, 185.

17. Other Cuban painters who gained familiarity with the new aesthetics were Wifredo Lam (a protégé of Picasso), Amelia Peláez (who studied the work of Picasso, Henri Matisse, and Georges Braque), Carlos Enríquez (who referenced the work of Francisco Picabia), Eduardo Abela (an adept of Marc Chagall), and Marcelo Pogolotti (an affiliate of the futurist group). See M. C., "Exposición Gattorno," *Revista de Avance* 1 (March 15, 1927): 15–16; and J. A. Martínez, *Cuban Art and National Identity: The Vanguardia Painters, 1927–1950* (Gainesville: University Press of Florida, 1994), 5, 14.

18. L. Garafola, "The Making of Ballet Modernism," *Dance Research Journal* 20, no. 2 (1988): 23–32.

19. A. Carpentier, *Recuento de moradas*, section 4, Fundación Alejo Carpentier, http://www.fundacioncarpentier.cult.cu/carpentier/recuento-de-moradas; J. A. González, "El ballet en Cuba hasta 1948," *Cuba en el Ballet* (Havana) 4, no. 3 (September 1973): 45–47; and F. Rey, "Siglo y medio de danza en el Gran Teatro de La Habana," in *Cuba en el Ballet* 7, no. 2 (April–June 1988): 2–9.

20. Carpentier writes about those magazines, but without indicating their names, in a letter from 1929 to his mother, Lina Valmont. A. Carpentier, *Cartas a Toutouche* (Havana: Letras Cubanas, 2010), 154–155.

21. A. Carpentier, "La última labor de Igor Stravinsky," *La Discusión* (Havana), July 15, 1923, 3.

22. A. Carpentier, "Las enseñanzas de Satie"; "El ballet moderno," *Chic* 12, no. 97 (September 1923): 18–19; "Ravel y la música descriptiva," *Chic* 13, no. 102 (February 1924): 34–35; and "Grandeza y decadencia del cubismo," *Chic* 13, no. 108 (August 1924): 36–37.

23. A. Carpentier, "Ordenado, disciplinado, trabajador y consciente," in *Amadeo Roldán: Testimonios*, ed. M. A. Henríquez and J. Piñeiro Díaz (Havana: Letras Cubanas, 2001), 50.

24. As Roberto González Echavarría argues, Carpentier was regarded more as a commentator on the arts than as an artist himself during the initial years of his career. R. González Echavarría, *Alejo Carpentier: el peregrino en su patria* (Madrid: Gredos, 2004), 76. Carpentier's nomination to the Nobel Award is reported in "Alejo Carpentier, propuesto para el Nobel de Literatura," *El País* (Madrid), October 9, 1979.

25. P. de Groote, *Ballets Suédois* (Ghent: Academia Press, 2002), 20–78.

26. Carpentier, "El ballet moderno"; Carpentier, "Actividades artísticas en Europa," *El Heraldo*, October 31, 1924, 7; and Carpentier, "Jean Cocteau y la estética del ambiente," *Social* no. 7 (July 1925): 41, 49, 59, 81.

27. A. Carpentier, "Las enseñanzas del murciélago," *El Heraldo*, November 11, 1924, 7; and "Hacia un teatro sintético cubano," May 22, 1925, reproduced in the website of the Fundación Alejo Carpentier, http://www.fundacioncarpentier.cult.cu/carpentier/hacia-un-teatro-sint%C3%A9tico-cubano, accessed July 17, 2015.

28. A. Carpentier to A. García Caturla, March 15, 1927, in *Obras completas* (Mexico City: Siglo XXI, 1983), 1:281–282.

29. When the information is available, I date Carpentier's librettos according to the year when he wrote them. Other studies have dated them by the year when the music was composed, published, or premiered, or when the librettos appeared in print. In his notes to the program for Ramiro Guerra's production of the ballet, Carpentier indicates that he penned *La rebambaramba* in 1926. In the same program, he states that *El milagro de anaquillé* dates from 1927. See Conjunto de Danza Moderna, *Auto sacramental, Suite Yoruba, El milagro de anaquillé, Concerto grosso, La rebambaramba*, souvenir program for performances on January 25, 1962, Teatro Nacional de Cuba, Havana.

33. For the libretto of *La rebambaramba* and my analysis of it, see A. Carpentier, *La rebambaramba*, in *Obras Completas*, 1:195–207; and L. Tomé, "Envisioning a Cuban Ballet: Afrocubanismo, Nationalism and Political Commentary in Alejo Carpentier and Amadeo Roldán's *La rebambaramba*," *Dance Research Journal of Korea* 71, no. 5 (2013): 157–181.

31. See A. Piñeiro, "Alejo Carpentier: Todo en la danza le fue cercano," *Cuba en el Ballet*, no. 94 (May–December 1999): 40–47.

32. A. Carpentier, *La hija del ogro*, ballet libretto, file MFP3, nos. 1–3, Fundación Alejo Carpentier.

33. Carpentier, "Un ballet afrocubano."

34. Frank Janney includes *Azúcar* and *Mata-cangrejo* in his bibliography of Carpentier's works, but it remains unclear whether the author ever completed these librettos. Janney, *Alejo Carpentier*, 133.

35. Letters exchanged between 1928 and 1931 confirm that Carpentier did not complete the libretto for *El embó*. When in 1931 the writer finally submitted a finished text to García Caturla, the project had metamorphosed into the comic opera for puppets *Manita en el suelo*. See García Caturla's letters from November 3, 1928, and April 29, 1931, and Carpentier's letters from July 6, 1931, and August 16, 1931, in A. Carpentier, *Obras completas*, 1:288, 294–300.

36. In later years, Carpentier would author three other ballet librettos. He wrote *Romeo y Julieta* and *Casa de baile* for composer Hilario González, who dates their collaboration to 1942. Both texts have been preserved, in addition to an untitled ballet libretto from 1960 allegorical of the history of Cuba since its colonization to the Revolution. See *Casa de baile*, folder 55; "Notas para ballet" [*Romeo y Julieta*], folder 194; and "Un ballet inédito, 1960," folder 41, in Fundación Alejo Carpentier. See also H. González, "Alejo Carpentier: precursor del 'movimiento' afrocubano," preface to A. Carpentier, *Obras completas*, 1:14–17; and L. Tomé, "Regreso al ballet: Un libreto de Alejo Carpentier," in *Cuba en el Ballet*, no. 125 (January–April 2013): 47–52.

37. Carpentier to A. García Caturla, March 15, 1927.

38. Tomé, "Envisioning a Cuban Ballet."

39. Carpentier to A. García Caturla, March 15, 1927.

40. Alberto Alonso produced *La rebambaramba* for the Havana television station CMQ-TV. The ballet aired on September 13, 1957. Ramiro Guerra staged *Milagro* with the National Theatre's Modern Dance Ensemble, also in Havana. It premiered on July 1, 1960. Guerra also choreographed *La rebambaramba* for that troupe, a production that was first seen on February 18, 1961. See Piñeiro "Alejo Carpentier," 42–43.

41. A. Carpentier, *La música en Cuba* (Mexico City: Fondo de Cultura Económica, 1946), 236, 252.

42. Citation from the English edition. A. Carpentier, *Music in Cuba*, trans. A. West-Duran (Minneapolis: University of Minnesota Press, 2001), 273.

43. A. Carpentier, "La evolución estética de los Ballets Rusos," *Social* 14, no. 4 (April 4, 1929): 37–39.

44. Carpentier, "Las enseñanzas de Satie" and "Grandeza y decadencia del cubismo." See also Carpentier, "Cocteau y sus teorías sobre el teatro"; "Jean Cocteau y la estética del ambiente"; "El arte múltiple de Picasso"; "Los dibujos de Jean Cocteau," *Chic* 15, no. 126 (February 1926): 16–17; and "Erick Satie, profeta y renovador," *Social* 12, no. 9 (September 1927): 28, 88.

45. The typed text, in the holdings of the Fundación Alejo Carpentier, lacks any indication of date and publication outlet. Its tone, similar to that of articles from 1924 to 1926 in which Carpentier's discussion of avant-garde art is well informed but still tentative, allows for dating it as one of those early texts. A. Carpentier, "El teatro futurista," file MPF5, nos. 1–3, Fundación Alejo Carpentier.

46. Guillaume Apollinaire authored the program notes upon witnessing rehearsals of the ballet. See the appendix with his text in D. Rothschild, *Picasso's "Parade": From Street to Stage* (New York: Drawing Center, 1991), 267–268.

47. Ibid.

48. For instance, Les Ballets Suédois's *Skating Rink* (1922) depicted the buzz of a contemporary city, with workers and fashionable characters sharing the stage. Another example was American-themed *Within the Quota* (1923), in which the present was vividly captured in Cole Porter's jazz score and Gerald Murphy's design for the backdrop—a blown-up newspaper's front page with headlines about the sale of a skyscraper, the flight of a new airplane model, and a police raid of a speakeasy. E. Näslund, "The Ballets Suédois and Its Modernist Concept," in *The Cambridge Companion to Ballet*, ed. M. Kant (Cambridge: Cambridge University Press, 2007), 204–206.

49. Cocteau intended the managers to verbally deliver these lines, but in its final version the ballet did not include the spoken word. The essence of the libretto was conveyed through the music, dance, and visual designs. Rothschild, *Picasso's "Parade,"* 76–81.

50. St. Lazarus is identified with the orisha Babalú Ayé in Cuban *santería*.

51. One instance of this was Carpentier's lecture, in collaboration with Cuban composer Moisés Simons, at the Club du Foubourg, Paris, in 1932. See A. Carpentier, "La consagración de nuestros ritmos," *Carteles* (Havana) 18, no. 15 (April 10, 1932): 20, 50, 54.

52. A. Carpentier, "Batouala—R. Maran," in *La Discusión*, January 21, 1923, 5, reproduced in *Crónicas caribeñas* (Havana: Letras Cubanas, 2012), 31–34.

53. F. Tobing Rony, *The Third Eye: Race, Cinema, and Ethnographic Spectacle* (Durham, NC: Duke University Press, 1996), 82–85, 239.

54. Ibid., 33, 47–49, 162.

55. J. Borge, *Latin American Writers and the Rise of Hollywood Cinema* (New York: Routledge, 2008), 49–50.

56. G. Mistral, "La película enemiga," *El Mercurio* (Santiago), June 6, 1926, 5, reproduced in J. Borge, *Avances de Hollywood: crítica cinematográfica en Latinoamérica, 1915–1945* (Rosario: Beatriz Viterbo, 2005), 105–109.

57. A. Carpentier, *Recuento de moradas*, sections 14 and 15.

58. Carpentier indicates the title of the documentary in Spanish as *Indios, hermanos míos*, and identifies the filmmaker by her nom de plume, Tytaina. See A. Carpentier, "México, según una película europea," *Carteles*, September 6, 1931, reproduced in *Obras completas* (Mexico City: Siglo XXI, 1985), 8:386–390.

59. Surprisingly, Carpentier does not indicate the title of the film or the names of its producers. Considering the year of the review, Carpentier might have referred to *Africa Speaks* (1930), shot during US explorer Paul Hoefler's expedition to Central Africa in 1928–1929. A. Carpentier, "Leyes del Africa," *Carteles* 17, no. 43 (December 27, 1931): 46–47, 50.

60. Tobing Rony, *Third Eye*, 27, 94.

61. Unruh, *Latin American Vanguards*, 66.

62. Additionally, the Afro-Cuban performers' opposition to the Business Man brings to mind the stories of Native Americans who in the United States had violently confronted photographers and moviemakers who tried to capture them on camera. Some Native Americans blocked the view of the cameras, threw rocks at the devices, destroyed them, or chased the individuals who had managed to record any footage. Tobing Rony, *Third Eye*, 239–240.

63. A contemporary restaging of this title by the Kirov Ballet is part of the program in *The Kirov Celebrates Nijinsky* (West Long Branch, NJ: Kultur, 2002), DVD.

64. Carpentier, "La evolución estética."

65. Tomé, "Envisioning a Cuban Ballet."

66. As a Cuban working in the European medium of classical music, Roldán critically assessed his position in an international context with preestablished notions of center and periphery. He realized that, for Latin American artists, working with the elements of local folklore was double-edged. It allowed them, on the one hand, to articulate original national languages that set them apart from the European tradition. On the other hand, to patronizing European eyes it reinforced the role of

Latin Americans as purveyors of the exotic, in a subordinate position of alterity within coloniality's cultural hierarchy. A. Roldán, "The Artistic Position of the American Composer," in *American Composers on American Music*, ed. H. Cowell (Stanford, CA: Stanford University Press 1933), 175–177.

67. Unruh, *Latin American Vanguards*, 21–23, 36.

68. Garafola, *Making of Ballet Modernism*, 26.

69. Metatheatricality, as Unruh explains, makes theater the ideal reflexive medium for "art to talk about art." Unruh, *Latin American Vanguards*, 173.

70. See A. Carpentier, "Panorama de la música en Cuba: la música contemporánea," *Revista Musical Chilena* (December 1947), reprinted in *Ese músico que llevo dentro* (Havana: Letras Cubanas, 1980), 3:272–284; and A. Carpentier, "Ordenado, disciplinado, trabajador y consciente," 51, and *La música en Cuba*, 236.

71. The publication of Malinowski's *Argonauts of the Western Pacific* in 1922 and Mauss's creation of the Institut d'Ethnologie in Paris in 1925 stand as landmark events in the professionalization of ethnographic fieldwork.

72. Carpentier, *La música en Cuba*, 244; "El recuerdo de Amadeo Roldán," 423; "Los Cuentos negros de Lydia Cabrera," *Carteles*, October 11, 1936, 40, reproduced in *Crónicas caribeñas*, 84–89; "El monte," *El Nacional* (Caracas), March 9, 1955, reproduced in *Crónicas caribeñas*, 267–69; *Tientos y diferencias* (Mexico City: Universidad Nacional Autónoma de México, 1964), 12; and R. Márquez, "Uno de los valores musicales de nuestra América," in *Amadeo Roldán: Testimonios*, 120–121.

73. Carpentier, "Lettre des Antilles," *Bifur* (Paris), September 3, 1929, 91–105; and "Images et Prières Nègres," in *Le Phare de Neuilly* (Paris), no. 1 (1933): 41–50.

74. Birkenmaier, *Alejo Carpentier*; and Maguire, *Racial Experiments*.

75. J. Clifford, "On Ethnographic Surrealism," *Comparative Studies in Society and History* 23, no. 4 (1981): 548.

76. Carpentier, "El monte."

77. Maguire, *Racial Experiments*, 16–21.

78. Carpentier, "Lettre des Antilles"; "Images et Prières Nègres"; "La musique cubaine," in *Documents* (Paris) no. 6 (1929), 324–327; and "Cuban Magic," *Transition* (New York), nos. 19–20 (1930): 384–390.

79. Birkenmaier, *Alejo Carpentier*, 55–79.

80. Anderson, *Carnival and National Identity*, 49–78.

81. Carpentier, *La música en Cuba*, 225–226, 231–232.

82. Carpentier, *Tientos y diferencias*, 12–13.

83. Carpentier, "Un ballet afrocubano," and preface to *Écue-Yamba-Ó* (Havana: Letras Cubanas, 2012), 45.

84. L. Cabrera, "Ritual y símbolos de la iniciación en la sociedad secreta Abakuá," *Journal de la Société des Américanistes* 58 (1969): 139–171.

85. Such divergences could also be attributed to variations in the performance of the ritual over time and across different Abakuá groups, as acknowledged by Cabrera.

86. I borrow the label "research-to-performance" from VéVé Clark, who applies it to Dunham's work. For analyses of Dunham's and Hurston's dance ethnography, see V. A. Clark, "Performing the Memory of Difference in Afro-Caribbean Dance: Katherine Dunham's Choreography, 1938–1987," in *History and Memory in African-American Culture*, ed. G. Fabris and R. O'Meally (New York: Oxford University Press, 1994), 188–204; and A. Kraut, *Choreographing the Folk: The Dance Stagings of Zora Neale Hurston* (Minneapolis: University of Minnesota Press, 2008).

87. While Hurston and Dunham integrated Caribbean dancers in their productions, they also worked with performers from the United States.

88. Conjunto de Danza Moderna, *Auto sacramental, Suite Yoruba, El milagro de anaquillé, Concerto grosso, La rebambaramba.*

89. Kraut, *Choreographing the Folk.*

90. Maguire, *Racial Experiments*, 47, 53.

91. Carpentier, "Images et Prières Nègres," 42.

92. Carpentier, "El recuerdo de Amadeo Roldán," 423–424.

93. The emphasis is mine. Carpentier's various observations, while underelaborated, support the notion that those ethnographers working within afrocubanismo in the late 1920s were self-conscious about the racial and social hierarchies mediating their engagement with the Afro-Cuban community, even if the lack of references to it in their texts from the period suggests the opposite. Carpentier, *La música en Cuba*, 225–226.

94. Marinello categorized Carpentier as a "Franco-Cuban writer" who spoke with "an irreducible Parisian accent" and was "taken for a foreigner in Havana." J. Marinello, *Literatura hispanoamericana: Hombres, meditaciones* (Mexico City: Ediciones de la Universidad Nacional de México, 1937), 168, 171.

95. Z. Gómez, *Amadeo Roldán* (Havana: Arte y Literatura, 1977), 22–28.

96. G. W. Stocking, *Victorian Anthropology* (New York: Free Press, 1987), 78–109.

97. To be sure, anthropology was not a monolithic field in the nineteenth century. I refer here to trends that were synergetic with dominant ideologies of racism and colonialism, but, as Marvin Harris demonstrates, nineteenth-century anthropologists developed diverging theories of race and, as a result of them, differing positions on the ethics of slavery and colonialism. M. Harris, *The Rise of Anthropological Theory: A History of Theories of Culture* (New York: Altamira Press, 2001), 80–141.

98. J. D. Moore, *Visions of Culture: an Introduction to Anthropological Theories and Theorists* (Walnut Creek, CA: Altamira, 2009), 30–41.

MARELYS VALENCIA

Por primera vez *y* Coffea Arábiga:
Dos poéticas documentales reflexivas
en el ojo de la tormenta revolucionaria
de los años sesenta

RESUMEN

El despliegue del documental cubano tiene lugar en los años sesenta. Los cineastas comienzan a experimentar con ideas y conceptos tanto de Europa Occidental como del llamado Bloque Comunista, que se referenciarán en este trabajo. A partir del análisis textual de dos documentales, exploramos la reflexividad como una herramienta conceptual y crítica utilizada por los cineastas para visualizar el proceso mismo de producción cinematográfica. Comparo este concepto en las obras *Por primera vez*, de Octavio Cortázar, y *Coffea Arábiga*, de Nicolás Guillén Landrián. El primero afirma la distancia entre espectadores urbanos y rurales, una brecha que intenta disminuir al transmitir el autodescubrimiento del campesino como audiencia. A pesar de que el documental revela al individuo detrás de las masas (a lo Ivens), el supuesto sujeto protagonista de la revolución está privado de agencia en ambos proyectos: el cine y la agenda del estado. En cambio, la reflexividad de *Coffea Arábiga* arroja luz sobre la falibilidad de las narrativas dentro y fuera del arte. Revela la naturaleza construida de los regímenes de la verdad, reivindicados por la revolución y el género documental.

ABSTRACT

The national and international display of the Cuban documentary has its place in the 1960s, when film makers began to experiment with ideas and concepts from both Western Europe and the so-called Communist Bloc. From the textual analysis of two documentaries, we grapple with reflexivity as a conceptual and critical tool used by cinematographers to visualize the very process of filmmaking. I attempt to compare this concept in the works *Por primera vez*, by Octavio Cortázar, and *Coffea Arábiga*, by Nicolás Guillén Landrián. The former affirms the distance between urban and rural spectators, a gap that it attempts to diminish by conveying the campesino's self-discovery as audience. Moreover, despite the fact that the documentary reveals the individual behind the masses (*a là* Ivens), the supposed subject or protagonist of the revolution is deprived of agency in both projects: the film and the state political agenda. On the other hand, *Coffea Arábiga*'s reflexivity sheds light on narrative fallibility both within and outside art;

it reveals the constructed nature of regimes of truth, entangled and claimed either by the revolution or the documentary genre.

¿Qué rupturas se manifiestan en la década de los sesenta con respecto al género documental en América Latina? ¿Qué influencia tienen el fenómeno revolución y su proyecto de nación en este cambio estético conceptual? ¿Cómo participa el documental de la agenda ideológica del nuevo gobierno revolucionario y, en particular, de su proyecto de democracia participativa?

La prioridad que la revolución estrenada en enero de 1959 otorga al documental se refleja en la producción vertiginosa del género en la década de 1960: de cuatro obras en 1959, a veintiuno el año siguiente y a cuarenta en 1965 (en Michael Chanan 2004, 35). El documental se convierte en vehículo del empeño ideológico y educativo del nuevo proyecto de nación, a la vez que en objeto de experimentación cinematográfica, en consonancia con el espíritu revolucionario y transformador del decenio. Como expresa Chanan, "the historical moment of the Cuban Revolution was also, by coincidence, a period of aesthetic revolution in documentary cinema" (184).

En este estudio enfoco dos obras documentales, *Coffea Arábiga* (1968), de Nicolás Guillén Landrián, y *Por primera vez* (1967), de Octavio Cortázar, las cuales pueden considerarse momentos cumbre del documental cubano y latinoamericano. Analizaré cómo estos documentales entran en diálogo con el proyecto de formulación de la nación del nuevo estado socialista que intenta reducir las múltiples posibilidades de la cubanía a una noción cultural-político hegemónica. *Por primera vez* refleja el proyecto de democracia integradora de la revolución, pero replica la actitud paternalista del estado (y del cine en América Latina y Cuba), ante los grupos subalternos. Por su parte, *Coffea Arábiga* propone una crítica al modelo de representación popular (dentro y fuera del arte), arrojando luz sobre los límites de la participación política dentro de la revolución. Como herramienta crítico analítica me centro en el concepto de reflexividad para contrastar las poéticas de Guillén Landrián y Cortázar, quienes desde distintas posiciones utilizan poéticas reflexivas autorreferenciales para hacer visible la pertinencia del cine en el proyecto de modernización y educación política de la revolución cubana.

Preludio

Para entender la vocación social y renovadora del documental en aquella primera década de la revolución, es necesaria la referencia a una obra anterior, *El Mégano*, a la que Ambrosio Fornet le confiere un carácter fundador (Paranaguá 1990). *El Mégano* fue producido en 1954, cinco años antes del triunfo de Fidel Castro, por un grupo de jóvenes primerizos: Julio García Espinosa, Tomás Gutiérrez Alea, Alfredo Guevara, José Massip y Jorge Haydú. Estos cineastas serían después los fundadores del Instituto Cubano de Arte e Industria Cinematográficos (ICAIC), creado el 24 de marzo de 1959 y primer decreto emitido por el gobierno en el plano de la cultura.

De estética neorealista, el corto reflejaba la explotación de los carboneros en la Ciénaga de Zapata. Sus veinte minutos de duración constituían una denuncia de la extrema pobreza en que vivían hombres, mujeres y niños dedicados a la producción de carbón en una zona cenagosa de la geografía cubana, olvidada por los gobiernos de la república. La aparición de los carboneros en diferentes facetas de su vida diaria otorgaba al filme una innegable fuerza realista y crítica, que no pasó por alto la censura del dictador Fulgencio Batista.

Una vez creado el ICAIC, y en busca de la representación de la vorágine de aquellos años iniciales a partir de un arte popular, el cine cubano de esa década se inspiró en varios movimientos o escuelas. El neorrealismo italiano constituyó uno de los referentes preferenciales, según apunta Alfredo Guevara, presidente del ICAIC, en el primer número de la revista *Cine Cubano* (junio de 1960), en torno a las perspectivas del nuevo cine, aunque también alude a la nueva ola francesa y a la cinematografía soviética. Sin embargo, el crítico Juan Antonio García Borrero considera que:

[. . .] el hecho de que los principales fundadores del ICAIC (Alfredo Guevara, Tomás Gutiérrez Alea, Julio García Espinosa) hubiesen estado vinculados [. . .] con el neorrealismo italiano, sobre todo a través de la relación de amistad establecida con Cesare Zavattini, y los estudios de Titón (Gutiérrez Alea) y Julio en Roma, ha dejado la impresión de que este movimiento estético alcanzó una fácil hegemonía en las prácticas fílmicas fomentadas por el ICAIC.

Más allá del progreso tecnológico en Europa y Estados Unidos y de su aprovechamiento por las nuevas estéticas, la renovación del documental cubano en la década de los sesenta obedece a la demanda creativa de un contexto marcado por transformaciones constantes y radicales en los órdenes económico, político y social. Tales preocupaciones aparecen en la reflexión del cineasta cubano Humberto Solás sobre el neorrealismo italiano que confirma la tesis de Borrero: "aunque sus filmes eran hermosos y a veces extraordinarios, constituían un testimonio pasivo de lo bueno y lo malo, del rico y el pobre —nada más. No le ofrecían a la gente las herramientas que le permitieran usar las oportunidades de la vida política en sí misma, para cambiar la sociedad" (citado por Julianne Burton 1986, 156–157). De ahí que los cubanos fueran más allá, expandiendo las visiones renovadoras de quienes les sirvieron de inspiración.

La aproximación a la realidad planteada por el documental cubano en los años sesenta también desplegó un arsenal de recursos técnico narrativos pensados para movilizar la subjetividad del espectador. El documentalista cubano Víctor Casaus, quien a su vez ha teorizado sobre la práctica de este género en el país, hace notar algunos principios prevalentes en estos documentales: un rápido y flexible acopio de imágenes sin seguir un plan o pre esquema de filmación (Santiago Álvarez sería el ejemplo más conocido, no seguía guiones o planes de filmación, sino que acopiaba imágenes y después el todo adquiría coherencia en el proceso de montaje); la inclusión de temas relacionados con las contingencias sociales y económicas de la época; el uso de un intuitivo estilo de montaje, y, por último, el uso de la entrevista directa con fines narrativos y como forma de incluir la voz popular en el discurso fílmico (Chanan 211).

A las observaciones de Casaus, yo añadiría la manipulación de la voz colectiva mediante la selección del individuo sin el cual no sería posible la colectividad por la que aboga el proceso revolucionario cubano, tal cual se desprende de los documentales de Joris Ivens. Para Burton, además de los aportes al cine de ficción que hiciera el soviético Mikhail Kalatozov,[1] quizá el extranjero que más directamente influyó en la creación documental fue el holandés Ivens, quien visitó la isla en 1960 y allí permaneció durante unos meses. Enfocarse en el individuo dentro de la multitud permite crear una "micronarrativa" dentro de la obra que realza "la riqueza emocional y plástica en los grandes momentos históricos e íntimos de la Revolución" (Sadoul 1983, 586).

Régimen de verdad

Mientras la literatura testimonial emerge en el panorama latinoamericano estableciéndose como género revolucionario por excelencia, en el cine otro género adquiere relevancia: el documental. Tanto en la literatura como en el cine, habían aparecido con anterioridad varios documentos artísticos que buscaban denunciar las consecuencias de regímenes de exclusión económica y social en el ámbito latinoamericano, y presentar las voces emergentes de cambio. Por ejemplo, en el mundo del llamado testimonio literario, había sido publicado *Operación Masacre*, de Rodolfo Walsh (1957),[2] y en el campo del cine, Glauber Rocha promovía un nuevo concepto de cine nacional en Brasil, desde la década de 1950, que contraponía la realidad social y las luchas de los trabajadores al cine comercial producido por las grandes compañías cinematográficas. Por su parte, el argentino Fernando Birri, creador de la Escuela de Cine de la Universidad de Santa Fe, defendía un tipo de documental que juzgara y rechazara la realidad de los sectores subalternos.

La premisa de Birri podría vincularse a la reflexión de George Yúdice (2003) sobre el testimonio, en cuanto a que este género interpela a un lector externo a la comunidad, situándolo en una posición en la que debe responder de forma solidaria. Como arma cultural, el testimonio denuncia relaciones de poder diferenciadas, dinámicas intersubjetivas que arrojan luz sobre las exclusiones de los proyectos de nación de las sociedades latinoamericanas. De esta forma, hace visible el silencio histórico sobre determinados grupos o sectores sociales; es más, el propio acto del testimonio pudiera entenderse como performance de descolonización.[3]

En el caso de Cuba, las agendas políticas de los otrora grupos sociales subalternos (negros, mujeres, clase trabajadora, campesinos) se diluyen en un programa totalizador, supuestamente común: la revolución. Su enfoque humanista incluye a ese conglomerado humano que comienza a partir de 1959 a presenciar la reestructuración del orden económico, social y político en función de la colectividad. Para expresar los intereses de esa colectividad en el cine, Gutiérrez Alea —e igualmente el Instituto Cubano de Arte e Industrias Cinematográficos (ICAIC) recién creado— aboga por un cine popular. El cineasta lo define no como un cine aceptado por la comunidad, sino como uno que exprese "los intereses más profundos y auténticos" del pueblo (Gutiérrez Alea 1982, 15).

Tal carácter popular debe expresarse igualmente en la forma. Lógicamente, los subgéneros explotados durante el capitalismo (musical, melodrama, comedia) no tienen cabida en la nueva sociedad; quedan descalificados por la nueva crítica cinematográfica, al ser reducidos a "producciones banales" con fines estrictamente comerciales (Juan-Navarro 2015, 4). En este contexto, la cuestión de lo auténticamente popular residirá en reflejar una realidad coherente con las supuestas necesidades del alegado yo origen de la revolución, por el que debe entenderse el pueblo. Pero si el estado, como aparato rector del nuevo sistema, expresa la voluntad de ese yo origen, entonces serán las instituciones (como el ICAIC), y determinados individuos dentro de esas instituciones, quienes decidan qué y quién habla por y para el pueblo, o mejor, qué es un arte auténticamente popular. Consecuentemente, esto generó un debate en torno a la función del artista en la sociedad, discusión que no comenzó a partir de la adhesión a las políticas estalinistas hacia el final de la década, sino antes.

La prohibición del documental *PM* (1961), de Sabá Cabrera Infante y Orlando Jiménez Leal sobre la vida nocturna en los bares del puerto de La Habana, sería el primer evento en atisbar el rumbo futuro del compromiso de los artistas y los límites de la libertad creativa. Se adujo que el alejamiento del reflejo de la actividad productiva y de los valores de la nueva Cuba en construcción no era compatible con la responsabilidad de un artista revolucionario. El evento suscitó el interés de Fidel Castro, quien se reunió en la Biblioteca Nacional con intelectuales y artistas durante tres días en junio de 1961, para dejar sentada la política cultural en una frase aparentemente clara: "Dentro de la Revolución todo, contra la Revolución nada." Otra vez, la ambivalencia y las oposiciones: dentro/fuera, como en el caso anterior de pasado/presente del cine. ¿No es acaso la vida nocturna del puerto habanero parte de la realidad?, ¿por qué dejar fuera de la revolución al segmento del pueblo reflejado en el documental?, ¿queda fuera el documental de la categoría de popular si muestra al púlpito lejos de las marchas revolucionarias, las consignas y la faena constructiva?[4]

Tales interrogaciones rezuman el conflicto del intelectual y el artista de aquellos años, entre quienes pudiéramos incluir a Guillén Landrián.

Dentro de la revolución

En esta sección propongo leer *Por primera vez* a partir de su reflexividad, para ilustrar el vínculo simbólico entre diégesis (texto), aparato cinematográfico y proyecto de nación revolucionario. Robert Stam (1992) define reflexividad como el proceso mediante el cual textos literarios y fílmicos ponen en primer plano su propia producción, su autoría, sus influencias intertextuales, su recepción o su enunciación (30). El procedimiento autorreferencial despliega una serie de relaciones entre el público y lo visible/invisible del proceso fílmico. En otras palabras, la reflexividad revela los factores que forman e informan sobre la subjetividad del espectador y el propio acto de ver cine. No quiere decir que los filmes reflexivos sean capaces de mostrarse de forma completamente penetrable a nuestra percepción —hay que recordar que se trata de un régimen de mediación donde intervienen elementos heterogéneos que generan distintas formas de subjetividad.

Lo que hace Cortázar es poner en circulación la noción cinemática de proyección dentro del nivel textual con la incorporación del montaje del aparato de proyección y luego la exhibición fílmica de *Tiempos modernos* (*Modern Times* 1936), de Charles Chaplin. Esta referencialidad al aparato de proyección y al cine mismo establece un diálogo con el otro espectador, el del documental, proceso que revela varios niveles de connotación: estético, político e ideológico.

El documental comienza con una entrevista a los técnicos que forman parte del equipo de cine móvil; los entrevistados dicen que viajan sin descanso veintiséis días del mes, y muestran a la cámara los componentes de su camión, convertido en una sala de proyección itinerante, para después hablar de la función social del programa. El documental hace viajar al espectador desde la perspectiva de la cámara por el sinuoso camino que conduce a *Los Mulos*, sumergiéndose en un panorama desconocido por los habitantes de la ciudad: lomas, paisajes deshabitados, ausencia de infraestructura social. Se trata de un viaje al pasado, cuya huella no ha sido completamente eliminada; es decir, el camino hacia la transformación social, cultural y económica del campo que busca la revolución se presenta como un viaje sinuoso y extenso. Aunque las primeras leyes del gobierno se encaminaron al mejoramiento de la vida del campesinado, con la proclamación de dos reformas agrarias que abolieron el latifundio y distribuyeron las tierras entre los campesinos, las montañas cubanas todavía muestran un paisaje humano subdesarrollado. El cine, por tanto, constituiría la metáfora del cambio, la revolución misma que ahora instaura un nuevo tipo de modernidad en el campo.

Esta reverencia hacia la modernidad y la civilización, reflejada en el cine mismo, puede percibirse en las entrevistas con algunos campesinos (de sexos y edades diferentes), quienes responden en *off* a las preguntas del realizador sobre si han visto cine alguna vez. Una mujer dice que debe ser algo muy "bonito y de mucha importancia." El énfasis en el atraso se palpa en los bohíos habitados por los entrevistados, desolación y pobreza que subrayan la respuesta negativa de los campesinos: sólo uno dice haber visto cine una vez. Consecuentemente, la frase de la campesina sobre el cine se corresponde con la perspectiva del realizador (y de la revolución) que reverencia la modernidad y la civilización, representadas por el cine y el equipo de cine móvil.

Burton destaca el aspecto democrático del filme no sólo al centrarse en sujetos privados de derechos durante épocas anteriores a la revolución, en particular mujeres y niños, sino al mostrarlos con sus propias voces, lo cual acentúa la agenda equitativa del proyecto social revolucionario (como había reflexionado Casaus). En tanto que material etnográfico, *Por primera vez* revaloriza a su objeto de representación y escudriñamiento al otorgarle una plataforma de expresión. Sin embargo, aunque sus voces no sean reinterpretadas por el cineasta, sí son conducidas en la dirección objetivo deseados por este último: mostrar su exclusión de los proyectos anteriores de modernización del país. De este modo *Por primera vez* acentúa la introducción a una modernidad proveniente de la ciudad, de sujetos ajenos a la comunidad rural.

Tal separación observador objeto de estudio tiene su clímax en la escena que antecede la exhibición de *Tiempos modernos*. Así, aunque se intenta velar la distancia entre realizador etnógrafo y objeto de representación mediante la interacción del primero con el segundo en la sección de entrevistas, el documental indicia que la modernización humanista (mediante el proyecto de cine móvil) descarta al campesino como portador de algún conocimiento o sabiduría. Mientras el equipo de cine móvil se ocupa del montaje del aparato de proyección al anochecer, rostros curiosos e impacientes se aglomeran y actúan inconscientes de la presencia de la cámara. Este segmento del documental (el de mayor carga emotiva) utiliza los presupuestos del *free cinema*, que perseguía además de la renovación estética, un cine más humanista. Tanto el *free cinema* como el *cinéma vérité* y el *direct cinema*, surgidos entre los años cincuenta y sesenta, intentaban registrar la realidad, mediante el uso de una cámara portable, escudriñadora, que no influía en las acciones o eventos. Se trataba de una sinceridad que sus adeptos atribuían al cine y que en *Por primera vez* se despliega hacia este contrapunteo visual entre los dispositivos técnicos y las formas de funcionamiento de la tecnología de proyección, y los rostros de los campesinos.

Finalmente aparece *Tiempos modernos* frente a la mirada sorprendida de los campesinos, y con Chaplin surgen lágrimas, carcajadas, sonrisas, mientras los dedos apuntan y los ojos parecen tocar la pantalla. El público de Los Mulos se funde de pronto con el espectador de la ciudad. Mientras los campesinos descubren a Chaplin (metáfora del cine y de la modernidad), el público del documental descubre al campesino a través de una cámara omnisciente.

Así, la reflexividad engulle el texto visual y lo lanza hacia afuera, mediante trazos que descubren el propio acto de enunciación.[5] Dicho de otra manera, se devela el mecanismo de proyección y el sistema de producción del documental, desde dónde, cómo y por qué se hace este cine, así como distintos niveles de audiencia. Una sincronía mitificadora hace patente el acto de ver desde dentro y fuera del documental, a la vez que establece ciertas diferencias de perspectiva: la inocencia en el espectador primerizo de Los Mulos frente a *Tiempos modernos*, y la mirada alerta (de naturaleza *voyeur*) del espectador que en cualquier sala de cine del país asiste (tal vez no menos asombrado) a la exhibición de *Por primera vez*. Hacer patente esta diferencia en formas y privilegios de y al ver, afirma la propia distancia entre el espectador de la ciudad y el del campo que intenta acortar el filme de Cortázar, que por momentos, como explicamos anteriormente, es atenuada mediante estrategias de sinceridad.

En efecto, Ann Marie Stock (2002) apunta que el documental "casts campesinos in a subordinate position relative to their habanero (people in Havana) counterparts" (84), crítica que ella extiende a la mayoría de la producción documental dedicada a reflejar la vida de los campesinos en Cuba, en la cual —observa— se reproduce una otredad ambivalente. Para otro crítico, Nicholas Balaisis, las apreciaciones de Chanan y Burton en cuanto al valor democrático del filme entran en contradicción con el carácter paternalista notado por Stock. En su opinión, estos criterios expresan la naturaleza ambivalente del proceso de modernización en la etapa posrevolucionaria (3).

Al socialismo reivindicar la modernidad, en este caso mediante el cine, nos remite a la paradoja del programa socialista cubano, reflejada en *Por primera vez* (mi traducción):

Si bien la campaña de cine móvil destinada a "civilizar" una gran parte de la población cubana a la que se le había negado la modernización, esta modernización amenazó lo que era supuestamente inherente a estos mismos temas: el estado auténtico (de los campesinos) como "hombres" naturales (19).

En este punto Balaisis (2014) desatiende la naturaleza del socialismo cubano. Como afirma Duanel Díaz Infante (2014), "a la etapa humanista de los primeros años," había seguido "un proceso de radicalización conocido como 'construcción simultánea del socialismo y el comunismo'" que buscaba el crecimiento de la producción y a la vez la creación del hombre nuevo (28). No obstante, en la práctica, el gobierno revolucionario enfocó el aspecto político y perdió de vista el perfilamiento de estrategias económicas. Según Carmelo Mesa-Lago (1975)

La política económica revolucionaria de la segunda mitad de la década del 60, dio prioridad al desarrollo del 'hombre nuevo' ignorando muchas leyes económicas básicas. Esa política se caracterizó por un idealismo extremo, movilización de trabajo, igualitarismo, incentivos morales, y zafras gigantes mientras se dejaba de lado la planificación central, la productividad del capital y del trabajo, y la estabilidad financiera (7).

Por tanto, en los años que nos conciernen, la prioridad del proyecto revolucionario no se dirigía a mantener el estatus natural de uno de los componentes de la nación (el campesino). El estado se trazó un objetivo de aliento robespierano: la construcción de un nuevo modelo de ciudadano, útil a las demandas de un gobierno asediado por amenazas externas e internas, y por su propia ineficiencia para sacar adelante la producción de bienes materiales. En otras palabras, los esfuerzos del estado se concentraron en la concientización política y en la educación de las masas para mantener un sistema de gobierno que dos años antes había fundado y elegido al Partido Comunista de Cuba como rector sempiterno de los destinos de la nación.

Es más, precisamente el impulso de planes de cooperativas de producción agropecuaria, con el fin de socializar aún más el proceso productivo en el país y formar individuos cultivados en la colectividad, tendría repercusiones desastrosas para el presente y el futuro de la economía cubana. El cambio de las condiciones de producción y de propiedad trajeron consigo el alejamiento de las futuras generaciones con respecto a la tierra. En efecto, la población rural cubana decreció continua y notablemente entre 1970 y 1990 (Oliveros Blet 2009).

Es justamente en este contexto que Guillén Landrián realiza uno de sus más polémicos documentales, *Coffea Arábica*, el cual ridiculiza la improductividad de esas movilizaciones de los sectores urbanos hacia la agricultura (ya mencionadas por Mesa-Lago), en particular, hacia el cultivo del café, como discutiremos más adelante.

Parafraseando a Walter Benjamin (2010/1936), se trataría de la estetización de la política o la politización del arte como equivalentes, mecanismo que, a diferencia de Guillén Landrián, en el documental de Cortázar se intenta velar mediante la sinceridad referida anteriormente, y producida por la reflexividad fílmica, descubridora de misterios cinematográficos y extra-artísticos.[6] *Por primera vez* intenta establecer, como propone Benjamin sobre el fascismo, la alineación entre la humanidad y la tecnología de reproducción masiva (a esta correlación capitalismo, tecnología, alienación sí hace alusión Balaisis). Esta última es productiva en el fascismo, según Benjamin, en cuanto sistema del que emerge la factibilidad del encuentro de la masa, cara a cara, consigo misma: el aura de la naturaleza única y eterna de la masa, transformada en la obra de arte. Pero esta masa objeto de representación que luego se contempla a sí misma en el acto de recepción de la obra, no puede devolver o retornar su mirada al ojo que la capta. La masa se convierte en objeto de contemplación sin agencia propia. De cierta forma, esta conversión del arte elitista al aura mítica de la masa se evidencia en varios documentales cubanos de la década del sesenta como *Historia de una batalla* (1962), de Manuel Octavio Gómez; *Patria o Muerte* (1960) y *Sexto aniversario* (1959), de Julio García-Espinosa.

Por primera vez transmite al espectador el mensaje de la misión redentora de la revolución al incluir al campesino en sus programas de reformas sociales. No obstante, se constata una agenda estatal como han expresado Stock y Balaisis. Regresamos aquí a la imposibilidad de representación del subalterno, a su apropiación desde la empresa artística, en este caso cinematográfica, que al final de *Por primera vez* pone en tela de juicio la supuesta relación horizontal entre el arte revolucionario y comprometido, y el sujeto al que representa. La voz del campesino en el documental sólo emerge a partir de las preguntas del realizador; el campesino aparece en mayor parte desprovisto de iniciativa, objeto apropiable y parte de un proyecto exterior a él: el cinematográfico y el de la revolución. El socialismo, como el último de los macro relatos del progreso y la racionalidad moderna, se perfila como otra modalidad colonizadora, representada en este nuevo estado que, al mismo tiempo que elimina relaciones de subordinación racial y clasista, se impone de forma hegemónica y paternalista.

Lo que está en juego en este documental es precisamente su nivel de reflexividad, de la que emerge una dialéctica fílmica basada en el diálogo con el proceso de recepción (dentro y fuera del documental) en función de la maquinaria ideológica del estado cubano y su proyecto de creación de un sujeto sensible a sus demandas. El espíritu interactivo de *Por primera vez* acerca a realizadores (parte de la comunidad letrada y urbana) y campesinos (nuevos agentes sociales), pero esta estrategia muestra ciertas tensiones que resultan de la propia mediación artística entre ciudad y campo. En otras palabras, en el documental cubano de la década (y posteriormente), no se ensaya, como apunta George Yúdice en torno al género testimonio (229), una práctica poética en la que participe de forma política el objeto de representación (la comunidad). Es decir, la representación no se convierte en una práctica comunitaria. Queda el documental como huella de la realidad representada en la que convergen diferentes capas de tiempo (pasado explotador y presente liberador) sin hacer uso del sermón político; pero también queda el rastro de las condiciones de representación, sus regímenes de verdad. A la comunidad campesina no le es permitida la posibilidad de observarse a sí misma, de evaluarse o al menos identificarse en la obra en la que es seducida a participar, pues es siempre objeto de la mirada de otros (aparato fílmico y público receptor). No se cuenta con la comunidad campesina filmada para completar el carácter reflexivo del cine que este documental propone: los campesinos continúan al margen de la misma lógica de revelación interna del documental en su apuesta autorreferencial. Permanecen atrapados en una inocencia provechosa para la agenda ideológica del filme, en última instancia pensada para un público citadino.[7]

Guillén Landrián: ¿dentro o fuera de la revolución?

En *Coffea Arábiga* (1968), de Nicolás Guillén Landrián, asoma la mirada crítica del realizador a una de las iniciativas del gobierno: el cultivo de café en el llamado Cordón de La Habana. Guillén Landrián asume también el modo reflexivo, pero para desestabilizar la propia concepción objetiva de la historia y del género documental. *Coffea Arábiga* despliega la condición de constructo del género, estimulando el cuestionamiento del espectador en torno a la pretensión de verdad en ambos espacios —en el medio artístico y su objeto (la realidad exterior). El artificio del documental queda expuesto: el público puede percibir el proceso de montaje y desmontaje de la imagen y el sonido, a la vez que asiste a la manipulación poética y caótica de sus códigos. Guillén Landrián despliega una reflexividad anticelebratoria del acto cinematográfico como experiencia cognitiva y dadora de certezas en torno a la realidad. La reflexividad expresada en la edición y el montaje, principalmente, permite asociaciones, contigüidades, imágenes, metáforas, que desmantelan la idea del documental como dador de certezas y verdades. Al mismo tiempo, se produce una noción de la Historia como constructo, ficción embaucadora que se repite para dejar fuera de sí a la propia multitud que la celebra y muere por ella, épicamente.

Encomendado a Guillén Landrián como proyecto didáctico del ICAIC, *Coffea Arábiga* nunca se proyectó en las salas de cine, por el contrario, pasó a las bóvedas, al mundo del silencio diseñado por la censura oficial hasta que a finales de los noventa el nombre de su autor fue resucitado por jóvenes cineastas —irónicamente, luego de su muerte en Miami. El documental abre con una imagen de las olas batiendo contra los peñascos, mientras se escucha en *off* la voz del poeta nacional cubano Nicolás Guillén, declamando que "el lagarto verde" —la isla— saca sus "uñas del mapa." La metáfora del lagarto despierto hace notar la acción rebelde de la isla en el mapa geopolítico de la modernidad. Guillén Landrián escoge, concienzudamente, a un poeta mulato (nada menos que a su tío) quien canta a la negritud en la mayor parte de su obra, para dialogar con un tema tabú en la sociedad: las tradiciones afrocubanas y el lugar de este grupo étnico en la nación y la cultura cubanas.

Su elección contrasta con un momento en que la discriminación racial se pretende eliminada por decreto gubernamental, con el objetivo de integrar a los afrodescendientes al nuevo proyecto social, pero a su vez, silenciando el trauma histórico y la cuestión racial en el ámbito político. De hecho, en 1965 la Unión de Escritores y Artistas de Cuba cesa su respaldo (¿político?) a Ediciones El Puente (1961–65) ante la Editorial Nacional de Cuba (María Isabel Alfonso 2012). El cierre de Ediciones El Puente, que había publicado varios autores afrocubanos, se ha explicado tanto a partir de argumentos raciales como de su independencia en términos económicos y estéticos con respecto a la agenda cultural de la revolución. Según Alfonso, "Con el surgimiento de las Ediciones se consolidan por primera vez las ansias generacionales de refundar y de cuestionar ciertos referentes culturales por parte de un número más visible de actantes de esa alteridad" (111).

Por su parte, en "Conspicuous Absences: Representations of Race in Post-1959 Cuban Film," Ana Serra observa que (mi traducción) "Debido a las necesidades urgentes de los primeros años de la revolución, el enfoque en clases sociales recibió el apoyo de escritores afrocubanos eminentes, así como de muchos realizadores de películas y documentales. La idea de la cultura afrocubana a menudo se proyecta como una investigación sobre los orígenes históricos de la nación revolucionaria, o se reivindica como la representación de un viejo ser que Cuba moderna necesita dejar atrás" (134).

Efectivamente, al indagar en el cultivo del café en el llamado "Cordón de La Habana,"[8] Guillén Landrián primero rescata el sustrato afrocubano de la identidad cubana, y luego lo lanza a dialogar con las políticas económicas y sociales que intentan solapar la brecha racial. Ante todo, la incorporación del estrato afrocubano se ubica de forma paralela a la incierta genealogía del cultivo del café: "Se supone, se dice, que en el Wajay se cultivó por primera vez el café en Cuba." Este elemento de la agricultura cubana constituye una narrativa periférica, imprecisa; el café, marginado por la triada "azúcar/poder/texto" que estudia Benítez Rojo con referencia al discurso hegemónico del azúcar a lo largo de la historia nacional, es imposible de representar sin titubeos, al mismo tiempo que hablar del aporte cultural y económico del negro es constatar el silencio.

Guillén Landrián opta por mostrar imágenes breves de prácticas culturales afrocubanas (religiosas) que se imbrican con la incertidumbre del itinerario del cultivo: el poblado del Wajay (en el occidente de la isla), donde no hay trazos del negro, y luego del Museo de la Gran Piedra en Santiago de Cuba (en la zona oriental), donde se destaca la huella de los franceses. Entonces surge el texto: "los negros como mano de obra" y en seguida: "los negros, ¡¿Cómo?! ¡¿los negros?!!" La pregunta gráfica sin sonido emula un efecto sonoro, al trasladar a la visualidad una construcción oral del texto escrito. Guillén Landrián se deshace de efectos sonoros para inscribir la palabra en el orden del sonido, a la vez que sitúa el texto en una doble posición: la del enunciador y la del receptor. El texto es origen y destino, juega con la premisa de que el sujeto del documental debe apuntar al yo origen, el pueblo, figura central de la revolución. Sin embargo, ese yo origen se asombra ante la palabra fantasma negro. El texto destaca, entonces, una aporía: la palabra negro provoca un ruido dentro del plano del discurso, es decir, el de la memoria y la historia nacional. La negación de una significación encierra una connotación: el desplazamiento o la borradura del negro y sus prácticas culturales de la construcción de la nación.

Esta primera secuencia de imágenes conforma una narrativa tejida entre el origen del cultivo y su aceleración, la esclavitud que le sirvió de fuerza productiva y el tabú en torno a la raza negra y sus tradiciones en el discurso hegemónico. No obstante, también habría que hacer notar que la borradura de tales tradiciones en esta década se entronca con la entronización del marxismo como ideología política institucional, y por tanto, con la desaprobación y el desaliento de las prácticas religiosas. El nuevo Partido Comunista resalta la lucha por una sociedad libre de prejuicios y superstición, objetivo subordinado a la construcción de una nueva sociedad, es decir, a una nueva formación social ateísta (Jorge I. Domínguez 1978). Consecuentemente, la cultura afrocubana se resiente en el reconocimiento de sus valores y legado cultural a la nación cubana. En efecto, la sección de apertura del documental de Guillén Landrián abre y cierra con un sol radiante rodeado por un fondo negro, al que le sigue la voz del poeta mulato sobre el mar bravo.

Elementos dispares se relacionan por analogía mediante el montaje. A la preparación de la tierra para recibir la semilla, la secunda la sintonía de la estación Radio Cordón de La Habana, creada para orientar y educar a los miles de trabajadores voluntarios de la ciudad movilizados en el cordón cafetalero. Al analizar la secuencia de la siembra, asistimos al extrañamiento de la imagen: en pantalla aparecen caracteres sin conexión contigua con la realidad diegética, ni correspondencia con el discurso de la voz en *off*. La imagen y la voz en *off* se superponen y crean un ruido explícito entre el éxito de la siembra directa del café (voz) y las consignas revolucionarias del momento que se visualizan: "cubanos, seguros"[9] y "pin, pon, fuera, abajo Caimanera" (base naval de los Estados Unidos en la isla). Así, las fórmulas y los informes de los ingenieros sobre el éxito de la cosecha se confunden con la propaganda política, como si una cosa y otra emanaran del mismo fenómeno: la retórica improductiva. El ruido en la comunicación apunta a la interconexión absurda de ambos mundos (el político y el agrario). El discurso épico de la revolución muestra una capacidad movilizadora, pero no necesariamente productiva en términos económicos. La productividad de la imagen invoca la improductividad del mundo exterior, particularmente cuando la transmisión radial dirigida a los cordoneros no se escucha sobre el manto de los cafetales, sino sobre una ciudad fría, moderna, y desprovista del elemento humano.

El documental, supuestamente un material didáctico pensado para instruir sobre el cultivo del café, utiliza otras estrategias discursivas para entrar en controversia con el momento histórico. El realizador hace énfasis en el extrañamiento con respecto a la realidad. Si Casaus destacaba la inclusión de la entrevista en el documental de estos años como forma de insertar la voz del pueblo, Guillén Landrián la utiliza sólo una vez, para crear cierto distanciamiento paródico de la realidad. Se trata de una puesta en escena que desestabiliza el referente extra diegético: las nuevas iniciativas económicas y la alianza con el eje soviético. En la entrevista, una mujer búlgara que aparece protegiéndose del sol con unos lentes oscuros, reproduce de memoria en lengua búlgara la definición de "umbráculo."[10] Así, además del elemento nuevo dentro del paisaje cubano vinculado a la gravitación de Cuba en el campo socialista, se cuestiona el trasplante de un sistema político ajeno a la cultura cubana y su posibilidad de traducción; la búlgara sólo puede repetir automáticamente lo que escucha en la radio, un adoctrinamiento que parece familiar (en cualquiera de sus formas), tanto en la Europa del Este como en La Habana, donde sólo hay lugar para la recitación, pero no para el pensamiento crítico o la libre creación. Por último, sus lentes de sol, tomados en *close up*, destacan el filtro separador del documental en relación con el mundo exterior, la *mise-en-abyme* o experiencia recursiva de la modernidad repetida en Cuba con el experimento socialista.

Luego, regresa Fidel Castro subiendo al estrado para pronunciar un discurso épico, mientras miles de personas lo aclaman. Su barba, como un prop (motivo) cinematográfico,[11] se diluye en flores de café bajo el sonido de "The Fool on the Hill," que da paso a una pantalla negra (sin el sol que anteriormente ha marcado el corte entre secuencias narrativas). Guillén Landrián combina imágenes documentales de la época prerrevolucionaria en las que sobresalen anuncios comerciales, el neón de la ciudad consumidora y dinámica, en contraste con las imágenes del negro maltratado y la miseria de los campesinos, entre ellos la fotografía de un hombre viejo que, sentado en un taburete, muestra sus manos callosas por el trabajo, pero vacías. La fotografía como medio se hace patente, se inscribe dentro del documental en busca de una memoria afectiva que mediante el montaje se perpetúa en el presente.

La fugaz sucesión de imágenes documentales dentro del documental (otra vez la autorreferencialidad que propone *Por primera vez*) permite igualmente el contrapunteo de tiempos históricos y niveles de discurso. Por ejemplo, presenta una secuencia de sabotajes, muertes y destrozos cometidos por la contrarrevolución, y seguidamente, en un fondo negro se interpela al espectador con una pregunta: "¿Prefieren ustedes tomar café Regil? O ¿Pilon? O ¿Tu-py?" (marcas de café publicitadas antes de la revolución). La supuesta respuesta a la pregunta se ofrece mediante una imagen documental de los milicianos con los fusiles en alto. Al parecer, la historia no permite el retorno al capitalismo consumista. La multitud frenética agita los brazos en una plaza cubana que un sol radiante, pero un fondo negro lo desplaza lentamente, hasta devorar toda la imagen como el hongo nuclear. Reaparece Fidel Castro (por dos segundos), luego, una danza afrocubana y otro texto: "En Cuba todos los negros, y los blancos, y todos tomamos café." La multitud se agita, esta vez durante unos segundos más y se simula un cierre, clásico entre los documentales épicos de la revolución. Pero no. Vuelve la infografía: "Un momento, por favor, para terminar Los Beatles, en "The Fool on the Hill." Suena la música, y se lee: "Todos creían que era un tonto el hombre que sobre la colina veía la tierra girar y el sol caer." La infografía retorna a la pantalla apelando al receptor: "¿El cierre?, todavía no."

No se trata sólo de reflexionar sobre regímenes de verdad reclamados por el discurso en cuanto a su adherencia a la realidad, sino sobre el cine en sí mismo y el proceso de representación. ¿Es posible representar? Guillén Landrián performativiza una crisis de representación en un momento histórico donde al arte y a los artistas les es demandado el acercamiento realista al mundo que les rodea. El reclamo de la realidad transformadora del nuevo gobierno como última constancia de verdad es denegado mediante la reflexividad que parodia al propio género del documental didáctico. Consecuentemente, se nos interpela a reflexionar sobre los límites de la representación, no sólo como empresa política, sino artística.

Guillén Landrián juega con el tiempo, mediante el montaje y la manipulación de la imagen. De las manos rudas y callosas del campesino comienza a emerger un sol (el mismo de las secuencias previas) que, una vez instalado en su eterno fondo negro, se pone lentamente. Esta colisión o encuentro de imágenes (manos callosas de las cuales emerge —reflejo obstinado— el sol oscurecido) recalca un movimiento temporal que no rinde cambios. En esta recurrencia, la isla caimán a la que le canta Nicolás Guillén y que acaba de sacar "sus uñas del mapa" revela un destino trágico donde coinciden pasado y presente; esta manipulación del tiempo evoca una especie de eterno retorno que se proyecta igualmente hacia el futuro, con el sol negro sobre el horizonte.

El sol de *Coffea Arábiga* nos recuerda del acercamiento peligroso a la verdad, un exceso de aproximación que la consume y nos deja sin referentes ni búsquedas. Pero se percibe también cierto matiz fenomenológico, como si las percepciones aparecieran descritas de golpe, de modo que no pueden ser enunciadas por el documental. Cuando la palabra se escucha es mediante fragmentos de programas radiales o en el texto musical. Incluyendo a Fidel Castro, todos los sujetos son silenciados. Consecuentemente, la promesa del discurso siempre es frustrada; pero queda la promesa de otro discurso deconstruido: el cinematográfico. La palabra felonía seductora y falsa de multitudes nos puede arrastrar al horror o al absurdo indecible. Sólo permanece la imagen —signo prehistórico—, abolida y renacida simultáneamente, con la propuesta estética, transgresora e irreverente de Guillén Landrián.

Coffea Arábiga desmantela el discurso de cualquier proyecto de nación (pasado, presente o por venir). El joven Guillén Landrián rompe con la premisa de la identificación del ojo del espectador con la cámara, la premisa que su maestro Ivens utilizó prolíficamente. No obstante, Guillén Landrián parece haber tenido en alta consideración a Ivens, como expresa en una entrevista con Lara Petusky para *Cubaencuentro* (publicada en 2005, después de la muerte del realizador cubano):

Ivens era un tipo con un amor hacia los demás y con una pupila cinematográfica extraordinaria. Fue quien me nombró director de cine a mí. Lo habían contratado en Cuba para formar la escuela de cine de documentalistas. Entonces él me aprobó como asistente de dirección. Era un salto de la cosa administrativa a la cosa artística. Yo le hice un guión sobre un cuadro de Van Gogh... Con ese guión él me logra nombrar en el departamento artístico, no administrativo, que fue por donde empecé.

Cabe aclarar que con *Coffea Arábiga* la acción sólo es posible a partir del arte, ya sea en la resistencia cultural y religiosa de los negros que se muestra a lo largo de esta obra documental, o en la propia manipulación de la imagen cinematográfica que se erige en desafío, provocación directa. Se trata, en palabras del crítico Santiago Juan-Navarro (2015), de: "[. . .] a popular, nonofficialist perspective, aimed at revealing the contradictions between the revolution's dreams and the geographical and social margins" (3). Pero, deberíamos añadir, están en juego también las formas en las que el cine puede experimentar para expresar esa contradicción social y política.

Podemos decir que aunque el documental de la década de los sesenta buscó expresar la compleja realidad social y participar de la construcción de una identidad nacional en función de un ideal socialista donde el individuo y el arte debían someterse a la colectividad, las propuestas estéticas variaron, y algunas contrariaron este compromiso ideológico. Las imágenes y los sonidos del documental sirvieron para corporeizar poéticamente ese proyecto de nación concebido desde arriba (el estado), pero también para desafiarlo e impugnarlo poéticamente. Como afirma Burton (1990):

El documental es una fuente de "contrainformación" para aquellos que no tienen acceso a las estructuras hegemónicas de comunicación en el mundo; un medio para la reconstrucción de los acontecimientos históricos y para desafiar las interpretaciones hegemónicas y, a menudo elitistas del pasado; un modo de producir, preservar y utilizar el testimonio de los individuos y grupos que de otra manera no tendrían ningún medio de grabación de su experiencia; un instrumento para la captura de la diferencia cultural . . . (6–7).

En los documentales analizados, los realizadores utilizan la reflexividad fílmica con intenciones, técnicas y medios diversos, ya sea para marcar el compromiso con el discurso hegemónico oficial o anunciar su separación de él. Al mismo tiempo, se arroja luz sobre cómo los realizadores de cine documental repiensan el género. Mediante la autorreferencialidad cinematográfica las imágenes de Cortázar persiguen la sutura al medio cinematográfico y al proyecto estatal de ambos espectadores (el citadino y el campesino de Los Mulos que observa la película de Chaplin), en el esfuerzo por reducir la brecha entre las masas de la ciudad y las del campo, pero también su diferencia y separación. Si bien Chanan celebra la posibilidad de que en *Por primera vez* la audiencia gane una visión de su "own self-discovery as audience" (29), este autodescubrimiento no es extensible al campesino de Los Mulos, al que sólo se le permite revelarse a otros como audiencia. El documental de Cortázar descubre a la masa y a unos individuos específicos dentro de esta (a lo Ivens), pero a estos supuestos sujetos de la revolución se les excluye de la reflexividad que el documental despliega, no se perfila un espacio para el auto reconocimiento de los campesinos en tanto que audiencia.

Mientras, en Guillén Landrián las múltiples imágenes experimentales intentan desmantelar cualquier intento de fijar el lenguaje, de atraer al espectador a una zona familiar y de lograr una identificación. Su reflexividad, desplegada en las referencias intertextuales e inter-mediáticas así como en el montaje y desmontaje del sonido y la imagen, busca informar sobre el propio proceso de construcción discursiva del documental con el fin de dejar una productiva reflexión postcinematográfica: la falibilidad de las narrativas fuera y dentro del arte, al igual que la noción de constructo de cualquier régimen de verdad.

NOTAS

1. Kalatozov realizó en 1964 la película *Yo soy Cuba* con la asistencia del cineasta cubano Enrique Pineda Barnet.

2. *Operación Masacre* se publicó primero como una serie de artículos entre mayo y julio de 1957 en el periódico *Mayoría*. Luego los artículos, considerados una sólida investigación periodística sobre los asesinatos clandestinos contra civiles peronistas durante la llamada Revolución Libertadora que derrocó a Perón en Argentina, fueron convertidos en un libro. En Cuba, se considera como antecedente del género las vivencias en prisión de Pablo de la Torriente Brau, publicadas primero como serie bajo el título "La isla de los 500 asesinatos" en el periódico *Ahora* en 1934, y después convertidas en el libro *Presidio Modelo*, al que le añadió otros capítulos y terminó en Nueva York en 1935. Pero su primera edición no ocurrió hasta 1969. Se habla también de la literatura de campaña escrita por el Che Guevara, y un siglo antes por los próceres de la independencia de Cuba quienes dejaron en cartas y diarios sus reflexiones sobre las contiendas contra España.

3. Al presentar una realidad a la que las convenciones del género (y expectativas de la audiencia) adjudican un carácter testimonial, el documental se convierte en herramienta de concientización social. La imagen de una realidad irrebatible se utiliza para vehicular agendas ideológicas de grupos sociales y políticos. Esto se advierte, por ejemplo, en *La hora de los hornos* (1968), de los argentinos Fernando Solanas y Octavio Getino, documental en el que según Chanan (2004), "the aim of teaching is not immediately to inspire action, but to impart the means for the acquisition of more and better knowledge upon action may be premised" (206). Por tanto, el compromiso del documental latinoamericano será en aquellos años con los sectores invocados para transformar el sistema de exclusión social en la región.

4. Estas preguntas coinciden con las de Desiderio Navarro sobre "Palabras a los intelectuales," título bajo el cual luego fue publicado el discurso de Fidel Castro en la reunión de marras. Se cuestiona Navarro (2001, 112):

¿Qué fenómenos y procesos de la realidad cultural y social cubana forman parte de la Revolución y cuáles no? ¿Cómo distinguir qué obra o comportamiento cultural actúa contra la Revolución, qué a favor y qué simplemente no la afecta? ¿Qué crítica social es revolucionaria y cuál es contrarrevolucionaria? ¿Quién, cómo y según qué criterios decide cuál es la respuesta correcta a esas preguntas? ¿No ir contra la Revolución implica silenciar los males sociales que sobreviven del pasado prerrevolucionario o los que nacen de las decisiones políticas erróneas y los problemas no resueltos del presente y el pasado revolucionarios? ¿Ir a favor de la Revolución no implica revelar, criticar y combatir públicamente esos males y errores? Y así sucesivamente.

5. Esta simultaneidad de narrativas que a su vez iluminan el proceso fílmico, la expresa Dziga Vertov, quien utiliza la reflexividad de una manera magistral; baste citar su documental *Man with a Movie Camera* (1929), en donde el propio realizador aparece en simulacro de filmación itinerante por toda la ciudad.

6. Vale la pena recordar la diferencia que establece Benjamin entre el receptor de la obra de arte y la reproducción masiva, separación que destaca el desplazamiento de la soledad ritual del espectador al "culto a la audiencia."

7. El público de la ciudad era numeroso. Como recuerdan De la Grange y Rico (2009) en *Letras Libres*, La Habana de los años cincuenta era "una de las capitales mundiales del séptimo arte." Y añaden: "La ciudad, alardeaban los cubanos, tenía más cines que Nueva York: 135 salas para una población que no llegaba al millón de habitantes. Grandes estudios como Warner, Twenty Century Fox, Columbia o Metro habían abierto centros de distribución y talleres donde se formaban decenas de técnicos. El cine no era sólo un motor cultural sino una industria de primer orden."

8. Una de las fracasadas iniciativas económicas impuestas por Fidel Castro. Al final de esa misma década, casi paraliza la producción de otros renglones económicos para conseguir la imposible meta de diez millones de toneladas de azúcar.

9. Consigna nacida durante los primeros años de la revolución, y que se completaba con "a los yanquis dales duro."

10. Sitio cubierto de ramaje o de otra cosa que da paso al aire, para resguardar las plantas de la fuerza del sol.

11. Stam amplía la función y traslación de los motivos literarios en el cine en un estudio ya clásico sobre la relación entre ambos medios: *Literature and Film: A Guide to the Theory and Practice of Adaptation* (2004).

BIBLIOGRAFÍA

Alfonso, María Isabel. "Ediciones El Puente y dinámicas raciales de los años 60: un capítulo olvidado de la historia literaria cubana." *Temas* 70 (abril–junio 2012): 110–118.

Balaisis, Nicholas. "Modernization and Ambivalence in Octavio Cortázar's *Por primera vez*." *Cinema Journal* 54.1 (Fall 2014): 1–24.

Benítez Rojo, Antonio. "Azúcar/poder/literatura." *Lectura crítica de la literatura americana*: La formación de las culturas nacionales. Selección y prólogo de Saúl Sosnowski. Biblioteca Ayacucho (1996): 80–104.

Benjamin, Walter. *The Work of Art in the Age of Mechanical Reproduction*. Charleston: CreateSpace Independent Publishing Platform, 2010.

Burton, Julianne. *Cinema and Social Change in Latin America: Conversations with Filmmakers.* Austin: University of Texas Press, 1986.

Burton, Julianne. *The Social Documentary in Latin America.* Pittsburgh, PA: University of Pittsburgh Press, 1990.

Chanan, Michael. *Cuban Cinema.* Minneapolis: University of Minnesota Press, 2004.

De la Grange, Bertrand, y Maité Rico. "La Habana, ruinas y revolución." *Letras Libres*, 31 de enero de 2009. http://www.letraslibres.com/mexico-espana/la-habana-ruinas-y-revolucion.

De la Torriente Brau, Pablo. *Presidio Modelo.* La Habana: Editorial de Ciencias Sociales, 1969.

Díaz Infante, Duanel. *La revolución congelada: Dialécticas del castrismo.* Madrid: Editorial Verbum, 2014.

Domínguez, Jorge I. Cuba: *Order and Revolution.* Cambridge, MA: Belknap Press of Harvard University Press, 1978.

García Borrero, Juan Antonio. *Cine cubano, la pupila insomne* (blog). https://cinecubanolapupilainsomne.wordpress.com/author/virgen1964/page/60/.

Gutiérrez Alea, Tomás. *Dialéctica del espectador.* La Habana: Unión de Escritores y Artistas de Cuba, 1982.

Juan-Navarro, Santiago. "En el vórtice de la enajenación: Nicolás Guillén Landrián y la implosión del documental científico-popular cubano de los 60." *Studies in Latin American Popular Culture* 33 (2015): 3–26.

Mesa-Lago, Carmelo. "La economía cubana en la década del 70: Pragmatismo y racionalidad." *Caribbean Studies* 14.4 (enero 1975): 7–39.

Navarro, Desiderio. "In media res publicas. Sobre los intelectuales y la crítica social en la esfera pública cubana." *La Gaceta de Cuba* 3 (mayo–junio 2001): 40–45.

Oliveros Blet, Arnoldo. "El crecimiento de la población rural cubana en el período 1990–2006." *Revista Novedades en Población* 5.9 (2009): 15–43.

Paranaguá, Paulo Antonio. *Le cinéma cubain.* París: Centre Georges Pompidou, 1990.

Petusky, Lara, Alejandro Coger y Manuel Zayas. "El cine postergado." *Cubaencuentro.* 2 de septiembre de 2005. http://arch1.cubaencuentro.com/entrevistas/20050904/74540a9e00385c591a45bac12d946245/1.html.

Sadoul, Georges. *Historia del cine mundial: Desde los orígenes.* México, DF: Siglo XXI, 1983.

Serra, Ana. "Conspicuous Absences. Representations of Race in Post–1959 Cuban Film." *Confluencia* 20.1 (Fall 2004): 134–146.

Stam, Robert. *Reflexivity in Film and Literature: From Don Quixote to Jean-Luc Godard.* Nueva York: Columbia University Press, 1992.

Stam, Robert, y Alessandra Raengo. *Literature and Film: A Guide to the Theory and Practice of Adaptation.* Oxford, Inglaterra: Wiley-Blackwell, 2004.

Stock, Ann Marie. *On Location in Cuba.* Chapel Hill: University of North Carolina Press, 2009.

Walsh, Rodolfo. *Operación Masacre.* Buenos Aires: Ediciones de la Flor, 1972.

Yúdice, George. "De la guerra civil a la guerra cultural: testimonio, posmodernidad y el debate sobre la autenticidad." Sara Castro-Klarén (Ed.). *Latin American Women's Narrative: Practices and Theoretical Perspectives.* Madrid: Iberoamericana; Frankfurt: Vervuert, 2003. 111–142.

LAURA REDRUELLO

Cine e Iglesia en el Período Especial cubano

RESUMEN

Esta ponencia analizará la relación entre el cine y la Iglesia católica en Cuba durante el revolucionario, para mostrar cómo a través del audiovisual, la iglesia recupera una plataforma de difusión de su pensamiento y logra paulatinamente salir de su involuntario enclaustramiento. Después del alborozo inicial de 1959, las relaciones de la Iglesia con la revolución se deterioran, y tras el cierre de todos los colegios y universidades religiosas, la iglesia queda totalmente relegada del nuevo panorama cultural del país. Sin embargo, la Iglesia se refugia en el cine y consigue mantener contacto con la sociedad civil a través de cineclubes, su participación en festivales nacionales y la publicación de revistas fílmicas desde sus propios centros.

ABSTRACT

This article analyzes the relationship between the cinema and the Catholic Church in Cuba during the revolutionary period, to show how through the audiovisual, the church recovered a platform of diffusion of its thought and gradually managed to leave its involuntary cloister. Following the initial excitement of 1959, the church's relations with the revolution deteriorated. After the closure of all religious colleges and universities, the church was completely relegated to the country's new cultural landscape. However, the church took "refuge" in cinema and managed to maintain contact with civil society through cinema clubs, participation in national festivals, and the publication of film journals from its own centers.

Desde comienzos de la Revolución cubana la Iglesia católica en Cuba ha buscado ansiosamente recuperar y mantener su presencia entre la población. El cine ha sido un elemento clave para retomar un proyecto de evangelización malogrado desde los primeros años de la revolución. Este ensayo analiza cómo durante el período revolucionario la Iglesia católica cubana se acerca a la sociedad a través del audiovisual y cómo la década de los noventa, debido a las circunstancias económicas y políticas del país, se convierte en una etapa clave para que la Iglesia vuelva a proyectarse públicamente en la cultura nacional.

En 1936 la encíclica Vigilanti Cura de Pío XI apunta al cine como uno de los medios de comunicación determinantes para ejercer influencia sobre las masas. La encíclica expone con todo detalle cómo la Iglesia debe manejar este potencial e insiste en la necesidad de "coaliarse" con el cine, por ser éste "un factor valioso de instrucción y educación" (Ramos 2006). La Iglesia cubana acata estas directrices, convirtiéndose Cuba en el país latinoamericano donde se establecen las relaciones más estrechas entre Iglesia y cine. Según el historiador Raúl Rodríguez La O, Cuba es "el primer país de América Latina en que la Iglesia se ocupa del cine y sus efectos" (Ramos 2006).

Lo cierto es que antes del triunfo de la Revolución cubana en 1959, la situación en que se encuentra la Iglesia católica cubana con respecto al medio audiovisual es inmejorable. En 1935 se inaugura la sección "Cine, Teatro" escrita por Leopoldo Barroso Molero en la revista de los padres franciscanos *San Antonio* donde se publican críticas y una clasificación moral de las películas. Al mismo tiempo el Comité de Damas Católicas comienzan a distribuir un volante al que denominan Guía Moral del Cine. Más tarde, en 1946 la Organización Católica Internacional de Cine y Audiovisual (OCIC) aprueba la creación de oficinas nacionales fuera de Europa para ejercer "un apostolado de presencia y animación de los medios con vistas a la producción de obras que alienten el pleno desarrollo de los valores humanos" (Piñera 1999, 109).

La Comisión del Cine cubana, dirigida por América Penichet es aceptada como una de las sedes principales, pasándose a llamar Centro Católico de Orientación Cinematográfica (CCOC), con la misión de ofrecer a los cubanos los "elementos indispensables para incentivar un juicio inteligente que les lleve a apreciar los valores morales sin despreocupar el criterio artístico y valorar el cine como arte" (Ramos 2006). Ese mismo año y en apoyo a esta medida, el cardenal Arteaga Betancourt hace construir en el Palacio Cardenalicio una sala de proyecciones (más tarde denominada Cine Club Félix Varela) que se constituye como el primer cine club católico. A la creación de este centro le sigue una importante y amplia red de cineclubes distribuidos por todo el país en los que se exhiben regularmente películas seguidas de comentarios y debates sobre la filmación. El Centro Católico en 1953 comienza a editar su primera revista cinematográfica denominada *Cine Guía*, que por su audacia y contenido compite con similares publicaciones europeas e incluso supera a la mayoría de sus pares americanas. También se organizan con éxito cursos de formación cinematográfica para educadores y estudiantes de las escuelas católicas y laicas (Piñera 1999, 112). Todo este esfuerzo se traduce en una interacción positiva con el mundo de la cultura cinematográfica del país. A fines de los cincuenta, el balance no podía ser más satisfactorio: el Centro Católico de Orientación Cinematográfica, denominado ahora Organización Católica Internacional de Cine-Cuba (OCIC-CUBA) integraba, junto a la Sociedad Cultural Nuestro Tiempo y el Departamento de Cine de la Universidad de La Habana, el trío de instituciones a la vanguardia del estudio y la apreciación cinematográfica en Cuba (Ramos 2006).

La Revolución de Fidel Castro triunfa en 1959, y las relaciones entre la Iglesia cubana y el nuevo poder político se deterioran gradual y por largo tiempo irreversiblemente. Del alborozo inicial, se pasa a un fuerte enfrentamiento tan sólo un año después, en 1960. Con la radical estatización emprendida por el nuevo régimen, la Iglesia cubana pierde una sensible parte de sus propiedades, incluyendo centros de educación, hospicios, asilos de ancianos y sedes de órdenes religiosas, quedándose tan sólo con la propiedad de la mayoría de los templos en el país. Para finales de 1961, en un estado ya declarado marxista-leninista y tras una expulsión masiva de clérigos continúa el éxodo, la prisión temporal y el silencio de gran cantidad de dirigentes y militantes seglares.

El proceso iniciado en los sesenta produjo en Cuba un marcado debilitamiento de la significación social de la religión. Actuaron, en tal sentido, diversos factores, entre ellos el mencionado enfrentamiento de las iglesias a las profundas transformaciones que beneficiaban al grueso de la población, lo que les restó aceptación popular; la salida definitiva del país de los sectores sociales más acomodados, que constituían el referente social principal de la mayoría de estas instituciones, así como de una parte considerable de dirigentes de culto (sacerdotes, pastores, monjas . . . etc.). Por otra parte, la política de confiscación de medios de producción y de servicios por parte del Estado afectó a las iglesias, en especial al privarlas de sus principales vías de influencias, los colegios y los medios de comunicación. (Ramírez 2015).

Esta nueva situación afecta dramáticamente a la Organización Católica, pues la mayoría de sus integrantes toman el camino del exilio. La prestigiosa revista *Cine Guía* saca a la luz su último número. En ese mismo año, al comenzar la nacionalización de los cines comerciales y de las escuelas privadas, se clausuran los cineclubes religiosos. Buena parte de lo conseguido por la Organización Católica se viene abajo en pocos años, y transita durante las décadas del sesenta y setenta como un centro semifantasma, limitándose su labor.

Pasados los conflictivos años sesenta y transitados los represivos setenta,[1] la Iglesia comienza a experimentar una gradual, aunque lenta recuperación en los años ochenta. Esta década es considerada por una parte considerable de los cubanos como la verdadera primavera de la Revolución cubana, debido al notable bienestar económico que se experimenta durante esos años. El dogmatismo cultural se reduce y hay un espacio de libertad impensable una década antes. En el ambiente intelectual, amén de la censura de siempre, se permiten obras literarias, revistas cinematográficas, piezas teatrales y plásticas de cierta osadía que transmiten frescura y diversidad y que nada tienen que ver con el anquilosado arte panfletario anterior. La Iglesia católica cubana no queda ajena a estos cambios. Si la década de los setenta se considera la etapa más silenciosa y represiva para la Iglesia, los ochenta representan un renacer con mejores condiciones para comenzar a proyectarse públicamente. En el panorama audiovisual comienzan una serie de pronunciamientos que rompen con la etapa de silencio. La década comienza con la llegada del misionero canadiense Denis Castonguay, quien crea en un ala del antiguo Palacio Cardenalicio el departamento de medios audiovisuales de la entonces Diócesis de La Habana. Castonguay logra importar equipos de video, caseteras, cámaras y diaporamas con los que se distribuyen en las diferentes parroquias cintas audiovisuales afines a los valores que defiende la Iglesia, pero también películas que por diversos motivos se encontraban censuradas por el oficialismo (O'Farril 2015). Este hecho marca la primera vez que una institución privada distribuye películas en la era de la revolución, y en particular filmes de temáticas religiosas, los cuales casi todos estaban estrictamente censurados por los canales oficiales de distribución y programación cinematográfica. Las primeras producciones llegan junto al primer grupo de empleados que tiene la Iglesia en esta área compuesto por personas del mundo profesional cubano, entre los que se encontraban los actores y directores Rodolfo Valdés Sigler, Alís García, Luis Felipe Bagos, Marlén Diaz y Evelio Taillat, quienes al presentar su deseo de salida definitiva del país son inmediatamente expulsados de su trabajo y comienzan a trabajar en el obispado habanero (O'Farril 2015). Cabe destacar de esta época las dos producciones que Rodolfo Valdés Sigler y Alis García dirigen en 1985 tituladas *La Virgen de la Caridad* y *La Muralla*. Aunque se trata de obras todavía con problemas en el lenguaje cinematográfico, obstan por ser la primera vez que los católicos cubanos pueden reconocerse y expresarse a través del medio audiovisual.

A mediados de los años ochenta, las actividades de la Organización Católica Cinematográfica también comienzan a reactivarse con algunos cursos para seminaristas y jóvenes laicos en el Seminario de San Carlos y San Ambrosio con profesores provenientes del Instituto Cubano del Arte e Industria Cinematográficos (ICAIC), iniciativa que marca el comienzo de un significativo acercamiento entre la Iglesia y la más importante institución oficial productora del cine cubano. Este comienzo de colaboración es determinante para que en 1984 se produzca el nombramiento del primer jurado internacional de la Organización Católica en el prestigioso Festival del Nuevo Cine Latinoamericano de La Habana. En general se puede decir que la participación de un jurado católico en un evento de estas dimensiones y su reconocimiento oficial en el periódico *Granma* se percibe como un avance sin precedentes en la incursión de la Iglesia en el mundo cultural cubano. Este logro consigue que se levanten muchos prejuicios y estereotipos con respecto a un catolicismo rancio y contribuye decisivamente a darle visibilidad a la enjuta presencia de la Iglesia en el ámbito cinematográfico nacional (O'Farril 2015).

En 1986 se organiza el Encuentro Nacional Eclesial Cubano (ENEC), "probablemente el evento más comprometedor y abarcador que la Iglesia ha celebrado en Cuba en toda su historia" (Céspedes 2003, 95). En el acto participan todas las comunidades católicas del país y sectores eclesiales de dentro y fuera de Cuba. Uno de los tópicos que requiere más atención es la cultura y su evangelización, con especial mención a los medios de comunicación social. Entre muchas de las conclusiones del encuentro se destaca la necesidad de la Iglesia de influir en la cultura y la continua búsqueda de un espacio en el medio intelectual (Céspedes 2003, 96). Ese mismo año al calor del ENEC se revitalizan las publicaciones católicas cubanas dedicadas al cine y al audiovisual, surgiendo el Boletín OCIC-CUBA. Paralelamente se crea la videoteca diocesana de La Habana, cuya función es prestar cintas a los feligreses, siendo la mayoría títulos que giran sobre la representación del hecho religioso o filmes que por diversas razones se censuran en el país.[2] Otro evento audiovisual importante es que de nuevo OCIC-Cuba es invitado a un festival cultural importante en la oficialidad del panorama cultural cubano, el festival Caracol, que auspicia la sesión de radio, cine y televisión de la oficialista Unión de escritores y artistas de Cuba (UNEAC), dirigida por Lizette Vila, funcionaria y promotora cultural. Lo religioso va tomando fuerza y la década termina con un hecho significativo: El ICAIC produce el documental, *El sacerdote comandante* (1989), dirigido por Guillermo Torres, que relata la vida del Padre Guillermo Sardiñas, quien fue capellán del ejército guerrillero de Fidel Castro, falleciendo en los primeros años de la Revolución. Se trata del primer documental producido por el Instituto cinematográfico cubano que aborda la vida de un religioso.[3]

Todos estos acontecimientos confirman el despertar de la Iglesia y auguran un panorama prometedor en el ámbito del audiovisual eclesial. Los noventa, con nuevos acontecimientos políticos, se presentan como idóneos para el avance de una Iglesia decidida a retomar posiciones en su misión de evangelizar a través de la cultura. Esta nueva etapa se inicia con la confirmación de la futura visita del Papa Juan Pablo II y el viaje de Fidel Castro a Brasil y su encuentro con las comunidades cristianas de base.

En 1991 la Unión Soviética amenaza con desaparecer y Cuba con quedarse aislada, por lo que el estado enfrenta nuevas inquietudes, como la legitimación política y la integración social de muchos segmentos de la población excluidos del gran cuerpo revolucionario, lo que provoca plantearse cambios en la Constitución, hasta ahora construida en términos de su identificación con el proyecto socialista (Bobes 2003, 175). En el IV Congreso del Partido Comunista de Cuba, celebrado en octubre de 1991, se plantea reformar la Constitución vigente estableciendo a Cuba como un estado laico no confesional, lo que se aprueba un año más tarde, entrando en vigor la nueva Constitución de 1992 que omite todas las expresiones explícitas o implícitas que comprometen al estado revolucionario con el ateísmo (Bobes 2003, 176). De los estatutos del PCC se excluye que las creencias religiosas sean un obstáculo para la militancia del Partido. La labor de la Oficina de Asuntos Religiosos del Comité Central del PCC, encargada de las relaciones con las organizaciones religiosas desde los años setenta, redobla esfuerzos por superar distancias y acercarse a instituciones y grupos religiosos nacionales y extranjeros. Tras el colapso de la Unión Soviética, toda la infraestructura económica de la nación se viene abajo, desapareciendo muchos alimentos, medicinas y una gran parte del transporte, y con ello la afluente vida cultural del país: espectáculos, obras teatrales, cinematográficas, impresión de libros y publicaciones periódicas llegan a sus mínimos. La crisis económica, traducida también como crisis de valores, afecta a las conductas de los ciudadanos que buscan nuevos espacios de realización personal que les ayude a compensar los males y ansiedades generados por la crisis (Perera 2014). Iglesias y templos se llenan más que nunca y la Biblia se comienza a vender en las ferias del libro. La Iglesia católica ve nuevas oportunidades para continuar avanzando tanto en sus proyecciones en el terreno social y político, como en su incursión en el espectro cultural del país. "Durante estos años el fenómeno religioso comenzó a crecer lenta pero sostenidamente en la sociedad. Las prácticas silenciosas de los cultos sincréticos y cristianos empezaron a salir a la luz, y se elevó la asistencia a los servicios católicos" (Bobes 2003, 185).

El audiovisual vuelve a convertirse en un recurso necesario para acercarse a una sociedad que atraviesa una situación social de incertidumbre y que ha experimentado una sensación de derrumbe de un mundo orientado por el marxismo y el socialismo. La crisis de los noventa, conocida como el Período Especial cubano, trae la necesaria apertura al exterior y la llegada de extranjeros y ciudadanos en el exilio. La incipiente comunicación con el exterior beneficia a las diversas comunidades presentes en el país. Con las visitas y los encuentros llegan las computadoras, caseteras y nuevos equipos. El departamento de medios audiovisuales de la arquidiócesis habanera se reestructura con nuevo material y a partir de 1992 vuelve a poner en marcha el noticiero diocesano "Aquí la iglesia", presentando el reportaje que se realiza testimoniando la recepción pública que tuvo el polémico documento eclesial "El amor todo lo espera".[4] Lo más llamativo de la primera mitad de esta década, y que será clave para las relaciones de la Iglesia con la cultura en lo que al panorama audiovisual se refiere, es el inicio de colaboración con la Organización Católica de algunos intelectuales representantes de instituciones culturales oficiales. En medio de la debacle económica e ideológica, muchos miembros del panorama cultural cubano toman el camino del exilio. Los que deciden quedarse en Cuba, por opción o sin ella, se aferran a muchas de las instituciones que hasta el momento habían quedado fuera del espectro oficial de la cultura. A la Iglesia católica se acercan varios miembros importantes de la intelectualidad y con OCIC —Cuba comienza a colaborar con el director de cine Fernando Pérez, uno de los más importantes de la isla en ese momento; Reynaldo González, director de la Cinemateca de Cuba; Luciano Castillo, director de la Mediateca de la Escuela de Cine y Televisión de San Antonio de Los Baños (EICTV); los directores Tomás Piard, Belkis Espinoza y Carlos León; los profesores Pablo Ramos, Raúl

Rodríguez La O, Caridad Abascal, y los promotores y especialistas cinematográficos Caridad Cumaná, Mayra Álvarez y Jesús Francisco Yagues.

Lo que hace aún más interesante esta nueva etapa, es que la religión, de
una forma u otra, comienza a tener un espacio en las obras que se realizan
bajo el auspicio de instituciones estatales. Hasta comienzo de los noventa, el
cine cubano había silenciado a actores sociales y políticos que consideraba en
los márgenes o políticamente incorrectos. Entre los excluidos se encontraban
evidentemente los religiosos. La realizadora Lizette Vila es quizás la primera
persona no vinculada a la Iglesia y con un cargo directivo en una institución
tan oficial como la UNEAC (Unión Nacional de Escritores y Artistas Cubanos)
que realiza en 1991 un insólito tríptico documental sobre la Iglesia católica
cubana, comenzando con el documental *Aquí en la tierra*, sobre el dedicado
trabajo de la orden religiosa Hijas de la Caridad con discapacitados y ancianos. En 1992, dirige *Cambiando vidas*, sobre los frailes de la orden San Juan
de Dios y su servicio a enfermos mentales. El tríptico termina en 1996, con
Confesiones, sobre la orden religiosa Hermanitas de Jesús, consagrada a la
atención de barrios pobres y marginales del país.

El sincretismo entre catolicismo y religión yoruba, logra su inclusión en
1994, cuando Félix de La Nuez dirige *La Virgen del Cobre*, documental dedicado a la Virgen de la Caridad, filmando el testimonio de los variopintos
creyentes que adscribe a esta deidad y la advocación de la Virgen María. La
devoción a la figura de San Lázaro queda recogida en el documental *A veces
nos encontramos*, filmado en 1997 por Ramón Estevanell. Aunque el documental no profundiza en la realidad socioreligiosa de la celebración, sí sirve de
respuesta al ingenuo documental de Octavio Cortázar *Acerca de un personaje
que unos llaman san Lázaro y otros llaman Babalú* realizado en 1968, que
auguraba que con los avances de la Revolución esta devoción pasaría a ser algo
del pasado (O'Farril 2015).

Ese mismo año Idelfonso Ramos dirige *Misa cubana*, documental que
recoge momentos de la misa dirigida y compuesta por José María Vitier, dedicada a la Virgen de la Caridad. La misa se celebra en la catedral de La Habana
y participan músicos como Silvio Rodríguez interpretando el tema "Déjame
tomar asiento" con letra del poeta cubano Emilio Ballagas. La cultura nacional
representada por músicos y escritores adheridos a la oficialidad se involucra
por primera vez en un proyecto de clara temática religiosa.

El cine comercial de la gran pantalla producido por el Instituto Cubano
de Cine (ICAIC) comienza a enfocar la religión desde un ángulo diferente al
que se había visto anteriormente, y es en esta década cuando paulatinamente
la cinematografía nacional decide dar un papel protagónico a aquellos que se
identifican con los valores y prácticas del catolicismo. Si hasta el año 1989
el cine promovido por la revolución se limitó a asociar la religión católica a
los sectores oligárquicos y reaccionarios del país, a partir de los noventa se

constata que el fenómeno religioso comienza a formar parte de la resolución de los conflictos sociales con nuevas "miradas que incorporan la religiosidad como un componente más de la cubanidad y que articulan un discurso de inserción de la religión en los sistemas de valores culturales e ideológicos de los individuos" (Leiva 2013, n.p.).

La película *Fresa y chocolate* del año 1994, dirigida por Tomás Gutiérrez Alea, se estrena en todas las salas de la isla, presentándose como uno de los filmes más controversiales en la historia del cine cubano. El filme denuncia la represión que sufrieron muchos de los intelectuales a finales de los setenta y comienzos de los ochenta por razones políticas, de género y también de religión. En la película, el papel protagónico lo desempeña Diego, un intelectual marginado por el sistema debido a su homosexualidad, pero como él también reconocerá, por ser religioso. Tanto él como Nancy, otra de las protagonistas de la película, tienen altares dedicados a santos cristianos (y a la vez yorubas): la Virgen de la Caridad del Cobre u Ochún, en el caso de Diego, y Santa Bárbara o Changó en el caso de Nancy (Ramblado 2006, 88). Ambos personajes dialogan en instancias cruciales con la Virgen o San Lázaro. La práctica religiosa se representa como expresión de la identidad cubana y además ya no recibe atención política (Ramblado 2006, 89). "La abundante iconografía religiosa presente en las viviendas de Diego y Nancy refiere de inmediato al sincretismo y a la dificultad de trazar los límites entre la manifestaciones de la religiosidad de diferentes sectores sociales, algo que también ocurre en la relación de los personajes con esos elementos iconográficos. Por vez primera el cine muestra a los personajes viviendo, todavía de puertas adentro, su religiosidad" (Leiva 2013).

Aunque la película no muestra como políticamente conflictivo la práctica privada de la religión, sí que llama la atención sobre la censura que el estado ejerce sobre varias esculturas de figuras católicas que el protagonista del filme, Diego, guarda para preparar una exposición que el gobierno prohíbe. Las esculturas que aparecen forman parte de un conjunto cuyo tema es la religión. Es ese el motivo por lo que, supuestamente, no pueden ser expuestas. Aunque lo polémico de este arte se extiende más allá de contener figuras religiosas, ya que al menos una de ellas tiene el rostro de Karl Marx, lo cierto es que se muestra (a la vez que se critica) abiertamente la represión gubernamental que sobre la expresión pública tienen los temas religiosos hasta la década de los 80 (Núñez 2016, 87). Núñez de la Paz (2004) estudia el movimiento de la cámara en la secuencia en que el creador de las figuras, Germán, y el protagonista de la película discuten sobre cómo actuar ante la prohibición del gobierno. En un primer plano aparecen dos de las esculturas, la de Dios con varias hoces en su cuerpo y la de Marx, con la frente bañada en sangre como si llevara una corona de espinas, y cargando también una hoz y un martillo. En el análisis secuencial de Núñez, el crítico interpreta el hecho de que al principio de la discusión Dios salga de la cámara y Marx entre en el plano, como una expulsión de Dios que es tirado fuera para que Marx, el otro dios, ocupe su espacio. Sin embargo el crítico señala cómo al finalizar el enfrentamiento de Diego con Germán, la figura de Dios sigue viva y en cambio la de Marx pierde la cabeza (o las ideas): "La secuencia parece señalar que, a pesar del intento de acabar con la religión, ella siempre estuvo presente y en contante enfrentamiento. Denuncia al Marx que llegó para que Dios no continuara siendo opio del pueblo, el Marx que usurpó su espacio y continuó repartiendo la dosis" (Núñez 2016, 98). La exposición es reprimida, lo cual queda claramente condenado en la película. El dogmatismo revolucionario parece afectar las libertades artísticas, pero también las religiosas (Núñez 2016).

Cinco años más tarde se estrena el filme *La vida es silbar* (1999) del prestigioso director Fernando Pérez. La película reflexiona sobre la búsqueda de la felicidad y presenta la religión como un elemento clave en esta búsqueda. Bebé, es el personaje guía de las cuatro historias que conforman el filme. Bebé aparece portando un crucifijo y explica que ella es feliz y que quiere que el resto de los personajes, Mariana, Elpidio y Julia, encuentren también su felicidad (Álvarez 2014, 124) . La muchacha del crucifijo, una figura mística y casi sobrenatural, abre, guía y cierra la trama. Los dos personajes centrales, Elpidio y Mariana recurren a la religión en una Cuba en plena crisis y dividida por emigraciones constantes (Álvarez 2014, 125). La película por primera vez se refiere abiertamente a la práctica de religión católica en el espacio público a través de una de sus protagonistas, Mariana, una estudiante de ballet que tiene una vida sexual desenfrenada. Durante los ensayos se entera que habrá audiciones para interpretar a Giselle, un papel que quiere representar con toda su alma. Su deseo le lleva a involucrarse en un compromiso de castidad con Dios. La película muestra imágenes de Mariana visitando regularmente la iglesia, orando y prometiendo a Dios una vida más recatada si consigue el papel de Giselle. Las imágenes del templo como espacio de refugio y recogimiento, abierto no sólo para Mariana, sino para una población en búsqueda de nuevos valores, se repiten en la pantalla grande. La fe de Mariana arrodillada ante el Cristo crucificado, sus oraciones y sus conversaciones con el sacerdote de la iglesia, muestran el comienzo de una práctica abierta del catolicismo. Sus visitas a una iglesia, prácticamente vacía, se hacen frecuentes. La película consigue alertar de cómo tanto la santería, en el caso de Elpidio, como el catolicismo, en el de Mariana, ayudan a una sociedad en crisis a entenderse mejor a sí misma (Álvarez 2014, 136).

El acercamiento de la población civil a la Iglesia se hace visible no sólo dentro de la pantalla, sino también fuera de ella. A partir de 1996, con las expectativas creadas con la visita a Cuba del Papa Juan Pablo II, las relaciones con el estado se relajan en buen grado, lo que incrementa la posibilidad de exhibición de los filmes realizados por la propia Iglesia. La Organización Católica de Cine organiza con gran éxito el ciclo "Jesucristo en el cine" con dos funciones semanales durante todo un mes. En abril de 1997 el centro cultural Yara, que alberga al cine más popular de la ciudad y por ende del país, decide homenajear a OCIC-CUBA y organiza una festividad en la que se nombra a la organización miembro de honor del citado centro, distinción que sólo se le había otorgado a personalidades seculares del mundo de la cultura cubana como Alicia Alonso, Tomás Gutiérrez Alea y Alfredo Guevara, o a instituciones nacionales como el Ballet Nacional de Cuba o el ICAIC (O'Farril 2015). Por primera vez, el área audiovisual de la Iglesia como institución vinculada a la cultura recibe un reconocimiento público que la ubica en el mismo nivel que las más prestigiosas instituciones culturales promovidas por la revolución.

Ante la inminente llegada del Papa Juan Pablo II la producción también se retoma con la realización de dos documentales sobre la figura del pontífice visitante: *Habemus Papa*, dirigida por Carlos León, que analiza el significado de la figura del sumo pontífice romano, y *Hacedor de puentes*, documental realizado por Caridad Abascal que gira sobre los viajes apostólicos del citado pontífice y las posibles expectativas que la visita genera en el ciudadano común, incluyendo en las entrevistas a cubanos no católicos y a marxistas. Aunque se prevé que ambos documentales se muestren en la televisión cubana, esto nunca sucede, aunque se programan exhibiciones públicas en sitios espaciosos pertenecientes a la Iglesia con un gran número de asistentes (O'Farril 2015). Ambos trabajos atraen a un público masivo y cumplen su objetivo de presentar a un segmento importante de la población cubana a la extraña figura que venida del Vaticano pronto estaría con ellos. Los documentales son reconocidos públicamente por su calidad fílmica y consiguen que por primera vez en todo el período revolucionario dos producciones religiosas se incluyan y premien en los principales festivales cinematográficos del país.

Tras concluir la visita del pontífice Wojtyla a Cuba, la Iglesia local trata de preservar el espacio que se había propiciado dentro de la sociedad cubana con varias producciones y publicaciones post-papa. Así, Enrique Grana, arma un documental titulado *Mensajero de la verdad y la esperanza* donde condensa los cinco días de la visita papal. Por su parte OCIC-Cuba produce una serie sobre el magisterio del Papa en Cuba dirigida por Caridad Cumaná quien con el documental *Cuba, cuida a tus familias*, retoma los debates públicos académicos sobre la Iglesia católica cubana y el entorno político social eclesiástico. Por su parte, Carlos León vuelve a la dirección con un nuevo proyecto, *Camino, verdad y vida, sobre la vocación sacerdotal* y Abascal centra su trabajo en los jóvenes y la enseñanza papal con el documental *La esperanza de la iglesia*.

Pese a que muchos de estos documentales tienen poca relevancia, OCIC-Cuba busca mantener un espacio público y continuar moviéndose con fuerza en la esfera cinematográfica nacional. A ello contribuye las proyecciones del cine club Feliz Varela, dirigido por Gina Preval, que logra mantener una programación mensual en la que comparten roles de presentadores miembros de OCIC-Cuba con profesionales del mundo del cine, consiguiendo atraer a un gran número de ciudadanos. La actividad del cine club alcanza cierta notoriedad en los círculos cinematográficos nacionales recordando en parte la labor de los antiguos cineclubes católicos de antes de la revolución.

En lo que se refiere a las publicaciones, y aprovechando el auge y las buenas relaciones con el estado, la Iglesia procede a una reorganización de su publicación oficial dedicada al cine y el Boletín OCIC-Cuba pasa a convertirse en la revista *ECOS* con un nuevo formato y secciones fijas que incorporan textos y autores de prestigio que ahondan en el hecho cinematográfico cubano. Con el cambio, la revista empieza a ganar más adeptos e incluso se distribuye en instituciones oficiales relacionadas con el cine, como la UNEAC o el ICAIC. La transmutación del boletín OCIC-Cuba a *ECOS* se puede considerar el mayor logro de la organización en el final de la década. La nueva revista *ECOS* surgida en 1997, aparece en un momento en el que las publicaciones oficiales, culturales o no, apenas ven la luz. *Cine Cubano*, la revista oficial del ICAIC, deja de publicarse en los primeros años de la década, por lo que *ECOS* queda prácticamente como la única publicación dedicada a la cinematografía nacional e internacional. Los ocho números que *ECOS* publica hasta el año 2000, dirigidos por Gustavo Andújar, y que tienen como principal artífice al filólogo Armando Núñez Chiong, suponen un nuevo logro de la Iglesia para acercarse a la población más cinéfila. La revista reseña en profundidad los estrenos nacionales y cubre exhaustivamente el Festival Internacional del Nuevo Cine Latinoamericano, con un discurso, que sin ser totalmente disonante, se aleja bastante del oficial. Directores, artistas, guionista y productores como Néstor Almendros, Cecil Blount DeMille, Elia Kazan, Gloria Estefan o Frank Sinatra, que habían pasado desapercibidos durante años en las publicaciones oficiales, aparecen en algunos de los artículos de *ECOS* (O'Farrill 2015). A la vez, algunos críticos conocidos en el ámbito cinematográfico nacional, como Lourdes Pérez, Mayra Álvarez, Mercedes Santos Moray o Santiago Villafuerte colaboran con la publicación reseñando los principales estrenos del país y contribuyendo a hacer de *ECOS* un referente nacional en materia cultural (Núñez 2016).

Continuando en el ámbito de las publicaciones, merece la pena resaltar también la edición e impresión en el año 1999 del primer libro que historiara el cine cubano, escrito por Walfredo Piñera y Caridad Cumaná, dos miembros activos del área audiovisual de la Iglesia. El libro titulado, *Mirada al cine cubano*, realiza un recorrido histórico de la cinematografía nacional desde sus inicios hasta el año 1999 incluyendo varios ensayos sobre la relación entre la Iglesia y el cine.

La evangelización a través del uso de la imagen llega también al público infantil. A finales de los noventa se incorpora plenamente a OCIC-Cuba, Pablo

Ramos Rivero, la máxima autoridad en Cuba con respecto al audiovisual y la niñez. Ramos Rivero es el encargado de organizar el taller internacional "El universo audiovisual del niño latinoamericano," para posteriormente presentar en la revista *ECOS* el texto "Educom: De los medios a los fines" donde expone las características del llamado Plan DENI, un programa desarrollado por la Iglesia en varios países con el objetivo de acompañar a los niños en el conocimiento del audiovisual. En Cuba se pone en práctica en ese año 1998 y se comienza a impartir a los niños que asisten a la catequesis de varias comunidades parroquiales.

La década se cierra para la Iglesia con un esperanzador programa repleto de nuevas oportunidades para recuperar a través del audiovisual un espacio social que se había perdido en 1959. Sin embargo, el panorama cambia ligeramente en el nuevo siglo, donde la Iglesia enfrenta una situación muy diferente a la vivida en el Período Especial. Por un lado, la presencia religiosa en la gran pantalla se incrementa, con un enfoque mucho más desprejuiciado que refleja la apertura ideológica y el debilitamiento de los patrones ideológicos marxistas de décadas anteriores (Leiva 2013). Sin ánimo de entrar en detalles, podemos citar filmes que hacen referencia al arraigo del sentimiento religioso como *Miel para Oshún* (2001), *Entre ciclones* (2003), *El premio flaco* (2008), *Habanastation* (2011) o *Los dioses rotos* (2008) y que pueden tener como antecedente a *La vida es silbar* (1998). Pero paralelamente los avances tecnológicos contribuyen a que el cine deje de ser uno de las principales atracciones que mueva a la población hacia los círculos religiosos. Los cineclubes y muchas de las proyecciones que la Iglesia organiza para la comunidad, quedan desplazados por las memorias "drive" en un principio, y "el Paquete"[5] después, ambos cargados de series, shows de la televisión de Miami y estrenos cinematográficos que permiten el acceso cómodamente y desde casa a las últimas producciones audiovisuales. La actividad de los cineclubes queda reducida a las exhibiciones de la sala de cine Walfredo Piñera del Centro Padre Félix Varela, o la del centro Loyola de la compañía de Jesús (O'Farrill 2015). Sin embargo, dentro de los esfuerzos por seguir creando producciones propias, hay que destacar la producción *Historias de familia* (2010), una serie de siete capítulos dirigida por Javier Pérez y producida por el Padre Pedro González Llorente, un sacerdote jesuita de origen cubano que regresa a Cuba en el año 2006 y crea el JECUB, centro de audiovisuales de la compañía de Jesús. La serie que pretende guiar al cubano desde los valores católicos a enfrentar las variadas situaciones y problemas que surgen en la vida cotidiana de las familias, nunca se exhibe en televisión y su difusión queda reducida a los miembros de la comunidad católica. Respecto a las publicaciones, la revista *ECOS* reduce su salida hasta que deja de editarse en papel en el año 2011, pasando a ser una publicación digital y de difícil acceso para la población.

No sólo los avances tecnológicos cambian el panorama del audiovisual en Cuba. Los nuevos cambios económicos a los que se enfrenta el país en la segunda década del año dos mil, y una mejora de las relaciones con el estado, contribuyen a que la Iglesia católica pueda dedicar más esfuerzos y espacios a la educación. A través de cursos de creación de empresas, computación e idiomas, se retoma el contacto con una gran parte de la población civil, católica o no, que encuentra en la Iglesia un lugar para la formación y el estudio que le permitirá confrontar las necesidades de un país que parece abrirse a nuevos retos.

El esfuerzo de la Iglesia en los años posteriores a la revolución para expandir su rol en la sociedad cubana a través de cineclubes, publicaciones, producciones propias, exhibiciones públicas, junto al incremento de la presencia de lo religioso en el cine nacional, contribuye a que la década de los noventa se vislumbre como una etapa clave para la Iglesia en su objetivo de influir en la cultura, recuperar visibilidad en la esfera pública y abrir nuevos canales de comunicación con la población civil. La situación de la Iglesia católica y las necesidades del país cambian según avanza el nuevo siglo, lo que abre nuevas posibilidades y vías de comunicación con la población que desplazan al audiovisual del primer plano que la Iglesia le otorgó durante décadas, y especialmente durante el Período Especial.

NOTAS

1. La primera mitad de la década de los setenta se conocen como el período dogmático o "quinquenio gris" término utilizado por el intelectual cubano Ambrosio Fornet para referirse al contexto cultural entre los años 1971–1975 de la cultura cubana, donde el realismo socialista marca una represiva política cultural y social, siendo especialmente afectada la población católica.

2. Lo interesante es que una de las mayores fuentes de suministro de la videoteca era la entidad estatal Omnivideo, una distribuidora que se encargaba de suministrar películas a las llamadas diplotiendas habilitadas para el turismo o para residentes extranjeros. En las cubiertas de los casetes que suministraba Omnivideo se podía leer que radicaba en Los Ángeles, California pero en realidad se encontraba en un lugar oculto de Cuba y lo que hacía era copiar vía satélite películas de la televisión norteamericana, que preparaban con subtítulos para su explotación comercial (O'Farril).

3. En 1985 se había publicado el libro *Fidel y la religión*, formado por una serie de entrevistas del sacerdote dominico brasileño Frei Betto con el gobernante cubano Fidel Castro, donde éste expresa su interés por los cambios en la Iglesia Católica latinoamericana. Las resonancias universales que toma la publicación del libro anima al ICAIC a producir este documental.

4. El amor todo lo espera es el documento publicado por los Obispos católicos en el año 1993, en pleno clímax de la crisis social, económica y política más aguda del país, donde las autoridades religiosas hacen un detallado análisis de la situación del momento, revisando las causas y consecuencias de la crisis y debatiendo temas hasta el momento tabú como el partido único, la doble moral, el exilio o la necesidad de un diálogo nacional.

5. "El Paquete Semanal" o "El Paquete" es una colección de material digital distribuido aproximadamente desde el año 2008 en el mercado clandestino de Cuba como sustituto del Internet de banda ancha. A partir del año 2015 la Iglesia católica consigue incorporar también en "El Paquete" material religioso.

BIBLIOGRAFÍA

Álvarez Álvarez Luis. "Ciudad letrada y ciudad sumergida." Fernando Pérez. *Cine, ciudades e intertextos*. Ed. Luis Álvarez Álvarez y Armando Pérez Padrón. La Habana: Letras Cubanas, 2014, 121–143.

Bobes, Velia C. "Cubanidad, identidad nacional y narrativas de la sociedad civil." *Cuba: Sociedad, cultura y política en tiempos de globalización*. Ed. Mauricio de Miranda Larrondo. Cali, Colombia: Centro Editorial Javeriano, 2003, 171–200.

Bobes, Velia C. *La nación inconclusa: (Re)constituciones de la ciudadanía y la identidad nacional en Cuba*. México, DF: FLACSO México, 2007.

De Céspedes García Menocal, Carlos Manuel. "La Iglesia católica en Cuba: Cultura y medios de comunicación social." *Desafíos de cara al nuevo milenio en tiempos de globalización: Cuba, sociedad, cultura y política en tiempos de globalización*. Ed. Mauricio de Miranda Larrondo. Cali, Colombia: Centro Editorial Javeriano, 2003, 95–125.

Fresa y chocolate. Dir. Tomás Gutiérrez Alea y Juan Carlos Tabío. La Habana: ICAIC, 1994.

La vida es silbar. Dir. Fernando Pérez. La Habana: ICAIC, 1998.

Leiva Lájara, Edelberto. "Imaginería, folclor y religión en el cine cubano contemporáneo." Universidad de La Habana–Aberystwyth University, Aberystwyth, London, March 19, 2013. Discurso principal.

Núñez Chiong, Armando. Entrevista personal. 12 de junio de 2016.

Núñez de la Paz, Nivia Ivette. *El anquilosamiento del proceso revolucionario cubano: Una interpretación socio-teológica del cotidiano enfatizando en el filme Fresa y Chocolate*. São Leopoldo: Escola Superior de Teologia, Instituto Ecumênico de Pós-Graduação, 2004 (disertación de maestría).

O'Farril, Arístides. Entrevista personal. 19 de marzo de 2015.

Perera Pérez, Maricela. "Subjetividad y religiosidad entre los cubanos: Apuntes para el debate." 4 de junio de 2014. http://bibliotecavirtual.clacso.org.ar/ar/libros/cuba/cips/caudales06/fscommand/44P1322.pdf.

Piñera, Walfredo. "La Iglesia católica y el cine en Cuba." *Mirada al cine cubano*. Ed Walfredo Piñera y María Caridad Cumana. La Habana, Edición OCIC, (1999): 109–118.

Ramos, Alberto. "Cine, medios, comunicación: El apostolado de la imagen." 6 de julio de 2006. http://www.espaciolaical.org/contens/07/ind_main7.htm.

Ramblado Minero, María de la Cinta. "La isla revolucionaria: El dilema de la identidad cubana en *Fresa y Chocolate* y *La nada cotidiana*." *Letras Hispanas* 3, no. 2 (2006): 84–94.

Ramírez Calzadilla, Jorge. "Las relaciones iglesia-estado y religión-sociedad en Cuba." 30 de julio de 2015. http://bibliotecavirtual.clacso.org.ar/Cuba/cips/20120824041639/ramirez.pdf.

YVON GRENIER

The Politics of Culture and the Gatekeeper State in Cuba

ABSTRACT

According to the dominant interpretation of political development and cultural policy in Castro's Cuba, artists and writers now enjoy more autonomy and freedom than ever before, and more than any other group in society. The literature suggests this is due to two factors: the relentless and extraordinary insistence of artists and writers on gaining more "space" to express themselves, and the capacity of La Revolución (i.e., the political leadership) to amend the totalitarian aberration of the past and "reinvent" itself. This article proposes a different interpretation. First, it explains how the pendulum between "closing" and "opening" in cultural policy is not new, nor is it a reliable indicator of liberalization. Rather, it is part of the governing strategy of the regime. Second, I propose that artists and writers typically seek recognition by the state and participation "within the revolution" at least as much as they want autonomy or freedom.

RESUMEN

Según la interpretación dominante sobre el desarrollo político y la política cultural en la Cuba de Castro, los artistas y escritores gozan ahora de mayor autonomía y libertad que nunca antes, y más que cualquier otro grupo en la sociedad. La literatura sugiere que esto se debe a dos factores: la incesante y extraordinaria insistencia de los artistas y escritores en ganar más "espacio" para expresarse, y la capacidad de "La Revolución" (es decir el liderazgo político) de enmendar la aberración totalitaria del pasado y "reinventarse." Este artículo propone una interpretación diferente. En primer lugar, explica cómo el péndulo entre "cerrar" y "abrir" en la política cultural no es nuevo, y tampoco es un indicador fiable de liberalización. Más bien, es parte de la estrategia del régimen. En segundo lugar, propongo que los artistas y escritores buscan el reconocimiento por el Estado y la participación "dentro de la revolución" por lo menos tanto como quieren la autonomía o la libertad.

> Mi trabajo es empujar los límites de la institución; el de ellos, preservarlos, y en esa "danza," todos sabemos lo que hacemos y que la música se acaba, pero estoy orgullosa de la tolerancia de la institución y de mi exigencia como artista.

Tania Bruguera, *Encuentro en la red*, April 24, 2009

According to the dominant interpretation of political development and cultural policy in Castro's Cuba, artists and writers now enjoy more autonomy and

261

freedom than ever before and more than any other group in society (Miller 2008; Weppler-Grogan 2010; Geoffray 2015).[1] The literature suggests this is due to two factors: the relentless and extraordinary insistence of artists and writers on gaining more "space" to express themselves, and the capacity of La Revolución (i.e., the political leadership) to amend the totalitarian aberration of the past and "reinvent" itself (Brenner 2008). This article proposes a different interpretation. First, it explains how the pendulum between "closing" and "opening" in cultural policy is not new, nor is it a reliable indicator of liberalization. Rather, it is part of the governing strategy of the regime. Second, I propose that artists and writers typically seek recognition by the state and participation "within the revolution" at least as much as they want autonomy or freedom. Actors at the margins (e.g., some theater companies, rappers, performance artists, projects like Estado de Sats, even a few economists) may be pushing harder than mainstream colleagues (Burnett and Neumandec 2014; De los Angeles Torres 2015). Indeed, there are notable exceptions. Yet, the typical relationship between the regime and the "cultural field"[2] is essentially one of mutual accommodation (Bruguera's "danza" in the opening quote), based on what Cuban sociologist Haroldo Dilla (2007) aptly called "subordinación negociada."

In an insightful article on economic reforms and the "gatekeeper state" in Cuba, political scientist Javier Corrales (2004) argues that "behind the pretense of market reforms, the Cuban government ended up magnifying the power of the state to decide who can benefit from market activities and by how much" (Corrales 2004, 46; see also Cooper 2002). It deployed a system of "formal and informal controls," alternatively using tactics of "openness and rigidity" to achieve its goals (Corrales 2004, 50–51, quoting Aguirre 2002). This interpretation is useful to explain tactics of openness and rigidity in the cultural field. Here, too, the state decides who can benefit from market activities, and by how much: who can publish, sell, and travel abroad, who can be visible on the island and by how much, who can be pardoned and reintegrated and when. What is more, the Castro regime has often alternated between openness and rigidity to achieve its political goals, and not just in the cultural field; this is well documented and analyzed for the economic field, for instance.

Much of the published material on the public role of artists and writers in general suggests that they are hard-wired to seek freedom from constraints and freedom to express their unique individuality (e.g., Steiner 1998). Since at least Plato it has been assumed that artists and writers tend to be critical of dominant values and institutions, if only because they can imagine a better world. In the same way, the literature on cultural policy in Cuba is almost unanimous in concluding that Cuban artists and writers continuously strive to acquire more space for expression, outsmarting censors with ingenious artistic and discursive strategies (Collmann 1999; Johnson 2003; Howe 2004; Miller 2005; Fernandes 2006; Geoffray 2008; Geoffray 2015). In doing so, they manage to disseminate critical perspectives on politics and society in a country where this is normally not allowed. Thus, Cuban writers and artists finally accomplish the mission that other Latin American "intellectuals" (mostly writers and artists) gave themselves back in the 1960s (while Cubans thought their mission was to support their government), becoming, by default, the voice of the voiceless, the critical conscience of society (Fuentes 1969; Navarro 2002; Mosquera 1999).

In one of the most convincing analyses from this perspective, sociologist Sujatha Fernandes (2006, 40) writes: "with formal political activities prohibited, critical debate began to be relegated to the sphere of arts and culture, where, perhaps surprisingly, the state tolerated greater diversity and freedom of cultural expression." She examines what she calls the semiautonomous "artistic public sphere," where artists can "negotiate with the state" and make gains unobtainable for other non-state agents. In doing so, they not only "amplify the scope of what is possible in cultural politics"; they also "[help] to delineate the boundaries of what is officially permissible" in the polity as a whole (151). Cultural policy is about more than "culture" narrowly defined: it concerns public expression more generally and affects the legitimacy and sustainability of a regime that, at least nominally, presents itself as the avant-garde of a genuine cultural revolution. After the late 1990s, she argues, "there were increasing attempts to use the arts as a way of reincorporating and reintegrating the Cuban people into a new hegemonic project" (40).

Fernandes's interpretation is interesting but it underestimates the willingness of most artists and writers who stay in Cuba to fit in, to be recognized, and to participate. In other words, the picture is more complete when one factors in both the propensity to push for more space and the inclination to participate, with some individuals and periods being more likely to correspond to one or the other option. Furthermore, her interpretation does not adequately consider the possibility that selectively liberalizing the cultural field, within uncodified but generally well-understood parameters, can serve the best interests of authoritarian rulers. The so-called "artistic public sphere" can be seen as "semi-autonomous" in the sense of Bourdieu's theory of fields: it is a social arena with its own logic and set of agents, all connected horizontally with other fields and vertically with the overarching field of power. While it can be conceived as a semi-protected space, it is still penetrated—one is tempted to say "curated"—by the state.[3]

This is not to deny that some writers and artists do benefit from the regime's occasional laissez-faire tactics. In fact, they are a privileged group in Cuba. The point is to see, as Geoffray (2008, 112) aptly concluded, how these tactics make it possible "to control those dynamics in a different and less costly way." Geoffray explains that in the cultural sphere, "it means that artists and intellectuals can express themselves quite freely as long as they do not structurally criticize the socialist regime." It would be preferable to say: *some* of them can express themselves *more* freely. The regime decides who can do that and by how much. It makes the newly acquired autonomy a privilege that individual artists and writers earn and are grateful for, rather than a conquest for the field as a whole.

Opening, Closing, and Uncertainty

> "Few countries have changed as much as Cuba has since then [the end of
> the Soviet Union] while remaining essentially the same."
> Ambrosio Fornet (1997, 3)

The new scholarship on authoritarian regimes takes a close look at practices and institutions where agents enjoy an increasing level of autonomy, negotiating with the regime and pushing for change (Gandhi 2010). This happens typically in so-called "hybrid" regimes of one sort or the other: late socialist, posttotalitarian, soft/competitive/electoral/semi-authoritarian (or semi-democratic). The key policy area is often the electoral system, looking at the possible benefits and perils for a regime to open the doors to opposition parties (Greene 2007). The case of Cuba suggests that political relaxation can take place in a policy area or field, too (e.g., the economy, culture, politics), and not just in what Jennifer Gandhi (2010, xviii) calls "nominally democratic institutions" such as legislatures or the electoral system. The rationale is the same: as Gandhi points out, autocrats need "compliance" but also "cooperation" from key sectors of society. That may require some give and take.

Authoritarian regimes are typically monistic but they are not monolithic. For their own stability they need to deal effectively with factions (in Madison's sense) of various kinds (ideological, institutional, clannish). In the domain of policies, there are typically two main factions or tendencies: the hardliners and the "liberals" (though they rarely are). In the cultural field, this translates into an opposition between "ideological" and "cultural" tendencies, based on views of how free cultural production should be from what visual artist Flavio Garciandía calls "contenidismo programático" (quoted in Weiss 2010, 11–12). Liberal/cultural actors seek more autonomy from official politics, though not necessarily more room for explicit political opposition. Hardliners reject both autonomy and willful depoliticization of cultural production. Over the past fifty-five years, hardliners and liberals have competed for recognition in the field and its subfields (cinema, literature, visual arts, music, theater). No one tendency has prevailed forever and each has felt the squeeze of the state at one point or another.[4]

In addition to tolerating those tendencies in its midst, the regime can reject them both and emerge as an overarching uniting force, thereby confirming its supreme authority in the field of revolutionary wisdom. Hence Alfredo Guevara (2003, 173) examines the tendencies of "dogmatismo y liberalismo" from his position as cultural apparatchik, and comments that "ambas han pretendido siempre hablar en nombre de la revolución, introduciendo así sus puntos de vista antirrevolucionnarios en un debate donde cada cual halla la justificación de su existencia en su contrario." Another power broker, Carlos Rafael Rodríguez, once stated "aunque el liberalismo es peligroso y la complacencia inaceptable, más peligrosos todavía, en el terreno de la cultura y la ciencia, son la intolerancia y el dogmatismo" (*Documentos*, 7). The first Minister of Culture Armando Hart (1976–1997) talked about his opposition to both the "dogmáticos" and the "librepensadores" (1987, 3).

The broadening of the parameters for policy discussions provides leaders with a wider range of publicly recognizable and legitimate policy alternatives to choose from.[5] The very fact that the field (any field in fact) can open and close at the Comandante's whim keeps the various groups guessing and competing in a climate of uncertainty.[6] Again, no faction or trend has remained dominant forever and what is tolerated is often just tolerated "by omission" (Dilla 2005, 36–37).[7]

Opening up allows rulers to turn the page on the Revolution's past "errors" (i.e., not directly their own) (Santí 2011). It gives the green light to some sectors in the field of culture (primarily academia)[8] to examine problems that the government is publicly committed to solve. Furthermore, a carefully calibrated thaw makes possible reconciliation with, and reintegration (even celebration) of, individuals (dead or alive) previously censured on the Procrustean bed of *parametración* (Antón Arrufat, Miguel Barnet, Pablo Armando Fernández, César López, Nancy Morejón, Virgilio Piñera, and Delfín Prats, among others).[9] Last but not least, any opening helps to polish the regime's image abroad. In sum, opening up lets some steam out, allowing the leaders and their winning coalition of the moment to regroup and to mend fences with key sectors of the cultural field.

After several years (even decades) of fairly erratic, partial, and capricious swings between opening and closing in the cultural field, and not only over time but horizontally from one subfield to the next, individuals and groups become risk averse. This is a mixed blessing at best for rulers, for they want *participation* from cultural agents, not total apathy. In his closing speech at the first National Conference of the Cuban Communist Party (February 2012), Raul Castro (2012) condemned what he called the "false unanimity" in the media (which of course are completely controlled by his government), taunting people to "tell the truth" and to be more critical. Fidel and other top officials made similar statements repeatedly in the past. For instance, in a speech to members of the Unión de Artistas y Escritores de Cuba in 1988, the secretary of the Central Committee and director of the Department of Revolutionary Orientation of the CCP Carlos Aldana denounced the UNEAC's "parálisis y [el] anquilosamiento," decried the fact that until recently "la UNEAC virtualmente actuaba como un apéndice del Partido," and denounced the "tenaz marasmo a la mayoría de nuestra prensa diaria." How to get out of all this? By fostering an intense debate, which according to Aldana was already taking place everywhere on the island, this originating "en los reiterados planteamientos críticos y tesis que el compañero Fidel ha venido desarrollando y en las transformaciones que se han derivado de ellos, cuya esencia es el perfeccionamiento de nuestro socialismo" (in *Documentos*, 8). There is no shortage of examples of artists and writers adopting ostensibly critical views that merely echo the most recent *mot d'ordre* formulated by the government.[10]

The challenge for agents is always to assess how much space the Comandante allows at any given time. Indicators of hardliner versus liberal tendencies can be hard to pin down in regimes where, contrary to appearances, the official ideology does not stand on its own. It is, in fact, a malleable resource in the hand of rulers. Years ago, sociologist Jeffrey Goldfarb (1978, 921) looked at the interplay between various politico-cultural tendencies in communist Poland and concluded that the line "between officially supported propagandistic expression and officially repressed dissident expression" could not be drawn neatly. He found that "public expression supported by the party and state does not necessarily mirror party values, and public expression repressed by the state is not necessarily dissident. Official policies with direct influence on public expression do not simply have the one dimensional consequence of promoting supportive expression and repressing politically dissident expression."[11] In Cuba, individual factors such as personal connection and international recognition can trump ideology in defining what crosses the line and what doesn't.

In economic policy it is common to divide Cuba's history under Castro as a pendulum between idealist and pragmatist periods (Mesa-Lago and Pérez-López 2004). It seems convenient to think in similar terms for the cultural field, with the "liberal" 1960s (at least up to 1968) and the dogmatic 1970s (at least up to 1976), followed by not so clear-cut periods. Arguably, even the contrast between the 1960s and 1970s can be overstated. In *Bowling Alone*, Robert Putnam (1995) writes that in the United States most of the 1960s took place during the 1970s. In Cuba, much of what is associated with the infamous 1970s started right away in 1959.[12] The fact that "realist socialism" was not imposed as the only possible paradigm in the cultural field mightily impressed many intellectuals of the time (Susan Sontag and Jean-Paul Sartre for instance) as a sure sign that Cuban communism was open and tolerant. But the presence of many groups and tendencies (think of the *Lunes* group versus the old PSP), vying for recognition by Fidel, never meant that the cultural field was genuinely open and pluralistic (Luis 2013). Che Guevara (1968, 93) was clear on this point in *El socialismo y el hombre en Cuba*: "No se puede oponer al realismo socialista 'la libertad,' porque ésta no existe todavía." The cultural field in the early 1960s was suffused with fanaticism, and artists were often "caught in the ideological crossfire at the beginning of their careers," some with tragic consequences (Howe 1994, 186).[13] The revolutionary enthusiasm of the 1960s made many observers forget or downplay that these were years of strident intolerance and civil war.

Similarly, it is acceptable in Cuba to identify the five years from the Congress on Education and Culture of 1971 to the creation of the Ministry of Culture in 1976 (the so-called *Quinquenio Gris*) as the only or main interlude of harsh cultural repression in Cuba (Kirk and Padura 2001; Weppler-Grogan 2010). Whether those years were "gray" or "black," lasted for five, fifteen (Mario Coyula's Trinquenio Amargo), or many more years, is open to discussion. But the consensus in Cuba seems to be that those particularly repressive years constituted a deviation from the blueprint enunciated in Fidel's 1961 speech "Palabras a los intelectuales." And yet, one could argue that the advent of Soviet-like orthodoxy in the 1970s, like the commencement of socialist realism in the Soviet Union in the 1930s, marked the *decline* of strident altercations and the beginning of a more predictable politico-cultural environment (Fitzpatrick 1992, 10–11).[14] All in all, only La Revolución, meaning the top political officials, meaning Fidel and now Raul, always prevail, deciding at any moment what the proper revolutionary orientation is, even retrospectively (the *Quinquenio Gris* for instance). For all practical purposes, with their use of both the conservative and liberal tendencies, letting one prevail and then censuring it, Fidel (and now Raul) have managed to be the leaders of both the government *and the opposition* for more than half a century.

Change and Continuity in *La política cultural de Fidel*

Leaders of self-proclaimed revolutionary regimes typically see themselves as enablers of an authentic cultural revolution. This has been true whether they were communist, fascist, or fundamental Islamist (in 1986, Ayatollah Khomeini established the Supreme Council for the Cultural Revolution in Iran). In Cuba since 1959 the ambitious goal of the revolution has been to create "a new man in a new society." Official documents talk about La Revolución as "the most important cultural fact of our history." And as the first minister of culture said, cultural policy in Cuba is "la política cultural de Fidel" (Hart 2002, 20). The motto of the First Congress of Cuban Writers and Artists in 1961 was To Defend the Revolution Is to Defend Culture. Or vice versa: to defend culture is to defend the Revolution (Gordon-Nesbitt 2015). Heberto Padilla (1990, 50) recalled: "The congress ended its sessions by giving unanimous approval to the new government." For years the Armed Forces and the Ministry of Interior awarded literary prizes, a sensible policy if the mission of cultural agents is to "defend" the regime.

Communist parties rarely make their top positions available to artists, writers, or intellectuals—the Italian Communist Party being the exception.[15] When in power, they put in place institutions to control the cultural field, which prevents rather than promotes the emergence of genuine intellectuals. As Czeslaw Milosz (1988, 206) wrote in *The Captive Mind*, communist cultural policy "strengthens modest talents and mutilates great ones." For all their professed commitment to culture and *l'humanité*, communist leaders mostly see cultural policy as a tool for mass mobilization and indoctrination. Artists and writers are "engineers of the soul" (Stalin's Soviet Union), "soldiers on the Cultural Front" (North Korea), or "soldiers of art" (Vietnam). They defer to authority.

Communist countries typically grant some privileges to their elite, and the cultural field is no exception.[16] In Cuba today successful artists are arguably part of the wealthiest 1 percent of the population. This seems unusual, although the idea of luring writers and artists with material incentive is not unique to Cuba.[17] Since the 1990s, trends in the economic and cultural fields mirror each other. In both fields, the gatekeeper state selectively relaxed control for the benefit of some. Dollarization, the luring of foreign capital and the expansion of touristic enclaves in the economy, corresponds to the selective opening of the cultural field to global market forces, creating what Guillermina De Ferrari (2009) called Cuba's "curated culture." After the collapse of the Soviet Union, the government was too preoccupied with the economic situation (not to mention the *balsero* crisis, the sinking of a tugboat in Havana Bay, and the riots in Havana) to spend much time micromanaging artistic production. Many artists (more so than writers) left the country during that period (though some managed to return part time recently), which in a way simplified the situation for the government but created the challenge of sustaining a strong and loyal cultural field.

As usual, the objective for the regime was to adapt to the new circumstances. Thus changes were implemented, while being mindful of the fact that, as former minister of culture (1997–2012) and president of UNEAC, Abel Prieto wrote in *La Gaceta de Cuba* in 1997, "no existe ninguna política cultural alternativa a la política martiana y fidelista que se inauguró en 1961 con *Palabras a los intelectuales*'" (quoted in Lucien 2006, 144).

For two decades, visual artists and writers have been able to sell (and publish) their works abroad. The best-known Cuban writers from the island (Marilyn Bobes, Daniel Chavarria, Pedro Juan Gutiérrez, Leonardo Padura, Senel Paz, Ena Lucía Portela, Guillermo Rodríguez Rivera) have been able to publish abroad before they are published in Cuba by a Cuban press. In fact, their work is not easily available on the island. Art has not been covered by the US embargo since the Berman Amendment of 1988 (though artists and curators continue to face restrictions, red tape, and uncertainty about visas.)[18] Artists have benefited from sales in hard currencies—and the state from taxation. Living in Cuba with dollars and CUCs, better living conditions, and a considerable safety net provided by state cultural institutions (e.g., state galleries and museums, "biennales" every three years since 1994, UNEAC, Brigada Hermanos Saíz, ICAIC, Fondo Cubano de Bienes Culturales, Consejo Nacional de las Artes Plásticas, Cuban rap agency) may make living in Cuba an attractive alternative to either the dim and more competitive world of exile or the *ninguneo* of internal exile (Arango 1997; Johnson 2003; Geoffray 2008). Be that as it may, as Rachel Weiss (1990, 219, 223) explains, "The complicity of this softer and more tactical alliance [between the state and artists] largely replaced the need for a continuing censorship of the harsher variety." For her, "commerce was the new politics in the new Cuban art, and, as before, artists found themselves both critical and complicit. What was perhaps different than before, though, was that they no longer seemed angry."

What is offered to artists and writers is a comfort zone, which as Antonio José Ponte explains, translates into *time* to step back and focus on one's oeuvre. Though this seems unlikely at the present time, the pendulum can swing back to a period of "rectification." If and when this happens, writers and artists can be mobilized again. As Haraszti (1987, 97) wrote in an insightful essay on culture under communism: "the artist, a soldier armed with paint-brush or pen under Stalinism, is, after de-Stalinization, demobilized and returned to civilian life. He remains, however, very much on active duty, in the reserves, as it were, always aware that his status might change the moment war is declared."

Today's artists and writers who are interested in political themes (there are fewer of those since the 1990s)[19] do it in part for external consumption and in an anesthetized way that may provoke a frisson for the few aficionados but have very limited public impact in Cuba. For decades Cuba exported its opposition (about 15 percent of the population, roughly the same percentage in East Germany's exodus from 1949 to 1961, or Somalia since 1991); now it also exports mildly critical art and literature, thereby defusing tensions on the island and reaping both political capital and dollars through taxation. Artists who play by the rules have been able to leave *and return* to their country, on their own, for two decades.[20] Ordinary Cubans were only granted this basic universal right (see Article 13 of the Universal Declaration of Human Rights) last January, while "exiled" Cubans are still denied the right to return to the island.

The case of artist Alexis Leyva Machado (1970–), known as Kcho, is a particularly interesting example of an official artist with a critical edge and yet favored by the gatekeeper state. Celebrated as Cuba's most internationally established artist since Wifredo Lam (1902–1982), Kcho almost instantly became an international star in his mid-twenties, winning numerous international prizes. In his short career he has had more than ninety solo exhibitions and 200 group exhibitions in thirty-five countries. His work has been exhibited in major museums and galleries around the world. Kcho is mostly known for his installations, an artistic genre (pioneered by Marcel Duchamp almost a century ago) that came to prominence, at the expense of the conventional media of painting and sculpture, during the 1970s and 1980s. Kcho has been called Fidel Castro's favorite artist. "I'm proud that Fidel calls me his brother," he said. (Fidel Castro's last public appearance was in January 2014, when he attended the inauguration of an art gallery devoted to his work and the work of Wifredo Lam.) He is a Stakhanovite who called upon fellow Cuban artists to join him in working harder to build socialism. He was elected deputy of the Popular Power National Assembly in July 2003 to represent the people of the Isla de la Juventud and he was reelected in January 2008. In 2012 he urged Cuban artists to continue working "gratuita y voluntariamente para el pueblo," and to pay taxes like any other private entrepreneurs in Cuba (which seems fair enough). Kcho's very public loyalty to the regime and exclusive personal connection to the heart of the "revolution" (Fidel himself) afford him an extraordinary level of recognition by the political leadership. He was given his own museum, gallery, and cultural center in Havana, where his work is presented along with a permanent collection of Wifredo Lam's works. In 2015 the state telecom agency Etecsa granted Kcho approval to open the country's first public wireless hub at his cultural center.[21] In an Internet-starved country like Cuba, the inauguration in March 2016 of the Google+Kcho.Mor Internet center at his Romerillo studio, free of charge for users and sponsored in part by Google, gives a measure of how "connected" the artist is with the powers that be.

Kcho's scavenged or improvised materials (beach debris, rocks, driftwood, twigs, pieces of rubber) conjure up the situation of scarcity on the island. Manuel E. González, a Cuban exile and current director of the art program for Chase Manhattan Bank in New York, said: "Kcho is the quintessential Cuban artist of the 'Special Period.'" More important, virtually all of his work deals with the eminently political topic of migration. He uses boats, docks, inner tubes, and oars, assembled with "unexpected grace" (Fusco 2001, 162). These are all potent symbols, in the Cuban context, not merely of travel and migration, but of *escape*. Perhaps his most famous work, *La Regata* (1994), an installation shown at the Fifth Havana Biennial (May–June 1994), consists of small wooden toy boats, old shoes, and other beached debris assembled in the shape of a larger boat. *La Regata* was one of the most prominent pieces of the exposition and it appears on the cover of the very official *Revolución y Cultura* magazine in Cuba (issue 5, 1994). It now belongs to the collection of the Museum Ludwig in Cologne, Germany. For Fernando Castro (n.d.), "the title camouflages with a very Cuban sense of humor what may be going on when a flotilla of vessels suddenly takes a definite direction. 'The world is made of migrations,' wrote Kcho. What might be a reference to 'Marielitos,' to Elián González, or other local attempts of emigration and exile, Kcho understands as a more general case of the human condition."

During the summer of 1994, some thirty-four thousand Cubans fled Cuba on makeshift *balsas*; from 1985 to 1993, according to Cuban migration expert Silvia Pedraza, close to six thousand *balseros* managed to reach the United States safely. Thousands drowned. González said about *La Regata*: "People went into that gallery and cried, thinking about how the installation evoked the tragic fate of so many Cubans who have taken to the seas over the years." But as Julian Stallabrass points out, "Much of this art, while it draws on the resonance of political issues, takes no stand, and is characterized by ironic or mute politics." As Cuban American artist and writer Coco Fusco (2001, 162) puts it, "while 30,000 rafters were trapped in camps in Guantánamo and other parts of the Caribbean, serving as pawns in a tug of war between Fidel Castro and Washington, the Cuban cultural ministry accelerated its export of raft art." For her, "Kcho's floating rafts are a perfect morsel of Havana Lite. His light-weight boats have been emptied of a massive human drama that is his people's deepest wound."

Kcho does not discourage political interpretation of his work. The titles of his exhibitions are politically suggestive: *El camino de la nostalgia* at Centre Wifredo Lam in Havana; *Tabla de salvación* at the Espacio Abierto Gallery, in Havana; *Todo cambia* for the Museum of Contemporary Art in Los Angeles; *Speaking of the Obvious Was Never a Pleasure for Us* at the Israel Museum, Billy Rose Pavilion, in Jerusalem; *No me agradezcan el silencio* at Casa de las Américas in Havana. But really, it is up to the (mostly foreign) viewer to decide for herself what the "content" of Kcho's art might be. It is political and even critical but in a disengaged way that sits comfortably within the parameters.

Testing the Parameters

One can distinguish between two types of parameters (Grenier 2013). The *primary* parameters shield the meta-political (foundational) narrative of the Fidelista regime from cross-examination. In Cuba the master narrative revolves around the notion that the Revolution continues and the government's opponents are counterrevolutionaries. Furthermore, the Revolution is teleologically embodied in the persona of Fidel Castro and now, by extension, Raul.[22] The *secondary* parameters delimit political participation within the regime, i.e., what can be said and done, how, where, and when.[23] To quote Fidel Castro's most famous admonition in *Palabras a los intelectuales*: "With the Revolution, everything, against the Revolution, no rights at all." Within the secondary parameters, it has been generally possible to publicly 1) deplore mistakes made in the past by fallen bureaucrats; 2) lament the poverty of criticism and debate as a consequence of internal problems within the cultural field and because of a misunderstanding of Fidel and Raul's policy; and 3) constructively highlight problems in Cuba without discussing their political root causes. Government officials can make mistakes and the population can help identify those, as long as culprits are "dogmatists ensconced in the cultural institutions" (Weppler-Grogan 2010, 146).[24] Fidel and Raul can also admit mistakes and "rectify" them; La Revolución is adaptable, grows from its lapses, and can never be wrong on the fundamentals. Finally, constructive criticism should always foster unity so it goes down better with praises of Fidel and La Revolución, denunciation of the United States and Cuban dissidents, and comforting words on how things have already improved. In sum, some criticism is possible within secondary parameters, and criticism is a seed that can grow and have unforeseen implications. But at face value, "within the revolution," no genuine criticism is possible in Cuba. Writers and artists who are in the fast lane of criticism on the island (say, a Leonardo Padura or a Tania Bruguera) are like sports cars: they need to have good brakes (i.e., they need to know how far they can go). To be a bona fide *public intellectual* in Cuba is virtually impossible.[25]

From discussions this author had with Cuban visual artists living in Cuba, it seems that censorship is not as overt as it used to be. They are typically not told directly and explicitly that their work is being censored or banned, since "Fuera de la estricta conversación policial, las autoridades evitan siempre pronunciarse" (Ponte 2010, 234). The works are censored rather than the writers or artists, especially if they are well established. Censorship is largely made of "reglas no escritas" (74) and takes many forms. Official cultural institutions can simply ignore a writer or an artist (Mexicans use the verb *ningunear*), like Wendy Guerra or Pedro Juan Gutiérrez, while allowing them to publish abroad.[26] Some artists or genres are favored in the media (reggaeton, for instance, in music), while others are not (singers and songwriters Frank Delgado or Pedro Luis Ferrer). Writers and artists who are somewhat critical of the status quo and who are well known abroad or well connected on the island (*trova* singer Silvio Rodríguez's son Silvito) are given a more comfortable niche from which they can do their work and get some exposure. For instance, author Leonardo Padura is celebrated on the island (he received the Premio Nacional de Literatura in 2012) and abroad, but his books are almost impossible to find in bookstores.[27] One finds cautiously critical and thoughtful literary reviews and art criticism in venues such as *La Gaceta de Cuba, Revolución y cultura*, or *Arte cubano*, but most publications and especially the official blogs (*La Jiribilla, Cubadebate, Cubahora, La pupila insomne*) are written by the regime's "soldiers on the cultural front."

The number of individuals involved in censorship is seemingly unlimited. Once a case goes up the chain of decision it is not clear where it stops. One painter told this author that in one particular case involving a work featuring Fidel and other survivors of the *Granma* landing in December 1956 as the "twelve apostles," Fidel himself probably approved the decision to present it to the public.[28] The safe decision for someone at the bottom of the censorship chain is simply to reject projects. Once the project is approved at a lower level, it can subsequently be rejected at a higher level. In this case those involved in the original decision will be in trouble, probably more so than the artist. In fact, for the artist, modest reprimand is the homage paid by the state to the artist for producing a work of significance. In this game the artist and his government contact/censor work together rather than against each other, to find a "space" for artistic expression that would be adequate and safe for both.[29] And to repeat, if anything goes wrong, the top leadership can always blame bureaucrats.

Even though artists are generally pretty shrewd and cautious when guessing the parameters, it is still perilous to "play with the chain." "You never know how far you can go," said Cuban writer Leonardo Padura, adding: "Sometimes it seems as if spaces open and then close again" (quoted in Burnett 2015). Art exhibitions have been censured and canceled; artists are reprimanded and sometimes jailed. After signing a public letter calling for democratic reforms in 1991, poet María Elena Cruz Varela was dragged out of her house by police and pages of her political writings shoved down her throat. The performance artist Ángel Delgado got six months in jail for publicly defecating on a copy of the daily *Granma*, during the exhibition *El objeto esculturado* (1989). In another case, according to artist and academic Luis Camnitzer, the exhibition at the Castillo de La Real Fuerza in February 1989 was closed "when it was found to include a portrait of Fidel Castro in drag with large breasts and leading a political rally, and Marcia Leiseca, the vice-minister of culture, was relocated to the Casa de las Américas" (quoted in Fernandes 2006, 139). The graffiti artist Danilo Maldonado was arrested in December 2014 for walking toward the Central Park to present a "performance" with two pigs named "Fidel and Raúl Castro." And most spectacularly, on December 30, 2014, less than two weeks after the historic agreement between presidents Castro and Obama, the government denied performance artist Tania Bruguera permission to stage an open-microphone event in the Plaza de la Revolución, detaining her (and confiscating her passport) along with up to dozens of government opponents. The performance, called *El susurro de Tatlin #6*, was a sequel to a similar one staged without incident at the Wifredo Lam Center, during the Havana Biennial, in 2009. The crackdown took place after negotiations between Bruguera and the authorities broke down concerning the site for the event and who could participate. This was a test for the Castro government after the announcement of normalization of relations with the United States on December 17. The government, via the Consejo Nacional de las Artes Plásticas de Cuba, showed its ability to renew its rhetoric, if not its behavior, by denouncing her for attempting to disrupt the negotiations with the United States and siding with elements reproved by President Obama! Bruguera and the supportive dissidents were released after a few days. Bruguera, who lives mostly in the United States and has performed there and in Europe, went further than ever before to test the parameters, but her status as an internationally known artist who lives mostly abroad gave her (so far) a shield unavailable to most artists on the island. It is noteworthy that although Bruguera saw some of her work censured in the past, she had managed until then to have a working relationship with cultural officials.

The case of writer and filmmaker Jesús Díaz (1941–2002) is particularly illuminating for he was repeatedly *parametrado* until he was finally pushed to exile.[30] A major player on the politico-cultural scene in Havana and Madrid, Díaz was a pure product of the Cuban revolution: he benefited from it, but he was also victimized by the regime he wanted to serve. At the age of twenty-four and with a few friends and collaborators, Díaz founded and became the first editor of the cultural magazine *El Caimán Barbudo* (1966–1967 under his directorship), the monthly supplement of the communist youth daily *Juventud Rebelde*. Díaz had been in charge of the cultural pages of this newspaper since 1965. After seventeen issues under his directorship (the last issue being August 1967), he and his collaborators were removed from their positions—according to Díaz (2000), for breach of political orthodoxy. The other major journal in which Díaz was directly involved in a leadership position was *Pensamiento Crítico* (nos. 1–53, February 1967–June 1971). *Pensamiento Crítico* (motto: *Pensar con cabeza propia*) was produced by a handful of young intellectuals in and around the Department of Philosophy of the University of Havana. It was directed by Fernando Martínez Heredia, who also was department director between 1966 and 1969. Up to fifty-three issues were published in forty-nine volumes (double issues: nos. 2–3, 18–19, 34–35, 49–50). Díaz points out that *Pensamiento Crítico* was an "autonomous" journal, in the sense that it was never an official organ of the Communist Party of Cuba, as many observers (especially in communist countries) wrongly assumed. In the summer of 1971 *Pensamiento Crítico* and the entire Department of Philosophy of the University of Havana were shut down by the Politburo of the Communist Party, according to Díaz, for "diversionismo ideológico." Even the building where it had its offices (K and 27th Street in Havana) was destroyed. The political leadership liquidated both *El Caimán Barbudo* and *Pensamiento Crítico* because they lost the battle for recognition within the cultural field at that particular time, not because its contributors consciously sought to challenge the rules of the game. In 1971 Díaz was sent to the countryside to work in a sugar mill, an unpleasant experience he describes in his great novel *Las iniciales de la tierra* (1987). Díaz became ill and depressed, but he recovered when Alfredo Guevara, director of the cinema institute (and a close friend of Fidel Castro since before the revolution), offered him employment and some protection. Díaz then joined the Communist Party. For the second time in his young career as a public intellectual in Cuba, Díaz joined the long cohort of writers and artists in the process of political rehabilitation. In 1987 his novel was finally published, after being rejected for publication by the *Dirección ideológica* of the Communist Party in 1973. Nobody ever explained to him why the novel was censured for fourteen years. When he asked he was told: "If you want your novel to be published, never repeat that question" (Maspéro 1998).

Díaz left the island in 1992 and became a prominent dissident (first in Berlin and then in Madrid) at a time when artists were leaving the country en masse. Jesus Díaz's rupture with the Fidelista state came as a result of a public speech he gave in Switzerland on February 2, 1992. He was participating in a roundtable organized by the left-leaning Swiss publication *Woken Zeitung*. Somewhat unexpectedly the event turned into a debate on Cuba between Díaz and Uruguayan essayist Eduardo Galeano (Simmen 2002, 67). Several weeks later, his text "Los anillos de la serpiente" (The Snake's Rings) was printed in the Spanish daily *El País* (March 12) and reproduced in several newspapers in other countries as well. It was even published in the UNEAC's *La Gaceta de Cuba*, followed by a blistering rebuttal by (this is typical) one of Díaz's old collaborators in *El Caimán Barbudo* and *Pensamiento Crítico*: Fernando Martínez Heredia. Then came an "unofficial" letter of condemnation by the Minister of Culture Armando Hart, in which Díaz was called a traitor who deserved nothing less than the death penalty. For his "treason" Díaz was expulsed from the Communist Party and the UNEAC. That letter made Díaz a Cuban exile. As Díaz put it: "No me quedé. Me dejaron, detalle no mínimo, creo yo" (in Collmann 1999, 164).

In his text Díaz condemns the "criminal" US "blockade," but he also condemns tourism "apartheid" on the island and calls "criminal" the official slogan "Socialism or Death." Last, he calls for an end to the "blockade" *in exchange for* the convocation of a plebiscite on the island on the political future of the country. This was (and still is) taboo in Cuba, and it put him squarely *fuera del juego* (out of the game). Díaz said he knew that the Cuban government wouldn't like his talk, "Pero yo no creía que la respuesta iba a ser la carta de Armando Hart. Eso no me lo imaginaba" (in Collmann 1999, 151–52). Again, in retrospect, he said that "en esa época, 1991, 1992, yo creía que había un margen mayor dentro de la isla que el que realmente existía." In a letter to Miguel Rivero, Díaz (2002) wrote: "No vine decidido a quedarme. Es más, si hubiera una mínima posibilidad de debate en Cuba habría regresado. Intenté abrir ese espacio con 'Los anillos de la serpiente,' que conoces. Sin embargo, Galeano, Hart y en última instancia el gobierno cubano se interpusieron en mi camino. Después de la carta del Ministro quedé colgado, volver era hacerlo a la cárcel y te confieso que no tuve valor. Muchas veces me reprocho el no estar preso en Cuba y me deprimo." This was the last (but not the first) time Díaz unwittingly crossed the line of the permissible, which is fascinating since conceivably, he, of all people, should have known better.

The literature on the cultural scene during the 1990s never fails to mention the importance of Tomás Gutiérrez Alea's movie *Fresa y chocolate* (1994), based on Senel Paz's short story *El Lobo, el bosque y el hombre nuevo* (1990), as a breakthrough. The movie is invariably presented, even by Minister of Culture Abel Prieto (1997–2012), as *the* evidence of liberalization of culture in Cuba during the 1990s. The film, which was only presented once on Cuban television, was definitely a sign of progress in Cuba, but one should remember that Gutiérrez Alea uncommonly met both conditions for getting a bit more space within the cultural field: he was internationally renowned and he enjoyed Fidel's personal recognition. In authoritarian regimes, the political is personal.[31] Furthermore, the movie itself meets an important condition: the action takes place during the 1970s, so it denounces past errors. Gutiérrez Alea, who was never a member of the Communist Party, always said that he was neither a counterrevolutionary nor a dissident (in Chanan 1996, 76). Asked what can be done to address the irremediable "crisis" he sees looming in the country, he answered like a teen in a beauty contest: "Bueno, una situación de crisis genera a veces una reacción, una respuesta. Yo creo que la única manera de superarla sería —y quizás estoy respondiendo a un sentimiento cristiano muy idealista— a través de la comprensión y el amor entre los hombres" (76).

In 2011, visual artist Pedro Pablo Oliva, winner of the National Arts Award in 2006, publicly stated his preference for a multiparty system. This comes close to crossing the line of the primary parameters. With this intervention he instantly (though maybe not permanently) became persona non grata in the art establishment. He was stripped of his position in the Provincial Assembly of People's Power (mostly an honorific position). More important, he had to close his popular art workshop. As his case became well known in Cuba and abroad, he received some support from fellow artists, from the vice minister of culture (Fernando Rojas) and from *Juventud Rebelde*.[32] The government tried not to provoke a complete and spectacular rupture with a prominent and much-loved artist from Pinar del Rio. On his blog, Oliva insisted that he supports the Revolution, that he is not a dissident and never accepted support from abroad.[33] All he wanted was the right to express his views, which he obviously thought was his natural right within La Revolución. In September 2014, censorship struck Oliva again. This time the president of the Consejo Nacional de las Artes Plásticas (Rubén del Valle) came in person to announce the "decision" made (typically, Oliva is not told by whom) to cancel his upcoming exhibition *Utopías y disidencias*. Del Valle was sad to say that "el contexto actual . . . no ofrecía la garantía de condiciones favorables desde un punto de vista que subrayaba como subjetivo." Oliva's public declaration on the episode is revelatory: "Me pregunto si esto no es una muestra más de la necesidad de cambiar nuestras políticas culturales."[34] As if the government's assault on freedom of expression could be addressed by fine-tuning cultural policy!

In 2013, the leader of the Cuban jazz-fusion combo Interactivo, Robertico Carcassés, improvised lyrics calling for "direct presidential elections," "freedom of information," and "the end of the blockade and the auto-blockade" during a televised concert in front of the US Interests Section in Havana. Cuban officials suspended Carcassés from performing on the island "indefinitely," but he was not incarcerated, perhaps because other musicians, including Silvio Rodríguez, publicly defended him.[35] Carcassés's criticism was bold, considering where and when it happened, even when weighted against his declaration on not being a "dissident" and condemning both the US "blockade" and the incarceration of the five "heroes." Other members of the music establishment have made public comments about the need for change in Cuba over the past few years: Rodríguez himself, Pablo Milanés, and Carlos Varela, to name a few. But irreverence toward officialdom is much more common in the fringe of the music industry in Cuba: e.g., rappers, hip-hop, and punk rock artists more or less marginalized or persecuted by the government (Fernandes 2006; Alberto 1997, 203–204; Burnett and Neumandec 2014). In fact, music being the most popular art form in Cuba, singers and musicians are probably best positioned in the cultural field to act as agents of change in the country.

A type of censorship that is apparently destined to prosper in the age of the gatekeeper state is highlighted by the recent case of Rafael Alcides, a well-known poet from the 1950s generation. He recently renounced his UNEAC membership and returned the Medalla Conmemorativa he received as a founding member of the organization. He did this when Cuban authorities censored him, preventing entry into the country of his own books published abroad. "En vista de que ya a mis libros no los dejan entrar en Cuba ni por la Aduana ni por el correo, lo que es igual a prohibirme como autor, renuncio a la UNEAC," Alcides wrote in a letter to UNEAC's president Miguel Barnet.[36] Books deemed undesirable in Cuba can still be published and circulate abroad, generating fame for their authors and revenue for both the writer and the state. This often (but not always) makes tolerable the restrictions placed on their circulation on the island.

These few examples illustrate how the regime's master narrative (La Revolución as an open-ended movement) can be used to test the parameters (Geoffray 2008). All of these writers and artists claimed to be expressing their views from within the revolution. This suggests that the revolutionary rhetoric can be a double-edged sword for the regime in place. Looking at the Soviet Union, political scientist Ivan Krastev (2011) argues that "the USSR's collapse showed that ideology corrodes autocratic regimes in two ways: it feeds the reformist delusions of the elites, and it gives the regime's opponents a language and a platform by holding up an ideal against which the regime can be measured and found wanting." The revolutionary tradition in Cuba is older than the current generation of rulers and it cannot be completely monopolized by them. And yet, the evidence suggests that the regime's manipulation of this historical revolutionary tradition works as a mechanism of control. The cases mentioned above are typical: all these individuals wanted to fit in, to participate, and to be recognized within the revolution. None are "counterrevolutionary." They can find legitimacy within the dominant ideology by asking the government to do more to fulfill its own ideals, but by doing so, they are trapping themselves into an ideological construct designed to legitimize the permanent tenure of the Revolution's self-appointed avant-garde. In Central Europe, according to historian Tony Judt (2007, 426–7), virtually all "dissidents" framed their opposition to the communist regime "from within" the socialist tradition. Unlike the New Left in the West, "the intellectual revisionists of the East continued to work with, and often within, the Communist Party. This was partly from necessity, of course; but partly too from sincere conviction." All of this vanished very quickly after the downfall of communism in the region. With the possible exception of the Czech Republic, writers, artists, and public intellectuals played a very limited role in the downfall of these regimes and even less so in the transition period.[37] Sujatha Fernandes talks about the artists' role in the emergence of "new revolutionary cultures" in Cuba. In fact, only the emancipation *from* the revolutionary mythology could truly be . . . revolutionary in Cuba.[38]

Conclusion

It is easy to wax eloquent about the art scene becoming a substitute for a genuine civil society and a scene of "symbolic resistance" (Geoffray 2008, 111) and "resistance to authoritarianism" (Mosquera 1999, 37). The signs of "resistance" are far less evident than the signs of participation and renovation of state control. Pockets of resistance come mostly from the margins of the cultural field, not from the cultural establishment.

What does the limited but unique government's opening in the cultural field tell us about Cuban governance as a whole? Is the milieu of art, as Rachel Weiss suggested, a "laboratory in which the security machinery could gain experience in dealing with unrest, something it had not really had to contend with previously"? Possibly, but another interpretation is at least equally plausible: after the collapse of the Soviet Union, the government seemed to have learned, perhaps from what Mario Vargas Llosa called the "perfect dictatorship" (i.e., twentieth-century PRI regime in Mexico), that to maintain a monopoly of power a regime does not need to control everything, especially not in the highbrow corners of the cultural field. The writers and artists who are still in Cuba are mostly there because they want to be. Some of them have experienced periods of banishment and agreed to turn the page. Others have carved for themselves a niche that is comfortable by Cuban standards and allows them to express themselves freely enough, if mostly among themselves and for foreign audiences. In Cuba, it is worth recalling, the art and literary scene is tiny and its debates almost never receive attention from the media.[39]

This opens the discussion on comparative post-totalitarian regimes. One can think of Cuba as a tired, "post-utopian" totalitarian regime, a totalitarianism with some teeth knocked out, as Solidarity leader Adam Michnik once said about Jaruzelski's Poland. But Cuba may well be an illustration of a different type: post-totalitarianism as a renovation of totalitarianism. In sum, to rephrase Weiss's hypothesis, the security machinery can gain experience in dealing not with unrest but with *ambition*. As Margaret Thatcher might say, give folks something to lose and they'll become conservative.

A possible counterhypothesis, implicit in this article, can be formulated based on the double intuition that political development is rarely one-dimensional and that openings and reforms can have unanticipated consequences (Van Delden and Grenier 2009). For all their quests for recognition and participation, writers and artists (and probably scholars in social sciences and humanities too) are engaged in an activity that is at least potentially disruptive for dominant values and institutions. If they don't seem to push very hard for democratization, at least not explicitly, their disengagement from propagandistic schemes may still contribute to the detotalitarianization of the cultural field, which in turn can have an impact on the overall political system.

NOTES

1. Writer Leonardo Padura recently said in an interview: "Por muchos años en Cuba se promovió la unanimidad como única alternativa. En los últimos años se ha abierto la posibilidad de la pluralidad. Si bien eso no se ha concretado en la existencia de partidos políticos (. . .) sí ha significado la posibilidad de comenzar establecer puntos de vista diferentes sin que eso signifique ser un opositor. Es muy importante entender eso y ponerlo en práctica." In *Diario de Cuba*, Dec. 26 2014.

2. Pierre Bourdieu's (1992) theory of fields is applied loosely in this article. Cuba's political regime is post-totalitarian; consequently, the "fields" cannot be assumed to be as autonomous from the general field of power as they would be in the liberal democracies examined by Bourdieu. With that proviso, the theoretical framework is still useful: i.e., fields have their own logic, they are connected horizontally to each other and vertically to the general field of power; finally, "agents" have "habitus" (I prefer to say "positions and dispositions").

3. Marie-Laure Geoffray (2015, 10), in her insightful analysis of the various "micro-arenas of contention" in Cuba, talks about their "heteronomy, despite their claim for autonomy, vis-à-vis the Cuban state."

4. Though one could assume that totalitarian regimes always prefer hard-core ideologues and mistrust detachment and moderation, Richard Wolin reminds us that the Nazi regime preferred to deal with public intellectuals who were broadly in agreement with Nazi's principles rather than with pure ideologues. Pure ideologues may in fact be harder to control than more flexible, pragmatic, and detached "public intellectuals." See Wolin 2006, 93.

5. Rafael Rojas (1997, 132) wrote, "las polémicas económicas y culturales de la década del 60 le fueron muy útiles a Fidel Castro y sus colaboradores después de la institucionalización."

6. Similarly, Marie-Laure Geoffray (2015, 12) observes a certain "logic of competition" among groups.

7. Ryszard Kapuściński (1989, 29) captured this apparently common practice in dictatorships in this comment about Emperor Selassié's regime in Ethiopia: "The Palace divided itself into factions and coteries that fought incessant wars, weakening and destroying each other. That is exactly what His Benevolent Majesty wanted. Such a balance assured his blessed peace. If one of the coteries gained the upper hand, His Highness would quickly bestow favors on its opponents, restoring the balance that paralized usurpers. His Majesty played the keys—a black one and then a white one—and brought from the piano a harmonious melody soothing to his ears."

8. For an analysis of how the gatekeeper state regulates higher education in particular, see Grenier (2016).

9. What Antón Arrufat (1987, 19) says about writer Virginio Piñera could apply, with some minor adjustments, to many other writers and artists, starting with himself: "Si estuvo marginado durante nueve años, no fue, como se ha afirmado en el extranjero, un perseguido. Siguió en su trabajo de traductor en el antiguo Instituto del Libro, en su apartamento, paseando por las calles . . . [. . .]. Fue rasgo permanente de su persona, desde que, en los primeros meses del triunfo se integró al proceso, hasta su muerte, *al estar dispuesto a participar*" (my emphasis).

10. Cuban social scientist and intellectual Esteban Morales Domínguez recently wrote on his (official) blog: "La televisión tampoco utiliza de manera suficiente el potencial de que dispone dentro de la intelectualidad, para debatir y esclarecer los temas de mayor interés de la población." Then he adds: "Es necesario que la crítica abierta, como la ha proclamado Raúl Castro, deje de ser algo más que una orientación política y una consigna. Para pasar a convertirse en el modo de existir político" (*El reto de la intelectualidad* (blog), http://www.estebanmoralesdominguez.blogspot.ca/, August 2, 2012). Also on his (official) blog, writer and film director Eduardo del Llano supports the idea of a "una prensa opositora libre y legal," only to add that it would be good for Raul, who himself called for a more vigorous press. Del Llano takes the opportunity to maul independent journalists, pitching in for an old government favorite: the distinction between good and bad opposition. Another example: in an interview, writer Senel Paz (1997, 85–86) says: "Remember that Soviet and Eastern European socialism did not crumble or collapse because of the undeniable social and other achievements that were publicized, as ours were too, in marvelous positive images. It collapsed for reasons that were never discussed. There was an aspect of reality the expression of which was prohibited; there was no image or, rather, only a captive image amounting to the fallacy that such a reality didn't exist because it couldn't be expressed." In other words, talking about problems gives a chance to solve them and prevent the regime's collapse.

11. In North Korea, admittedly an extreme case of totalitarianism, one finds no real aesthetic or political difference between artists who are purged and those who are not, according to Tatiana Gabroussenko (2010, 168–169). For her, "the degree of ideological dissent in the activity of the North Korean literary 'soldiers' was virtually zero. Close investigation of supposedly heretical texts whose authors were purged for alleged ideological transgressions provides no proof of any ideological defiance. North Korean literature appeared to be remarkably homogeneous in terms of ideological and Party loyalties, and all writers, including the victims of the political campaigns of the 1950s, eagerly responded to Party demands."

12. To recall: by the end of 1961, independent cultural institutions or media no longer existed on the island. In the first years following the downfall of Batista, cultural institutions (e.g., the art schools) and universities were thoroughly purged of their politically undesirable elements (Loomis 2011). Independent or semi-independent cultural magazines were shut down during the first half of the decade (*Lunes de Revolución* in 1961; *El Puente* in 1965). Even dissonant *malgré lui* cultural supplement *El Caimán Barbudo* (under Jesús Díaz) and *El Sable* (a graphic weekly

supplement to *Juventud Rebelde*) misjudged the parameters and were taken down. In theater, art, and architecture repression and intimidation had already wreaked havoc by the middle of the decade (Loomis 2011). The infamous Luis Pavón of the *Quinquenio Gris* had his counterpart in the first half of the 1960s: former leader of the Partido Socialista Popular (PSP) Edith García Buchaca. The UMAP (Military Units to Aid Production) were put in place in 1965 and lasted until 1968. Some authors acknowledge that the *grande noirceur* started at the end of the 1960s rather than in 1971 (Rojas 1997a, 130–131; Hernández 2009; Farber 2012, 81). But the myth of the liberal 1960s (incidentally, not unlike the myth of the nontotalitarian Lenin in 1917–1922 in the Soviet Union) is tenacious.

13. An interesting comparison can be made with the Soviet Union during the 1920s, with radical groups like Proletkult (Proletarian Culture) and RAPP (Russian Association of Proletarian Writers).

14. As *trova* singer and cultural ambassador Silvio Rodríguez once said, "the 1970s were in fact kinder than the 1960s" (in Kirk and Padura 2001, 11).

15. In 1936 Stalin started to use the term *intelligentsia* to represent one of the three main entities in society (aside from the workers and the peasants). However, by intelligentsia he meant the cultural and administrative elite of society (himself included) (Fitspatrick 1992, 15).

16. For instance, Kim Il-sung "gave filmmakers and crews preferential food rations and housing" (Fischer 2014).

17. Vietnam, according to Nguyen Qui Duc (2014), "has entered yet another era in its history of cultural control. Forget apparatchiks with comb-overs and coordinated suits trying to protect the revolution against degenerate thought. The people who now run Vietnam's publishing houses, film festivals and cultural exchange programs are artists—many of whom were once censored under Communism—and they have been co-opted by the lure of condos, cars and washing machines." He adds that "the new enforcers of these old restrictions are driven less by ideological purity than by a mixed bag of political correctness and market-driven concerns."

18. In 1997 Cuban artist Kcho was denied a visa to attend an exhibition of his work at the Museum of Contemporary Art in Los Angeles. For a discussion on the legal dimension of the embargo on Cuban art, see Whitfield 2009.

19. During the 1990s "most artists chose not to directly collide with revolutionary ideology, strategically insisting instead on the separation of art from politics" (Hernandez-Reguant 2009, 11). An interesting comparison could be made here with Mexico's post-muralist *Generación de la ruptura* (e.g. José Luis Cuevas, Alberto Gironella, Juan Soriano, Pedro Coronel, Fernando García Ponce, perhaps Vlady, among others).

20. Granting freedom to travel has turned out to be a smart policy move in post-communist Russia, according to political scientist Ivan Krastev (2011).

21. See "Cuba Approves First Public Wi-Fi Hub in Havana," *BBC News*, March 16, 2015, http://www.bbc.com/news/technology-31905794.

22. As Raul Castro said in his opening speech to the sixth congress of the CCP (April 2011): "el Partido Comunista de Cuba podrá estar en condiciones de ser, para todos los tiempos, el digno heredero de la autoridad y la confianza ilimitada del pueblo en la Revolución y en su único Comandante en Jefe, el compañero Fidel Castro Ruz, cuyo aporte moral y liderazgo indiscutible no dependen de cargo alguno." Consequently, it is strictly counterrevolutionary and anti-Cuba to criticize the "único Comandante en Jefe" and both writers and artists make sure they never do that explicitly. For instance, Pablo Milanés recently said (typically, to a foreign journalist) that in his youth he was sent to a "Stalinist camp" (meaning the UMAP). Everybody understands what he meant but couldn't say: he was sent to a Castrist camp.

23. Primary and secondary parameters correspond broadly to what authors Baogang He and Mark E. Warren (2011) called "regime level" and "governance level."

24. Thus, after affirming that censorship no longer exists in Cuba, John Kirk adds: "This does not mean, unfortunately, that there are not still 'hard-liners' seeking to limit cultural expression, nor functionaries determined to protect their sinecure by criticizing any work they might consider the least bit unorthodox" (Kirk and Padura 2001, xxiv).

25. For Cuban writer Arturo Arango (2009, 16): "La figura del intelectual clásico a lo Zola, o, en términos más contemporáneos, a lo Monsiváis, Poniatowska, Saramago, Benedetti, Galeano, entre los de izquierdas, o Paz, Vargas Llosa, entre los de derechas, creadores de opinión, poseedores de una vasta audiencia ciudadana, no ha sido permitida en la política cubana."

26. For writer Wendy Guerra: "One of the ways Cuba's socialist system has to disqualify you has always been to disappear your name" (quoted in Anderson 2013).

27. The film *Regreso a Ítaca* by French filmmaker Laurent Cantet, with a script written by Leonardo Padura (based on his novel *La novela de mi vida*), was initially scheduled for showing at the 36th Festival del Nuevo Cine Latinoamericano in Havana (2014) before it was excluded (some would say "censured") from the program. Apparently Padura didn't protest (not publicly anyway) (Ponte 2014).

28. "Although Fidel deliberately mythified the figure after 1959 by casting his followers in the apostolic role of 'The Twelve' and himself as Jesus, survivors originally numbered twenty" (Guerra 2012, 16).

29. For Cuban curator Gerardo Mosquera: "Since the [1980s], censorship has become more cynical, and some officials even discuss with artists what is allowed in their works—almost as if it were a technical problem" (quoted in Weiss 2011, Note 97, 299–300).

30. For a more detailled analysis, see Grenier (2017).

31. Hedrick Smith (1984, 511) wrote that the mildly critical movie *The Red Snowball Tree* (1974) by Vasily Shukshin was released in the Soviet Union "because Brezhnev was moved to tears by it."

32. http://www.diariodecuba.com/derechos-humanos/5067-el-caso-de-pedro-pablo-oliva -abre-un-debate-sobre-la-intolerancia-en-la-isla.

33. http://www.pedropablooliva.com/home.php.

34. http://www.diariodecuba.com/cultura/1411145496_10479.html.

35. For Marie-Laure Geoffray (2015: 17, Note 44), "The fact that singer Robertico Carcassés voiced criticisms of the Cuban political system during an open air concert on 13 September, 2013, in favour of four Cuban spies imprisoned in the United States, clearly shows that there is a shift in discursive norms as far as criticism. Moreover, the fact that Cuban authorities did not really sanction the singer (a few threats of censorship) also demonstrates that such criticism has become more tolerated (thus blurring the distinction made by Grenier between first and secondary parameters)." Geoffray is right about the fluidity of the secondary parameters, but Carcassés did not really infringe on the primary parameters. Direct presidential elections does not necessarily mean free and fair competitive elections. Auto-blockade may or may not refer to the dictatorial nature of the regime. And Carcassés's courageous public statements spared Fidel or Raul.

36. http://www.diariodecuba.com/cultura/1404334956_9336.html.

37. "The intellectuals who *did* make a successful leap into democratic public life were usually 'technocrats'—lawyers or economists—who had played no conspicuous part in the dissenting community before 1989. Not having performed a hitherto heroic role they offered more reassuring models for their similarly un-heroic fellow citizens" (Judt 2007, 695).

38. Cuban artist Tania Bruguera makes an interesting comment about the Plaza de la Revolución in Havana as a place for her December 2014 performance involving an open mike for anybody to use and speak their mind. She says: "Como artista creo que la Plaza es un símbolo gastado; no estoy segura que pertenezca al pueblo, sino a los órganos del poder, me debato si es el lugar correcto y tengo dudas." In *Diario de Cuba*, Dec. 29 2014. Couldn't the same comment be made about the concept of revolution itself?

39. Arturo Arango (2009, 16) draws the same conclusion: "Nuestra actuación política suele ocurrir sólo dentro del campo cultural, y se trata, en lo posible, que esté referida exclusivamente a él."

REFERENCES

Aguirre, Benigno E. 2002. "Social Control in Cuba." *Latin American Politics and Society* 44, no. 2 (Summer): 67–98.

Anderson, Jon Lee. 2013. "Private Eyes." *New Yorker*, October 21.

Arango, Arturo. 1997. "To Write in Cuba, Today." *South Atlantic Quarterly* 96, no. 1 (Winter): 117–127.

———. 2009. "Una travesía desde los márgenes, entrevista a Arturo Arango." Interview by Elizabeth Mirabal Llorens y Carlos Valazco Fernández. *Revolución y Cultura* 4: 7–16.

Arrufat, Antón. 1987. "Lanzando un fogonazo." *La Gaceta de Cuba* (July): 18–19.

Bourdieu, Pierre. 1992. *Les régles de l'art: Genèse et structure du champ littéraire.* Paris: Le Seuil.

Brenner A., Phillip, ed. 2008. *Contemporary Cuba Reader: Reinventing the Revolution.* Lanham, MD: Rowman and Littlefield.

Burnett, Victoria. 2015. "In Cuba, Artistic Freedom Remains an Open Question." *New York Times*, January 23.

Burnett, Victoria, and William Neuman. 2014. "Sudden US Thaw Worries Cuban Dissidents." *New York Times*, December 26.

Castro, Fernando. n.d. "Kcho: Some Man Is an Island." *Literal Magazine* 3. http://literalmagazine.com/kcho-some-man-is-an-island/.

Castro, Raúl. 2012. First National Conference, Cuban Communist Party, February 2, Havana. http://cubadebate.cu.

Chanan, Michael. 1996. "Tomás Gutiérrez Alea entrevisto por Michael Chanan." *Encuentro de la Cultura Cubana*, no. 1 (Summer): 71–89.

Collmann, Lilliam Oliva. 1999. *Jesús Díaz, el ejercicio de los límites de la expresión revolucionaria en Cuba.* New York: Peter Lang Publishing.

Cooper, Frederick. 2002. *Africa since 1940: The Past of the Present.* Cambridge: Cambridge University Press.

Corrales, Javier. 2004. "The Gatekeeper State: Limited Economic Reforms and Regime Survival in Cuba, 1989–2002." *Latin American Research Review* 39, no. 2: 35–65.

De Ferrari, Guillermina. 2007. "Cuba: A Curated Culture." *Journal of Latin American Cultural Studies* 16, no. 2 (August): 219–240.

De los Angeles Torres, María. 2015. "Teatro Buendía: Performing Dissent 'Dentro de la Revolución.'" *Cuban Studies* 43: 169–189.

Díaz, Jesús. 2000. "El fin de otra ilusión: A propósito de la quiebra de *El Caimán Barbudo* y la clausura de *Pensamiento Crítico.*" *Encuentro de la cultura cubana* 16–17 (Spring–Summer).

———. 2002. "Correspondencia especial." [Correspondence with Miguel Rivero]. *Encuentro de la cultura cubana* 25 (Summer).

Dilla Alfonso, Haroldo. 2005. "Larval Actors, Uncertain Scenarios, and Cryptic Scripts: Where Is Cuban Society Headed?" In *Changes in Cuban Society since the Nineties*, edited by Joseph S. Tulchin, Lilian Bobea, Mayra P. Espina Prieto, and Rafael Hernández, with Elizabeth Bryan. Washington, DC: Woodrow Wilson International Center for Scholars.

Dilla, Haroldo. 2007. Letter published in *Consenso desde Cuba, Revista Digital.* http://www.desdecuba.com/polemica/articulos/101_01.shtml.

————. 2012. "Padura: Indolente, mirando para abajo." *Cubaencuentro*, July 2.

"Documentos fundamentales del IV Congreso de la Unión de escritores y artistas." 1988. Supplement of *La Gaceta de Cuba* (March).

Farber, Samuel. 2011. *Cuba since the Revolution of 1959: A Critical Assessment*. Chicago: Haymarket Books.

Fernandes, Sujatha. 2006. *Cuba Represent! Cuban Arts, State Power, and the Making of New Revolutionary Cultures*. Durham, NC: Duke University Press.

Fischer, Paul. 2014. "North Korea's Fear of Hollywood." *New York Times*, July 3.

Fitzpatrick, Sheila, 1992. *The Cultural Front: Power and Culture in Revolutionary Russia*. Ithaca, NY: Cornell University Press.

Fogel, Jean-Francois, and Bertrand Rosenthal. 1993. *Fin de siècle à la Havane, les secrets du pouvoir cubain*. Paris: Le Seuil.

Fornet, Ambrosio. 1997. Introduction to special issue on Cuba. *South Atlantic Quarterly* 96, no. 1 (Winter): 1–15.

"From Cuba." 2002. Special issue of *boundary 2*, 29 (Fall): 3.

Fuentes, Carlos. 1969. *La nueva novela latinoamericana*. Mexico City: Joaquín Mortiz.

Fusco, Coco. 2001. *The Bodies That Were Not Ours, and Other Writings*. London: Routledge, 2001.

Gabroussenko, Tatiana. 2010. *Soldiers on the Cultural Front: Developments in the Early History of North Korean Literature and Literary Policy*. Honolulu: Center for Korean Studies, University of Hawai'i, University of Hawai'i Press.

Geoffray, Marie Laure. 2008. "Symbolic Emancipation in Authoritarian Cuba." In *Changing Cuba/Changing World*, compiled by Mauricio A. Font. New York: Cuba Project, Bildner Center for Western Hemisphere Studies.

————. 2015. "Transnational Dynamics of Contention in Contemporary Cuba." *Journal of Latin American Studies* (February): 1–27.

Gandhi, Jennifer. 2010. *Political Institutions under Dictatorship*. Cambridge: Cambridge University Press.

Gillman, Claudia. 2003. *Entre la pluma y el fusil, debates y dilemas del escritor revolucionario en América latina*. Buenos Aires: Siglo XXI.

Goldfarb, Jeffrey C. 1978. "Social Bases of Independent Public Expression in Communist Societies." *American Journal of Sociology* 83 (4): 920–939.

Gordon-Nesbitt, Rebecca. 2015. *To Defend the Revolution Is to Defend Culture*. London: PM Press.

Greene, Kenneth. 2006. *Why Dominant Parties Lose: Mexico's Democratization in Comparative Perspective*. Cambridge: Cambridge University Press.

Grenier, Yvon. 2013. "The Politics of Culture in Cuba." In *Handbook of Contemporary Cuba: Economy, Politics, Civil Society and Globalization*, edited by Mauricio Font and Carlos Riobó, 1:173–190. Boulder, CO: Paradigm Press.

————. 2016. "*Temas* and Anathemas: Depoliticization and 'Newspeak' in Cuba's Social Sciences and Humanities." *Revista Mexicana de Análisis Político y Administración Pública* 10 (July–December): 155–182.

————. 2017. "Jesús Díaz (1941-2002): The Unintentional Deviationist." *Cuban Studies* 45: 115–131.

Guerra, Lillian. 2012. *Visions of Power in Cuba: Revolution, Redemption, and Resistance, 1959–1971*. Chapel Hill: University of North Carolina Press.

Guevara, Alfredo. 2003. *Tiempo de Fundación*. Sevilla: Iberautor Promociones Culturales.

Haraszti, Miklos. 1987. *The Velvet Prison: Artists under State Socialism*. New York: Basic Books.

Hart, Armando. 1987. "Intervención del compañero Armando Hart, Ministro de Cultura, en la inauguración del Forum de Crítica e Investigación Literaria." *La Gaceta de Cuba* (March): 2–3.

———. 2002. "Prólogo." In República de Cuba, *Protección del Patrimonio Cultural, Compilación de textos legislativos.* Havana: Consejo Nacional del Patrimonio Cultural, Ministerio de Cultura.

He, Baogang, and Mark E. Warren. 2011. "Authoritarian Deliberation: The Deliberative Turn in Chinese Political Development." *Perspectives on Politics* 9: 269–89.

Hernández, Rafael. 2002. "Looking at Cuba: Notes toward a Discussion." *boundaries 2* (Fall): 125–126.

———. 2009. "The Red Year." *ReVista: Harvard Review of Latin America* 8, no. 11 (Winter): 21–24.

Hernandez-Reguant, Ariana, ed. 2009. *Cuba in the Special Period: Culture and Ideology in the 1990s.* New York: Palgrave Macmillan.

Howe, Linda S. 2004. *Cuban Writers and Artists after the Revolution.* Madison: University of Wisconsin Press.

Johnson, Peter T. 2003. "The Nuanced Lives of the Intelligentsia." In *Conflicts and Change in Cuba,* edited by Enrique A. Baloyra and James A. Morris, 137–163. Albuquerque: University of New Mexico Press.

Jones, Derek, ed. 2001. *Censorship: A World Encyclopedia.* London: Fitzroy Dearborn.

Judt, Tony. 2007. *Postwar: A History of Europe since 1945.* New York: Penguin.

Kapuściński, Ryszard. 1989. *The Emperor: Downfall of an Autocrat.* New York: Vintage International.

Kirk, John M., and Leonardo Padura Fuentes. 2001. *Culture and the Revolution: Conversations in Havana.* Gainesville: University Press of Florida.

Krastev, Ivan. 2011. "Paradoxes of the New Authoritarianism." *Journal of Democracy* 22, no. 2 (April): 5–16.

Loomis, John A. 2011. *Revolution of Forms: Cuba's Forgotten Art Schools.* Rev. ed. Foreword by Gerardo Mosquera. New York: Princeton Architectural Press.

Lucien, Renée Clémentine. 2006. *Résistance et cubanité: Trois écrivains nés avec la Révolution cubaine, Eliseo Alberto, Leonardo Padura, Zoé Valdés.* Paris: L'Harmattan.

Luis, William. 2013. *Lunes de revolución.* Madrid: Verbum.

Maspéro, François. 1998. Review of *Parle-moi un peu de Cuba.* Le Monde, May 29.

Mesa-Lago, Carmelo, and Jorge Pérez-López. 2004. *Cuba's Aborted Reform: Socioeconomic Effect, International Comparisons, and Transition Policies.* Gainesville: University Press of Florida.

Miller, Nicola. 2008. "A Revolutionary Modernity: The Cultural Policy of the Cuban Revolution." *Journal of Latin American Studies* 40: 675–696.

Milosz, Czeslaw. 1988. *La pensée captive.* Paris: Gallimard, Folio.

Mosquera, Gerardo. 1999. "La isla infinita, introducción al nuevo arte cubano." In *Contemporary Art from Cuba: Irony and Survival on the Utopian Island,* edited by Marylyn A. Zeitlin. New York: Arizona State University Art Museum, Delano Greenidge Editions.

Navarro, Desiderio. 2002. "In *Medias Res Publicas*: On Intellectuals and Social Criticism in the Cuban Public Sphere." Special issue, *boundary 2* (Fall).

Nguyen Qui Duc. 2014. "The New Censors of Hanoi." *New York Times,* April 27.

Paz, Senel. 1997. Interviewed by Magda Resik in "Writing Is a Sort of Shipwreck: An Interview with Senel Paz." *South Atlantic Quarterly* 96, no. 1 (Winter): 84–93.

Ponte, Antonio José. 2010. *Villa Marista en plata: Arte, política, nuevas tecnologías.* Madrid: Editorial Colibrí.

———. 2012. ¿Cómo gestionar desde La Habana la literatura del exilio? *Diario de Cuba* (Madrid), February 17.

———. 2014. ¿Donde está Leonardo Padura? *Diario de Cuba* (Madrid), December 15.

Protección del Patrimonio Cultural, Compilación de textos legislativos. 2002. Havana: Republica de Cuba, Consejo Nacional del Patrimonio Cultural, Ministerio de Cultura.

Putnam, Robert D. 1995. "Bowling Alone: America's Declining Social Capital." *Journal of Democracy* 6, no. 1: 65–78.

Rojas, Rafael. 1997a. "Entre la revolución y la reforma." *Encuentro de la Cultura Cubana* 4–5 (Spring–Summer).

———. 1997b. "Políticas invisibles." *Encuentro de la Cultura Cubana* 6–7 (Fall–Winter).

———. 2000. "El intelectual y la revolución Contrapunteo cubano del nihilismo y el civismo." *Encuentro de la cultura cubana* 16–17 (Spring–Summer).

———. 2006. *Tumbas sin sosiego.* Barcelona: Anagrama.

———. 2009. *El estante vacío, literatura y política en Cuba.* Barcelona: Anagrama.

Rosenberg Weinreb, Amelia. 2009. *Cuba in the Shadow of Change: Daily Life in the Twilight of the Revolution.* Gainesville: University Press of Florida.

Santí, Enrico Mario. 2011. *Fresa y chocolate: The Rhetoric of Reconciliation.* Miami: Institute for Cuban and Cuban-American Studies.

Simmen, Andrés. 2002. "Tras la muerte de Jesús Díaz." *Encuentro de la cultura cubana* 25 (Summer).

Smith, Hedrick. 1984. *The Russians.* Rev. ed. New York: Ballantine Books.

Steiner, George. 1998. *Real Presences.* Chicago: University of Chicago Press.

Van Delden, Marteen, and Yvon Grenier. 2009. *Gunshots at the Fiesta: Politics and Literature in Latin America.* Nashville, TN: Vanderbilt University Press.

Weiss, Rachel. 2011. *To and from Utopia in the New Cuban Art.* Minneapolis: University of Minnesota Press.

Weppler-Grogan, Doreen. 2010. "Cultural Policy, the Visual Arts, and the Advance of the Cuban Revolution in the Aftermath of the Gray Years." *Cuban Studies* 42: 143–165.

Whitfield, Esther. 2009. "Truths and Fictions: The Economics of Writing, 1994–1999." In *Cuba in the Special Period: Culture and Ideology in the 1990s,* edited by Ariana Hernandez-Reguant, 21–36. New York: Palgrave Macmillan.

Wolin, Richard. 2006. *The Seduction of Unreason: The Intellectual Romance with Fascism from Nietzsche to Postmodernism.* Princeton, NJ: Princeton University Press.

ECONOMY

CARMELO MESA-LAGO, ROBERTO
VEIGA GONZÁLEZ, LENIER GONZÁLEZ
MEDEROS, SOFÍA VERA ROJAS, AND
ANÍBAL PÉREZ-LIÑÁN[1]

Voices of Change from Cuba's Expanding Nonstate Sector

ABSTRACT

Analysis of the emerging nonstate sector (NSS) in Cuba (self-employed, usufruct farmers, members of new cooperatives, and sellers/buyers of dwellings) based on eighty intensive interviews taken in Cuba between September 2014 and November 2015. The interviews identify the characteristics of the interviewees (age, gender, race, and education) and search for key NSS aspects such as: satisfaction level, employees hired, profit and its distribution (investment and consumption), time to recover investment, taxes, plans to expand the activity, reception of remittances, state microcredit and other types of aid, competition and price reduction, publicity channels, sources of inputs, problems faced, and improvements or changes desired. It ends with suggestions for the NSS improvement extracted from the interviews.

RESUMEN

Análisis del emergente sector no estatal —SNE— en Cuba (cuentapropistas, usufructuarios, socios de nuevas cooperativas y compraventa de viviendas) mediante ochenta entrevistas intensivas tomadas entre septiembre de 2014 y noviembre de 2015, las cuales identifican características de los entrevistados (edad, género, raza y educación) e indagan sobre aspectos claves: nivel de satisfacción, número de empleados, ganancias y su distribución (inversión y consumo), tiempo para recuperar la inversión, impuestos, planes de expansión de la actividad, recepción de remesas, microcrédito estatal y otro tipo de ayuda, competencia y reducción de precios, vías de publicidad, fuentes de insumos, problemas enfrentados y deseos de cambio o mejora. Termina con sugerencias para desarrollar el sector extraídas de las entrevistas.

This article summarizes the main conclusions from a forthcoming book by the authors studying the nonstate sector (NSS) in Cuba, which has a growing dynamism capable of transforming the predominant state economy (72 percent of the labor force), which is undergoing a difficult situation (Mesa-Lago, Veiga, González, Vera, and Pérez-Liñán 2018). We explain the composition of the

289

NSS and identify four of their key groups: self-employed; usufruct farmers; members of the new nonagricultural and production cooperatives; and home buyers, sellers, and real estate agents. In each of the four groups we provide antecedents based on all the available information: size and trends, progress, obstacles, and impacts. The most innovative and relevant element in the book is the analysis of the answers from interviews conducted in Cuba in 2014–2015 to collect the NSS "voices." The principal objective of the book and this article is to offer key data not available on the NSS: its characteristics of age, gender, race, and education; important economic aspects such as level of satisfaction, profits, investment, employees hired, reception of foreign remittances, state microcredit and other aid, competition, publicity, and expansion plans; and the NSS's own perceptions of their problems and desires for change. We compare such aspects and perceptions among the four groups, and extract suggestions from the "voices" to improve the sector and contribute to the economic and social development of the country.

NSS Definition, Expansion, Restrictions, and Impact

What Is the Nonstate Sector?

The term *nonstate sector* (NSS) is used for two reasons. First, the government loathes the term *private*. Second, NSS embraces both private activities (self-employment and home buying and selling) and mixed types of ownership. For instance, in the NASC the state keeps ownership of the structure and leases it (often selling the equipment) to co-op members who have to pay rent and public utilities, buy inputs, and refurbish the locale. In the usufruct, the state also keeps the land ownership and leases a parcel to the farmer (without paying rent) through ten-year contracts that may be canceled or renewed, whereas the farmer works the land and keeps the produce.

Expansion

The expansion of the NSS in Cuba is one of President Raúl Castro's key structural reforms initiated since 2007 (Mesa-Lago and Pérez-López 2013; Mesa-Lago 2014). The NSS is mainly composed of four groups: the self-employed (498,000), usufruct farmers (312,300), and members of new non-agricultural and services cooperatives—NASC (5,500) and buyers and sellers of private dwellings (about 100,000). The total NSS in 2014 was 1.16 million, tantamount to 23 percent of the labor force. Self-employment and usufruct began during the severe economic crisis of the 1990s ("Período Especial"), but they have been significantly expanded since 2011, while NASC and buying/selling of dwellings started in 2011–2012.

Restrictions

All four groups are closely regulated and supervised by the state, which imposes other obligations: (1) usufruct farmers must sell part of the crop at state-fixed prices below the market price—if this duty is not met, the state cancels the contract; (2) self-employment is limited to 201 occupations, most of which are unskilled or low skilled (e.g., fortune-tellers, clowns, restroom attendants, cart sellers of produce) with very few skilled occupations (e.g., translators, real estate and insurance agents), university graduates are banned from practicing their profession as self-employed; (3) NASC have to pass four instances to be approved and the final decision is left to the Council of Ministers; and (4) no one can have more than two homes—a principal residence and a second residence at the beach or in the countryside for recreational purposes (very few Cubans can afford the latter)—and home sellers must update the dwelling inscription at the real-estate registry (neglected for half a century) and follow a complex procedure while buyers must prove the legal origin of the money to buy the property.

In addition, heavy taxation is imposed on the NSS. For instance, the self-employed must pay sales tax, labor force tax, monthly and annual income tax and social security—the labor tax increases gradually with the number of employees hired. They are also submitted to frequent inspections and sanctions for legal infractions (e.g., an usufruct farmer for investing in the parcel without state permit, a self-employed person for selling goods not specifically authorized, or a home buyer for relying on a third party). Confiscation of assets is often imposed for those violations.

Impacts and potential

Despite these restrictions and obstacles, the NSS has the potential to transform the Cuban economy, increase GDP growth, raise agricultural output, expand exports and reduce the $2.5 billion of annual imports, and improve worker income and living standards. Furthermore, in 2011 the government estimated that there were 1.8 million state employees (36 percent of the labor force) that were not needed and had to be dismissed to reduce high wage costs and the fiscal deficit. The only way to accomplish that task is by developing the NSS but the cited restrictions have obstructed its expansion.

Current economic impacts of NSS are difficult to assess due to the lack of systematic statistics. The self-employed are 10 percent of the labor force (but only 5 percent of GDP due to their low skills and productivity) and 54 percent of total produce sales. Usufruct farmers are 6 percent of the labor force, the major reason for the expansion of sowed land and reduction of idle land. Together with private farmers and agricultural co-ops (usufruct is not disaggregated), they generate 83 percent of agricultural production compared with 17 percent by the state. NASC members have the least impact, making up only 0.1 percent of the labor force and 4 percent of produce sales. Private builders of dwellings represent 52 percent of the total compared with 48 percent by the state—no data are available on the value of sales (based on ONEI 2015; Pons 2015).

The Literature

The literature on the NSS is growing fast—Feinberg 2013; Peters 2014; González-Corzo and Justo 2014; Piñeiro 2014; CSG 2015; Padilla 2015; Pérez Villanueva and Torres 2015; Pons 2015; Ritter and Henken 2015; Morales 2016—and yet the available work still doesn't provide comprehensive systematic data on the four groups, based on intensive interviews on key relevant issues of the NSS.

This vacuum is largely filled by gathering NSS "voices" through eighty intensive interviews in the provinces of Havana, Artemisa, and Mayabeque between September 2014 and November 2015. Four questionnaires were elaborated, one for each of the four NSS groups, tested in a pilot, and subsequently revised; each interview took from ninety minutes to two hours, most questions were open ended to allow the interviewees to say what they wanted. About 60 percent of the questions were similar to compare answers among the four groups. Results were tabulated to prepare comparative tables. Chapters of the book systematically deal with the four NSS groups: antecedents such as size and trends, characteristics, progress, obstacles, and impact; the presentation and analysis of the interview results; the conclusions that provide aggregate data for all the NSS on the key issues investigated; a selection of most relevant/interesting answers, and suggestions extracted from the interviews. This article summarizes the book major findings.

New Light on Crucial Issues

Characteristics of Interviewees

Table 1 shows the percentage distribution of the four characteristics in the sample (age, gender, race and education), among all 80 interviewees.

The average interviewee is 41 years old (the population average), male, and white with mid-technical or university education. An accurate comparison of the sample with national averages is difficult because of lack of data on the latter. Age and identification as black representation seem to be similar. On the other hand, women are underrepresented (26 percent in the sample versus 37 percent nationally); whites are overrepresented (80 percent versus 64 percent) and mulattoes underrepresented (11 percent versus 27 percent);

TABLE 1. Characteristics by age, gender, race and education

Characteristics	Percentage	Characteristics	Percentage
Age		**Skin color**	
22–30	21	White	80
31–40	37	Mulatto	11
41–50	15	Black	9
51–60	16	Total	100
61–75	11	**Education**	
Total	100	Primary/secondary	16
Gender		Middle technician	19
Male	74	Pre-university	24
Female	26	University	41
Total	100	Total	100

education is higher in the sample particularly at the university level (41 percent and 22 percent). The youngest group in the sample is the self-employed (average of 34 years old), followed by home buyers/sellers (40) and usufruct farmers (51)—despite the physically demanding work, 28 percent are in the 61–75 age bracket (ONEI 2015, 2016). All usufruct farmers are white and male, the latter probably due to the type of work involved, and they are the least educated; the best educated are the self-employed and home buyers/sellers.

Satisfaction Level

Fifty-five interviewees (self-employed, usufruct farmers, and NASC members) were asked to measure their level of satisfaction in what they do and earn, based on a scale from 1 (least satisfied) to 10 (most satisfied); they ranked themselves without any instructions: 80 percent were highly satisfied (8–10), 15 percent were ambiguous (4–7), and 5 percent (3) were dissatisfied (1–3) (table 2 and figure 1). The most satisfied were the self-employed (72 percent in the highest three levels and only 8 percent in the lowest three levels), followed by usufruct farmers (64 percent and 12 percent respectively); NASC members were only five but ranked least satisfied.

Some voices: "I love what I do and the business income is comfortable"; "my work helps me to develop both professionally and personally"; "I am satisfied with what I do but not with what I earn"; "it is much better than to work for the state, but still I don't fulfill my expectations and want to improve them."

TABLE 2. Level of satisfaction

How satisfied/unsatisfied you are? *(1 = least, 10 = most)*	*Percentage*
Satisfied (8–10)	80
Ambiguous (4–7)	15
Unsatisfied (1–3)	5
Total	100

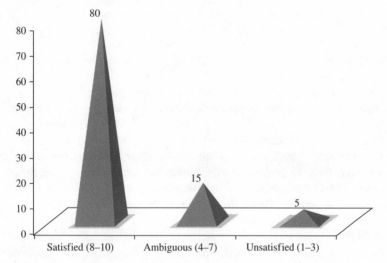

FIGURE 1. How satisfied are you with what you do and earn?

Employees Hired

The self-employed, usufruct farmers, and NASC members hire wage earners to help them. Out of 55 interviewees, 43 percent (24) don't hire and 4 percent (2) don't know or did not answer; there is evidence that some don't declare their employees (employees hired by one self-employed person average 0.6 percent nationally). Out of the remaining 53 percent (29): 36 percent hire between one and five employees, 13 percent between six and ten, 2 percent between eleven and fifteen, and 2 percent between sixteen and twenty. Therefore, a large majority (79 percent) either do not hire or have less than five employees. The self-employed contract more employees (68 percent) than the usufruct farmers (44 percent). Among those with employees, 31 percent pay a

TABLE 3. Number of employees hired

How many employees do you have?	Percentage
None	43
Have	57
1–5	36
6–10	13
11–15	2
16–20	2
Other	4
Total	100

daily wage, 13 percent monthly, 5 percent weekly, and 11 percent at another frequency. It was impossible to tabulate wages because of the huge variety of payment methods and their sums. Among those who hire, one-third—mainly the self-employed—have problems with their employees.

Profit and Its Distribution

Among 55 interviewees (self-employed, usufruct farmers, and NASC members), 93 percent had profits and only 7 percent did not, which explains the high satisfaction level, despite bureaucratic restrictions. Investment went to build or repair, buy inputs and equipment, or acquire a dwelling. Associations showed that the more educated invest more, and vice versa. The young assigned more of their profit to investment than the elderly. The self-employed invested much more than usufruct farmers, because the former are more educated, have higher profits, and hire more employees, and vice versa.

Sixty-five interviewees (the same number as above plus home sellers) were asked how they allocate their profits (including the previously excluded selling value of their dwellings): 35 percent (23) invested the entire profit, 29 percent (19) mixed investment and consumption, and 14 percent (22) used all for consumption; 14 percent (9) didn't know, didn't answer, or had no profits (table 4 and figure 2). Despite legal authorization, usufruct farmers have not built a house or stable in the parcel, either because they have a dwelling close to the parcel, the building cost is too high, or it takes time away from working the land; 56 percent of usufruct farmers sell their crop to the state, which sets the price below the market price (*acopio*); among those farmers, 40 percent sell between 51 percent and 100 percent of their crops to the state.

TABLE 4. Profit allocation

How do you allocate your profits?	Percentage
Investment	35
Consumption	22
Both	29
Other	14
Total	100

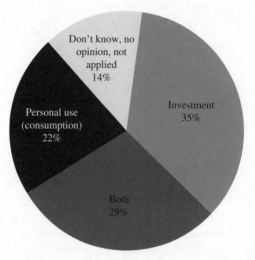

FIGURE 2. How do you allocate your profits?

Time to Recover Investment

Among the self-employed, 68 percent invested; 29 percent of them recovered their investment in less than one year, 18 percent recovered it between one and two years, and 53 percent recovered it between two and four years (table 5). The Kellogg study of nine self-employed persons found that seven (78 percent) had the potential to recoup the investment in less than one year, much more than in our study, but those nine self-employed were enrolled in the Cuba Emprende training program and hence had more potential to recover the investment more quickly (CSG 2015).

Taxes

Cuba has a dual currency: the national peso (CUP) and the "convertible peso" (CUC)—not really convertible because it is not traded in the international mar-

**TABLE 5. Time to recover
investment (self-employed)**

How many years did it take to recover your investment?	Percentage
Less than 1	29
More than 1 and less than 2	18
2–4	53
Total	100

ket. CUC is similar in value to the dollar and equal to 25 CUP. Amid many tributes, there is a monthly and annual progressive income tax; the monthly one was impossible to tabulate due to its huge diversity. In the NSS, save for buyers/ sellers, 58 percent pay the annual tax: 20 percent from 300 to 1,000 CUP; 18 percent from 1,001 to 5,000 CUP, and 15 percent from 5,000 to 20,000 CUP (the last is three times the median state annual wage). The remaining 42 percent either did not know or did not respond. The more educated pay more annual tax than the less educated, possibly because the former have higher profits.

Reception of Foreign Remittances

Among 55 interviewees (excluding buyers/sellers), 76 percent (42) do not receive remittances from abroad and 34 percent (13) get them. Usufruct farmers receive proportionally more remittances (32 percent) than the self-employed (12 percent), possibly because they have less income (table 6). Out of the five NASC members, three receive remittances and two do not.

An average of 24 percent receive remittances, considerably less than the average 65 percent among the population. Recipients might be underrepresented in our sample, and some recipients might be reluctant to report. Reception of remittances seems to depend on the recipient's age: older people receive more remittances and younger people receive fewer, possibly because the elderly have children and grandchildren abroad who send remittances, whereas the young live off their own earnings.

TABLE 6. Reception of foreign remittances

Do you receive remittances?	Percentage
No	76
Yes	24
Total	100

Reception of State Credit or Loans

This question was asked to 75 interviewees (excluding real-estate agents) and all answered negatively for the following reasons: does not want the microloan, does not need it, requested and did not get it, too much bureaucracy, complex and long process (*papeleo*), or too small sum for the demanded effort: "I tried but walked out in the third week because of too much bureaucracy."

Other Types of Aid

Among 65 interviewees (excluding buyers/sellers/real estate agents), 68 percent (44) received aid and 32 percent (21) did not. Aid comes from family and friends, mostly domestic but some from abroad (sending inputs). The younger the interviewee, the more aid they receive, and vice versa, an indication of solidarity.

Figure 3 compares reception of remittances, state microloans, and other types of aid.

Competition and Reduction of Prices

This question was only asked to 30 interviewees (self-employed and NASC) as it was not germane to the rest. Seventy-seven percent (23) faced competition and 23 percent (seven) did not (table 7). Then we asked 55 interviewees (all save for buyers/sellers/real estate agents) if they cut prices: 84 percent (46) answered no and only 16 percent (9) answered yes. All self-employed argued that their product or service is different or better. All usufruct farmers said that

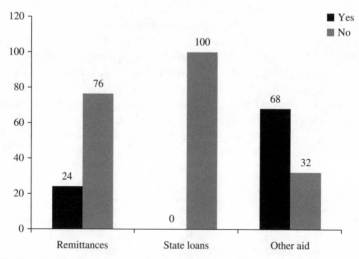

FIGURE 3. Reception of remittances, state loans, and other aid

TABLE 7. Competition

Do you have competition?	Percentage
Yes	77
No	23
Total	100

they could not reduce prices because of the very high cost of inputs and the low price paid for their produce by state *acopio*.

Sources for Acquisition of Inputs

Fifty-five interviewees (self-employed, usufruct farmers, and NASC members) were asked where they obtain their inputs. Categories were not exclusive and there were 80 mentions (table 8 and figure 4): 25 percent (20), all self-employed, bought inputs in the hard-currency state shops (TRD) at very high prices because TRD charge a 200 percent markup; 25 percent (20), all usufruct farmers, got inputs in credit and service cooperatives (CCS); 16 percent (13), both self-employed and usufruct farmers, bought on the black market (*por la izquierda*) also at high prices; 9 percent (7) bought from other usufruct producers or self-employed; 4 percent (3) didn't buy (usufruct farmer) or resorted to relatives (self-employed); 4 percent got inputs in the free agricultural market also at high prices but lower than TRD and black market; 4 percent, all self-employed, got inputs from abroad, through persons that buy abroad and sell in Cuba at lower prices than the TRD (*mulas*) or from relatives: "most inputs are bought abroad with somebody that travels here because they are cheaper." Only 2 percent (2), all self-employed, bought in the only wholesale market, El Trigal, which is notoriously insufficient, and 10 percent (8), all NASC members, bought in multiple places.

TABLE 8. Sources for inputs

Where do you get inputs?	Percentage
State shop (TRD)	25
Cooperative (CCS)	25
Black market (*izquierda*)	16
Other producer or self-employed	9
Don't buy or family	4
Agricultural market	4
Abroad	4
Wholesale market	2
Other	11
Total	100

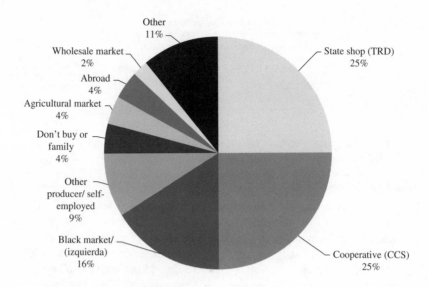

FIGURE 4. Where do you buy your inputs?

The lower the age the fewer that buy in the TRD and vice versa; women buy in the TRD more than men because men have more access to diverse sources (e.g., usufruct farmers in CCS).

Publicity Channels

This question was asked to 55 interviewees (all save for usufruct farmers because they don't advertise); there were 100 mentions as categories are not exclusive: 33 percent (33 mentions) advertise mouth-to-mouth; 19 percent by Internet (all except NASC members); 13 percent with personal cards (except buyers and sellers); 11 percent with posters on the façade of the business (all interviewees); 10 percent with flyers (self-employed); 12 percent by other means such as fairs, telephone directory, radio, and television; only 2 percent do not advertise (table 9 and figure 5).

Rudimentary means of publicity: word of mouth (predominant), personal cards, flyers, and posters are the large majority (67 percent), whereas Internet and other modern means are a minority (31 percent)—albeit rising—because only 5 percent of the population has Internet access at $2.50 an hour. Revolico. com and the "weekly package" (an external disc with movies, TV shows, and ads) are the most used means.

TABLE 9. Publicity

How do you advertise?	Percentage
Word of mouth	33
Internet	19
Card	13
Poster	11
Flyers	10
Other	12
Don't advertise	2
Total	100

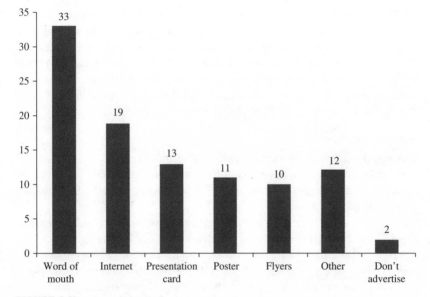

FIGURE 5. How do you advertise?

Expansion of the Activity

Proof of the Cuban entrepreneurial spirit is that 92 percent of the self-employed that were posed this question answered that they want to expand their micro-business and only 8 percent said they don't: "It is important to keep a low profile in this activity because if I expand, I would have to hire employees and then pay the annual income tax that would take most of my profits."

Among the 92 percent that plan an expansion, 44 percent would do it geographically, 16 percent by hiring more employees, and 32 percent by other means

TABLE 10. Plans to expand
(self-employed)

Do you plan to expand?	Percentage
Yes	**92**
Geographically	44
More employees	16
Other	32
No	**8**
Total	100

such as adding another room to rent to tourists and pursuing more educated clients that pay higher prices for quality services. Of the 44 percent that want to expand geographically, 16 percent would expand in Havana, 8 percent in other provinces, 8 percent abroad; among 12 percent of others plan to generate more products or services, to buy more cars to transport tourists, and to acquire houses to rent (table 10). Two noteworthy answers: "I would like to have a virtual office on the Internet to sell my services abroad" and "I can see a container leaving for the Caribbean, to sell in the Bahamas or in the Cayman Islands."

Main Problems Faced

This and the following question were posed to the 80 interviewees; questions were open ended and the large majority answered in detail, therefore what appears here and in the next section are exactly the voices of the NSS identifying their problems and desires.

There were 116 mentions because categories were not exclusive: 97.4 percent (77 mentions) reported major problems and only 2.6 percent (3) did not report problems. Identified problems were: 31.9 percent (37 mentions) cited poor access and high prices of inputs (all interviewees except NASC members); 26.7 percent (31) complained about bureaucracy, obstacles, and excessive state interference (all interviewees); 7.8 percent (9) pinpointed high prices (including those of houses) and low income or salaries (especially among buyers/sellers); 4.3 percent (5) noted the scarce access and high prices of Internet or technology (self-employed); and 26.7 percent (31 mentions) referred to other problems specific to each group: insufficient skilled personnel (self-employed); high transport cost, inefficient distribution, low *acopio* prices, and lack of water (usufruct farmers); expensive building repairs and equipment (NASC members); high tariffs charged by notaries public (also bribes) and real estate agents (buyer/sellers), and lack of professionalism and improper competition (real estate agents) (table 11 and figure 6).

Some voices: "here everything is difficult and expensive"; "there are no seeds, fertilizers, pesticides"; "today I ran 30 kilometers looking for malt and

TABLE 11. Major problems

What major problems do you face?	Percent
Limited access, expensive inputs, and wholesale market	31.9
Bureaucracy, obstacles, and state interference	26.7
High prices and low salaries	7.8
Internet: limited access and high cost	4.3
Other	26.7
Don't have serious problems	2.6
Total	100.0

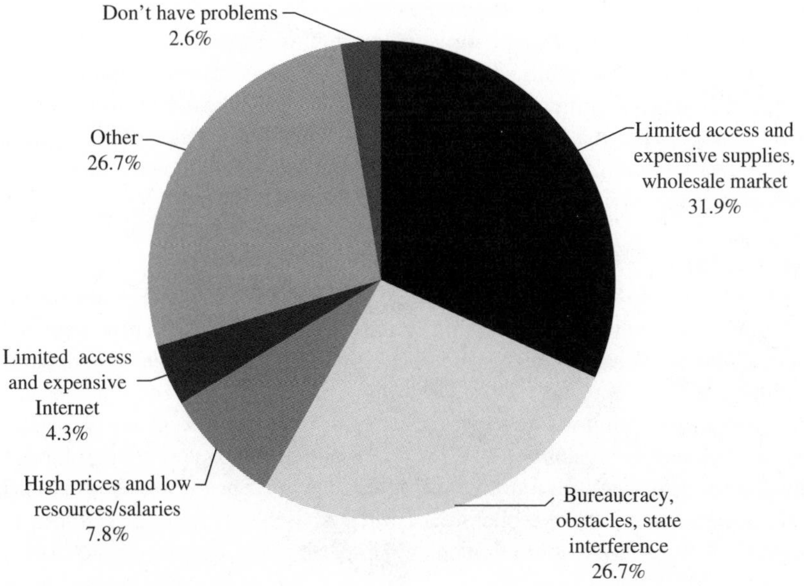

FIGURE 6. What major problems do you face?

did not find it"; "if you don't buy right away there is nothing left afterward"; "the legislation changes constantly, every month they enact two or three regulations, those unable to be up-to-date are lost"; "I wished that all my clients would have Internet or could check my page on Facebook."

Desires to Improve or Change

This question, asked to 80 interviewees, had 104 mentions as categories were not exclusive. Desires matched the main problems noted (table 12 and figure 7):

TABLE 12. Desire of improvement and change

What things you would like to improve or change?	Percentage
Higher access and lower prices of inputs and wholesale market	24
More liberty and fewer state obstacles, regulations, and interference	24
More state incentives, guarantees and recognition, lower taxes	10
Higher income or wages	9
Better Internet access and lower prices	6
More professionalism, no bribes	4
More access to microcredit	3
Other	20
Total	100

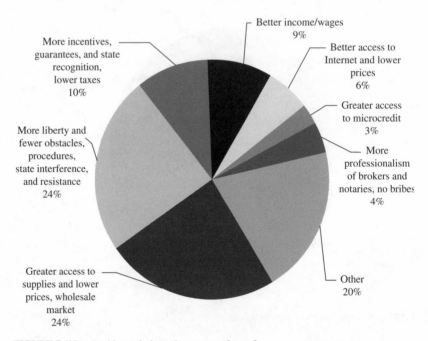

FIGURE 7. What would you desire to improve or change?

24 percent (25 mentions in all four groups) wanted more access to inputs (including construction materials) and lower prices. Another 24 percent claimed more liberty, fewer state obstacles, regulations, and interference; furthermore, the third desire for change (self-employed and usufruct farmers) is related to the previous one—10 percent (11 mentions) asked the government to offer incentives, guarantees, and recognition, and to cut taxes—hence these two add up to 34 percent.

Another 9 percent (buyers/sellers/real estate agents) request higher wages; 6 percent (self-employed and buyers/sellers) want more access to Internet and lower prices; 3 percent (self-employed and buyers/sellers) demand more access to state credit and fewer requisites; and 4 percent (buyers/sellers/real estate agents) desire more professionalism from notaries public and real estate agents.

Lastly, 20 percent (21 mentions) point to other specific wishes related to the group: the self-employed would like to freely associate among themselves to create a structure that would defend their interests and improve the area where they live; usufruct farmers want to stop the *acopio* distributing everything and to receive higher state prices for their produce; NASC members would like to have a better relationship with state enterprises, to end the "experimental" nature of their co-ops, and to directly import inputs; home buyers and sellers want to have more and cheaper dwellings built; and real estate agents would like to receive salaries commensurate with the prices of dwellings in order to sell more.

Some voices: "what I would like mostly is not to spend so much time to seek even for minimum things"; "I would like to be able to buy without the preoccupation later on how to justify from where the things came from"; "more liberty to private businesses to do other things"; "more liberty to work directly with a foreign client"; "more liberty to negotiate with state enterprises"; "more clear regulations concerning what can the private sector do."

Suggestions from Interviewees

These suggestions are extracted from the interviewees' answers:

- Eliminate excessive bureaucracy: "the state should eradicate all absurd obstacles, allow people to do with their goods what they want to do, and oblige bureaucrats to do their work properly without demanding bribes to get rapid results."
- Expand self-employed activities, especially skilled ones: "have more flexible definitions of occupations to allow others not specifically determined, as well as more clear and lenient rules on what the private sector can do."
- Include university graduates in self-employed: "authorize self-employment university graduates to halt the professional exodus from state employment due to its poor wages, develop micro- and middle-size businesses, use the highly underutilized human capital, and raise income of professionals."
- Reduce excessive, high taxes on the NSS: "foreign investors are granted eight years free on profit taxes but a self-employed trying to survive can be taxed as much as 59 percent on profit"; a lower tax burden would promote NSS development and raise its fiscal contributions.
- Abolish the tax on self-employment that charges an increasing rate according to the number of employees hired, thereby penalizing those that create more

jobs, encouraging the underreporting of employees and obstructing the target of eliminating unneeded state employees.

- Authorize the NASC to hire permanent employees (instead of for one year only) as well as outside the co-ops in order to increase their services/production.
- Comply with the often-infringed rule that authorizes the NSS to sign contracts with state enterprises; the latter "want to do business mainly with other state enterprises and not with the private ones or the NASC," "we can't sell to or buy from a state factory or market."
- Create more wholesale markets throughout the country and reduce their prices, as well as the TRD prices, to eliminate the black market and stimulate production: "the state should try to gain more in volume rather than in the price of each product."
- Extend the usufruct contract from ten to fifty years or an indefinite period to provide stability and incentives for investment in the land: "the period of usufruct is too short," "more time should be given to the contract," "provide guarantees that the land will not be taken away."
- Extend the lease period for NASC coming from state enterprises: "the period concerns us because most of our things are leased . . . we are afraid to invest and that later all would end."
- Terminate state resistance and the experimental nature of NASC in order to provide security and stimulate investment: "the persisting resistance places us in constant risk of bankruptcy," "the NASC is an experiment that could end tomorrow," "tell us when it will end."
- End the *acopio* and raise state purchase prices of produce: "I don't want the *acopio* because the government keeps everything that one produces," "sell what we need and cheaper to reduce selling prices to the public."
- Make the process to get microcredit easier, which has been a worldwide success in promoting micro-businesses and development: "I started to ask for a loan and gave up because it never ended," "I tried and at the third week walked out because of too much bureaucracy."
- Abolish the requisite for the NSS to prove where the inputs are bought, a serious barrier for its expansion: "I want to buy without worrying later to justify from were inputs came."
- Allow expansion abroad of self-employed and co-ops to increase exports and reduce imports and the trade deficit: "I see a container leaving for the Caribbean, why I can't sell in Bahamas or Cayman Islands?"
- Expand Internet access and reduce its cost: "there is very little access to Internet," "I would like all my clients to have e-mail and be able to see my page in Facebook."
- Permit the self-employed to associate among themselves to better look after their interests: "We are affiliated to a trade union, it would be better that we group ourselves," "if there were a framework to get together systematically, I am sure we could contribute more and better."

Voices of the NSS in Cuba

The following comments summarize the attitudes of those in the nonstate sector:

- "Allow free rein to the fertile imagination that Cubans are showing, which should be done without obstacles and in a free manner; the government should facilitate that flow; don't obstruct it, and control only what must be controlled" (self-employed).
- "The current way of thinking must be changed, not only among us but by our leaders, they have to give us more freedom to grow" (NASC partner).
- "The state should give us more support in order to produce more and better . . . give more opportunities to the peasants (*guajiro*)" (usufruct farmer).
- "I would like that those who govern think more on how to make life easier to us and less on how to preserve the ideas that have been proved only offer penury" (home seller).

NOTE

1. The authors are responsible for this article but gratefully acknowledge the financial support for the research from Vanderbilt University and the University of Pittsburgh, as well as the seminar held at Harvard University to present the results and Alejandro de la Fuente's encouragement to submit this article to *Cuban Studies*. This article was submitted on April 26, 2016, and includes data available through that date.

REFERENCES

Cuba Study Group (CSG). 2015. *Suministrando el crecimiento: Retos y oportunidades para emprendedores cubanos*. Notre Dame, IN: Kellogg School of Management.

Feinberg, Richard. 2013. *Soft Landing in Cuba? Emerging Entrepreneurs and Middle Classes*. Washington, DC: Brookings Institution.

González-Corzo, Mario, and Orlando Justo. 2014. "Cuba's Emerging Self-Employed Entrepreneurs: Recent Developments and Prospects for the Future." *Journal of Development Entrepreneurship* 19, no. 3.

Mesa-Lago, Carmelo. 2014. "Institutional Changes in Cuba's Economic and Social Reforms." In *Cuba Economic Change in Comparative Perspective*, ed. Richard Feinberg and Ted Piccone, 49–69. Washington, DC: Brookings Institution and Universidad de La Habana.

Mesa-Lago, Carmelo, and Jorge Pérez-López. 2013. *Cuba under Raúl Castro: Assessing the Reforms*. Boulder, CO: Lynne Rienner Publishers.

Mesa-Lago, Carmelo, Roberto Veiga, Lenier González, Sofía Vera, and Aníbal Pérez-Liñán. 2016. *Voices of Change in Cuba from the Expanding Nonstate Sector*. Pittsburgh, PA: University of Pittsburgh Press, 2018.

Morales, Emilio. 2016. *Estudio sobre real estate en el mercado cubano, informe anual 2015*. Miami: Havana Consulting Group & Tech.

Oficina Nacional de Estadísticas e Información (ONEI). 2010, 2011, 2012, 2013, 2014, 2015. *Anuario Estadístico de Cuba 2009, 2010, 2011, 2012, 2013, 2014*. La Habana: ONEI.

ONEI. 2013. *Informe final del censo de población y viviendas*. La Habana: ONEI.

ONEI. 2016. *El color de la piel según el censo de población y viviendas*. La Habana: ONEI.

Padilla Pérez, Maybell. 2015. "Self-Employment in Cuba: Results of a Survey." *Cuba in Transition* 24. Miami: Association for the Study of the Cuban Economy.

Pérez Villanueva, Omar Everleny, and Ricardo Torres Pérez, eds. 2015. *Miradas a la economía cubana: Análisis del sector no estatal*. La Habana: CEEC, Editorial Caminos.

Peters, Philip. 2014. *Cuba's New Real Estate Market*. Washington, DC: Brookings Institution.

Piñeiro Harnecker, Camila. 2014. "Diágnóstico preliminar de las cooperativas no agropecuarias en La Habana, Cuba." *Cuba y la Economía* (Havana), May 30.

Pons, Saira. 2015. *Tax Law Dilemmas for Self-Employed Workers*. La Habana: CEEC, Universidad de La Habana.

Ritter, Archibald R. M., and Ted Henken. 2015. *Entrepreneurial Cuba: The Changing Policy Landscape*. Boulder, CO: First Forum Press.

PREMIO NACIONAL DE ARTES PLÁSTICAS 2016

JOSÉ MANUEL FORS
HOJARASCA, 1982

Instalación. Cubos de plexiglás y hojarasca. Medidas variables. Photo courtesy of Panamerican Art Projects.

PRIMARY SOURCES

LILLIAN GUERRA

"Lo mismo que hay que separar la Iglesia del Estado, hay que separar la política de la academia": Entrevista a Carmelo Mesa-Lago

Autor de 94 libros o monografías y de 318 artículos o capítulos traducidos a siete idiomas y publicados en 34 países, el Catedrático Distinguido Emérito en Economía y Estudios Latinoamericanos de la Universidad de Pittsburgh Carmelo Mesa-Lago es uno de los más reconocidos, admirados y distinguidos economistas en el mundo.[1] Nacido en el reparto habanero de La Víbora de Rogelio Mesa Naranjo, procurador, y Ana María Lago, maestra de piano y kindergarten, el doctor Mesa-Lago se educó en la escuela San Pablo de la Cruz y en los Escolapios de la Víbora y La Habana, antes de graduarse de la Escuela de Leyes de la Universidad de la Habana en 1956, año en que la facultad clausuró el recinto para protestar contra la violencia desatada por la dictadura de Fulgencio Batista. Viajó a España para hacer un doctorado en derecho especializado en seguridad social; Mesa-Lago volvió a Cuba en 1958, semanas antes de la fuga de Batista y la toma de poder del gobierno revolucionario de Fidel Castro. Por haberse dedicado al estudio de la seguridad social (campos que siguieron siendo mayores enfoques de interés académico y pasión personal durante su larga y distinguida carrera), con un análisis de las pensiones en Cuba, el joven intelectual fue reclutado inmediatamente en enero de 1959 por el Ministro del Trabajo para reformar el sistema y crear el Banco de Seguros Sociales de Cuba. Mesa-Lago cumplió con ánimo este papel hasta que la transformación del gobierno revolucionario en estado autoritario hizo insoportable la continuación de su aporte. Dejó Cuba en junio de 1961 e hizo de nuevo su carrera universitaria, esta vez en Estados Unidos, donde obtuvo títulos de maestría en economía por la Universidad de Miami (1965) y de doctor en relaciones laborales y seguridad social de la prestigiosa Universidad de Cornell (1968). Por adoptar posiciones críticas, siempre apoyadas en abundantes fuentes documentales, tanto de las políticas de la Revolución cubana como de Estados Unidos hacia Cuba, Mesa-Lago enfrentó repetidas veces las visiones binarias y la hipocresía de muchos observadores, activistas, políticos y personas de ambos países, en búsqueda de análisis más profundos y soluciones más razonables sobre la actualidad y el futuro de Cuba. Tan innegables y objetivas fueron sus contribuciones y perspectiva que Mesa-Lago fue elegido presidente de Latin American

313

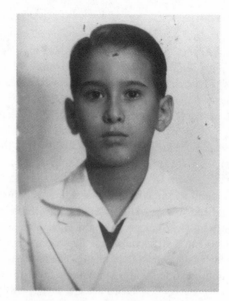

FIGURA 1. Foto escolar de Carmelo Mesa-Lago en Cuba

Studies Association (LASA) en 1980 y fue el primero en invitar a académicos cubanos para participar en el congreso celebrado en Pittsburgh, siguiendo una larga trayectoria de tender puentes con Cuba. Entre sus muchos logros se encuentra la fundación en 1970 de esta revista, *Cuban Studies*, y su publicación como anuario, desde 1986, por la imprenta de la Universidad de Pittsburgh, donde Mesa-Lago ejerció su profesión como catedrático e investigador de la economía y de estudios latinoamericanos desde 1968. A finales de febrero de 2015, Carmelo Mesa-Lago compartió conmigo muchas de las experiencias claves de su trayectoria como individuo y académico comprometido con la misión de ahondar en la economía y la política social en la isla.

Carmelo Mesa-Lago: Entré en la Universidad de La Habana en 1951 y el 10 de marzo de 1952 fue el golpe de estado de Batista, por lo que nuestros estudios siempre estuvieron en el aire. Cada vez que cerraban la universidad [por culpa de la violencia casi constante de la policía contra manifestaciones de estudiantes], no sabíamos si iba a abrirse de nuevo, fue muy inestable la situación, pero fue también una época muy positiva para mí. Yo había sido un estudiante regular en el bachillerato, incluso un par de asignaturas las llevé a "arrastre," que quiere decir que las suspendes y las llevas al año siguiente; a algunas gentes les digo eso y no me lo creen. En la universidad me hice amigo de un grupo de alumnos muy estudiosos, y creo que por osmosis, yo que sé, empecé también a estudiar. Me presenté a los exámenes de premio que había después de que se pasaban los exámenes de los cursos con sobresaliente. Había una docena que íbamos al premio, nos metíamos en la biblioteca del Colegio de Abogados de La Habana, que estaba situada en La Habana Vieja y no tenía aire acondicionado, uno sudaba a mares pero ahí podías encontrar tesoros para prepararte a las preguntas de los premios. Al final terminé tercero en el curso y como Premio Dolz me daban un puesto de abogado de oficio en una audiencia en Cuba. Los dos primeros siempre escogían La Habana, entonces el tercero que fui yo, seleccioné Matanzas. Pero gané otro premio y me fui a España [en 1956], terminé un doctorado en derecho especializado en seguridad social, y mi tesis analizaba las pensiones de Cuba y recomendaba unificarlas; regresé a Cuba en octubre de 1958. El 8 de enero del 1959, el Ministro del Trabajo Manolo Fernández me llamó y me dijo: "Sé que usted ha escrito una tesis sobre la unificación de los seguros sociales en Cuba, ¿quiere encargarse de hacer esto aquí?". Eso era como un sueño, yo tenía veinticinco años, había escrito una tesis, y me pedían llevar mis recomendaciones a la práctica, así que acepté inmediatamente. Yo había retornado al puesto de abogado en la Audiencia de Matanzas, y mientras tanto trabajaba gratis para el Ministerio del Trabajo donde las reuniones terminaban a veces a las tres de la madrugada, entonces tomaba mi auto y me iba para Matanzas para ejercer mi trabajo de abogado de oficio. El gobierno revolucionario nos asignó la defensa de criminales de guerra de Batista ya que no había abogados que querían tomar esos casos. Esa encomienda fue extremadamente difícil porque cuando entrábamos en la Audiencia —éramos varios abogados de oficio—, la gente nos gritaba e insultaba, por defender a criminales de guerra, pero ese era nuestro deber.

Lillian Guerra: ¿Y cómo eran los juicios durante el año que estuviste trabajando en ambas capacidades, como asesor del Ministro de Trabajo y como abogado de oficio? ¿Hubo un caso que te impresionó más que los otros?

CML: Había un acusado de criminal de guerra que, por todo lo que yo pude averiguar en el poco tiempo que tenía, creía que era inocente. No era un tribunal de abogados sino de oficiales del Ejército Rebelde. En vista que lo consideraba inocente, estaba muy preocupado porque fueran a fusilarlo. Otros no me preocupaban porque era obvio que habían sido unos asesinos. En mi caso, yo tenía que preguntarle a los testigos si reconocían que el acusado no era el que había cometido el crimen, pero estaba muy nervioso porque si me decían que sí, el tipo iba al paredón. Por suerte, me dijeron todos los testigos que no había sido él y el hombre salió libre, pero eso fue un solo caso, al resto lo fusilaron.

LG: ¿Cómo ordenabas la defensa? ¿A base de qué evidencia?

CML: Te daban muy poco tiempo e información sobre el caso y teníamos muy poco tiempo para estudiar el expediente y hablar con los acusados. Los juicios se basaban esencialmente en testigos y en un ambiente muy emotivo:

habían muchos testigos que lloraban, por ejemplo, porque era el padre al que habían asesinado. Hubo uno que lo colgaron de un árbol, lo ahorcaron y el policía le disparó varios tiros en la cabeza, ¡horroroso! Había testigos presenciales, pero en muchos casos era un *hearsay*, o sea, un familiar al que alguien le había dicho que el acusado era el asesino. Yo era entonces revolucionario pero enfrentaba un serio conflicto porque los juicios no se ajustaban a todos los requisitos legales establecidos en la Constitución y en las leyes. No obstante, creo que la mayoría de los acusados que fusilaron era culpable. La mayoría de ellos estaba impávido no reflejaba sentimientos, algunos confesaron; los condenaban y los fusilaban esa misma madrugada.

LG: ¿Fuiste afectado por esa experiencia?

CML: Si me afectó, fue una de las cosas más difíciles de mi vida, muy difícil porque, de nuevo, yo era revolucionario, sabía que muchos acusados eran culpables, pero al mismo tiempo me daba cuenta de que podían fusilar a uno que era inocente, por la forma en que se conducía el juicio, por tribunales que no eran de abogados y el ambiente tan apasionado. Además nosotros no teníamos suficiente tiempo para preparar la defensa, nos daban un expediente unas horas antes del juicio, entonces no podías buscar un testigo, nada de esas cosas, tenías que trabajar con lo que había allí, y todos los testigos en contra del acusado.

LG: ¿Y cómo era el ambiente en las oficinas del Ministerio del Trabajo?

CML: El Ministro del Trabajo, Manolo Fernández era un hombre peculiar, un tío feísimo, le faltaban unos dientes [risas], y le decían "el anarcoloco", apodo porque parece que había sido anarquista. Pero era muy sagaz, inteligente y justo, siempre me apoyó en mi labor. No sólo era Fidel, sino también sus ministros los que trabajaban en horas estrambóticas, a veces una reunión empezaba a la una de la mañana, en una oficina que habían estado fumando todo el día, y donde tu entrabas ahí y tenías una intoxicación de nicotina [risas].

LG: ¿Y tú fumabas?

CML: No, yo de vez en cuando me fumaba un tabaco, pero los cigarros no me gustaban. Lo interesante del Ministro es que él quería hacer lo correcto, no fue a buscar a un político, me buscó a mí, pero la primera vez que él me entrevistó le dije: "Mire, Ministro, quiero decirle una cosa, en el bufete donde estaban mi padre y dos abogados [durante la revolución contra Batista] estuvo escondido y hacía reuniones Armando Hart, el [entonces] Ministro de Educación, pero yo no tengo credenciales revolucionarias, yo estuve estudiando en España", la España de Franco; aunque yo era antifranquista estaba afuera cuando ocurría la revolución en Cuba. Pero el ministro respondió, "No lo hemos escogido a usted porque sea un político, lo hemos escogido a usted porque sabe del tema", entonces eso me dio seguridad. Luego yo contraté a la Organización Internacional del Trabajo [OIT] para que nos asesorara en la elaboración de la ley y esta pasó, ¡pero yo no tenía absolutamente ninguna experiencia política y enfrenté serias dificultades! Había tres mil empleados en unos cincuenta fondos o cajas de retiro e hicimos un estudio de racionalización de personal, porque dijimos: si unimos a todas estas cajas no necesitamos a toda esta gente, vamos a ahorrar ese dinero y usarlo para aumentar las pensiones, pues había pensiones de quince pesos al mes así que concluimos que se podían despedir unos novecientos empleados innecesarios, se les trataría de buscar un puesto en otro lugar. Pero todos los empleados se fueron en manifestación frente al edificio donde estaba el Banco de Seguros Sociales pidiendo nuestras cabezas. La segunda dificultad es que Fidel Castro en persona se apareció y dijo que necesitaba cuarenta millones de pesos para la Reforma Agraria. Yo era secretario general del banco, miembro de la junta directiva, y ese dinero era para las pensiones de los trabajadores, ¡tremendo problema!; yo conocía a Felipe Pazos, que era entonces el presidente del Banco Nacional. Lo fui a ver y le dije: "Mire, tenemos este problema, nosotros queremos cooperar pero necesitamos garantías para ese dinero". Felipe Pazos escribió un contrato de préstamo en que el Banco Nacional era colateral, o sea, daba garantía de que se devolvería el dinero. A los dos meses volvió a aparecer Fidel pidiendo sesenta millones de dólares más, ahí decidí: "Yo no sigo aquí" [risas]. Estuve trabajando seis meses gratis y en el puesto creo que unos seis meses, además la mitad de mi sueldo la doné para la Reforma Agraria [risas].

LG: Entonces, te quedaste sin poder trabajar, me imagino, porque renunciar un puesto asignado por el gobierno revolucionario era mal visto, como una ofensa a la causa definida por Fidel Castro.

CML: Mi puesto en el Banco de Seguros Sociales era la ilusión de mi vida y fue muy duro dejarlo. Trabajé en el bufete de mi padre, di clases en la Universidad de La Salle y en la de Villanueva y escribía una columna para el periódico *El Mundo*. En 1961, después de Bahía de Cochinos,[2] el gobierno nacionalizó todas las escuelas privadas y las universidades, además incautaron *El Mundo*, así que yo no podía dar clases ni escribir en el periódico. Me quedaba el bufete pero en realidad a mí no me interesaba el derecho civil, yo quería seguir en el tema de la seguridad social. En aquel entonces, yo era un devoto católico, y en mayo de 1961, al declararse ateo el gobierno, empezaron las acusaciones contra la Iglesia de que su clero y creyentes estaban conspirando contra la Revolución.

LG: Sin duda, la Iglesia era uno de los pocos lugares en Cuba donde se podría protestar contra la adopción del comunismo por el gobierno. Ya para 1961, no quedaba ni prensa ni protecciones para ningún tipo de asamblea, ni crítica pública del gobierno o las decisiones de sus líderes. Hasta los sindicatos habían rendido el derecho a la huelga como medida temporal para ayudar a crecer la economía en marzo de 1959, luego vieron que su "medida tem-

FIGURA 2. Esta imagen de Carmelo Mesa-Lago, sentado en el escritorio de su habitación en el Colegio Iberoamericano en Madrid, fue tomada después de recibir el premio a la mejor disertación doctoral escrita en la Universidad Complutense por un miembro del Colegio en 1958

poral" se había convertido en prohibición permanente. La iglesia entonces aprovecha su derecho aun existente de publicar ideas *independientes* —fueran o no fueran contrarias al gobierno—. Eso empezó a ser visto como acto contrarrevolucionario en sí, ¿verdad?

CML: Yo estuve copiando en mimeógrafo las pastorales de los obispos y distribuyéndolas en las iglesias. Una mañana teníamos la maletera de mi auto lleno de esas copias, y esa noche le di el auto, porque estaba muy cansado, a uno que trabajaba con nosotros para que él hiciera la distribución y luego dejara el auto frente a mi casa. Por la mañana vino la policía y me dice: "Abra el auto". Parece que alguien vio y denunció y yo estaba temblando porque ignoraba si se había quedado algún papel allí, así que abrí la maletera del auto y no había nada, de todas maneras me llevaron a Los Maristas y me tuvieron allí como unas seis o siete horas sin decirme absolutamente nada y después me dejaron ir.[3]

LG: ¿Y esos papeles se consideraban…?

CML: Si, esos se consideraban propaganda contrarrevolucionaria. Yo tenía muchos conflictos [con la política de la Revolución] en términos de la libertad de prensa, lo que pasaba con la Iglesia, y otras cosas que estaban haciendo, así que empecé a desencantarme rápidamente. Además, no tenía futuro en Cuba, ¿qué iba a hacer? Entonces vino la invasión de Bahía de Cochinos, alguien me dijo que yo estaba en una lista, me fui de la casa, a un apartamento de un pariente. Los policías me fueron a buscar al bufete de mi padre y empezaron a buscar [evidencia contra mi] por todas partes y no encontraron nada por suerte; después fusilaron a un amigo mío y a otros los pusieron presos. A un maestro mío de los Escolapios lo detuvieron y estuvo nueve años preso, uno de los mejores maestros que he tenido en mi vida. Yo no quería asilarme en una embajada y decidí jugármela. Había un barco que venía de las Antillas inglesas llevando trabajadores afrocaribeños para trabajar en las minas del sur de Inglaterra, era un barco del apartheid negrero, eso era lo que era. Justo en ese momento había centenares de sacerdotes y de monjas que se iban de Cuba y la embajada española pidió al barco que cambiara de ruta y pasara por La Habana. Mi padrino me compró un pasaje en el barco. Cuando iba a embarcarme, vi a un miliciano que era un ex-alumno de los Escolapios donde yo había estudiado, que sabía quién era yo, así que esperé hasta el último minuto por miedo que me detuviera. Fui el último que entró en el barco, ya se había ido el miliciano y no pasó nada. [. . .] Salí el 13 de junio de 1961, un martes trece (risas): ¡ni te cases ni te embarques, ni de tu casa faltes!, mi madre que era muy religiosa dijo: "No te preocupes porque es el día de San Antonio… [risas] que te va a proteger". En España pronto me di cuenta que no tenía futuro. Varios antiguos compañeros de la Facultad de Derecho llevaban años estudiando para hacer "oposiciones" a una sola cátedra de derecho del trabajo y seguridad social. Además me fui de Cuba por una dictadura y vivía bajo otra.

LG: ¿Y qué hizo tu familia? ¿Tú le pagaste los pasajes para que se pudieran ir?

CML: En Madrid me dedicaba a escribir artículos, porque increíblemente pagaban alrededor de cien dólares por publicarlos en las revistas de derecho y empecé a reunir plata para sacar a toda la familia de Cuba, que eran nueve porque mi padre decía que se iban todos o no salía nadie. Además yo había sido alumno de un profesor muy famoso en la Facultad de Derecho, un experto en derecho del trabajo y de seguridad social y él me contrató como asistente de su cátedra, y al final me dio una billetera con tres mil pesetas, unos doscientos dólares. Con ese ahorro pude comprar todos los pasajes pero después los perdí, porque ocurrió la Crisis de los Misiles y se cerraron todas las salidas de Cuba directas a los Estados Unidos. Entonces decidí irme de España y venir a los Estados Unidos, para Oklahoma a enseñar inglés en una universidad. Tomé un avión que le llamaban el ataúd volante [risas] porque era muy viejo, de hélices. Tomó como quince horas en llegar. Arribé en Nueva York y hablé con mi hermana que estaba en Miami y ella me dijo: "En la Universidad de Miami se ha abierto un puesto en el Grupo

Cubano de Investigaciones Económicas y necesitan un experto en derecho del trabajo y seguridad social"; esto era como un retrato. Así que cambié mi pasaje de Oklahoma y me vine para Miami en julio de 1962.

En el Grupo [Cubano] de la Universidad de Miami todos éramos cubanos y, por supuesto, teníamos unos prejuicios enormes, aunque habíamos dos que nos decían que éramos de "izquierda", en broma ¿no?, pero también medio en serio. El asesor del Grupo Cubano era el Profesor James Vadikan, el decano del Departamento de Economía, fue la primera persona que me enseñó que tenía que controlar mis prejuicios ideológicos y políticos, trabajar basado en cifras e información verídica, a fin de que hablaran por sí mismas. Vadikan sembró esa semilla en mí y fueron los primeros trabajos en que intenté ser lo más objetivo posible y documentado. Intenté hacer una licenciatura en derecho pero con siete años de estudio en esa disciplina, me aceptaban sólo un año y, además, no me gustaba; también quería ahondar en mis estudios de seguridad social. Como el Grupo estaba afiliado al Departamento de Economía y no me costaba la matrícula, decidí estudiar economía desde cero y terminé la maestría. Entonces Vadikan me animó y escribió una carta de recomendación para un doctorado en la Universidad de Cornell, en la Escuela de Relaciones Industriales y Laborales en la que hay una especialización en seguridad social y también podía tomar cursos de economía; esa es la única universidad que yo apliqué, me aceptaron con matrícula gratis y me ofrecieron una beca, te vas a reír de la cantidad: ¡mil dólares al año! [risas] Yo había ahorrado para pagar los pasajes de mi familia y salieron por México donde pasaron dos meses esperando la visa. Cuando ya estaba listo para irme a Cornell, *por fin todo el familión* —mi abuelo, mi tía abuela, mi padre, mi madre, cuatro tíos, mi padrino, una prima—, diez en total llegaron a Miami.

LG: Tiene que haber sido muy difícil optar por el doctorado en Cornell, pues las familias cubanas, tal vez por la trauma de la separación impuesta por la Revolución, no quieren que sus hijos se vayan lejos; prefieren que se queden en Miami o dónde sea, aunque pierden un futuro mejor, una educación mejor en el norte de Estados Unidos, porque sus familias no los quieren dejar ir.

CML: Sí, yo estaba en una disyuntiva, si quedarme o irme y fue Vadikan quien me dijo que estaba tirando mi futuro. Ocurrió un accidente de automóvil que me dejó con varias costillas y la nariz rota y un abogado consiguió tres mil dólares de compensación. Así que cuando llegaron mis padres les dije: "Yo me tengo que ir, mira les dejo a ustedes dinero, la casa" [lo que se pagaba al mes era una basura, unos cien dólares], y el auto, pero me tengo que ir", y ellos me dijeron: "No, no, no, vete", me fui, y eso me cambió mi vida. La verdad que no fue fácil, pero mi padre estaba orgulloso de lo que yo hacía y quería que yo siguiera. Él estaba contento con mis éxitos en las universidades de La Habana y Madrid, especialmente cuando me dieron el premio del Colegio de Abogados de La Habana por el mejor libro publicado sobre derecho en 1959.

LG: ¿Y ese premio te lo dio Fidel?

CML: Me lo dio Fidel, la única vez que lo he visto tan de cerca, él era un tipo altísimo y corpulento, me entregó el diploma y me dio la mano, blanda, fofa, lo cual me sorprendió.

LG: ¿Y cómo te casaste con tu esposa, Elena? Ha sido una gran relación matrimonial y profesional que ha durado décadas, ¿no?

CML: Bueno, ella vivía, ¡tú no vas a creer esto!, a una cuadra de mi casa, yo en Concepción entre Delicias y Diez de Octubre y ella en Delicias. Había estado en su casa, pero le llevo cinco años, ella era muy delgada y lucía muy jovencita, como una niña ¿no? Así que no me llamó la atención. Después nos reencontramos en Miami y entonces ya era otra cosa [risas]. Seguía delgada, pero más llenita, muy elegante y vistosa, además habían pasado varios años, así que la diferencia no era tan importante como cuando ella tenía quince y yo veinte, así que empezamos a salir pero yo no tenía un centavo y me iba a estudiar a Cornell, con una beca que era una basura, a más que tenía que mandarle dinero a mis padres. Estuve un año entero a base de *hamburgers* y *hot dogs* y no tenía un refrigerador. Para que la leche [no se echara a perder] y porque siempre había frío allí, la ponía afuera, en la ventana de la habitación; ponía también unas galletas de dulce, y había una ardilla que venía y se las comía [risas]. En fin, nos escribíamos y yo llegué a la conclusión de que era absurdo, ¡yo no podía hacerlo solo!, la necesitaba a ella y bueno nos casamos en septiembre de 1966. La mejor decisión de mi vida, Elena ha sido extraordinaria y a ella le debo lo que soy. Nos fuimos a Cornell, alquilamos un duplex que habían construido para los veteranos de la Segunda Guerra Mundial, era una pequeña choza dividida en dos, por lo que tu oías todo lo que hablaba la gente de al lado y nosotros tratábamos de no hablar alto [risas]. Antes de casarnos, Elena aprendió una cosa que se llamaba *keypunch operator*, las operadoras que llenaban tarjetas para las computadoras, pero ella salió en estado durante la luna de miel. Nosotros pensábamos que íbamos a tener todos los hijos que nos mandara Dios, después nos quedamos con tres hijas. Lisa, la mayor nació en Ithaca.

LG: ¿Y a qué tú debes tu conciencia política? ¿Igual, hay que preguntarte cómo tú lograste salvar tu trabajo académico de las presiones por politizarlo que predominaban en la época en que comenzaste tu carrera en Estados Unidos?

CML: Mi padre estuvo muy metido en política en contra de [Gerardo] Machado, él acusó al policía que mató a Rafael Trejo, que sabes, fue el primer mártir de la Universidad de la Habana que murió por un disparo de la policía en 1930 y su muerte lanzó el movimiento estudiantil contra Machado.[4] ¡Papá estaba completamente loco! Le dijeron [a mi padre] que lo iban a matar y se escondió y cuando yo nací él estaba escondido; mi familia, por supuesto era Auténtica, Grau era el Mesías, que así es que le decían en Cuba, mi padre lloró cuando fue elegido presidente en 1944, pero fue un desastre, después fue elegido Prío y nunca se me olvida que mi padre estaba oyendo el radio y decía: "¡Pero es que el Directorio está ahora en el poder!" y Mamá que era mucho más pragmática le advertía: "No te vuelvas a ilusionar".[5] Papá que había sido político y arriesgado su vida, se volvió antipolítico y siempre me decía: "Cuando tu entres a la universidad no te metas en política", pero ¡qué va!, yo me metí y fui elegido delegado del curso en tres años consecutivos a la Federación Estudiantil Universitaria, y hacía un periodiquito en que escribía artículos, que se llamaba *Lex*, que quiere decir "derecho," y el segundo era *El Siboney*. Mi papá no sabía nada y, por supuesto, yo no se lo decía. A pesar de todo eso yo tenía cierto desprecio por la política, una cosa era la política universitaria y otra cosa era la política nacional.

LG: Hasta cierto punto, se podría decir que ganarte el puesto en la Universidad de Pittsburgh en 1967 fue una bendición porque allí te apartaste de la cultura política de los cubanos del exilio, ¿no? Esa época de finales de los sesenta y setenta fueron muy violentos, muy extremistas, años en que los cubanos de la ultra-derecha de Miami imponían a los demás una sola posición frente a la Revolución —la de rechazo total, hostilidad total— y a su vez, una sola posición frente a los que pensaban diferente, de intolerancia y hasta represión total. Como dice María de los Ángeles Torres en su excelente libro *In the Land of Mirrors: Cuban Exile Politics in the United States*, se convierten en espejos, uno del otro.[6]

CML: Sí, en parte fue una bendición, porque había muy pocos cubanos en Pittsburgh, casi todos eran médicos que debido al frío gradualmente se fueron a Miami, lo que quedaba de cubanos era básicamente universitario y algunos médicos que permanecieron. Así que en Pittsburgh no existía la presión social de Miami donde había libertad para expresar tus puntos de vista pero tenías que pagar un precio, esto para mí fue muy importante porque pude decir lo que yo pensaba basado en mi investigación, sin preocuparme de que pudiera traer repercusiones políticas. Por otra parte en Pittsburgh y otras partes había otro tipo de presión opuesta de aquellos que creían ciegamente en la Revolución y no admitían ideas diversas. Cuando empecé a trabajar en la Academia, yo estaba hablando animadamente con una persona y me preguntaba: "¿Y tú de dónde eres?", yo decía: "Soy de Cuba"; inmediatamente esa persona terminaba la conversación o cambiaba el tema o se marchaba. Yo me daba cuenta inmediatamente del cambio, porque tener un punto de vista aunque fuera académico fundamentado, crítico de muchas cosas, especialmente de la economía, pero al mismo tiempo alabando ciertas cosas de la Revolución, ¡era un problema tremendo! Yo recuerdo el congreso de LASA en 1970 en que el moderador de la sesión era Joe Kahl, un sociólogo internacionalmente famoso por su trabajo cuantitativo sobre México; el tópico era la zafra de los diez millones de toneladas y yo había seguido por la radio y por los periódicos el avance de la zafra, había hecho unos cálculos y expliqué los problemas que había y predije que no iban a alcanzar los diez millones de toneladas. Entonces, aquel público —había gente sentada hasta en las escaleras—, se volvió contra mí y Joe que era amigo me dijo: "Si, comprendo lo que tú dices, pero los diez millones de toneladas van" y yo le repliqué: "Joe, te admiro por lo que tú has hecho sobre México, pero esto no tiene nada que ver con tu labor académica". En la Universidad Libre de Berlín, cuando su gobierno estaba controlado por marxistas, yo critiqué la política económica de Cuba ¡y la reacción fue despampanante! Pero nunca en mi vida me he amilanado, siempre he dicho lo que creo pero con fundamento, claro que pagando un precio. Así que veo la política como un obstáculo en la búsqueda de la verdad, esto no quiere decir que yo tenga la verdad, pero toda mi vida he tratado de encontrarla, y tengo dudas en muchas cosas, y siempre estoy buscando e investigando. Esa ideología, ese fanatismo que tiene alguna gente me golpea. Yo me he pasado más de medio siglo estudiando un tema y entonces viene una persona y me dice: "Déjame decirte lo que yo creo" y me da un *lecture* con absoluta certeza, y yo pienso, ¡cómo es esto posible!

LG: Sí, mi experiencia es muy semejante. A veces parece que él que ha estado una semana en Cuba sabe más que él que hizo un doctorado y se ha pasado años viviendo e investigando en Cuba. Es porque el *brand* de la Revolución Cubana le funciona muy bien al que no tiene que vivir la realidad cubana; comprueba sus credenciales de izquierdista sin tener que hacer nada por modificar su modo de vida en Estados Unidos ni tampoco lidiar con los límites absolutos sobre la libertad de pensamiento, de autonomía económica, de casi todo, que exige un estado comunista.

CML: Eso nos pasó con un vecino nuestro que era médico, que nos conocía hacía cuarenta años, se fue a Cuba una semana con la mujer y volvió diciéndome maravillas de lo que había visto sobre salud. Yo traté de compensar esa andanada, de una manera diplomática, contándole lo que había sufrido una prima hermana en Cuba para tener una operación y él me miró y me dijo: "I don't think so", no te creo, y yo le riposté: "Esto me duele mucho porque tú me conoces hace cuarenta años, hemos sido vecinos, tú sabes que yo he escrito mucho sobre la salud en Cuba y con una sola semana que tu estuviste allá, eres capaz de decir una cosa como esa." ¡Terrible!

LG: Tú fuiste uno de los pioneros en tratar de abrir las puertas hacia el debate intelectual y acabar con la tendencia de sustituir el análisis por la demagogia, tanto en Estados Unidos como en Cuba. ¿Cuándo empezaste esa lucha?

CML: Sobre esto tengo que hablar de María Cristina Herrera y del Instituto de Estudios Cubanos, el cual fundamos un grupo de académicos cubanos en

Miami creo que en 1969, cuyo objetivo era que cubanos que trabajaban en universidades o *colleges*, pudieran hablar seriamente sobre Cuba sin tirarse los trastos a la cabeza, ¡esa era la idea! El Instituto tuvo una importancia enorme, a mí me influyó extraordinariamente, y llegó un instante en que nosotros llegamos a la conclusión: ¡ya podemos hablar entre nosotros, pero ahora tenemos que hablar con los cubanos! y entonces se hicieron reuniones con los cubanos, en Cuba y en los Estados Unidos. María Cristina era una mujer única, era parapléjica y [los cubanos del exilio extremista] le pusieron una bomba en su casa [donde vivía] con la madre de ochenta y tantos años [en 1983], algo increíble. [Esa cultura de violencia y de intolerancia del exilio] nos hizo comprender que el diálogo no podía ser sólo entre nosotros, sino tenía que ser también con los cubanos de la isla. Cuando viene la invitación al diálogo en 1978, hay un grupo nuestro que va a La Habana y le sigue otra reunión en 1979 que incluyó una serie de profesores que después cambiaron de posición. En aquel entonces tenían unas grandes barbas y ahora están muy afeitados [risas].

LG: Esa serie de reuniones es mejor conocida como "El Diálogo", ¿no? Era un "diálogo" que se quería establecer entre el gobierno de Castro y el ala del exilio que quería participar de alguna manera positiva en la formación de la política *hacia* Cuba y *dentro de* Cuba.[7]

CML: La primera reunión importante en La Habana fue organizada por el Instituto de Estudios Cubanos en 1980 porque por primera vez había académicos o funcionarios cubanos reuniéndose con un grupo de cubanos exiliados (de Estados Unidos, España y otros países). En esa reunión ocurrió una cosa muy interesante. Los del gobierno cubano me habían prometido darme estadísticas de Cuba para yo poder hacer un análisis sobre el plan quinquenal de 1976–1980. Cuando llegamos había una fiesta y yo me dirigí a la contraparte cubana y le pregunté: "¿Dónde están las estadísticas?" y me dijo: "Ah, aquí están" y entonces yo me fui a mi habitación y estuve trabajando hasta las dos de la mañana. Todos nosotros nos levantamos temprano y fuimos al lugar donde iba a ser la reunión [se ríe]. Los cubanos habían arreglado el aula, había una tarima en que se sentarían ellos y después nosotros estaríamos sentados abajo en línea de sillas. Varios de nosotros, entre ellos estaban Pepe Prince, Kike Valoira, todos estos grandes que han muerto desgraciadamente jóvenes, ¡cambiamos todo el arreglo y pusimos una mesa redonda! Entonces yo en la pizarra puse todas las cifras para demostrar que el plan quinquenal había fracasado. Cuando llegó un funcionario de JUCEPLAN [Junta Central de Planificación] y vio aquello, se puso pálido porque habíamos cambiado todo el escenario y estaba aquello puesto en la pizarra. No pudieron rebatir porque no estaban acostumbrados a que se le presentara evidencia que era imposible de refutar.

LG: ¿Y quién habló para defender al gobierno cubano?

CML: Habló Alfredo Guevara, el jefe del Instituto Cubano de Artes e Industrias Cinematográficos [ICAIC]. El jugó un papel muy negativo, porque trató de dividirnos. Nosotros éramos quince y todos pensábamos diferente y ellos eran un bloque unido, aunque hubiera diferencias entre ellos no la expresaban. En su trabajo de división Guevara usó todo tipo de triquiñuelas, hubo un momento en que me preguntó: "Pero, ¿cómo tú puedes saber todas estas cosas?, tú andas revoleteando por aquí buscando y nos sorprendes"; insinuaba, aunque nunca lo dijo, que yo tenía algo que ver con la inteligencia norteamericana, ¡sabe Dios qué!, yo nunca he tenido relación alguna con esa gente; fue muy duro. [También] estaba Nelson Valdés, él que escribió el libro famoso sobre El Che con Bonachea.[8] Estaba hablando el famoso poeta cubano Cintio Vitier, y Nelson con su entrenamiento norteamericano le advierte: "Me da mucha pena tener que interrumpir, pero ya usted terminó su tiempo", entonces Guevara se disparó y nos amonestó: "Ustedes que vienen con esa mentalidad americana, este es un tesoro de Cuba". Así, que Cintio habló todo lo que quiso y lo que decía era muy interesante pero el punto era que se habían roto todas las reglas. Al final de la reunión, nunca se me olvida, [de la parte del exilio] estaba Manolo Fernández que había sido un dirigente de Acción Católica en Cuba [antes de la Revolución] y había publicado muchas cosas históricas sobre la Iglesia, ya murió. Él era amigo de Guevara, lo conocía de Cuba antes, por la afinidad mutua al cine. Manolo publicaba un boletín para el Instituto [de Estudios Cubanos] que se llamaba *Unidos* y le dio una copia a [Alfredo] Guevara. Este lo leyó y le dijo a Manolo, que era ¡contrarrevolucionario! Mientras que el boletín nos creaba problemas en Miami.

LG: ¿Guevara lo acusó de contrarrevolucionario en su cara?

CML: Se lo dijo en su cara frente a todos nosotros y nunca se me olvida, no me lo puedo quitar de la cabeza, que cuando nuestro ómnibus se iba, Guevara se reía, se reía. Fue muy difícil esa reunión, sumamente difícil, pero mantuvimos nuestras posiciones y se produjo la discusión. Con respecto al Diálogo, yo nunca me engañé, sabía que eso no era un diálogo. Fidel entró en el auditorio en que están sentados los cubanos de afuera y comenzó a hablar; había mucha gente importante en el estrado, como Antonio Núñez Jiménez,[9] el moncadista Juan Almeida y Armando Hart, el Ministro de Educación y de Cultura en esos momentos. Todos esos estaban allí, ¡pero nadie abrió la boca!, el único que habló durante todo el tiempo fue Fidel.

LG: ¿Un monólogo total?

CML: Era un monólogo, ¡yo sabía que no era un diálogo!, pero lo más importante para mí era que hubiese esa reunión, y que como resultado de ella se liberaron ¡3.600 presos políticos!, sobre los cuales nos mandaban listas con los nombres de donde habían estado para comprobarlo. Además comenzó la reunificación de la familia cubana, las visitas de los cubanos a los Estados

Unidos y viceversa y con esas visitas vino uno de los traumas más grandes que ha tenido la Revolución, que es el efecto de demostración: los cubanos pensaban que todos nosotros éramos maleantes y que estábamos muriéndonos de hambre y la mafia, qué se yo, y entonces de pronto vieron que los familiares llegaban cargados de regalos (algunos se endeudaron para hacer eso), pero lo más importante es que se restableció el lazo familiar que se había perdido.

LG: ¿Y tú estuviste muchos años sin ir a Cuba?

CML: Desde 1990, la última reunión de discusión en Cuba, pasaron veinte años sin poder ir porque no me daban visa. No obstante, yo expandí mi relación académica con economistas y científicos sociales cubanos, las cuales mantengo. Nosotros nos mandamos los trabajos para comentarlos, yo he escrito cosas con ellos, hemos estado en muchas reuniones, hemos escrito libros juntos. ¡Yo aprecio el enorme valor que tienen ellos!, porque es muy fácil despotricar desde aquí cuando tú estás seguro, pero vivir allá y hacer críticas, a veces fuertes, otras leves o entre líneas, implica tener un coraje a toda prueba.

LG: ¿Cómo hacían ustedes cuando estaban en Cuba en 1980 para poder reunirse sin ser grabados y vigilados por las fuerzas de inteligencia del gobierno cubano?

CML: En el año ochenta en esa reunión del Instituto de Estudios Cubanos, estaba María Cristina Herrera, Jorge Domínguez, Nelson Valdés, Pepe Prince, Sergio Roca y otros intelectuales de la emigración. Estábamos en el Habana Libre y lo primero que decidimos es que no podíamos hablar nada allí, porque te imaginas que estábamos planeando todo lo que íbamos a hacer en la reunión, entonces decidimos irnos al malecón [se ríe] ¡y discutimos todo el plan en el malecón!

LG: ¿Y los cubanos de la isla encubrían en público lo que pensaban y decían en privado?

CML: Había gente, por ejemplo Luis Gutiérrez, Julio Carranza y Pedro Monreal, que tenían posiciones que no se conformaban completamente con la visión oficial, luego publicaron el libro famoso y, después, fueron todos sacados de sus puestos.[10] Había gente que en privado te decía algunas cosas, pero una vez que estaban en público eran una roca sólida, unida, no había posibilidad, tú sabías que era un teatro. Sin embargo, ¡lo importante es que estábamos hablando! y eso nos lleva al actual proceso de normalización, ¡yo creo que eso está muy bien! En 1968 desde el teatro de la Universidad de Miami, en un programa de televisión costa a costa que se llamaba *The Advocates*, y coordinaba Richard Fagen, yo estuve en el programa, dije que estaba en contra del embargo y di las razones por las que tomaba esa posición, ¡en el año sesenta y ocho!, la mitad de los amigos no me habló después de eso. Una amiga, ¡pero del alma!, me comentó que yo parecía un sueco y yo le dije: "Pues sabes qué, me alegro de tu percepción, pues mi deseo era ser lo más imparcial posible".

LG: ¿Y qué te inspiraba a seguir tratando de abrir puertas en Cuba si sabías que todo era o teatro o monólogo?

CML: Yo creo que tender puentes y establecer lazos académicos han tenido resultados positivos, como las relaciones crecientes entre científicos sociales de aquí y de allá, incluso la generación de consensos en puntos importantes. En 1974 parecía que iban a permitir a algunos académicos ir a Cuba, pero la revista *Visión* me pidió un artículo sobre Cuba y yo lo escribí, lo publicaron y eso cayó como una bomba y ahí mismo se terminó todo, porque el problema fundamental es que Cuba espera una especie de compromiso de tu parte, ¿te das cuenta?, yo te dejo entrar pero tú vas a moderar el tono o tú vas a apoyar cosas. Yo nunca he aparecido en un periódico o actividad pública en Cuba diciendo contra el embargo pero nunca he firmado un papel, tampoco en el exilio. No quiero envolverme en la política. Esto no significa que soy neutral o sin visión política. Al contrario, ¡yo soy un demócrata ferviente! pero ¿entiendes? Lo mismo que hay que separar la Iglesia del Estado hay que separar la política de la academia. Hay intolerancia en ambos lados: Cuba quiere que tú digas sólo cosas buenas del régimen y un grupo influyente de cubano americanos en Miami, quieren que tú digas que todo es un desastre, o sea, paraíso e infierno a la vez, lo cual está en contra de la realidad. Si tu alabas alguna cosa de allá, ¡eres fidelista o castrista! Y si escribes algo que le molesta al lado de allá, entonces ¡eres un contrarrevolucionario! Cada vez que me han negado una visa en Cuba ha sido porque ha salido un libro mío que no les gustó, pero ya ellos saben que yo no voy a cambiar [se ríe], ¡yo no voy a cambiar!

LG: ¡Menos mal! A estas alturas, qué tú cambiaras: ¡Imagínate! [Risas].

CML: Una de las cosas que más me duele es que no puedo ofrecer a Cuba mi conocimiento y experiencia de medio siglo. ¿Cómo es posible que el gobierno socialista de Michelle Bachelet en Chile me nombre en la Comisión Presidencial de Reforma de Pensiones y yo en Cuba no pueda hacer nada sobre eso? En 2003 me habían invitado al primer seminario internacional de seguridad social en La Habana y tenía concertada una reunión con dos funcionarios para discutir la reforma de las pensiones allá y no me dieron la visa. Es verdad que he recomendado asuntos que después han seguido en Cuba, pero no sé si porque lo dije yo o porque ellos llegaron a la conclusión por ellos mismos. Algo increíble, cuando en 2007 me dieron el premio internacional de la OIT al "trabajo decente", la delegación cubana en la Asamblea General en Ginebra estaba ausente y en Cuba no salió absolutamente nada.[11]

LG: ¿Cuál tú dirías que es el legado de la larga época de apoyo soviético a la economía y la cultura política de Cuba? Te pregunto porque si hay silencios enormes y estratégicos en la forma que el gobierno cubano representa la realidad contemporánea, es aun mayor la amnesia total sobre el pasado soviético. Hasta se ha convertido en una especie de tabú hablar de eso en Cuba.

CML: Yo he estimado que entre 1960, cuando empezó la relación con la Unión Soviética, y 1990 cuando terminó, Cuba recibió 65.000 millones de dólares, más que la Alianza para el Progreso a toda América Latina, hasta 1985 recibían por lo menos seis mil millones anuales. De la suma de ayuda total, el 60 por ciento fue en subsidios de precio, porque Cuba le compraba el petróleo a la Unión Soviética por debajo del precio mundial y le vendía el azúcar y el níquel por encima del precio mundial (el azúcar hasta siete veces el precio mundial), o eran créditos para pagar déficits en la balanza comercial o eran donaciones. Un 40 por ciento eran préstamos de los cuales Cuba solamente pagó quinientos millones de dólares. Yo le pregunté una vez a Carlos Rafael Rodríguez, en una conversación de una hora y media: ¿y qué va a pasar con la deuda soviética?, Y me contestó: "¿Qué deuda?" [risas]. Uno se pregunta ¿qué se hizo con esa enorme cantidad de plata? No pasó nada, fue un período relativamente bueno pero no hubo una transformación de la estructura económica de Cuba.

LG: ¿Y cómo tú me explicas eso?

CML: Cuba siempre ha sido dependiente de una potencia extranjera, primero fue de España, después de los Estados Unidos, después de la Unión Soviética y hasta hace poco de Venezuela, que no es una potencia como las otras, pero que tenía el petróleo y además el deseo de apoyar a Cuba. A pesar de todo lo recibido no ha habido realmente una transformación de la estructura económica de Cuba, se cambió del azúcar a los servicios. Hoy la mayor entrada en divisas de Cuba es el pago de los servicios profesionales, especialmente por Venezuela pero también por Brasil y otros países, el segundo es el turismo. En el producto interno bruto [PIB] de Cuba, alrededor de dos tercios son servicios, lo cual parece que es una economía desarrollada, pero no lo es. La agricultura genera un porcentaje minúsculo del PIB y es de una productividad muy baja, mientras que en la industria ha habido un proceso de decapitalización, en la última cifra que tengo, de 2013, la producción industrial de Cuba estaba 45 por ciento por debajo de 1989, lo que ha habido es un largo proceso de declive. Generalmente, los países primero desarrollan la agricultura, después la industria y después los servicios; en Cuba hay un enorme desarrollo de los servicios pero sin pasar por los procesos anteriores, o por lo menos han sido truncados.

LG: ¿Pero eso no es porque el Estado monopoliza precisamente esas esferas para que el ciudadano no pueda hacerle competencia al Estado?

CML: El problema es que, además de eso, hay un sistema económico que ha sido terriblemente ineficiente, que ha desperdiciado recursos y no hay que olvidar que Fidel inventó toda una serie de proyectos que luego fracasaron.

Por ejemplo, decidió que en vez del forraje tradicional, había que alimentar al ganado con yerba pangola y melazas, un subproducto de la caña de azúcar, porque el bioquímico y granjero francés André Voisin lo entusiasmó con esa idea. Además a Fidel se le ocurrió, eso no fue influencia de un extranjero, que había que mezclar el ganado Cebú, muy extendido en Cuba, pero de carne dura y muy difícil de manejar, con la Holstein que estaba siendo importada, de ahí saldría un híbrido, que le pusieron "F1", ¡por Fidel por supuesto! que iba a dar mucha leche, la carne iba a ser más suave y estaría aclimatado al trópico. Por último, Fidel impulsó la inseminación artificial masiva del ganado, tenían los instrumentos para hacerlo pero no el conocimiento de cómo y cuándo hacerlo; cuando la practicaban los campesinos, ellos sabían cuando la vaca estaba en celo, mientras que los inseminadores no tenían la menor idea y se gastó una gran cantidad en este proyecto que no dio frutos. Después hubo en Cuba un congreso internacional de ciencia animal en que participaron genetistas británicos y dijeron en una ponencia científica, que esos programas habían sido un desastre, los británicos probaron que la vaca no daba mucha leche, que el ganado había bajado de peso y que la masa de ganado había caído. El número de cabezas de ganado vacuno en Cuba llegó a 7 millones en 1967, pero bajó a 3,9 millones en 2009. Cuando los genetistas británicos terminaron de dar su ponencia en el congreso científico, Fidel se paró y los criticó, los denunció; después de varios años se publicó un artículo en la revista *Desarrollo Económico*, en que un experto cubano en ciencia animal, explicó que es lo que había pasado, cómo había adelgazado el ganado, cómo había muerto, et cetera. Otra "gran idea" de Fidel fue la zafra de los diez millones de toneladas, pero iba más allá porque él pretendía que eventualmente alcanzaría veinte millones de toneladas, Cuba haría un *dumping* de azúcar en el mercado internacional y se convertiría en casi el único gran productor de azúcar. El problema es que el azúcar no es igual que el petróleo que solo existe en ciertos lugares, el azúcar se puede cultivar en muchísimas partes. Además toda la economía cubana se puso en la zafra de 1970 al servicio de producir diez millones de toneladas, sacaron transporte, sacaron mano de obra, sacaron energía, ¡de todo!, y ocurrió que no llegaron a los diez millones, fueron ocho y medio, pero a costa de un declive en el resto de la economía que terminó en una recesión en ese año. Hay otras muchas grandiosas ideas, como que Cuba sería ¡mejor productor de queso que Holanda! Pero hay una diferencia interesante entre Fidel y Raúl, porque a Fidel se le ocurría una cosa y después que la anunciaba, le decía a los planificadores: háganme un plan para hacer la producción, algo totalmente irracional y, además, a escala nacional sin hacer experimentos pilotos, ver cómo funciona y después extenderlo. Raúl hace lo contrario pero va muy lento.

LG: ¿Y el papel de la gente?

CML: Ha habido un desperdicio enorme de recursos físicos y humanos; otra cosa es la falta de mantenimiento del equipo. Al no sentirse dueños de los medios de producción, a los trabajadores no les importa el mantenimiento y el cuidado, entonces se rompen los tractores, se rompen los autobuses chinos, se rompe todo. La mejor prueba de que la producción agrícola estatal nunca funcionó, está en que los agricultores pequeños, porque en Cuba no les llaman agricultores privados una mala palabra, tienen un seis por ciento de la tierra cultivable y por muchísimos años han sido los que suministran el grueso de la producción agrícola.

LG: Como no pudiste ir a Cuba por períodos largos, diste saltos de diez años entre 1980 y 1990, y luego de veinte años hasta 2010, ¿qué es lo que más te impactó?

CML: En los diez años entre 1980 y 1990, noté un deterioro considerable de los edificios, calles, etc. en La Habana, ¡pero cuando volví en 2010, veinte años después ¡fue impactante! Algo muy curioso, es que cuando estaba [en Centro Habana] en Galiano y San Rafael, no sabía dónde me encontraba, porque habían hecho una calle peatonal y las tiendas se habían convertido en viviendas que estaban muy deterioradas. Después me fui a la Plaza Vieja, que la habían completamente demolido y reconstruido por [el Historiador de la Ciudad] Eusebio Leal y su equipo ¡y tampoco sabía dónde estaba! Lo más horrible fue cuando fui a La Habana Vieja y vi los edificios, fuera del área reconstruida, caminas media cuadra y ves aquello apuntalado, ruinas de edificios [que eran] bellísimos.

LG: ¿Y cuándo fuiste más recientemente, en 2010 y 2011?

CML: Estas visitas fueron después de la elección de Obama, la cual constituyó un choque enorme en Cuba porque la gente no podía creerlo; los afrocubanos decían: Me presentan a los Estados Unidos como discriminadores raciales, pero han elegido un presidente negro y aquí, ninguno de ellos tiene posiciones importantes de poder, ni como empresarios. En 2010 volví para participar en la Semana Social Católica en la que había 150 profesionales de toda la Isla y me reuní con todo el equipo del Centro de Estudios de la Economía Cubana y con otros colegas, todo esto fue muy fructífero, aunque el deterioro de la ciudad se había agravado. En 2011 regresamos Elena y yo con nuestras hijas que nunca habían estado en Cuba y fue la primera visita como turista, aunque hubo momentos muy traumáticos, como cuando visitamos La Víbora que está irreconocible.[12]

LG: ¿Cuál es el factor más importante que tú ves dentro de Cuba que determinará su futuro?

CML: Una juventud que no cree. Un factor importante en la caída del comunismo en la Unión Soviética y la Europa Oriental fue que la juventud estaba completamente desencantada y alienada con el sistema. Otro factor crucial es el desarrollo del sector no estatal (cuentapropistas, usufructuarios de la tierra, miembros de las nuevas cooperativas, y compradores-vendedores de viviendas), estos microempresarios están creciendo y parte se hace independientes del Estado, a pesar de todas las trabas, altos impuestos y sanciones que sufren. La expansión de medios de comunicación en que se intercambian opiniones muy diversas y se hacen críticas a las fallas del sistema, así como de los blogs de disidentes, y una más espontánea crítica popular. Por último, la llegada de cientos de miles de visitantes y, sobre todo, estudiantes americanos podría jugar un papel al intercambiar con el pueblo cubano.

LG: ¿Cuál va a ser el legado tuyo, Carmelo?

CML: Mira, de lo que me siento más satisfecho en mi vida académica es que muchos de mis estudiantes ocupan hoy posiciones importantes en todo el mundo. Tengo antiguos alumnos por todas partes, en los Estados Unidos, en España, en Suiza, en Alemania, en el Reino Unido, en Argentina, en Brasil, en Chile ¡eso es una satisfacción enorme! Para mí eso es crucial porque tu pensamiento sigue vivo, se reproduce y expande.

LG: Muchos dicen que has creado una nueva escuela de pensamiento económico-social.

CML: Frente a la escuela de Chicago y la escuela marxista, una nueva manera de hacer economía y política social, algunos nos llaman "los Pitt Boys". En Cuba, también hay seguidores, mucha gente que me lee, y dos generaciones que de una manera u otra, han sido influenciadas por mis ideas, la metodología que he desarrollado, el deseo de buscar la objetividad y el equilibrio, el uso de las fuentes de Cuba sometiéndolas a un juicio justo, y por respetar y aprender de los académicos cubanos. Yo me siento muy feliz con todo eso.

NOTAS

1. Para apreciar en detalle la impresionante y prolífica carrera del Doctor Mesa-Lago, véase su curriculum completo y biografía en *http://www.mesa-lago.com*.

2. Se refiere a la invasión militar de la isla por Bahía de Cochinos en abril de 1961 en que participaron más de dos mil cubanos exiliados, en su mayoría ex-batistianos, reclutados y entrenados por la CIA. No obstante el apoyo y confianza absoluta de sus patrones en la administración del Presidente John F. Kennedy, el intento rotundamente repulsado por las fuerzas armadas y milicias voluntarias del gobierno revolucionario. Mejor conocido en Cuba por el titular de "Playa Girón", lugar donde desembarcó la expedición, el evento en sí representó un eje en la radicalización del proceso revolucionario, tanto por el apoyo casi incondicional que rindió el pueblo cubano inspirado en un profundo nacionalismo histórico, como por la decisión de Fidel Castro de abrazar abiertamente a la Unión Soviética y el comunismo en los días subsiguientes al triunfo de Cuba. A partir de abril de 1961, los líderes y activistas revolucionarios comenzaron a justificar la pérdida de todos los derechos de asamblea, protesta, libre pensamiento y crítica pública en la idea que Cuba era una plaza eternamente sitiada y que cualquiera "duda" expresada con respecto a las políticas y actitudes del gobierno amenazaba la seguridad nacional y por lo tanto, la soberanía nacional.

3. Durante la primera década de la Revolución hasta que se formalizaran los sistemas de vigilancia sobre el pueblo basado en la asesoría soviética, este antiguo colegio católico para varones

se convirtió en un centro secreto del Ministerio del Interior para interrogaciones y detenciones oficiales y extraoficiales de ciudadanos sospechados de actuar o promulgar ideas y movimientos contrarios al gobierno revolucionario.

4. El General Gerardo Machado, dirigente del Partido Liberal, fue elegido Presidente de Cuba en 1925 a base de una plataforma que prometía consolidar la soberanía nacional frente a los crecientes intereses e intervención directa de Estados Unidos en la economía y proyectos legislativos de Cuba. Famosamente, Machado no solo traicionó de inmediato sus promesas de campaña a embarcar en un largo tour por el noreste de Estados Unidos en que se reunió con los grandes inversionistas y magnates americanos para asegurar la protección de su privilegios en la isla, sino que promulgó la odiosa Prórroga de Poderes en 1928, una ley que arbitrariamente extendía su estancia en el poder sin elección, al igual que el mando de los congresistas. Presionado por protestas masivas estudiantiles, periodísticas y laborales, Machado optó por el camino del terror y la vigilancia contra sus opositores. Eventualmente, tras una larga huelga general y total degeneración política, tuvo que huir de Cuba en agosto de 1933, dejando el caos económico y las fuerzas revolucionarias de la oposición en el poder.

5. El Directorio Revolucionario fue una organización armada nacida de las protestas estudiantiles y del sector progresista de la facultad de la Universidad de la Habana. Organizado primero en 1928 y de manera más radical en 1931, el Directorio nutrió el gabinete del gobierno revolucionario bajo el líder y ex-profesor Dr. Ramón Grau de San Martín desde septiembre de 1933 hasta enero de 1934, cuando el gobierno de Estados Unidos apoyó el golpe de estado de Fulgencio Batista, ex-sargento del ejército de Machado que encabezó la afiliación inicial de los rangos menores y soldados a la Revolución del 1933 y luego su ruptura (y propia promoción) bajo un estado militar contrarrevolucionario fiel al autotitulado General Batista. Unidos por la traición de Batista y el proyecto común de consolidar una democracia constitucional y país soberano, los mayores activistas y miembros del Directorio luego fundaron el Partido Auténtico con el pleno respaldo de la mayoría del pueblo. A pesar de fomentar una inmensa corrupción gubernamental que provocó la división de sus filas y el establecimiento de un partido opositor de "limpios" que se nombraron "Los Ortodoxos", El Partido Auténtico dominó la esfera política electoral desde 1944 hasta el segundo golpe de estado y dictadura del mismo Batista (marzo 1952 a diciembre 1958).

6. Véase María de los Angeles Torres, *In the Land of Mirrors: Cuban Exile Politics in the United States* (Ann Arbor: University of Michigan Press, 2001).

7. Torres ofrece la mejor discusión y análisis publicado de este intento desde su doble óptica de académica y de partícipe en los hechos. Véase *In the Land of Mirrors*, 84–104. Basado en múltiples archivos públicos y privados, la tesis doctoral de Michael Bustamante representa una importante y profunda investigación sobre el Diálogo, la identidad política transnacional cubano y su legado para las estrategias del gobierno cubano por desacreditar y, a su vez, explotar la visión progresista de jóvenes exiliados, muchos de los cuales fueron blancos tanto para grupos terroristas basados en Miami luego de su activismo en Cuba. See Bustamante, "Cuban Counterpoints: Memory Struggles in Revolution and Exile," Tesis doctoral de la Facultad de Historia, Yale University, 2017.

8. Nelson Valdés and Rolando Bonachea, eds., *Che: Selected Works of Ernesto Che Guevara* (Cambridge, MA: MIT Press, 1969). También ambos habían editado una selección impresionante de escritos de Fidel Castro, muchas de las cuales documentaban su obvia, aunque ya negada, dedicación anterior a la causa electoral y constitucional como base de todo gobierno legítimo cubano. Véase *Revolutionary Struggle (1947–1958): The Selected Works of Fidel Castro* (Cambridge, MA: MIT Press, 1972).

9. Largo militante del Partido Comunista en Cuba desde 1938 cuando se cambió el nombre por Partido Socialista Popular, Núñez Jiménez participó en el Festival de la Juventud Comunista en Berlín del Este en 1951, evento patrocinado por la Unión Soviética como representante y fotógrafo oficial de la delegación cubana encabezada por Nicolás Guillén, entre otros. Núñez Jiménez

también participó en el Festival de la Juventud organizado en Praga en 1953. Como todo militante fiel a la línea soviética durante la lucha contra Batista, Núñez Jiménez rehusó apoyar las fuerzas revolucionarias de Fidel Castro hasta noviembre de 1958 cuando el Partido Comunista cambió de posición, consciente de la necesidad de no quedarse fuera y del lado de la dictadura en el momento inevitable de su caída del poder. Luego Fidel Castro lo nombró director del Instituto de Reforma Agraria, la agencia estatal más poderosa en los primeros años de la Revolución, a pesar de negar que ninguno de sus políticas debía ser orientadas hacia el comunismo. Véase Lillian Guerra, *Visions of Power in Cuba: Revolution, Redemption, and Resistance, 1959–1971* (Chapel Hill: University of North Carolina Press, 2013).

10. Julio Carranza Urdaneta, Luis Gutiérrez González y Pedro Monreal Valdés, *Cuba: Restructuring the Economy, A Contribution to the Debate* (London: Institute for Latin American Studies at the University of London, 1996).

11. En junio de 2007, la OIT otorgó su primer premio al trabajo decente al ex-Presidente sudafricano y ganador del Premio Nobel de la Paz Nelson Mandela y a Carmelo Mesa-Lago "como reconocimiento a sus aportes para mejorar la vida de las personas en el mundo." Véase el comunicado de prensa disponible en el sitio http://www.ilo.org/global/about-the-ilo/newsroom/news/WCMS_083098/lang--es/index.htm.

12. Después de negarle tres veces una visa académica en 2014–2016 para participar en eventos a los que fue invitado en Cuba, incluyendo un homenaje por sus ochenta años y su obra, Mesa-Lago regresó a La Habana con una visa familiar, a fines de 2016, acompañado de toda su familia (por primera vez con sus nietos).

JOSÉ ABREU CARDET

La United Fruit Company: La visión de un historiador cubano

En 1976 la editorial cubana Ciencias Sociales publicó el libro *United Fruit Company: Un caso del dominio imperialista en Cuba*, un texto bastante singular en el universo intelectual cubano. Por primera vez se hacía el estudio de una empresa transnacional estadounidense, establecida en la mayor de Las Antillas. Otro hecho que marcaba aquel acontecimiento era que la obra fue el resultado de un trabajo en equipo de varios investigadores, asunto no muy frecuente en la historiografía cubana en aquellos momentos. El grupo estaba dirigido por Alejandro García y Óscar Zanetti, lo integraban además, los estudiantes de la Escuela de Historia de la Universidad de La Habana: Sergio Guerra, Rosa Pulperio, Concepción Planos, Josefina Ballester, Manuel Rodríguez, Vivian Peraza, Francisco Román García, María del Carmen Maseda, Armando Vallejo y Rafael García.

El doctor Óscar Zanetti Lecuona tuvo la amabilidad de responder un cuestionario que le hicimos llegar sobre el referido libro. Uno de los historiadores cubanos de mayor prestigio, especialista en historia económica e historiografía, con una vasta obra sobre la industria azucarera en Cuba. No se puede pensar en el pasado azucarero de las Antillas españolas sin traer a colación a este colega, y mucho menos referirnos a los estudios historiográficos sin tener en cuenta sus enfoques originales sobre el tema. A los cuarenta años de la publicación de *United Fruit Company: Un caso del dominio imperialista en Cuba* el profesor Zanetti, un apellido que ha escapado del entorno de una familia para convertirse en adjetivo de lo que se debe hacer en la historia, se somete voluntariamente a este pequeño proceso sobre un libro que marco los estudios del pasado económico de la mayor de las Antillas.

¿Cuándo nació y sus padres en qué trabajaban?

Nací en La Habana, en 1946. Mi padre era médico; vinculado a la lucha contra Batista en el Movimiento 26 de Julio,[1] después del triunfo de la revolución se hizo médico militar. Cuando ya yo había crecido un poco e iba al colegio, mi madre comenzó a trabajar como operadora de IBM en unos equipos de tarjetas perforadas, que de cierto modo fueron antecedente de la actual tecnología digital.

Motivaciones de usted para estudiar historia. Me interesaría una valoración suya sobre lo que fue la carrera de historia que se inició en 1962.

En otra ocasión he contado que tanto mi padre como mi abuelo materno eran amantes de la historia y grandes lectores. Yo empecé desde temprano a leer la literatura infantil y juvenil de la época (Salgari, Dumas, etc.), y como sus novelas tenían base histórica, sobre todo mi padre me alentó a buscar detrás de ellas; así fui leyendo libros de historia y sintiéndome atraído por esa disciplina. Claro que en aquella época la historia no era una profesión, quienes la escribían se ganaban la vida en otras actividades, eran abogados, profesores, periodistas, etc., por lo cual no se me ocurría pensar que pudiera hacerme historiador. Tras el triunfo de la revolución la situación cambió y se creó una carrera universitaria de historia.[2] Así todo, yo me sentía más inclinado a la economía, pero como no era bueno en matemáticas opté finalmente por estudiar historia. Ingresé en el tercer curso de esa carrera a principios de 1963. Era una carrera nueva con un amplio abanico de profesores de muy disímiles características; predominaban antiguos profesores de instituto (bachillerato), como Hortensia Pichardo, Estrella Rey, Aleida Plasencia o el propio Sergio Aguirre, director de la escuela, pero había intelectuales de otras características como Manuel Galich, Pelegrín Torras y hasta Alejo Carpentier que impartió un par de cursos de historia de la Literatura. También enseñaban algunas jóvenes profesoras recién graduadas de filosofía y letras. El currículo era de notable amplitud cultural, pero cojeaba en lo relativo a la formación profesional, al desarrollo de las habilidades del oficio, casi limitado a la asignatura Técnicas de la Investigación Histórica que impartía la Dra. Pichardo.

¿Por qué en un período tan rico en la historia militar, de la revolución de independencia, de la lucha contra Batista se especializó en historia económica? ¿Qué preparación le dio la universidad en ese sentido? ¿Cómo se formó usted como historiador de la economía?

Los temas que apuntas son sin duda los más tradicionales dentro de la historiografía cubana; el grueso de las obras publicadas durante algo más de un siglo se han dedicado a esos asuntos. Cuando yo inicié mi formación universitaria en la década de 1960, estaba sobre el tapete la necesidad de una reelaboración de nuestro discurso histórico nacional desde una perspectiva marxista, lo cual no podía resolverse con una simple relectura de la historiografía tradicional aderezada con los conceptos del materialismo histórico. Obras entonces pioneras como las de Julio Le Riverend y Manuel Moreno Fraginals hacían patente la necesidad de una profunda indagación sobre problemas económicos y sociales de nuestro pasado que apenas se habían estudiado.

La preparación universitaria en ese sentido resultaba bastante deficiente, pues apenas consistía en cursos de economía política, cuyo acercamiento a los problemas económicos era generalmente abstracto y hasta dogmático. Más adelante se introdujeron cursos de estadística y demografía, pero quienes la impartían no solían aplicarla a situaciones históricas. Así, los métodos y otros recursos apropiados para estudio de fenómenos económicos se adquirían principalmente en la propia práctica de la investigación.

Cuando leemos lo publicado en los sesenta, setenta y parte de los ochenta nos encontramos con una historia heroica pese a que el marxismo debía de incentivar el estudio de la economía. ¿Usted cree que ha faltado un impulso a los estudios de historia económica?

Creo que esa historia heroica, trabajada desde una perspectiva nacionalista, se ha cultivado siempre, no sólo en esas décadas —y se ha visto estimulada en la medida en que ha contribuido al afianzamiento de la conciencia nacional. Sin embargo, creo que algunas de las obras más relevantes y reconocidas internacionalmente de nuestra historiografía en la segunda mitad del siglo pasado corresponden a la historia económica. O mejor, socioeconómica, pues esa especialidad entre nosotros ha sido más cercana a los paradigmas marxista y de la escuela de los *Annales* que a la historiografía más estrictamente económica, de inspiración neoclásica, que se fue imponiendo a escala mundial durante las últimas décadas.

Creo que es precisamente en los pasados veinte años que la historiografía económica ha perdido impulso en nuestro país, aunque no le falten obras sobresalientes. Los factores de esa declinación son diversos; han estado ausentes las contribuciones de nuestros economistas, poco atraídos por el análisis histórico —incluso de épocas recientes—, que son los mejor preparados para el trabajo con estadísticas y otros aspectos deficitarios en nuestra historia económica. Por el lado de los historiadores, ha sido sobre todo la inclinación hacia los problemas socio culturales y otros temas en boga a escala mundial lo que ha restado adeptos a la historiografía económica. Claro que dicha situación es también reflejo de la paupérrima cultura económica de los cubanos en las últimas generaciones.

Tengo entendido que usted es un gran lector de ficción; ¿para su formación como historiador de la economía le ha reportado algo útil en el sentido académico?

Sí, soy un lector asiduo, tanto de la narrativa como de la ensayística. Además de investigar principalmente temas económicos y sociales —también trabajo la historiografía—, como docente impartí por mucho tiempo Metodología de la Investigación Histórica, materias todas poco atractivas para el alumnado y el público general. Por ello para lograr captar la atención del auditorio en clase, así como ganar lectores, siempre me he preocupado por emplear recursos literarios y de otro tipo —que faciliten la comunicación—, algo que lamentablemente descuidan colegas que cultivan temas más potables.

¿Cómo se acercó a los estudios del azúcar? ¿Alguna lectura de un texto sobre el tema le impresionó mucho? ¿La investigación de la United Fruit influyó en su decisión de dedicarse a ese tema de la historia del azúcar? ¿Ya lo había decidido?

El azúcar ha sido durante dos siglos la base de la actividad económica en el país; si se quiere entender la economía cubana, su formación y sus problemas hay que entrar por ella. Por otra parte en los años en que estudié y me gradué, los que rodearon a la famosa zafra de los diez millones,[3] el azúcar era el centro de la vida social; hasta la música, el deporte y la literatura aunque no fuesen dulces estaban azucarados. De hecho, antes de la experiencia sin duda decisiva —de la investigación sobre la United Fruit, durante la zafra de 1970 había participado con un nutrido grupo de estudiantes de la Escuela de Historia de la Universidad de La Habana en una investigación— *tournee* que durante varios meses recorrió centrales por todo el país, combinando el corte de caña con el acopio, de manera un tanto pintoresca, de información sobre la historia azucarera. Una vez graduado, la Yunai, fue una suerte de replanteo en serio de aquel proyecto y su realización me abrió la mente a una comprensión bastante más profunda de los problemas del azúcar y de la economía cubana.

¿Cómo surgió la idea de la investigación sobre la United Fruit? ¿Por qué la United Fruit y no otras empresas de los Estados Unidos como los centrales azucareros la Chaparra, Delicia o las plantas de níquel? ¿Se discutió esa posibilidad?

En la selección específica de la United Fruit influyó sobre todo Oscar Pino Santos. Periodista económico reconocido, Pino tenía una relevante trayectoria política en el Instituto de Reforma Agraria, como embajador en China, etc., —y acababa de ganar el premio de Ensayo de la Casa de las Américas con una obra, *El asalto a Cuba por la oligarquía financiera yanqui*, que ofrecía un singular acercamiento al proceso de penetración imperialista en nuestro país. Con buenas conexiones en el Ministerio del Azúcar, Pino se acercó con una propuesta a la Escuela de Historia de la Universidad de La Habana, que acababa de tener la experiencia que te he apuntado y que desde su creación no había conseguido solucionar adecuadamente la formación investigativa de sus estudiantes. Se decidió entonces hacer de la investigación de la United Fruit el ejercicio de graduación para un gran grupo de estudiantes del último año de la carrera, al cual dirigiríamos Alejandro García y yo bajo la coordinación del Dr. Carlos Funtanellas, que era el subdirector de Investigaciones de la Escuela. ¡Ah!, un detalle crucial: Pino era de Banes[4] y sabía que la documentación de la United allí estaba relativamente bien conservada, eso determinó la selección.

¿El aseguramiento material cómo se logró? ¿Fue necesario convencer a muchos para esa investigación o encontraron caminos de plata?

El aseguramiento material fue proporcionado básicamente por el MINAZ, con cierto apoyo del PCC regional de Banes y Mayarí[5] y de la Universidad de La Habana. Nos alojábamos en casas proporcionadas por las administraciones de los centrales Nicaragua (Boston) y Guatemala (Preston)[6] y comíamos en los comedores de los trabajadores. Esto último, como te imaginarás, era bastante flojo, y el partido [PCC] en Banes nos facilitó una reservación en el restaurant del único hotel del pueblo; esa posibilidad, rotándola entre los estudiantes, permitía que estos comiesen razonablemente bien al menos un día a la semana. Los movimientos entre los dos centrales lo hacíamos en carritos de línea o mediante un lanchón que viajaba entre Antilla y Guatemala.[7] Como ves, los caminos no fueron precisamente de plata, pero si transitables.

¿Cómo se organizó el equipo? ¿La selección de los estudiantes en base a qué se hizo?

Ya te adelanté que fueron los estudiantes del último año de la carrera; casi todos, porque había algunos que eran becados de organismos con los cuales ya tenían comprometido su trabajo de graduación. Luego propiamente no hubo selección, aunque algunas muchachas que ya eran madres no pudieron moverse a los centrales y trabajaron desde La Habana. El equipo se organizó sobre la marcha, en la medida en que pudimos agrupar las fuentes y determinar los temas de investigación; en la selección de estos últimos dimos cierto margen a las preferencias de los estudiantes.

El papel de Carlos Funtanellas.[8]

Fue la máxima autoridad del proyecto. No era historiador económico, sino especialista en historiografía, pero se había formado en el Colegio de México y tenía conocimientos sobre técnicas de investigación y organización archivística que resultaron muy útiles. Pero su papel fue sobre todo de organizador y de coordinación institucional.

¿Qué conocimiento tenían usted y Alejandro sobre la industria azucarera y en especial la United Fruit?

Específicamente sobre la industria azucarera nuestros conocimientos eran bastante elementales; manejábamos lo fundamental de la escasa bibliografía disponible sobre el tema y algunos saberes prácticos derivados de la experiencia en los centrales durante la zafra de 1970. Alejandro había estudiado un par de años Ciencias Comerciales y tenía conocimientos de contabilidad y otras materias económicas que resultaron decisivos para encauzar el trabajo.

En Cuba había un antecedente aunque fuera mucho más modesto de investigación sobre la industria del azúcar en el siglo XX. ¿Alguna investigación anterior, algunos libros les sirvieron de orientación metodológica?

Antecedentes sobre historia de empresas no existía ninguno. Sobre la economía azucarera disponíamos de dos obras clásicas, ambas de Ramiro Guerra, *Azúcar y población en las Antillas* y *La industria azucarera de Cuba*, útiles por demás, sobre todo la segunda que presentaba un cuadro general de la organización del sector a finales de la década de 1930. Estaba, por supuesto, *El ingenio* de Moreno, que a pesar de referirse a otra época ofrecía múltiples sugerencias y otras obras de alcance más parcial, como el *Contrapunteo* de Ortiz, que enriquecían el contexto cultural del estudio. Ademá, existían otras obras no históricas sino más o menos técnicas, como la *Introducción a la tecnología del azúcar de caña*, de Jenkins o la utilísima *Contabilidad de ingenios azucareros*, de Fernández Cepero, o los trabajos de Pedrosa Puertas, todos muy valiosos para poder entender el funcionamiento de la industria y sus problemas. También habían publicaciones seriadas como el *Anuario azucarero de Cuba* o la revista *Cuba económica y financiera*. Ello se explica en un acápite relativamente extenso sobre las fuentes de la Introducción del libro.

¿Alguna investigación, anterior algunos libros les sirvieron de orientación metodológica?

La literatura disponible sobre investigaciones parecidas en otros países era muy pobre. Pudimos consultar alguna obra de la *business history* norteamericana y estudios de historia económica que sugerían e ilustraban la aplicación de técnicas como el análisis estadístico y aportaban explicaciones sobre el funcionamiento de la economía y empresas capitalistas. También dispusimos de alguna obra general sobre historia azucarera Noël Deerr —y de dos o tres monografías sobre la United Fruit en Centroamérica y otras partes, pues era una empresa muy notoria en la historia latinoamericana de la primera mitad del siglo XX.

¿Sostuvo conversaciones con técnicos o especialistas de la industria del azúcar? ¿Con quienes, su interés sobre qué giraba?

Si, la ayuda de técnicos y conocedores fue muy valiosa. En Banes, por ejemplo, Ángel Ricota, un viejo trabajador de las oficinas del Central Boston, en Macabí, nos orientó respecto a fuentes, además de proporcionarnos información indispensable sobre la organización y las prácticas funcionales de la compañía; en Preston contamos con el químico Augusto Cornide, cuyas explicaciones nos sirvieron para adentrarnos en el complicado terreno de los índices de eficiencia. En menor escala, también tuvimos apoyos similares en Preston. Fue igualmente importante la ayuda de viejos dirigentes obreros, todos ellos relacionados como testimoniantes en las fuentes del libro. Ya en La

Habana, durante el proceso de análisis de la información y la redacción de la obra, pudimos hacer consultas puntuales a reconocidos técnicos del MINAZ como Henderson, el creador de la primera cosechadora cañera cubana. Ellos fueron de mucha ayuda.

¿Desde cuándo se comenzó a preparar el proyecto? ¿Quienes lo elaboraron?
¿Consultaron con colegas por ejemplo Moreno Fraginals?

El proyecto se preparó básicamente entre Funtanellas, Pino Santos, Alejandro y yo. No creo que se haya consultado a Moreno, con quien la Escuela —particularmente Funtanellas— no tenía una buena relación; quizás Funtanellas haya consultado a Le Riverend, a quien lo unía una antigua amistad. Entre la formulación del proyecto y la ejecución de la investigación transcurrió muy poco tiempo, apenas un par de meses. Por ello muchas situaciones debieron solucionarse sobre la marcha.

¿Estudió o indagó sobre la tecnología de esa industria?

Desde luego, consultamos manuales sobre tecnología azucarera, en particular el de Jenkins, así como sobre agricultura cañera. Fueron igualmente útiles las revistas de la Asociación de Técnicos Azucareros de Cuba (ATAC) y en general la biblioteca de esa institución que es excelente.

¿Usted era profesor en la universidad; de que especialidad?

Tres o cuatro años antes, cuando aun estudiaba historia, yo había impartido cursos de filosofía, como profesor del Departamento de Filosofía de la Universidad de La Habana. Al graduarme de historia fui seleccionado junto a tres o cuatro compañeros de mi curso para integrar un equipo de investigación adscrito a la subdirección que desempeñaba el Dr. Funtanellas, con quien Alejandro, graduado un poco antes, ya venía colaborando. Creo que nos seleccionaron para el proyecto de la UFCo. porque éramos dentro de aquel equipo los más interesados en historia económica y Alejandro, además, tenía amistad personal con Pino Santos.

¿Visitaron previamente a Banes antes de elaborar el proyecto?

Quizás Funtanellas lo haya hecho, y también Pino, pero no conozco ese detalle. Alejandro y yo llegamos junto con el grupo de estudiantes.

¿Qué investigaciones había realizado antes?

Años atrás yo había realizado alguna investigación arqueológica; excavaciones y un estudio ceramográfico, pero eso no tenía relación alguna con el proyecto de la United, salvo que casualmente las excavaciones se habían realizado en Banes y Mayarí, así que ya había estado en la zona. Mi primera investigación histórica dentro del equipo, realizada un año antes, fue un estudio sobre el comercio exterior de Cuba en el período republicano, para el cual conté con la asesoría de un profesor francés, Guy Bourdé, que fue vital para mi formación, sobre todo en lo relativo al análisis estadístico a partir de fuentes históricas. Esa pequeña monografía se publicó un par de años después en el primer número de un *Anuario de Estudios Cubanos*, de breve existencia.

El apoyo de la localidad, es decir de, las autoridades en Banes, Holguín.

Ya te he dicho algo al respecto. Entonces Banes era un regional de la provincia de Oriente, igual que Holguín, por tanto este último fue sobre todo un lugar de paso, aunque teníamos contacto con algunos historiadores holguineros, particularmente Hiram Pérez, pues su hermano Hernán era profesor en nuestro departamento universitario.

Sus recuerdos sobre el Holguín de la época y sobre Banes. ¿El movimiento de activista de historia de esa localidad los apoyó?

En mi memoria de habanero recuerdo a Banes como un pueblo relativamente modesto y todavía segmentado por la presencia de la United Fruit apenas una década atrás. En este sentido las diferencias eran muy notables entre las instalaciones de la compañía casas y almacenes, así como entre los barrios. Durante nuestro trabajo contamos con el auxilio en diversos sentidos —de Pedro Martínez, quien estaba a cargo de la Comisión de Historia del Partido regional en Banes; también se nos acercaron algunos historiadores locales, en modo alguno profesionales, pero que en ciertos casos colaboraron con nuestras investigaciones mediante testimonios y explicaciones sobre todo en lo relativo al movimiento obrero y la política local— así como con necesidades más prácticas de la vida. En Guatemala fue más o menos igual, aunque en aquel momento un movimiento de activistas de historia como tal, no lo recuerdo.

Estado de la documentación. ¿Se vieron obligados a darle una organización mínima o ya la tenía, es decir era un material que se podía trabajar o el estado de organización original se había perdido?

La situación fue distinta en ambos centrales. En Banes y Macabí se conservaba mucha documentación,[9] sin duda la mayor parte de la dejada por la compañía. En Macabí estaban las oficinas operativas del central Boston que conservaban pequeños archivos todavía organizados. Pero el grueso de la documentación de la División Banes la encontramos convertida en un enorme montón de papeles en el suelo de una de las áreas del gran almacén de la compañía en Banes. Recuerdo que abrimos un espacio en el medio y pedimos a un estudiante que se metiera en la masa de papeles, que le llegaba hasta el cuello, para sacar una foto que no se por dónde andará. Luego el primer trabajo fue rehacer el archivo, recogiendo la documentación y agrupándola según su naturaleza en grandes anaqueles colocados en el mismo local; había libros de nóminas, expedientes de personal, libros de contabilidad, reportes de fabricación, copiadores de cartas de los administradores, etc. Nos pasamos como un mes rehaciendo el archivo para poder iniciar la explotación de esas fuentes. Meses después, al terminar el trabajo, mudamos ordenadamente toda la documentación para un pequeño local de mampostería a un lado del pequeño patio ferrocarrilero que había detrás del gran almacén, pues nos parecía que estaría mejor conservada ya que allí sólo cabían los anaqueles de documentos. Según me contaron, un tiempo después el local lo destinaron a barbería y se sacaron los documentos que fueron trasladados al sótano del museo municipal. Ignoro su estado posterior. La documentación conservada en el central Guatemala era mucho menor, pues sus administraciones no la cuidaron e incluso nos contaron de un administrador que envío papelería a los hornos porque ocupaba espacio y era imperialista. Sin embargo, la que quedaba estaba relativamente ordenada e incluso se conservaba un espectacular archivo fotográfico.

Las entrevistas, ¿su importancia en el trabajo tenían alguna experiencia en historia oral?

Las entrevistas fueron muy importantes, sobre todo para las incidencias del movimiento obrero, pero también para ciertos aspectos funcionales de la compañía. Nosotros teníamos alguna experiencia con ese recurso por la anterior investigación de los centrales en 1970, pero afinamos ciertos aspectos técnicos a partir de manuales de sociología. No creo que pudiera hablarse aún de historia oral, pues ella requiere un diseño específico y un empleo más exhaustivo de las fuentes; se trataba más bien de recogida de datos a partir de testimonios verbales. De hecho, en las fuentes relacionadas, las entrevistas que se mencionan fueron las que se desarrollaron como tal, pero contamos también con testimonios breves y aclaraciones que sin constituir entrevistas aportaron información útil. Las técnicas de entrevista aplicadas a la historia se irían perfilando posteriormente en otras investigaciones, como la de los ferrocarriles.

Dificultades en las entrevistas.

Las usuales, fallos de memoria de los testimoniantes que había que manejar con cuidado, pues era posible despertar sus recuerdos a partir de otra información disponible pero evitando contaminar las respuestas. También, por supuesto había quien sesgaba el testimonio por determinado interés y resultaba necesario percatarse de ello mediante la crítica y otros medios.

¿Se habían utilizados las fuentes orales con anterioridad en un estudio de historia económica?

El grueso de la información procedente de testimonios nutrió la historia del movimiento obrero y otros aspectos sociales de nuestro estudio. Ya te advertí que en la investigación sobre la United Fruit, al igual que la de ferrocarriles y otras posteriores, lo económico era la columna vertebral para dilucidar los problemas centrales de la historia de la empresa, pero ella abarcó diversos asuntos sociales y políticos sin los cuales la reconstrucción histórica hubiese quedado incompleta, e incluso ciertos problemas económicos no hubieran podido entenderse a cabalidad. Claro que también alguna información oral de empleados y obreros calificados contribuyó a esclarecer asuntos económicos.

¿Había trabajado anteriormente con estadísticas y gráficas? ¿Quién las elaboró?

Ya te dije que yo había hecho una investigación anterior sobre el comercio exterior cuyo análisis era fundamentalmente estadístico, con reconstrucción de series, cálculos diversos y representaciones gráficas. Alejandro también tenía experiencia al respecto. A él y a mí ese aspecto nos correspondió casi por entero.

¿Los estudiantes fueron recopiladores de datos o realmente redactaron sus respectivos capítulos?

Los estudiantes redactaron informes temáticos dedicados a aspectos específicos, algunos con un notable nivel de terminación. Recuerdo, por ejemplo, los de Sergio Guerra sobre aspectos demográfico o el de Manuel Rodríguez que había estudiado un año de ingeniería y se familiarizó bastante bien con los aspectos tecnológicos. Posteriormente, Alejandro y yo, con esa información sintetizada, los cientos, miles de fichas que le daban sustento, otra información adicional recopilada directamente por nosotros sobre aspectos que, como la contabilidad, no estaban al alcance de los estudiantes. Con más bibliografía, prensa y otras fuentes consultadas en La Habana, desarrollamos el análisis, trazamos la estructura del libro y redactamos sus capítulos.

¿Algunos de los estudiantes continúo investigando historia económica?

Dos de ellos, Francisco Román y Armando Vallejo derivaron hacia la economía, aunque no propiamente a la historia económica sino a la enseñanza de economía política.

¿Había redactado un texto anterior al de la United Fruit?

Sí, el estudio sobre comercio exterior que te he mencionado y también alguno que otro texto, pero no de carácter histórico.

¿El trabajo de redacción que tiempo duró? ¿Cómo lograron coordinar o hacer coincidir todos esos capítulos escritos por tantas personas, la mayoría estudiantes de poco experiencia?

Como te expliqué, la confección del libro estuvo a cargo de Alejandro y yo; nos tomó casi dos años. El análisis de los problemas y la guía general para la redacción, el capitulario y los asuntos a tratar dentro de cada capítulo, los precisamos en conjunto, después nos distribuimos los capítulos. Cada cual redactaba el suyo y después lo pasaba al otro, que daba la redacción final. Así tratamos de evitar que se notasen grandes diferencias en la redacción de los diferentes capítulos.

La relación estudiante profesor en este asunto de una investigación es compleja, pues hasta qué límite confiar en la seriedad del estudiante. ¿Usaron mecanismos de comprobación?

Yo entonces tenía veinticinco años y no estaba muy lejos de los estudiantes; me había graduado un par de años antes así que para mí eran en buena medida compañeros de carrera. Alejandro era mayor y graduado de otra promoción, pero por su personalidad y larga experiencia docente resultaba muy accesible y eficaz en el plano pedagógico. Por otra parte, el grupo era bastante serio y asumió la tarea con responsabilidad. Además, trabajamos hombro con hombro con los estudiantes; participamos en sus primeras entrevistas y al finalizar analizábamos con ellos la experiencia. Estábamos a su alcance durante la explotación de las fuentes y nos consultaban. Al final del día revisábamos las fichas confeccionadas; incluso en los primeros momentos esa revisión era contra el documento para evaluar la calidad de la recogida de datos. Durante la redacción de sus trabajos también interactuamos con frecuencia, revisamos los borradores y sugerimos enmiendas antes de recibir la redacción final.

¿Fue necesario retornar a Banes, consultar los archivos y hacer entrevistas mientras se realizaba ese trabajo de redacción?

Este es un detalle que no recuerdo bien; me parece que sí, pero no estoy absolutamente seguro.

¿Por qué no continuaron a Chaparra, Delicias, Nicaro u otras empresas de los Estados Unidos en Cuba?

Como lo indica el subtítulo del libro, la investigación sobre la United Fruit era un estudio de caso sobre la penetración imperialista y la actuación de las empresas norteamericanas en Cuba. Aunque nos dimos cuenta que la United en más de un sentido resultaba un tanto atípica entre las empresas azucareras, no tenía sentido repetir la experiencia. Quizás trabajar otro central o compañía azucarera norteamericana hubiese ampliado la perspectiva pero no nos añadiría mucho más, por eso preferimos movernos a otro plano y abarcar en una investigación de características similares todo un sector de la economía: el ferroviario. Esta era una de las ramas más antiguas de la moderna economía cubana, se inicia casi a principios del siglo XIX, y nos reportaría una visión más amplia y diversa de la evolución económica del país y del funcionamiento empresarial, como así fue.

¿En caso de hacerlo de nuevo, que le agregaría y qué cree usted que sobra del libro, si es que sobra algo?

A cuarenta años de distancia y con toda la experiencia acumulada sería un libro distinto. Creo que la estructura temática básicamente se mantendría, aunque habría que dar espacio a asuntos que entonces no atendimos, como el impacto ecológico. También sería necesario acercarse más a la vida de las comunidades en los bateyes, tanto de los ingenios como rurales y seguir en esa misma cuerda la interacción de la compañía con la comunidad banense que quedó un tanto limitada a lo político. Claro, ahora prácticamente no podríamos contar con testimonios directos, pero si resultase posible consultar los archivos de la United en Boston que al parecer aún no son muy accesibles —el libro ganaría muchísimo. Ciertas interpretaciones y explicaciones sin duda cambiarían, mejoraría la calidad de la redacción; todo lo que podría aportarle casi medio siglo de experiencia profesional y la propia evolución de la historiografía. Por eso cuando nos han hablado de una segunda edición hemos tomado la idea con reserva, pues podría ser una edición revisada pero difícilmente ampliada; habría que mantenerla casi como una reliquia.

Pese al peso de la industria azucarera no hay muchos estudios regionales sobre el azúcar. Tanto la historia de centrales como de regiones azucareras. ¿Por qué?

Sí, sin dudas la industria azucarera no se ha estudiado aquí en correspondencia con su importancia sobre todo en el siglo XX, a pesar de haber captado una buena proporción de los estudios de nuestra historiografía económica. Pero en los estudios de centrales y empresas azucareras estamos, por ejemplo, detrás de Puerto Rico. Desde el ángulo de la historia regional algo se ha hecho, en Guantánamo, Cienfuegos y otros lugares, en el propio Holguín; pero por lo general se trata de monografías breves sobre algún central.

Las razones no son difíciles de explicar; es un déficit generalizado de nuestra historiografía económica, esa pérdida de impulso a la cual aludía una de tus preguntas. En un momento en que se hace evidente que la economía está en el centro de los problemas del país, al igual que sucediera en otras etapas de nuestra historia, cabe esperar que se despierten las inquietudes de los historiadores y economistas, que se revitalice la historiografía económica, incluyendo la investigación de los problemas de nuestra historia reciente, apenas estudiados.

¿Usted cree que la United Fruit Company marcó en lo cultural a Banes? ¿Era palpable esa influencia? Quiero su criterio de lo que vio y sintió.

Cuando estuve allí en 1971 y 1972 la presencia de la Compañía era muy viva; se apreciaba en el orden urbano, en la arquitectura, en las conversaciones de la gente. Había componentes étnicos incomprensibles sin la presencia de la United. No sé pasados cuarenta años cuánto de ello se mantendrá, resultará perceptible. Quizás ocurra como en tantas otras situaciones en las cuales se manifiestan rasgos y fenómenos cuyo origen histórico se ignora. Está, por otra parte, Guatemala, que a diferencia de Banes con su autonomía de gran población, era sólo un gran batey en torno al central cuya supervivencia no sé en qué se fundamentará una vez demolido este, con un polo de atracción tan cercano en la minería.

Ustedes trabajaron en una zona azucarera, unos historiadores, que en esa época no eran tantos, de La Habana por demás metidos en el poblado y el central, ¿cómo eran mirados por los obreros, los vecinos? ¿Dejaron algún tipo de huella?

Eso tendrías que preguntarlo allí, aunque me imagino que probablemente ya nadie lo recuerde. Quizás en Guatemala, que era un pueblo más pequeño. Las relaciones fueron buenas con quienes tuvieron que ver con nuestro trabajo más o menos directamente y también con gente del pueblo que se acercaba; por supuesto que hubo interacción con los pobladores y hasta su amorcito efímero con algún estudiante, pero ya ha pasado demasiado tiempo para que se recuerde. Tanto para los estudiantes como para nosotros creo que fue una experiencia inolvidable.

Creo que la mayoría de los trabajos que usted realizó después de la United Fruit fue en solitario. ¿Por qué no repitió la experiencia?

No, en realidad no fue así; Alejandro y yo repetimos la experiencia de la United Fruit en escala ampliada en la investigación sobre la historia de los ferrocarriles, cuyo resultados quedaron plasmados en *Caminos para el azúcar*, una obra premiada internacionalmente y publicada también en inglés por una editorial universitaria norteamericana. Ya en la segunda mitad de los setenta, con los grandes cambios que experimentó la educación superior, los ejercicios de graduación se individualizaron en los trabajos de diploma y la conducción de los estudiantes adquirió otras características. Con ello cambiaron también nuestras propias investigaciones, más aún cuando comenzaron a realizarse las tesis de doctorado.

¿La investigación de la United Fruit qué le reportó de positivo a su experiencia de investigador?

Creo que fue un sólido fundamento de mi formación como historiador, sólo un par de mis trabajos posteriores, el ya mencionado de los ferrocarriles y el más reciente *Esplendor y decadencia del azúcar en las Antillas hispanas*, han superado en amplitud y alcance la investigación sobre la United Fruit. Sin esa experiencia inicial no habría podido emprender posteriores investigaciones sobre el azúcar, como el análisis comparativo plasmado en *Esplendor...* o el estudio sobre la regulación de la industria que titulé *Las manos en el dulce.* Creo que para Alejandro fue también importante en su posterior investigación sobre la economía bananera.

En el libro de la United Fruit Company la fotografía es interesante. Da la impresión que es como un libro pequeño dentro del libro. ¿Cómo se pensó en eso?

Siempre consideramos que el libro debía tener ilustraciones, además de mapas y gráficos estadísticos. Ya te dije que en Preston encontramos una excelente colección fotográfica. Sobre todo fotos de los años veinte y treinta. Pudiéramos haber incluido más fotos pero las limitaciones editoriales lo impidieron. Seleccionamos las fundamentales para ilustrar los diversos aspectos de la actividad de la compañía.

¿Al terminar el libro quedó algo en el tintero como por ejemplo un estudio de la inmigración, una compilación de documentos, que hubiera sido muy valiosa?

Recogimos algunos documentos en un anexo del libro, pero más bien con finalidad ilustrativa. La obra constituye un análisis de conjunto, que trató de abarcar todas las facetas de la actividad de la United Fruit en Cuba; en consecuencia cada asunto fue abordado con profundidad, pero dedicándole el espacio apropiado para mantener el equilibrio general de la monografía. Es por ello que algunos temas serían susceptibles de estudiarse de manera específica con un mayor detalle si las fuentes accesibles lo permiten.

¿Cómo se produjo la publicación del libro, fue necesaria una evaluación fuera del área académica por la implicación del tema?

El libro no era un texto docente, luego su publicación por los canales editoriales universitarios no resultaba factible. La gestión editorial la hicimos Alejandro y yo, pues ya Funtanellas había fallecido. La editorial de Ciencias Sociales del Instituto Cubano del Libro que entonces dirigía Frank Pérez se mostró interesada en la publicación y esta pudo llevarse a cabo. El proceso de edición y corrección de los textos resultó bastante flojo y se escaparon un montón de erratas. Recuerdo que Alejandro y yo preparamos una fe de erratas en esténcil que tenía como cuatro o cinco páginas y la distribuimos a quienes regalamos el libro.

Siempre cuando se termina un libro se expone el criterio de que no se ha agotado el tema, hay muchos senderos que recorrer. Pero este libro es un mazazo por su peso como obra académica a todo el que se acerque al tema. Parece que todo está dicho sobre la United Fruit Company ¿qué aspecto usted aconsejaría a quienes pretendan estudiar la empresa y no hacer una copia?

Ya te he dicho algo al respecto. Creo que las mayores posibilidades de ampliación y corrección radican en la consulta de fuentes norteamericanas, tanto del archivo de la compañía en Boston, como de los *Confidential files* que recogen la documentación operativa de la embajada norteamericana en La Habana desde las décadas de 1930 a 1950, hoy día todos microfilmados y accesibles, pero cuya consulta no estuvo entonces a nuestro alcance.

Usted me dijo en una ocasión al mirar los archivos de la Chaparra "¡Aquí hay un libro!" ¿Piensa usted en la posibilidad de otra experiencia similar sobre empresas azucarera de Estados Unidos u otras? ¿No cree usted que podrían universidades o instituciones cubanas emprender ese camino, adelantarse a los vecinos que de seguro lo harán?

Habría que localizar qué archivos de centrales azucareros quedan por ahí con una documentación capaz de informarnos sobre la historia de estos. Sinceramente, no soy nada optimista. Vi bastante completa la documentación del central Manatí en el archivo provincial de Santiago y supongo que allí se conserve. También debes tener en cuenta que la administración de los centrales por el estado socialista cubre una etapa casi tan prolongada como el tiempo de operación de las empresas norteamericanas, un proceso que también necesita estudiarse. Aunque tampoco soy optimista respecto a las fuentes, a pesar de ser más recientes y de que esos centrales no cambiaron de propietario, aunque muchos de ellos hoy están demolidos.

¿Usted no cree que el azúcar se mira como un asunto un poco apartado de la sociedad? No se ven los vínculos de casi todo lo cubano con el azúcar. Por ejemplo la esplendorosa Haba, esa descripción que hace Dulce María Loynaz de la magnificencia de la ciudad en Fe de vida *y otras muchas descripciones de otros autores, ¿no necesitan un recordatorio que detrás está el azúcar? El fin de la guerra de 1868 se habla de divisiones internas entre los independentistas etc., etc., pero no se dice del poder del azúcar en sufragar la guerra. Incluso hasta que no se eliminó la plantación esclavista azucarera no se invadió el occidente de la isla. La plantación azucarera le da sentido urbano a la sociedad cubana; el azucar propaga pequeñas ciudades que son los bateyes. ¿Cree usted que existe esa falta de conexión en los estudios de la sociedad y el trasfondo azucarero?*

Creo que el azúcar constituyó en Cuba el eje de toda una civilización; ese fue el enfoque de Moreno que hizo tan innovador a *El ingenio*, una perspectiva que yo traté de mantener en *Esplendor y decadencia*, con las limitaciones impuestas por la finalidad comparativa. Me parece que para otros importantes autores cubanos como Reinaldo González o Miguel Barnet, eso también ha estado claro. Los colegas de Patrimonio han actuado con parecido espíritu, aunque no tengan a la mano los recursos para conservar plenamente joyas urbanísticas como el batey de Jaronú.[10] El riesgo es que al perder el azúcar su protagonismo en nuestra sociedad esa perspectiva se esfume y la realidad que tú apuntas tenga que ser redescubierta por los historiadores de aquí a cincuenta o cien años.

NOTAS

1. Movimiento clandestino fundado en 1955 que combatía a la dictadura de Batista.

2. La carrera de Historia se inició en la Universidad de La Habana en 1962.

3. Zafra azucarera iniciada el 14 de julio de 1969 pretendía producir diez millones de toneladas. No se alcanzó esa cifra y en general fue un fracaso.

4. La dirección de la United Fruit Company radicaba en el poblado de Banes, cabecera del municipio del mismo nombre, en la costa norte del oriente de Cuba. En ese municipio se encontraba el central Boston de la referida compañía.

5. MINAZ es el Ministerio de la industria azucarera de Cuba. PCC, el Partido Comunista de Cuba. En esa época Cuba estaba estructurada en provincias, regiones y municipios. En el municipio Mayarí de la costa norte del oriente de Cuba radicaba el central azucarero Preston.

6. Después de su nacionalización por el gobierno cubano en 1960 les pusieron el nombre de esos dos países.

7. Antilla es un puerto situado en la bahía de Nipe en las costas de esa bahía estaba el central Preston o Guatemala como se le llamo después de 1960.

8. El libro esta dedicado a Carlos Funtanellas.

9. Nombre con que era conocido el central Boston por el lugar donde se construyó.

10. Central azucarero situado en la provincia de Camagüey.

Book Reviews

HISTORY

Alejandro Leonardo Fernández Calderón. *Páginas en conflicto: Debate racial en la prensa cubana (1912–1930).* **La Habana: Editorial Universidad de La Habana, 2014. 222 pp.**

Este libro, *Páginas en conflicto*, premio Catauro Cubano por la Fundación Fernando Ortiz de conjunto con el Instituto Cubano del Libro, es la segunda obra de Fernández Calderón, precedida por *Sobrevivir a la masacre del doce (1912–1920)*. El tópico fundamental del autor, como bien señala María del Carmen Barcia en el prólogo, resulta cuanto menos expectante, considerando que establece un diálogo con las opiniones y reflexiones emitidas en la prensa cubana durante las primeras tres décadas del siglo XX.

La obra rescata las voces de actores sociales representativos y polémicos, quienes desafiaron las leyes gravitacionales que había impuesto la "raza" como eje de distinción social y cultural. Sus palabras preliminares muestran algunas de las claves historiográficas del debate racial, atendiendo a cada periodo histórico y a la impronta en el uso de términos o conceptualizaciones para referirse al mismo. Establece el autor diferentes pautas analíticas enfocadas en las heterogéneas actuaciones de la "raza" como línea divisoria, incluyendo algunas de las resoluciones que afloraron en los diarios de la primera década republicana en torno a temas como el Partido de los Independientes de Color.

El estudio dialoga con varias aristas, concentradas en "la consolidación y reorganización de la élite negra para poder proyectarse a la revaluación de las formas de enfrentamiento al racismo y la lucha por sus derechos ciudadanos, desarrollando como estrategia, al igual que había ocurrido a finales del siglo XIX, su participación en el circuito periodístico a través de los diarios, para impactar en la opinión pública con un discurso propio." El análisis se plantea a partir de la interlocución con diversos actores involucrados, con referencias al estatus social, filiaciones ideológicas —representadas en las clientelas políticas—, pertenencia generacional, mecanismos de sociabilidad (sociedades negras), discurso de género y actividades de ocio como el deporte. Esto se conecta además con mecanismos de articulación eminentemente racistas, que se materializaban en prácticas discriminatorias aceptadas en la vida económica, política, social y cultural del país.

En el libro se muestra el protagonismo periodístico de una élite negra de intelectuales, profesionales, políticos y veteranos de las guerras de independencia, a través de las asociaciones como el Club Atenas (1917) y sus órganos de prensa. Por este medio fomentaron unas propuestas a favor de la igualdad racial y los derechos ciudadanos, en las que gana peso la participación política, pero a la vez se posicionaban a partir de varios puntos contradictorios.

Era recurrente la promoción de un modelo de ciudadano negro con patrones de comportamiento y civilidad de cierto "refinamiento." Según el autor, "Se acercaban en sus códigos de conducta a los valores sociales promulgados por la cultura hegemónica blanca, elitista y racista, evidenciando sus deseos de cumplir con los requisitos establecidos para ser aceptados."

Por otra parte, fue patente la pugna generacional en cuanto a la manera de encauzar la lucha contra la discriminación racial, con énfasis en el estatismo social que caracterizaba al viejo liderazgo de activistas negros y mestizos. Un tercer elemento lo constituyó el debate en torno al papel de las mujeres que por su condición racial y de género estuvieron sumidas en el anonimato. El autor reabre un tema poco abordado por la historiografía y resalta como los antagonistas del dialogo intergeneracional mantuvieron una actitud conservadora, pues muchos jóvenes o viejos defensores del papel del negro en la sociedad sostuvieron una postura abiertamente machista y misógina al referirse a las mujeres negras y mestizas.

En este apartado se echa en falta que aunque el autor reconoce la participación de mujeres negras y mestizas en los proyectos periodísticos, no establece algún tipo de nexo con la revolución feminista que acontecía entonces en la sociedad cubana. Y en otro orden, desarrolla ideas donde emplea erróneamente el término *fémina*, cuestionado desde los estudios de género por su invocación a una condición biológica.

Otra novedad del libro está relacionada con el tema del deporte. Esta actividad brindó alternativas para el ascenso social; sin embargo, a pesar de la popularidad alcanzada, varios de los diarios examinados patentizaron como: "Los prejuicios contra los negros y los actos de exclusión continuaron siendo parte de los códigos sociales, y el deporte, [. . .] fue en más de una ocasión escenario de confrontaciones denigrantes y prejuiciosas."

La investigación atiende a las rígidas interpelaciones del racismo imperante en ámbitos de la sociedad republicana, siendo la prensa uno de los principales vehículos en la promoción de prejuicios y estereotipos, enzarzando el debate sobre la brujería y la denominada "inmigración indeseable". Para ambos casos se establecía un racero de jerarquía racial con un basamento pseudocientífico tendente a legitimar la "inferioridad del negro". De esa forma se instituyó un baremo que pretendía catalogar determinadas manifestaciones culturales como "cosas de negros", tesis que paulatinamente fue complementada con nuevos análisis culturales.

La obra trae a coalición tópicos relevantes del debate racial en la historia de Cuba a partir de la prensa, poniendo de relieve los diferentes argumentos que utilizó un sector para mirarse a sí mismo en su práctica cotidiana, aunque en la mayoría de las referencias se asumieran con vehemencia los valores de la cultura occidental. Se intentaba así erigir una "imagen civilizada" del ciudadano negro en la que quedaban fuera, desde una visión más progresista, las mujeres negras y mestizas o los valores culturales de raíz africana. Y aunque también hubo un claro enfrentamiento contra los prejuicios y la desigualdad racial, la manera de interpretar las prácticas racistas se generó a partir de unos límites en la convivencia, lo que hacía evidente la necesidad de insistir en su total redefinición.

MAIKEL COLÓN PICHARDO
Universidad de Barcelona

John A. Gronbeck-Tedesco. *Cuba, the United States, and Cultures of the Transnational Left, 1930–1975.* **Cambridge: Cambridge University Press, 2015. 307 pp.**

The past few years seem to have inaugurated a transnational turn in the growing scholarship on Cuba's 1959 revolution.[1] John Gronbeck-Tedesco's *Cuba, the United States, and Cultures of the Transnational Left* is a welcome addition to this trend. In this sweeping exploration of US-Cuban cultural and political relations, Gronbeck-Tedesco describes a shared long-term dialogue, "a larger transnational space of Left culture," constructed between Cuban and US activists (45). Yet this is not necessarily a story of unity. Gronbeck-Tedesco is sensitive to aspects of disagreement or mutual incomprehension—what he calls "gaps in the transnation" (68)—that make this a story of conflict as well as solidarity. Eschewing a teleological tendency to see 1933 as "prelude" to the 1959 revolution, Gronbeck-Tedesco argues instead for conceptualizing the "Cuban revolutions as *a* historical period—bridging what is usually historicized separately as the 'thirties' and the 'sixties'" (4). This broader historical scale captures intriguing continuities and parallels.

Organized chronologically and thematically, the book moves from the internationalism of the old left and popular front to the rise of the new left and "tricontinentalism." Along the way we meet activists, writers, and intellectuals representative of the Generación del 30, *afrocubanismo*, the Harlem Renaissance, the black power movement, first- and second-wave feminism, and the US "third world left." Throughout, the book pays significant attention to race and gender, two areas where we find perhaps the greatest "gaps" between island and mainland activists. Some of the material covered here may feel familiar, as Gronbeck-Tedesco is building on work by Van Gosse, Frank Guridy, Mark O. Sawyer, and others. But the book's ambitious scope, long historical period, and careful research provide new insights.

The chapters on the 1930s are particularly enlightening, adding significantly to the perennially underdeveloped historiography on the 1933 revolution. Here Gronbeck-Tedesco usefully reconstructs the enormous impact that 1933 made on progressives in the United States and beyond. Cuba's 1933 revolution, he shows, became a touchstone in left-wing literature alongside other global conflagrations such as the Spanish Civil War, the Scottsboro case, and the peasant rebellion in China. Carlton Beals's widely read work *The Crime of Cuba* (1933) was particularly influential in this regard. In a thoughtful analysis of the book's text and photos, Gronbeck-Tedesco shows how Beals launched a powerful denunciation of Machado while also mobilizing certain condescending constructions of Cuban exoticism and racial difference that echoed tropes from tourist literature and social science. Thus the US left reproduced neocolonial language while professing authentically felt solidarity—an observation equally applicable to the 1960s and beyond.

In other ways, too, it is striking how trends we often associate with the 1960s were anticipated in the 1930s. The author shows that, already in the 1930s, Cuba provided an idealized trope of agrarian revolution and mass uprising. Here he carefully reconstructs the way Pablo de la Torriente Brau's 1934 exposé of the agrarian conflict in Realengo 18 entered wider transnational circulation when the US journalist Josephine Herbst published a similar series of articles in *New Masses* one year later in which she positioned Realengo 18 as "a kind of agrarian vanguard, believing that she [had] discovered in the Cuban hinterland seeds for revolution" (66). Cuba's 1933 revolution seemed to provide an appealing alternative to the Soviet Union, then beset by bureaucracy, political purges, executions, and famine, just as the 1959 revolution initially raised hopes for a "humanist" revolution that might forge a third way in the polarized Cold War world.

After 1959, it proves somewhat harder to flesh out individual Cuban cultural figures of the period, as Gronbeck-Tedesco does so well for writers and intellectuals of the 1930s such as de la Torriente Brau, Nicolás Guillén, Mariblanca Sabas Alomá, and Regino Pedroso. In these sections the book largely provides insight into the way US activists or organizations like the Venceremos Brigades interpreted the Cuban revolution or interacted with Cuban officialdom. As Gronbeck-Tedesco notes, these post-1959 connections often produced disenchantment, as black power and second-wave feminist activists found the Cuban model increasingly restrictive, while for gay rights activists Cuba would prove more dystopian than utopian. Yet these very divergences forced US activists to sharpen their own ideas. As this book shows convincingly, US-Cuban conversations could be deeply productive even if discordant.

MICHELLE CHASE
Pace University

NOTE

1. While diplomatic historians have long addressed interstate relations, especially US-Cuban relations, recent publications shed light on other forms of cultural and political interaction, combine attention to state and nonstate actors, and move beyond the Western Hemisphere. For merely

a few recent examples, see Manuel Barcia, "Locking Horns with the Northern Empire: Anti-American Imperialism at the Tricontinental Conference of 1966 in Havana," *Journal of Transatlantic Studies* 7, no. 3 (2009): 208–217; Anita Casavantes Bradford, *The Revolution Is for the Children: The Politics of Childhood in Havana and Miami, 1959–1962* (Chapel Hill: University of North Carolina Press, 2014); Anne E. Gorsuch, "'Cuba, My Love': The Romance of Revolutionary Cuba in the Soviet Sixties," *American Historical Review* 120, no. 2 (2015): 497–526; Teishan Latner, "Take Me to Havana! Airline Hijacking, U.S.-Cuba Relations, and Political Protest in Late Sixties' America," *Diplomatic History* 39, no. 1 (2015): 16–44; Jacqueline Loss, *Dreaming in Russian: The Cuban Soviet Imaginary* (Austin: University of Texas Press, 2013); Rafael Rojas, *Fighting over Fidel: The New York Intellectuals and the Cuban Revolution* (Princeton, NJ: Princeton University Press, 2016); and Sarah Seidman, "Tricontinental Routes of Solidarity: Stokely Carmichael in Cuba," *Journal of Transnational American Studies* 2 (2012): 1–25.

Karen Y. Morrison. *Cuba's Racial Crucible: The Sexual Economy of Social Identities, 1750–2000*. Bloomington: Indiana University Press, 2015. 372 pp.

Karen Y. Morrison's *Cuba's Racial Crucible: The Sexual Economy of Social Identities, 1750–2000* argues for the centrality of the family in the *longue durée* of race making in Cuba. Morrison's ambitious project tackles a long chronological scope, starting in the eighteenth century, moving through the illegal slave trade, the Wars of Independence, and emancipation in the nineteenth century, and concluding with the twentieth century and the Cuban Revolution. Morrison argues against an explanation of interracial family formation in Cuba, as being a simple matter of *blanqueamiento*, or a shared and straightforward project of whitening. Instead, she argues that "this study highlights the inextricable links between 'family,' 'race,' and 'nation' in the competing nationalist visions of Cuba that have existed since the eighteenth century" (xvi).

To bridge so many eras and examples, Morrison develops an analytical concept that she refers to as "the sexual economy of race." Rather than focusing on the discourses of race and nation as articulated by intellectuals and politicians, she grounds her study in baptismal, marriage, and census records to examine how family formations shaped Cuban racial norms and, in turn, how Cuban women and men's reproductive choices shaped race. She argues that "the emergence of Cuba's current multi-racial nationalism was not solely a product of twentieth century revolutionary agendas; nor did it emerge exclusively from political acts[;] . . . it was also born out of Cuba's reproductive and familial past, Cuba's uniquely evolving sexual economy of race" (xx). This "on-the-ground" approach adds significantly to the historiography on race and race making in Cuba, which has often privileged (the disproportionately male) political and military experiences.

Morrison begins her analysis in the eighteenth century, and she illustrates how the practices of the Catholic Church, the military, and the increasingly capitalist-oriented economy reshaped family relationships for Cubans of color in the wake of the Bourbon Reforms. During this era, Morrison identifies that white men could and did recognize their children with women of color, and that legitimacy rates for baptized children were quite high. She concludes that despite the changing norms and limited opportunities for Cubans of color, their rates of marriage and legitimate births generally matched those of families the church identified as white (72).

The book then moves into the nineteenth century, for which Morrison notes multiple strategies by which women could control the sexual and racial implications of their reproductive lives. She demonstrates the mutability of race through a close reading of church records. For example, by examining baptismal records, she demonstrates how some white women might have "become" women of color to legitimate their relationships with Cuban men of color, or how women of color might have abandoned their children (even temporarily), allowing the church to claim them and baptize the babies as white (115–116). In addition, she rejects the classic literary icon of the tragic *mulata*, as represented in the Cuban classic *Cecelia Valdés*. In this vein, it might be valuable to read these chapters alongside Emily Clark's *The Strange History of the American Quadroon*, which also argues against taking this fictional female character as representative of women of color in the eighteenth and nineteenth centuries.

Morrison's chapters on the twentieth century move away from a close reading of baptismal, marriage, and census data, and instead rely more on literary and intellectual texts on the politics of *afrocubanismo*. She concludes the book with fascinating interviews with elderly Cubans who speak freely about their families and racial identities, providing vivid detail and tantalizing possibilities for rich lives that are often only hinted at in the eighteenth- and nineteenth-century census and clerical archives.

Morrison's work is best when she plums the archival and oral history sources to reveal race making on an individual and family level. For example, she mines the nineteenth-century baptism records from the Espíritu Santo Parish in Havana, noting trends in legitimacy and baptism rates for children based on their parents' color and labor status (64–69). In another chapter, she uses baptism records to note patterns of paternal recognition for children born out of wedlock, alongside exceptional moments such as when African royalty were written into the documents (153). This close attention to detail and variation in the sources enables the reader to imagine the possibilities and constraints on families of color over time. This material outshines her analyses of the more traditional intellectual history sources. It would have been valuable if Morrison had also been more explicit about the limits of her archival sources and the potential changing definition of "whiteness" in the Cuban context. In addition, I would have been interested in a more nuanced discussion of how the different bureaucratic regimes she examines, the church, the colonial government, and then the independent state constructed and recorded racial identities. However, given the immensity of the task, this archival work stands as one of the key strengths of the book.

She includes thirteen testimonies in the final chapter, each illustrating the intimate and family politics of race. This material provocatively produces more questions than it answers. For example, several of the testimonies are from individuals with fathers of color and mothers they identified as white, signaling many more such couplings than may be apparent in the written record. In addition, she includes oral histories in which individuals were irritated by her questions about race and others in which individuals spoke openly about the norms of respectability that governed many Afro-Cuban women's lives.

Despite the book's strengths, there are some key questions the book leaves dangling. In particular, the book gives the twentieth-century short shrift, particularly the postrevolutionary period. While the Cuban decision to stop notating race on government documents may have precluded the same type of close analysis Morrison devotes to the eighteenth and nineteenth centuries, she does not grapple with the family racial and sexual choices that Cubans have made since the 1959 revolution. Instead, she looks at Fidel Castro's rhetoric and language rather than considering how the revolution has (or has not) changed the sexual economy of race. Given the limited nature of this material, it would have been better to end the book in 1959 and not promise an analysis of postrevolutionary Cuba.

Morrison's book opens up several new avenues for research on sexuality and family formation in Cuba, and she does so with a masterful grasp on colonial sources and raises critical questions for the twentieth century. While most scholars accept the primacy of race and sexuality in Cuban history, Morrison succeeds at excavating these questions on a micro-level, providing new insights into the choices and family formations forged by both enslaved and free Cubans over time.

JANA LIPMAN
Tulane University

Katia Figueredo Cabrera. *Cuba y La Guerra Civil Española: Mitos y realidades de la derecha hispano-cubana (1936–1942)*. **Havana: Editorial Universidad de La Habana, 2014. 465 pp.**

Katia Figueredo Cabrera's *Cuba y La Guerra Civil Española: Mitos y realidades de la derecha hispano-cubana (1936–1942)* broadens our understanding of the sizable Spanish community living on the island during the Spanish

Civil War and at the onset of World War II. The monograph is divided into six chapters that analyze the diplomatic relationship between Havana and Madrid from 1936 to 1942, Spanish pro-right-wing organizations in Cuba, and economic factors that motivated Cuba's responses. Figueredo's work underscores the Cuban state's contradictory reactions to Francisco Franco's rebellion: initially, state diplomacy and rhetoric externally supported the Republic while remaining internally tolerant of right-wing pro-Franco forces. Figueredo fills a void in the study of the right-wing pro-Franco movement in Cuba by challenging previously held assumptions that gave right-wing forces a more prominent role in the spread of fascism in the Caribbean. Instead, Figueredo emphasizes economic factors as essential motives for the diplomatic rapprochement between the island and the peninsula. Moreover, Figueredo accurately surmises that Cuban scholarship has overtly emphasized the impact of Spanish Republican exiles without a careful corresponding analysis of the pro-Franco right. The paucity of scholarly monographs on the right-wing Spanish community in Cuba is a testament to the scarce attention it has received from the Cuban academy and Anglophone scholarship.

Figueredo is conversant with existing scholarship dealing with both pro-Republican and pro-Falangist forces in Cuba. To that end, she compares Cuban state responses to pro-Republican and pro-Falangist organizations, concluding that the Cuban government—in contrast to the majority of the Cubans on the island—allowed the pro-Falangist forces greater flexibility in skirting Cuban laws that limited advocacy for Cuba's involvement in foreign ideological struggles. However, the author challenges the notion put forth in Allan Chase's *Falange: The Axis Secret Army in the Americas* (1943), Consuelo Naranjo Orovio's *Cuba: Otro escenario de lucha* (1988), and Juan Chongo Leiva's *El fracaso de Hitler in Cuba* (1989) that "seconded and defended . . . an exaggerated image of the real reach and continental activism of the Spanish Falange in the Cuba" (39). Figueredo asserts that these monographs, though commendable works of scholarship, encourage a myth of peninsular power on the island. This myth distorts our understanding of the anti-Republican forces in Cuba on its own terms.

Figueredo employs right-wing publications like *La Discusión* and *El Diario de la Marina* instead of relying heavily on *Noticias de Hoy*, the official organ of the communist party, as prior scholarship has done. By analyzing pro-right-wing discourse and underscoring the role of pro-Franco Spaniards and Cubans on the island, like the role played by Jose Ignacio Rivero (100–101), she solidifies her claim that to understand the pro-right community one must look to the pro-right publications that she masterfully employs. Moreover, she challenges assumptions that right-wing groups in Cuba were exclusively of the elite classes, utilizing records from the Tribunal de Urgencia that demonstrate that pro-right forces had some working-class support (99). As Figueredo admits, the dearth of sources have made the scholarly investigation of the Spanish right difficult. To this end, Figueredo conducted an exhaustive analysis of the documents in the Cuban National Archive's Fondo Registro de Asociaciones and Cuba's Ministry of Foreign Relation's Fondo de España, as well as, press sources. Figueredo's plethora of sources are evident in her annex where she publishes more than twenty-five visual, statistical, and documentary sources. Figueredo utilizes archival and press sources from the three main Spanish pro-right organizations in Cuba: Falange Española Tradicionalista, the Juntas de Ofensivas Nacional Sindicalista, and the Comité Nacionalista Español, as well as other less prominent organizations, to understand the responses of the Spanish-Cuban right wing to events on the peninsula and Cuban state policy. As a result, Figueredo depicts the pro-right Spanish community's desire for a return to a "spiritual empire," exalting the past glories of Spain, as well as the universalist ideologies of the Catholic Church. Pro-right Spaniards perceived Franco as a symbol of "freedom, morality, tradition," in their fight against Moscow (38).

Although Figueredo's monograph will no doubt become the standard for understanding the right wing of the Spanish community in Cuba, the monograph reads more like a collection of essays, rather than a single narrative, which can make the chronology confusing. In addition, whereas she does a fine job presenting Republican mobilization against Franco's regime within the island, she implicitly accepts the role of the Catholic Church as pro-Franco without recognizing the pro-Republican elements within the Cuban church. Although few in number, these pro-Republican priests caused a rift within the church during this period. However, *Cuba y la Guerra Civil Española* gives the reader a real sense of the issues facing the Cuban government which was struggling with a new experiment with democracy, precarious commercial relationships with Spain, fears of a "fifth column," US influence, and an attempt to isolate Cuba from totalitarian ideologies. The Spanish right wing in Cuba played an important role in exacerbating these issues and Figueredo masterfully presents this phenomena. Figueredo's book gives us a fuller picture of the Spanish community in Cuba from 1936 to 1942 and the Cuban state's responses to the spread of fascism in the Caribbean through a dispassionate analysis of pro-Franco support in Cuba.

DANIEL FERNANDEZ GUEVARA
University of Florida

Dayron Oliva Hernández. *¿La nación secuestrada? Machismo y racismo en la política inmigratoria cubana (1902–1933).* La Habana: Casa Editora Abril, 2016. 172 pp.

Resulta cada vez más complejo repensar las primeras décadas del siglo XX cubano, dado el cúmulo de minuciosas investigaciones alrededor de la primera república (1902–1933). Los científicos sociales que se dedican al estudio de dicho periodo, han acometido una ardua tarea de replanteos. Al respecto, los estudios de género y dentro de ellos la masculinidades, pudieran ubicarse como parte de las nuevas miradas historiográficas a partir del tratamiento a la (de)construcción de la masculinidad hegemónica y sus relaciones con otras identidades.

La investigación de Dayron Oliva Hernández se enmarca en tales propósitos con su ensayo *¿La nación secuestrada? Machismo y racismo en la política inmigratoria cubana (1902–1933)*, merecedor del Premio Calendario 2015. En este se conecta la categoría masculinidad a las problemáticas de inmigración y raza, aspectos más abordados en otros resultados investigativos; al igual que sucede con los estudios de género, recolocado en las últimas décadas desde la Historia de las Mujeres, temática donde queda mucho por problematizar. Desde estas variables, el autor analiza el universo de las masculinidades migratorias que llegaron a Cuba a inicios del siglo XX —europeos, antillanos, asiáticos— y que influyeron en los debates científicos e intelectuales dentro de un contexto social racista y machista. Sus reflexiones ofrecen un panorama más dinámico de las desigualdades sociales, la subalternidad y las representaciones alrededor de la nación.

La obra aborda en un primer momento el contexto histórico del siglo XIX colonial, desentrañado las formulaciones en torno a los binomios de las razas superiores —modernas, blancas y civilizadas— versus las supuestamente inferiores —primitivas, salvajes e irracionales—. Igualmente destaca la entonces propuesta de la elite intelectual en favor de la inmigración blanca como solución al problema de las razas en Cuba, como alternativa al empleo de esclavos africanos, a lo que contribuyeron los discursos de las ciencias y sus corrientes de finales del XIX —positivismo, darwinismo social, higiene social— en función de la legitimidad del diseño de la raza cubana. Las formulaciones de la *intelligentsia* blanca permitieron la operatividad de la racionalidad instrumental del cuerpo masculino en vista al control del proyecto de modernidad.

En el segundo momento se centra el autor al interior de la temporalidad de su objeto de estudio. Lentamente hilvana las identidades de los inmigrantes, sus problemáticas particulares y distintos imaginarios. Aquí se reflexiona en particular sobre el arquetipo del canario, generalmente catalogado de inmigración favorecida, quedando matizado dentro de la escala social denostadora de los blancos de orillas y sus calificativos —bruto, inculto, persistente—etiquetas más visible y señaladas tradicionalmente para otros sujetos —negros antillanos y chinos— que conviven en el seno de las ambigüedades de la igualdad racial y las prácticas racistas. También es notable el acercamiento al cuerpo femenino blanco de la inmigrante canaria a partir de los roles conservadores de madre y esposa, mediados por la impronta del movimiento feminista, las polémicas de los derechos sociales de la mujer y la lucha contra el machismo. A esto se vinculan otras temáticas como el matrimonio, la prostitución, la maternidad y la familia. Igualmente se le presta atención al caso de los chinos y braceros antillanos, siendo los segundos más abordados en otras investigaciones desde las relaciones del mercado laboral y su carácter de inmigración indeseable, aspectos revaluados desde la óptica de la construcción de las masculinidades subalternas

La propuesta del libro cuenta entre sus méritos la elaboración del proceso de masculinización del cuerpo de la nación desde el vínculo poder-saber, en pos del modelo ciudadano masculino —blanco, civilizado, citadino— representativo de la modernidad insular. Desde la revisión de fuentes documentales visibiliza en el espacio de la inmigración los cuerpos observados desde los *hombres de ciencia y política* en función de los mejoramientos/retrocesos de la nación cubana. Así articula el universo de las identidades inmigrantes dentro del contexto del racismo y machismo, ambas prácticas sociales de larga duración y persistencia. Por ello, establece una propuesta teórica metodológica para la evaluación de la problemática de las masculinidades en el diálogo hegemónico-subalterno.

La obra invita también a la reflexión de algunas aristas en el texto tratadas insuficientemente: podemos mencionar la problemática de tales identidades en el contexto de la apertura a la etnografía y la antropología cultural producida en la década de 1920, disciplinas que recomendaron la reincorporación de sujetos tenidos hasta ese instante como marginales y reinterpretados dentro del folklore cubano. De igual manera, se ubica la necesaria indagación de los inmigrantes desde las voces de los Otros, localizando sus testimonios, mecanismo de escapismo social y sus reevaluaciones frente a un ambiente hostil de control social. De esta forma, se reflejarían los lugares comunes y diferentes del intercambio contradictorio de la dinámica con otros cuerpos del *nosotros* social —negros, mestizos, mujeres— que pugnan igualmente contra la masculinidad hegemónica blanca, civilizada y heterosexual.

Sirva este ensayo de Olivas Hernández para alentar muy pronto futuras contribuciones en torno a la reescritura de la historia de Cuba, cada vez más necesitada de desdibujar las trampas de secuestradores discursos machistas y racistas. De esta forma, estamos rescatando la nación cubana y volviéndola más inclusiva en cuanto a equidad e igualdad social.

ALEJANDRO L. FERNÁNDEZ CALDERÓN
Historiador cubano residente en Alemania

Jorge Núñez Vega. *La danza de los millones: Modernización y cambio cultural en La Habana (1915–1920).* **La Habana: Ediciones Imagen Contemporánea, 2015. 244 pp.**

En *La danza de los millones*, novela de Rafael Cisneros publicada en 1923, su autor describía la realidad cubana como un "carnaval de la locura y la risa." Expresiones como esta podían indicar los complejos procesos materiales y psicológicos a los que se enfrentaba la sociedad habanera del momento. Esta realidad es analizada a profundidad en *La danza de los millones: Modernización y cambio cultural en La Habana (1915–1920)*, de Jorge Núñez Vega. Con relación a este libro la expresión inicial funciona como la metáfora que describe la expectativa y desorientación de los sujetos frente a las nuevas transformaciones que se experimentaban en la sociedad cubana de la época y de los cuales son generadores conscientes o inconscientes. Esta celebración se proyecta, entonces, como una inversión del orden en el continuum del tiempo-espacio que se expresa como un cambio de los sentidos interpretativos y vivenciales de los sucesos. El ejercicio de parafrasear el título de Cisneros constituye una forma no solo de enmarcar un espacio temporal, sino también de construir un acercamiento a la sociedad descrita por el novelista desde la ficción.

La aparición de este libro se produce por coincidencia en el contexto del centenario de la Primera Guerra Mundial, y por tanto representa una excelente contribución para comprender mejor las repercusiones para Cuba de ese acontecimiento global. El mismo trasciende los abordajes tradicionales acuñados por la historiografía en torno a la economía y la política en Cuba durante el período en cuestión, para así redimensionar sus significados tradicionales.

El propio subtítulo "Modernización y cambio cultural" marca los temas centrales que explicarán las dinámicas interpretativas y que guiarán las conclusiones del autor. El libro se adentra en los móviles y objetivos del proceso modernizador, en sus actores y en las percepciones del mundo y del ser de los mismos para construir los caminos de la modernidad en la capital cubana, la que es entendida a la americana, pero indiscutiblemente anclada en un pasado distinto, lo cual implicó la aparición de un grupo de contradicciones y la ocurrencia de múltiples mecanismos de simulación.

En esta línea, la apariencia se convierte en realidad trastocando los sentidos y dando un significado innegable a la expresión de Ambrosio Fornet: "La entrada de Estados Unidos en la guerra no alteró el tren de vida de los viejos y nuevos ricos cubanos, pero sí su imagen pública." El hombre moderno tal y como lo presenta Núñez Vega en su libro debe ser ante todo un actor donde la modernidad constituye por sí misma un espectáculo de luces y sombras, que disimula o expone a conveniencia sus esencias en pos de la puesta en escena del sujeto moderno y sus atributos modernizadores.

La danza de los millones está dividida en tres capítulos que recorren los distintos procesos de construcción, asimilación y diálogo con la modernidad entendida desde el *American style*. Los dos primeros capítulos se dedican al análisis de los cambios ocurridos en la escena social habanera y a sus repercusiones económicas y culturales. Son estudiados los objetos y espacios que configuran los significados de la modernidad. Objetos tales como el automóvil y la ropa redimensionan sus posibilidades adquiriendo independencia y definiendo a sus portadores en múltiples procesos de simulación, ocultamiento o puesta en escena.

Los espacios de placer —repartos, clubes, cines o teatros— son conceptualizados como los lugares de configuración y representación de las aspiraciones de este grupo, constituyendo para los mismos tanto el escenario como los actores. Ocurre así la objetivación del sujeto de la modernidad, convirtiéndolo en un modelo arquetípico más que real, por tanto, apetecible y deseable. Lo mismo se produce en cuanto a la subjetivación de los espacios y objetos de la modernidad, adquiriendo éstos cualidades y características perfectamente definidas e identificables.

El tercer capítulo se dedica a la construcción discursiva de esa modernidad y al papel de los intelectuales en el proceso de construcción y arbitraje de la misma. En este sentido la última parte cierra el ciclo al moldear, modular y expresar esas aspiraciones al cambio cultural y las incertidumbres y carencias que hacen presa de ella.

El autor realiza un estudio acucioso de la producción literaria de la época ya sea novela, cuento o la propia crónica social y de espectáculos para construir el discurso de la modernidad de los distintos grupos sociales. Cada obra muestra configuraciones psicosociales del mundo y del ser tanto del escritor como de la sociedad en su conjunto capaz de decodificar y clasificar los símbolos contenidos en el texto. Ese tipo de literatura se comporta como un mecanismo generador de los significados de la modernidad.

La obra de Núñez Vega es atravesada constantemente por la noción de distinción de Pierre Bourdieu entendida como "diferencia, separación, rasgo distintivo, en fin, propiedad relacional que no existe sino *en* y *por* la relación con otras propiedades." Alcanzar el status de moderno implica distinguirse (diferenciarse en positivo) frente a un grupo significativo de sujetos. De tal manera la relación entre modernidad y distinción ocurre en ambos sentidos, convirtiéndose en una operación biunívoca que define las características y alcance del proyecto modernizador para la capital.

El texto construye la modernidad como proceso y como proyecto con múltiples implicaciones discursivas. Como proyecto trasciende su escenificación y proyección física y material para reconfigurarse en un producto simbólico que marca el proceso traumático de cambio cultural. La obra demuestra con acierto como estos cinco años constituyeron un cambio cultural profundo y un punto de no retorno para la sociedad en su conjunto, pero sobre todo un choque psicológico para los implicados.

LAURA VÁZQUEZ FLEITAS
Universidad de La Habana

Enrique López Mesa. *Tabaco, mito y esclavos: Apuntes cubanos de historia agraria.* **La Habana: Editorial de Ciencias Sociales, 2015. 238 pp.**

El libro de Enrique López Mesa *Tabaco, mito y esclavos* constituye un relevante ejercicio de ingenio y erudición. La obra no solo discute y valora la bibliografía relativa al cultivo del tabaco en Cuba y a los mitos raciales que se formaron en torno a sus propietarios, arrendatarios y fuerza de trabajo, sino que reconstruye pasajes de la evolución histórica de los vegueríos cubanos de los siglos XVIII, XIX y primeras décadas del XX. El objetivo central del autor es desmontar las fabulaciones de la historiografía cubana de la primera mitad del siglo XIX, a propósito de la composición étnica de la mano de obra en el cultivo de la aromática hoja.

Quizás lo más original, en el contexto del mutismo crítico preponderante en la historiografía cubana, sea precisamente la recensión que efectúa de los prestigiosos fundadores de la historia agraria nacional. El cuestionamiento comprende a la obra de Fernando Ortiz, autor de la primera investigación histórica comparativa sobre el cultivo del tabaco y la caña de azúcar (1940), de Jorge García Gallo, historiador marxista de los vegueríos cubanos (1959), de Heinrich Friedlaender, estudioso alemán cuya visita a la isla nos dejó la primera historia económica de Cuba (1944), de José Rivero Muñiz, el más importante historiador del tabaco, y de Julio Le Riverend, cuyas primeras investigaciones sobre los vegueros cubanos en el decenio de 1940 siguieron las pautas trazadas por Ortiz.

La impugnación a los supuestos de los que partía la historiografía cubana de las décadas de 1940 a 1950, no se limitó a una simple objeción con relación a la ausencia de fuentes estadísticas que acreditasen sus aseveraciones, sino que supuso por parte del autor una evaluación de la mentalidad dominante en la sociedad. Parte de los resultados parciales de investigaciones realizadas por la hornada de historiadores que irrumpió en la década de 1970. La nueva historiografía económica y social, a diferencia de la que le precedió, se caracterizó por la amplia utilización de padrones y censos de población. En las nuevas investigaciones aparecían eslavos, gente "de color," en una proporción igual o mayor a la de los blancos en regiones aisladas del país.

Luego de consultar recientes investigaciones regionales, López Mesa emprendió una prolongada investigación en la documentación del siglo XVII y XVIII cubanos en busca de testimonios y evidencias de la presencia del "otro" ignorado o relegado por los historiadores de la primera mitad del siglo XX. El hecho que haya podido recoger decenas de documentos en los que se da cuenta de la temprana aparición de esclavos y negros libres en algunas vegas arroja luz sobre la forma superficial en que se había historiado el asunto. Los testimonios consultados informan también sobre la el interés de la Factoría del tabaco y la Real Compañía de Comercio en que los vegueros tuvieran esclavos y el beneficio que se obtenía de la explotación de su trabajo.

Por esa razón, López Mesa sintió la necesidad de explicar las razones por las que los vegueros apelaron desde épocas tan remotas al trabajo cautivo para el cultivo de las tierras que poseían o arrendaban. A esos efectos consultó una variedad de cálculos de rentabilidad del trabajo esclavo y libre realizados en los siglos XVIII y XIX por funcionarios de la factoría de tabaco y por propietarios de plantaciones tabacaleras. La escasez de mano de obra asalariada determinaba que a los vegueros les resultase más rentable comprar esclavos a plazos o alquilarlos, que emplear trabajo libre y pagar jornales. Algunas fuentes citadas indican que los jornales en Cuba a mediados del siglo XIX duplicaban los europeos. La tendencia a emplear esclavos en plantaciones de tabaco se acentuó aún más con la ruina de las plantaciones de café cubanas desde la década de 1840, a causa de la competencia del café brasileño y la caída de los precios del producto.

De acuerdo con la investigación, la fuerza de trabajo esclava y de "color" libre era mayoritaria en la mayor parte de los empadronamientos de vegas de tabaco efectuados en la isla en 1820, 1853, 1861 y 1899. El censo de 1861 confirma esa presencia mayoritaria de ambos sexos en las vegas sobre los hombres blancos, aunque estos predominas en algunas regiones. Ahora bien, de acuerdo con el autor, cambios radicales en la composición étnica de la población rural a fines del siglo XIX y principios del XX contribuyeron a la aparición del mito sobre la ausencia de gente "de color" en las vegas. La abolición de la esclavitud provocó la emigración de los emancipados y los negros libres a las ciudades. Paralelamente la emigración de canarios a la isla en remplazo de los esclavos y libres de "color" para la cosecha dio comienzo al blanqueamiento del trabajo en las vegas.

López Mesa enunció la incidencia que tuvo la política migratoria alentada por la intelectualidad reformista blanca desde el siglo XIX, en la generación del mito de una población blanca predominante en las vegas durante el periodo esclavista. De ahí la conveniencia de exaltar la tradición de luchas de los vegueros "blancos todos o casi todos" desde comienzos del siglo XVIII con sus primeras sublevaciones contra el estanco del tabaco. De ese modo, "si se aspiraba a 'blanquear' el presente era recomendable comenzar a blanquear el pasado."

Los problemas más interesantes del libro guardan relación con la génesis del mito racial. El autor presume que en su origen tuvieron lugar "lo espontáneo y lo inducido, lo que equivaldría a decir la ignorancia y la conveniencia." El factor espontáneo en una primera fase, se consolida cuando interviene para su conformación final el factor inducido, o voluntario, "aportado en una segunda fase por la clase dominante nacional que supo comprender la conveniencia del mito para sus intereses políticos y, consecuentemente, lo capitalizó en beneficio propio, lo divulgó y promovió su aceptación como una verdad absoluta exenta de comprobación." Se trata, de una petición de principio: los expositores del mito no son descritos como representantes de la clase dominante. Los ejemplos que se citan de autores que promovieron y divulgaron el mito racial del veguero fueron no solo Fernando Ortiz e historiadores referidos anteriormente, sino el periodista estadounidense Charles Popper, el autono-anexionista cubano Francisco Figueras y el caricaturista Torrente, autor del personaje de Liborio, representación del campesino cubano blanco.

La primera pregunta que debemos hacernos sobre los relatos míticos de estos autores está relacionada con su carácter inducido e intencionalidad, pues como explica López Mesa la clase dominante "divulgó y promovió su aceptación." Si bien en las exposiciones de Pepper y Figueras se trasluce el designio racista de sus apreciaciones sobre los negros y la sobrevaloración del canario, en el caso de Ortiz y los historiadores republicanos, no se advierte un propósito de denigrar al negro o de ocultar deliberadamente su presencia en los vegueríos cubanos.

El autor ha tenido el cuidado de no atribuirles a estos el papel de voceros de la burguesía, ni de ningún tipo de interés político manifiesto. De ahí que convendría aclarar que estos más que forjadores premeditados de un mito, en función de los intereses de una clase, como parece sugerir el texto, pudieran ser expositores involuntarios o inconscientes de figuraciones generalizadas en la sociedad. El hecho de ser prestigiosos historiadores y estudiosos del hombre en sociedad nos lleva a preguntarnos ¿cómo es posible que no se plantearan comprobar en la documentación del siglo XIX la presencia de los esclavos y los libres "de color" en los cultivos de tabaco? Solo el hecho que compartiesen de manera inconsciente las creencias infundadas de sus contemporáneos sobre el pasado podía inhibir a Ortiz y a sus colegas de investigar en los testimonios y fuentes estadísticas de la época. Desde luego, puede alegarse también que eran tan solo juicios presentistas sobre el pasado colonial.

La residencia de esclavos y libres "de color" en las vegas del periodo colonial demandaba la elucidación de sus condiciones de trabajo y vida. El autor se ocupa de reconstituir de algún modo su rentabilidad, su productividad, el índice de masculinidad, las tasas de mortalidad, la duración de la jornada laboral, la alimentación, vestuario y el trato diferenciado que recibía la fuerza laboral en las distintas regiones del país. De manera parecida efectuó comparaciones sobre condiciones de vida y explotación de la fuerza laboral en las pequeñas vegas y las plantaciones tabacaleras de Vuelta Abajo, introduciendo un análisis comparativo con las plantaciones de Virginia y Brasil. En el libro se analiza también la formación de familias de esclavos y la correlación existente entre esclavos criollos y africanos en las plantaciones de tabaco.

Una de las cuestiones sugeridas por la investigación es que los esclavos y libres "de color" eran explotados con más rigor en las plantaciones de tabaco que en las vegas, pero no tanto como en las de azúcar y café. Esclarecida de algún modo la génesis del mito, López Mesa cuestionó la noción de que la población rural criolla procedía en gran medida de los inmigrantes canarios, en tanto, tal aseveración constituía otra de las ficciones del siglo XIX sobre el cultivo del tabaco.

Una cuestión conceptual de primero es formulada en los siguientes términos: ¿Eran las grandes vegas donde trabajaban intensamente decenas de esclavos para el mercado exterior plantaciones? ¿Se conciliaba la realidad de la explotación del trabajo esclavo en las vegas pinareñas con el concepto de plantación en boga en la historiografía de la esclavitud americana? El autor rechaza la noción de que para que existiera la plantación se requerían "grandes extensiones de tierras y nutridas dotaciones de esclavos." Luego de revisar las definiciones en la historiografía de la esclavitud americana y tomar solo los elementos que consideraba presentes en las plantaciones de tabaco cubanas, reitera su criterio de que lo esencial era el carácter forzado y no calificado de los trabajadores, la intensidad de la explotación del trabajo y el destino de la producción al mercado externo. Una última característica de la plantación de tabaco cubana, nos dice, es que no se explotaba el trabajo tan brutalmente como en las otras plantaciones, pero considerablemente más que en los cultivos destinados al consumo interno.

En el curso de su exposición el historiador interrogó en más de una ocasión la obra de sus colegas y la suya propia. Más que una respuesta a sus sensatas inquietudes, el libro constituye una invitación a discutir críticamente problemas de la disciplina histórica. La importancia de su propuesta radica más en el procedimiento empleado en su exposición, que en su objeto. Esta obra debe desbrozar nuevos caminos a la investigación histórica en Cuba.

JORGE IBARRA CUESTA

ECONOMY

Archibald R. M. Ritter and Ted A. Henken. *Entrepreneurial Cuba: The Changing Policy Landscape.* **Boulder, CO: First Forum Press, 2015. 373 pp.**

The small business sector, under many different guises, often has been, since the 1960s, at the center of Cuban economic policy. In some ways it has been the canary in the mine. As ideological winds have shifted and economic conditions changed, it has been repressed or encouraged, morphed and gone underground, surviving, if not thriving, as part of the second or underground economy. Along the way, it has helped satisfy consumer needs not fulfilled by the inefficient state economy. This intricate, at times even colorful, trajectory has seen the 1968 Revolutionary Offensive that did away with even the smallest private businesses, modest efforts to legalize self-employment in the 1979s, the Mercados Libres Campesinos experiment of the 1980s, and the late 1980s ideological retrenchment associated with the late 1980s Rectification Process.

Of much consequence—ideologically and increasingly economically— are the policy decisions implemented since the 1990s by the regime, under the leadership of both Castro brothers. Initially as part of Special Period, various emergency measures were introduced to allow Cuba to cope with the economic crisis precipitated by the collapse of the communist bloc and the end of Soviet subsidies. These early, modest entrepreneurial openings were eventually expanded as part of the deeper institutional reforms implemented by Raúl upon assuming power in 2006, at first temporarily, and then permanently upon the resignation of his brother as head of the Cuban government.

In keeping with the historical zigzag policy pattern surrounding small businesses activities—euphemistically labeled these days as the "non-state sector"—while increasingly liberal, they have not been immune to temporary reversals. Among the more significant reforms were the approval of an increasing number of self-employment occupations, gradual expansion of the number of patrons restaurants could serve (as dictated by the allowed number of chairs in privately owned *paladares*), and the gradual, if uneven, relaxation of regulatory, taxing, and employment regulations. Absent has been the authorization for professionals (with minor exceptions, such as student tutoring) to privately engage in their crafts and the inability to provide wholesale markets where self-employed workers could purchase inputs for their small enterprises.

The authors of this volume, an economist and a sociologist, have combined their talents and carefully documented this ever-changing policy landscape, including the cooperative sector. They have centered their attention on post–Special Period policies and their implications, specifically to "evaluate the effects of these policy changes in terms of the generation of productive employment in the non-state sector, the efficient provision of goods and services by this emergent sector, and the reduction in the size and scope of the underground economy" (297).

While assessing post-1990 changes, *Entrepreneurial Cuba* also generated a systematic examination of the evolution of the self-employment sector in the early decades of the revolution in light of shifting ideological, political, and economic motivations. Likewise, the contextual setting is enhanced by placing Cuban self-employment within the broader global informal economy framework, particularly in Latin America, and by assessing the overall features of the second economy in socialist economies "neither regulated by the state nor included in its central plan" (41). These historical and contextual factors are of prime importance in assessing the promise and potential pitfalls the small enterprise sector confronts in a changing Cuba.

Rich in its analysis, the book is balanced and comprehensive. It is wide ranging in that it carefully evaluates the many factors impinging on the performance of the small business sector, including their legal and regulatory underpinnings. The authors also evaluate challenges in the Cuban economic model and how they have shaped the proclivity for Cuban entrepreneurs to bend the rules. Present is a treatment of the informal social and trading networks that have sustained the second economy, including the ever-present pilfering of state property and the regulatory and transactional corruption so prevalent in Cuba's centralized economy.

While none of the above is new to students of the Cuban economy—as documented in previous studies and in countless anecdotal reports—Ritter and Henken make two major contributions. First, they summarize and analyze in a single source a vast amount of historical and contemporary information. The value of the multidisciplinary approach is most evident in the authors' assessment of how the evolving policy environment has influenced the growth of *paladares*, the most important and visible segment of the nonstate sector. By focusing on this segment, the authors validate and strengthen their conclusions by drawing from experiences documented in longitudinal, qualitative case studies. The latter provide insights not readily gleaned from documentary and statistical sources by grounding the analysis in realistic appreciations of the challenges and opportunities faced by entrepreneurial Cubans. Most impressive is the capacity of Cuban entrepreneurs to adapt to a policy regime constantly shifting between encouraging and constraining their activities.

Commendable, too, is the authors' balanced approach regarding the Cuban political environment and how it relates to the nonstate sector. Without being bombastic, they are critical of the government when they need to be. One of their analytical premises is that the "growth of private employment and income represents a latent political threat to state power since it erodes the ideals of state ownership of the means of production, the central plan, and especially universal state employment" (275).

This dilemma dominates the concluding discussion of future policy options. Three scenarios are considered possible. The first entails a policy reversal with a return to Fidel's orthodoxy. This scenario is regarded as unlikely, as Raúl's policy discourse has discredited this option. A second scenario consists of maintaining the current course while allowing for the gradual but managed growth of the nonstate sector. While this might be a viable alternative, it will have limited economic and employment generation effects unless the reform process is deepened by, for example, further liberalizing the tax and regulatory regimes and allowing for the provision of professional services.

The final scenario would be one in which reforms are accelerated, not only allowing for small business growth but also capable of accommodating the emergence of medium and large enterprises in a context where public, private, and cooperative sectors coexist (311). As Ritter and Henken recognize, this scenario is unlikely to come to fruition under the historical revolutionary leadership, it would have to entail the resolution of political antagonisms between Washington and Havana, and a reappraisal by the Cuban government of its relationship with the émigré population. Not mentioned by Ritter and Henken is that eventual political developments—not foreseen today—may facilitate the changes they anticipate under their third scenario.

In short, *Entrepreneurial Cuba* is a must-read for those interested in the country's current situation. Its publication is timely not only for what it reveals regarding the country's economic, social, and political situation but also for its insights regarding the country's future evolution.

SERGIO DÍAZ-BRIQUETS

CULTURE AND SOCIETY

Iraida H. López. *Impossible Returns: Narratives of the Cuban Diaspora.*
Gainesville: University Press of Florida, 2015. 312 pp.

Sabemos que todo libro se puede leer de múltiples maneras. Pero usualmente creemos que esa aseveración es válida sólo para las obras llamadas de creación y no para una estudio crítico. Estos los leemos como un texto con una sola posible lectura, casi como si fuera un manual de ciencias. Pero creo que hasta un estudio académico puede tener múltiples lecturas. Intentaré explicar mi propuesta y tomaré *Impossible Returns*, el nuevo libro de Iraida López, como ejemplo.

La lectura más directa y menos controvertible de este libro convertiría sus palabras en una especie de vidrio transparente que nos dejaría observar las obras que se estudian como objetos definidos, sin distorsión. Visto de esta forma la autora desaparece, pero nos hace ver, aunque arregladas para servir de prueba de su tesis, sólo las piezas que estudia. Visto de esta forma, el libro de López ofrece una argumentación lógica y personal de un hecho que ha marcado a muchos cubanos: el regreso a Cuba tras años fuera del país.

Visto así, *Impossible Returns* es un caso ejemplar de crítica académica. Su estructura es lógica. Abre con una introducción donde se presentan los postulados críticos que se emplearán. López se vale de múltiples acercamientos teóricos. Dentro de ese contexto, su empleo del viejo concepto de generación es, para mí, excesivo y hasta peligroso. Pero es, como veremos, de gran importancia para su argumentación.

En los seis capítulos que forman el cuerpo del libro, López agrupa obras que comparten estructuras formales —autobiografías, novelas, películas, obras de arte visual, piezas musicales— para presentar el tema central del libro. Estudia, entre otras, obras de Emilio Bejel, Ruth Behar, Cristina García, Achy Obejas, Jesús Díaz, Gustavo Pérez-Firmat, Nancy Alonso, entre muchos otros artistas de la isla y de la diáspora. En el epílogo resume en unas seis páginas lo dicho en esos seis capítulos.

Una lectura tradicional de este libro se centraría en ese cuerpo y trataría de ver cómo la autora es capaz de crear un argumento coherente e innovador. Pero esa no es la lectura que propongo. Sólo diré, para cumplir con los requisitos de una reseña académica, que el libro es un excelente ejemplo de crítica cultural, que cumple con todos los requisitos de ese género y que ofrece una visión innovadora del tema que estudia.

Pero quiero acercarme a *Impossible Returns* desde otra perspectiva; quiero ver el libro como si fuera otro texto más que narra el retorno a la Isla. En otras palabras, quiero ver este libro como un artefacto estético, como una obra de arte que se podría estudiar como otro ejemplo más de la narrativa del problemático retorno a Cuba. Lo que propongo es usar las herramientas críticas que

López misma utiliza para estudiar su propia obra. *Impossible Returns* es, visto de esta forma, otro testimonio de ese retorno a Cuba, sólo que López presenta el suyo como si fuera un "collage" de otros testimonios.

Como señalaba, López emplea las ideas de la llamada teoría de las generaciones, un acercamiento que ha marcado profundamente los estudios culturales en España e Hispanoamérica. Pero la autora no acepta pasivamente esas ideas, como lo hace evidente en su trabajo. Su interés en estas viejas herramientas críticas le viene por el impacto que ha tenido el concepto de "one-and-a-half generation," concepto que divulgó Gustavo Pérez Firmat en *Life on the Hyphen: The Cuban-American Way* (1994). Y es que ella misma es parte de esa generación que llegó a los Estados Unidos muy joven y por ello, contrario a la anterior, la de sus padres, pudo convertirse en sujeto bilingüe y bicultural, pudo convertirse en ser híbrido. Es el impacto y el constante empleo de ese término lo que me lleva a proponer esta lectura poco tradicional de un libro como este.

Si leemos el libro de esta manera —y aunque lo leamos como tradicionalmente se lee un libro de crítica cultural— el mejor capítulo de *Impossible Returns* es el tercero, el que le dedica a Ana Mendieta, otro miembro de la "one-and-a half generation." En ningún otro capítulo del libro es tan evidente la presencia de López como en este ya que aquí narra su propio regreso a Cuba en busca de las esculturas rupestres que Mendieta creó en parajes aislados de las Cuevas de Jaruco. Aunque el capítulo también se acerca a la obra de Mendieta de manera crítica y la ve a través de la erudición de otros críticos de arte, especialmente desde las perspectiva ofrecida por Gerardo Mosquera, el centro del capítulo es la narrativa del propio regreso de la autora. Fue la lectura de este que me hizo pensar en la posibilidad de leer todo el libro como una muestra más de lo mismo que López estudia: la morfología y la complejidad del retorno a Cuba. Por ello el libro abre con una epílogo del poeta griego Constantino Cavafis y por eso mismo en el último párrafo del libro López parece poner cierre a la aventura de su generación: "The return of the one-and-a half generation, the children of post-1959 exile, may well be a chapter that has run its course in the history of returns" (229).

Leamos *Impossible Returns* como un libro de crítica académica o como un testimonio autobiográfico, no me cabe duda de que Iraida López ofrece con este una importante contribución a los estudios de la cultura cubana y de la cubanía.

EFRAÍN BARRADAS
University of Florida

Olga Portuondo Zúñiga. *¡Misericordia! Terremotos y otras calamidades en la mentalidad del santiaguero.* **Santiago de Cuba: Editorial Oriente, 2014. 285 pp.**

Los últimos dos decenios de la producción historiográfica cubana han estado signados, entre otras cuestiones, por el desfasaje "natural" entre los "centros" del saber histórico y su "periferia," o lo que es lo mismo, los historiadores de la Isla han intentado acortar la brecha que separa lo que ellos investigan de lo que actualmente realizan sus colegas desde otras latitudes. La apertura y renovación historiográfica que existió durante los noventa condujo a replantear los referentes teóricos y metodológicos empleados en nuestras investigaciones, mucho de los cuales se convirtieron en "obsoletos," tras la crisis de los paradigmas y la "moda" de otras formas de hacer historia.

Veinte años después, los que escriben la historia insular, siguen delante de esa encrucijada, cada vez más alarmante, porque el tiempo solo profundiza la distancia. *¡Misericordia! Terremotos y otras calamidades en la mentalidad del santiaguero*, de la investigadora Olga Portuondo Zúñiga, es un buen asidero para dialogar con estas problemáticas. Texto que se incorpora al reducido número de los estudios cubanos realizados sobre las actitudes colectivas, el imaginario popular o las mentalidades, cuya matriz analítica nos permiten descubrir otras "realidades," que contrapuntean, con la visión totalizadora del decursar nacional.

A pesar de una estructura desigual en relación con los contenidos que aborda, la lectura se torna ágil, pues los capítulos a manera de viñetas, permiten descubrir esos "desastres naturales" que han acompañado a los pobladores de la región oriental del país. Seis capítulos a través de los cuales el lector podrá transitar desde los primeros años de la villa hasta la actualidad (2013), siendo *¡Misericordia!* el hilo conductor para enlazar las temporalidades diversas con las cuales se mueve el discurso histórico. La autora demuestra como el sentido común de los sectores subalternos codifica una coyuntura amenazante, la que desborda muchas veces el núcleo de su religiosidad. Sin embargo, no solo se registra esta perspectiva, pues Portuondo Zúñiga no obvia la importante labor de los científicos y naturalistas "cubanos" que desde el siglo XIX indagan sobre las causas de estos eventos, así como su posible predictibilidad.

Esta apoyatura bibliográfica, se refuerza con el uso de las fuentes, donde cobran particular interés las provenientes del Archivo General de Indias y las conservadas en las instituciones santiagueras, las cuales enriquecen la exploración realizada. Como se había mencionado con anterioridad, el texto se subdivide en seis acápites capitulares que desglosan casi cinco siglos de reacciones colectivas ante terremotos, epidemias de cólera u otras calamidades. En este sentido, se encuentra una desconexión entre la temporalidad que abordó la autora (1515–1692, 1693–1794, 1795–1852, 1853–1932, 1932–1947 o 1947–

2013) y la paginación que le dedica a las mismas. No en balde, las centurias coloniales son las privilegiadas en cuanto al tratamiento argumentativo, o al menos desde lo escrito, la diferencia entre los análisis de uno u otro periodo aparece marcada por la abundancia o la escasez de los documentos originales como asideros del ejercicio intelectivo.

Un aspecto que llama la atención de *¡Misericordia!* es la ausencia de los referentes teóricos y metodológicos que permiten el acercamiento al complejo campo de las mentalidades colectivas. No creo que peque de irreverente si incluyo en este caso la omisión de la producción historiográfica francesa, la cual tuvo entre sus nodos el abordaje de estas cuestiones. Ya sea desde la firma de los *Annales* de la tercera generación, que hizo de la *mentalidad* un lugar común en la práctica histórica de una década, o de los estudios sobre el miedo en Occidente, realizados desde los setenta por Jean Delumeau, los cuales hubiesen aportado, sin dudas, otras claves interpretativas.

No se trata de interpretar con otros anteojos un contexto que difiere mucho de los presupuestos que le dieron origen a ese universo conceptual. Mas resulta imprescindible, acotar al menos en una nota al pie la existencia de los mismos, para luego si se prefiere, instrumentarlos o no en nuestra narrativa, o diseñar en relación con el objeto de estudio y de acuerdo a los resultados investigativos los términos propios para describir o nombrar esa realidad.

Además la obra se mueve en una dinámica de larga duración, o al menos así se infiere de las fronteras temporales definidas, lo cual no obsta a una mención de los aportes braudelianos, aunque la autora no haga uso de los mismos. De igual manera, el libro podría haber hecho un empleo más extenso de la abundante producción historiográfica que existe sobre los "desastres naturales." A pesar de que algunos de estos estudios aparecen en la bibliografía consultada por la autora, su instrumentación hubiera permitido encontrar respuestas similares o no a estos fenómenos ambientales, lo cual desde una perspectiva comparativa enriquecería de modo sustancial la investigación.

No obstante los aspectos señalados acerca de este libro, constituye este una sugerente propuesta historiográfica, sin que esto impida manifestar de nuestra parte ese desajuste con el cual se dio inicio a esta reflexión. El cautivante universo que descubren los documentos utilizados por la autora, infieren la utilización de un arsenal teórico diferente o al menos reducir los marcos temporales. Sin dudas, esto hubiese facilitado visibilizar la compleja madeja de sentimientos, instintos de supervivencia o religiosidad reflejados en esa *¡Misericordia!* que más de una vez los santiagueros tuvieron que gritar.

DAVID DOMÍNGUEZ CABRERA
Universidad de La Habana

Rebecca M. Bodenheimer. *Geographies of Cubanidad: Place, Race, and Musical Performance in Contemporary Cuba.* Jackson: University Press of Mississippi, 2015. 308 pp.

Recientemente escuché un chiste que recoge el desdén común de los habaneros hacia los habitantes de otras provincias cubanas. El chiste formula la pregunta: "¿qué es un pinareño?" —es decir, un habitante de Pinar del Río—. La respuesta: "un palestino [oriental] al que se le pasó la parada de guaguas [autobuses] en La Habana." En Cuba, la percepción prevaleciente es que las regiones de Pinar del Río y Oriente son mucho más "atrasadas," rurales y pobres que la ciudad capital. La creciente migración de personas del extremo oriental de la isla —de donde provienen los "palestinos"— hacia La Habana ha sido objeto de rechazo y burla, según evidencia el humor popular.

La obra provocadora, incisiva y bien fundamentada de Rebecca Bodenheimer aborda un tema poco explorado en la bibliografía sobre la música popular cubana: las diferencias —y a veces rivalidades— entre la vertiente occidental y la oriental de la identidad nacional en la isla. Sobre todo, se trata de la tenaz bifurcación entre habaneros y santiagueros en la historia cultural, económica y política de Cuba, desde la época colonial española hasta el presente. El libro es una versión revisada y actualizada de la tesis doctoral en etnomusicología de la autora, que giró en torno a la rumba contemporánea en Matanzas y La Habana, y luego se amplió a Santiago de Cuba y Guantánamo. Su propósito básico es destacar el papel de las prácticas musicales en la construcción de identidades locales, regionales y nacionales en la Cuba actual. En particular, se examinan la rumba, el son, la timba, el changüí, el reggaetón y otros géneros populares en la isla.

Bodenheimer parte de la premisa de que el discurso dominante sobre la cubanidad ha sido racializado y regionalizado, antes y después de la Revolución cubana de 1959. El origen de dicho discurso puede trazarse a la utopía esbozada por José Martí de una "nación para todos," sin reparar en las fisuras étnicas y geográficas dentro de la emergente república cubana. Siguiendo a teóricos como Doreen Massey y Stuart Hall, la autora escudriña la "política espacial" que vincula ciertos lugares y prácticas musicales con grupos étnicos particulares, como la representación habitual de Matanzas como "la cuna de la cultura afrocubana." Un tema recurrente del libro es la racialización de la rumba matancera como ícono de la negritud y del son santiaguero como género mulato. A lo largo de su argumentación, Bodenheimer incorpora los aportes de la geografía y la antropología cultural para interpretar cómo la música popular se entrelaza con los espacios físicos en la formación de identidades colectivas.

Geographies of Cubanidad se asienta en el trabajo de campo etnográfico de la autora en La Habana y Matanzas entre agosto de 2006 y mayo de 2007, seguido de una estadía más corta en Santiago de Cuba durante el verano de 2011. El proyecto se centró originalmente en los circuitos rumberos de La Habana y Matanzas, donde Bodenheimer aprendió a bailar y tocar el género con el grupo folclórico Los Muñequitos de Matanzas. Bodenheimer había conocido a su esposo santiaguero, Lázaro Moncada Merencio, en el famoso Callejón de Hamel en Centro Habana en el 2004, y se casó con él en el 2008. Esta relación sentimental probablemente incidió en su decisión posterior de extender su investigación a Santiago. Su metodología consistió primordialmente en la observación partícipe en ensayos y representaciones musicales, así como en entrevistas no estructuradas con miembros de varios grupos musicales, como el Ballet Folklórico de Oriente. También recurrió al análisis textual de las canciones y a la investigación de archivos históricos como los del Centro de Investigación y Desarrollo de la Música Cubana en La Habana y la Casa del Caribe en Santiago.

El hallazgo principal de la investigación fue que, al contrario de la noción hegemónica de la cubanidad, la identidad nacional sigue estando atravesada por divisiones geográficas, especialmente entre La Habana y Matanzas y el resto de la isla. La región oriental es considerada demográficamente como la más "negra" de la isla, mientras que Camagüey suele verse como la más "blanca." Matanzas, como ya se mencionó, supuestamente representa la negritud más auténtica en cuanto a tradiciones musicales y religiosas. A su vez, La Habana aparece en el imaginario popular como la ciudad más híbrida racial y culturalmente, así como la más cosmopolita y moderna del país. El análisis de las letras de canciones de orquestas bien conocidas como Los Van Van y NG La Banda muestra la persistencia del regionalismo en la música popular contemporánea. Sin embargo, los estudios especializados han tendido a privilegiar los ritmos asociados con la región occidental como la rumba y la timba, y a marginar las tradiciones populares orientales como la conga o la tumba francesa. Incluso, algunos ensayos recientes han cuestionado los orígenes del son cubano en la región oriental de la isla.

Bodenheimer plantea un asunto clave para los estudios culturales cubanos: la perseverancia de desigualdades regionales y raciales en la producción, distribución y consumo de la música popular. Su meticulosa investigación documenta las fracturas de la narrativa convencional sobre la identidad nacional, especialmente a partir de la crisis económica de la década de 1990 en Cuba. Su experiencia de campo, realizada en tres ciudades de la isla, le permitió contrastar las prácticas musicales en diversas regiones. Dado el tamaño limitado de su muestra y el análisis mayormente cualitativo de los resultados, resulta difícil replicar un estudio como este. Además, es prácticamente imposible evaluar el efecto subjetivo de la presencia de una investigadora estadounidense (blanca) y su relación con un cubano (negro) en los hallazgos. No obstante, *Geographies of Cubanidad* contribuye sustancialmente a identificar y analizar un problema válido y pertinente para mayor reflexión académica, que el choteo criollo ya ha reconocido cuando se mofa de los estereotipos de habaneros, orientales y pinareños.

JORGE DUANY
Florida International University

Irina Pacheco Valera. *Imaginarios socioculturales cubanos*. La Habana: Editorial José Martí, Instituto Cubano del Libro, 2015. 337 pp.

Si cada generación debiera interpretar su historia, entonces está obligada a una formación intelectual que le permita descubrir lo esencial. Las condicionantes suelen ser infinitas. Nadie podría atraparlas. Sin embargo, para dejar a un lado el esquematismo, las descripciones rígidas, el voluntarismo, el teleologismo y dogmatismo que ha padecido la disciplina histórica a nivel mundial y nacional, pese a los ejemplos de consagración científica, resulta determinante una mirada múltiple en la que intervengan el mayor número de ciencias posibles relacionadas con el estudio del hombre y la sociedad. Sería lo que ya en nuestro siglo XIX se nombrara, como gesto fundador, una antropología filosófica. Esta concepción surgía entonces cuando ganaban la batalla, en el terreno intelectual, los "constructores" de la ciencia del hombre a través del análisis de su conciencia individual. Lugar privilegiado, sin dudas, se concedía a la sicología —ciencia en ciernes todavía— en detrimento de la ideología que ya había comenzado a dar sus frutos en el siglo XVIII.

Desincrustar conceptos, fundar otros nuevos que permitan la comprensión de las sociedades pasadas y presentes, no es tarea de un día. Los estudios culturales, especialmente, se rebelaron contra el status de una academia cuya furia clasificatoria, y de "verificabilidad," perpetuaba la distancia —ínfima, por cierto— que se establecía entre el modo de producir en una época y las expresiones subjetivas de sus mentalidades, las representaciones simbólicas de los imaginarios socioculturales.

El concepto de inconsciente colectivo o imaginario colectivo sienta la precedencia, después de largas discusiones entre las más diversas tendencias dentro de esta escuela historiográfica, desde las concepciones idealistas de Philippe Ariés hasta las más sensibles a las estructuras socioeconómicas como George Dubby, y las más totalizadoras en la cosmovisión de Robert Mandrou. Aparecería el concepto de imaginarios sociales en la obra *La institución imaginaria de la sociedad* (1975) de Cornelius Castoriadis para interrogarse nuevamente sobre la independencia de las ideas con relación a lo económico y explicar, con mayor expansión, el funcionamiento de lo social. De estos referentes teóricos, implícita o explícitamente, parte el libro de la investigadora y profesora Irina Pacheco Valera: *Imaginarios socioculturales cubanos*, recientemente publicado por la editorial José Martí del Instituto Cubano del Libro.

El primer capítulo del libro: "Mujeres, música e itinerarios del pensamiento pedagógico-musical cubano," comprende los aportes a la música nacional de Ana Aguado y Ursulina Sáez Medina, fruto de la pedagogía renovadora del Conservatorio de Música y Declamación de La Habana, fundado, en 1897, por los hermanos Carlos Alfredo y Eduardo Peyrellade Zaldívar. Reconoce, además, el escenario musical habanero de los años cuarenta: La Sociedad Pro-Arte Musical, la Sociedad Coral de La Habana —responsable de la existencia de la Cantoría de Beneficiencia, de la Cantoría del Instituto Cívico Militar, del Coro de Dominicas Francesas y de la Coral de la Universidad de La Habana—, la Sociedad Lyceum y Lawn Tennis y la Sociedad Universitaria de Bellas Artes. Centra su interés también en la Confederación de Conservatorios y Profesionales de la Música (1940), el Grupo de Renovación Musical (1942) y la Sociedad de Música de Cámara de Cuba (1944) para concluir con una entrevista —recurso utilizado más de una vez por la autora— al director de la orquesta Sierra Maestra, Eduardo Himely, cuyas aseveraciones permiten esa cercanía necesaria al conocimiento del son como género musical identitario de la nación cubana.

Del mismo modo reúne la investigadora sus textos —bajo el sugerente título "Voces y miradas socioculturales cubanas," en calidad de segundo capítulo otorgándole una estructura temática—, consagrados a revelar los proyectos identitarios culturales de Miranda y Bolívar en la modernidad de José Martí por el equilibrio del mundo, su visión de Argentina en la modernidad de *Nuestra América*, el imaginario sociocultural cubano en la República y la presencia de la mujer culminando su exposición con un recorrido por el campo intelectual cubano en la Revolución. Este último matizado por las realizaciones de aquellas décadas marcadas, y diferenciadas, por la realidad económica y social del país. Si se tiene en cuenta lo difícil de este período histórico, convendríamos en que, por ahora, sólo constituye un punto de partida.

Como puede apreciarse, se trata del rescate de un conjunto de trabajos publicados por la autora, en su mayoría, en soporte digital para ofrecer un arsenal de fuentes históricas y recursos teórico-metodológicos que incitan a nuevas investigaciones orientadas a descubrir la espiritualidad y la racionalidad cubanas en aras del ascenso cultural del pueblo. Es ahí donde reside, a mi juicio, su mayor mérito.

La profesora Irina Pacheco se habría de enfrentar, desde hace unos años atrás, a la generosa labor de visibilizar a las mujeres en la construcción de la nación. Resulta sumamente elocuente el hecho de que esta actitud se hace cada vez más notoria en nuestras ciencias sociales —sobre todo por las mujeres que configuran progresivamente una nueva mirada de la historia nacional—, y alcanza un prestigio todavía no equiparable a su verdadera eficacia.

A su estudio *La Sociedad Pro-Arte Musical: Testimonio de su tiempo*, merecedor del Premio Memoria 2007, y publicado en el 2011 por Ediciones Memoria del Centro Cultural Pablo de la Torriente Brau, añade, en esta nueva propuesta, nombres desconocidos por generaciones enteras como los de la soprano Ana Aguado (1866–1921), la pianista Ursulina Sáez Medina (1918–1967), las profesoras graduadas en el Conservatorio Peyrellade (1897), cuya contribución a la pedagogía musical posibilitaría el desarrollo de esta expresión artística definitoria del alma cubana.

Por su empeño, cristalizado en este libro, se agradece a la autora esa mirada ineludible que apenas asoma en un camino todavía por andar de nuestra cultura nacional.

ALICIA CONDE RODRÍGUEZ
Instituto de Historia de Cuba

Contributors

Ana Amigo studied undergraduate courses in Madrid, Florence, and Granada, and then fulfilled a master's degree in Spanish art. In 2012 she started a PhD program at Universidad Complutense de Madrid. This scholarship has allowed her to enrich her dissertation process by carrying out research in Havana (2014), at New York University (2015), and at the OpenSpace Research Centre in the United Kingdom (2016). She is currently finishing her PhD dissertation "Looking for a Modern Identity: Urban Leisure in Nineteenth-Century Havana (1844–1868)." Her research interests are cross-cultural and urban studies, postcolonial theories, and the trope of modernity.

Ruth Behar is Victor Haim Perera Collegiate Professor of Anthropology at the University of Michigan and the recipient of a MacArthur Fellows Award. Ruth's recent books include *An Island Called Home: Returning to Jewish Cuba* and *Traveling Heavy: A Memoir in between Journeys.* She is the editor of the pioneering anthology *Bridges to Cuba* and coeditor, with Lucía Suarez, of *The Portable Island: Cubans at Home in the World.* Her documentary *Adio Kerida/Goodbye Dear Love: A Cuban Sephardic Journey,* has traveled the world. With poet Richard Blanco, she runs a blog that offers a forum for Cuban stories that engage the heart as the island moves into a new era of its history (www.bridgestocuba.com).

Devyn Spence Benson is an assistant professor of Africana and Latin American studies at Davidson College. She is a historian of nineteenth- and twentieth-century Latin America, with a focus on race and revolution in Cuba. She is the author of articles and reviews in *Hispanic American Historical Review, Journal of Cuban Studies, Journal of Transnational American Studies,* and *PALARA: Publication of the Afro-Latin/American Research Association.* Benson's book *Antiracism in Cuba: The Unfinished Revolution* (University of North Carolina Press, 2016) is based on more than eighteen months of field research in Cuba, where she has traveled annually since 2003. Follow her on Twitter @BensonDevyn.

Takkara Brunson is an assistant professor of Africana Studies at California State University, Fresno. Her research examines gender and women of African descent in Latin America and the African diaspora. Her articles have appeared in *Gender & History* and *Meridians: Feminism, Race, Transnationalism.* Currently, she is preparing her manuscript, "Constructing Black Cuban Womanhood: Gender and Racial Politics between Emancipation and the Cuban Revolution, 1886–1950s."

Roberto Veiga González is an interviewer and compiler of interviews in Cuba. He earned his bachelor's in law from the University of Havana and enrolled in doctorate courses in political science at the University of Florence; he is the former editor of *Espacio Laical*; currently he is coeditor of *Cuba Posible* (Havana), and he has published many articles on Cuba (rveigagonzalez@gmail.com).

Lenier González Mederos is an interviewer and compiler of interviews in Cuba. He earned his bachelor's in social communications from the University of Havana; he completed doctorate courses in sociology at the University of Florence; he is former vice-editor of *Espacio Laical*; currently he is coeditor of *Cuba Posible* (Havana), one of the most important and influential magazines in Cuba, and he has published many articles on Cuba. (lenioglez@gmail.com)

Yvon Grenier is professor of political science at St. Francis Xavier University in Nova Scotia, Canada. He is the author of *Guerre et pouvoir au Salvador* (Les Presses de l'Université Laval, 1994), *The Emergence of Insurgency in El Salvador* (University of Pittsburgh Press and Macmillan, 1999), *Art and Politics: Octavio Paz and the Pursuit of Freedom* (Rowman and Littlefield, 2001; Fondo de Cultura Económica in 2004), and coauthor with Maarten Van Delden of *Gunshots at the Fiesta: Literature and Politics in Latin America* (Vanderbilt University Press, 2009, 2012). He edited a book of political essays by the Mexican Nobel laureate Octavio Paz, entitled *Sueño en libertad, escritos políticos* (Seix Barral, 2001). Grenier was editor of *Canadian Journal of Latin American and Caribbean Studies* and is contributing editor of *Literal, Latin American Voices*.

Jenna Leving Jacobson completed her PhD in Romance languages and literatures from the University of Chicago in 2014. Her dissertation, "Confessing Exile: Revolution and Redemption in the Narratives of the Cuban (Re)encuentro," explored the relationship between Cuban exiles and their homeland as articulated though literary and filmic narrative. Her essay "Nation, Violence, Memory: Interrupting the Foundational Discourse in Sab," is forthcoming from the University of Minnesota Press's Hispanic Issues Series.

Laura Lomas (PhD, Columbia University, 2001) teaches Latina/o and comparative American literature in the English Department at Rutgers University–Newark. Her first book, *Translating Empire: José Martí, Migrant Latino Subjects and American Modernities* (Duke University Press, 2008), won the MLA Prize for Latina/o and Chicana/o literature and an honorable mention from LASA's Latina/o Studies Section. Coeditor of the forthcoming *Cambridge History of Latina/o American Literature*, Lomas also has published essays and book chapters, most recently in *Small Axe*, *Latino Nineteenth Century*, and *Cambridge Companion to Latina/o American Literature*. She is currently working on a monograph on Lourdes Casal and interdisciplinarity in between states.

Iraida H. López, a professor of Spanish and Latino/a and Latin American studies at Ramapo College of New Jersey, is the author of *Impossible Returns: Narratives of the Cuban Diaspora* (2015) and *La autobiografía hispana contemporánea en los Estados Unidos* (2001). She collaborated with Cuban writer Ena Lucía Portela in the annotated editions of *El viejo, el asesino, yo y otros cuentos* (2009) and *Cien botellas en una pared* (2010). Her essays on literature and linguistics have appeared in edited volumes devoted to Cuban American and Latino/a literatures, as well as in peer-reviewed journals and publications in the United States and abroad. López is currently cochair of the LASA Cuba Section.

María Elena Meneses Muro es licenciada en historia con Diploma de Oro por la Universidad de La Habana en el año 2013 e investigadora del Instituto de Historia de Cuba. Ha participado en eventos científicos nacionales e internacionales con ponencias relacionadas con la temática de la esclavitud en Cuba. Ganó el Premio Relevante a la mejor ponencia presentada en el XVIII Encuentro de Estudios sobre las Guerras de Independencia en Cuba (2016). Ha impartido conferencias en centros culturales de la Oficina del Historiador de la Ciudad de la Habana.

Carmelo Mesa-Lago is coordinator of this project; Distinguished Service Professor Emeritus of Economics and Latin American Studies, University of Pittsburgh; visiting professor or researcher in eight countries and lecturer in 39; and author of 96 books and monographs and 303 scholarly articles and chapters in books published in seven languages in 34 countries, about half of them on Cuba. He is founder and has been editor of *Cuban Studies* for 18 years. His most recent book is *Cuba under Raúl Castro: Assessing the Reforms*, with Jorge Pérez-López (Lynne Rienner, 2013). He won the International Prize on Decent Work from the ILO, shared with Nelson Mandela (cmesa@usa.net).

Aníbal Pérez-Liñán is an adviser on the processing and tabulation of interviews; professor of political science at the University of Pittsburgh; editor of *Latin American Research Review*; distinguished researcher at the Kellogg Institute for International Studies, University of Notre Dame; visiting professor in seven countries; author of two books and more than sixty scholarly articles or chapters in books on political institutions and democracy (anibal.perez.linan@gmail.com).

Yolanda Prieto is professor emerita of sociology at Ramapo College of New Jersey. She specializes in the study of migration, in particular the post-1959 Cuban exodus to the United States. She has written numerous articles and coedited books on the experiences of Cuban immigrant women in the United States. Prieto has widely researched and written about religion in US Latino communities as well as the relations between Cuban Catholics on the island and those abroad. She is the author of *The Cubans of Union City: Immigrants and Exiles in a New Jersey Community* (Temple University Press, 2009).

Laura Redruello is an associate professor at Manhattan College. She received her PhD in Hispanic literature from Vanderbilt University. Her primary research interests are Cuban fiction and essay, film studies, and popular music. Related to these topics she has published several articles, such as "Escribir en Cuba: ¿Creer, mentir o callar? Una entrevista con el escritor cubano Arturo Arango," "Diferencias genéricas en el discurso fílmico cubano: El caso de Suite Habana," "La intertextualidad como trasgresión:

Nicolás Guillén en el rap cubano," "Habana Abierta: El reencuentro en el documental cubano," "Algunas reflexiones en torno a la película Alicia en el Pueblo de Maravillas," "Touring Havana in the Work of Ronaldo Menéndez," "Confrontaciones de la ciudad en la narrativa cubana contemporánea" y "El lobo, el bosque y el hombre nuevo: El fin de tres décadas de dogmatismo soviético." She currently is working on the book *La Iglesia Catolica en Cuba: Poder y cultura*.

Sofía Vera Rojas is a processor and tabulator of interviews; she received her PhD in political science from the University of Pittsburgh with a specialization in comparative politics; her research interests are Latin America political parties, electoral behavior, and democracy (sbv2@pitt.edu).

Lester Tomé, PhD, is an assistant professor in the Dance Department and the Latin American and Latino/a Studies Program at Smith College. He is also a faculty member in the Five College Dance Department. He has been a fellow of the National Endowment for the Humanities and a Peggy Rockefeller Visiting Scholar at Harvard University's David Rockefeller Center for Latin American Studies. He is at work on a book manuscript that examines the development of ballet in Cuba in the 1960s and 1970s. His articles have appeared in *Encuentro de la Cultura Cubana*, *Dance Chronicle*, *Dance Research Journal*, *Dance Magazine*, and *Cuba en el Ballet*.

Marelys Valencia es candidata a doctora en estudios romances por la Universidad de Miami. Tiene una maestría en español de la Universidad de Oregón. Ha trabajado como periodista para importantes medios de prensa en América Latina y Estados Unidos, como *Radio Cooperativa*, de Chile; el diario *La Prensa*, de Bolivia; el semanario cubano *Granma Internacional*, y Yahoo Noticias en español, donde mantuvo una columna semanal fija hasta hace un año. Sus artículos en el campo de los estudios cubanos han aparecido en espacios académicos de Estados Unidos y Europa, como *Latin American Theatre Review*, *Cuadernos AISPI*, y *Letras Femeninas*. Ha obtenido becas de la Fundación James Madison, en Washington DC, así como del Instituto Goethe y del programa InterNations de Alemania.

On the Cover

Ángel Delgado, *Límite continuo XII*. 2009. Digital print, wax pencil and dry pastel on canvas, 39" × 78".

Born in Havana in 1965, Ángel Delgado is a multifaceted and multidisciplinary artist who, since the early 1990s, has created a vast body of work around one central theme: freedom. Angelito, as he is familiarly known among colleagues and friends, will be forever remembered in the history of Cuban art for his imprisonment in the infamous Combinado del Este prison in 1990, an action that showcased the hopelessly repressive nature of the Cuban regime. In *Hope Is the Last Thing That We Are Losing*, Angelito staged a performance in which he defecated on a copy of *Granma*, the official daily of the Cuban Communist Party, while surrounded by a circle of little prints with green bones. Many Cubans at the time actually used *Granma* in lieu of nonexistent toilet paper and joked that this was the newspaper's main purpose, but state security officials failed to appreciate the multiple layers of Angelito's artistic intervention and sent him to jail for six months.

Prison would provide themes, visual cues, and an appreciation for certain media and materials that stayed with him ever since. It was in prison that Angelito began to sculpt in soap, a material that was available and that has remained important in his creative work. He also began to draw on handkerchiefs, another medium he continues to use. "Prison was like a school to me," Delgado has stated. "The Elementary School of Plastic Art, [the Academy of] San Alejandro, the Instituto Superior de Arte, and prison. Materials were those appropriate to my extreme circumstances."

From this experience, the artist also drew a catalog of personal reflections and visual references that have come to dominate most of his work. He has become something of a complement to Michel Foucault's studies on punishment, knowledge, and surveillance. Angelito provides visual deliberations of what Foucault called the history of the "soul on trial," of how bodies are constituted by modern technologies of power and of the transformation of offenders into serial pathological subjects who become legible and visible to the state. His faceless, generic subjects are the creation of modern disciplinary regimes. He paints Foucault's panopticon and its creatures.

A prolific and renowned artist, Delgado has participated in countless collective and solo exhibitions, and his works are part of numerous public and private collections all over the world. Recent collective public exhibitions include

New Vision (Till Richter Museum, Germany, 2013), *Citizens of the World: Cuba in Queens* (Queens Museum, New York, 2013), *La Revolución no será televisada* (Bronx Museum, New York, 2012), *Cuban Video* (Rubin Museum of Art, New York, 2011), *Arte no es vida: Actions by Artists of the Americas, 1960–2000* (Museo del Barrio, New York, 2008), *Killing Time* (Exit Art, New York, 2008), and *Cuba Avant Garde: Contemporary Cuban Art from the Farber Collection*, which has toured extensively around the country. Recent solo exhibits include *Revision* (Aluna Art Foundation, Miami, 2015), *Constancy*, (Amanda Harris Gallery, Las Vegas, 2014), *Uncomfortable Landscapes* (Nina Menocal Gallery, Mexico City, 2013), and *Inside Outside* (Jonathan Ferrara Gallery, New Orleans, 2011).

Additional information on Ángel Delgado's work can be found in José de la Fuente's edited volume *Ángel Delgado, 1990–2007* (Ciudad Real: Colección La Balsa, 2008) (available at https://www.artnexus.com/StoreView .aspx?id=469).